TO END

M000306029

MARK SALTER

To End a Civil War

Norway's Peace Engagement in Sri Lanka

HURST & COMPANY, LONDON

First published in the United Kingdom in 2015 by
C. Hurst & Co. (Publishers) Ltd.,
41 Great Russell Street, London, WC1B 3PL
© Mark Salter, 2015
All rights reserved.
Printed in India

Distributed in the United States, Canada and Latin America by
Oxford University Press, 198 Madison Avenue, New York, NY 10016,
United States of America.

A Cataloguing-in-Publication data record for this book
is available from the British Library.

978-1-84904-574-2 *paperback*

This book is printed using paper from registered sustainable
and managed sources.

www.hurstpublishers.com

CONTENTS

ACKNOWLEDGEMENTS

The list of people to whom thanks are due in one way or another is considerable. First, major thanks are owed to the Norwegian Ministry of Foreign Affairs for supporting the production of this book. Kristine Höglund and colleagues at the Uppsala University Peace & Conflict Department provided invaluable support to the overall project as well as helpful, informed comments on much of the draft manuscript. Individual thanks are due, in the first instance, to Erik Solheim and Vidar Helgesen; in Oslo to Wegger Christian Strøm men, Tore Hattrem, Hilde Haraldstad, Tone Allers, Bård Ludvig Thorheim, and Jon Westborg—the original Norwegian diplomatic presence in Colombo; in Chennai, to *The Hindu*'s Editor N. Ram; in Colombo to Jehan Perera, Saravanamuttu (Sara) Paikiasothy for comments on parts of the draft text, and to Dominic and Nazreen Sansoni for friendship and support; in New York to Shimali Senanayake; in London to Frances Harrison, Mark Ellingham and Nat Jansz; and in Stockholm to colleagues at Internationella Byrån for their constant support and advice.

I owe a special debt of gratitude to Manisha Gangahar in Chandrigarh for her swift, accurate transcriptions of many of the interviews; to Jonathan Buckley for both his acute observations and customarily sterling editorial work on the draft manuscript; and to the team at Hurst—publisher Michael Dwyer and editor Rob Pinney in particular—for their central role in bringing this book into being.

Finally, thanks and gratitude from way below the baseline go to my family: Sofia, Hannah, Jonathan, Leah and Joseph for their patience (mostly), love and support in the marathon process of researching and writing this book. It wouldn't have been possible without them.

This book is dedicated to the memory of Tomas Stangeland and his critical role in the Norwegian peace engagement in Sri Lanka.

LIST OF ACRONYMS

ANC	African National Congress
BJP	Bharatiya Janata Party, India
BSS	Bodhu Bala Sena (Buddhist Power Force)
CFA	Ceasefire Agreement
CPA	Centre for Policy Alternatives
CSO	Civil Society Organisation
CWC	Ceylon Workers' Congress
ENLF	Eelam National Liberation Front
EPDP	Eelam People's Democratic Party
EPRLF	Eelam People's Revolutionary Liberation Front
EROS	Eelam Revolutionary Organisation of Students
FoF	Forum of Federations
GoSL	Government of Sri Lanka
HMG	Humanitarian Monitoring Group
HoM	Head of Mission
HSZ	High Security Zone
ICRC	International Committee of the Red Cross
IDP	Internally Displaced Person
IPKF	Indian Peace Keeping Force
IPU	Inter-Parliamentary Union
IRA	Irish Republican Army
ISGA	Interim Self Governing Authority
IWG	Sri Lanka International Working Group
JHU	Jathika Hela Urumaya (National Heritage Party)
JPC	Joint Peace Council
JTF	Joint Task Force for Humanitarian and Reconstruction Activities

JVP	Janatha Vimukhti Peramuna (People's Liberation Front)
LLRC	Lessons Learnt And Reconciliation Commission
LRRP	Long–Range Reconnaissance Patrol
LTTE	Liberation Tigers of Tamil Eelam
MFA	Ministry of Foreign Affairs
MoU	Memorandum of Understanding
NACPR	National Advisory Council for Peace and Reconciliation
NERF	North East Reconstruction Fund
NORAD	Norwegian Agency For Development Co-operation
NPC	Northern Provincial Council
OHCHR	Office of the High Commissioner for Human Rights
OISL	Office (OHCHR) Investigation on Sri Lanka
PA	People's Alliance
PFLT	People's Front of Liberation Tigers
PLOTE	People's Liberation Organisation of Tamil Eelam
PTA	Prevention of Terrorism Act
PTK	Puthukkudiyiruppu
P-TOMS	Post Tsunami Operational Management Structure
RAW	Research and Analysis Wing, India
RDA	Reconstruction and Development Agency
RDC	Reconstruction and Development Council
RNG	Royal Norwegian Government
SCOPP	Secretariat for Coordinating the Peace Process
SDN	Sub-Committee on De-Escalation and Normalisation
SGI	Sub-Committee on Gender Issues
SIHRN	Sub-Committee for Immediate Humanitarian and Rehabilitation Needs
SLA	Sri Lankan Army
SLAF	Sri Lankan Air Force
SLFP	Sri Lanka Freedom Party
SLMC	Sri Lanka Muslim Congress
SLMM	Sri Lanka Monitoring Mission
SLN	Sri Lankan Navy
SPA	Sub-Committee on Political Affairs
STF	Special Task Force
TELA	Tamil Eelam Liberation Army
TELO	Tamil Eelam Liberation Organisation
TID	Terrorism Investigation Division

LIST OF ACRONYMS

TMVP	Tamil Makkal Viduthalai Pulikal (Tamil People's Liberation Tigers)
TNA	Tamil National Alliance
TNF	Tamil National Force
TRO	Tamil Rehabilitation Organisation
TOSIS	Tiger Organisation Security Intelligence Service
TRO	Tamil Rehabilitation Organisation
TULF	Tamil United Liberation Front
UNF	United National Front
UNHCR	United Nations High Commissioner for Refugees
UNICEF	United Nations Children's Fund
UNP	United National Party
URNG	Unidad Revolucionaria Nacional Guatemala (Guatemalan National Revolutionary Unity)
UPF	Upcountry People's Front
UPFA	United People's Freedom Alliance
UTHR-J	University Teachers for Human Rights-Jaffna
WTO	World Trade Organisation

Sri Lanka

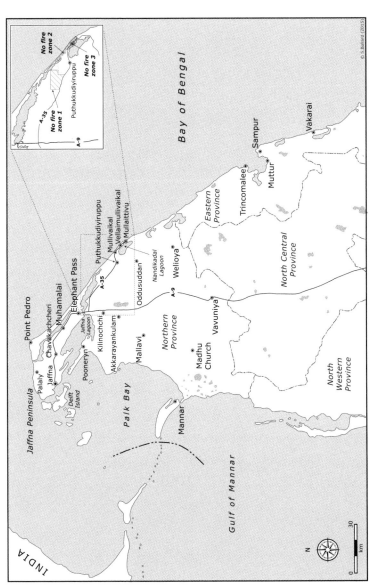

The Vanni and Northern Sri Lanka

INDIA

Jaffna Peninsula
Palaly
Point Pedro
Jaffna
Chavakachcheri
Muhamalai
Elephant Pass
Delft Island
Pooneryn
Jaffna Lagoon
Kilinochchi
Akkarayankulam
Puthukkudiyiruppu
Mullivaikal
Vellaimullivaikal
Mullaittivu
Oddusuddan
A-35
Nandikadal Lagoon
Mallavi
A-9
Weliova
Northern Province
Madhu Church
Vavuniya
Eastern Province
Trincomalee
Sampur
Muttur
Vakarai
North Central Province
North Western Province
Bay of Bengal
Palk Bay
Mannar
Gulf of Mannar

No fire zone 2
No fire zone 3
Puthukkudiyiruppu
A-35
No fire zone 1
A-9

© S. Ballard (2015)

N
0   30
km

INTRODUCTION

For 26 years the main story in Sri Lanka has changed little: bombs, bullets, carnage and suffering. LTTE suicide bombs on buses, at train stations, suicide trucks at the Temple of the Tooth, the Central Bank, the assassination of one president, the wounding of another, and government military campaigns with increasing fire-power and increasing casualties, terrifying air strikes and massive bombardment ... In those 26 years the great map of the 20th century was transformed: the Berlin wall came crashing down, Germany was reunified, the Soviet Union disappeared, China became the factory of the world and India boomed. But in Sri Lanka, the story remained the same.

Romesh Gunesekera[1]

After some hesitation, I finally gave in. Unexpectedly finding myself with time on my hands towards the end of a research trip, I decided to make the journey to the North. The last time I had travelled by plane to Jaffna was 2002. At that stage, even with a ceasefire in place, security controls were oppressive—even for a foreigner. But, as a Tamil colleague pointed out to me as we drove into town, 'try being a Tamil and see what you have to contend with'.

In 2012, three years after the Sri Lanka Armed Forces' victory over the Liberation Tigers of Tamil Eelam (LTTE), the trip northwards was an alto-gether different proposition. Having visited a downtown Colombo office to buy my ticket and made a guest house reservation in Jaffna by phone, I turned up early next morning at Ratmalana, the smaller of Colombo's two airport-cum-military bases. Security was not much beyond the expected, and as I and a dozen fellow passengers made our way towards the modest propeller-driven plane awaiting us on the tarmac, I fell into conversation with a family group from Sydney.

Like thousands of other Sri Lankan Tamils, at a certain point during the war they had decided that enough was enough and had elected to get out of Sri Lanka for good. After everything that had happened since then, the mother explained, they were making a return visit chiefly to see relatives—but also, I got the impression, to check the pulse of life back in the homeland. I say 'homeland' because the more we talked, the more obvious it became that despite having uprooted themselves many years previously, the Northern Lankan territory known as the Vanni remained a fundamental point of emotional orientation for this family, older and younger members alike.

We said our goodbyes at Palali airport—the body searches and methodical baggage searches of the past replaced by paeans to the 'Victory over Terrorism' emblazoned across the arrivals hall—and I headed for my guesthouse. Not long after checking in I was picked up by N, a local guide recommended to me by a Colombo contact. N was a sprightly, grey-bearded Tamil who had lived in Jaffna all his life. In the course of an initial bike excursion round town, I learned a number of important things about N.

First, that thanks to a combination of foresight and no small amount of fortune, N and his immediate family had survived the war years unharmed. Their house had been bombed, they had avoided forcible evacuation by the LTTE in 1995, and family members had fled the country in the aftermath of the 1983 riots.[2] But miraculously no one had been killed. Second, that whenever delicate issues relating to the war arose in our conversations—as they often did over the next two days—N's reflex response was to laugh, shrug his shoulders and lapse into silence. Third, that like many Tamils (and indeed Sinhalese), N was an ardent Anglophile. He never went so far as to suggest (as one Jaffna Tamil academic had once intimated to me) that things had been better for Sri Lanka under British colonial rule, but my nationality, combined with my willingness to engage in extended discussions of that most important of issues—the state of the English and Sri Lankan national cricket teams—certainly helped to remove his initial caution.

That process was further helped by an afternoon visit to his imperial-era alma mater, which ended in a leisurely half-hour spent watching one of the school teams slogging it out against local opposition. I have to admit I felt quite at home. So much so that I forgot to ask if N could take me to the site of the sprawling LTTE cemetery—or *Mavira Thuyilim Illam* (Martyrs' Sleeping House) as it was known—at Kopai to the north of the town.

This memorial had stayed with me since I had first visited it ten years earlier. Partly because, as with the First World War cemeteries in Flanders, the size of the place conveyed the scale of the casualties in a way that no list of figures could ever match. Partly, too, because it was my introduction to the reality of the child soldiers that had been compelled to fight for Tamil Eelam—an independent Tamil state. The absence of dates on a headstone was the giveaway, I had learned, and sure enough there they were: row after row of tidily kept graves with a name and a youthful face to identify them—but no ages or dates.

It was probably just as well that I forgot to enquire about the Kopai cemetery. I was already aware that following the end of the war in 2009 the Sri Lanka Army had destroyed all LTTE cemeteries. What I didn't know at this point was that the ruins of the Kopai cemetery had already given way to the new headquarters of the Sri Lanka Army 51st Division, opened amid much fanfare in early 2011.

Our leisurely amble round Jaffna was in any case simply a prelude to the main purpose of the visit. The following morning N picked me up in a van driven by S, a Batticaloa Tamil. I had explained my plans earlier. Again the quizzical laugh and shrug of the shoulders from N, this time followed by a cheerful 'Yes, I think we can do that'. I wanted to head south over Elephant Pass, on to Kilinochchi and continue towards Puthukkudiyiruppu (PTK), Mullaitivu and the coastal area where the final stages of the war were fought in May 2009. Whereas a year earlier the journey would have been impossible for a foreigner, I had been told in Colombo that restrictions were beginning to ease. Army checkpoints remained ubiquitous, but it was at least possible to travel there.[3]

We made our first stop at Elephant Pass, the epicentre of several battles throughout the conflict. Overlooking Jaffna lagoon from a raised mound adjoining the entry to the causeway was a monument: four metallic hands holding aloft a teardrop-shaped Sri Lanka, sprouting flowers from its coastline. Of greater resonance, however, was the surrounding set of stone lions and the national flag fluttering high above them—symbols that for many Tamils are associated exclusively with the Sinhalese nation. Moving on, our next stop was Kilinochchi, the de facto LTTE capital for more than ten years, until the Army pushed the Tigers out at the beginning of 2009 after a long and bloody siege.

Since then, Kilinochchi has undergone a complete makeover, and while the results are hardly beautiful, it is at least good to see that it has become a functioning town again. Somewhere among the new construction, the former LTTE administrative headquarters and peace secretariat buildings are still standing, but instead of looking for them we stopped at a couple of the established 'war tourism' sights. First, another monument, this one a concrete slab with a large golden bullet lodged into its surface and topped by a lotus flower emerging from one of a series of fissures created by the projectile. Second, the wreck of the town's water tower, a huge bullet-scarred cone that was blown up by the Tigers prior to evacuating the town and now lies like a beached concrete whale near the side of the road. A small shop—Souvenir Galore—stands close by.

While much of the rest of Kilinochchi has been rebuilt, the water tower remains as it was, a testament to the evils of the LTTE. As the Ministry of Defence's website puts it, 'LTTE terrorists destroyed the tank that supplied water to the whole Kilinochchi area ... before they fled their self-proclaimed capital. Water being one of the most basic human needs ... the LTTE once again demonstrated its callous disregard for the Tamil people.' A plaque next to the site tells you: 'The tower is a silent witness to the brutality of terrorism ... a monument to the futility of terror ... terrorism shall never rise again in our great land. We are free.'[4]

As we moved further towards Mullaitivu and the coast we were joined at the memorials and sights by a large group of Sinhalese. N, who had already seen quite a bit of this kind of tourism, explained that most of the sightseers came from military families, or at least had a relative who had fought in the war, and generally came on Army-subsidised package tours. And while happy to see Sinhalese taking the opportunity to visit the North, I couldn't help feeling that we were likely coming at things from very different angles.

From Kilinochchi we drove north along the A9 to Paranthan junction—the scene of a bloody battle during the final stages of the assault on Kilinochchi—and turned east along the A35 towards PTK. While the A9—which connects Jaffna with the rest of the country—had mostly been repaired, the A35 had not. As we continued, the increasing frequency of potholes was mirrored by the regularity of the checkpoints and military installations ranged along the roadside. In places these were offset by sections of new housing, shops and restaurants. The government never tires of repeating that it is rebuilding the country, and here was the evidence.

Yet rebuilding is only part of the story. Along the A35, for every new housing plot there are dozens of shattered buildings still bearing the scars of war: bullet-riddled walls, gaping roofs, mangled pillars. In many cases

Tamil civilians—the former occupants, presumably—were camped in shacks thrown up right next to their smashed-up houses. It's hard to imagine that the construction of a sparkling new barracks close by had done much to bolster faith in the new political dispensation among these dispossessed people.

Outside many of the barracks, and at other stations along the Vanni 'war tourism' circuit, garish statues of the Buddha flashed their presence. It was unnerving to see Siddhartha Gautama, that apostle of compassion and non-violence, press-ganged into military service. Taken together with the Army installations themselves, these statues struck me as nothing so much as the 'under new management' signs pasted across a building to announce a change of ownership.

The military-run cafés and souvenir shops that have sprouted up next to established stops on the war tourist itinerary are something of a puzzle. While I was as pleased as anyone to pick up a thirst-quenching soda in the scorching heat, I could not help wondering what soldiers were doing running the places that serve them. The short answer, I suspect, is that while regional neighbour Myanmar attempts to extract the military from its previously dominant role in the national economy, in Sri Lanka the Rajapaksa government elected to deal with the issue by moving things in precisely the opposite direction: more, not less, military involvement in Sri Lankan public life.

As we approached PTK we stopped at a series of former LTTE installations, now transformed into memorials and museums. I remember with great clarity a gruesome set of metal cages used by the Tigers. Lined with spikes, they forced the prisoner to remain bolt upright. The cages were a terrible testament to the cruelties that the Tigers were capable of visiting on their own people. And yet, by the fourth or fifth display of AK-47s, uniforms bearing the Tiger insignia, grenades, claymore mines, 'suicide boats' and improvised submarines, all complete with relentlessly pedagogical anti-LTTE labelling (in both English and Sinhalese, but not in Tamil), I began to switch off. Chiefly because I have never been an enthusiast for exhibitions of war paraphernalia, but also because of what seemed to me to be their implicit message.

From what I could see, there is both an absence of Tamil perspectives in these places and—most critically—a profound silence over the Tamils' wartime suffering, except to the extent that it can be viewed as confirming the justice of the great military 'humanitarian rescue operation' of 2009. In this sense it is very much of a piece with the overall national memorialisation project pursued by the Rajapaksa government after the fighting ended. And until this critical issue is properly addressed, the soldiers who guard the monuments and sell refreshments at the adjacent cafés will continue to be viewed by Vanni Tamils as an army of occupation, not of liberation. Casting yourself in the role of liberators is rarely an easy assignment: try asking the Americans, or before them Soviet forces in Afghanistan. But sensitivity to local feelings, some measure of public recognition for how things look from their side, generally helps. Especially when the people concerned are citizens of your own country.

Our next stop was Prabhakaran's underground bunker complex at Vishwamadu—a truly eerie experience. Under the watchful eye of a Sinhalese soldier, we surveyed the somewhat motley collection of assembled LTTE memorabilia, all of it meticulously labelled to emphasize 'The Evils Of The LTTE': here a terrorist gadget, there—to quote—an 'example of the luxury life style of the LTTE leader's family', and so on. (Whether Prabhakaran's insulin cooler, on display in one of the bedrooms, fits that categorisation is debateable.) We descended to the dimly lit lower floors, their sturdy hatch doors encased in reinforced concrete, and peered into the semi-darkness with bats swooping round us.

I found myself thinking about another dictator's bunker that I had visited twenty-five years earlier when researching another book: Hitler's *Wolfsschanze*—'Wolf's Lair'—buried deep in the forests of Ostpreußen, now northeast Poland. To prevent the complex falling into the hands of the advancing Red Army, in January 1945 the Nazis blew up this extraordinary piece of defensive architecture—a complex they had constructed less than four years previously. When I visited its ruins in 1989, at the heart of the *Wolfsschanze* I found huge slabs of concrete scattered at all angles amidst the forest greenery, their entrails disgorging huge iron tendrils that flailed up towards the enveloping canopy. The Nazis needed over a ton of explosives to finish the demolition job, but finish it they did. Vishwamadu, by contrast, is a well-established sight, complete with a nearby café—'Café 68', named after the Army division based there. Why would anyone want to put a stop to the tourist trade here?

But somebody clearly did. Later in 2013, reports emerged that the Army had decided it was high time to blow up the LTTE leader's bunker. Interviewed by a BBC reporter, a military spokesman suggested that visits to Vishwamadu had only ever been a 'temporary phenomenon', and now that the area had been de-mined, there was really no reason to 'keep the ghosts of terrorism' alive.[5]

After all the monuments I was almost looking forward to reaching the coast. Before getting there, however, my eye was caught by a couple of fields we passed on the way through Mullaitivu. What seized my attention was mound after mound of the wrecks of every imaginable kind of vehicle: cars, pickup trucks, vans, scooters, three-wheelers, even buses—and, above all, bicycles. All had been abandoned by civilians fleeing the fighting in May 2009, N explained. At one point scrap metal dealers had descended and made off with the best stuff, and in an outburst of civic propriety the local authorities had recently issued an appeal for people to remove their wheeled property from the area. But the likelihood of that ever happening seemed highly remote.

On the coast north of Mullaitivu, in the area in which the final stages of the war were fought, we gazed on the wreck of the *Farah III*, a Jordanian cargo ship that ran into trouble off the Mullaitivu coast in December 2006. The Sea Tigers eventually boarded the *Farah III*, and a few months later the deserted vessel ran aground. Prior to Mullaitivu's capture in May 2009, the rusting hulk served as target practice for the Tigers. Today it remains where it has lain since early 2007, to be photographed by the tourist parties who swarm over the terrain where so many soldiers, Tiger cadres and terrified Tamil civilians died in the war's final stages.[6]

Here, amid the customary detritus of war—the burnt-out shells of houses, pockmarked tracks and broken palmyra-like stumps which are all that remains of the coastal village of Vellaimullivaikal—we came across several open fields covered with more intimately human traces. It is alleged that the Army buried mounds of bodies here when the fighting was over. But what we found were not graves—we saw fields littered with clothes, suit-cases and other mundane tokens of human existence, all abandoned by civilians attempting to flee the Army's remorseless shelling of its own self-proclaimed 'No Fire Zone', and the Tigers' efforts to prevent them escaping. Nearly four years later it was all still there, a little weather-beaten but otherwise undisturbed, as if in a fit of absent-mindedness some-one had simply forgotten to clear them up.

It was an eerie, unforgettable sight. Stunned, I made to climb out of our vehicle, only to be stopped by N: 'Best not get out: it might attract the Army's attention,' he said. At the edge of the field two young girls emerged from their makeshift shack to greet our vehicle—I don't imagine this par-ticular corner of the war tourist circuit receives too many visits.

The vision of those fields flecked with clothes remains branded in my memory, as the image of the ordinary lives that were uprooted or ended by the final stages of a conflict that wreaked havoc in Sri Lanka for two and a half decades, and has served as a constant reminder of my chief reason for deciding to write this book.

Which is what? Simply put, that important aspects of the conflict's final decade seemed to me to have remained untold, or at the very least, under-examined. Of these aspects, the Norwegian effort to facilitate a peace agreement during the last decade of the conflict was paramount: an effort that, if it had succeeded—as it nearly did in its early stages—could well have prevented the death and destruction of 'Eelam War IV', the conflict's final phase. If the carnage had been successfully prevented with Norwegian assistance, we would be looking not only at a very different Sri Lanka today but also, perhaps, an important example for others seeking a peace-ful, negotiated means of overcoming protracted ethnic conflict.

But that, as we know, is not how things turned out. Right to the very end of its term in office the Rajapaksa government continued to trumpet its triumph over terrorism and the rescue of the inhabitants of the Northeast from the clutches of a cruel dictator. Others, both inside and outside the country, were telling a very different story. Whatever victory there was, it was achieved at an extraordinarily high human cost—as many as 70,000 lives by some UN estimates for the final stages of the war alone. And while some may be pleased to see the back of the LTTE, six years after the end of the war the Tamil population continue to demonstrate little enthusiasm for the de facto military occupation of the Vanni.

This, then, is the story of the Norwegian effort to facilitate an end to the Sri Lankan conflict—in the first instance as seen by the Norwegian facilita-tion team, but also as perceived by others involved in the process.

This is not an academic study of the Sri Lankan conflict. There are already a number of those, and I have no wish to repeat what others have said. And despite my own long-standing engagement in Sri Lanka and particular interest in Norway's role, the original idea for this book is not strictly mine. Credit for that is due to two central figures in the Norwegian involvement, Erik Solheim and Vidar Helgesen, who went on to become household names in Sri Lanka on account of their role in their country's peace facilitation effort.

In 2012 Vidar approached me about an idea he and Erik had been discuss-ing for some time. Ever since the Sri Lankan conflict's bloody finale they had been focused on the need to set the record straight concerning Norway's engagement—a feeling doubtless heightened by the ardour with which Oslo continued to be blamed in nationalist circles in Sri Lanka for just about anything and everything that had gone wrong in the country.

Vidar asked if I would be interested in participating in such a venture. Intrigued by the suggestion, we discussed matters with Erik to determine whether a book on the subject would be a feasible proposition. The answer was a definite 'yes'. Thereafter, spurred on by the Norwegian Foreign Ministry, the project began to take shape. Work then began—I undertook the research and writing, and Erik and Vidar served as prime interviewees.[7]

We began by drawing up a wider list of people to interview, the idea being that the narrative would base itself on the views and experiences of a range of participants in and close observers of the peace process that unfolded following the signing of the February 2002 Ceasefire Agreement between the government of Sri Lanka and the LTTE. While for several reasons it proved impossible to talk to everyone on the list, a remarkable number of people agreed to be interviewed (a full list appears at the end of this book). For that I must chiefly thank the Norwegian Foreign Ministry, and Erik and Vidar in particular, since it was their connections, combined with the remarkable degree of respect with which they are held both inside Sri Lanka and beyond, that made this happen.

The only places in which my Norwegian calling card failed to elicit a favourable response were in certain isolated corners of the Indian foreign affairs establishment and large sections of the Rajapaksa government. If there are names some readers are surprised not to find in the list of interviewees, in most cases the explanation is that the persons in question were either unwilling to speak to me or uncontactable. One official explained Colombo's position nicely when he told me, 'listen: your book is going into the past; these days we prefer to look forwards.'

I would argue, of course, that the main point of 'going into the past' is precisely in order to improve our actions both now and in the future. But that is beside the point. In the end, any omissions, major or otherwise, are the author's responsibility, and for these, along with any errors, I beg advance forgiveness.

1

BEGINNINGS

Where does the story of Norway's engagement in Sri Lanka's civil war start? On the face of it the answer seems relatively straightforward. On 1 January 2000 President Chandrika Kumaratunga gave a New Year speech in which she announced that Norway had accepted a formal invitation to facilitate the process of initiating peace talks between the government of Sri Lanka and the LTTE. News of the speech, relayed to Oslo by Ambassador Jon Westborg in Colombo, came as a major surprise to the Norwegian Foreign Ministry, which up until this point had been operating in the strictest confidentiality, on the assumption that the Sri Lankan government would continue to do the same.[1]

In reality, however, the story is not quite that simple. The closer you look into the origins of the Norwegian engagement in Sri Lanka, the more complex the antecedents to Kumaratunga's New Year speech appear.[2] Like its Northern European neighbours, over the last few decades Norway has become a significant provider of development assistance to a wide range of countries in the global South. Up until the mid-1960s, Sri Lanka did not feature on the list of recipient countries for Norwegian aid. In 1966, however, some modest NGO development programme funding was initiated, and a decade later, in 1977, a bilateral co-operation agreement was signed between the two countries.[3]

How this came to be is described by Arne Fjørtoft, a Norwegian journalist and development activist:

At that time I was a radio journalist and my boss asked me to interview three visiting students from Sri Lanka. They came from a fishing community on the

11

Jaffna peninsula, and their dream was to start a project. I got them on board with a Norwegian youth organisation and found them some money. They went back home but in 1966 we had reports that things weren't going so well for them. I took leave and went to Sri Lanka to help reorganise their project.[4]

So began what became for Fjørtoft a long-term connection with Sri Lanka:

I managed to turn around the fishery project, which was located on a small island called Karanika, twelve miles off Jaffna. We ended up with 2,000 employees all over the country. It was a success. The strategy was to get support from everyone, the government included.

Transitioning from individual project support to broader bilateral co-operation, however, involved new challenges, and the vital role that Fjørtoft played in reaching that point is abundantly clear. He explains:

After Mrs Bandaranaike won the 1970 [Presidential] elections I became close to her nephew Felix Bandaranaike, [which meant that] I could get things done. Sri Lanka opened an embassy in Stockholm in the 1970s, and the Ambassador Rex Koelmeyer and I became good friends. I invited Felix to Norway and we met the Director General of NORAD.[5] We were told that Sri Lanka was not a priority country. I thought that we could mend this, so in 1975–6 I fixed with Felix to invite three key Norwegian foreign relations people to come to Sri Lanka. I told them that they couldn't come to the country empty-handed. They were impressed during their visit. Norway decided to focus on Sri Lanka, and in 1977 Norad opened its office there.

Even at this early stage, however, domestic political considerations had a significant impact on NORAD's work. Fjørtoft explains:

They [NORAD] started with a major project in Hambantota:[6] we were told clearly by Mrs Bandaranaike that we had to start in the South and only then go into the North. We had fifty million kroner at our disposal—a big amount at the time.[7]

Norwegian officials maintain that this pattern continued over the following decades, with the majority of development assistance continuing to flow to the South, to be disbursed through government-run channels. Of the widespread belief that the majority of Norwegian assistance went to Tamils, Jon Westborg states:

It's a straight misconception, which has been utilised with considerable effectiveness by the nationalists. They continuously put it out whenever they felt like gaining [some political] mileage. But if you look at economic facts, the majority of Norwegian development funds went to the South.

Even at these early stages, the conflict-related dimensions of Norway's engagement in Sri Lanka were readily apparent. As Jon Westborg describes it:

In 1981, when Prabhakaran came out of simply robbing banks and started to build a military force, I had an interesting approach from a government official responsible for development issues.[8] He argued that there was an urgent need to create employment for the younger generation in the North.

If this were not done, the government official added, 'things were going to blow up there'.

However, in the context of the Sinhalisation policies that had been pursued by successive Sri Lankan governments from the 1950s onwards, it was difficult for a government of any political stripe to offer political or economic support to Tamils in the North. As Westborg puts it:

At that point the government had a two-thirds majority: if they had started doing active development work in the North they would have lost their overall mandate. So the official said to me 'Tell your government in Oslo that we want [you to undertake] a proper development programme in the North'. Oslo got the message, but felt that what was being asked was way beyond what they should be doing.[9]

Thinking back on it now, however, Westborg regrets that he and others did not lobby harder for an assistance programme in the North. As well they might, for the 1980s proved to be the decade when ethnic tensions between the island's majority Sinhalese and minority Tamil communities erupted into violence and destruction.

Simmering Conflict

A clear sign that relations were deteriorating came in May 1981 when the Jaffna Library was burnt to the ground—allegedly by a combination of local police and paramilitary forces, and under direct instruction, many believe, from the United National Party (UNP) government of J.R. Jayawardene. More than 90,000 books, many of historical value and cultural importance to Tamils, were reduced to cinders. Cultural symbolism aside, the Jaffna Library's destruction is credited with having persuaded many Sri Lankan Tamils of the futility of a parliamentary approach to protecting their rights—an approach taken by the Tamil United Liberation Front (TULF), which in 1977 had won the majority of seats in Tamil regions on a platform advocating independence.[10] Popular support for the separatist agenda—the creation of a separate Tamil Eelam advocated by the LTTE and other militant groups—began to increase.[11]

In July 1983, continuing its campaign of assassinations of government officials, police and army personnel in the North, LTTE cadres launched an ambush on a Sri Lanka Army (SLA) checkpoint just outside Jaffna, killing thirteen soldiers. Outrage at the incident prompted fury among sections of the majority Sinhalese population—a fury that found expression in a series of pogroms directed against the Tamil community in Colombo and elsewhere around the country.

Anywhere between 400 and more than 3,000 Tamils are thought to have died during the bloodletting of what came to be known as 'Black July'.[12] Large numbers of Tamils also fled Sinhalese-majority areas as a result of the violence directed against their communities. Many moved to the North, while those who could afford to do so joined an exodus to India, Malaysia, the UK, Canada, Australia and other countries with significant Tamil communities. The shocking events of Black July are usually considered the starting point of the country's civil war.

The Jayawardene government's lacklustre response to Black July shocked many, both inside and outside Sri Lanka. It is abundantly clear that if the president had reacted by ordering an immediate clampdown by the security forces, the violence would have fizzled out with only a few casualties. The reality was quite the opposite. For some days Jayawardene simply disappeared from the public eye. Eventually he made a televised appearance in which he appealed for all sides to stop the violence. Tellingly, however, the president blamed the violence not on organised attacks on Tamil civilians by Sinhala mobs but on what he called the 'deep ill-feeling and suspicion' between the two communities that had been fuelled, he contended, by Tamil calls for an independent state.

After two years of escalating combat between government forces and the LTTE, a first Indian-backed attempt to broker talks between the two sides took place in Thimpu, Bhutan in July–August 1985.[13] Prior to the talks there had been two important developments. First, the LTTE had elected to join forces with the Eelam National Liberation Front (ENLF), a united front of Tamil groups that had been formed the previous year. Second, a mutual ceasefire between government and Tamil forces was declared on 18 June. Following intensive discussions—and under strong pressure from India, which had been providing funding and military training to the LTTE and other Tamil militant groups[14]—the ENLF decided to drop its earlier demand that the government table a set of substantive proposals prior to the talks.[15]

In response to the government's offer of devolution for the Northeast, which they rejected, the Tamil coalition tabled a set of four key principles as the basis for negotiation. Known thereafter as the 'Thimpu Declaration', these principles—recognition of Sri Lankan Tamils as a nation; the existence of an identified Tamil homeland; the Tamil nation's right to self determination; and the right to citizenship and fundamental rights of all Sri Lankan Tamils—remain the bedrock of Tamil nationalism. In response, all but the fourth element of the Thimpu Declaration was rejected as incompatible with the Constitution of Sri Lanka by the government delegation led by H.W. Jayawardene, brother of the president. After two rounds of discussions, the talks broke down and the war continued.

Following a spate of civilian massacres in 1986 and the dissolution of the ENLF as an alliance of Tamil forces, government troops succeeded in pushing LTTE fighters back to the northern city of Jaffna in early 1987. At the same time the government tabled a series of accords setting up new district councils in majority Tamil areas in the North and East.

Sensing the opportunity to make a decisive advance, in May 1987 the army launched a full-scale offensive, dubbed 'Operation Liberation' (*Vadamarachchi*), with the aim of wresting control of the Jaffna peninsula from the LTTE. The SLA's military push proved successful, and both Prabhakaran and Soosai, commander of the Sea Tigers,[16] made only the narrowest of escapes from the advancing forces.[17]

Soon after, in July 1987, the LTTE carried out the first of what would become the organisation's best-known and grimmest tactic—the suicide attack. A member of the 'Black Tigers' squadron drove a truck carrying explosives through the wall of an army camp in the Jaffna area. More than forty SLA soldiers were killed in the blast.[18]

The Indian Peace Keeping Force (IPKF)

From an early stage India became deeply involved in the Sri Lankan conflict. Two key factors underpinning this involvement are worth emphasising: first, India's status (and self-perception) as the major regional power; second, its concerns about the potential impact of developments in Sri Lanka on India's own Tamil population. The latter concern was particularly pronounced in connection with the state of Tamil Nadu, where a Tamil population of more than sixty million soon brought the plight of Sri Lanka's Tamils into the realm of domestic Indian politics. Throughout the conflict, at different times and in different ways, the Indian government and the Tamil Nadu state governments have supported both sides—the government and the LTTE.[19]

In the initial stages of the conflict, at President Indira Gandhi's behest, Indian support was focused on the Tamil insurgents. Between mid-1983 and summer 1987, Research and Analysis Wing (RAW), India's foreign intelligence agency, provided financial support, weaponry and military training to no fewer than six Sri Lankan Tamil militant groups: the LTTE; the pro-India Tamil Eelam Liberation Organisation (TELO); the People's Liberation Organisation of Tamil Eelam (PLOTE); the pro-LTTE Eelam Revolutionary Organisation of Students (EROS); the leftist Eelam People's Revolutionary Liberation Front (EPRLF); and the Tamil Eelam Liberation Army (TELA), previously part of TELO.

Erik Solheim on Tamil Nadu and the LTTE[20]

In the 1980s Tamil Nadu was dominated by M.G. Ramachendran, the Indian Ronald Reagan, a former actor turned politician. MGR, as he was affectionately known, was immensely popular among Indian Tamils, a popularity that stemmed partly from his having played the hero underdog in many films ... MGR 'adopted' Prabhakaran and gave massive support to the LTTE. Later, Balasingham told me how he and Prabhakaran had become the darlings of MGR, and received vast amounts of money as a result.

On one occasion, for example, Bala told me how by chance the LTTE had refused to attend a meeting of Tamil militant groups called by MGR's main political rival Karunanidhi. That was to the taste of MGR. The day after Prabhakaran and Balasingham were called to him. The Tamil Nadu first minister simply asked them: 'How much do you need?' Prabhakaran mentioned an amount in millions of rupees and MGR apparently replied, 'That's far too little, you need more.' Then he went to his bookshelf, picked up a huge pile of cash and put it into Prabhakaran's hands—ten times the amount that Prabhakaran had asked for. Later, when the weapons had been purchased and delivered to Chennai harbour, MGR again came to the LTTE's rescue. The military hardware was loaded into cars and taken with police escort to the safe house where Prabhakaran and Balasingham were hiding. Later it was transported across the Palk Strait to Sri Lanka.

In all probability, however, Indian support to Tamil militants was more complex than it appeared. By backing a range of different militant groups, some argue the Indian government aimed to keep the Tamil independence movement divided and to put itself in a position to exert control over it—precisely as India did, for example, in the run-up to the Thimpu talks.

Regardless of Indian support, during the course of the following decade all other Tamil militant groups were either merged with or wiped out by the LTTE. The most notorious of these murderous operations was carried out in April 1986 after Prabhakaran turned against TELO leader Sri Sribaratnam and his followers. In a series of co-ordinated attacks on TELO camps in Tamil Nadu, over 100 of their cadres were wiped out on Prabhakaran's orders. Over time, there came to be no space for Tamil militancy outside the LTTE.

The turning point for Indian involvement in the Sri Lanka conflict, however, came as a result of the full-scale siege of Jaffna launched by the advancing SLA in May 1987. In response to the looming humanitarian crisis in Jaffna, the Indian Air Force airdropped twenty-five tons of food and medicine into LTTE-held areas on 5 June 1987. The message from India seemed clear: military victory would not be tolerated unless a political solution to the Sri Lankan conflict had been reached.[21] A proposal for bilateral governmental negotiations was put forward by India, and Sri Lankan President Jayawardene was in no position to decline. The outcome, the Indo-Sri Lanka Peace Accord, was signed by Prime Minister Rajiv Gandhi and President Jayawardene on 29 July 1987.

Under the terms of the Accord the government agreed to implement what were seen as a number of important concessions on key Tamil demands, including: devolution of power to the provinces; the merger—subject to a referendum—of the Northern and Eastern provinces into a single entity; and official status for the Tamil language. All these measures were included in the 13th Amendment to the Constitution, pushed through parliament by President Jayawardene against strenuous opposition. Most importantly for the immediate future, India undertook to establish the Indian Peace Keeping Force (IPKF), whose job would be to maintain order in the North and East. It also agreed to stop assisting Tamil insurgents.

The most significant and immediate impact of the IPKF's arrival in the North of the country, however, was that it enabled the government to move its forces south to quell mounting protests against the arrival of Indian forces. The most important of these was the uprising launched in 1987 by the Janatha Vimukthi Peramuna (JVP), a major upheaval that was brutally crushed two years later.

The JVP Uprising of 1987–89

During the 1980s the JVP had gravitated away from its Marxist roots and supportive attitude towards the Tamils in favour of a more intolerant, nationalist political agenda. Exploiting the arrival of the IPKF as an opportunity to ramp up opposition to what they saw as an elitist and authoritarian regime,[22] the JVP began a campaign of terror aimed against both the state apparatus and sections of civil society opposed to its thinking.[23]

Operating from its base in the southern coastal town of Matara, between 1987 and 1989 the JVP killed thousands of people, crippling the country's economy via a succession of ruthlessly enforced *hartals* (general strikes). JVP leader Rohana Wijeweera and his deputy were eventually captured and executed by government forces in November 1989, and by early 1990 the remaining JVP politburo had been either killed or imprisoned, and a further 7,000 party members detained. The government was thus able to declare victory over forces that were seemingly bent on its destruction. What received markedly less attention, however, were widespread claims of a systematic campaign of beatings, torture, disappearances and extra-judicial killings carried out by government security forces during the course of the insurrection.

Credible domestic sources contend that over 60,000 people were killed during the upheavals of 1987–89—a figure that makes the continued absence of political recognition of the killings all the more troublesome. Some would argue, moreover, that the official reaction to the defeat of the JVP in 1989 prefigured the Rajapaksa government's response to the LTTE's military destruction twenty years later. Some also point to the precedent for such brutal repression—and avoidance of accountability—that was created by the Bandaranaike government's suppression of the first JVP uprising in May–June 1971. Ironically, too, allegations of widespread atrocities committed by army troops during the final months of the 1980s uprising were the reason former President Mahinda Rajapaksa, then a human rights activist, travelled to Geneva in March 1990. His destination: the UN Human Rights Council.[24]

While most Tamil militant groups laid down their weapons and agreed to seek a peaceful solution to the conflict, the LTTE soon made it clear that it would not disarm its cadres. Keen to ensure the Accord's successful implementation, the IPKF attempted to demobilise the LTTE by force. Their efforts failed and rapidly escalated during October 1987 into an all-out conflict between the Indian Army and the LTTE.[25]

An important side-effect of this military confrontation was that the IPKF was soon being accused of human rights abuses against both the local Tamil civilian population and LTTE cadres—a fact that did little to endear them to either. Over time, the IPKF came to be viewed as a foreign occupation force and was met with growing opposition from the Tamil community as a whole. At the same time, nationalist sentiments led many Sinhalese to oppose any continued Indian presence.

Encouraged by rising opposition to the IPKF on all sides, the Sri Lankan government began to make increasingly vocal calls for Indian forces to leave the island. From the start, President Ranasinghe Premadasa, elected in January 1989, demanded the IPKF's withdrawal. At a mid-July meeting with B.G. Desmukh, then envoy of Indian Prime Minister Rajiv Gandhi, Premadasa went so far as to tell him that he would go to any lengths, including even suicide, if the IPKF did not cease all operations against the LTTE by the end of July 1989.[26] Most ominously, in April 1989 Premadasa issued a secret order to the Army to deliver weapons to the LTTE in order to assist them in their fight against the IPKF and its proxy, the Tamil National Army (TNA).[27] Although IPKF casualties continued to mount and calls from all for its withdrawal grew in intensity, Gandhi refused to remove his forces from the country. For his part, Premadasa elected to open negotiations. His initial step was to declare a unilateral ceasefire—a move with which the Indian forces also complied. An invitation to talks was sent to the LTTE and in April 1989 a positive response was received from Anton Balasingham in the Tigers' office in London.[28]

Between May and November 1989, three rounds of talks were held in Colombo with high-level participation from both the LTTE and the government (though without Prabhakaran). Eventually the LTTE acceded to Premadasa's request that it form a political party to contest future elections for the Northeast Provincial Council—a significant move that appeared to signal the Tigers' willingness (under the right conditions) to enter mainstream democratic politics.[29] In return the LTTE received a steady flow of arms and other military equipment from the government, thereby strengthening its ability to carry out attacks on both IPKF forces and Tamil militias loyal to the Indians.[30]

Following Gandhi's electoral defeat in December 1989, the new Indian Prime Minister V.P. Singh ordered the IPKF's withdrawal, and the last ship carrying troops back to India left on 24 March 1990. At it its peak four Indian Army divisions and nearly 80,000 men had been deployed in the country, and during the course of its thirty-two-month engagement in Sri Lanka more than 1,100 Indian soldiers and 5,000 Sri Lankans had been killed.

Long after its departure, the repercussions of the IPKF's deployment—often described as 'India's Vietnam'—continued to be felt in both countries. On the Indian side fallout from the IPKF fiasco manifested itself in a number of ways. First, subsequent Indian administrations were cautious of criticising the Sri Lankan government of the day's actions. Second, India steered clear of any further direct military involvement in the conflict. Third, for all its regional superpower status, India remained a largely background presence in subsequent peace efforts in Sri Lanka.

There seems to be little doubt that the IPKF episode was a key factor in the selection of Norway as a third-party mediator—a preference, as one commentator put it, for a 'light touch facilitator'.[31] While officially not involved in the process of selecting the Norwegians, as we shall see later the Indians were far from absent from the story.[32] Suffice to say for now that there can be little doubt that President Kumaratunga and her government consulted closely with their Indian counterparts on the subject during the late 1990s. Tellingly, too, the first country that the Norwegian facilitation team visited after their initial mission to Sri Lanka in early 2000 was India.

Ceasefire and Talks

With the IPKF in the process of withdrawing, the LTTE unleashed a campaign of ethnic cleansing to force the Sinhalese and in particular the Muslim population out of the North and East, and proceeded to exert control over much of the land forcibly vacated as a result. In similar fashion, following the IPKF's full withdrawal, the LTTE rapidly began the process of setting up its own governance structures in the areas now under its control. A tentative ceasefire held in the first part of 1990—the final months of the IPKF's presence—as the LTTE occupied itself with eliminating a number of rival Tamil groups and government forces sought to crush the JVP uprising in the South.

Meanwhile, starting in early 1990 a Sri Lankan government delegation led by the Foreign Minister Abdul Hameed began a fresh series of peace talks with the LTTE. The talks, held as previously in Colombo, initially appeared to be moving forward. In the end, seemingly under pressure from hard-line elements within Premadasa's government, agreement stalled on the core issues of dissolving the Northeast Provincial Council and amending the Sixth Amendment to the 1978 Constitution, as demanded by the LTTE as a precondition.[33, 34] Tensions further heightened after Sri Lankan Minister of State for Defence Ranjan Wijeratne demanded that as a prelude to any elections to the reconstituted Northeast Provincial Council, all LTTE weapons should be decommissioned. Unsurprisingly, the LTTE refused.

The final straw, however, came in June 1990 when hundreds of police—some put the number as high as 750—who had been ordered by Colombo to surrender to the LTTE were murdered in cold blood.[35] The radical change in mood this provoked in Colombo is evident in Wijeratne's statement in parliament soon afterwards; 'No half-way house with me,' he stated. 'Now I am going all out for the LTTE. We will show no mercy. We annihilate terrorists.'[36]

Eelam War II

In June 1990 the increasingly fragile ceasefire broke down when government forces launched an offensive aimed at retaking Jaffna. What came to be known as Eelam War II—a phase of the conflict notorious for its sheer brutality—had begun. A week into the resumption of fighting, government minister and chief peace negotiator Abdul Hameed made a last-ditch attempt to strike a deal with the LTTE at a meeting in Jaffna with LTTE deputy commander Mahattaya, ultimately to no avail.

Norwegian Peace Moves

In parallel with the meeting with Mahattaya, it appears that Hameed—at President Premadasa's direct request—contacted Arne Fjørtoft to ask if he would be willing to explore the possibility of back-channel negotiations with the LTTE, using the Norwegian's established links with the Tigers. After sounding out Foreign Minister Kjell Bondevik on the request, Fjørtoft went ahead.[37]

> I worked directly with Premadasa ... He was keen to find a solution but he had a terrible deputy minister of defence, Ranjan Wijeratne. He told me: 'we will crush these beggars within three months, I am not willing to talk to these criminals'. I went to Jaffna again two months later, in December [1990]. The LTTE called me and said they were willing [to have] a ceasefire at the end of the year—if the government was also ready ... My impression was that Premadasa was willing to do it, but he was scared of Wijeratne. I was waiting in Norway for news from Colombo, but in the end they did not accept [a ceasefire]. Ranjan lost his life. He was heavily protected, but he was assassinated.[38] They say Premadasa got him killed, no one knows for sure.[39]

Government forces imposed an embargo on food and medicine entering the Jaffna peninsula while the air force relentlessly bombed LTTE targets in the area. The following months were marked by a series of atrocities and massacres on both sides, and in most instances civilians were the victims. Charred corpses became a common sight along the roadsides of the North and East. Throughout the country, government death squads hunted down Sinhalese and Tamil youths suspected of being either JVP or LTTE sympathisers. Perhaps most notoriously of all, in August 1990 the LTTE butchered more than 300 Muslims, including 120 in a single attack on a mosque. Two months later, Tiger forces expelled the entire Muslim population of the Northern Province.[40] More than 72,000 Muslims were given twenty-four hours notice to leave their homes.[41]

Analysts suggest that among the factors that sparked these brutal moves against the Muslim population was LTTE anger over the good relations maintained by Muslim political leaders with both the EPLRF-dominated North Eastern Provincial Council and Indian forces during the IPKF's presence.[42] In addition, some suggest that the LTTE's resort to ethnic cleansing may have been triggered by increasingly vocal calls from Muslim political leaders—notably the SLMC's Mohammed Ashraff—for the setting up of a separate Muslim administrative entity in the Northeast.[43]

In May 1991, former Indian Prime Minister Rajiv Gandhi was killed by an LTTE suicide bomber. The carefully planned assassination took place at an election rally held on 21 May 1991 in a town close to Chennai, capital of the southern Indian state of Tamil Nadu. Although the LTTE never formally acknowledged responsibility for Gandhi's assassination, it is widely believed that Prabhakaran directly ordered the killing. He did so, it is suggested, partly in revenge for Gandhi's role in establishing the IPKF, and partly to provide a graphic demonstration of the LTTE's ability to reach anyone, even at the highest levels, should it so choose.[44] In the final analysis, however, the political fallout from Gandhi's assassination was one that the LTTE in general, and Prabhakaran in particular, would later come to regret.

A major military confrontation took place in July 1991, when the SLA's strategic base at Elephant Pass, controlling access to the Jaffna Peninsula, was encircled by some 5,000 LTTE troops. Casualties during the month-long siege were high: more than 2,000 soldiers on both sides had died by the time 10,000 SLA troops arrived to relieve the base in August 1991. In February 1992 a determined government offensive once again failed to capture Jaffna.[45] Just over a year later (1 May 1993), the LTTE again demonstrated the lethal power of its most deadly weapon—the suicide bomber—

when a member of the Black Tigers assassinated President Premadasa at a May Day rally. Later the same year, in November 1993, the LTTE secured a notable victory over government forces at the Battle of Pooneryn, an encounter that left hundreds dead on both sides.

In the meantime, behind the scenes Arne Fjørtoft continued his efforts to persuade both sides to restart negotiations. On the Norwegian side his efforts were supported by Jan Egeland, appointed Secretary of State in 1992. Egeland, whose enthusiasm for Norwegian engagement in conflict mediation efforts around the globe was already well known, recalls their initial contact regarding Sri Lanka.

> [Arne] came and said, 'Listen, I have contact with the LTTE, directly on the highest level.' So I said, 'Arne, if you can come with both sides, I am interested.' A while later he came back saying, 'Yes, Hameed is interested.' At that point I think Hameed was Justice Minister—the Muslim minority are not at the centre of power in Sri Lanka really: but he was in government and a minister, so there seemed to be positive signals from both sides. The LTTE international secretary in London flew over to see me. We met with the LTTE a number of times in 1992–93: government contact was through Arne Fjørtoft. The ICRC helped with letters to Prabhakaran, messages and calls to him: I never spoke to him. The only ones who had contact with Prabhakaran at that time were the ICRC. With my Red Cross background I could call the ICRC and they said yes, we are willing to transmit messages from you. So I wrote to Prabhakaran saying that we were ready to facilitate a meeting between him and the government, and that Arne Fjørtoft would be facilitating this. Our embassy in Geneva was ready.

As a result, in 1993 at least one highly confidential meeting between the two sides took place at the Norwegian Ambassador's residence in Geneva.[46] It appears, however, that there were few tangible results. 'There was a plan for some follow-up', Egeland recalls. 'But then Hameed went out of government and things halted as far as the Geneva connection went.'

New peace initiative

The 1994 parliamentary elections constituted a landmark in the country's political evolution. By this stage, UNP rule—which had continued uninterrupted for seventeen years—had become characterised by empty nationalist rhetoric, arbitrary suppression of political opposition and intimidation of the press. An additional hallmark of both Jayawardene's and Premadasa's rule was frequent disappearances and extra-judicial killings carried out by death squads, often operating in unmarked white vans—a notorious local trademark. Ostensibly deployed in the battle against the JVP and the LTTE, in reality the death squads appeared to be directed as much against domestic political critics as armed threats in the North and South.

Opposing the UNP in the 1994 elections was the People's Alliance (PA), a recently-formed coalition between the Sri Lanka Freedom Party (SLFP) headed by Chandrika Kumaratunga and a number of smaller leftist parties. Most importantly, Kumaratunga campaigned on a pro-peace platform that emphasised a commitment to dialogue with the LTTE and the promotion of national unity and reconciliation. The message appeared to chime with popular feeling: having secured just under 49 per cent of the vote, with support from a few smaller parties the PA were able to form a working government, and Kumaratunga assumed the position of Prime Minister. True to her word, efforts to clear the way for talks with the LTTE were initiated at the earliest opportunity.[47] An initial exchange of letters between Kumaratunga and LTTE leader Prabhakaran ensued, with the focus shifting rapidly to the modalities for an opening round of talks.[48]

A first round of talks was duly held in LTTE-controlled Jaffna on 13–14 October 1994, resulting in little substantive progress beyond an agreement to hold a second round of talks ten days later, a fortnight before the presidential election. The day before talks were due to resume, however, a bomb at a UNP election rally eliminated the entire party leadership, UNP presidential candidate Gamini Dissanayake included.[49] While it did not openly point a finger at the LTTE, the government nevertheless ordered an investigation into the killing and postponed the talks.

In the November 1994 presidential elections Kumaratunga received a decisive popular endorsement, securing 62 per cent of the vote. On the day she assumed the presidency (12 November) the Tigers issued a statement welcoming her victory and announcing a one-week 'goodwill' ceasefire effective immediately.[50] A week later the new president responded by proposing a two-week long cessation of hostilities.[51] After an intensive exchange of letters, a second round of talks was held in Jaffna on 2 January 1995, resulting in a formal 'Declaration of Cessation of Hostilities', signed on 5 January and effective three days later.[52] Importantly, the Declaration—the first ever formal agreement between the two sides—envisaged the setting up of local committees, based at strategic locations throughout the North and East,[53] whose job would be to monitor implementation of the terms of the Declaration.

Each committee was to have five members, appointed by mutual agreement: two representatives each for the government and LTTE and one 'international', who would also serve as Chair. Finally, it was proposed that the internationals be drawn from the International Committee of the Red Cross (ICRC) and three identified countries—Canada, the Netherlands and Norway. As Kumaratunga later put it:

> My policy was, just bring in small countries or countries that do not have direct interest in Sri Lanka ... And also those who have had some kind of experience in peace making. Canada we brought in as a big player. Although they did not have that much experience, there is a huge contingent of Tamil diaspora there, so we thought we could pressurise the LTTE through that. The fact that Norway had been involved in the Oslo agreement, that they had some skills, was something we also took into consideration.

Following what appeared to be a promising start, circumstances on the ground began to deteriorate. By the time the committees were due to begin operation, only four internationals—two from Norway and one each from Canada and the Netherlands—had arrived in Colombo.[54] On 10 January two of them headed to their designated regions, Trincomalee and Batticaloa-Amparai. The LTTE, which had not been consulted on the choice or placement of the internationals, reacted furiously, with Prabhakaran reportedly insisting that the committees would not be allowed to start functioning until their heads had briefed him personally on proposed operations.[55] Following a third round of talks on 14 January, military and economic issues relating to the cessation of hostilities increasingly came to the fore.

Teresita Schaffer on President Kumaratunga

Teresita Schaffer, US Ambassador to Colombo at the time of the Kumaratunga presidency, offers an interesting insight into the factors that contributed to the failure of peace efforts.

> Another of Chandrika's initiatives was with the French, and she also had the effort with the monitoring group, the Canadians, Dutch and Norwegians. It was a Chandrika brainchild, which was why the LTTE hated it. Every time she hatched a brainchild she simply reached for the phone. She never gave anyone a chance to buy into it. This impulsiveness, which makes her a rather endearing character, served her very ill here. ... She was a very amateurish manager of the peace process. For starters, [the monitors] were three people. What kind of monitoring can you do with three people? Eventually they increased it to six. But they had no conceivable way of verifying whose story contained the greater amount of nonsense.

On 5 February, the four internationals were given the go-ahead by the government to travel to Jaffna to talk to the LTTE, which they did, supposedly even briefly meeting Prabhakaran himself.[56] A first-hand account of the meeting indicates that discussions focused on the inadequacies of the Declaration and the need to supplement it with a more comprehensive document.[57] Hereafter, Kumaratunga again took charge of the dialogue with the LTTE. On 20 February she sent a letter to Prabhakaran proposing direct talks, using the offices of an intermediary. In this context she proposed François Michel, a former French diplomat, as an intermediary.[58] The proposal was politely but firmly rejected in writing by the LTTE, who neither trusted Kumaratunga's motives nor believed that a retired French diplomat, acting in his personal capacity, was an appropriate third party.[59]

However, this was not the end of the story. Over the following weeks the exchange of letters between Kumaratunga and Prabhakaran regarding the French intermediary was leaked to the Colombo press, which the LTTE saw as an attempt to cast them as spoilers of Kumaratunga's peace efforts. Inevitably, media-fuelled controversy continued for some time, but Kumaratunga made a renewed effort to get talks going, proposing two days of further negotiations in Jaffna in early April.

With frustration mounting on both sides, the LTTE issued an ultimatum: by 28 March their core demands—including freedom of movement for LTTE cadres in the East and an easing of economic restrictions on the Jaffna peninsula—had to be met. Following another round of correspondence between the two leaders, the deadline for the LTTE's ultimatum was moved back to 19 April, and after further wrangling a fourth round of talks was held in Jaffna on 10 April, with few tangible results. Finally, the LTTE announced that from 19 April the ceasefire would no longer hold. On the same day it blew up two Sri Lankan Navy gunboats moored in the high-security harbour at Trincomalee. The next phase of the conflict, known as Eelam War III, had effectively begun.

Chandrika Kumaratunga on the 1994–1995 peace talks

My political opponents often say [the talks] were not a success because I did not use professionals to manage the process. But the Norwegians used professionals and that did not work either. I don't agree with that view. I used some people who are good at negotiating. And besides, what do you mean by professionalism when negotiating with terrorists? Prabhakaran and I exchanged 42 or 43 letters, and what I learnt was that he was not willing to accept anything other than Eelam.[60] I suggested that before we chalk out Eelam we want to do some work in the North. It was devastated by then, already before the war the North was neglected, and this was one of the major reasons why Tamil people followed Prabhakaran. So I said, we will work out a package for repairing roads, hospitals, university, schools, fisheries, harbours; will you let us come and do it? And he wrote back saying, 'I shall do the development when we get Eelam'. ... He wanted to continue to say that no government would ever do anything for the Tamils. That is what he convinced the people, so he could then say 'give me your children as cannon fodder'.

Secondly, Prabhakaran got worried because as I came into government offering peace there was huge euphoria. Even in market places they were selling Chandrika bangles, and devout Hindus apparently put a picture of me in the shrine rooms where they worshipped. So he got worried, wanted to show Chandrika as a devil. [The LTTE] used to publish leaflets from time to time and they would represent me as a she-devil, with long teeth and blood pouring from my teeth.

Like the cynics said, the whole lesson learned was: don't you think you are wasting your time? He won't accept anything less than Eelam. But because I wanted to end the war as fast as possible my point was that, even if Prabhakaran was not willing to accept anything other than separate state—which we were not willing to give at all—by constantly knocking at their doors we would convince increasing numbers of Tamil people of our *bona fide* intentions, that we really wanted to do something for them. They didn't want awards but only their rights, not a separate state. Once they knew that we were willing to give them their rights and this man was not willing, then they would move away from him.

Eelam War III

Following the breakdown of peace talks, the Kumaratunga administration adopted a policy dubbed 'war for peace'.[61] The first target was Jaffna: having pushed large numbers of troops into the area, SLA forces initially succeeded in cutting the Jaffna peninsula off from the rest of the island, and after two further months of heavy fighting, government forces entered Jaffna in early November 1995, the first time in nearly ten years.

Recognising that their position was fast becoming untenable, LTTE forces had withdrawn, forcing almost the entire local civilian population— some 350,000 people[62]—to evacuate Jaffna with them and head for the Vanni. (Most of these refugees were able to return home during the course of the following twelve months). As a contemporary reports notes, 'for the first time in 600 years ... the city of Jaffna ... was completely empty'.[63]

The LTTE's response to the loss of Jaffna was to launch a major offensive, codenamed Operation Unceasing Waves, in July 1996, which resulted in the capture of the strategically located town of Mullaitivu and the death of between 1,000 and 1,600 SLA troops—several hundred of them reportedly executed after their surrender or capture.[64] In response, the SLA initiated a large-scale offensive of its own in August 1996. Thousands of civilians fled the fighting, and at the end of September the town of Kilinochchi was seized from the LTTE.[65]

In May 1997 government forces began what was known as Operation Secure Victory (*Jaya Sekuri*). A 20,000-strong force of government troops was deployed with the objective of wiping out LTTE jungle bases and securing a major section of the main A9 road northwards, thereby opening up a supply line to Jaffna through the LTTE-controlled Vanni region. By the time the SLA called off the offensive eighteen months later, almost 1,500 government soldiers had been killed and another 10,000 wounded.[66] Within two weeks of the start of the 'Unceasing Waves III' offensive that was launched a year later in November 1999, the LTTE had managed to retake every mile of the A9 road lost to the SLA during the previous campaign.

While violence continued in the North, the LTTE deployed its Black Tiger squadron and timed bombing devices in urban areas in the south of the country, killing hundreds of civilians and creating a pervasive climate of fear.[67] In January 1996 the LTTE carried out one of its deadliest suicide bomb attacks on the Central Bank in Colombo: 90 people were killed and an estimated 1,400 injured in the blast. In October 1997 the Sri Lankan World Trade Centre was bombed, and in January 1998 an audacious attack was carried out on the Temple of the Tooth in Kandy.[68] In response, the Sri Lankan government proscribed the LTTE and strenuously lobbied governments around the world to do the same, with some success.

Enter Norway

Despite its growing role as a provider of development assistance to Sri Lanka, until the mid-1990s Norway had no diplomatic representation in the country. All this changed in late 1996, with the establishment of an embassy in Colombo.[69] The man chosen to be the first Norwegian Ambassador to Sri Lanka, Jon Westborg, was already intimately familiar with the country, having spent four years there as a local representative for Save The Children (1978–82).[70]

Westborg explains how bilateral relations developed steadily in the aftermath of the setting up of the Colombo embassy. 'Starting in 1997 we held an annual round of discussions with the Sri Lankan government regarding our development cooperation with the country. In these discussions our clear message was that Norwegian development cooperation should be utilised primarily for work that facilitated peaceful negotiation and development in the country.'

Even at this relatively early stage in their efforts to support the government's peace-directed agenda, the Norwegians came in for some strident political criticism. 'In 1997 we took heavy flak from the UNP', Westborg explains, 'because we, among others, funded a campaign in the southern part of the country to make people understand the need for a negotiated settlement.[71] The flak came from Ranil, on the grounds that we were interfering in the country's internal affairs.'[72]

The same did not apply in the case of Foreign Minister Kadirgamar, a man otherwise known to be highly sceptical about outsider involvement in efforts to end the country's civil war. Westborg's explanation for Kadirgamar's silence on the growing Norwegian presence is straightforward. 'He knew that was what the president wanted: a negotiated settlement, which was actually what he wanted as well. In spite of what many people said, Kadirgamar had strong views on the need for Tamil rights within a united Sri Lanka. But he loathed and had no belief in the LTTE with its demand for a separate state and its violent, anti-democratic methods.'

Jon Westborg on redefining development assistance

Norway was at the end of a process of disbanding the separation between our embassies and our NORAD aid missions abroad. This was generally done by upgrading the missions to fully-fledged embassies with a resident ambassador. This was a process in which I was heavily involved. In Sri Lanka, however, voices were raised in the Norwegian parliament asking whether it would not more be appropriate to close down our aid programme, because they felt it could be viewed as a smokescreen for the ongoing war—leading nowhere—and the country's poor track record on human rights. Others felt that there was now a new president in power who had a different vocabulary on human rights and democracy, and who had at least attempted to reach out to the rebels. Dialogue was thus viewed as a better option.

In the event a compromise was reached under which traditional development cooperation would continue as per existing agreements, while the funds released when those agreements expired would be used to support government and civil society in their efforts to find a negotiated solution to the conflict. Initially this did not necessarily imply that Norway would aspire to take a central role [in peace efforts], but neither did it rule this out. In confidential meetings with Professor G.L. Peiris, I put forward the basis for Norwegian interest in providing financial assistance to government efforts aimed at creating public support and an overall foundation for a negotiated solution to the conflict.

At that point Peiris was minister of law and constitutional affairs, and Deputy Minister of Finance, and in the latter capacity he handled all development cooperation with the country. In his opinion, the ongoing war was the single most detrimental factor to both economic and social development, and accordingly he found our offer interesting.

He therefore proposed to raise the Norwegian offer with President Kumaratunga and suggested that our annual bilateral development discussions be raised to a political level, and in future encompass issues of human rights and the war. This subsequently became reality. In our discussions in January 1997 the Norwegian delegation was led by Knut Vollebæk, who later that year became foreign minister.[73] As a result of Professor Peiris' active involvement, the meeting minutes as well as the final press statement included a paragraph stating that Norwegian development assistance would also emphasise support for activities that sought to create an enabling environment for a negotiated solution to the conflict.

The extent to which others were aware of the peace-making role for which Norway was being groomed remains an interesting question. Recalling this period, an international NGO activist with a long-standing involvement in Sri Lanka noted: 'During 1997 there were rumours that trips were being made to Oslo. I met Bala[singham] regularly, I knew him quite well. I also knew Jon Westborg and the Norwegian Aid people who were based in Colombo. It was a really good mission, both in developmental and political terms. At this stage I thought the Norwegians were probably exploring the possibility of a bilateral dialogue, and were shifting [the focus of] their development support to back up their overall political approach.'[74]

Finally, an account of Norway's engagement in Sri Lanka during this period would not be complete without noting that its peace efforts assumed a number of forms. In the civil society sphere, for example, in February 1996 the Foreign Ministry sponsored a small high-level conference, hosted by the Christian Michelsen Institute in Bergen, on the prospects for peace in Sri Lanka and the role of the international community. Participants on the Norwegian side included Jan Egeland and Erna Solberg, then a Conservative MP and since October 2013 the country's Prime Minister. Also present were Sarath Amunugama, a senior Sri Lankan parliamentarian and V. Rudrakumaran, a US-based LTTE adviser. The participation of an MP with good links to the government and a senior LTTE representative from the Tamil diaspora underlined the conference's unofficial objective of fostering renewed dialogue between the parties to the Sri Lankan conflict.

Enter Solheim

It is at this point that Erik Solheim enters the story of the Norwegian peace engagement in Sri Lanka. After resigning as leader of the Socialist Left Party in 1997,[75] Solheim turned his attention towards writing a book about his experience in politics.[76] At his old friend Arne Fjørtoft's invitation, in January 1998 Solheim made his first visit to Sri Lanka, the aim being, as he puts it, 'just to go and write, disappear from Norwegian media, focus on the book'.

In between intense periods of writing he engaged in meetings arranged by Fjørtoft with a number of domestic political figures: ex-Foreign Minister Abdul Hameed, Neelan Tirulchelvan and Colombo Mayor Karu Jayasuriya, who later became deputy leader of the UNP.[77] At this stage, these encounters were viewed by Solheim as no more than an 'interesting side affair'. At the same time, however, Solheim began reading about the country and in particular the JVP uprising—a major political upheaval whose consequences in terms of lives lost were at the time at least as profound as those of the continuing war in the North.

For all this, Solheim maintains that at this point he had 'absolutely no idea' that he would soon be playing a central role supporting efforts to end the Sri Lankan conflict. Returning to Norway in spring 1998, he remained focused on his book. Meanwhile, on the international stage events in the Balkans—Kosovo in particular—dominated the headlines. In Norway, as all over Europe, NATO military intervention firmly divided public and political opinion. Solheim and Kristin Halvorsen, his successor as Socialist Left Party Leader, supported the intervention, leading to severely heightened political tensions and even the threat of a split within the party.

During the same period, Solheim's international political focus began to shift towards Sri Lanka. First he initiated an all-party parliamentary group visit, headed by the speaker Kirsti Kolle Grøndahl. Later the chairman of the foreign affairs committee, Haakon Blankenborg visited the country with Solheim. 'The aim was to build a broader platform for Norwegian-Sri Lankan relations,' Solheim explains. Recalling these visits, Jon Westborg suggests that they were 'of considerable value, both in Sri Lanka and in relation to the *Storting* (parliament). Even if they did not meet the president the parliamentary group met with senior ministers, notably G.L. Peiris. Blankenborg also met with Kadirgamar ... The visit of Ms. Grøndal as president of the parliament, and second only to the King in the Norwegian political hierarchy, together with an all-party delegation, and of Blankenborg: both were exemplary guests and ambassadors for the *Storting*. This was certainly not lost on the few individuals in the Sri Lankan leadership who really mattered, and demonstrated the seriousness with which the Norwegian side treated our relationship with Sri Lanka in the middle of an ongoing war. It certainly demonstrated Erik's abilities as a politician, out of the box thinker and builder of relations.'

Solheim's first contact with the LTTE occurred in late 1998. As he explains, 'In October I went to Paris to meet some of the Tamil political leaders in order to become more informed about their views.[78] We went to a working class district of northeastern Paris, close to Porte de la Chapelle where they had an office, and there were quite a few Tamils living in the area as well.'

The kidney saga

The makings of a qualitatively new phase in Norway's engagement in Sri Lanka, however, emerged the following month. Solheim describes events as follows:

> In September 1998, Chelliah [Rajakulasingham], a leader of the Oslo Tamil community and subsequently a well-known TV journalist, who also had a close relationship to the Tamil Tigers, came to me one day in Parliament. His message was very concrete. They [the LTTE] had a proposal: Balasingham needed treatment for diabetes, and the LTTE wanted to know if Norway would help in getting him out of Sri Lanka for medical treatment. He explained that Balasingham would be the key person in a new Sri Lankan peace process, and would establish himself in Europe for that purpose.

Why did the LTTE choose Solheim as the target of their request for help? Solheim explains:

> I think they came to me as a kind of backup proposition. I was a well-known Norwegian politician, had shown some interest in Sri Lankan affairs and had indicated an interest in meeting the LTTE international's Paris-based leaders. Chelliah had been to the Norwegian Ministry of Foreign Affairs, but had been given a low-level reception. They were not sure their important message would

even get through to minister Vollebæk. By involving me they could feel confident that their 'proposal' would be taken directly to the foreign minister and not forgotten. So they wanted me to contact Foreign Minister Knut Vollebæk directly to make sure he understood the importance of the proposal.

Solheim's response to the request was immediate.

> I called Vollebæk up and told him this was potentially big, and had to be dealt with in complete confidence ... Vollebæk was eager to seize this opportunity. He told me that his special adviser Wegger Strømmen would be the contact point on this issue. Wegger was special adviser to Vollebæk, his Sancho Panza—his closest confidant and front man. After a while it became clear that it would be difficult to run peace processes without direct formal authority within the bureaucratic structure of the Ministry.

> So I went to the Prime Minister Kjell Bondevik and convinced him that parliament would not oppose it if he added another deputy foreign minister to the government payroll—and he did.[79] So from then on Wegger Strømmen became a State Secretary[80] and took charge of everything relating to Sri Lanka'.

Getting Balasingham out of the Vanni implied the need for some form of co-operation with the Sri Lankan authorities. Conscious of the proposal's political sensitivities, discussions with Colombo were conducted by the Norwegians in secret, and at the highest levels—directly and exclusively with Kumaratunga and Foreign Minister Lakshman Kadirgamar. Of this, Solheim recalls:

> There was absolutely no way we could take Balasingham out without the government's blessing ... So Jon [Westborg] went to Kadirgamar. It helped that they were neighbours in Colombo. He [Kadirgamar] did most of his business from his house, as he was a top target on the LTTE hit list. He rarely went to his office in the ministry. Jon and Kadirgamar could visit each other simply by slipping through the fence between the two properties. Only the security guards would know. We floated a number of ideas for how Balasingham could be taken out of the country.

In the process a division of labour was established on the Norwegian side, an arrangement that was to continue for some time. As Solheim describes it, 'Jon was in contact with the government while I dealt with the Tigers. It was extremely helpful that Jon built such a good relationship with Kadirgamar. I felt they were similar personalities, both deeply rooted in South Asian traditions. They for sure found a common tone.'

Solheim's report on events leading up to the Norwegian attempt to get Balasingham out of Sri Lanka is complemented by the version provided by Adele Balasingham in *The Will To Freedom*, her account of her twenty-year connection with the LTTE.[81] According to her, Balasingham's deteriorating health became obvious towards the end of August 1998.[82] Reports of Balasingham's condition were relayed to Prabhakaran on a regular basis. After some deliberation, it was decided that they should approach Norway, via the LTTE's Paris-based international secretariat, with a request for assistance.[83]

Following the Oslo meeting with Solheim, in mid-September 1998 Westborg approached G.L. Peiris with a request to let Balasingham out of the country for medical treatment. Peiris immediately discussed the request with President Kumaratunga and, as Westborg describes it, agreed that Kadirgamar would be the appropriate person to handle an issue 'involving a foreign government on a sensitive issue'. Initial reports of the government's response were positive, including the suggestion—conveyed to the LTTE via the Norwegians—that the logistics of Balasingham's evacuation were already under discussion in Colombo.

The exact timeframe of subsequent events is contested. According to Adele Balasingham it was two months before the LTTE received a formal response from the government.[84] The response, moreover, was not encouraging. The Norwegians informed the LTTE that after intensive discussions the government had put together a list of demands that the LTTE would have to fulfil in return for official assistance with evacuating Balasingham.[85] Predictably, the government's list of demands was rejected outright by the LTTE as both unreasonable and unrelated to the 'humanitarian' request for Balasingham's safe passage.

By contrast, Jon Westborg maintains that the government reacted a good month earlier. Having already been instructed by Oslo to move ahead rapidly on the LTTE's request, Westborg says he met Peiris on 13 October, Kadirgamar on 18 October, and Kumaratunga and Kadirgamar jointly the following week, on 26 October. 'The reality was that from mid-October onwards the Norwegian side was communicating Kadirgamar's and Kumaratunga's reactions to the LTTE and vice versa.'

What is clear is that by mid-November an impasse had been reached. Solheim's analysis of the underlying political dynamics is characteristically blunt: 'At the end of the day what stopped Colombo was that if it [Bala's departure] came out, it would have been used by [then opposition leader] Wickremasinghe in campaigning against the government—though they [the government] were very positive initially, and saw it as an opportunity. All this was known to Balasingham as well', he adds. Solheim cites one further domestic factor that may have influenced the government's handling of this issue. 'Chandrika was somewhat afraid of her uncle, Anuruddha Ratwatte, who was Deputy Defence Minister and chief architect of the military campaign against the LTTE. We got the impression that she was somewhat afraid that he might even go after her life.'[86]

To the question of why the LTTE did not bring medical specialists over to the Vanni to perform dialysis, Solheim responds:

> I think they wanted to establish Balasingham abroad. And when you ask people to die for the cause it's hard to justify spending enormous amounts on the treatment of one single person. ... the government side made endless demands that the LTTE should satisfy as a precondition for Balasingham getting out—in other words, basically a non-starter. At some point we came to the conclusion that there was nothing more we could do. The Tigers said it was outrageous, that this was a humanitarian thing, not politics.[87]

Jon Westborg views things differently. 'One should bear in mind that Kumaratunga and Kadirgamar never actually rejected the idea of providing Balasingham with the required assistance—they simply had difficulties in giving things the final go ahead.' Elaborating on this theme, another Norwegian official argues: 'In their official functions [Kumaratunga and Kadirgamar] made or participated in decisions that they were well aware would cost hundreds of lives on both sides. But when it came down to known individuals asking for help to save their lives, they had serious problems in refusing them. That would basically amount to murder and in a different manner burden their own consciences.'

Interestingly, Solheim's account of the impasse is corroborated in its essentials by a government 'insider'. Bernard Goonetilleke, a senior Sri Lankan Foreign Ministry official who later became directly involved in the peace process,[88] has the following to say on the subject:

> I remember Kadirgamar talking to Westborg. I told [Kadirgamar] that we were dealing with a humanitarian situation, and he asked me to prepare a letter to the president on the subject. A discussion took place in the president's circle and they decided to make certain demands on the LTTE that I thought were inappropriate. As a result Balasingham had to make use of other means to get out of the country.

With the official exit route effectively blocked, as Goonetilleke observes, the LTTE decided to make its own arrangements. On 23 January 1999, amid an emotional farewell, Anton and Adele Balasingham left Sri Lanka.[89]

Westborg points out that there are 'reasons to believe' that Balasingham received 'some medical assistance' with the government's full knowledge—this came after it had enlisted the medical expertise of a 'well-reputed organisation' to verify 'the reality of Balasingham's situation. If not he would likely not have got out alive', he suggests. In a similar vein, Westborg contends that Kumaratunga and Kadirgamar were both very much 'aware of when the LTTE moved him out of the Vanni'. Having followed their response to the situation closely, Westborg is at pains to emphasise that in his view, Kumaratunga and Kadirgamar 'lost a great opportunity to build credit for the negotiations that later developed'.

Solheim again picks up the story:

> Next we were informed that the LTTE had brought Balasingham out on their own to a Southeast Asian country.[90] The ability of the Lankan navy to intercept boats was limited at that time. Balasingham was a British citizen. He received health treatment in Bangkok and stayed there for two or three months,[91] recovered, and then went to London with his wife.[92] She was his nurse, his best friend, lover, his everything. I've rarely met a couple who were so close. They established themselves in London. After this they asked us to come over [in order to] start discussions.

First encounter

Solheim's first encounter with Balasingham—the first of what proved to be many meetings—came not long after his arrival in London.

> I went there in the summer.[93] The kidney treatment Bala had had in Bangkok was enough to keep him alive. During our meeting, however, he was clearly not well. I took his medical data, went back to Norway and gave it to Norway's foremost kidney specialist, Dr. Per Fauchald from the National Hospital. After studying the medical papers, Fauchald concluded that dialysis would keep Bala alive but that he would not be in a position where he could really participate in a peace process where you need to travel, sit in long meetings and so on.

A kidney transplant appeared to be the obvious solution. Solheim continues:

> In Norway there are two ways to get an organ: through a close relative, or you sit in line and wait for one as a result of a traffic accident or some such event. There is a long queue for such procedures and it would be difficult to argue that a foreigner should be given priority. So Balasingham had to identify a relative. The LTTE found a Vanni Tamil with the right blood type who offered a kidney. They said he was a 'relative': we did not want to check.

During the course of autumn 1999 the transplant was arranged at the university hospital in Oslo. Solheim notes:

> At a certain point Balasingham informed us that the kidney donor transport had been organised, but he requested that the donor should be allowed to stay in

Europe afterwards. 'At our request the young man was brought to Jakarta by the LTTE. We had a very able ambassador there, Sjur Torgersen, with wide experience of 'out of the box' diplomatic activities. Sjur took care of him and put him on a plane to Europe. It was the man's first trip outside Sri Lanka and I still recall his surprise over the escalators at Amsterdam airport. He gave his kidney at the Norwegian national hospital, and later went to the UK, where I think he remains to this day. The British were helpful here, as always.

The transplant took place in Oslo in February 2000.[94] In the light of later developments, Solheim suggests that the operation 'led to him [Balasingham] living a number of additional years and contributing immensely to the peace process, but may also have increased his chances of getting cancer. So in this sense it may eventually have resulted in his death.' After the operation Balasingham spent a month recovering in Oslo. As Solheim explains, the operation itself was kept secret,

> basically [out of deference to] Colombo. But the news was out in the Tamil community in Oslo within hours of his arrival in town. There were Tamils working at the hotel where he was staying as well as at the national hospital. They recognised him in a second, while no Norwegian even blinked. It speaks loudly for the discipline of the Tamil community that no one leaked this to the media.

What was the reaction to all this from Colombo? 'We kept them informed', says Solheim. 'They had no difficulty with the way in which Balasingham had managed to get out of Sri Lanka. Chandrika said it was a humanitarian issue. And after she announced the peace process, news of Balasingham's kidney transplant was taken positively.'[95]

The kidney saga: another view

An interesting angle on the story of Balasingham's transplant is provided by Wegger Christian Strømmen, deputy foreign minister in the Christian Democrat-led government formed following the September 1997 elections, to whom Solheim initially answered on Sri Lankan affairs.[96] Strømmen's first encounter with Solheim over Sri Lanka came in 1998—a year before his appointment as deputy foreign minister. He offers a vivid description of the occasion:

> One day Erik walks into my office. I already knew him a little bit—he had previously been chairman of the Socialist Left Party. Before this the prime minister had said to me, "Erik has got a wild idea about something so see him, and speak to the foreign minister afterwards. He has this grand story

that out of the blue, the LTTE walked into his office one day recently." Personally I didn't really believe it, but in any case ...

In the background there was a man called Chelliah, who was the local LTTE representative. We had had our eyes on him for quite some time. He was a smart guy, but we knew he was collecting funds from the Tamil community, which numbers some 13,000 people. He came along with Erik to the meeting with me. They claimed that they could prove that Prabhakaran was interested in restoring a political process of dialogue with the government ... So I did the obvious thing: I said you have to prove it. Through a complicated system we managed to confirm that it was true, that Chelliah really had come with a message from Prabhakaran. We managed to get a satellite phone into the Vanni fairly quickly. I raised the issue with Jon Westborg. He knew the foreign minister well. Kadirgamar confirmed that this was worth pursuing—and he was also helpful in getting the satellite phone into the jungle.

We developed a kind of back and forth diplomacy with Erik relating to the LTTE, and I and Jon [Westborg] to the government. In the Vanni we looked around for information about the LTTE. It turned out that they did not have a political wing. Instead they had a kind of in-house philosopher, essayist-at-large, master of rhetoric, history professor, big talker, a very smart man—Anton Balasingham. I'm not sure I've met anyone who was cleverer with the English language. We were told that he had previously been a translator at the British High Commission in Colombo.[97] ... And he was no threat to Prabhakaran.

Erik kept coming back to [the fact] that we had to get Balasingham out of the jungle. I was holding back on the issue. We knew he had serious health problems. We had lengthy discussions on ways to get him out, but it came to nothing. Eventually Balasingham made his way out of the Vanni and reached Thailand. Everything became much easier for us when he came out, as now we had someone to relate to on a political level. He was a British citizen married to an Australian. They settled in South London in a Tamil-dominated area, where Erik and I went to see him. The Brits were very interested in what we were up to: they were definitely following us.

Balasingham's kidney surgery had a number of important consequences. First, in addition to saving the life of the LTTE's chief ideologue and political thinker, it brought him to London and put him in a position to function as the LTTE's main point of international contact. Second, despite the ultimate breakdown of negotiations over the conditions for Balasingham's exit from the country, the saga served to establish the Norwegians' credentials as an efficient interlocutor—with both the LTTE and the government. Third, it highlighted the strategic foresight of the decision to establish a full embassy in Colombo. As Solheim put it, 'It was through the kidney operation that the important contacts were made. And Jon [Westborg] is right to say that if there had not been an embassy in Colombo with a competent ambassador then we would have had to send an envoy—which would have been incredibly difficult.'

Meetings with Balasingham

Subsequent to Balasingham's arrival in London, Solheim—usually accompanied by Kjersti Tromsdal from the Norwegian Foreign Ministry—made a series of regular visits to the UK to consult with him, always with Adele in attendance. Reflecting on those initial encounters in 2000, Solheim recalls:

> Balasingham was a rather impressive figure. He had a wide knowledge of the world, and right the way through was very frank with us, including admitting to the LTTE's mistakes. He believed that Tamils had a superior culture, was very proud of what they had achieved in general, of the LTTE as a military machine and so on. He saw himself as carrying a heavy responsibility for the ordinary Tamil and a historic destiny for the Tamil nation. Over time I came to regard Bala highly and to consider him both as a great human being as well as a good friend.

With regard to the LTTE's ideological roots and proclivities, Solheim states:

> I was fascinated by the LTTE because I had had a lot of contact with Indian the leftist movements in the early 1990s. They saw the LTTE as a fascist, deeply reactionary and ultra-rightist group—far away from the left, in other words. It became clear to me that this was not a Marxist or left-wing movement but a staunch nationalist group, much like the Serb or Croat nationalists. It was all about being a Tamil in other words, nothing to do with left or right.

In this context Solheim notes that Balasingham was clear that in his view the LTTE was not a leftist political force. Rather he saw it as a social movement that 'aimed to transform the Tamil community, lifting up people who had never had a chance to play a role in traditional Tamil society.' From Balasingham's perspective, 'everything was about India. He saw Tamil culture as an extension of Indian culture. He saw the Tamil struggle as part of the South Asian or Indian struggle.'

Perhaps most controversially, in terms of official LTTE policies, Balasingham conceded that the killing of Rajiv Gandhi was the biggest mistake the LTTE had ever made made.[98] Solheim recalls Balasingham stating that Prabhakaran and LTTE intelligence chief Pottu Amman had initially 'tried to hide it from him', but had changed their line after a few weeks. Balasingham put the decision down to Prabhakaran's desire for revenge for Tamils killed by Indian troops, and a belief that Gandhi was ready to send Indian troops back to Sri Lanka—an obvious misinterpretation of the situation. In terms of LTTE policy, and in particular international relations, Solheim suggests that Balasingham took a 'pragmatic overall view. He wanted to reach out to the US and Europe, but his real affinity was with India.' Thus at the end of his life in 2006, Balasingham went so far as to try and 'apologise' to India for this misdeed.

When speaking with Solheim, the impact of his initial meetings and discussions with Balasingham is abundantly clear. As he puts it, 'I came to accept the key underlying demands of Tamils for equal rights in Sri Lanka. The right to use your own language, to cultivate your own culture and way of life. Add to that the right to self-rule, self-government in Tamil-dominated areas.' Overall, Solheim believes that 'the underlying issue of the Tamil struggle in Sri Lanka is a just cause', but—and it is a critical 'but'—should not have been 'taken to the extremity of the LTTE, not using their completely unacceptable methods'.

Official discussions

In parallel with Norwegian efforts to facilitate Balasingham's medical treatment, discussions began with key Sri Lankan government ministers on the outlines of a political settlement to the conflict. In particular, two key members of the Norwegian team—Jon Westborg and Wegger Strømmen—held a series of confidential meetings with Foreign Minister Kadirgamar.

Strømmen offers a vivid account of these encounters:

> I met Kadirgamar many times in secret meetings in London and Switzerland. We developed close ties. He liked me. It so happens we also had the same profession.[99] He was a Tamil so was considered a kind of traitor, but he was always very curious about the LTTE. I related to him all the time. We decided very early on that I could not go to Sri Lanka, which is why we used to meet in London and a place outside Geneva. Very movie-like ... We had a nice villa at our disposal— the Swiss took care of that.

Strømmen's account of parallel efforts to open up Norwegian lines of communications with the LTTE goes a long way towards explaining their focus on Balasingham. 'We quickly lost interest in the LTTE's representative in Paris. There was also an LTTE man in the UK, which has a large Tamil community. For our purposes you couldn't use either of them, however.'

As Strømmen emphasises, even at this exploratory stage it was not all plain sailing for the Norwegians. A moment of particular tension came in July 1999 following the murder of Neelam Tiruchelvam.[100] Tiruchelvan had long advocated a negotiated settlement to the Sri Lankan conflict, and had most recently been involved in discussions with the government on the so-called 'devolution package' put together by G.L. Peiris. Strømmen recalls:

> When Neelam was killed we went straight to London, as we were very angry with the LTTE. Erik was very upset since he had met him a number of times, and together we confronted Balasingham directly. And he told us point-blank 'Yes, we killed him and if you listen to me I will tell you why.'

According to Solheim, 'His explanation was basically that Tiruchelvam had given public support to the devolution package developed by G.L. Peiris, and that this was not sufficient from the Tamil perspective. The LTTE had warned him that supporting the devolution package was a betrayal of Tamil interests, and told him to quit.' Tiruchelvam had understood the warnings, Solheim reports, and had decided to go to the US for a period to 'cool down'.

Solheim offers the following interpretation of Balasingham's stance.

> As far as I understood he was never into military or terrorist-type decisions. But he would explain to us why they occurred: in this sense he became enormously useful to us because we got to understand why the LTTE did such things ... It was clear to us from the very beginning that all killings in Sri Lanka were carried out by the two sides, the Sri Lankan state and the LTTE. There were no freelancers and when someone said that the other side had done it in order to put the blame on you, it was hardly ever true.

On the basis of their meetings in Europe and Sri Lanka, Solheim had come to regard Tiruchelvam as an impressive individual. 'He was offered a government position by Chandrika but refused. He was absolutely sincere in wanting to find a peaceful solution. But the LTTE simply did not accept any other Tamil voice. Since the 1980s, competing groups were either brought into the LTTE or simply wiped out. Neelam definitely represented the old Tamil elite—very different from the LTTE boys.'[101]

Devolution in focus

At this point, from the government's perspective the main issue for discussion was the devolution package put together by G.L. Peiris, who had been working on different versions of it ever since Kumaratunga's SLFP government was elected in 1994. To date none of them had made much headway and opinions among the Norwegian team regarding its usefulness as the basis for a new peace initiative differed significantly.

Solheim was sceptical. Recalling the period, he says 'the LTTE had made it clear that in no way would they start the discussion on the basis of that document. I can understand that ... They wanted a peace process between equals, not to discuss a document written without their participation. Remember that G.L. Peiris developed the first such reform package in 1995—Neelam had played a role in that—right after talks with the LTTE broke down and Chandrika launched a major attack on the Jaffna peninsula.'

Despite this background, Solheim argues that the devolution package should be considered a 'good faith proposal. It included wide-ranging suggestions on Tamil self-rule.' In his view the LTTE did not 'reject the government's right to present proposals' as such, but felt they should be tabled 'only after a ceasefire and confidence-building measures. Then the LTTE would also produce its own proposals.'[102]

On the domestic political front, as we shall see later, discussion of the devolution package continued for another two years. Solheim admits, however, that the Norwegian team 'didn't follow it very closely because we thought it highly unlikely that the LTTE would involve themselves in a process to which they were not a party. It was an endless process in Parliament, but it was simply a non-starter. If [the] LTTE were not a party, there would be nothing to it.' Wegger Strømmen offers a contrasting perspective:

> My view was that with this devolution package thing, we can write and rewrite it, but there had to be a basic understanding and trust that we are not discussing anything formally that could lead to [the creation of] a separate state. And if we can get to that, we could start a political process based on the devolution package.

Parallel to these discussions, the Norwegians initiated a more informal dialogue with Kadirgamar and Balasingham on the conceptual outlines of a peace agreement.[103] Strømmen explains:

> Kadirgamar was very comfortable as long as I stayed within international language—sovereignty and so on. He knew the issues very well, and mostly left the semantics to me. Balasingham was the best English speaker I've ever met, which made him difficult. He clearly thought that an independent Tamil state wouldn't be viable unless there was massive support from Tamil Nadu. But I was making the argument to him that the sovereignty you are asking for—self-determination—has to be interpreted in a very different way today. It doesn't mean that you are a separate people, that you have a right to your own state: those days are clearly gone. Today people in all quarters talk of sovereignty—like American

Indians, for example, and the US federal government accepts it. We are in a time where the notion of sovereignty and self-determination is floating: so your claim comes too late.

I wanted to get the discussions of sovereignty to the point where a devolution package would flow naturally, not unnaturally like Peiris always seemed to want it. *Then* we could begin to discuss how many Tamil policemen there should be in the Eastern province, things like that. I wanted a kind of framework: but we never got to that, we only had bits and pieces.

Nevertheless, Strømmen maintains that 'we really thought we had something going in 1999. I was amazed how we were able to keep things secret.'

Strømmen was certainly right, not least when it came to establishing Norway's credentials as a third-party facilitator between the government and LTTE. As Westborg explains, the Norwegians never received a written mandate to assist in bringing the two parties together. Rather, he suggests, it was a gradual process developing out of the contacts that had been established in connection with Balasingham's kidney problems. Before 1999, Kumaratunga had initiated exploratory discussions of a third-party role with France,[104] the Vatican and the UK[105]—with the latter reportedly still an option as late as May 1999.[106] By Kumaratunga's own account:

I needed time to get the people to be with us. We did a two-year programme, we took Sinhalese public opinion from 23 per cent to 68 per cent saying yes to a negotiated peace. And also telling Tamil people all this, which is why Prabhakaran was stopping any information from getting to them. I realised Prabhakaran was not going to agree, so I thought let's try a foreign party. We chose Norway as we knew that some Norwegians were close to the LTTE; and [Jon] Westborg had worked on this for years—goodwill and all that.

For the Norwegians it was during early autumn 1999 that things really began to move. Jon Westborg describes developments as follows: 'In August Wegger [Strømmen] and I shuttled between meetings with Kadirgamar in Geneva and Balasingham in London. These meetings ... gradually cemented the impression that the government had decided to try us out as a go between.' In a follow-up meeting in mid-September, Kadirgamar communicated to Westborg that the government had finally come to the conclusion that Norway was the most reliable potential facilitator. It was a conclusion that the Norwegians appear to have accepted readily.

The international context of Norwegian 'peace diplomacy'

What was the wider international context that led to Norway's mediation between the parties to one of the most intractable contemporary conflicts?

Solheim proffers a number of reflections on the subject: 'Norwegians are missionary by instinct, and we have not faced a serious threat since 1945. We believe that we have something to contribute worldwide—that instinct is a basic starting point.' However, with the end of the Cold War, other uses emerged:

> The national foreign policy elite realised that [peace diplomacy] was potentially a very important foreign policy tool. The Cold War is over: why would anyone talk to Norway or take an interest in the country now? So it became a foreign policy tool, to help ensure that the main world powers would be interested in talking to Norway.

Summarising the evolution of a new post-Cold War Norwegian 'peace ideology', Solheim points to three stages in its development:

> First came the idea that we want to engage globally, to make the world a better place, to assist in peace. Then came practical experience from the Oslo channel in the Middle East, and other places. Only third came the broader theory—that peace diplomacy is the promotion of enlightened Norwegian self-interest. It took many years to get this broader view rooted in the Ministry of Foreign Affairs and in Norwegian foreign policy thinking as a whole ... Civil servants and the foreign policy elites had been groomed in the Cold War era, and were deeply pro-American, pro-western in their approach ... They were also disappointed that Norway had not joined the EU. It took time to understand the new world emerging in the aftermath of the Cold War and the rise of the South, China in particular.

Yet, as Solheim points out, even traditionalists in the foreign policy elite reacted positively to the most celebrated of Norway's 1990s peace initiatives—the Oslo Process.[107] 'Involvement in [the] Middle East was seen as successful', he maintains, 'not least the 1993 Nobel Peace Prize and the signing of the deal between Peres and Arafat outside the White House.' After the Oslo Process, bureaucratic-institutional support for the new peace diplomacy was, Solheim argues, paralleled in the political sphere. 'Even after changes of government, like that in 1997 to a Christian Democrat-led government and foreign minister, it was a case of complete continuation: they eventually came to the same conclusions as us on [the direction of] foreign policy.'

A highly placed UN official who dealt with Sri Lanka for many years offers a viewpoint that complements Solheim's:

> The UN has its potential when there is a readiness of the parties to accept international mediation. At the same time, there is also a lot of wariness among governments, and asking the UN in is seen as internationalisation of the issue. As far as the Norwegian involvement in Sri Lanka is concerned, the Norwegians

did not have a legacy, they are not a big power, did not have strategic interests, so the acceptance of them as an honest broker was heightened.

The official added that 'very often, the Norwegians are the natural ally of the UN.'

Jan Egeland on the origins and approach of Norwegian 'peace diplomacy'

I became political advisor to Foreign Minister Thorvald Stoltenberg in 1991, and from 1992 until October 1997 I was state secretary. This was the period when many of the things that shaped Norwegian peace and humanitarian work were established. I came with a human rights background and perspective. One of the things that had already started was the Guatemala peace process. Church organisations had suggested the possibility of hosting talks between the government of Guatemala and the *Unidad Revolucionaria Nacional Guatemalteca* (URNG) guerrillas. This was in 1990, just before we took over government. The first Guatemala contact meeting was in Oslo, and to me that was the first step in our 'peace diplomacy'.

I was very much a risk taker. I came from that tradition, was in a network of many NGOs. I was accessible, so people came with ideas, they knew that our policy was one of not instinctively saying 'No' as everybody [in the Foreign Ministry] would have done in the past; there was a good chance of getting a 'Yes'. The Guatemala talks are known. But even earlier on Norwegian Church Aid were involved in the Mali peace agreement.[108]

One way or the other I must have been part of about ten peace processes. The Oslo agreement was the most spectacular, of course: it surpassed anything that Norwegian diplomats had achieved previously. At that time things became crazy. At least once a week I must have had parties, or facilitators or the media coming to me and saying, 'can you take this peace process on as well?' This was wrong of course, and it led us into processes that led nowhere–including Sri Lanka.

Initially this was not a consensus thing: it was a thing we did. Stoltenberg saw that the world was changing and he appointed me as an NGO activist. We got the Oslo agreement and many others, people saw we could deliver agreements. This was criticised by the Conservatives in Parliament. I remember we were criticised for dealing with a 'Banana Republic', as they called Guatemala.

Consensus is important for foreign expenditure: we Norwegians are very good taxpayers. Even the Conservatives are willing to pay taxes and fight for justice internationally. Peace mediation became a consensus much later, because it seemed to be working. I have always argued that we need to be in it because it is good in itself. Others argue it is not just

---

about ideals, it is in our interest, it gives us access, credibility, contacts and so on. But if a moment came when neither Washington nor London nor Brussels were interested any longer, [on this argument] we would stop fighting for peace. In my view we should still continue, because it is the right thing to do.

It is also important to have professionalism: you can't have too much amateurism and perhaps we had too much of that in some cases. But the number one thing is contacts. I think that contacts are more important than knowing the context, which you can learn later—although you need to learn that so that you do not make mistakes, of course.

Military offensive

The fact that efforts to lay the ground for a new round of peace negotiations were underway in 1999 in no sense implied the cessation of hostilities—in fact, quite the reverse. In March 1999, government forces attempted to overrun the Vanni from the South. Despite some territorial gains, they were unable to dislodge the LTTE from the region. Now it was the LTTE's turn to go on the offensive, unleashing 'Operation Unceasing Waves III' on 2 November 1999.[109] Nearly all of the Vanni rapidly fell back under LTTE control and—perhaps most importantly from a strategic perspective—its forces then advanced north, eventually capturing the strategic Elephant Pass in spring 2000 (see Chapter 2), before moving on towards Jaffna, the Tamil-dominated regional capital that had been seized by government forces in December 1995.

In a move that presaged later political scapegoating over the conduct of the war, the government attempted to blame these military setbacks on the opposition UNP, with some ministers even going so far as to suggest they were part of a plot to unseat the government hatched between senior army figures and retired officers now involved in opposition politics.[110]

Elections and bombs

It was in this highly charged context that Kumaratunga called early presidential elections. As Solheim recalls, 'In late 1999 everything was about the presidential elections in Colombo. Chandrika was confident of being re-elected. Throughout the peace process, she was far more negative towards Ranil [Wickremasinghe][111] than Prabhakaran. She detested him. [I think] it was a case of two competing elite figures. She didn't like Ranil: she thought he was gay, not a "real man". If she had an option to bring one of them into her cabinet it would have been Prabhakaran. This is what I concluded at least: that she really did detest Ranil on a personal level.'[112]

Kumaratunga's eventual victory aside, the 1999 campaign is remembered largely for the LTTE's attempt to assassinate her at the final election rally held in Colombo Town Hall on 18 December, three days prior to polling. Fortunately for Kumaratunga, the official car that brought her to the rally took much of the force of the blast. A badly shaken Chandrika was rushed to hospital, where she eventually lost vision in her right eye. The day after the attack, in a radio broadcast from her hospital bed, Kumaratunga appealed to Sri Lankans to remain calm, emphasising that it was the duty of all 'to protect all Tamil citizens of this country'—an action that was hailed as a 'sharp and laudable contrast to the behaviour of Jayawardene in July 1983'.[113]

If the resolve displayed by Kumaratunga in the aftermath of the attack was in some measure predictable, her next move, on the day before the elections, was a good deal more unexpected. Solheim relates: 'After coming out of hospital, she told the BBC that Norway was the preferred peace facilitator. Until then, there was complete secrecy about this. Her announcement came as a complete surprise to us.' Solheim's analysis of the announcement is that Kumaratunga was determined to ensure 'that peace efforts were not derailed because of the assassination attempt ... Chandrika wanted peace. There's no doubt about that.'

These events had a decisive political impact: 'I had got an inkling [of the Norwegian involvement] from Westborg who said "we are talking",' says Tyrone Ferdinands, a peace activist. 'And then Chandrika opened it up in her BBC interview. That wrecked Ranil's chance of winning the elections: whether admitting it or not, the LTTE intervened decisively in southern politics. The interview and the attempt on her life both had a decisive effect on the elections, which she could have lost.'[114]

Jon Westborg offers a further perspective. 'After Chandrika came out of hospital I had a five hour-long conversation with her, and she was adamant on going forward with negotiations. For somebody who had gone through what she had it would have been natural to be vindictive: so her actual attitude was quite a reaction.' Westborg also confirms Solheim's contention that Kumaratunga had never indicated that she was planning to go public on the role envisaged for Norway. 'When I met her afterwards Chandrika apologised', he states. With regard to the foreign minister's reaction to the BBC interview, Westborg indicates that Kadirgamar was 'taken aback, and stressed that this was not how it should have been done'.

Perhaps the most intriguing reading of the impact of the announcement comes from Kumaratunga herself.

> I knew it wouldn't really bother the Norwegians: they were surprised that I said it without telling them, but they were also doing things without telling me. The Tamil diaspora started saying to the LTTE, why the hell do you not take up this process? Actually, I said it not to get personal and even at that stage I was hoping that the Tamil people would force Prabhakaran by saying well, we didn't know about all this: why aren't you taking this offer? And that was happening to some extent.

Whatever secrecy surrounding Norway's role remained, it was definitively shaken off by the president's New Year speech. Thereafter Norway's direct involvement in attempts to resolve the conflict was a matter of public knowledge. Both the Norwegians' ability and resolve to navigate the murky waters of Sri Lankan ethnic politics would soon begin to be put to the test.

2

2000

Following President Kumaratunga's announcement of Norway's involvement in efforts to kick-start a new round of talks between the government and the LTTE, Erik Solheim travelled to Colombo with Norwegian Foreign Minister Knut Vollebaek in mid-February 2000.[1] They were joined for the talks by Ambassador Jon Westborg. On the government side the line-up was newly re-elected Chandrika Kumaratunga, Foreign Minster Lakshman Kadirgamar, Sri Lankan Ambassador to Delhi Mangala Munasinghe and Foreign Secretary S. Perera.

From the start, Solheim reports, it was clear that Kumaratunga was running the proceedings—a perception that chimed with earlier impressions of what he terms the country's 'highly centralised' political culture.[2] 'Everyone wanted to ask the president about everything', he recalls, 'So when Chandrika gave us her blessings, at least everyone would co-operate. We were broadly accepted—though there must have been scepticism', he concedes.

Kumaratunga repeatedly returned to a single question: did the Norwegians think the LTTE were really serious about starting talks with the government? Complicating matters here was the fact that at this stage, as Solheim admits, 'We [the Norwegians] had little knowledge about that question.' Their response was simply to 'try and put everything in a positive light.' At the same time, he says, the Norwegians fully acknowledged that both sides had 'bitter past experiences, and thought the other was to blame for the conflict'.

Solheim's strongest recollection of the meeting, however, concerns an altogether different matter. 'What I really remember is the atmosphere when Chandrika claimed that the LTTE were dangerous Marxists and that we should take care. After a while I admitted cautiously that I had been one in younger days, and that maybe it was not *so* big a reason for concern. Then Munasinghe chopped in, mentioning that he too had previously been a Marxist, even a Trotskyite. Eventually Chandrika herself admitted that she had also been one during her student days in Paris. We all laughed over this somewhat unexpected meeting of (past) minds. It greatly reduced the tension of the gathering, although my friend Knut Vollebaek, a Christian Democrat, was somewhat left on the sidelines of this exchange.'

Formally speaking, the main outcome of the talks was agreement on a public statement regarding Norway's third-party role in Sri Lanka. At the subsequent press conference Kumaratunga emphasised that her overriding objective was to bring peace—notwithstanding her oft-voiced scepticism regarding the LTTE's sincerity.[3]

Reflecting on his initial meetings with both sides, Solheim recalls: 'We told the government that the LTTE felt that the peace process must be based on a ceasefire and that assassinations are part of war—[in their view] there was no distinction between top leaders and soldiers when it came to killings. The government of Sri Lanka did not want to declare a ceasefire. They thought talks and war could go on in parallel initially, and that de-escalation in the fighting would come as a result of progress on the political track. They were constantly afraid of being fooled by the LTTE. By contrast, Balasingham thought that the peace process would be a protracted affair, and that it would be very hard to sustain it if there was war [going on] at the same time.'

The view from India

One outsider with a particularly good vantage point from which to observe the early stages of the Norwegian facilitation effort was Gopalkrishna Gandhi, Indian High Commissioner to Sri Lanka (2000–2):

> From my discussions with Kadirgamar and President Kumaratunga, I could gather that they wanted this process to work. They had their own set of misgivings and reservations, but I felt that they were none the less cautiously optimistic about the process. They were also in need of what could be called a reprieve from the ballistics. So, there was both a short term and a long-term view that they were taking. If there could be reprieve without a long-term solution, fine. If there

was a long-term solution without a reprieve, then perhaps. But they needed both. Reprieve in the sense of relief from the daily bloodletting.

India is an important point of reference at this stage because from Colombo Solheim and Westborg flew directly to Delhi for a first meeting with Indian government representatives. This, as Solheim recalls, proved to be something of a baptism of fire.

> We travelled to Delhi to meet Foreign Secretary Lalit Mansingh, a foreign policy hotshot who later became Indian Ambassador to Washington ... He asked us to sit down and then began a third-degree interrogation, without any pleasantries. 'Why do you think you can contribute at all in this part of the world?' he asked. There was no protocol, [it was] like a police interrogation. After an hour and a half, we left.

Solheim continues, 'Then we met Jaswant Singh, the BJP leader and Minister of External Affairs.[4] He was pleasant, nice and kind. I felt that we had obviously passed the test. Then he said, "I have just one question for you: are you patient?"' In reply, Solheim 'admitted that Norwegians are not patient', contending that they intended to 'solve this conflict fast'. Singh's response was blunt:

> If that's the case, take the fastest taxi to the airport, get on a plane, make certain you have a one way ticket, go back to Europe and stay there. Because if you think this conflict can be solved rapidly you will just complicate matters. Only if you take a long-term historical perspective, if you think you can spend ten years on it—and even then it will be very difficult—then perhaps you can make a contribution.

'All in all we really got the treatment', muses Solheim. 'But, of course, he was right. And it was very good advice.'

It should be pointed out that Lalit Mansingh himself describes his first meeting with the Norwegians in somewhat different terms: 'When Erik met me I had read the Sri Lanka briefs carefully because I was not dealing with the country officially before. I was informed that there had been many mediatory missions prior to [the Norwegians]—the number given to me was thirty-three. I told Erik that from my point of view, forgive me for being a little sceptical, but many mediatory efforts have preceded yours. And India, as a matter of policy, does not invite mediation. But I told him, you have our best wishes.'

Solheim confirms the substance of Mansingh's recollections. 'There was clearly great reluctance to see third party involvement in the region', he says. '[The Indians] simply did not like the idea of third party intervention. But they accepted it and gradually started working with us.'

Moreover, it was clear to Solheim that the Indians felt that 'this was their part of the world, that they were the big power here. ... they were afraid that if a third party succeeded in Sri Lanka then the next thing to come up would be the issue of Kashmir.' And capping it all, 'They thought we were amateurs [who did] not really understand the place ... Norway was small, had no colonial past, so we wouldn't be able to change anything.' This first visit underscored the fact that, as Solheim puts it, 'there was no way we could achieve anything without India ... In a final peace agreement India— or someone India trusted—would have to be some sort of guarantor.'

Further talks

A week after their return to Norway in mid-February 2000 Vollebaek and Solheim were back in London for further discussions with Balasingham. The Norwegian team reported on their recent visit to Colombo, but overall nothing substantial appears to have emerged from the meeting. 'He said he needed to discuss matters with Prabhakaran: everything was about whether he could bring Prabhakaran with him or not,' Solheim reports. 'But he was also clear that no ceasefire meant no talks, and that the LTTE also wanted initial confidence-building measures.'

By contrast, says Solheim, the government 'wanted to move straight to the core issues, because they were afraid of being dragged into drawn-out processes where they would sooner or later be attacked by the opposition.' And yet, for Solheim the key difficulty at this stage was what he calls 'foot-dragging on the government's side over petty issues'. In their discussions about easing the economic embargo on Jaffna and the Vanni, for example, Kadirgamar 'emphasised that a number of products could have a double use: cement could be used for buildings, military installations and even trenches; fertilizers could also be used for bombs, and so on.' As Solheim observes: 'Kadirgamar was for sure right in a formal sense. But why would a movement with access to highly advanced bombs and military technology focus in on fertilizer?'

As a result of this approach, Solheim suggests, 'nothing really substantial happened before Ranil [Wickremasinghe] came into office. In the end, the government did accept more goods being allowed [into the Vanni]. But to me this was a huge weakness of Kadirgamar's—his capacity for letting such petty issues become major obstacles ... His approach added to the [prevailing] lack of confidence.'

Norwegian Facilitation: the early road map

From interviews with Solheim it is apparent that from an early stage of the engagement in Sri Lanka, the Norwegians were operating on the basis of a basic 'road map'. Solheim outlines it as follows: 'Some parameters were absolutely clear. There would be no new separate [Tamil] state, because that could come only from an LTTE military victory. There was [no way that] Sri Lanka would accept that, nor would India allow a new state in its hemisphere.'

At the same time, 'a unitary state run from Colombo was also out of the question. So as a compromise [we felt that] there had to be some sort of federation, or confederation, or self-rule—whatever term you want to use.' At this stage the Norwegians 'did not touch on the complexities. There were so many layers—the Muslim factor, dispersed Tamil populations, the Sinhalese living [in majority Tamil regions], federal or confederal units, the land problem, the police: all these issues came up.'

Overall the Norwegians were thinking in terms 'some sort of a federal solution where as a starting point, powers would be devolved to a Tamil entity in the North. There would be some [form of] Tamil representation at the centre: a two-chamber system—something like that.' And when describing the parameters of Norwegian involvement, Solheim notes that 'facilitator was the term used, though both parties undoubtedly demanded that we should be negotiators in all but name'.

A change of government

As they were embarking upon the first steps of the negotiation process in Sri Lanka, the Norwegians had a major political distraction of their own to attend to—the collapse of the Christian Democrat-led minority government and the formation of a new minority Labour coalition administration.

The new Foreign Minister Thorbjørn Jagland began work by emphasising Norway's continuing commitment to advancing the Sri Lankan peace process. With the change of government, Wegger Strømmen was replaced as deputy foreign minister—the minister immediately responsible for the Sri Lanka 'file'—by Raymond Johansen, an experienced politician and friend of Solheim. According to Johansen the outgoing Strømmen handed the Sri

Lanka file to Johansen and informed him that Solheim was 'the key figure'. Thus his first item of business, Johansen recalls, was to 'get Erik out of parliament and into the foreign ministry. He had already moved to the foreign service as a civil servant. This was tricky: no one had ever made a similar move from parliament to the foreign service before.' Tricky or not, Solheim was duly given leave from parliament and formally appointed as the government's special adviser on Sri Lanka.

He immediately began another round of intensive consultations: on 17–18 March he and Westborg met Balsingham in London, and the following week the pair were in Colombo for discussions with Kumaratunga. Internal reports indicate a number of important developments. First, discussions of the modalities for beginning peace talks were advancing steadily. The government side, for example, had already provided a list of proposed negotiators, and through the Norwegians had asked the LTTE to do the same. On the LTTE side, Balasingham had asked the Norwegians to inform the government that he was in good health and fully prepared both for 'substantial discussions' and a suggested parallel review of modalities for [military] de-escalation.

Second, Solheim lodged a request with Kumaratunga for the government to facilitate a meeting with Prabhakaran. In reply the president affirmed that the army would provide helicopter transport up to the Vanni—a clear sign, in the Norwegians' view, that she was 'eager to make the meeting happen'.

Soon after this Norway faced the first public test of its role in Sri Lanka. Doubtless roused by Sri Lankan media reports of the recent meetings in London and Colombo, on 11 April an estimated 300–400 protestors gathered outside the Norwegian Embassy in Colombo to express their opposition to talks between the government and the LTTE, and to Norway's attempts to facilitate such a process. In a sign of things to come, the protest, organised by the 'National Movement Against Terrorism', attracted a sizeable number of Buddhist monks to its ranks.

LTTE offensive

In the culmination of the 'Unceasing Waves III' offensive,[5] on 22 April the LTTE overran the Army military bases at Yakachchi and Elephant Pass, which jointly guarded the narrow stretch of land joining the Jaffna peninsula to the Vanni mainland.[6] The government forces made a hasty retreat towards Jaffna, sustaining serious losses as they withdrew. For the first time in nearly twenty years the strategically located Elephant Pass base, sur-

rounded by what had effectively been a no-man's land ever since government forces seized the area in 1983, was now under LTTE control.
Commenting on the Tigers' victory, a seasoned Colombo journalist went
so far as to suggest that the battle for Elephant Pass had 'transformed the
LTTE from a guerrilla force to a conventional fighting force capable of
conducting operations on multiple fronts'.[7]

In response the SLA launched a desperate—and ultimately unsuccessful—attempt to take back the southern part of the Jaffna Peninsula, again
suffering significant losses. The LTTE continued to press towards Jaffna,
and as heavily armed combat forces made their way into the suburbs, many
feared it was simply a matter of time before the town centre fell to the
LTTE. But whatever advantages they possessed over government forces at
this point, the estimated 7,000-strong Tiger army was massively outnum-
bered by the 40,000 SLA troops garrisoned in Jaffna town, and by mid-June
the SLA had succeeded in pushing LTTE forces some way back southwards
along the Jaffna peninsula.[8] With the immediate military threat to its position seemingly removed, over the following weeks the focus of government
attention shifted away from emergency plans to evacuate forces stationed
inside Jaffna, towards domestic political concerns.

Norwegian perspectives

During this period Erik Solheim and his Norwegian colleagues were both
closely following developments in the Jaffna peninsula and actively consulting with the parties and other key actors. On 1 May 2000, Westborg met
President Kumaratunga in Colombo and the following day Solheim visited
Balasingham in London.[9] A day later Solheim met US Under Secretary for
Political Affairs Thomas Pickering and briefed him on recent developments
in Sri Lanka as well as the Norwegian peace efforts.[10] Finally, the following
week (11 May) Solheim and Westborg were in Delhi again.[11]

Commenting on this period, however, Solheim's focus is very much on
events in the Jaffna peninsula. '2000–1 was a very successful period for the
LTTE. Later it became common wisdom in some quarters that the LTTE
had used [the peace process] to arm themselves and weaken the government'—a view that he believes was 'absolutely contrary to the truth. The
LTTE was at the peak of its power in 2000–1—exactly the point at which it
first declared a ceasefire.'

'Elephant Pass was captured and Jaffna was isolated after a civilian aircraft
was shot down by the LTTE. It gave them enormous confidence,' he states.

On a more sombre note, Solheim recalls: 'The LTTE did not take prisoners. Balasingham was open about this because [he argued that] they had no means to take care of them. They were simply killed off.' But despite the LTTE's known ruthlessness with regard to prisoners, Solheim maintains:

> no one seriously thought that 40,000 soldiers would be killed ... From the town outskirts the LTTE issued a demand that '[the SLA] should leave all their military equipment behind, and ships could pick up the soldiers and take them to Colombo ... The Indians were ready to rescue the soldiers by ship, but wanted no part in the fighting. We worked closely with Delhi on this offer. The LTTE were ready to let the soldiers go, but insisted they should leave their equipment.

However, the discussion lost its urgency once government forces were able to stabilise the military situation and relieve the immediate threat to the air base. Pakistan's provision of military supplies—mainly rocket launchers—played a part in this, while India looked the other way as it happened.

Impact of the offensive

With military operations in the North at the forefront of national and international attention, Norwegian efforts to kick-start a new peace process were effectively put on hold. The government's focus was now squarely on military matters. In particular, it embarked on a major arms purchasing spree aimed at providing an immediate boost to the SLA's capacity to counter LTTE operations on the Jaffna peninsula.[12] As India was refusing to sell arms to the Sri Lankans, the government turned to more willing sellers—China, Pakistan and Israel in particular.[13] Commenting on India's refusal to supply arms, Solheim notes that the Norwegians had 'long discussions' during which the Indians were clear that they would not provide Colombo with military assistance.[14] 'They said they had no sympathy with the Tigers whatsoever. But they were tired of the government too: India did not want to be dragged in [to Sri Lanka] once again.'

The impact of this influx of weapons was immediate and significant. From early June, the SLA had a clear edge over the LTTE, and in the face of sustained SLA pressure the LTTE forces began a gradual but inexorable retreat southwards. In his annual Heroes Day speech on 27 November,[15] Prabhakaran implicitly acknowledged the role of the government's new weaponry in forcing the LTTE to abandon the assault on Jaffna.[16]

The Jaffna offensive had an effect on Sri Lanka's international focus too. As had been the case in 1987, when faced with military threat, Sri Lanka

turned to India. In addition to the request for military assistance and discussion of military evacuation plans for Jaffna, during a visit to Colombo
in May 2000 Foreign Minister Jaswant Singh mooted the possibility of
Indian mediation, 'if invited' to do so. Though nothing ultimately came of
this idea, it none the less served to underscore the fact that for the time
being at least, the Norwegian facilitation initiative was not at the forefront
of Sri Lankan attention.

With India now seemingly in the driving seat, the Norwegians' initial
investment in building relationships with key people in Delhi came to the
fore. As Solheim describes it, 'we got oral updates from [the] Indians about
their thinking. During the first phase [that is, up until 2005] there was a BJP
coalition government. The key person was the head of the intelligence
service.[17] I would go to Delhi and meet him every time I went to Sri Lanka.
We would talk about the latest developments ... We were also in close
contact with the Indian ambassador in Colombo, [first] Nirupam Sen and
[later] Gopalkrishna Gandhi.'

However, as Solheim notes, despite being evidently well informed about
developments, 'even they were not able to penetrate the top LTTE leadership. It's hard to say why', he notes, before adding that it should be recalled
that in 1994 'Mathaya[18] was accused by Prabhakaran of being an Indian
agent and liquidated.'[19]

The devolution debate

With the immediate military threat to Jaffna somewhat reduced, Kumaratunga's government turned its attention to the parliamentary elections due
to be held that autumn. In particular, what had long been a central element
of Kumaratunga's strategy for ending the conflict—a raft of constitutional
reforms popularly known as the 'devolution package'[20]—now came to the
fore. Initially, Kumaratunga's aim was to try and get the reforms through
parliament before it was dissolved in late August 2000.

Securing the necessary two-thirds parliamentary majority required
Kumaratunga to reach out to her political opponents, notably opposition
leader Ranil Wickremasinghe. Accordingly, in an unprecedented effort to
build cross-party consensus, in particular between the two main Sinhala-
dominated parties, during the course of June 2000 Kumaratunga's ruling
People's Alliance (PA) initiated an intensive series of consultations with
the UNP.[21]

The consultations focused on three aspects of the devolution package: the
unit of devolution; the structure of the state; and control of land. On the

first aspect, it was agreed that for a specified period an Interim Council would be established in the Northeast, after which a referendum on a merger of the two provinces would be held. If it proved impossible to hold the referendum at that point, the North and East would automatically become two provinces, a provision viewed as a safeguard for the minority Muslim and Sinhalese populations in the East, both of which were much more comfortable with the idea of a separate province. On the nature of the state, a compromise was hammered out, stressing the preservation of Sri Lanka's territorial integrity while also promoting federalism. On land issues, too, a compromise that acknowledged the state's control over land while not overemphasising its 'ownership' was agreed.

An overall PA-UNP agreement on the devolution package was reached on 30 June, a development widely hailed as a historic 'first' in post-independence politics. Problems with the deal, however, were already beginning to emerge. For example, a meeting between the Tamil political parties represented in parliament,[22] convened by Kumaratunga herself, rejected the idea of a referendum on the status of the two provinces on the grounds that the Northeast constituted the Tamil homeland and that the merger of the North and East was thus non-negotiable. Concerning the structure of the state, the Tamil parties argued for a return to Kumaratunga's earlier,[23] more radical proposal to redefine Sri Lanka constitutionally as a 'union of the regions'. Finally, they proposed that control of state land should be vested firmly with the regions, chiefly as a means of protecting the Tamil homeland from what was seen as creeping Sinhalese colonisation.

Furthermore, the fragile edifice of bipartisan consensus now began to crumble. In particular, disagreement concerning the form in which the proposals were to be presented to parliament came to the fore. While Kumaratunga aimed to transform the proposals directly into a new Constitution, Wickremasinghe argued they should go forward in the form of a white paper that would form the basis for new negotiations with the LTTE.

In addition, the UNP objected to a key transitional provision due to be included in the bill, which Kumaratunga announced it was her intention to take to parliament before the impending pre-electoral recession. While the new constitution proposed a move to a prime ministerial governance system, under transitional provisions the presidency would continue its functions for the full duration of the present incumbent's term of office: not only that, it would also take over all the powers assigned to the prime minister under the new constitution. In this proposal, many felt it was hard not to see an attempt by Kumaratunga to extend her own political powers.

Political tensions heightened further with the intervention of senior Buddhist clergy and a number of hard-line religious-nationalist groups. The former argued publicly that the Maha Sangha—the Buddhist clergy—had not been consulted and accordingly wrote to all Buddhist MPs asking them not to support the proposals in parliament. The latter took to the streets of Colombo in a series of vocal protests against what they viewed as a sinister attempt to divide the country.

Undeterred, Kumaratunga pressed on, and on 3 August tabled her 'Draft Bill to Repeal and Replace The Constitution of the Democratic Socialist Republic of Sri Lanka',[24] just three weeks before parliament was due to be dissolved. After a day of fierce debate, to which the opposition UNP's most incendiary contribution was for its leader Ranil Wickremasinghe to set alight a copy of the draft constitution in the main parliamentary chamber,[25] the government announced that it had decided not to put the bill to a vote. Suggestions from senior government figures that the vote was simply being postponed did little to disguise what many saw as a full-scale retreat.

Sri Lankan perspectives on devolution

Jayanpathy Wickremaratne, current advisor to the Ministry of Constitutional Affairs[26]

> I came into the process in October 1996, during talks between the government and Tamil parties, and the Tamils pushed for a 'union of regions'. In the final 2000 constitutional draft there is no description of the state as 'unitary' or 'federal'. A 'union of regions' was dropped because it was so divisive.
>
> In 1999 we had a strategy workshop, and thought we should propose something different: 'Sri Lanka shall be one' (this taken from South Africa). An independent state consisting of institutions of the centre and the regions, who shall exercise power in accordance with the constitution. Which makes it clear that it is a federal state, but without the label.
>
> If Gamini[27] [had been leader of the UNP], things would have been different. Chandrika had won with the support of Tamils and Muslims, and any right-thinking person would have believed that she had the potential to bring peace. Gamini proposed the same thing. He wouldn't have done what Ranil [Wickremasinghe] did, dragging the process out. For three years, not a single written proposal was put forward by Ranil. Out of frustration we put forward our own. After that he said that he needed three months to respond. And still he wouldn't take a position on the nature of the state. That was Ranil all over—even now he makes the same mistake, doesn't respond to people, doesn't interact.

Ranil Wickremasinghe, ex-prime minister (2002–4).[28]

> We decided that there [should] be a devolution package, but it had to be broad-based, accepted by all. And there was some aspects of [the package] which were not acceptable to us. Sri Lanka being called a 'union of regions', some things which were going even further down [that] road, and trying to use the 'Indian model', on which there would be questions in Sri Lanka. Finally on [the issue of the] executive presidency, where [the government] went back on the agreement reached with us.

Tyrone Ferdinands, peace activist. The key thing was that Chandrika kept the LTTE out of it ... the problem was that all Sri Lankan peace processes were bilateral, between two parties, and whoever facilitated or negotiated or supported these processes refused to see the value of multi-party inclusivity. ... I couldn't see how devolution could have been the driver of change: it could have been a component if Chandrika had managed to push it through and then she had persisted. Balasingham himself said that her 1995 devolution proposals were actually the best, although at the time [the LTTE] rejected them. Somehow the whole devolution approach itself was problematic. This was a political problem no doubt, but to have [it as] the central focus was not appropriate.

> Paikiasothy Saravanamuttu, Director, Centre for Policy Alternatives. Ultimately the devolution package—in all its variants—was doomed to failure for one basic reason: the Sinhalese attachment to the notion of a unitary state was, and is, simply too strong. Despite Kumaratunga's best efforts to educate the ordinary population in the advantages of devolution, of a devolved political order, the attachment [to a unitary state] was just too strong. This—not Wickremasinghe's and UNP opposition—is fundamentally the reason that it failed.

Devolution's failure: a Norwegian analysis

In the view of the Norwegians, the reform package was bound to fail partly because, as Solheim puts it, it was 'highly unlikely that the Tigers would involve themselves in a process to which they were not a party.' He suggests, however, that 'the main hindrance was the animosity between the two main political parties.' Wickremasinghe, he argues, would 'rationalise' his knee-jerk political antagonism, claiming the devolution package 'would not bring peace anyhow, because the Tamils would not accept it. It gave Ranil an excuse not to work on a bipartisan basis: but an excuse that was basically correct.' In that sense at least, he notes, 'Ranil had a much more realistic perspective that the Tigers had to be accepted as a partner.'

Jon Westborg offers the following analysis of the government's decision to withdraw the bill: 'I think Chandrika's devolution package was dropped mainly because she thought [the proposals] meant she wouldn't be able to keep power. She needed the presidency to keep power. So she manipulated and changed the proposals in such a way that they no longer included the proviso that she would step down immediately.'[29]

Solheim on Ranil Wickremasinghe

Erik Solheim had first met Wickremasinghe in 1999, during a visit to Sri Lanka with the leader of the Norwegian Parliament's Foreign Affairs Committee. Solheim describes this initial encounter:

> It felt as if [Ranil] was not really interested in us boring Norwegians, who in any case didn't understand anything. With us it was like this was one of the meetings he had to attend ... Compare this to the charisma of Chandrika, who encompasses every human feeling from the best to the worst—nice, hospitable, warm, and sometimes devious as well.

> Later we also came to see Ranil's greatness. He has a strong sense of Sri Lanka's place in history, a deep insight [into the situation in the country]. He wants to uplift his nation economically and socially, to make it the Singapore or Korea of South Asia.

> [Our visit] was before Chandrika made the announcement of Norway as a peace facilitator ... Later, of course, Ranil was always interested [in us], he had a changed approach. But it's a weakness for a politician not to seem interested. Before he could hardly stay awake; later he was deeply interested. Ranil couldn't play that game of politics where you give people the impression that you are interested in everybody.

Reviewing the years 2000–1, when Wickremasinghe remained in opposition, Solheim says, 'These were early days. Basically we wanted Ranil to be informed about what was happening. We held the view that Norway should be bipartisan. Chandrika didn't like it but didn't say absolutely no—in fact she didn't want us to inform anyone in her own party either,' he adds. And when 'Ranil started running the show', in 2002, moreover, the Norwegians also 'kept Chandrika informed ... We would by and large speak favourably about Chandrika in the presence of Ranil and vice versa. And we were careful not to go behind the back of either.'

Parliamentary elections

With the conflict in the North seemingly reaching a stalemate, the next major development in the aftermath of the devolution package furore was the parliamentary elections of 10 October 2000. In the event, the ruling PA coalition triumphed, albeit with a slightly reduced slice of the popular vote (45.1 per cent), six seats short of the number required to avoid a hung parliament—not the most auspicious outcome. The emergence of the nationalist JVP as a parliamentary force (ten seats on 6 per cent of the vote) was also significant. Ominously, soon after her victory Kumaratunga proceeded to state that the government would prosecute the war against the LTTE with renewed vigour, while Kadirgamar suggested the Norwegian peace facilitation initiative had now been put on hold.[30]

First meeting with Prabhakaran

Undeterred by the discouraging noises emerging from Colombo, the Norwegian team were busily engaged in setting up their first encounter with LTTE leader Velupillai Prabhakaran. After consultations with all concerned, the meeting was set for 1 November at an undisclosed location in the Vanni. Solheim explains: 'The meeting was suggested and encouraged by Balasingham. Chandrika was OK with it and kept it a secret. Kadirgamar, of course, knew all about it.'

On the morning of 1 November, the Norwegian delegation—Solheim, Westborg and Kjersti Tromsdal—left Colombo in an Air Force helicopter. According to Westborg, 'We landed west of Vavuniya and drove [in an embassy car] to Madhu Church', where they were met by LTTE cadres, among them the later head of the LTTE peace secretariat, Pulidevan. 'Then we drove up along the coast and ended up in this place—nice plants, Indian Army style.[31] [There are] no rocks in that part of the country so it was brick built. It had a big TV screen, satellite TV. I was not so surprised that they had a setup like that', he adds. 'They wanted to show that they were not some ordinary outfit, that this was a serious government-in-waiting sort of thing.'

Having no information as to when and where the meeting with Prabhakaran would happen, the Norwegians sat tight and waited—as it turned out, until the following day. Solheim picks up the story: 'He suddenly arrived by car with a huge security detail. The LTTE was eager to treat us in a dignified manner', he notes, 'but for Prabhakaran security was paramount, the rest was secondary.'

Solheim describes the initial interaction as 'friendly, business-like'. At the same time, he indicates that Prabhakaran 'did not give out the impression of a very military person—more like a teacher'. Overall, says Solheim, Prabhakaran 'simply did not come across as particularly great. There was not really a foreigner who met him who was really impressed. He was not an intellectual type of man, he was much more interested in practical matters.'

Discussions were conducted entirely through an interpreter. Solheim records that '[i]t was a small group, the three of us and three of them: there was Prabhakaran, Shankar (who was later killed by the Army)[32] and Tamilselvan[33]... [We] discussed the sanctions, how many bags of cement, rice [were being allowed] into LTTE areas. The meeting lasted three hours to half a day.' Beyond the meeting, however, there was 'no chance to meet [anyone] except for those people surrounding us.' In this sense, he notes, 'I can't say we gained much of an impression of life in the area.'

Westborg's account suggests that discussions were more wide-ranging. 'There was substance to the discussion', he states. '[Prabhakaran] used quite a bit of time trying to get an impression of why the rest of the world would not acknowledge the Tamil right to self-determination. And basically, why couldn't they accept [Tamil] independence? He got a straightforward answer: nobody wants that to happen. India doesn't want it—nobody wants it. The [next] question was [what about] Eritrea? And we told him that Eritrea was an independent country that should have had its freedom long ago. So, they got clear answers. Then of course we also discussed practical issues such as confidence-building measures (CBMs).'[34]

In contrast to Solheim, Westborg appears to have been impressed by the LTTE leader and his subordinates. 'They argued their case', he says, 'but it was not the type of argument that you could have with Balasingham ... They were not insistent, because they recognised that our role was not to convince the other party to change their stand completely.'

Interestingly, Balasingham—who was not present—suggests that the focus of Prabhakaran's remarks was on the modalities for any future negotiations with the government. According to Balasingham, the LTTE leader underscored the fact that from the Tigers' perspective, 'a process of de-escalation and normalisation was a necessary prerequisite for talks'. Moreover, de-escalation was defined as meaning 'the total cessation of armed hostilities, the removal of the economic embargo and the restoration of conditions of normalcy in the Tamil homeland'.[35]

The last word on the meeting, however, goes to Westborg.

> What kind of man is Prabhakaran? That's the kind of question the Sinhalese asked me, and a lot of people still ask me even today. My reaction was that I can't really say what kind of a man he was. But I can tell you what he decided to try and project to me—a listening person responding calmly through an interpreter.

Return to Colombo

On returning to Colombo, Solheim held a press conference at which he described the encounter with Prabhakaran as 'serious, frank, open and useful'—without revealing any of the substance of the discussions.[36] Solheim's recollections of this episode are instructive. '[The] prime minister was furious that we had gone to Vanni.[37] He went ballistic in the media, understandably so given that he had not been informed. Chandrika never felt it necessary to inform even the prime minister.' Of the press conference, he recalls that there was 'enormous curiosity about Prabhakaran. How could we be certain that it was him and no one else? ... There was such mystery surrounding Prabhakaran: he had not been in the public gaze for more than ten years.' As they soon discovered, Kumaratunga herself was very curious about Prabhakaran. 'Even Chandrika was eager for confirmation that we had not met his doppelganger.'

Subsequent debriefings and exchanges with government officials were of course more focused on the issues that needed to be addressed if a peace process were to recommence. Solheim's assessment is that the government side now 'wanted to move towards a peace process. Recognising that they had lost a significant number of soldiers, but also that the LTTE were more serious than in the past—while also keeping their guard very, very high at the same time.' As Solheim puts it, 'Besides being fooled militarily [the government] were also afraid of being fooled in the fight for the votes of the Sinhalese.'

As Solheim also notes, underlying everything was the fundamental question of 'whether Prabhakaran would accept anything other than a separate state. And whether his promises could be believed. Trust was the key word here.' All of which, Solheim suggests, initially put the Norwegians in a tight spot. 'Later on we could argue that technically Prabhakaran had kept his word. But in those early days this wasn't possible. Our argument to Colombo was, why are you so involved in petty issues like cement sanctions?' As they pointed out to the government, 'if the LTTE needed weapons they would get them from anywhere.'

On the other side, de-proscription was a high priority issue for the LTTE, but Kumaratunga refused to countenance such a move. This, as Solheim acknowledges, was a 'major hurdle, because the LTTE demanded that the two sides should be seen as equal, and how could they be equal when the LTTE was proscribed?' In fact, in his view this could be seen as 'the key [issue] for the LTTE: it was all about pride and status.' On a related note, there was 'the need the LTTE felt to gain international support, because they knew they were up against a much stronger adversary. Proscription may also have made the collection of money, procurement of weapons more difficult,' Solheim contends—even though it 'for sure didn't stop it.'

Solheim summarised the difficulties of moving forward with a peace process as follows: 'The government wanted to discuss the "core issues", the settlement of the Tamil problem. Everyone agreed that the core issues were the core issues. It was just that the LTTE wanted confidence-building measures first.' On this issue, however, it was evident that the government was 'afraid of being dragged into a process that would give the LTTE recognition and material benefits, without them in the end being ready for a political settlement.'

The Memorandum of Understanding

The meetings with the two sides spurred the Norwegians to table a written proposal with the stated objective of easing the humanitarian situation, in particular in the North, and contributing to 'an atmosphere conducive to negotiations'.[38] In mid-November 2000 Oslo produced a draft 'Memorandum of Understanding on Humanitarian Measures'.[39] The MoU focused primarily on the kind of confidence-building measures sought by the LTTE, in particular facilitating what it called the 'unimpeded flow of non-military goods to the civilian population in the Vanni'.[40]

The MoU also tabled detailed proposals for how the sale and transport of two of the items of greatest concern to the government side—fuel and cement—would be regulated. Finally it proposed the establishment of what was called a 'Humanitarian Monitoring Group' (HMG), whose mandate would be to 'ensure the implementation by Parties of their obligations under this Agreement.'[41]

In many respects the MoU's proposal for a monitoring structure, as well as the language used to outline its role and function, mirrors the 'Monitoring Committees' proposal tabled by President Kumaratunga in 1994–5. Moreover, the MoU's detailed proposals for ensuring the flow of 'non-military goods' into the Vanni provided the basis on which the 2002 Ceasefire Agreement's even more detailed provisions for the movement of goods into LTTE-controlled territory were framed. However, as Solheim points out, 'critics who say that the Ceasefire Agreement came as a complete surprise in 2002 may be right in a sense, because the whole MoU process was basically kept exclusively between Chandrika and Kadirgamar on the Sri Lankan side and us Norwegians.'

In a belated response to the Norwegians' meeting with Prabhakaran, on 17 November a crowd gathered outside the Norwegian Embassy in Colombo to express their opposition to this development. A crude effigy of Erik Solheim was ceremonially burned—the first, but certainly not the last time he was to be attacked in such a way.

More significantly, on 27 November Prabhakaran gave his annual Heroes Day speech. After giving a positive evaluation of the MoU proposal, to which he said the LTTE would respond positively 'if the government takes the initiative', Prabhakaran also announced that the LTTE was prepared for 'unconditional peace talks'. Though seemingly marking a step forward, the speech provoked mixed reactions. The international community's response was largely positive, with US Assistant Secretary of State for South Asia Karl Inderfurth stating that the speech offered 'hopeful signs' that the LTTE were 'willing to forgo the idea of an independent Eelam.'[42] The response in Colombo, however, was altogether more guarded.

As if to demonstrate his sincerity, on 21 December Prabhakaran declared a unilateral one-month ceasefire, effective from 24 December, describing the move as a 'genuine expression of goodwill indicating our sincere desire for peace and a negotiated peaceful settlement'. Reaction was again mixed, with some suggesting that it was little more than an attempt by the LTTE to force the government to accept its stated preconditions for talks—de-escalation of the war and a lifting of the economic embargo on the North.[43]

This at least is how Kadirgamar appears to have interpreted the ceasefire declaration. In response, he emphasised that the government would consider the LTTE's conditions only after negotiations on the 'core issues' had begun and were progressing satisfactorily. From the government's perspective, the 'core issues' were: stopping the war; ending terrorist attacks; a negotiated settlement of the problems afflicting the Tamil people; devolution of power; and speedy resolution of the plight of the country's internally displaced people (IDPs).[44]

The gulf between the two sides' positions—one that was to manifest itself on numerous subsequent occasions—was stark. On one side, the Tigers' preconditions—a ceasefire, the LTTE's de-proscription and lifting the economic embargo on the North prior to the opening of talks—were not accepted by the government. On the other, the government's assertion that the implementation of these measures was dependent on the progress of talks on a political settlement was rejected by the Tigers. The LTTE's ceasefire offer was thus dismissed by the government, and the country entered the new year in a state of limbo.

3

ELECTIONS AND CEASEFIRES

Seemingly unperturbed by the Sri Lankan government's rejection of the unilateral ceasefire it had declared just before Christmas 2000,[1] in late January 2001 the LTTE announced that it was extending the ceasefire by a further month. It went on to do so on two further occasions—each time without a response from the government—until 24 April, when the unilateral truce was finally called off. Even if the LTTE initiative failed to solicit a positive reaction from the government, it did appear to achieve two other important goals: it helped to bolster the LTTE's image as a responsible, peace-orientated actor in the Sri Lankan conflict; and it provided the backdrop for Anton Balasingham's efforts to persuade the UK not to proscribe the LTTE under domestic anti-terrorism legislation. In the event, London put off a final decision on the issue, an outcome viewed as a victory of sorts by the Tigers.

On the government's side, the early months of 2001 saw renewed efforts to move forward with negotiations. An official visit to India by President Kumaratunga and Foreign Minister Kadirgamar in late February, during which the state of the peace process as well as the constitutional reform package were the main issues, was described as a potential 'prelude to peace talks'.[2] In early April, moreover, Kadirgamar made a statement to the Sri Lankan parliament in which he noted that with the help of Norwegian facilitation there had been 'very considerable progress' towards the objective of 'the LTTE coming to the negotiating table', and informed the House that he expected to be able to announce the dates and venue of talks by the end of the month.

The LTTE statement calling off the ceasefire from midnight on 24 April, however, makes it seem as though the two sides were at times operating in parallel worlds. The decision to return to armed hostilities was described as a 'painful' one, compelled by the government's 'hard-line, intransigent attitude', and in particular by what is referred to as the 'serious military setbacks' the LTTE had suffered during the previous four months.[3]

From the facilitators' perspective, the LTTE's ceasefire initiative had presented some difficulties. 'We preferred mutually agreed ceasefires,' says Erik Solheim. 'We thought such unilateral initiatives were not always help-ful because they created suspicion. Suspicion apart, the government would also not provide a propaganda victory for the LTTE by responding to a Tiger initiative.' Despite this, Solheim notes that the Norwegians 'were asking them [the government] to reciprocate. They said it could be a public ploy and not serious but gradually admitted [there had been] a substantial reduction in the fighting. And at the end, Chandrika acknowledged that the LTTE had done it in a serious fashion.'

Hostilities resumed soon thereafter. In an offensive dubbed Operation Agni Khiela 1 (Fire Flame 1), launched only hours after the LTTE ceasefire expired, two divisions of SLA troops began a major assault from the defen-sive lines recently established north of Elephant Pass.[4] After making sub-stantial advances towards LTTE fortifications, SLA forces encountered stiff resistance. The Tiger counterattack is described by Anton Balasingham: 'The invading Sri Lankan troops marched straight into the Tiger trap. Without knowing the perils that lay ahead, they were jubilant at having captured 8 km^2 of territory within three hours, with little resistance. Then suddenly the LTTE combat units struck back in fury with formidable fire-power ...The formation broke and fled into the minefields.[5] It was a night-mare for hundreds of Sri Lankan troops caught in these killing fields.'[6]

Alarmed by the extent of their losses and realising that it had encoun-tered seemingly insurmountable obstacles to further progress, on 28 April the SLA announced that military operations on the Jaffna peninsula were being 'suspended'. While the exact casualty figures on both sides are dis-puted, at the SLA's own admission around 250 soldiers were killed during the offensive and more than 1,100 injured. After stumbling into LTTE mine-fields, a large number needed emergency amputations, while others filled most of the hospital beds in Jaffna, Colombo and regional hospitals in the aftermath of the fighting.[7]

Recalling what at the time must have seemed to be a serious setback for Norwegian peace efforts, Solheim states that the campaign was a 'military disaster' for the government. He admits, too, that the facilitators were aggrieved, 'because Chandrika had made a clear promise to me that as long as the LTTE had declared a ceasefire and did not resume fighting, the government would not launch any offensives.' This, he says, was one of the 'very few times during the peace process that I felt personally betrayed'. Later on, he recalls, 'Chandrika blamed it on the Generals, saying they had pushed [the operation] against her will.' But 'we didn't believe this in the formal sense. No General would dare to start a major operation without the president accepting it.'

By way of explanation for her actions, Solheim suggests that Kumaratunga may have calculated that if she could 'push the LTTE back it would weaken them in the peace process. And this could be a huge benefit [to her] in the coming elections—and a parliamentary election was very close at that point.' Overall, however, he concludes, 'we considered [her] behaviour to be the exception rather than the rule. Normally speaking, she could be trusted.'

Ceasefire in focus

With the military option seemingly closed off for the moment, the focus swung back towards negotiation. During the course of the following month, Solheim made visits to Sri Lanka and London. In London he conferred with Balasingham, and in Colombo there were lengthy meetings with Kumaratunga and Kadirgamar, the second (18 May) preceded by a visit to LTTE-held territory for a meeting with Tamilselvan rather than Prabhakaran—a development that met with protests from Solheim and a request that the LTTE not repeat the perceived slight.[8]

Ominously, the meeting with Tamilselvan was preceded by an apparent attempt on his life. On the way to Malavi, the vehicle in which Tamilselvan usually travelled was ripped apart by a landmine. Several LTTE cadres died in the blast, but Tamilselvan himself was not on board that day. While the government vehemently denied responsibility for the attack, the LTTE pointed the finger at an SLA 'deep penetration unit' they claimed was active in the region.[9] Wherever responsibility for the attack lay, it can only have hindered Norwegian efforts to bring the two sides closer. Solheim returned from the meeting with Tamilselvan with the news that the LTTE were continuing to insist on de-proscription as a precondition for talking to the government. The gap between the LTTE and the government remained unbridged—and was perhaps, some felt, unbridgeable.[10]

Solheim under fire

Towards the end of May, Solheim travelled to the USA to brief Richard Armitage, Deputy Secretary of State in the recently formed Bush Administration, on current developments in Sri Lanka. In the course of the visit, Solheim also took the opportunity to brief members of Congress. For Solheim this was a move that had some unexpected—and unpleasant—consequences.[11] At the beginning of June 2001, Norwegian Foreign Minister Thorbjørn Jagland received an urgent request from Kumaratunga to come to Colombo for talks. No explanation was offered, and Jagland and Solheim travelled to Colombo on 7 June with little idea of the meeting's real purpose.

Reports of the ensuing discussion indicate there were three key issues Kumaratunga and Kadirgamar wanted to discuss with Jagland—but not, it turned out with Solheim, who was excluded. First, the thorny issue of LTTE de-proscription; second, the government's assessment of Solheim's performance as a facilitator; and third, as one report put it, a 'request to alter the structure, substance and style of Norway's mediatory efforts'.[12]

After the meeting, the outcome that gained most attention was Jagland's announcement that, at the government's request, Norwegian involvement in Sri Lanka was being 'upgraded'. He also took the unprecedented step of adding a rider to the joint declaration to the effect that he did this in his capacity as leader of the Norwegian Labour party—thereby seemingly bringing domestic party politics into the equation. As a consequence, Jagland stated, from now on he would himself be taking a more direct, hands-on role in the facilitation of peace talks. He concluded by stating that he would soon be seeking to schedule meetings with the LTTE leadership.

Solheim himself picks up the story. The fact that Kumaratunga now began to voice criticism of him at this particular juncture was, as he sees it, 'very much related to the issue of the [Agni Khiela 1] offensive. She may have recognised that she had given a promise and had not lived up to it. Much more important', he continues, 'I went to the US to give the State Department a fair picture of what happened [over the last few months]. I also went to Congress. They never betrayed our trust ... But people reported back to Chandrika on what I had said in Congress—that the offensive was not needed, was a military disaster and that the LTTE had gone for a ceasefire. She was angry.'[13]

Solheim is non-committal as to whether the Sri Lankan government had decided in advance to call for his removal from the facilitation effort, but states that Jagland did not 'consult properly with us beforehand'. In Solheim's view, Jagland's most serious error was that 'he accepted a meeting with the president without bringing Westborg, me or anyone with knowledge of Sri Lankan affairs'. Consequently, he was 'brought into a situation he did not understand—he had not even been to South Asia previously. In the event he spent thirteen hours of his life on the island, believing he had become a world champion in Sri Lankan affairs.'

Solheim and Westborg sat kicking their heels in Colombo waiting to hear the outcome of the meeting. Eventually they got their answer in the form of a brief press statement issued by the Norwegian Embassy in Colombo and—a few hours later—the Sri Lankan Foreign Ministry. Solheim recalls the three-line statement as simply noting that the foreign minister, in his capacity as Labour Party chairman, had met Kumaratunga, and that as a result, a decision had been taken that from now on Norway would be represented 'at a high level'.

'Jagland did not inform either me or Westborg about the content of the talks,' says Solheim. 'He did not dare to do that. I first came to understand what had happened when I landed in Frankfurt on my way home and the US embassy in Oslo called me and asked what the hell had been going on down there.' Even back in Oslo, it seems, there was no discussion of developments in Colombo between the two men.

A dimension that did not previously appear to have figured in Kumaratunga's calculations now began to make itself felt—the LTTE's response to these developments. Before leaving for Colombo, Solheim had called Balasingham in London and told him that he would brief him on his way back to Oslo. As things turned out, Solheim was not in a position to do this. After news of the outcome of Jagland's meeting with Kumaratunga and Kadirgamar reached him, Balasingham reportedly told a Colombo media outlet that the LTTE considered the government's attempt to replace Solheim as chief facilitator to be completely unacceptable—not least because it had been taken without any consultation with them.[14]

According to Solheim, the LTTE responded to the situation by 'simply breaking off conversation with Norway'. They did so for two principal reasons, Solheim suggests: 'First, that they had spent a lot of time talking to me and had trust in me; and second, if the Foreign Minister could make an agreement with the government without even informing or consulting them, what would be next? Can such a third party be trusted in a peace process?'

The immediate impact of the LTTE's displeasure was dramatic. According to Solheim, Balasingham 'simply ended all contact'.[15] 'I sent emails, they did not respond—even to telephone calls—for half a year. This went on until the Labour government left office in Norway in September 2001. Wickremasinghe came to power in December, and at some point the communication reopened'. But Solheim states that the row 'never affected my relationship with Chandrika'. As he puts it, 'She is known for throwing people out if it proves politically useful to do so, then taking them in through the backdoor after some months. We have a close relationship today.'

Parliamentary manoeuvres

In the midst of the uncertainties regarding the Norwegian facilitation effort, in mid-June a new political crisis erupted in Sri Lanka. Following the October 2000 elections, Kumaratunga had cobbled together a government led by her People's Alliance (PA) Party by securing support from two political parties outside her coalition. Of these, the Sri Lanka Muslim Congress (SLMC) led by Rauff Hakeem was particularly successful in extracting maximum compensation for their support—in this case a number of ministerial posts.

The relationship between the two leaders was not easy, however, and on 19 June Kumaratunga sacked him from the cabinet following a public outburst from Hakeem criticising the PA. In solidarity, the other SLMC ministers then tendered their resignations. With the government now reduced to a minority in parliament, the UNP submitted a no-confidence motion: suddenly, it appeared, Kumaratunga had a full-blown crisis on her hands.[16] Her response came a couple of weeks later. In a move designed to scupper a vote on the UNP no-confidence motion, on 10 July Kumaratunga prorogued Parliament and announced that a referendum on a new Constitution would be held in late August.[17] Amid all this political wrangling in the South, peace negotiations were effectively consigned to the back burner. But then, in late July, an event took place that shook the Sri Lankan political establishment to the core.

Airport assault

In the early morning of 24 July—the anniversary of the appalling anti-Tamil riots of 1983—a Black Tiger suicide squad penetrated the high-security complex surrounding Colombo airport and carried out a devastating attack on it and the nearby Sri Lankan Air Force (SLAF) base at Katunayake. The LTTE strike team succeeded in destroying three Sri Lanka Airlines planes, badly damaging two more and knocking out no fewer than eight SLAF aircraft before they were eventually killed by SLA troops.

A third of the country's commercial fleet and a quarter of the SLAF's fighter force had been destroyed, and losses to Sri Lankan Airlines were estimated at USD $350 million. Moreover, the impact of the attack on tourism, foreign investment and the country's overall image was severe—in 2001 Sri Lanka recorded a negative growth rate of 1.4 per cent, the only time this has occurred since the country achieved independence.[18] For the LTTE, the incident was proof of its extended military capabilities and its ability to strike at the heart of the Sri Lankan military machine at will.[19]

Solheim recalls that on the day of the attack he was in Alabama. 'I picked up a local newspaper—*The Tuscaloosa Times* I think. They had a one-page article on the attack. ... It was a huge setback for the government. It made it clear that all the talk of the LTTE being close to defeat was wishful thinking. It led to a complete breakdown of the economy. Most air companies stopped flying to Colombo.' No less significantly, Solheim suggests, 'it had an enormous impact on Tamil morale. They felt uplifted. There has been no parallel to this since.'

Elections in Norway

Parliamentary elections were due in Norway in September 2001, and a month beforehand opinion polls suggested that a change of government was likely. Polling took place on September 10 and 11—a sombre experience, Solheim notes, on account of the news of the Al-Qaeda attacks on New York and Washington.

In the event, while Jens Stoltenberg's Labour Party gained the highest number of seats in parliament—albeit on a radically reduced share of the vote—it was unable to form a government. Instead, a centre-right coalition comprising the Conservatives, Liberals and Christian Democrat parties was formed, with Kjell Magne Bondevik nominated as the new prime minister. From the perspective of the Sri Lanka facilitation effort, the new administration brought two fresh faces to the Norwegian team: Conservative leader Jan Petersen, nominated as foreign minister, and his party colleague Vidar Helgesen, the new deputy foreign minister and the person tasked with direct oversight of the Sri Lanka brief.

With elections soon due in Colombo, Helgesen had a few weeks during which to, as he puts it, 'contemplate the Sri Lanka issue'. Petersen had already made it clear that he would be leaving it to Helgesen to choose the team with which Norway would re-engage with Sri Lanka, and Helgesen soon concluded that 'we needed to continue with Erik involved.[20] Primarily because he had done a good job, particularly on building trust with the LTTE.'

In the meantime, Petersen had met his Sri Lankan counterpart and Kadirgamar had insisted that there should be 'no freelancing' in the facilitation effort in future.[21] The Sri Lankans 'did not insist that Erik should be removed', Helgesen says, but it was clear 'that I would have to spend a lot of time on the issue.'[22] Helgesen also recalls that during this period Petersen met his British counterpart, Jack Straw, in London. The first item on Straw's agenda was an urgent enquiry as to whether Norway would now be 're-engaging with Sri Lanka'.

Sri Lankan elections

While Norway was gearing up for parliamentary elections, President Kumaratunga was fighting a rear-guard action to try and prevent her PA government from falling. The immediate solution to her political problems came in the form of a one-year pact with the Janatha Vimukthi Peramuna (JVP).[23] In exchange for securing backing in parliament from the JVP's ten MPs, Kumaratunga agreed—among other things—to put her plan to bring forward the 'devolution package' on hold.[24]

The pact with the leftist JVP came as a surprise to many, not least because in February 1988 the JVP had ordered the assassination of her husband Vijaya Kumaratunga, a popular film star turned politician. Chandrika herself witnessed the crime. Equally suspicious of the JVP was Mahinda Rajapaksa, a rising SLFP star from the southern coastal town of Hambantota, who knew the party all too well from the terror it had inflicted in and around its southern strongholds during the 1971 and 1987–89 uprisings. The JVP's anti-devolution stance and generally hawkish approach to talks with the LTTE made them far from natural allies of the SLFP.

It proved to be a short-lived alliance. The day before the UNP no-confidence motion was due to be debated in parliament, nine MPs from the ruling PA, including three ex-ministers, announced their resignations and decision to cross the floor to join the UNP. With her slim parliamentary majority effectively removed, Kumaratunga responded by dissolving parliament and calling fresh elections for 5 December.[25]

In Norway, ideological factors lent a particular complexion to the administration's interest in the impending election in Sri Lanka. As Helgesen explains, 'The UNP—a sister party of the Norwegian Conservatives and a member of the global group of conservative parties—was expected to win. So in a sense it looked as if a party that on paper at least had some similarities with the Norwegian Conservatives was going to come into power.' Ahead of the elections, the new government in Oslo announced that Solheim would continue to be the Special Envoy for Sri Lanka.

Throughout the election campaign, the LTTE maintained a noticeably low profile—a striking contrast to the attacks carried out during the elections of the previous year. Commentators speculated the Tigers' quiescence was attributable to the global fallout from the September 11 atrocity, and their desire to avoid the ubiquitous label of 'terrorists'.[26] If the LTTE exercised some self-restraint, the same cannot be said for the main political parties, who launched into what one report described as a 'bloody, no holds barred campaign'. Scores of people were killed during the campaign, including twelve on polling day itself, and vicious slanging-matches between the two major parties were commonplace, with the PA in particular adopting a tough nationalist stance of a kind that made of a mockery of Kumaratunga's past commitment to seeking a negotiated settlement with the LTTE.[27]

Describing the run-up to the December elections, Indian journalist Nirupama Subramanian, then based in Colombo, notes, '[After] the airport attack ... you could see the mood in Sri Lanka change. That really scared people ... the mood became "let's make peace with the LTTE".' In addition she recalls, 'the mood was set against Chandrika. She had been in power since 1994 [and] there's always an anti-incumbency tendency.'

As for Wickremasinghe's campaign, Subramanian argues that he had 'given enough indication before that that if he won the elections, he would stop the war. It just became stop the war—what after, that he never spelt out. And everybody bought into that.' Beyond his general commitment to seeking a negotiated settlement with the LTTE, Wickremasinghe announced his intention to set up an interim administration for the Northeast in which all political parties represented in the region would have a place. It was a clear nod to a key longstanding Tamil demand, and carried with it an implicit incentive for the LTTE to abandon the military path in favour of democratic politics.

As if working in tandem with Wickremasinghe, in his annual Heroes Day speech, delivered on 27 November, Prabhakaran declared that the 'basic aspiration' of the Tamil people was to live in their ancestral homeland with 'peace and dignity'. They wanted 'neither separatism nor terrorism', he maintained, and as such did not constitute a 'threat to the Sinhalese people'. In addition Prabhakaran underlined the necessity of de-proscribing the LTTE and recognising them as the 'legitimate representatives of the Tamil people' before peace negotiations could commence.

As widely anticipated, the elections resulted in a decisive, if not overwhelming, victory for the UNP-led United National Front (UNF) coalition, which gained a little over 45 per cent of the vote and 109 seats in the 225-member parliament. Securing a parliamentary majority required allies, and one emerged in the form of the SLMC, whose five seats took the government over the 50 per cent mark.[28]

Post-election peace moves

Regarding the overall Norwegian response to the elections, Solheim states, 'We were tired of [Kumaratunga], because we felt we had spent an enormous amount of time on petty details that in the end amounted to little. Now there was a new government, with a completely different, forward-leaning approach. Ranil's movement looked very strong. The media portrayed him as the new saviour. But support for the SLFP was still very widespread.' In terms of the LTTE's reaction, he notes that they 'always had more confidence in the UNP. They believed that when they had worked with Hameed and Premadasa in 1989–90, [the UNP] were much more serious than Chandrika. Hameed was their favourite Sri Lankan politician. Balasingham always gave the impression of trusting the UNP more than the SLFP.'

Helgesen recalls that, 'On election night or a day after, Ranil Wickremasinghe met Jon Westborg and formally asked for Norwegian re-engagement. I then travelled to London with Erik, we secured formal acceptance from the LTTE to re-engage, and we started working on a ceasefire.' Reflecting on the same period, Solheim indicates that there had been 'clear signals that Ranil would win. Ranil and the LTTE sent signals to each other through us.[29] Balasingham and Ranil may have met very briefly during the 1990 peace talks.' He also stresses that, once elected, Wickremasinghe wasted no time. 'He made it clear that the time had come for a peace process, and the LTTE reciprocated by announcing a new ceasefire at Christmas.'

Alongside the reciprocal ceasefires announced by both sides, Wickremasinghe lost no time in anchoring the new peace initiative with key partners. With Norway's facilitative role secured, the next country to attend to was India.[30] An invitation from Indian Prime Minister A.B. Vajpayee was quickly secured and a three-day official visit took place over Christmas. Unsurprisingly, negotiations with the LTTE were the centrepiece of discussions, but another critical topic was Norway's facilitation role—an important issue in view of Delhi's long-standing scepticism. In line with his broader emphasis on the revival of the Sri Lankan economy as the basis for sustained peace, Wickremasinghe also stressed that the country could no longer afford the estimated USD $1 billion it spent annually on defence—approximately a quarter of total government spending.[31]

In another important development, Wickremasinghe announced the establishment of a new governmental committee tasked with working out a 'political solution' to the conflict. The committee consisted of just two people, Constitutional Affairs Minister G.L. Peiris and Economic Reforms Minister Milinda Moragoda. While Moragoda was a new face for the Norwegians, Peiris most certainly was not. As Solheim observes, '[Peiris] had been writing the devolution document for Chandrika. He was disappointed with her; but jealousy over Kadirgamar was also a key factor. Although Peiris was number one on the devolution question, over time Chandrika increasingly preferred Kadirgamar's counsel. So Peiris changed parties.'

London, Colombo and Oslo

Describing the developments of early 2002, Solheim says, 'Ranil had responded favourably to the LTTE's ceasefire. He was communicating with Jon [Westborg], I was communicating with Bala, and I went to London every week.' On 4 January Solheim and Helgesen travelled to London for what was Helgesen's first meeting with Balasingham. Helgesen describes his impressions of the LTTE spokesperson. 'We met in his living room. Erik had told me that I should be ready for a long lecture about the historical grievances of the Tamils and their legitimate struggle for freedom. That didn't happen—it was right down to business. Erik was very surprised. Clearly there was an urgency on their part, a wish not to waste time.'

'He was obviously a man with a big ego, but not in a truly negative sense. He did have a very strong position, an ideology ... But I was impressed with the focus on the issues ... I found him quite business-like,' says Helgesen. 'He had experience with the previous government, and it had not been that helpful from his perspective. But we could relate, and he was also happy that Erik would be retained.'

Having clarified the parameters of the LTTE's approach to transforming the current temporary ceasefire into a more permanent arrangement,[32] the

Norwegians flew to Colombo on 10 January 2002—Helgesen's first visit to the country. He recalls that there was 'some discussion' of 'substantive issues [relating to the] ceasefire', and evidence of a 'strong desire to see a ceasefire agreement come into force'. The Norwegians insisted that they 'needed to talk to everyone'. In particular, they asked for a meeting with the president. They got one, and with it a strong indication of the political tensions already afflicting the new government.

Helgesen says he sensed that Kumaratunga was 'testing' him. Initially, like others he encountered in his new ministerial role, she was surprised by his youth—he was just thirty-four. 'Then I got to experience her habit of lecturing,' he continues. 'Essentially about how she had started the peace process and Ranil had sabotaged it, how generous and benevolent she had been to Tamils, and how the Tamil people had appreciated it. She expressed support for the new peace efforts', he says, 'but spent much more time talking about the awful new prime minister.' Recalling this aspect of the discussion, Helgesen states that his strongest impression from the whole trip was the realisation that 'one of the big challenges would be to deal with the absence of bipartisanship. Clearly we had to make a choice as the facilitator.'

There was also a first meeting with the new prime minister. For Helgesen, as for others, first impressions were of a 'weak handshake and some-what unimposing presence'. But also that he appeared 'honest, interested, willing to get down to business'. Moreover, Helgesen came away with the impression that Wickremasinghe's basic agenda was to 'let the Tamils have whatever is needed, short of independence', so that the government could 'get on with the business of making Sri Lanka the new Singapore'. Wickremasinghe's essential agenda was to 'get the economy going—liberalise, privatise'. And in this context, Solheim recalls, the fact that both he and Helgesen were conservatives 'definitely helped'.

Japanese engagement

Solheim explains how Japan came to be involved at an early stage of the peace process.

There was a visit to Norway in late 2001, and the Japanese demanded a role in the peace process ... There was a high-ranking civil servant coming and he said that up to now Japan had been seen as the great wallet of peace processes around the world, treated by the Americans and

Europeans as a nation that should provide money, but get no respect or honour and certainly no influence. So [this had to] stop. The time had come for Japan to be treated as a major partner ... We felt this was fair, so it was the start of the Japanese involvement in the peace process. Later Akashi was appointed the Japanese peace envoy to Sri Lanka, and we engaged with him.[33]

At the same time the Norwegians knew that India was reluctant to involve a major power such as Japan in Sri Lankan affairs. Accordingly, they felt that they should not promise more than they could deliver. 'I made suggestions as to what role Japan could play', Solheim recalls. 'The answer from them was always the same—"Very good, but not good enough".'

The Ceasefire Agreement (CFA)

Over the following weeks the tempo of developments quickened. In early February Helgesen and Solheim returned to Colombo—accompanied as often by Kjersti Tromsdal, and joined on the ground by Jon Westborg—to discuss a 'Memorandum of Understanding' (MoU) for a permanent cease-fire, which had been drafted following the recent round of discussions with both sides. Although the Norwegians designed the document's structure, its content was based on inputs provided by the government and LTTE. Two visits to London followed to iron out the details of the memo-randum with Balasingham.

Two weeks after Solheim's latest trip to London—and just before the temporary ceasefires expired—a fully-fledged Ceasefire Agreement (CFA) between the government and LTTE went public in the form of a signing ceremony held in Vavuniya on 22 February 2002.[34] Getting to that point had required a herculean effort by the Norwegian facilitators. Solheim picks up the story: 'I was mainly in contact with Balasingham, Jon [Westborg] was in Colombo talking to the people there. I had no legal or semi-legal experi-ence with formulations, so we consulted closely with the Foreign Ministry's legal department.' Additionally, he recalls, 'we brought in people recom-mended by the Ministry of Defence, in particular officers with experience of ceasefire agreements in the Middle East and the Balkans. Two of them went on to become leaders of the monitoring mission in Sri Lanka.'

Tomas Stangeland, First Secretary at the Norwegian Embassy in Colombo, who became an important figure in the facilitation effort, recollects the drafting process. 'I was quite involved in drafting the agreement. I was writing and so was Erik. We studied other ceasefire agreements. We had a list—I remember that we looked at a UN website with all the [existing] ceasefire agreements.' Even though the final CFA document is fairly extensive, the process of formulating it took place within a remarkably short period of time. By way of explanation, Solheim emphasises that the drafting process was 'driven by the parties, and it was basically about what Balasingham proposed and what the government could accept. In a sense, Bala was the driving force on political proposals.'

Helgesen offers a wider explanation for the speed with which the document was finalised. 'The reason things went fast was that there was a strong political determination on both sides to get a ceasefire agreement', he says. While the government side did forward the occasional proposal, 'the dynamics were that the government or the military had red lines on [certain] issues, whereas on the confidence-building measures, Balasingham's demands were essentially accepted—for example on the list of embargoed items[35]—because the government did not have strong objections on the civilian front.'[36]

The CFA: an overview[37]

Following a preamble that outlines the overall objective of finding 'a negotiated solution to the on-going ethnic conflict in Sri Lanka', the CFA is divided into four Articles:

Article 1, which chiefly deals with military matters, covers such issues as:

- Military stance (1.3). While continuing to perform the 'legitimate task' of 'safeguarding' the country's 'sovereignty and territorial integrity', the Sri Lankan armed forces will do so 'without engaging in offensive operations against the LTTE'.
- The separation of forces (1.4—1.8). Specifically a zone of 600 metres between each side's forward lines is to be maintained (1.4). The monitoring mission will provide assistance with demarcating lines 'in areas where localities have not been clearly established' within thirty days of the CFA coming into force. (1.6). The government will disarm 'Tamil paramilitary groups', also within thirty days ('D-day +30').[38]
- Freedom of movement (1.9—1.13). Provisions include the right, as

---

of 'D-day +60', for 'unarmed government troops' to 'unlimited passage' between Jaffna and Vavuniya using the A9 highway, that is through LTTE-held territory, and for a specified number of LTTE members, 'freedom of movement in 'areas of the North and East dominated by the government for the 'purpose of political work'.[39]

Article 2 focuses on confidence-building measures to be taken by the parties with the aim, as the introduction states, of 'restoring normalcy for all inhabitants of Sri Lanka'.

- An undertaking by both parties, 'in accordance with international law', not to engage in 'hostile acts against the civilian population' including torture, intimidation, abduction, extortion and harassment' (2.1).
- Vacation of a number of civilian buildings—places of worship, schools, public buildings—currently occupied by 'either Party' by a specified time limit ranging from D-day +30 (places of worship) to D-day +160 (schools) and publication of a schedule for their vacation by D-day +30 (2.2–2.4).
- Measures to ensure the 'unimpeded flow' of 'non-military goods to and from the LTTE-dominated areas' (2.6). Exceptions for 'certain items' are detailed in Annex A to the Agreement.[40]
- With the same stated aim, measures to open checkpoints on the parties' 'lines of control' at a series of locations—seventeen in total—listed in Annex B to the Agreement (2.7).
- Opening up of the A9 (Kandy-Jaffna) road to 'non-military traffic of goods and passengers' (2.10). Modalities to be worked out 'with the assistance of the Royal Norwegian Government (RNG)' by 'D-day +30'.[41]

Article 3 outlines the modalities for establishing the Sri Lanka Monitoring Mission (SLMM), the body tasked with overseeing adherence to and implementation of the CFA once it came into force. The opening section of the Article indicates that the Head of Mission (HoM) will be appointed by Norway; s/he will have the 'final authority' regarding 'interpretation of the Agreement'; the SLMM will 'liaise with the Parties and report to the RNG'; the Mission will be composed of 'representatives from Nordic countries'; and it will be headquartered in Colombo, and have a local presence in six designated locations.[42] It further outlines:

- Setting up of local monitoring committees in all locations with an SLMM presence, consisting of five members: two appointees each from the government and LTTE and one 'international monitor appointed by the Head of Mission (HoM)', that is an SLMM member (3.7).
- Freedom of movement for SLMM members in 'performing their tasks' will be ensured by the Parties (3.8).
- SLMM members will be responsible for taking 'immediate action on any complaint made by either party' (3.11).

Article 4 defines the terms under which the Agreement comes into force, and under which it can be terminated.

- The Agreement will remain in force until 'notice of termination' is given to the Norwegian government by 'either party' (4.4). Notice must be provided 14 days in advance of the 'effective date of termination'.

Annex A lists the non-military goods not covered by Article 2.6 that are subject to restrictions. These include: explosives, remote controlled devices, barbed wire, binoculars and telescopes, compasses and penlight batteries. Additionally, there is a list of goods 'restricted in accordance with a defined list of procedures and quantities', namely diesel, petrol, cement and iron rods.

Annex B lists the checkpoints between government and LTTE-controlled territory as agreed in Article 2.7—seventeen locations in total.

With respect to 'red lines' on the government's side, Solheim emphasises that in addition to proposals that were 'unacceptable to the military establishment', the government was sensitive to anything that might make it 'easier for the LTTE to continue with terrorist activities'. Of these 'red lines', the most sensitive concerned access to, and control of, the sea. Helgesen notes that at an early stage of the drafting process, the LTTE tabled a proposal that gave control of 'defined areas to the Sea Tigers. We clearly understood, however, that the government could not accept this.'

As Solheim recalls, the issue was as follows:

> Ranil did not accept that the two parties would not buy new weapons. Any government over time needs to replenish its arsenal. It would also have been a

hard sell to the Sri Lankan military establishment. But if the government could continuously modernise its armed forces, it would over time give them a definite advantage. For this reason, Prabhakaran reserved the right to smuggle weapons in by sea using the LTTE shipping fleet.

A related issue was the question of what the Sri Lankan Navy would do when they encountered the LTTE shipping in weapons. 'The informal agreement was that the LTTE would try to keep a low profile and reduce smuggling, and the Navy would look the other way. That was proposed by us', Solheim states. 'We thought it was the only way [things] could work.' In his view the arrangement 'worked well for at least a year—as long as Ranil controlled the armed forces and the LTTE behaved itself. Later, it became a major obstacle to the peace process', he concedes. 'We were depending on goodwill: and that was particularly the case at sea.'

Another paramount issue from the LTTE's viewpoint was the disarmament and integration into government forces of Tamil paramilitary groups such as Douglas Devananda's Eelam People's Democratic Party (EPDP). 'The existence of such formations was no secret ... none of these groups would have existed without government support. They were tools of the Sri Lankan state', Solheim says.

In terms of external involvement, the CFA's most important component was the proposed monitoring body, the SLMM. Here, Solheim notes that 'the monitoring mission was our idea: there were no objections.' With regard to the SLMM's composition, 'Ranil was quite flexible. He didn't want to offend the Indians who did not want large nations or former colonial powers involved. The LTTE would not accept any Muslim nation.' The Norwegians proposed three countries: Norway, Sweden and Finland. On hearing this, the Danish government apparently 'went ballistic', Helgesen recalls, '[so] we added them and Iceland'.[43] And eventually, despite initial reservations, the Indians accepted the Nordic team.

When it came to the right of unarmed Tiger cadres to move around outside the LTTE-controlled Vanni, Solheim notes, 'Ranil took the position that the Vanni region was outside the control of the state and so he was not too concerned about what happened there.' A related issue that occasioned a lot of discussion, Solheim recalls, was the CFA's stipulation that fifty unarmed LTTE members would be allowed freedom of movement for political work in areas of the North and East dominated by the government. 'The terms were complicated', says Solheim 'like [the definition of] "dominated". But Ranil and Bala[singham] were both practical: there was a certain meeting of minds.' A clause giving government troops the right to limited passage between Jaffna and Vavuniya using the A9 road—part of a broader scheme to allow provisions for the Jaffna peninsula to pass through LTTE-controlled areas by road was 'seen as a concession by the LTTE', he recalls. Finally, the restoration of public buildings and places of worship was seen as a key issue on the LTTE side. 'So many of these had been taken over by the army,' Solheim notes.

Signing the CFA

On 21 February Jon Westborg travelled to Kilinochchi to collect the document that had earlier been signed by Prabhakaran. The next day, amid much fanfare, a signing ceremony was held in Vavuniya with Wickremasinghe. At the same time the Norwegian foreign minister, accompanied by Helgesen, held a press conference in Oslo to go public with the CFA document.[44]

Recalling the occasion, Solheim says, 'We felt hope and pride: the momentum was powerful, and we had worked very hard. There were positive reactions everywhere.' That said, conspicuous by her absence from the Vavuniya ceremony was President Kumaratunga, who had effectively been sidelined from the drafting process. In fact, Kumaratunga had received a copy of the agreement only after Prabhakaran had signed it, thus depriving her of the few days to study the document in advance that she had requested.[45] 'Ranil didn't want [to involve her]', recalls Solheim. 'The LTTE had lost confidence in her, neither of the two parties wanted to bring her in.' But, Solheim says, 'I think today that not involving her more was the biggest single mistake of the entire peace process.' Her lack of investment in the CFA was clearly manifested in the statement that she reportedly issued within minutes of the agreement's official announcement in Oslo. While voicing her support for the peace process in general and the ceasefire in particular, Kumaratunga took the government to task for failing to consult her, and voiced concerns over specific provisions of the ceasefire document.[46]

Perspectives on the CFA

Bernard Goonetilleke

I was Ambassador to China at this point, and returned to Colombo before Christmas 2001 and was told what my task was. Sri Lanka had had negotiations with the LTTE on several occasions but did not have any institutional memory ... whereas Balasingham had been there throughout. Accordingly the intention was to establish an institution to serve as a resource centre for negotiations. I was asked to set up the Secretariat for Coordinating the Peace Process (SCOPP)— the government peace secretariat ... The draft of the CFA came into our hands by late January 2002. There were some rounds of discussions with regard to the contents where we were able to submit recommendations for amendments. Some were accepted, most were not, because the Norwegians had already discussed and obtained the consent of the LTTE to that particular text.

In an ideal situation there should have been considerable negotiations on the text. The deadlines—within thirty days, do this; within one hundred, do this—were nice on paper. But if we had had the ability to discuss those periods or dates we would have made other recommendations. One of the LTTE's complaints was that the deadlines were not met by the government. And for a good reason. This was not possible due to the ground situation ... But the Norwegians thought it was necessary to have these kinds of time limits so that things did not get dragged out.

Gopalkrishna Gandhi

I was not present in any discussions between the Norwegians and the government. But in my discussions with [Kumaratunga] and Kadirgamar,[47] I could gather that they also wanted this to work. They had their own set of misgivings and reservations, but without wanting to know more than was it required for me to know, I sought briefings from officials and responses from the political executive in Sri Lanka.

Ashley Wills

Jon [Westborg] and I talked about whether the Norwegians were willing—if the domestic political situation in Sri Lanka permitted, and if the Indians would allow it to unfold—to try and bring off a mediation, especially if we were prepared to help them behind the scenes. I consulted with Washington; this would have been in early 2001. And Washington said 'OK, as long as you do not commit US troops'. Elections took place and Ranil was brought to power. Jon and I had talked to him during the campaign about Norway's willingness to engage, and our willingness to support Norway. And Ranil, to his great credit, went along with it. I had been agitating in my telegrams home to get senior people in the Administration in on this enterprise, because for a while at least, it seemed to be pretty hopeful ... Richard Armitage and Secretary [of State] Colin Powell did get interested. They saw it as a possibility for a good example to be set. So they got involved, especially Armitage.

When it came to the drafting of the CFA, we were someway beyond an informed bystander and somewhere short of being directly consulted every single day. The Norwegians realised that [in order] for our support to continue, they needed to keep us informed. They also used to come to us—Jon [Westborg] in particular— and ask for our opinion on [a particular] approach or tactic. On the government side, Ranil was extremely sensitive to our point of view and always wanted to know what we thought. So we would hear from the Norwegians and the Lankans. We would try to be 'correct'. We didn't want to be seen to be bossing anybody around but we had opinions, and we would offer these occasionally.

Paikiasothy Saravanamuttu

There is a crying need for an account of how the CFA was designed and negotiated. The [main] problem ... was that the two sides went into it with very different objectives and intentions. That they went into it in the first place is probably [due to the fact] that they had to, rather than [because] they wanted to.

Second, the dynamics of the Sri Lankan political situation played out in a way that ultimately wrecked the CFA. Instead of blaming one side or the other, both should have realised that there was something valuable in using the CFA as a bridge towards a political solution. But the politics intervened.

Third, a complementary human rights agreement [was needed]. They came to recognise that rather late in the day. The LTTE always took the attitude that any kind of memorandum on human rights would be used to hammer them. The government felt that if we push it too far, these guys will return to the bunkers. Fourth, the UNF government did very little to go out to Sinhalese constituencies and explain what the CFA [and] the SLMM was all about. They didn't communicate their policy and vision with regard to the peace process—they expected civil society to do that. Civil society tried, but without political backing it is very difficult in this country.

Finally, from the point of view of the UNF government, the CFA was something they desperately needed. They assumed that sometime later they would also capture the presidency, and then they could move towards a political settlement. For the LTTE, the CFA was recognition of the reality on the ground: that they had won their place at the table by [military] means, and that the CFA would pave the way for control of the North and the East.

Tyrone Ferdinands

The CFA was worth supporting—it was workable, but then the parties started playing politics with it. The LTTE was very creative here. Regarding the forward defence line, the LTTE converted it into a border [and] used it for checkpoints. In retrospect, the other problem was the whole issue of parity. The Norwegians tried to create parity in the talks. But when it comes to a state and a rebel force, parity can't be conceded.

Nirupama Subramanian

I didn't like the LTTE, I thought they were totally fascist ... Even if Tamil Eelam were a separate country, if they ran it, it would have been a total disaster ... [the CFA] separated the country into two. The LTTE was seen as an equal partner with the government. They run the North and these guys run the South. And by removing groups like EPDP and TELO,[48] by stripping them of their arms, you have given LTTE its heart's desire, which is to be treated as the sole representative of the Tamil people.

A Norwegian analysis of the CFA

Some commentators argue that Prabhakaran wanted Tamil Eelam and nothing short of it: from that perspective, was the CFA a surprising development?

Vidar Helgesen

[The fact that] people and organisations develop is very important. Whatever Prabhakaran's intentions at the outset, as the peace process moved on the LTTE developed its Interim Self-Governing Authority (ISGA) proposal.[49] That was the first time that they had ever proposed anything. Had the government not dismissed that out of hand, but engaged with it, things may have evolved differently.

Overall there was a build-up of civilian capacity and civilian thought-process within the LTTE that could ultimately could have changed, or challenged, Prabhakaran. But you never know: he may have been stalling. Had the government made different choices, however, the dynamics might have been very different. After all, Prabhakaran started out by banning LTTE cadres from marrying, and then he fell in love. People change.

Erik Solheim

Ranil wanted a process that established the LTTE as a political entity. Selling this to the Sinhalese was the difficult part. Bala[singham] had the same view: the 'boys' have been fighting, they need to see something different, and the LTTE should make the transformation into a political entity. He was keen on this from the beginning.

At the same time, at quite an early stage [and in the context of] some unacceptable act of Prabhakaran's, Bala[singham] told me: 'please remember that he is a warlord. He has no real interest in all these [political] concepts.' Bala[singham] was referring to warlords in China in the 1910s and 1920s to make me understand better. And he also told me: 'you must never underestimate the capacity for violence of these guys.'

Was Balasingham effectively saying look at, for example, Sinn Fein in Ireland?[50]

Erik Solheim

Yes. He wanted to see the LTTE as a broad movement fighting with political and military means, like the ANC.[51] The military aspect was subordi-

---

nate. He had a clear vision of achieving the LTTE's aims through the peace process and also transforming it. Bala[singham] did indeed refer to Northern Ireland sometimes. Later on [the LTTE] identified with Kosovo, the southern Sudanese, because they achieved their own state. I told them that if you want to create a new state it is very useful to have the USA as your main backer. And if you want American backing you have to refrain from terrorism.

Norwegian tensions

Tensions within the Norwegian team never made headline news but they were a significant factor in the drafting of the CFA. This became particularly pertinent to two key relationships: between Solheim and Westborg; and—to a lesser degree—between Solheim and Helgesen.

Vidar Helgesen

You had Jon Westborg as ambassador: he was instrumental in preparing the ground for the peace effort and Norway's role before Erik came on board. And when you are the ambassador, you are the king's representative. Jon being born in India, being equally South Asian and Norwegian in style, had a profound understanding [of the situation]. Then along comes Erik, who defies ministerial culture. In a South Asian context, coming to meetings with the president without a tie, with a rucksack—it's all very odd. There was a cultural clash within the Norwegian team between Jon and Erik. Who would be leading the efforts on the ground? Who would be shaking hands with the president first? At times there was rivalry. That was part of the reason why there had been insistence on the part of the Sri Lankans that Norway engage at a political level.

Erik Solheim

There may have been an element of jealousy between me and Jon, although gradually we came to terms with each other, and are now good friends. Jon may have had the attitude that someone coming from the outside should not be in the [foreign] ministry, being a traditionalist in that sense. And if he thought I was too close to the Tigers, I thought he was too close to the government. Jon also basically thought that you should not speak to the media.

Vidar Helgesen

Erik wanted me to clarify that he would go [to Sri Lanka] as the special envoy and be in charge of the operation, whereas I had this political-level imperative from the foreign minister that I engage personally. Foreign Minister Petersen also shared the view of Lankan officials that Erik had previously had too high a media profile. So my job now was to manage media access. And with Jon, one could say that he thinks that the world would be a better place without the media.

Tomas Stangeland

Jon had a unique relationship with Kadirgamar, also with Milinda [Moragoda] and Ranil, and this was from [the time] when they had been in opposition. Kadirgamar trusted Jon, although he was generally sceptical towards foreigners … Because of his Asian background, Sri Lankans felt he understood them. Jon knew more about the country than people in Colombo because he had travelled extensively in Sri Lanka. That was unique.

I first met Erik when he came to Sri Lanka in August 2002. His enthusiasm and straightforwardness were important and something people respected. He had a good relationship with all the actors except Kadirgamar, who was suspicious of everybody apart from Jon. But I don't think people looked at Erik as neutral … Erik was sort of the face of the [peace] process, and it was easy [for him] to be labelled as friendly to the LTTE since he was the only one who met them. Maybe he should have had a lower profile: but it was difficult to keep a lower profile. [Both] Erik and Jon's perspectives were important.

Setting up the monitoring mission

A major task now confronting the Norwegians was to set up the SLMM as quickly as possible. The immediate issues were threefold: designing a structure for the operation; appointing a Head of Mission; and coordinating with the five Nordic co-sponsors regarding finance and staffing.[52]

The Norwegian facilitation team dealt rapidly with the most pressing challenges. On 2 March, Major-General Trond Furuhøvde arrived in Colombo as the Head of Mission (HoM), and within a week the first group of monitors arrived in Sri Lanka. On 13 March, the day on which the SLMM established its initial headquarters at a Colombo hotel, the HoM received its first complaint of an alleged breach of the CFA, in this instance from the government side. Two weeks later a group of monitors were deployed to Trincomalee—the first SLMM field office to become operational—and by 3 April all six local offices were up and running. A week later Furuhøvde opened the Kilinochchi–Jaffna stretch of the A9, making Jaffna accessible by road for the first time in twenty years. All in all, this was an impressive start for a mission that had formally been in existence for approximately six weeks. Lisa Golden, a senior Norwegian official who was centrally involved in establishing the SLMM, takes up the story:

From the time they hit the ground in March 2002, Trond and his Deputy Hagrup Haukland quickly built up the mission, from acquiring offices and vehicles to starting operations and phasing in new monitors as they arrived. Before they left for Colombo, one job was to take Trond and Hagrup to visit Balasingham—with Erik—in London. Much as they made their introductions to the government and to the LTTE in Sri Lanka ... Communication between the SLMM and both parties—at the leadership and local levels—was central to the way the SLMM was intended to work. In the meantime, we had to find funding. At that point, we did not have a Peace and Reconciliation section or related budget line in the Foreign Ministry, so we borrowed from the humanitarian section, and we agreed with the other Nordic countries on cost sharing.

Norway's original contribution to the SLMM budget was around 30 million kroner (USD $5 million). The SLMM was unquestionably the most expensive part of Norway's contribution to the peace process. Moreover, as Golden further notes:

The CFA and terms of reference for the SLMM agreed by the parties envisioned a civilian mission of unarmed monitors. Although the monitors were unarmed and working in a civilian capacity, the top two in the mission both had a military background. Trond was a retired general and Hagrup a colonel, I believe. That proved to be a good idea. Both parties seemed to respect their military experience. They in turn could understand the security situation and the security-related aspects of the CFA. And they were able to draw on their organisational and leadership experience from peacekeeping operations.

Hagrup gave a lot of input to the practical setup of the mission and seemed to get the logistics running smoothly in no time. Trond was more politically minded and the philosophical type. From the start, Trond seemed to establish a good rapport with both the government and the LTTE. To my mind, he came to embody the central principles of the SLMM, including ownership by the signatories themselves and their involvement in resolving disputes. He also shouldered the responsibility of making rulings on reported breaches of the CFA if the parties could not agree. That was definitely not easy, but he often managed to involve the government and LTTE in discussing breaches and to find ways to frame rulings that opened rather than closed options for resolution. He would often consult Oslo on issues of political importance, but kept his independence, as stipulated in the CFA.

The post-CFA period

The next step in Wickremasinghe's efforts to sell the CFA to the Sri Lankan people was a visit to Jaffna in mid-March—the first Sri Lankan leader to do so in twenty years. Popular enthusiasm for the visit of the man who had delivered peace, or at least an absence of war, was palpable, and was exemplified by the words reportedly addressed to him by a resident of Chavakchcheri, the Jaffna peninsula's second largest town, which had been razed to the ground during fighting in 2000: 'You are our saviour'.[53] While in Jaffna, Wickremasinghe also met Christina Rocca, US Assistant Secretary of State for South Asia, who travelled to the North to meet him there—a politically astute affirmation of Jaffna's place within a unified Sri Lanka and a clear message of US support for Wickremasinghe's peace efforts.

In advance of Rocca's visit to Sri Lanka, the US Embassy in Colombo put out a strongly worded statement which cited evidence that the LTTE were still engaging in activities expressly forbidden under the terms of the CFA, such as extortion, kidnappings and child soldier recruitment. During Rocca's visit to Jaffna she appeared to follow up on the statement, calling on the LTTE to give up terrorism, adhere to all provisions of the CFA and abandon the idea of Tamil Eelam as 'both unnecessary and unattainable' if it wanted the US and other countries to consider lifting the ban on the Tigers.[54] Responding to queries about a heightened US interest in Sri Lanka, Rocca noted that 'we have a much greater interest this time because this is at last a chance for a good news story to come out of South Asia'.[55]

Balasingham returns to the Vanni

In preparation for talks with the government, the LTTE had been agitating for some time for Anton Balasingham, based in London, to be able to confer with Prabhakaran and the LTTE leadership back in the Vanni. Following the failure of initial attempts to persuade India to allow the Balasinghams to relocate to Chennai in the southern state of Tamil Nadu, it was eventually agreed that they would fly to the Maldives, accompanied by Erik Solheim. From the Maldivian capital Male they were then due to fly north to the Vanni by seaplane, accompanied by Tomas Stangeland.[56]

On the morning of 25 March the Balasinghams' plane landed on the reservoir at Iranamadhu, in the Kilinochchi area. On arrival they were greeted by Soosai, the Sea Tiger Commander, and taken ashore, where Prabhakaran and his wife welcomed them. On the afternoon of the Balasinghams' arrival, Solheim and Westborg, who had travelled together to Colombo from Male the previous evening, flew to the Vanni with the SLMM's Furuhøvde. The next morning a meeting to review the state of the peace process was held with the LTTE leadership.[57]

True to its promises, on 8 April the government opened the final remaining stretch of the A9 linking the Jaffna peninsula with the Vanni—another symbolically significant event that was greeted by cheering crowds who lined the road. In the meantime it had also become apparent that a proposal from the Thai government to host the initial round of peace talks in the Bangkok area had been accepted in principle by both sides. In this context the Norwegians announced that Vidar Helgesen would be visiting Sri Lanka in mid-April for meetings with the government and Prabhakaran.

Prabhakaran meets the press

A couple of days later, on 10 April, Prabhakaran gave a press conference—the first time he had spoken directly to the media in over twelve years.[58] A Sri Lankan journalist who covered the peace process from an early stage provides a vivid description of the media encounter with the Tiger supremo.[59] 'After the A9 opened there was a sense of [being able to travel] into the truly unknown. At this stage I didn't know about what the LTTE were all about and I was completely friendly with them. But you could sense they didn't know what to make of friendliness ... The checking and body-searching on the way into the press conference was intense', she recalls. 'The press conference was held pretty late in the evening, in a long hall. We were all crowded into it ... Prabhakaran came in with bodyguards armed with SLA weapons. The translator, George, told us not to make any sudden moves, if we did not want to get shot.'

Prabhakaran did not impress. 'He was in a bush suit. And that voice will always stay with me: he just squeaked', she remembers. 'He himself seemed overwhelmed by the crowd. It was really Balasingham who conducted the press conference'—a view that is essentially backed up by other accounts. 'Bala[singham] was looking out for Prabhakaran the whole time. Prabhakaran would say something briefly and Bala[singham] would then answer.[60] At the time, we felt that maybe Prabhakaran was simply not familiar with crowds,' Looking back, the journalist goes on, she sees that he was 'too smart', for that—'it was just a strategy'. Overall, there was a feeling of 'optimism, willingness to take things forward.'

Nirupama Subaramaniam's memories of the event have a somewhat different flavour. 'First of all I remember it because they [the LTTE] were—sorry to use the word—racists. Suddenly the whole world had landed in the Vanni. And the white guys got all the good accommodation while the Indian male journalists had the worst of it. There were two or three of us women,' she recalls, 'and we were put up in women Tigers' bunks. The Indian men were left completely by themselves.' In Subramanian's view the differential treatment meted out to South Asian and Western journalists reflected the fact that the LTTE 'knew they were not seeking to influence India. Their attention was on the West: that was their target audience.' Not that this was how things seem to have worked out. 'The press conference was dominated by the Indians, because of our sheer numbers,' Subaramaniam says. 'They took over the press conference with questions about Rajiv Gandhi. 'Why did you kill him?' Prabhakaran didn't say anything. Balasingham answered and said it was an event in history. Finally she recalls a question to Prabhakaran from *Newsweek's* Alex Perry: "'If you think of yourself as a leader of Tamil Eelam, why do you surround yourself with these mafia goons, the guys in dark glasses?" There was almost shock over that one. I don't remember the answer.'

The Norwegians were not present at the press conference. Solheim says

> We Norwegians didn't want to be seen there. From the LTTE's side, the purpose of the conference was to give momentum to the [peace] process. Ranil too wanted it as a proof of [their] sincerity. It went well. The main problem was the questions on Rajiv Gandhi. Bala[singham]'s answer may have been that we should look forward.[61] Privately, he felt the murder was a complete disaster.

It seems reasonable to highlight a conclusion put forward by T.S. Subramanian, who as a native Tamil speaker (like Nirupama Subramaniam) is at a distinct advantage when it comes to decoding the Prabhakaran-Balasingham interaction: 'If the LTTE leader's replies—as opposed to Balasingham's translations of them—were any indication, political negotiations for a final settlement were very far from his thoughts,' he says. 'The formation of an LTTE or LTTE-dominated interim administration in the Northeast and, as a precondition for that, the lifting of Sri Lanka's ban on the LTTE seemed to engage his mind now.'

The Muslim dimension

A less widely reported aspect of Prabhakaran's press conference was Balasingham's remarks on the sensitive subject of the LTTE's relations with the Muslim population. Offering an apology to the Muslim people for 'what has happened in the past',[62] he assured them that they would be able to return to their 'homes in the North'. Shortly afterwards—on 13 April—Prabhakaran held a bilateral meeting with SLMC leader Rauff Hakeem in Kilinochchi, the first such encounter between the two. Issues discussed included measures to prevent the harassment of Muslims in LTTE-controlled territory,[63] and the position of the Muslim community in the interim administration proposed by the LTTE for a future unified

Northeast. Concluding the discussion, a Memorandum of Understanding (MoU) was signed by both leaders.[64] The meeting was widely seen as presaging a thaw in relations between the two communities—a view certainly encouraged by Hakeem, who in an interview soon afterwards stated that 'the rapprochement between the LTTE and the SLMC has ... elements which are very progressive'.[65]

However, as soon became apparent, the question of Muslim representation—not in a future northeastern administration but in peace talks—would prove a source of continuing tension between the leaderships of the two communities. In the meantime, some six weeks after the Prabhakaran-Hakeem meeting, the eruption of inter-communal mob attacks in the East underscored the importance of achieving a political *modus vivendi* between the Tamil and Muslim communities.

On one side, Muslims in the East now intensified their calls on the SLMC leadership to pressurise the government to ensure their safety through a strong military presence in the area. On the other, the LTTE were pressing the government to adhere to the CFA timetable for withdrawing the SLA from public buildings in the East and elsewhere, a move which Muslims of course felt would render them more vulnerable to LTTE attacks. Reflecting on LTTE-Muslim relations at this point, Solheim comments:

> Right from the beginning we knew that the LTTE had profoundly failed in creating Tamil-Muslim unity. There had been pure, simple ethnic cleansing: all Muslims were kicked out from Jaffna in 1990 at twenty-four hours notice. They lived in camps north of Colombo in very difficult conditions. They had lost everything,' he says. 'The only positive aspect was that not many Muslims were killed. Their properties were taken, and we anticipated that [this] would be the main issue.

The essential problem, he argues, was that the LTTE 'felt they had earned their position as the legitimate representatives of the Tamil people—that the conflict was between Tamils and the state. There was also an element of chauvinism. Balasingham claimed that Tamil was the mother language of all four South Indian languages. For them, Muslims were secondary.' Concerning the peace process, Solheim argues, 'the Muslims wanted tripartite talks. The LTTE would not accept that, but the government would not have been averse to it at all. The LTTE wanted it to be an uncomplicated, bilateral thing.' Demographically speaking, Solheim explains,

> the North was basically Jaffna, all Tamils, [but] the East was one-third Tamil, one-third Sinhalese, one-third Muslims. ... If you take the East as one entity, and you bring Sinhalese and Muslims together, they become a majority. So the LTTE

was always reluctant. They never included Muslims in their cause. For the Muslims in the East, while they spoke Tamil and felt some affinity with Tamils, it would have been logical to ally with Sinhalese to keep a separate identity.

Helgesen in the Vanni

At around the same time, Vidar Helgesen arrived in Colombo and joined Solheim for talks with both sides on moving forward with peace negotiations. The first stop on the trip was the Vanni for a meeting with Prabhakaran—Helgesen's first encounter with the LTTE leader. 'It was my first trip to Sri Lanka after the ceasefire', he recalls. 'I had read about Prabhakaran.[66] For the world's most ruthless terrorist leader, he was quite underwhelming,' recalls Helgesen.

As at the press conference a week earlier, 'Balasingham was the interpreter. Prabhakaran essentially spoke to Balasingham. We ended with lunch. He wasn't very conversant at [the] table either,' Helgesen says. 'He spoke about one of his favourite movies, *The Heroes of Telemark*—the heavy water sabotage operation [carried out by the Norwegian resistance] during the Second World War.' He also recalls there being a pervasive sense of the LTTE 'knowing what they wanted: this was very consistent through the years, whereas on the government side things were much more fluid.'

Back in Colombo there were meetings with Wickremasinghe and his team, and with President Kumaratunga. Helgesen's abiding memory from these discussions is the 'strong desire on the part of Ranil and his team to get to the negotiating table'. And if an internal Norwegian Embassy report on developments at the time is anything to go by, the government's sentiments closely mirrored those of the Sri Lankan populace. In particular, the embassy report quotes an opinion poll indicating that in mid-March 2002 as much as 85 per cent of the population supported the idea of peace negotiations.[67]

Post-CFA developments: the Norwegian take

Helgesen and Solheim have come to some broad conclusions regarding developments in the aftermath of the CFA. 'The main issue was to prepare the ground for talks', says Helgesen. 'And the main challenge was the implementation of confidence-building measures, because the LTTE insisted on the return of normalcy to the North and East. They felt that the government was moving too slowly. [And] as Erik often said, if you are in

Prabhakaran's shoes you are used to getting your way. So if you point to a site and say you want a school here, it will be there next week.' Whereas the government side 'would have wanted to start talks in late February', the LTTE 'first wanted a tangible improvement on the ground'.

Overall, Solheim maintains, 'there was a level of disappointment on the LTTE side that economic benefits did not materialise as quickly as they had envisioned. During the ceasefire period I would visit Sri Lanka every five weeks, going to Colombo and the Vanni. There was always an impression that the government wanted to use the momentum generated by the CFA. The LTTE went step by step, ensuring that everything was working well. They would always find something to complain about. And they were slowing down the speed somewhat, [in order] to prepare better for the peace process. Bala[singham] knew Prabhakaran better than anyone else. He did not want to make too many mistakes,' Solheim says.

Concerning the time factor in peace processes such as Sri Lanka's, Solheim argues, 'I tend to believe that momentum is essential'—which is precisely what he feels was amply present in the immediate aftermath of the CFA's signature. 'Ranil used the term asymmetrical federalism, which is federalism [but] with more powers given to the Tamil Northeast. At this point such a solution would have been acceptable to nearly all Tamils and a vast majority of Sinhalese as well. Then there could have been a referendum: police, land, other such powers would be given over. And Prabhakaran could have been the prime minister of that area.' Further, he suggests that 'Ranil took the view that Tamils are generally more successful, that the Sinhalese should learn from the Tamils, [and that that way] Sri Lanka would develop better. Economic prosperity was his agenda.'

The negotiators meet

Talks had been scheduled to begin in May, but the continuing emergence of issues requiring urgent attention meant that the date kept being nudged forward. At one point it was reported that Balasingham was refusing to meet Vidar Helgesen to discuss dates for the talks,[68] mainly because of the government's alleged failure to implement measures stipulated in the CFA. On 28 July, however, the Norwegians finally managed to arrange a meeting between Balasingham (who had returned to the UK in April) and Milinda Moragoda, chief negotiator for the government, at the Norwegian Ambassador to London's residence. This was the first high-level bilateral encounter between the two sides.[69] From Oslo, Solheim, Helgesen and Lisa Golden were present. 'There was an atmosphere of positive anticipation',

Helgesen recalls. 'Balasingham obviously liked Milinda', says Solheim. 'The meeting went very well. They talked about the most contentious issue: the desire of the government to go into the core issues versus the LTTE's step-by-step approach.'

'We tried to understand both positions', Solheim explains. 'We tried to convince the LTTE to accommodate the government because [otherwise] it would be very hard for them to sustain the peace process for a long time. The LTTE's main argument was that people were suffering in [the] North and East. They were also sceptical of Colombo's ability to deliver substantial concessions or wide-ranging powers.' At the same time, Solheim emphasises that Balasingham 'knew it would be very hard to convince Prabhakaran to take the last step: getting rid of the military. Prabhakaran was very suspicious. So Bala[singham] also needed time.'

Milinda Moragoda on the London talks

The basic problem for us was that the LTTE wanted various things to be done on the ground before engaging. We thought this could be a tactic just to drag things out. Bala[singham] argued that they were not ready [for talks], that they didn't have the experts. He was someone who could present his case very eloquently: and he [was] very flattering, saying we had so many experts. My argument was that we have to engage now, because that's what we want. At the first meeting I said that we can start in the baby pool, move to the shallow end and then go to the deep end. But we need to get into the baby pool.

After the meeting in London, already there were all these ceasefire violations, the process was not going anywhere and we felt they were not serious. The Norwegians could see it as well. On the LTTE's side there was a long list of ceasefire violations, on our side there was very little. It almost came to a breaking point. I suggested that we needed to meet again, and we insisted on starting negotiations. There was a fair gap after the meeting in London. The LTTE's argument was always 'we need to establish confidence on the ground'. Our approach was that when the ceasefire itself was being violated, the moral high ground was on our side.

At the London meeting it was agreed that Thailand would be an acceptable venue for talks. 'The LTTE wanted Thailand because they had significant operations there', says Helgesen, who flew to Bangkok to ask the Thai Foreign Minister to host the meeting. 'They were more than helpful',

Solheim adds. But the question of dates remained hanging in the air, so the Norwegians organised a second meeting between the two sides, held in Oslo on 14 August 2002, four days after the government had announced that the LTTE was no longer proscribed. Agreement on key practical matters was duly reached: the talks would take place between 12 and 17 September at Sattahip Naval Base, with Norwegian facilitation.

Securing international support

From an early stage of the process, securing international engagement in Sri Lanka was a critical aspect of the Norwegian peace effort.[70] Helgesen takes up the theme:

> It was important for us to mobilise other actors. With the US, we had the advantage that [Deputy Secretary] Richard Armitage had a personal interest in Sri Lanka. In his military days he had an Asian engagement and he had a strong personal interest in South Asia in general.[71] This was post 9/11', Helgesen points out, 'and Armitage was intrigued by exploring the potential of negotiating with terrorists in contrast to other means of dealing with them. Ten years ago he attended a donors' meeting in Oslo, where he sat in the same room with Balasingham.[72]

With respect to India, Helgesen relates that both before and after his first visit to Sri Lanka in January 2002, he went to Delhi. 'Foreign Minister Jaswant Singh said that this was a long-term endeavour, and that we had to understand what kind of a movement we were dealing with ... It was hard to judge whether they believed the [CFA would] stand a chance', he says. 'I thought the minister was much more sceptical than the security people we met.[73] The security people were much more understanding of the needs on the Tamil side, whereas the diplomats were dismissive and just wanted the LTTE to go away. But formally they expressed support for Norway's effort. The Rajiv Gandhi killing was a big part of it,' he points out. None the less his view is that 'the security people in many ways had a better understanding of the need for a balanced approach while negotiating.' In this context, as Helgesen notes, it is worth recalling that Indian security forces had been the ones who had equipped and trained the LTTE and other Tamil groups during the early phase of the insurgency.

ELECTIONS AND CEASEFIRES

Enjoying peace: voices on the post-CFA atmosphere

As might be expected following a decisive halt to a decades-long conflict, the immediate post-CFA period in Sri Lanka is remembered by many as a time of real and widespread hope. 'Post-CFA the atmosphere in the country was euphoric', says Frances Harrison, BBC Correspondent in Sri Lanka at the time. 'There were thousands going up the A9 to check out the North, even posing for photos with LTTE cadres. At a certain level there was engagement between younger people on both sides—in a sense it was the beginning of something quite magical.'

Sinhalese journalist Shimali Senanayake, then Associated Press (AP) and *New York Times* Sri Lanka correspondent, recalls a pre-CFA conversation that remained with her throughout the following months:

> My 'Aha!' moment came when I was talking to an Indian friend who was into business in Sri Lanka. She said: 'It's good if Ranil wins [the elections], then the war will end. Then at least there won't be anything going on here in the South: what happens in the North and East is of no consequence to us. At least the South will be peaceful and we can all get on with our lives.' And it suddenly came to me that this is *exactly* what Ranil was planning. In hindsight, maybe he thought the ceasefire would last forever, he would last forever, the LTTE would run that [northern] part of the country, he would run this part and everyone would be happy. And for the UNP, 'everyone' meant the business lobby.

'There was a lot of enthusiasm', Helgesen recalls, 'positive vibes about the [peace] process, Ranil's government and Norway. And a curiosity about the North, the LTTE, hence all the delegations. A lot of people, while cautious and afraid of [the] LTTE, were also curious about them', he says. 'The economy started picking up, the security arrangements in Colombo came down, you could travel without stopping at check-points', Solheim recalls. 'It made a huge difference to people's daily lives—especially no fear of [bomb] blasts. There was a positive atmosphere. Ranil would have been elected by a landslide if there had been an election during that time.'

Recalling this stage in the process, government negotiator Milinda Moragoda says, 'The CFA was a start, a good beginning. But it was never meant to be more than that. We wanted a quick conclusion to the [peace] process, because in a democracy people are not going to wait forever. But because of their unwillingness or whatever reason, the LTTE wanted to drag [the process] out: that was their tactic. If both sides had moved in tandem, the process would have gone to the next level.'

4

PEACE TALKS

By the evening of 15 September the delegates had gathered in Jomtiem, a coastal resort some 165 km southeast of Bangkok.[1] It was already evident that media interest in the talks was exceptionally high—by the following morning, some 250 journalists (including 35 from Sri Lanka) had arrived for the formal opening of the talks. At the inauguration ceremony, held at a plush city centre hotel, G.L. Peiris and Anton Balasingham, as leaders of their delegations, were scheduled to make the opening speeches, along with Vidar Helgesen. Before they took the floor, however, it fell to Erik Solheim to open proceedings. Though his speech was by some way the shortest of the three, its content captured plenty of media attention. In the course of welcoming the delegations, he turned towards the two leaders and addressed each of them, as 'Your Excellency'—precisely what diplomatic protocol demanded, as he understood it. The indignation this stirred in some quarters, in particular among Sri Lankan officialdom, was remarkable.

Following on from Solheim, G.L. Peiris emphasised the government's commitment to 'the amplest degree of devolution' and the establishment of 'institutions designed to achieve this purpose'. At the same time, he reiterated what was effectively Colombo's bottom line: that any reforms resulting from the peace process would have to be implemented within the framework of a state 'whose unity and territorial integrity is ensured in fact and in law'.[2] Peiris also signalled his appreciation of the LTTE's priorities by stressing the overriding need for efforts to ensure the 'resettlement, rehabilitation and reintegration of all displaced persons in their original areas'.[3]

Chiming with Peiris, Balasingham underscored the urgency of promoting economic recovery for the 'war-affected Tamil population', placing the need for an 'immediate programme of resettlement, rehabilitation and reconstruction' centre-stage.[4] As the 'legitimate and authentic representatives of the Tamil people', who had 'lived, fought and suffered with and for our people throughout the ... war', it was crucial, he argued, that the LTTE draw on the 'effective administrative structure' built up over 'more than ten years' and play a 'leading and pivotal role in administration [and] economic development of the Northeast'. The 'deepest aspiration of our people', he concluded 'is peace, a peace with justice and freedom: a permanent peace in which our people enjoy the right to self-determination and to co-exist with others.'[5]

Talks open

From the opening ceremony the two negotiating teams were driven to nearby Sattahip naval base for the afternoon's opening session. Once issues regarding the agenda and related modalities had been settled, substantive issues were broached. According to John Gooneratne, Deputy Head of the Government Peace Secretariat (SCOPP) and an observer at the talks, the LTTE side argued from the start that the key issue was the return of IDPs to their homes inside the High Security Zones (HSZ) from which they had been ejected—a priority duly noted by the government team.[6]

Unsurprisingly, Balasingham's own account of the discussions is somewhat different, focusing on the 'hostile behaviour and ... lack of co-operation of the armed forces' and the related complaint that the SLA had 'refused to comply' with the terms of the CFA and 'continued to occupy public buildings ... causing a huge humanitarian crisis of displacement'.[7] For the government team, leading negotiator Moragoda's response was to propose the setting up of a Joint Committee whose remit would be to address issues relating to the HSZ and the return of IDPs to the Jaffna peninsula—a proposal to which Balasingham eventually agreed.

When it came to the question of setting up an Interim Administrative Council in the North and East, which had been a central LTTE demand prior to the talks, accounts differ. Balasingham maintains that having pointed out that the creation of an Interim Council had featured in the UNP election manifesto, he went on to 'insist' that Wickremasinghe's government was now 'obliged' to set one up 'as early as possible'.[8] By contrast, Gooneratne says that an Interim Council was an issue that 'was not taken up by [the LTTE] with any consistency. Sometimes they blew hot on it ... sometimes cold'.[9]

Either way, it is clear is that steps to create an Interim Administrative Council did not follow the Sattahip negotiations. An important indication as to why Balasingham and his team elected to put the issue on the back burner is provided in the LTTE chief negotiator's account of the talks. G.L. Peiris, he says, gave a characteristically 'lengthy exposition' outlining the formidable constitutional obstacles to the formation of an administrative structure with the powers needed to address rehabilitation and development issues, and raised the possibility that any moves to do so would be struck down as unconstitutional by the president. In view of this, Peiris proposed the formation of a provisional mechanism that he termed a 'pre-interim' structure, which could, he argued, eventually evolve into an interim administration.[10]

Despite expressing concern that Prabhakaran would be 'seriously disappointed' by any delay in the formation of an interim administration, Balasingham conceded that Peiris had presented 'rational and convincing arguments' concerning the constitutional difficulties involved, and thus agreed to Peiris' alternative: the establishment of a 'Joint Task Force for Humanitarian and Reconstruction Activities' (JTF).[11] The two sides agreed that the JTF's primary task would be to assume responsibility for the 'identification, financing and monitoring of urgent humanitarian and reconstruction activities in the North and East.' It would consist of six members, three from each side, with one person on the government side representing Muslims.[12] Negotiations concluded with agreement on the dates for the next three rounds of talks, beginning with a second round in Thailand: this time, however, at a location considerably closer to Bangkok.

Solheim on the Sattahip Talks

There was a lot of behind the scenes wrangling needed just to get started. The day before the opening it became clear that when we had proposed opening statements of fifteen to twenty minutes, Bala[singham] had interpreted that as meaning a short introduction of perhaps five to ten minutes minutes, whereas G.L. Peiris had decided to speak for half an hour. Bala[singham] was both furious and nervous—fearing that he would look like a fool in the eyes of Tamils. So I rushed back and forth between their bungalows to get Bala[singham]'s remarks extended and Peiris's cut.

Then came the issue of who would speak first. The government, while accepting the LTTE as [an] equal partner, also wanted to distinguish between a government and a rebel group. I decided that Peiris should be allowed to speak first, since after all he was the government representative. But to placate the LTTE, I gave them the central seating position on the podium. So G.L. was allowed to speak first, and the LTTE were given the best seating position.

This was agreed, but when we came to the actual ceremony the Thais had placed the government centre stage. They refused to change this, arguing that according to Thai protocol a government ranked higher than a rebel group. In the end we found a solution to this dilemma. The Thais accepted that as long as I physically changed the name cards, it was not their decision and they could look the other way. So the LTTE got the centre stage seats. Whether anyone actually noticed, I cannot recall.

We also had a discussion [about] flags. Could the Tiger banner be treated as equal to the Sri Lanka national flag? In the end I suggested the obvious solution—no flags, the Thai and Norwegian ones included. That was accepted.

There was a lot of tension over such matters, and with the formal opening ceremony, nervousness about how it would look to the parties' constituents. [It was agreed that] Vidar would make the Norwegian opening statement, and I would be the moderator. The mistake was that I had no experience of or real interest in protocol—it was just to make people happy. I used the term 'Your Excellency' for both Balasingham and Peiris. That created an uproar: it was a bad and unnecessary mistake on my part, simply due to lack of experience. At the first meeting it was not much of an issue, but later on it was used [against us] again and again. But the opening ceremony was very positive ...

One of the reasons for being in the naval base was to try to shield the talks from the media. We thought they should be closed to the media during the actual discussions, and round[ed] off with a press conference at the end of the talks, but both parties were interested in pursuing their own interests. Peiris would go to the beach resort Pattaya to feed the press. He was very keen on the media, wanted to feed it all the time. I think this came down to a mixture of his personal ambitions combined with the fear that unless they were kept well fed, the media would simply spin their own stories. And the government wanted to have some good news to report, of course. The LTTE had its own media people. Every round ended with a statement—essentially a Helgesen-Bala[singham]-G.L. [Peiris] production.

Press Conference

In terms of media interest the concluding joint press conference almost eclipsed the Sattahip talks.[13] Responding to questions about what the LTTE was seeking from the talks by way of a final outcome, Balasingham stated that the Tigers wanted 'substantial autonomy and self government' in what he called the 'Tamil homeland'. They would only seek an independent state, he claimed, 'as a last resort'—that is, if their demand for regional autonomy was 'rejected and conditions of oppression continue'.

Elaborating further, Balasingham argued that 'the LTTE does not operate with the concept of a separate state [but] with [that] of a homeland and self-determination'. And homeland, he contested, 'does not mean a separate state as such. It refers to territory where the Tamil-speaking people live'. Thus, 'when we [speak of] self-determination ... [it] entails substantial autonomy or self-government in ... the historical areas where we live.' In conclusion, Balasingham expressed confidence that solutions could be achieved 'if both the parties agree to a particular political system or model.'[14]

This upbeat assessment of the prospects for a settlement appeared to be shared on the government side. When asked whether Balasingham's comments raised hopes regarding the possibility of resolving the conflict, G. L. Peiris responded, 'Definitely. We know that [separation] is not their objective ... [The LTTE's] aspirations can be fulfilled within one country if we set about it in the proper way.'[15] The content of these remarks may have offered nothing particularly new, but—as a number of commentators pointed out—the clarity with which the LTTE's proposed an alternative to an independent state was unprecedented.

Helgesen's account of the Sattahip talks

The official opening of the talks did nothing to dampen expectations. I made it clear in my opening statement that we had to be prepared for setbacks and breakdowns, walkouts. Our expectations were not that this would be a smooth process. I took care to quote Gandhi, a message to the Indians: we knew they were watching.

Then the talks started. Balasingham had his health issue, [which meant] a couple of hours in the morning and evening, with a long lunch break. In terms of designing the process, we had to agree the agenda with both sides. The parameters imposed by Balasingham's health were very clear. At the talks in Geneva in October 2006, I remember vividly his long speech, very agitated, which ended with some ferocious statement, after which he said: 'And now I need to rest.'

We always [tried to keep] the issue of implementation of the CFA as agenda item number one. [Sattahip] was essentially a continuation of discussions that had taken place prior to it, with the LTTE complaining, and over time the government complaining more and more about LTTE ceasefire violations ... The Tigers wanted the ceasefire to be implemented and very much took a step-by-step approach. The government was focused on economic reconstruction, wanted international attention. And while the government wanted to talk on political issues, they didn't push it.

We did suggest that it would have been better if we could have the talks first and then talk to the media, to which everyone consented in principle. The issue was essentially Peiris—he was not possible to control. To me, his [press statements] came as a surprise. I had thought we would complete the talks first and then issue a statement.

Overall, the Sattahip talks went well. There was a good atmosphere, but substantively they did not make a lot of progress, as reflected in the final statement: 'We fully agree to address all political issues, the full range of issues pertaining to a lasting political agreement, but that can only be achieved [through] a step-by-step approach, and the first step is improving economic conditions.' So everything else was about returning normalcy to the Northeast: the joint committee on HSZs and the humanitarian and reconstruction task force were established.

Post-Sattahip developments

The week following the conclusion of the Sattahip talks, after a lengthy debriefing between Kumaratunga and Morogoda, the establishment of a joint committee to review the peace process was announced. Each side agreed to nominate two members whose primary task was to assess the progress of the talks in meetings that preceded and followed each round.[16] The first meeting of the committee was held on 12 October. In addition to Morogoda and Defence Minister Marapana, Wickremasinghe himself attended from the government side, while Kumaratunga was accompanied by her foreign affairs advisor, Kadirgamar.

During the autumn, Wickremasinghe's administration introduced a piece of legislation—the 19th Amendment to the Constitution—that, it argued, would bolster the domestic political stability needed to pursue the peace process. As things stood, the Constitution gave the president discretionary power to prorogue or dissolve parliament a year after the last elections were held. The Amendment would remove this presidential prerogative, thus making it impossible for Kumaratunga to call fresh elections—which, it was suggested, she might now view as winnable.[17] The Amendment also included a so-called 'Conscience Clause' that gave MPs the right to vote in defiance of their party whip, thereby allowing them to cross the floor unimpeded and—it was hoped—vote with the government in sufficient numbers to secure the two-thirds majority required to get the constitutional amendment passed.[18]

In the event the 'Conscience Clause' was ruled illegal by the Supreme Court in late October,[19] and the Amendment itself was eventually withdrawn when it became clear that the government would not be able to muster the parliamentary support needed to get it through.[20]

In the meantime, unrest continued in the East of the country. Of a string of violent incidents, one that received widespread attention was a mid-October demonstration outside a Special Task Force (STF)[21] camp at Kanchirankudah in the Trincomalee area—one of a number of STF camps located in the East that the LTTE argued should be removed as part of the ceasefire deal.[22] The demonstration turned violent when troops opened fire on the protestors, killing up to ten people and injuring more. Further complicating matters, camps such as Kanchirankudah were precisely the ones that many Muslims insisted should remain in order to guarantee their safety.

Security challenges apart, continuing instability in the East also increased the pressure on Rauff Hakeem to maintain unity among the fractious ranks of the SLMC and the discontented Muslims of the region. But unity, particularly among the SLMC parliamentary group, remained elusive. Sharp differences between Hakeem and a rebel faction led by A.L.M. Athauallah over the latter's continued demand that a separate southeastern Muslim unit be included in any final settlement remained unresolved, and seemingly unresolvable.

With a little under two weeks to go until the second round of talks, on 21 October Anton Balasingham arrived in the Vanni for consultations with Prabhakaran and the rest of the LTTE leadership. At the same time, the Norwegian facilitation team—this time including Hans Brattskar, Westborg's successor as Ambassador in Colombo—travelled to the North to discuss the agenda for the forthcoming talks.[23] In his account of this return visit to the Vanni, Balasingham notes that despite his careful explanation of the arguments put forward by Peiris in Sattahip in favour of the JTF proposal as a viable alternative to pushing forward with an interim Northeast administration, Prabhakaran was 'not impressed'.

A similar pattern was played out, Balasingham suggests, when the Norwegian delegation met the LTTE leader in Kilinochchi on 22 October. By all accounts, Prabhakaran painted a 'gloomy picture of the plight of the Tamil people,' arguing that the 'terms and conditions of the [CFA] had not been implemented,' and suggesting that the power struggle between 'the Sinhala leadership,' particularly the president and prime minister, posed a serious threat to the peace process as a whole. Despite the more positive reading of the political situation in Colombo offered by Helgesen in reply, the Norwegian's optimism 'did not impress Prabhakaran'.[24]

To many observers, it already seemed clear that the JTF agreed at Sattahip would be the most critical item on the agenda for the second round of talks. In particular, attention would be focused on the key issues the task force was supposed to address: a re-settlement programme for the more than 70,000 internally displaced persons (IDPs) in the North, and the interlinked issue of HSZs in the region.

Second round

The second round of talks, held between 31 October and 3 November, took place at the Rose Garden Hotel in Nakhon Pathom, thirty-five miles west of Bangkok. Two members were added to both delegations: Major General Shantha Kotegoda and Deputy Defence Secretary Austin Fernando on the government side; and Tamilselvan, Head of Political Section, and Colonel Karuna, Commander of Eastern Forces, for the LTTE.[25] Commentators were quick to point out that Kotegoda and Karuna had led their respective forces during the unsuccessful Jaya Sekuri Operation launched by government forces in May 1997.[26]

The first item for consideration was the deteriorating security situation in the East. Karuna offered assurances that the LTTE would do its best to ensure that the violence was kept under control. At the same time, he argued that the Tigers were not solely responsible for clashes in the East. Pointing to the Muslims' role in feeding tensions, he remarked that it appeared as if sections of the SLMC were intent on keeping the situation in the East unstable.[27] At the end of this discussion, a statement on 'Agreed Measures to Improve the Security Situation in the East' was adopted. Proposed measures included the reconstitution of local SLMM Monitoring Committees as provided for in the CFA; the establishment of two additional SLMM offices in Batticaloa and Amparai; the setting up of local peace committees to address local inter-ethnic tensions and grievances; and an agreement between Hakeem and Karuna to work together more closely in future on the basis of the Memorandum of Understanding agreed between Hakeem and Prabhakaran in mid-April 2002.

Into the second round of talks the focus switched to the setting up of the two structures agreed in Sattahip: the Joint Task Force (JTF) and a Joint

Committee to address issues relating to the HSZs and return of IDPs. Initial discussion of modalities for establishing these structures focused on legal issues, with the government delegation asserting the need for both mechanisms to be 'anchored, however tenuously, to a constitutional framework'.[28] According to Gooneratne, the LTTE rejected this approach. As a liberation movement, the Tigers did not accept the overriding authority of the Sri Lankan Constitution—a document that would, they pointed out, in any case need to be revised if and when a final solution to the ethnic conflict was reached.

On a related, more directly political note, a draft proposal circulated by the Norwegians and based on consultations with both sides suggested that the JTF be set up under the auspices of the prime minister's Secretariat, the thinking being that under prevailing conditions and with a president seemingly hostile to the peace process, this would constitute an effective means of shielding the Task Force from unwanted political interference. While the underlying thinking was understandable, the LTTE rejected this proposal too, also because of their fundamental reluctance to accept the final authority of a Sri Lankan institution, in this instance the prime minister's office.[29]

In the end, the LTTE accepted a proposal from Moragoda to rebrand these bodies as 'Sub-Committees' and increase their number to three: a Sub-Committee for Immediate Humanitarian and Rehabilitation Needs (SIHRN); a Sub-Committee on Political Affairs (SPA); and a Sub-Committee on De-Escalation and Normalisation (SDN). It was also agreed that the sub-committees would report to plenary meetings of the peace talks, thereby removing any potential difficulties regarding their constitutional status.

Solheim and Helgesen on the Rose Garden Talks

Erik Solheim

> The format was the same as before, but the media came much closer. ... The Sri Lankan media created huge problems: the government and LTTE felt they had to feed them something or they would write some fabrication. Barring some exceptions, they were not trustworthy.

> On the LTTE side, everything was about Balasingham. Karuna, Adele Balasingham and Tamilselvan were also there. Only Bala[singham] spoke, however. ... Balasingham treated the others as young boys, students. The discussion was always in English ... The government were more interested in political affairs, the LTTE in economics and de-escalation. I think Balasingham was consulting Prabhakaran throughout. I am not sure how

they managed the phone calls, however: Prabhakaran would have been afraid of giving away his position both for fear of targeted attacks as well as the obvious chance of interception. They may have communicated through a middle-man or directly. I don't know.

The government side had General Kotegoda as an adviser at the talks. He made positive contributions and was well respected. Later, because of the good chemistry at the talks between the two men, he was accused of being behind Karuna's defection. [Overall], this round of talks brought a broad institutional framework to the peace process.

Vidar Helgesen

Normalisation was *the* theme: the LTTE was consistent [on that] throughout: the first agenda item was always implementation of the CFA. Initially there was no issue on the security front: the HSZ issue [was there] of course, because of the return of IDPs, but there were no clashes. The sole focus of the LTTE was on getting humanitarian and economic development restored.

The identification of problems came from the LTTE. In particular, they were concerned about the continued existence of the HSZs. The government was positive about addressing the issue, not realising how difficult it would be for the military establishment. There was no military representation at the talks, but it was agreed that the [SDN] would have high-level military personnel on both sides. A sub-committee on political matters was also established. It didn't actually meet, and didn't have to because the respective heads of delegation headed it. But it was a concession for the government to show that there would be progress on political issues. [Overall] we had reinforced architecture for the peace process, and that was significant.

The final statement also says 'The Sri Lankan government will support the LTTE in its efforts to access expertise and expand their international mobility for this purpose.' This was something that Ranil and his team understood, but Chandrika never did. The proposal came from the LTTE, and we argued strongly that it would be positive for the peace process if the LTTE were able to travel, learn from different experiences.

After the talks

While the issue of an interim administration for the North and East had not been discussed, immediately after the Rose Garden talks the LTTE made a number of moves that appeared to signal their intention to press ahead with consolidating their de facto administrative control over much of the region.

The opening of LTTE-run police stations in a number of locations in the East was announced, followed soon after by plans to open LTTE-controlled Courts of Law in the East, operating on the basis of their own Penal Code.[30] Unsurprisingly this news was greeted with anguish in Colombo: one respected commentator, for example, suggested that 'the LTTE have established, with UNF government concurrence by default, a parallel state which needs de jure recognition in a peace format. Failing this, these institutions are the de facto trappings for Eelam.'[31]

With the focus of attention shifting towards the international donors' conference scheduled for 25 November, Milinda Moragoda flew to Delhi for last-minute talks in an ultimately unsuccessful attempt to persuade the Indians to participate in the Oslo meeting. Although nothing was said formally, there seemed little doubt that a key factor was Delhi's refusal to appear on the same platform as the LTTE, which it had banned following the 1991 assassination of Rajiv Ghandi.[32] Moreover, India insisted on being treated as the paramount power in Sri Lanka, not simply one among many.

Oslo Donor Conference

The one-day donor meeting, held at the Holmenkollen Park Hotel in Oslo, attracted over 100 representatives—among them a number of high-level ministers—from some 37 countries. The meeting opened with speeches from Wickremasinghe and Norwegian Foreign Minister Petersen. The latter's emphasis on the need to build popular support for the peace process was echoed in Wickremasinghe's focus on the importance of international investment in the Sri Lankan 'peace dividend' in order to ensure that the 'momentum for peace' was maintained.[33]

As anticipated, however, the focus of controversy was US Assistant Secretary of State Richard Armitage's intervention. Urging the LTTE to give up 'violence and secession', he called on the Tigers to make a 'public renunciation of terrorism and violence' as the basis for clarifying to 'the people of Sri Lanka and indeed the international community' that the LTTE had 'abandoned its armed struggle for a separate state'.[34]

Balasingham said nothing publicly in response. In writing, however, he argued that 'the American conception of armed struggle was superficial and biased. Operating with the ill-defined category of political violence, [it] characterises all forms of conflict and popular agitation ... as 'terrorism', without taking into account the moral basis, political context and history of specific struggles fought against state terror and oppression.' Later in the day, on the margins of the main meeting, he had the opportunity to respond to Armitage 'in polite form, briefly explaining the political and historical background of the emergence of the armed resistance movement of the Tamils'.[35] Perhaps the most notable aspect of Balasingham's own speech was its emphasis on the joint nature of the appeal to the international community for financial support. While this was very much according to the script agreed at the Rose Garden talks, such a public display of government-LTTE unity made a considerable impression on the high-level donor representatives at the conference.[36]

By the conference's end, more than USD $70 million had been pledged in support for reconstruction and rehabilitation, particularly in the North and East. It was agreed that the funds would be disbursed via the newly-established North East Reconstruction Fund (NERF), which would be lodged with the World Bank. Capping what appeared to have been a productive meeting, that same evening Wickremasinghe and Balasingham met bilaterally for the first time, in the presence of Helgesen and Solheim. While nothing of substance was agreed, the fact of their discussion, and its reportedly amicable tone, was widely viewed as a further step forward.[37]

Rounding off a seemingly upbeat sequence of events, in his annual Heroes Day speech, delivered on 27 November, Prabhakaran echoed the approach to the issue of Eelam put forward by Balasingham during the Sattahip talks.[38] The Tamil people, he stated, 'want to live in freedom and dignity ... in their historically constituted traditional lands ... under a system of self-rule'. And this, he argued, is 'the political aspiration of our people' which in turn constitutes 'the essential meaning of self-determination'. In this context the LTTE was prepared to 'consider favourably' a political framework that offered 'substantial regional autonomy and self-government in our homeland' based on 'our right to internal self-determination' within Sri Lanka. If this demand were not met, however, the LTTE leader re-affirmed that the Tigers would have 'no alternative' but to 'secede and form an independent state'.[39]

Balasingham's broader assessment of the Oslo conference, however, is not entirely positive. The conference, he argued, had created an opportunity for 'powerful international governments ... with divergent economic and geo-political interests' to become involved in the Sri Lanka peace process. Previously the international community's role had been to 'encourage' both sides to 'seek the path of a negotiated settlement' with accompanying pledges to mobilise resources in support of the peace process. Following the Oslo Conference, he argued, the focus of international attention shifted towards pledges as a 'reward for the renunciation of armed struggle and the quest for secession'. In this sense, the 'international safety net' propounded by Wickremasinghe was perceived by the LTTE as a means of containment, 'imposing constraints and prescribing parameters … that began to shift the strategic equilibrium in Sri Lanka's favour'. This is why, Balasingham maintains, there was increasingly vocal LTTE criticism of what he describes as the 'excessive internationalisation' of the peace process.[40]

Perspectives on the Oslo Conference

Erik Solheim

Armitage came and met with Balasingham: they met on the margins but did not want a handshake photograph. That was very big, given US anti-terrorism rhetoric after 9/11. They claimed they would never talk to terrorists, yet Armitage did exactly that. … Armitage later told us that if he had actually asked whether he could talk to a group designated as 'terrorist', he would have got a resounding 'no'. So he phrased the question to the State Department lawyers a little differently: 'I want to go and speak to the LTTE. How can that be done?' Then he got the answers he wanted. I learned a lot from this behaviour when I became [a] minister myself. You need to ask the right question.

Ranil came too. To us the key element was creating political momentum. Ranil met Balasingham, and that went very well. There was positive feedback from other donors present; everything was positive. The main donor conference was the Japanese meeting.[41] The Oslo meeting was a political way of reaffirming support for the peace process—not really so much about money, as I see it.

Vidar Helgesen

The most important thing was [the fact that] Richard Armitage came and sat in the same room as Balasingham, even though the LTTE was a listed terrorist organisation. That was a very strong message. We did talk to Armitage in advance because we wanted him to come. There was a lot of discussion about the modalities—how to ensure that [Balasingham and Armitage] could sit in one room and that from no angle would it be possible to photograph the two of them together. The prime minister hosted a dinner, and the media gave the conference some coverage. Generally speaking Norwegian media had two angles on the entire peace process: breakthrough or breakdown. Anything in between was not seen as news.

Third Round of Talks: The 'Oslo Declaration'

Since the Rose Garden talks two of the three sub-committees had begun functioning.[42] Accordingly, the opening session in Oslo—for which the delegations remained the same on both sides—was devoted to a report on their activities.[43]

As in previous negotiations, a key issue was the Army-controlled HSZs in the North. The argument followed familiar lines. Led from the front by Balasingham, the LTTE complained about the pace at which the Army was vacating public buildings, emphasising the humanitarian consequences of denying the displaced local Tamil population the right to return to their homes. In response, the government emphasised the Sri Lankan military's continuing security concerns and the need for more time in which to identify appropriate locations for new army camps and construct them. No conclusions of substance were reached, and the gap between the two sides' positions on the HSZs and right of return to the Jaffna peninsula remained as wide as ever.

A decision was taken to set up a Sub-Committee on Gender Issues (SGI) consisting of four members from each side, whose remit was to explore ways and means of promoting the 'effective inclusion of gender issues in the peace process'. The idea of setting up the sub-committee came from Vidar Helgesen, with strong support from Adele Balasingham and others. There was also an agreement, reflected in both the 'Record of Decisions' and the Norwegian outcome statement, on the urgent need to 'improve the situation for children affected by armed conflict'. In this context, the LTTE agreed to 'engage in partnership with UNICEF'.[44]

Concluding the list of measures agreed in Oslo, the final outcomes document states that 'in order to arrive at the broadest possible consensus' regarding the peace process, the government would establish an 'appropriate mechanism for consultation with all segments of opinion'—an indication of growing awareness of the importance of keeping President Kumaratunga and the parliamentary opposition, as well as the population as a whole, on board with developments.[45]

Each of the elements detailed above were important to the peace process. The centrepiece of the Oslo negotiations, however, was explicitly political. The key issues discussed in this area are reflected in the talk's final outcome statement, in particular the section devoted to 'political issues' that led to it being dubbed the 'Oslo Declaration'.[46] The crucial section of the statement is reproduced below.

'Responding to a proposal by the leadership of the LTTE, the parties agreed to explore a solution founded on the principle of internal self-determination in areas of historical habitation of the Tamil peoples,[47] based on a federal structure within an united Sri Lanka. The parties acknowledged that the solution has to be acceptable to all communities.'

The statement goes on to identify a list of 'substantive political issues' it was agreed the Sub-Committee on Political Affairs would be considering in this context:

- Power-sharing between the centre and the region, as well as within the centre
- Geographical region
- Human rights protection
- Political and administrative mechanisms
- Public finance
- Law and order

In the event, it was one notion—federalism—that captured the headlines. Had both sets of negotiators really committed, people wondered, to 'exploring' a governance structure that many on both sides of the conflict had traditionally opposed? Responding to the suggestion that the LTTE had now given up its traditional demand for independence, Balasingham argued that this was not the case. Referring to Prabhakaran's 2002 Heroes Day speech, he emphasised the two-stage nature of the LTTE's position. As a first stage the LTTE demanded regional autonomy and self-government based on the principle of 'internal self-determination'. If the government were to take serious steps to implement these demands, Balasingham argued, then a final settlement to the conflict could, theoretically, take place within the framework of a unified Sri Lanka. If, however, the 'internal element of self-determination is blocked ... and the demand for regional self-rule is rejected' then the LTTE would view itself as having 'no alternative other than to secede and form an independent state'.[48]

In addition, Balasingham maintains that the LTTE's willingness to entertain federalist perspectives stemmed from the negotiators' discussions with the Forum of Federations (FoF), who, with the Norwegian's support, had organised a seminar on federalism on the sidelines of the Oslo negotiations.[49] Starting from the proposition that the LTTE needed to 'articulate concrete concepts that reflect the realities of the modern world', Balasingham says that FoF members argued that the LTTE's 'demand for regional self-rule' could only be accommodated within a 'federal system of government'—which in the LTTE strategist's interpretation essentially implied a 'political system combining self-rule and shared rule'.[50]

Having given 'serious reflection' to the FoF viewpoint, the LTTE—at this point most likely meaning Balasingham himself—decided to pursue the subject further, which in turn led to the joint decision that was presented in the final statement. As a piece of political narrative this is, of course, smoothly presented: its most striking lacuna concerns the Norwegian facilitators' absence from the account, an absence that is hard to square with Solheim's own version of events (see below).

Reaction to the Declaration

Responses to the Oslo talks varied widely. At the sceptical end of the spectrum, the Oslo statement's allusion to the parties' intention to explore federal options was seen as inherently questionable. 'What has evolved in Norway', suggested one leading commentator, 'is only an overall statement of intent to explore a federal solution without any specific note of unit or substance.'[51]

More fundamentally, the LTTE's apparent agreement to pursue federalist options was interpreted as evidence not of an opening up on the Tigers' part, but rather as a 'political ploy' intended purely for 'international consumption'. The LTTE, it was suggested, 'want the negotiating process to fail at some stage without any blame attaching to them. The peace process should not arrive at a logical conclusion; instead it should collapse without a satisfactory federal solution.' And at that point, the Tigers could play the trump card affirmed in Prabhakaran's Heroes Day speech: exercise their right to 'external self-determination' and resume fighting. The bottom line, in short, was that the LTTE's only genuine commitment was to the creation of an independent state.

Peace talks progress: an optimistic view

Jehan Perera suggested that the explanation for the apparent evolution in the LTTE's approach to 'final status' issues lay in the fact that 'in the engagement and dialogue taking place owing to the peace process, the reality of federalism was the only viable alternative [that had] made its presence felt.'[52] Perera emphasised that in a peace process

> the two sides are not negotiating in the spirit of bargaining ... Sustaining long-term relationships requires a different type of negotiation in which the interests of each side are met in a fair and reasonable manner. It seems that the government and LTTE negotiators have engaged in such interest-based negotiations. ... Those who pride themselves on being hard bargainers might get themselves a good bargain on one occasion. But the relationship is unlikely to survive.[53]

Perera continued with a rousing argument for what might be called the democratisation of the peace process. First, he stressed the strategic role of civil society organisations (CSOs) in public outreach, in particular in explaining the implications of federalism with respect to 'structures of governance and power sharing' to ordinary people—Sinhalese, Tamils and Muslims alike. Second he emphasised the critical importance of bringing the Southern political opposition on board, for example through setting up a joint committee to 'work out the content of the political solution'.

Recalling the fact that without Opposition support it would be impossible for the government to muster the two-thirds majority required to effect any constitutional changes resulting from the peace process, Perera argued that in the absence of bipartisan political consensus on a constitutional reform process it would be 'unrealistic' to think that the LTTE will make a 'full transition from a military organisation to a political one'.

Finally, Perera noted that prior to the Oslo peace talks President Kumaratunga had stated that the PA were the 'only party' to have spelled out their own 'devolution of power proposal', in the shape of the federalist 1997 constitutional reform bill.[54] Accordingly, he suggested that since the government and opposition appeared to be 'stand[ing] on common ground' with regard to a 'political solution based on federalist principles', it was time for them to put their traditional rivalries aside and collaborate on the project of making 'permanent and just peace a reality for all communities inhabiting Sri Lanka'.

This interpretation suggested that the LTTE's commitment to the peace process would be driven forward by a number of contingent factors. The Tigers, like the government, had a clear interest in securing financial assistance for the purposes of 'rehabilitation, reconstruction and development'. In addition, they were seeking to secure some kind of international legitimacy, with the ultimate aim of de-proscription as a terrorist organisation by countries such as the USA, UK, Canada and Australia. This was more than sufficient, it was argued, to keep the LTTE engaged in what was described as a 'tactical shift with both short- and long-term objectives, while retaining its basic ideological moorings'.

In contrast to Perera, other, more common responses to the Sri Lanka peace process were reminiscent of Cold War anti-communist rhetoric.

When faced with an indication of willingness to compromise by the Tigers, anti-LTTE commentators often responded by highlighting the discrepancy between Prabhakaran's apparent commitment to negotiating over Tamil Eelam and terrorism as a means of achieving that goal. On this basis, the commitment made in the Oslo Declaration to explore federal options was frequently dismissed as part of a broader strategy to hoodwink the government. In essence, such arguments reasserted the old adage that a leopard— or in this instance, a tiger—never changes its spots. By contrast, the viewpoint exemplified by Jehan Perera builds on assumptions not so much about the 'true nature' of the parties involved as the structure and functioning of successful interest-based negotiations processes. In emphasising the importance of building popular understanding of and support for the peace process, as well as developing a bipartisan political consensus behind any proposal for a final political solution to the conflict, Perera highlighted two of the central challenges that confronted the government as this point: challenges, however, to which neither the Wickremasinghe administration nor its successor proved able to rise.

Reflections on Oslo

Erik Solheim

> The government was pushing and pushing for some commitment [from] the LTTE side for a final solution. They for sure believed in this themselves, but the pressure to deliver some substance was also driven by the political need to show rapid results to sceptics in the South. And the government agenda at the talks was always in danger of falling hostage to their continuing competition with both the president and parliamentary opposition.

> I met with Milinda and we had a nice meal in a fish restaurant between the negotiation sessions. Over fish soup he drafted a text that would be helpful to moving things forward at the talks. The next day we showed it to Bala[singham]. He basically concurred, but made two changes. First, that [the text] was based on Prabhakaran's proposal made in his recent Heroes Day speech; second that they [the LTTE] would 'explore'—and had not accepted—a federal solution. That was agreed by both sides. The political discussions were not conducted with Bala[singham] taking direct instructions from Prabhakaran. Bala[singham] had much more flexibility on politics than on military affairs. I think Bala[singham] thought that he would bring Prabhakaran on board [over federalism] after the talks; [it was only] later it that became clear that he had gone too far. But [at the time] it was seen as a huge breakthrough.

> The six areas we were able to get into the document specify what the discussion about federalism meant. It was a breakthrough in the sense that [the] LTTE

accept[ed] a broad discussion about a federal structure short of a separate state. Read the first one: power sharing between the centre and the regions. This is what federalism is about. They also adopted a phrase used earlier: 'in the areas of historical habitation of Tamil-speaking peoples', which means the North and the East; and Tamil-speaking peoples can only mean Muslims and Tamils.

The push for the Declaration came from Ranil's advisers. It was a strong government political need: they were still in fierce competition with Chandrika, and they had a strong desire to get proof of the LTTE's acceptance of something other than a separate state. In the first two rounds they had accepted other issues, and now they felt was the time to get serious. Bala[singham] wanted to accommodate [them]. The Colombo and world media removed the nuances: 'explore' disappeared from the text and it was presented as an agreement, not a declaration. A lot of Tamils asked Prabhakaran whether it was true that they had accepted federalism, which irritated him. Overall, I now think that the timing was a mistake. Bala[singham] stretched his neck out, but it was a step too far at that time, given the psychology of Prabhakaran. Except for the impact it had on Prabhakaran, however, the Declaration was an enormous success.

Vidar Helgesen

Federalism was problematic on both sides because the nationalists preferred a unitary state. But we ended up with a declaration to explore a solution for internal self-determination based on a federal structure within a united Sri Lanka. ... It was very clear to us that this was only about exploring—[the Declaration] doesn't say [the parties] are committed to it. But nonetheless, the word federalism had not been on paper between the two parties prior to this. Four days later I was at the UN in New York—December was Norway's last month on the Security Council—and a secretary came to me with a note. It said 'Congratulations on Sri Lanka, Kofi Annan'. So internationally it was seen as a breakthrough in the political process. But clearly we should have managed the fallout from the federalism declaration better. The word 'explore' should have been written in font size 26 and bold!

... The LTTE felt at this stage—or at least Balasingham did—that they had to move. [But] we know from later that the federalism 'thing' was not anchored sufficiently. We cannot know what really happened. Balasingham always consulted Prabhakaran, we thought, so he probably had his backing. Later, the LTTE discussed political and administrative mechanisms: after the breakdown of the talks, they came back with the ISGA proposal. I guess what may have happened was a profound backlash from [Tamil] diaspora groups. Balasingham was given a hell of a beating by the Tamils in Oslo after the declaration. And when that reached Prabhakaran it may have given him cold feet.

... We never got around to real discussion on the content of federalism. The agenda of Ranil's government was to resolve the conflict, give the LTTE or Tamils as much self-governing authority as they could within a united Sri Lanka, and move on with their economic ambitions. At later rounds of talks the LTTE studied these issues quite seriously, but after the change of President [in 2005], government delegations only scratched the surface.

Milinda Moragoda, government negotiator

The Oslo Declaration set an outer limit for the first time, which to some extent eased the pressure on us. Otherwise, it was kind of an open-ended journey. From the beginning we were seeking to set an outer limit. We had nothing to hide, we were transparent. It was the first time any administration in Sri Lanka had been this open in a negotiation. And when those negotiations failed, we saw that Prabhakaran was not sincere ... Kumaratunga was playing politics at the time: she was waiting for her moment to recapture office. But the way the LTTE handled things also contributed to that process. If they were sincere they would have approached it differently.

Bernard Goonetilleke

By the time of the second round of talks, it is clear now—but was hazy then—that the LTTE was not there to negotiate. They were playing for time. Their final objective was not to have an understanding with the government on the future of the North and East. That became clear after several rounds of negotiations when we went to Oslo in December. We ran out of issues to discuss. They wanted to make use of the time in each session to discuss 'existential needs of the Tamil population'. We agreed to do that in the morning, but we said that we needed to discuss substantive issues in the afternoon sessions, so we would be going parallel.

One afternoon, it almost came to a point where we had no discussion. The following day, we thought there would be nothing more to discuss. But in the evening the Norwegian team worked on Balasingham. Then in the morning there was a piece of paper, which surprisingly was listing certain issues that the LTTE were ready to discuss. That was improved, adapted and became the Oslo Declaration ... But we soon discovered that either Balasingham had been squeezed too much by the Norwegians, and had agreed to something for which he had no authority, or the LTTE thought that Balasingham had given away too much.

Following the Oslo meeting Bala[singham] came to the Vanni with the intention of staying for a week or so. Two days later I got a message saying that he was feeling sick. We sent a helicopter and brought him out: people said that he did not look sick. Subsequently we came to know that there had been a big confrontation with Prabhakaran, as a result of which Balasingham decided to cut all connections with the outside world, until somebody from the Norwegian side knocked on his door in London. But from there on his ability to negotiate was reduced. We also realised that Tamilselvan was not very happy about the Oslo outcome.

The government was pleased with the outcome: federalism is a dirty word in Sri Lanka because of the historical context. As we saw it, the Sri Lankan administration went beyond their historical position and agreed to a federal arrangement. And from the LTTE point of view, instead of asking for a separate state, they had come down.

V. Rudrakumaran

I was surprised when Bala[singham] mentioned the Oslo Declaration. Personally I believe in an independent state. It was too premature. If that was going to be the real end, that card should have been played at a later stage. I was really taken aback. Later I learnt that even other members were taken aback. But nobody had the guts to say anything to Bala[singham]. The perception was that he must have consulted with the leader.

High Security Zones

On 14 December 2002, immediately following the Oslo talks, a second meeting of the Sub-Committee on De-Escalation and Normalisation (SDN) was held.[55] As anticipated, the main issue was the vexed question of the HSZs. With the LTTE underscoring the urgency of resolving the problem in order to facilitate the return of displaced civilians, the committee agreed that Jaffna Commander Sarath Fonseka would submit a plan by 21 December for limited civilian resettlement within a specified area of the Jaffna peninsula HSZs.[56] In addition, the LTTE reasserted an earlier demand that the Douglas Devananda's Eelam People's Democratic Party (EPDP) vacate Jaffna in the wake of continuing 'civil disturbances'—allegedly Tiger-instigated protests over their presence.[57]

Fonseka duly submitted his De-escalation Plan on 20 December, for discussion the following day between himself, his LTTE counterpart Colonel Theepan and SLMM Head General Furuhøvde. In the document Fonseka proposed an Army withdrawal from two defined sectors of the HSZ. To make this possible, however, he indicated that it would be necessary to secure assurances that LTTE would 'disarm its cadres and decommission its weapons'.[58]

Not surprisingly, the LTTE was sharply critical of the proposal, as reflected in their official statement of 26 December. Describing the proposed pre-conditions for an Army evacuation of the HSZ as 'unacceptable and unrealistic', it suggested that the SLA was 'simply not prepared to ease urgent existential problems of the people of Jaffna', and also indicated that in the LTTE's view the Sub-Committee on De-escalation and Normalisation had been rendered 'irrelevant by the SLA's new conditions for de-escalation'.[59] Most unhelpfully of all, Fonseka's document also included a number of references to the LTTE as terrorists.

In his SLMM end of year review, released the same day, General Furuhøvde addressed the HSZ issue. 'In order to build peace, the forces on both sides must be kept stable. In Jaffna, simply dismantling HSZs for resettlement and handing over land for cultivation will decrease both security and combat potential of the government forces. The balance of forces is the basis of the ceasefire agreement.'[60] It was a viewpoint hardly calculated to endear Furuhøvde to the LTTE, a fact underlined by Balasingham's response, which characterised his 'comments and value judgements' on the security situation in Jaffna as 'unacceptable'. Taken together with Fonseka's 'hard-line position', Balasingham argued, it had rendered the Sub-Committee on De-Escalation and Normalisation 'meaningless'.[61]

Return to the Rose Garden

In the aftermath of the controversy generated by the Fonseka De-Escalation Plan, it was hardly surprising that the issue of the HSZs was very much in focus as the fourth round of talks, opened on 6 January 2003, again at the Rose Garden in Nakom Pathom. As had become established practice, each session opened with a report from one of the sub-committees. Day one began with a report from SIHRN convenors Bernard Goonetilleke and Tamilselvan about progress on humanitarian issues. Tamilselvan again emphasised the need to speed up the implementation of humanitarian and rehabilitation programmes in the North and East, suggesting that continued delays in this area were leading to a 'significant erosion of confidence among Tamil people in the peace process'[62]—a recurring LTTE complaint.

Following a lengthy discussion, a number of decisions were taken, all of them reflected in the talks' final outcome documents.[63] With respect to the SIHRN, the government undertook to ensure that the role of government institutions engaged in the North and East would be 'properly clarified and co-ordinated' in relation to the sub-committee. Second, as a basis for this effort at institutional streamlining, it was agreed that the SIHRN constituted the 'prime decision-making body' with respect to immediate humanitarian and rehabilitation needs in the North and East, and that its membership would be increased from five to seven on both sides. Finally, both parties welcomed the sub-committee's recent decision to select the World Bank as custodian of the nascent North East Reconstruction Fund (NERF).[64]

As if making a conscious bid to build up the stock of positives before dealing with the difficult issues on the table, the first day of talks also found time to discuss the Gender Sub-Committee, whose establishment had been agreed at the previous round of talks in Oslo. Both sides provided the names of their five designated committee members, and they agreed to hold a first meeting the following month. Additionally, Norway undertook to provide financial backing for the committee as well as a 'senior Norwegian resource person' for its work.[65] On human rights—another critical area that was first given formal attention at the fourth round of talks—a decision was taken to invite former Amnesty International Secretary Ian Martin to 'work out a schedule' on human rights issues.

Day two went straight into discussion relating to the Subcommittee on De-escalation and Normalisation—which at least initially meant an open confrontation over the recommendations in the Fonseka De-Escalation Plan. The LTTE restated its objections to the plan, principally focusing on the proposed linkage between humanitarian questions such as the resettlement of IDPs on the Jaffna peninsula and security issues, notably Fonseka's suggestion that any Army withdrawal from the HSZs should be matched by decommissioning measures on the LTTE side.

Referring to Prabhakaran's depiction of the Fonseka plan as a 'document of surrender' for the LTTE, Balasingham announced that the Tigers were suspending their participation in the SDN, and communicated the LTTE leader's position that in view of the politico-strategic issues at stake, from now on 'de-escalation' issues should be discussed in plenary sessions of the peace talks.[66] Despite this impasse, both sides agreed to move on to look at the issue of the significantly larger number of IDPs seeking return to areas outside the HSZs.[67] Here a measure of agreement was reached, as was reflected in both the final talks statement and a separate Action Plan for an Accelerated Resettlement Plan for the Jaffna District, which defined a series of resettlement-related activities to be carried out by the SIHRN in areas outside the HSZs, as well as their resourcing and timelines.

While stating that the parties had 'not reached agreement on the continuation of the SDN', the final talks statement nonetheless strove to conclude on an upbeat note. Following the completion of the Action Plan described above, a 'second phase' would focus on refugees displaced from within the HSZs.[68] To assist this process, it was announced that the government would undertake a review with the assistance of an 'internationally recognised expert' and 'taking into account relevant humanitarian and security needs'.[69]

Before looking more closely at the most contentious aspects of this round of Rose Garden talks, a few other aspects of the final outcomes statement also deserve mention. First, to reinforce 'respect for the provisions of the Ceasefire Agreement', it was agreed that monthly meetings between the government, LTTE and SLMM would be held to review issues arising from the Monitoring Mission's regular summary of CFA 'violations and complaints'. The meetings were to be organised by Austin Fernando and Colonel Karuna, who also undertook to report back on them to the peace talks. Second, the Norwegians undertook to ask the ICRC to table a proposal for an 'independent verification mechanism' for the large number of military personnel or civilians described as 'Missing in Action' and 'Involuntary Disappearances'. Third, it was agreed that a Muslim delegation would be invited to the peace talks 'at an appropriate time' for 'deliberations on relevant substantive issues'. Finally, while negotiations remained in a fundamental sense hostage to the two sides' contrasting priorities and approaches—the government side emphasising the desire to get to 'core' political issues, the LTTE focusing on 'immediate existential needs'—the final statement contained some interesting points of compromise. In particular, the agreement to begin a process of discussion on human rights issues was framed in the context of an 'agreement on basic principles for a political settlement', a reference to the Oslo Declaration.

The facilitators on the Rose Garden talks

Erik Solheim

> High-security zones were a big issue at this time. [It was our] first involvement with key actors like Fonseka, the Jaffna commander. The HSZ in Jaffna was huge. The LTTE demanded that Army forces withdraw to a limited parameter of military installations, but the SLA argued that would mean they were defenceless if the LTTE launched a surprise attack. Satish Nambiar was a retired Indian general. He was asked by the Sri Lankan government to prepare a report on how all this could be done.
>
> Nambiar's report came [see note 71]: it didn't satisfy the government, Fonseka or the LTTE. But the thing that really infuriated the LTTE was in fact Fonseka's report. It spoke of the LTTE as an inferior terrorist outfit, and basically argued that the Army can't give anything away because they need to protect their forces from these bastards. It was seen as an effort to spoil the peace process. Nambiar's report was made public.[70] He came under enormous criticism in Colombo. The LTTE was also unhappy but did not speak publicly about it. Nambiar simply withdrew: he was treated very badly by the Sri Lankan media.
>
> The government had good intentions on the HSZs, but the military blocked them. Exactly what Chandrika's role in all this was is hard to say. A man like Ranil did

not easily command the respect of the military establishment. They found him soft. The government had to convince the military that the CFA provisions—military personnel out of HSZs, vacating temples and so on—could be carried out without great risk to security. The CFA did not always specify exactly how to do this. [Bear in mind that] the LTTE also had HSZs and the government had no access to those. The LTTE had no intention of letting Army forces into them.

The gender sub-committee was basically Maitree Wickremasinghe's idea, which Vidar then took forward.[71] It came about because of criticism that the peace process was an all-male affair. Women's views were not taken or considered. For me it was a very good initiative.

Overall the atmosphere was starting to sour: there was a gradual downturn from the Rose Garden talks onwards. The reference to setting up an independent verification mechanism on disappearances [concerned the] huge number of people [who had] simply disappeared or were missing in action from the war, and were presumably killed. This was mainly a government issue, and the mechanism was a way of giving something to the Army. Remember that the LTTE had killed thousands of Sri Lankan soldiers, and their relatives wanted to know what had happened to their loved ones.

Vidar Helgesen

The HSZs were a continuous concern, and one where there was not much movement on the government side. That was why the LTTE pulled the plug on the Sub-committee on Normalisation and De-escalation: they simply did not see the government move.

This was also the first time the human rights issue was mentioned. This was partly because there was criticism that the SLMM did not have a human rights component to their mandate. Ian Martin was brought in to advise, and he attended the Berlin talks. It was one of the issues that we had agreed to discuss in Oslo. After the declaration from Oslo, the human rights constituency was also watching us, so there was pressure on the parties and on us to move on this issue.

[There were] two more agreements: on a gender sub-committee and that a Muslim delegation would be invited to participate 'at an appropriate time'. On the first, later I was told by Milinda Morogoda that Ranil's wife was behind the idea. On the second, the government side was quite happy with the proposal, but would also have been fine with three parties at the talks. From Balasingham's perspective, however, the main issue was that there could not be tripartite talks.

Fifth Round: Berlin, 7–8 February 2003

When it came to selecting a location for the fifth round of talks, Solheim notes that the LTTE were keen on using different venues in order to attract wider attention to the peace process. Balasingham, whose health was deteriorating, was also reluctant to travel to from London to Asia this time. So it was agreed that the talks would be held at the Norwegian Embassy in Berlin.

For reasons that the participants could hardly have anticipated, the opening of the Berlin talks was anything but quiet. The day before the first session, reports emerged of the Sri Lankan Navy (SLN) sighting two LTTE vessels—a speedboat and a trawler—off Delft island, close to the Jaffna peninsula.[72] The SLN approached the trawler and asked to inspect the vessel. The LTTE crew refused and informed the SLN that in order to do this they would have to wait for the arrival of the SLMM. In a bid to avert an escalating crisis, 'as an exception' the government delegation in Berlin agreed to allow the SLMM to conduct a search of the vessel unaccompanied.[73] This they did and duly uncovered a quantity of arms and ammunition concealed below deck—the first time since the CFA that arms had been discovered on board an LTTE vessel.[74]

Amid frantic efforts to resolve the standoff, news came through on the morning of 7 February that the three Tiger cadres on board had blown themselves up, sinking the trawler. The SLMM monitors had narrowly escaped, diving overboard just as the vessel was about to go down.[75] The LTTE delegation vehemently protested over the incident, but it was agreed that the parties would arrange a tripartite meeting between the government, LTTE and SLMM to work out ways of avoiding such episodes in future.

Solheim and Helgesen concur that the Delft island incident overshadowed the rest of the Berlin talks. Bravely attempting to put a positive spin on the affair, however, Solheim suggested that the fact that the talks had survived this upset was indicative of the fact that the parties were not allowing such 'incidents to destroy the peace process'.[76] More controversially, today Solheim states that at the time, 'there was a strong suspicion that the Navy orchestrated [the Delft sea incident] to time it with the talks. I can't prove this. And [it] may just have been coincidence.'

Human rights

Naval dramas aside, perhaps the most notable feature of the Berlin talks was the attention devoted to human rights issues,[77] a development reflected in two headline elements of the Final Decisions document.

First, following a 'thorough discussion', it was agreed to follow through on the decision taken at the fourth round of talks to invite Ian Martin to 'draw up a roadmap' for 'human rights issues relating to the peace process' for discussion at the next round of talks. The draft roadmap was to include 'substantive human rights activities and commitments to be implemented throughout the negotiation process'; effective mechanisms for human rights monitoring; and training for LTTE cadres and government officials in human rights and humanitarian law. With regard to child soldiers, the LTTE agreed to 'work with' UNICEF on an 'action plan' for 'children affected by the conflict in the North east'. The Tigers also agreed to a 'complete cessation' of its recruitment of 'persons under 18 years of age'.[78]

Child soldiers

On the discussion of child soldiers—an issue that was given considerable attention in the outcome documents[79]—Helgesen notes that 'UNICEF had already engaged with the LTTE ... And there was some progress made. The LTTE also knew it was a key issue [for them in order] to give a better impression to the international community ... They were serious about the issue. A lot of people joined [the LTTE] because of their support for the cause, but also [because of] poverty. Whether pressurised or volunteered, however, many were very young.'

Anne Sender, SLMM Field Monitor

For us Norwegian do-gooders the child abduction thing was awful ... [LTTE-controlled territory] was run by fear. They took people and banged them up. But the poorest people were quite happy to give their children away to the LTTE. They would have discipline, education, learn English. There was a 15-year-old boy who was taken. I went to his house, but the mother said he had gone voluntarily. When he came back we helped him with school, bought him books, shoes. He was a bright lad. We said you have to finish school, move forward. He was there for a few months and then ran back to the LTTE. Half a year later I met him, and he was an LTTE soldier. He was guarding a Heroes Graveyard inside the LTTE area. I saw him again, he looked around, and then sometime later, he looked me up, saying thank you for trying to help but I like it here, I've chosen this life. I've learnt English, I'm learning marketing.

So the whole child soldier issue is much more complicated than we think. Many were doing much better there, especially those from poor families. The LTTE educated them and they learnt fast.

In his account of the discussion, Balasingham notes that the LTTE officially rejected the accusation that they had been recruiting child soldiers, with Tamilselvan arguing that the Tigers were 'maintaining thousands of war-affected children in orphanages and child welfare centres', because conditions of 'war, economic deprivation and extreme poverty [had] driven the children into the fold of the LTTE', which in response was 'spending huge amounts of money for their welfare and rehabilitation.'[80]

Other outcomes

The Berlin talks also produced other outcomes which, although not headline news, were nevertheless important in the context of the peace process. First, a decision was taken to set up three committees—one for each district of the Eastern province—to 'address land issues and other areas of mutual concern'. The committees' composition would be six representatives each from the Muslim population and the LTTE. The committees would start work 'immediately' and similar structures would be appointed to 'address such issues relating to other communities as and when required'.[81] This was a 'very positive development', notes Solheim. 'We visited Muslim communities and there was huge optimism.' Helgesen takes a more sanguine view of the issue. 'Over the course of the talks [Rauff] Hakeem kept moaning [about the situation of Muslims], and the LTTE had to give him something.'

Second, it was announced that the next round of talks—due to be held 18–21 March in Japan—would include a discussion of 'the fiscal aspects of a federal structure'. In this context it was also noted that the LTTE had 'already taken action' to establish a 'Political Affairs Committee with a view to addressing in depth issues pertaining to alternative structures of power sharing'.[82]

After the fifth round

Two weeks after the end of the Berlin talks, a date of symbolic importance for the peace process occurred: the first anniversary of the CFA's signing (22 February). In Colombo, public focus was on the celebrations led and encouraged by Prime Minister Wickremasinghe. In stark contrast, towns throughout the North and East were the focus of a day of LTTE-led shutdowns (*hartal*), in protest at what was described as 'unsatisfactory progress' with implementation of the CFA, exemplified by the lack of practical rehabilitation measures and the Army's continuing occupation of the HSZs.[83]

The day after, under pressure from the LTTE, Jaffna Mayor Cellian postponed the planned reopening of the town's symbolically important public library, which had been burned to the ground in 1981. Cellian was quoted as saying that he had been threatened with 'serious consequences' if the ceremonial re-opening went ahead—ostensibly the LTTE's objection was that other Tamil parties such as the EPDP might gain public credit from their presence at the event.[84] More fundamentally, however, LTTE opposition to the library's reopening was attributed to their resistance to any extension of central governmental powers in the region.[85]

Yet the two sides continued to participate in the thematic committees that had been established during the talks. Thus, at the end of the month, a fourth meeting of the Sub-Committee for Immediate Humanitarian and Rehabilitation Needs was held in Kilinochchi. Commenting on the sub-committee, one commentator notes the complications that appeared to dominate its workflow: 'projects were being prepared [with an] elaborate overlay of study processes, assessment processes, and the balancing of government and LTTE members in any panel or group.' The bureaucracy, he says, delayed work on 'the main activity at hand'.[86]

On 5–6 March the first meeting of the Sub-Committee on Gender Issues (SGI) was held at the LTTE Peace Secretariat in Kilinochchi, an event highlighted in Balasingham's own account, whose wife Adele had long identified herself with the struggle for womens' equality and rights within Tamil society.[87] In the course of the meeting the sub-committee decided to focus its efforts on a range of issues including resettlement, personal safety and security, infrastructure and services, livelihood and employment, political representation and decision-making, and reconciliation. In addition, it announced its intention to 'formulate Gender Guidelines for the Sub-Committees and other mechanisms associated with the peace process'.[88]

The next major development on the ground, however, was ominous. Following an intelligence tipoff, the biggest vessel in the Sri Lankan fleet set out from the Trincomalee naval base during the night of 9 March in search of an LTTE vessel suspected of shipping arms to the island. Early the following morning, a 60-metre tanker was intercepted.

Having been told that the tanker was carrying cargo from Kenya to Bangladesh, naval personnel were refused permission to board. Following the arrival of four additional Navy craft and a period of tense standoff, fighting eventually broke out. The LTTE vessel was sunk, with no survivors among the eleven crew. While no clear proof of the weapons cargo ever emerged, a few days later the LTTE admitted that three senior cadres had been killed in the incident—an admission that exposed the falsity of initial claims that the ship was simply a merchant vessel.[89] Publicly the Tigers protested that the SLN's action had violated the CFA, pointing to the section on 'military operations' which included a clause prohibiting the Sri Lankan armed forces as a whole from engaging in 'offensive operations against the LTTE'. As such, the episode was a 'grave violation of the truce agreement'.[90]

The SLMM came out of the incident looking somewhat powerless—as indeed they were in such situations. This was the first occasion that an LTTE vessel had been sunk by the Sri Lankan Navy since the signing of the CFA, and the incident reinforced the widely held perception that the CFA's maritime provisions were its weakest link.

Sixth Round: Hakone, 18–21 March 2003

In light of the dramatic incident that had taken place little more than a week earlier, it was of little surprise that the first day's discussions in Hakone culminated in an agreement to convene a meeting within three weeks of 'senior naval and political representatives from both sides' to work out how to 'prevent future incidents at sea that could threaten the stability of the ceasefire'.[91]

Day two of the talks, chaired by Yasushi Akashi in his capacity as Economic Advisor to the SIHRN, began by focusing on reconstruction and rehabilitation issues. As in previous rounds of talks, the discussion opened with a detailed progress report from SIHRN co-convenor Bernard Goonetilleke. The critical response this elicited from the LTTE side was indicative of differing perceptions and experiences in this area. In his own report, SIHRN co-convenor Tamilselvan emphasised that a combination of bureaucratic delays and 'government lethargy' in appointing members of the District Needs Assessment Panels were severely impeding the committees' functioning. Even where projects had been identified, he argued, the implementation funds were still not available. With respect to resettlement schemes, he reiterated the LTTE position that the Army's continued refusal to allow civilians to return to the HSZs remained a major stumbling block.[92]

The afternoon session was devoted to a discussion of the draft human rights roadmap circulated by Ian Martin.[93] The outcome was a request to Martin—reflected in the outcome documents—to further develop the following three aspects as the basis for a final statement the parties agreed should be adopted at the next round of talks, scheduled to be held in Thailand at the end of April:

- Drafting of a Declaration on Human Rights and Humanitarian Principles that reflected 'aspects of fundamental human rights and humanitarian standards, that the parties would undertake to ensure are respected in practice by their personnel'.
- Planning of a 'programme of human rights training' for 'LTTE cadres and government officials, police and prison officials' that would 'contribute to the respect of these principles in practice'. The programme was to include 'specialised training' by UNICEF in relation to the rights of the child; UNHCR in relation to rights of IDPs and refugees; and ICRC in relation to international humanitarian law.
- Proposals for strengthening the Human Rights Commission of Sri Lanka to enable it to 'develop the capacity for increasingly effective monitoring throughout the country'.[94]

On day three the focus shifted to political issues. The discussion took as its point of departure the need to determine 'how to give effect to the general principles of federalism in a final settlement of the ethnic conflict', with a specific focus on 'the essential elements of fiscal federalism'—a somewhat vague formulation that appears to have been accepted by both parties.[95] In addition, it was agreed that the existing 'framework for political matters' would be expanded into a 'complete plan' at the next round of talks. It was in this context that a proposal to invite Forum of Federations experts to participate as consultants in the next round was accepted.[96]

During the session Balasingham announced the formation of an LTTE Political Affairs Committee, consisting of twenty-one 'leading members' of the organisation. Over the coming months the Committee's remit, he explained, would be to undertake an 'in-depth study of systems of government, particularly federal models'. To this end, it would 'study federal systems in other parts of the world, arrange seminars for LTTE cadres, consult Tamil parliamentarians and academics and seek advice from lawyers and constitutional experts', all with a view to 'preparing the ground for the process of establishing internal self-determination within a united, federal Sri Lanka'.[97]

Following a discussion of reconciliation between the Tamil and Muslim communities, there was agreement that local LTTE and Muslim representatives in Batticaloa would meet in late April. Additionally, a request from Rauff Hakeem to organise a separate meeting between the LTTE and Muslim community leaderships in Kilinochchi to discuss 'political matters', specifically the 'participation of a Muslim delegation' in 'negotiations at plenary sessions', was accepted.[98]

During the final afternoon session Vidar Helgesen presented a review of the state of the peace process. Progress so far was highly uneven, he argued. While the talks were continuing, and a framework of sub-committees was in place, their practical functioning varied widely, he noted. Thus while the SIHRN was inching forward slowly, the SDN had stopped functioning and the Political Sub-Committee was yet to meet. The GSI, set up later than the other three committees, was still in its formative stages.[99]

Helgesen underlined the LTTE's dissatisfaction with the speed at which the 'existential needs' of the people of the North and East were being addressed, and the particular importance of addressing the issue of the HSZs. It was also a cause of regret, he stated, that the problems faced by the Muslim community—notably their land disputes—remained effectively unaddressed. While not as dark as the picture others might have painted, coming as it did from the facilitators, and more than a year after the signing of the CFA, this was still a less than optimistic survey of the situation.

The facilitators' perspectives on Hakone

Erik Solheim

The opening lunch was unbelievable. The Japanese wanted to make a magnificent start. Every dish was like a work of art—and hugely expensive no doubt—exquisite food, beautifully presented and brilliantly prepared. Everyone came, of course. The Sri Lankan government, our Japanese hosts, the Norwegian facilitators, some observers and other dignitaries. Everyone, that is, except the Tigers. [The] world media was full of articles about the Tiger snub to Japan. Why would they do this? It did not bode well for the talks ... No one seemed to be able to fathom the real reason for the Tiger 'boycott'. Which was that it was simply impossible either to tempt or to force Balasingham to eat Japanese food. No raw fish! Full stop. So Bala[singham] had simply organised local Tamils to bring rice and curry to him and the LTTE delegation in his room. The Japanese were in a frenzy; they thought it was a diplomatic issue. Then another 'diplomatic issue' came up. Balasingham invited some journalists over for drinks in his room and the Japanese, who were extremely generous hosts, refused to foot that particular bill, which ran to only a couple [of] hundred dollars. So Bala[singham] cancelled a tour of Japan that the Japanese had organised.

Nothing very much happened in the talks. Ian Martin came in as the human rights adviser. The Hakone talks [took place] exactly as the invasion of Iraq started. Ian was furious with Tony Blair and it was an emotional moment when he publicly cancelled his membership of the British Labour party after forty years.

The government was keen to show that it took the child soldier recruitment issue seriously. This was more of a political concern. I took the cynical view that you can't resolve this issue if you don't resolve the underlying problem. Neither party committed a lot of human rights violations during peacetime. Ian Martin provided advice and even spoke to the parties. Later he went on some missions to the Vanni. Child soldier recruitment by the LTTE was a key issue. Ian talked about globally accepted standards. The LTTE argued that in the USA, boys as young as seventeen could be accepted into the armed forces, in Australia even at sixteen, and that in this sense their practice was not that different.[100]

Vidar Helgesen

The key issues in Hakone were security and the continuing discussion of political matters. It was explicitly stated that the parties would invite federation consultants to the seventh session of talks—which never happened. The LTTE committed to exploring federalism and to having a political affairs committee. While there were increasing security concerns, we did not have a sense of the impending breakdown of the process. The LTTE committed to favourably considering supporting the holding of local government elections in the North and East. And the final statement included a commitment to develop a federal system. Because it all broke down, I haven't really revisited this. There are also some more things in the record of decisions: for example Balasingham and Peiris agreed to hold talks in London before the seventh session.[101]

Ian Martin

At Hakone, I presented my draft human rights roadmap. There were major discussions over it. There was no problem with the roadmap: I had met both Balasingham and Peiris by then. But the big issue was: what form of monitoring? The LTTE came out against any international monitoring. They were fine with monitoring by the Sri Lankan National Human Rights Commission, which was extraordinary, because they hated the commission. But it was a choice for something they were confident would be relatively ineffective. I was extremely disappointed. The government went along with that. You had the LTTE's desire to avoid anything that was too effective and on the government side, not wanting to open international doors. The only person who favoured international human rights monitoring was Rauff Hakeem.

Bernard Goonetilleke

In Hakone we tried to take up two issues. Ian Martin presented his paper and attempted to get the LTTE to agree to [a number of] human rights measures. Balasingham took an interesting stance: we are not in a position to enter into any international kind of arrangement, he said. There is a national human rights commission in Sri Lanka, however, and we would be ready to work with it. That took us by surprise. They found an escape route. Then we asked whether we could get back to one of the subjects agreed in Oslo.[102] Bala[singham] said he had no mandate to discuss it. Then he made a gesture, moving his fingers across his neck, to say that was what would happen if he discussed it. That made it clear to us that he had exceeded his authority in Oslo.

After each and every [round of talks], they would take a delegation out and meet with the local diaspora. The basic message was: our thirst is for a separate Tamil Eelam. And the LTTE delegation would respond, 'yes, we are discussing [it] with the government, but the diaspora should continue to support us and provide financial resources. We need to talk to the government on equal terms.'

Nordic tour

Following an earlier visit to European federal countries to study their political systems, a week after the Hakone talks more than twenty members of the LTTE Political Affairs Committee began a ten day tour of the Nordic countries. From the Norwegian organisers' perspective, the tour's objective was to expose the Tigers' political leadership to 'different democratic systems' as well as 'related issues such as civilian control of armed forces' and 'the Åland islands solution'.[103] The LTTE itself described the tour's goals as studying 'aspects of federalism, constitutional frameworks and administrative structures employed in those countries'.[104]

Delhi visit

By way of a reminder that more than one centre of political power existed in the country, in the second week of April President Kumaratunga made a four-day visit to India, during which the peace process was very much the focus of discussion. The president reportedly voiced her apprehension about the way negotiations were being conducted. Arguing that the UNP government had allowed the LTTE to establish a de facto separate state since the signing of the ceasefire agreement, she maintained that the Tigers had significantly bolstered their recruitment efforts, increasing the number of cadres from 6,000 to 18,000, and had continued to smuggle large amounts of weaponry into the country. At the same, maintaining her customary line, President Kumaratunga emphasised that she would do nothing to undermine the peace process.

In response, an Indian government spokesperson stated that there were many actors involved in the Sri Lankan peace process, all of whose views were taken into account—including that of the president.[105] As well as indicating how carefully India continued to tread over Sri Lankan affairs, the visit was a reminder of the importance of keeping President Kumaratunga within the peace process—something that Prime Minister Wickremasinghe did not always seem to take as seriously as the domestic political situation required.

Washington donor conference

The donor seminar hosted by the US in Washington on 14–15 April 2003— timed to coincide with annual meetings of the IMF and World Bank, and thus to enable the participation of key officials—proved to be something of a watershed, as it was the first major peace-process related event in which the LTTE did not participate. Its absence was not of its own choosing. Because the Tigers were officially designated as a terrorist organisation, the US State Department did not issue them with an invitation.[106] Despite the participation of representatives of twenty-five countries and sixteen international organisations—India, which had boycotted the 2002 Oslo donor conference on account of the LTTE's attendance, was a particularly notable presence—the LTTE's absence had a significant impact on the meeting.

The LTTE were not silent on the issue. A statement on 4 April underlined the Tigers' 'deep disappointment' at their exclusion, and a further one issued a week later indicated that the organisation was 'reviewing' its participation in the Tokyo Donor Conference scheduled for early June.[107] To help 'restore confidence and re-establish goodwill', the statement called for 'full implementation' of the 'normalisation aspects' of the CFA, as well as the implementation of 'agreements pertaining to resettlement of refugees and IDPs reached in the six rounds of talks.'[108]

In his opening address, US Under Secretary of State Richard Armitage emphasised that while the US was 'encouraged' by the LTTE's 'recent behaviour', its overall position remained clear: 'The LTTE must unequivocally renounce terrorism, in word and in deed, if we are to consider withdrawing the [terrorist] designation.'[109] Ignoring this highly sensitive issue, the head of the government delegation, Milinda Morogoda, chose to emphasise the parties' focus on the 'common goal of a political solution'. From the demand for a separate state, he argued, the LTTE had 'moved to consideration of patterns of devolution within a federal system'.[110]

Recognising that some donors might consider it 'desirable [to] postpone granting us assistance until the current negotiations are concluded and a peace accord has been signed', Morogoda underscored the critical importance of backing the government's ability to 'demonstrate now ... the dividend that peace will bring', or else risk the 'negative effects of frustration among the parties, a breakdown of the negotiations and a resumption of hostilities'.[111] He went on to stress the importance of securing funds to support measures intended to meet 'both the immediate needs of reconstruction, rehabilitation and relief as well as for laying the foundations for overall economic recovery after two decades of destructive and debilitating conflict'. Tasks identified as 'demanding ... immediate attention in this context' included:

- Locating and neutralising 'some one million land mines scattered in unmarked areas'.
- Rebuilding and restoring basic services to 'whole towns and villages'.
- Providing shelter and agricultural subsistence tools to 'an estimated one million internally displaced persons'.
- Rebuilding the many schools that have been 'destroyed or damaged in conflict-affected areas', and providing resources for schools in other parts of the country that have 'suffered severely from a chronic lack of funds'.
- Getting people back to work 'throughout the island'.[112]

By the seminar's conclusion, some USD $3.5 billion worth of assistance had been pledged by donors over a three-year period—the biggest aid pledge received to date by Sri Lanka, representing a significant portion of the official estimate of USD $6 billion needed for reconstruction purposes over the coming six years.[113]

Reactions to the Washington conference

Erik Solheim

> It was kind of a political support conference. The initiative [needed] to make it happen was taken by Milinda in consultation with Armitage. The intention—to get US support for the peace process, to create a safety net—was a positive one. [It also] sent out the message to the Sinhala public that you are not alone, you have big friends. However, it was unilateral thinking not to involve the LTTE. Neither the government nor we understood how seriously the LTTE would take this. Bala[singham] had objected earlier, but not very strongly. As I recall, the Sri Lankans may have mentioned it, and the LTTE did not really object. It was not a clash point. If that had happened, we would have said don't do it.

> To me, the meeting's substance was not important. The fact that the government went without the LTTE was problematic. Later the LTTE called and said that they had suspended [their participation in] the peace process and formal talks. The LTTE very clearly used the US event as an excuse. I think [the decision to

withdraw] was the result a chain of events, but this enforced it. But at the time it was not on my radar that the LTTE would take it very seriously. Prabhakaran strongly suspected that he was being pushed into a corner by the international community. The Washington conference exacerbated this suspicion, but in itself it was not the sole cause [of the LTTE withdrawal]. The Tamil diaspora was sceptical of federalism throughout the process. Bala[singham] called me up and said it was a suspension and not a break, and that we should have understood [their issues] about the Washington conference.

Vidar Helgesen

We did hear a voice of concern from Balasingham [over the fact] that the LTTE was not invited. We also emphasised that the Americans provided support for the process. I did not really realise this would have such an impact, because it was not [just] about a single meeting in Washington, it was part of a series of meetings. You had the Oslo conference, there was the Washington meeting, there was supposed to be a Brussels meeting, then the Tokyo conference. Washington was a preparatory seminar, not a pledging meeting. It was for mobilising political commitment ahead of the Tokyo meeting. Maybe the way the government sold the conference at home tilted the balance.

Milinda Moragoda

[The Washington conference] came up in Hakone. I was minister of economic reforms, the whole restructuring of the country was going on, so we were proposing a meeting in Washington after the annual meetings of the IMF and World Bank ... I mentioned that we were planning to have this meeting in Washington to discuss the overall development programme, and that part of it would be to discuss the North and the East, but that the substance of the [issues in the] North and East were going to be discussed in Tokyo ... At that stage it was Bala[singham] who jokingly said that they wanted to come. I said that was unlikely to happen. It was very clear that I did not make a commitment that they could come to Washington. Right after the Hakone meeting, Tamilselvan said that I had promised that they could come to Washington. I got quite annoyed. Then Bala[singham] formally apologised. That's why I said I had respect for him.

I told them our philosophy was summarised in one sentence: a warm heart—meaning we are sincere—and a cool head. This delicate balance was sometimes difficult to maintain on our side. Ranil was supportive, but there were different views within the government on the question of military preparedness. The LTTE was after all a military organisation. Concerning the 'international safety net', the idea was to be honest with everybody. Norway would facilitate, but it did not have muscle, so the safety net was with the US and Japan. Formally India was not [a] part of it, but they were briefed. It was a senior Indian minister who told me to add 'deep breath' to the philosophy as well. He felt that India was supportive, but they had lost men in the country after 1987.[114]

The US, Japan and Sri Lanka

Richard Armitage, US Deputy Secretary of State (2001–5), recalls that Vidar Helgesen first came to see him because 'he had heard there's this character who actually cared about Sri Lanka'. Armitage is candid about some of the factors animating his interest in the Sri Lankan conflict. 'I did think this was a situation that was resolvable', he says: and as he began to get more involved, moreover, 'with the nature of the child soldiers, the suicide killings—all these things that we were starting to face in Middle East—I thought this would be a perfect way to get a resolution on such issues, as a lesson [on how to do so].'

What of the LTTE's terrorist status? Even in the post 9/11 world, Armitage felt the fact the LTTE was already proscribed was 'less of a constraint than an opportunity to slowly move them away [from terrorism]. And 'if the LTTE could be induced to modify', he reasoned, 'then we could remove them from the [proscribed] list.'

Devinda Subasinghe, Sri Lankan Ambassador to the US at the time, confirms that Armitage had long taken a personal interest in developments. 'He had been in Sri Lanka in July 1983—Reagan sent him and Weinberger to Colombo when it was burning.' Moving forward to 2002, Subasinghe notes that 'Ranil had been cultivating Washington. He was already well known there'. Consequently, 'when Ranil came into office there was a lot of support and expectation. And Armitage made the decision to put the full weight and faith of the US government behind him.'

'One of the triggers', Subasinghe says, 'was an inter-agency review of Sri Lanka policy that Armitage requested. A US Pacific Command review evaluated the defence forces, their needs, gaps and so on. That became the foundation or benchmark to restart military–military relations, which had hit a low because of human rights issues … And it was all thanks to Armitage's leadership.'

With respect to military co-operation, the focus was on 'assistance with trying to track [LTTE] arms shipments, upgrading the Sri Lanka Navy (SLN)'s firepower, radar systems and intelligence sharing'. Not that all of the military co-operation occurred immediately. 'Much of [it] was over a period of time, and also much of it kicked in [in] 2007–8: so there was a time lag between request and delivery.'

US assistance was not, however, purely military. 'For example, Sri Lanka qualified for USD $1 billion in aid under the Millennium

Challenge Account', says Subasinghe. 'And Armitage took the lead in coordinating the conference in Washington. In that context the former diplomat recalls: 'I got a call during the Tokyo round of talks from Milinda, with Erik, Vidar and Balasingham on a conference line saying that Bala[singham] wanted to come to the Washington conference. Milinda explained that Bala[singham] knew he [wouldn't receive an invitation], but would still like to make a request through us.'

The other key component of economic aid to Sri Lanka at this point was Japan, Subasinghe explains. 'Ranil told me to ask Armitage to ask Japan to open up their cheque book. Armitage said, 'OK, done, what next?' But we all forgot to consult the Indians', he continues. 'Brajesh Mishra, the Indian National Security Adviser, blew his top: what are the Japanese doing in our front yard, he asked? So Akashi had to make a stop in New Delhi to try and calm things down. But Mishra went to Tokyo before he was finally re-assured. That was a slip-up on our part. Overall, there was a strong economic focus to the peace process', Subasinghe maintains, 'and without US leadership on that front we would not have made the near USD $4 billion mark that we achieved in Tokyo.'[116]

The LTTE suspends participation in the talks

Following a holiday week surrounding Sri Lankan New Year in which political attention was focused on reports from the Washington seminar, and more disturbing news of escalating Tamil-Muslim clashes in the Eastern coastal town of Muttur,[116] few if any were prepared for the LTTE's announcement on 21 April that they were suspending participation in negotiations 'for the time being', and would not be attending the Tokyo donor conference in June.[117]

In his account of the events leading up to the decision, Balasingham points to a number of factors. First, having undertaken its own evaluation of progress achieved to date following the Hakone talks, he suggests that the government—and indeed the facilitators—were continuing to prioritise 'progress at the political level, over and above the most critical and pressing humanitarian issues faced by the war-affected Tamil community'. As a result, he maintained, the 'project of de-escalation and normalisation had collapsed, closing the door for rehabilitation and reconstruction'.[118] Second, the government's current effort to 'engage the international community for the mobilisation of resources' was, Balasingham argued, 'primarily aimed at 'regaining' and 'developing southern Sri Lanka' as well as 'building up an effective international safety net to contain the LTTE'.[119]

Third, he suggested that the LTTE now found itself facing a 'new phenomenon': the excessive involvement of 'international custodians of peace' in the negotiating process. Combining 'political pressure' with 'economic assistance', the 'international actors' were intervening to 'promote the interests of the Sri Lankan state', the effect of which was to 'severely undermine the status and power relations between the protagonists'.[120] Consequently, as a 'non-state actor caught up in the intrigue-ridden world of the international state system', the LTTE was now 'compelled to free itself from the overpowering forces of containment'.

In a letter sent to Wickremasinghe on 21 April, Balasingham further spelled out the LTTE's analysis of the situation. Noting that the governemnt, in spite of the LTTE's 'goodwill and trust', had elected to 'marginalise' the Tigers in 'approaching the international community for economic assistance', Balasingham underscored that 'there had been no change in the ground situation'. More broadly, progress in key areas such as the 'agreement to explore federalism' had not been matched by any amelioration of the 'continuing hardships being faced by our people'. While poverty reduction had been given a central position in the government's economic strategy, Balasingham argues, centrepiece documents such as the 'Regaining Sri Lanka' manifesto failed to 'examine the causality of the phenomenon of poverty, the effects of ethnic war and the unique conditions of devastation prevailing in the Northeast'. Lacking any 'comprehensive strategy for serious development' of these regions, the government had undermined 'the confidence of the Tamil people and the LTTE leadership in the negotiating process'—hence the decision to suspend LTTE participation 'for the time being'. In order to restore Tamil people's faith in the peace process, the government was urged to fully implement 'without further delay' both the 'normalisation aspects' of the CFA and to permit the 'immediate resettlement of IDPs in the Northeast'.

It quickly became clear that 'suspended participation' extended to every aspect of the peace process. On 23 April, for example, Tamilselvan—recently returned from the LTTE Political Committee's Nordic study tour—wrote to Bernard Goonetilleke informing him of the need to postpone the next meeting of the SIHRN, due to be held on 25–26 April.[121]

In an exchange with US Ambassador to Colombo Ashley Wills, who had criticised the Tigers for 'walking away from the talks', Balasingham reiterated the view that the LTTE had not abandoned the negotiations but rather 'temporarily suspended the talks' in order to give 'time and space for the government to implement crucial decisions, particularly the normalisation aspects of the CFA'.[122]

The contested nature of the issues at stake was underscored by the media coverage of the LTTE's decision. Sinhalese political analyst Jayaveda Uyangoda, for example, was quoted as suggesting that the LTTE's latest pronouncement should primarily be understood as signalling the Tigers' desire for 'the international community to stop treating them as terrorists ... There has been asymmetry in favour of Colombo, for which the Tigers want redress by political means.'[123] Alternatively, the LTTE's move was interpreted as proof that 'the Tigers have their eyes fixed firmly on the objective of regaining Jaffna'—a priority expressed, it was suggested, in the statement's reiteration of the importance of government movement on the issue of 'resettlement of internally displaced persons' and reaffirmation of the injustice of the continuing 'massive military occupation of Jaffna'.[124]

Others shared the analysis of Senior Indian High Commission representative Taranjit Sandhu, imparted in a 24 April meeting with his US counterpart. 'He [TS] said he thought it was a "tactical" step by the Tigers, who wanted the government to cave in on various issues.'[125] In a similar vein, during meetings with the diplomatic community and other international representatives, Milinda Morogoda propounded the view that the LTTE were using 'shock therapy' in order to try and 'regain some control of the agenda'.[126]

Wickremasinghe's reply to Balasingham (29 April), taken to Kilinochchi by Jon Westborg and the new Norwegian Ambassador Hans Brattskar to ensure safe and rapid delivery,[127] attempted to answer him point for point and to present a more optimistic assessment of the negotiations to date, stressing that in overall terms there had been 'substantial progress towards peace and development throughout the country'. Responding to Balasingham's criticism regarding the LTTE's exclusion from the Washington donor seminar, Wickremasinghe argued that the decision to hold the meeting in the US capital was strongly influenced by the possibility of securing the participation of the major donors 'as participants in the ... spring meetings of the World Bank and IMF'. This was happening, moreover, at a time when the donors' attention was 'absorbed by the needs of Iraq'—a clear hint that both parties in Sri Lanka should be mindful of a broader international context in which there was stiff competition for donor resources.

Overall, Wickremasinghe's response—described by Balasingham as a 'feeble attempt to defend government policies'[128]—was indicative of a steadily growing gulf between the two sides. What for the government appeared to be a strategic, forward-thinking move intended to help maximise potential donor interest in Sri Lanka was perceived by the LTTE as calculated marginalisation, insult and public humiliation. If there was to be any chance of pulling the peace process back on track, it was vital to address this disparity—and quickly.

Reactions to the LTTE's withdrawal

Erik Solheim

> When Bala[singham] called to say the talks were suspended, we were certainly disappointed, and somewhat confused. We hoped it would be a short suspension and undoubtedly that was also Bala[singham]'s intention at that point. The LTTE had no plan for going back to war, nor of aborting peace talks for [a] long [period]. The fact that talks barely reopened later shows how dangerous such a 'break' can be: you let other forces come in and set the agenda. Two or three more rounds of talks were on the cards. We were very eager to link the LTTE with the international community because that would reduce the chance of terrorist attacks by the Tigers. We hoped that they would come to understand the federal system. We also believed—somewhat naively—that economic progress would have a major impact in [a] positive sense. Looking back, we thought we would try to convince the government to move more quickly on the LTTE's demands.

> Later we came to understand that the suspension of [the] talks also had to do with the relationship between Balasingham and Prabhakaran. Bala[singham] was not in favour of this move, but Prabhakaran had been discomforted by the federalism discussion. I think Prabhakaran did not doubt Ranil's readiness to make major efforts for the North and East, he just doubted his ability to do it [in practice]. Also, he did not underestimate the strength of Chandrika and the SLFP, which we may have done at this point. Prabhakaran was also worried by Ranil's talk of a 'security net', afraid it would spin the LTTE into a web, limiting their options. He did not see the international attention [given] to the peace process as what it was: a huge opportunity for the LTTE to break out of the isolation they had brought upon themselves as a result of the killing of Rajiv Gandhi.

> There is really nothing to the argument that introducing human rights to the talks was why the LTTE pulled out. That is the voice of westerners who think human rights are the overriding issue. European governments, civil society, Sinhalese civil society pushed the human rights issue. In reality, neither LTTE nor the government were so interested in this. The LTTE may have been pushed against the wall on the issue, but that could not have been the reason for pulling out of talks.

> There was no big benefit from the Washington meeting, so holding it was a mistake. But the meeting was well intended. Bala[singham] had much more understanding of the government's need to gain a strong position among the Sinhalese, otherwise they couldn't give real concessions to the Tamils. But

Prabhakaran did not understand that. The point of the Washington meeting was to build support for the peace process among the Sinhalese.

Vidar Helgesen

We were well aware of the LTTE's disappointment about their absence [in Washington], but we had no indication that this would be considered so grave that it would result in their pulling out. With fairly well informed hindsight, there is much to suggest that it was a convenient excuse for a decision that would have been taken in any case.

We now know that there were strong reactions in the diaspora, the hardliners within the LTTE, against federalism and related agreements [arrived at] during the talks. The follow-up to the Oslo Declaration was quite an ambitious list of issues to be addressed. There was a sense that Balasingham was running his own show, and that Prabhakaran was not happy with that. Prabhakaran had to trade off between military hardliners and those seeking a political process. And here he made the call that Bala[singham] had gone too far, and that they needed to suspend the talks. It also had to do with frustration that economic development wasn't happening, that the LTTE were not getting enough of a hand in on reconstruction activities; that the government was building this international safety net that Ranil talked about, but which from the LTTE's perspective was a safety net for the government, not the peace process as such. In that context, the Washington meeting played a role, but was not the full story.

I would not be surprised if reports of the LTTE imposing economic control, taxing everyone's earnings, imposing a kind of economic stranglehold over the North and East were true. They did establish political structures, from councils to courts, the emergence of a civil administration. I saw this as extremely positive because it had in it the nucleus for a political structure for a federal solution. They also established land registries to try to get economic control. It wouldn't surprise me at all because of the nature of the LTTE. We were not aware that they were cementing economic control; but we did see the evolution of a political structure.

Meanwhile, media reports carried massive claims that the LTTE were rearming and regrouping. The government side, in a way, was rearming more, but we did not know that. We were not there to design any outcome of the peace process. We were there to facilitate a discussion between the two sides.

Milinda Moragoda

In a general sense there was always a paradigm difference between the LTTE and the government in that their [the LTTE's] focus seemed to be consolidation on the ground. Maybe that was to protect themselves, or because they had intended to break out of the process at some stage and gain further advantage. Whenever political issues came up we had to come up with different, creative ways in which to handle them ... On the security side, they wanted to do things their own way, but we said no—we have to do it jointly. They always ignored the political side. If they had engaged more on the political side, and in a serious way, that would have built a lot more confidence.

Jehan Perera

At the time I thought it was a tactical ploy on the LTTE's part to pull out of talks, and that they would come back. I was sympathetic to their situation: things were moving slowly, they were losing ground, their cadres wanted to marry, go out to the movies and not fight, so they had to keep the pressure up. When they pulled out I saw it in that light: that things needed to move faster ... But I didn't think they would go back to war.

5

STALEMATE

From May to July 2003, following the LTTE's decision to suspend participation in the peace talks, a flurry of letters, proposals and counter-proposals flew between the two sides. The country had been here before, notably during the talks initiated by President Kumaratunga in 1994–5, when she and LTTE leader Prabhakaran exchanged no fewer than forty-three letters over a period of seven months, ultimately to no avail.[1]

Aware of the importance of maintaining domestic political support for the peace process, on 6 May Wickremasinghe made a statement in Parliament, informing the house of the letter in which Balasingham notified him of the LTTE's decision to suspend its participation, and disclosing his response to the LTTE chief negotiator. Already, a determined international effort to bring the LTTE back to the negotiating table had been launched. On 1 May, Norwegian ambassador Hans Brattskar and his predecessor Jon Westborg—now ambassador to Delhi—had travelled to Kilinochchi for talks with LTTE political wing leader Tamilselvan; their second visit in the space of a couple of days, the first being to deliver Wickremasinghe's letter of 29 April directly to the LTTE leadership.[2]

The following week, on 6 May, the Norwegian team—including Vidar Helgesen and Erik Solheim, who had arrived from Oslo following a stopover in Delhi for discussions with senior Indian officials—met Anton Balasingham immediately after his arrival in the country for consultations with Prabhakaran. Separately, but with the shared objective of trying to revive the peace process, Japanese envoy Yasushi Akashi also arrived in

Colombo. On 7 May in Kilinochchi, Akashi tried to persuade Prabhakaran to return to the talks, and specifically to send an LTTE delegation to the Tokyo donor conference scheduled for 9–10 June. At the end of his mission Akashi announced that he had given the LTTE a week in which to decide on their attendance at the Tokyo conference. 'The process of aid and the process of negotiations must go hand in hand, as nobody can simply receive aid without undertaking some responsibility for the peace process', he stated at a press conference. 'If [the LTTE] miss this opportunity then such a chance may not come again for a long time,' he concluded.

With regard to further talks, Akashi indicated that Prabhakaran had said that the LTTE would not return to the negotiating table unless the government took 'positive action' to ensure the effective functioning of the North East Rehabilitation Fund (NERF) and the Sub-Committee on Immediate Rehabilitation and Humanitarian Needs (SIHRN).[3] Media commentators speculated that the Tigers' covert objective was to secure a measure of control over the sizeable funds that these structures—the NERF in particular—were expected to receive in the wake of the forthcoming Tokyo conference.[4]

In the meantime, the full Norwegian team met with Balasingham again in Kilinochchi on 8 May. On this occasion, Solheim recalls, Balasingham called together a broad group of LTTE military commanders, including Soosai, Bhanu and Balraj,[5] to meet the Norwegians for the first time. A similar set of issues to those raised with Akashi was discussed, with the addition of the Nambiar Report,[6] the final version of which had been officially released earlier the same week. According to one analyst, the LTTE leadership also highlighted another area in which they wanted to see 'positive action' from the government. This was the recent set of proposals put forward by SLMM leader Tryggve Tellefsen for official recognition of the Sea Tigers as a 'de facto naval unit', and on this basis, the demarcation of areas at sea within which they would be permitted to conduct both training and live firing exercises.[7]

International pressure

Adding to the chorus of international voices calling for the peace process to continue, on a mid-May visit to Sri Lanka, US Assistant Secretary of State for South Asian Affairs Christina Rocca urged the LTTE to re-engage fully. 'It is in the best interest of the peace process, the Tamil people, and the Tigers themselves that the LTTE be at the table in Tokyo', she stated. At the same time, Rocca identified the ongoing dispute between the Prime

Minister Wickremasinghe and President Kumaratunga as something that could derail the process, and accordingly urged the two leaders to put aside their differences in an effort to present a united Sri Lankan front at the Tokyo conference.[8] As Solheim observes, Rocca's statement is an interesting reminder of 'how differently the US treated the Tigers, compared to Afghan and Palestinian "terrorist" groups. There were limits to US engagement', he notes, but there was also a 'willingness to support the peace process' that showed 'substantial flexibility' in relation to the 'guiding Washington doctrine of the time'.

A further obstacle emerged on 11 May when Anton Balasingham, with his wife Adele, was rushed from Sri Lanka to London for an urgent medical check-up. Though his departure prompted media speculation that the LTTE's chief advisor had been sidelined by Prabhakaran in favour of the more hardline Tamilselvan, it seems probable that his rapid exit from the country was for precisely the reason given.[9] International efforts to bring the Tigers back to the negotiating table reached a crescendo in mid-May when a heavyweight Norwegian delegation, led by Foreign Minister Jan Petersen, arrived in Sri Lanka. On 15 May the delegation travelled to Kilinochchi for a meeting with Prabhakaran, Tamilselvan and LTTE advisers Maheshwaran and Rudrakumaran.

During the meeting Prabhakaran repeated the essential elements of his message to Akashi, with one important addition: a request to the government in Colombo to put forward proposals for 'a new innovative structure for the reconstruction and development of the North and East'.[10] The government was quick to respond: two days after the Norwegians' visit to Kilinochchi, Helgesen returned to the Vanni with a set of proposals which he duly handed over to Tamilselvan. The tranche comprised a 'concept paper' on the establishment of a 'Reconstruction and Development Council' (RDC) for the North and East,[11] and a 'proposal for utilising locally elected bodies as a means to run development and reconstruction related affairs of the North and East'.[12]

On 21 May, reportedly at Prabhakaran's request, Balasingham—now recovered—sent a response to Helgesen that was then forwarded to Ranil Wickremasinghe.[13] Balasingham stated that the RDC proposed by the government fell short of the LTTE leader's expectations of a 'concrete framework for an interim administrative set-up'. The alternative proposed by the Tigers was an 'interim administrative mechanism' with 'greater participation [for] the LTTE in both decision making and delivery of the tasks of rebuilding the war-damaged economy and restoring normalcy in the Tamil-speaking homeland.'[14]

Continuing the exchange, a week later (27 May) the Sri Lankan Prime Minister responded to Balasingham amid unconfirmed reports that the government had invited Norway and Japan to come up with an alternative to the interim administrative mechanism demanded by the LTTE.[15] Although no one was saying so openly, there was a palpable sense of working against the clock as the deadline for the Tokyo donor conference, due to be held two weeks later, crept closer.

The government's revised proposals envisaged the establishment of a new interim arrangement dubbed a 'representative Apex Body' and a 'policy and advisory board', whose main role was 'decision making' with regard to 'all immediate and medium term rehabilitation, reconstruction and development work in the North-East and advising on policy development'.[16] The Apex Body would be constituted in such a way that it reflected the 'ethnic composition in the North-East, and comprised members who are truly representative of the ethnic groups' of the region. It was suggested that the new body would be headed by a special commissioner, appointed by the prime minister.

The LTTE's response was immediate and negative. In a four-page reply, dated 30 May, Balasingham criticised the government for failing to specify the nature of the role envisaged for the LTTE in the proposed Apex Body, which he also described as tantamount to a new 'apex bureaucracy', linked to 'several other inefficient and defunct state agencies and mechanisms' that would be incapable of carrying out the 'immense humanitarian tasks' of rehabilitation and development in the North-East in an efficient manner.[17]

The exchange continued at pace. Wickremasinghe's reply of 1 June attempted to clarify some of the issues raised by Balasingham and suggested that a meeting between the two sides should be held soon in order to achieve 'a practical resolution of this matter'.[18] But Balasingham was unpersuaded. Pointing to what he termed 'serious differences' between 'what the LTTE leadership proposes and what the government offers', he went on to argue that the LTTE were prepared to 'resume negotiations' on condition that the government tabled a 'draft framework for an Interim Administration structure along the lines proposed by our leadership'.[19]

The Tokyo donor conference

At this point, with only a week to go until the Tokyo donor conference, attention turned to the unresolved question of the LTTE's participation. Wickremasinghe offered to dispatch a 'special team' to sort out the remaining differences between the two sides, and thus—it was hoped—pave the way for the Tigers' attendance. The LTTE responded by demanding a guarantee on the establishment of an interim administration, a move that appeared tantamount to turning down the government's offer.[20] 'The Tigers just do not want aid with strings attached', remarked one commentator. 'Given its authoritarian, anti-democratic structure, the LTTE is in no mood to agree to the basic principles of peace and democracy as desired by the donor community. It would prefer to boycott Tokyo ... than agree to relax its iron grip on the Tamil people and help foster democracy and human rights.'[21] From the government's perspective, however, Prime Minister Wickremasinghe continued to insist that the two sides were 'not that far apart' on the contours of an administrative structure for the North-East, emphasising in this context the agreement on the foundational role of the federal solution reached at the Oslo talks.[22]

With or without the LTTE, preparations for the Tokyo Conference continued apace. The announcement that US Under Secretary of State Richard Armitage would be attending the meeting gave the organisers a much-needed fillip. In the event more than fifty countries and twenty-one donor or other international organisations attended the two-day meeting, which opened on 9 June.

By the end of the conference donors had pledged a total of USD $4.5 billion to the country, to be disbursed over the following three years.[23] They also made a concerted appeal to the LTTE to return to the table. As well as underscoring the need for long-term assistance to support the rebuilding of conflict-affected parts of the North and development throughout the country, the conference's final declaration noted that donors would be closely monitoring progress on the ground to ensure that the peace process moved forward in tandem with reconstruction efforts[24]—a point made by a number of keynote speakers, notably Japanese Prime Minister Junichiro Koizumi.[25]

In terms of future developments, an important by-product of the Tokyo conference was the emergence of the so-called 'Co-Chairs' structure, composed of three countries and one regional entity—the USA, Japan, Norway and the European Union. Initially established to assist with preparations for the Tokyo conference, over time the Co-Chairs came to play an increasingly central role in international engagement with the conflict in Sri Lanka.[26]

As anticipated, the LTTE's official response to the outcomes of the Tokyo conference was negative. In addition to emphasising the fact that they had not been 'involved in the deliberations or ... formulations of [the] existing declarations', the Tigers again took the opportunity to underscore their opposition to the proposal for a 'provisional administrative structure' out-lined in Tokyo by Prime Minister Wickremasinghe.[27] A 23 June statement issued by the LTTE suggested that the conference's Final Declaration was an attempt by the government to 'superimpose its own agenda on the LTTE'. The statement also argued that 'severe economic and political bank-ruptcy have compelled the government to seek the ultimate refuge in the so-called "international safety net" to resolve the economic and political crisis of the country.' Thus, 'the Colombo regime has shifted the peace process from third party facilitation to the realm of international arbitra-tion by formidable external forces.'[28] While the government had attempted to use the notion of an 'international safety net' to reassure the majority Sinhalese population of the viability of the peace process, it has been argued that for the LTTE this was taken as evidence that Wickremasinghe was 'using that net to trap it'.[29]

Summer of discontent

A week after the Tokyo conference there were two major military inci-dents. In the first, Thambirajah Subathiran of the Eelam People's Revolutionary Liberation Front (EPRLF), a leading Tamil political figure known for his consistent and public opposition to the LTTE, was assassi-nated while exercising on the roof of his office early on the morning of 14 June. A few hours later, an LTTE ship suspected of carrying a weapons cargo was sunk—or may have self-detonated—after engaging with the Sri Lanka Navy, at a distance from the Sri Lankan coastline hotly disputed by the two sides.[30] If the first incident underscored the reality that the LTTE continued to see members of alternative Tamil groups as prime targets for assassination, the second emphasised that the maritime dimensions of the ceasefire agreement remained fragile at best.

Further assassinations in the following weeks highlighted the continued vulnerability of non-LTTE Tamil groups in the Northeast. Under the terms of the ceasefire, all Tamil forces other than the LTTE had been disarmed. At the same time, the agreement gave the LTTE free access to government-controlled areas for 'political work'. Since the 'political work' proviso was being flouted openly by the LTTE—one of the assassinations had taken place in Colombo, for example—the situation for non-Tiger Tamil groups became incredibly difficult.[31]

Ten days later the political focus returned to constitutional matters as Prime Minister Wickremasinghe, chief negotiator Milinda Morogoda and

Attorney General Kandapper Kamalasabayon made an official visit to the UK in order to consult British constitutional experts on the interim administrative proposals that the government was preparing in response to the LTTE's demands. Reports from London of meetings between Solheim and Balasingham and then between Solheim and Wickremasinghe sparked optimism about the potential resumption of negotiations.[32] It was said that a critical factor here was Solheim's disclosure to Balasingham of the main elements of the government's revised proposal.[33]

However, Balasingham's statement after the meeting noted that the LTTE leadership 'is awaiting the government's proposal for an interim administration. If a concrete set of proposals is presented, the LTTE will study the framework and suggest amendments and improvements.' Regarding the possibility of talks, Balasingham returned to a well-worn LTTE theme, arguing that '[i]nstead of pursuing guidelines, milestones and roadmaps for an imaginary solution, the talks should address crucial issues related to the harsh existential realities of the ground situation.'[34]

On 27 June an estimated 25–30,000 Tamils, many carrying pictures of Prabhakaran, gathered in central Jaffna for a *Pongu Thamil* or 'Tamil Resurgence' rally. Reportedly the largest peaceful demonstration in Jaffna since the army retook the city in 1995, it was ostensibly organised by university students but was in reality very much a Tiger-orchestrated event.[35] The slogans chanted by the crowd and the resolution they 'adopted' at the conclusion of the demonstration reflected the LTTE's priorities and concerns at the time.

For its part, the government side appeared to be taking seriously the LTTE's demands for an interim administrative structure for the Northeast. A new proposal, titled 'Provisional Administrative Structure for the Northern and Eastern Province', was delivered to Kilinochchi on 17 July by Jon Westborg, with a further copy transmitted to Anton Balasingham in London.[36] The central element was the creation of a 'Provisional Administrative Council', in which the LTTE would have the majority of members. This Council was to have 'such powers and functions as are at present being exercised ... by the government in respect of regional administration—except [in] the area of police and security, land and revenue—but including rehabilitation, reconstruction and resettlement.'[37]

An initial LTTE response came on 27 July. Addressing a meeting of several thousand LTTE cadres held in the Battticaloa area, Tamilselvan stated that the government's document again fell short of the 'expectations of the Tamil people'. At the same time he noted that the LTTE was studying the proposals carefully, and in consultation with legal and constitutional experts would soon be submitting 'counter-proposals ... that would satisfy the expectations and reflect the interests of our people'. If the government accepted these counter-proposals, peace talks could recommence.[38] Three weeks later, it was announced that a team of LTTE legal experts would be holding a three-day meeting in Paris later that month to scrutinise the government's proposal and formulate the Tigers' counter-document.[39]

In the meantime, Erik Solheim made a three-day visit to Sri Lanka to try and resolve a row over a LTTE camp that had recently been established at Kinniya, close to Trincomalee. Despite an SLMM ruling that the camp was located in government-controlled territory and as such violated the cease-fire agreement, Tiger cadres were refusing to vacate it on the grounds that the surrounding area had, they asserted, been under LTTE control for the last ten years.[40] Military concerns aside, Solheim was alerted by local residents to the camp's potential to ignite already fragile inter-ethnic relations in the mainly Muslim area. Matters were hardly helped by the reported emergence of armed Muslim gangs created to protect the community against the perceived threat from the LTTE.[41] Solheim left Batticaloa the next day, having failed to persuade the LTTE to leave.[42]

From the Norwegian perspective, Helgesen recalls, 'Our main preoccupation was to avoid further slide-back—to ensure that the ceasefire was respected, and that we did not have [a] complete disintegration of the fabric of the peace process. Our second major priority was how to get the parties back to the table.'

LTTE deliberations

The LTTE's Paris meeting, described as a session of the LTTE Constitutional Affairs Committee, lasted three days, from 23–26 August. The participants included senior LTTE leaders—Tamilselvan, Karuna and Peace Secretariat Head Pulidevan—and constitutional and legal experts from the diaspora. Balasingham was notably absent, which further fuelled speculation that he had been sidelined for his 'moderate' views in favour of Tamilchelvan's more 'hard-line' approach. For the final day of discussions they were joined by Erik Solheim, Bob Rae and Professor David Cameron, the latter two from the Canada-based Forum of Federations (FoF).

Details of the Paris discussions, which were described as both 'positive and innovative',[43] were not disclosed, but informed sources suggested that the LTTE's new proposal would be based on a federative model of governance in which the Tigers retained all the powers they currently exercised in areas under their control, including the judiciary, police and revenue systems. In contrast to the government's 'minimalist' outline, the LTTE would thus be putting forward, as Jayaveda Uyangoda described it, 'a maximalist framework for a political settlement'.[44] But with the People's Liberation Front (JVP) at the same time launching a march across the South of the country to 'save the motherland from the clutches of the Tigers' and to protest that 'federalism is not the solution in Sri Lanka', it was evident that securing political support in the South for a federative governance model proposal would be highly challenging.[45]

In early October, six weeks after the meeting in Paris, the members of the LTTE Constitutional Affairs Committee convened for a second time, on this occasion at the Glencree Centre for Reconciliation near Dublin, Ireland, principally to discuss the Tigers' draft proposals with a group of international legal and constitutional experts.

The Glencree meeting

Peter Bowling of the Sri Lanka International Working Group (IWG) was involved in setting up the Glencree meeting.

> I went to the Vanni in summer 2003 and had discussions about getting the LTTE back into the process of negotiations. Although they spoke of [tabling] proposals based on constitutional provisions, they actually seemed more interested in meeting their constituency, raising money for a return to conflict—on almost anything else, apart from getting ready to return to peace talks. I told the LTTE: you have never developed your own constitutional proposals beyond five or six basic principles. I told them to start acting like a party to a peace process, and that I would work with them on thinking around what kind of constitutional amendments you would need [with respect to] devolution.
>
> Two weeks later I got a call from the Vanni saying [that they] would like to begin some discussions. This was in July 2003. They said [they would] first have a series of meetings with the diaspora in Paris, and then one at the Glencree Centre in Ireland. They asked us to put together a team of constitutional experts to meet with the political wing of LTTE. We had four days of meetings in Glencree.
>
> We brought in a highly respected constitutional lawyer who had worked extensively in Asia and the Pacific Islands. He acted as an external resource person, suggesting a methodology for developing thinking around constitutional forms and political demands by using a starting

point based in functions. In other words, what the constitution would provide to address the range of needs of the Tamil people—political, developmental, recognition-based—and not by examining models and cherry-picking from precedents and comparative examples.[46]

I had never seen them work so hard. I had never seen Tamilselvan engage so profoundly, directly, in English. At that stage the LTTE leadership was committed to finding a set of proposals that was workable for them [so they] could restart talks, and could just about be acceptable to the South ... The other factor that became significant was increasing dissatisfaction with the diaspora support, [the sense] that in the end it was very much down to [the Vanni leadership] to come up with the proposals. Before that, they had consistently looked to the diaspora for the answers.

Back in Colombo, long-standing tensions between Kumaratunga and Wickremasinghe over the security situation spilled into the open in the form of a furious exchange of letters, prompted by media reports of a growing LTTE strategic threat to the naval base at Trincomalee. These reports were forcefully countered by the government,[47] but in early October Kumaratunga dispatched a fiery missive accusing the prime minister of seriously damaging the country's security and urging him to put the country before personal or political interests. The president ended by emphasising that she stood 'ready to assist, advise and give leadership, if you are willing'.[48]

Controversy over military matters continued later that month when, on the back of a recent incident in which information had allegedly been leaked to the Sea Tigers by the SLMM, President Kumaratunga questioned the impartiality and 'willingness to be objective' of SLMM Head Tryggve Tellefsen, requesting that he be replaced in a letter to Norwegian Prime Minister Kjell Bondevik.[49]

At the same time, facilitators were planning a visit to Sri Lanka with a view to kick-starting talks between the two sides—a move sparked by an LTTE statement indicating willingness to participate in negotiations 'at any time'[50] and the government's positive response.[51] A new round of talks, it was suggested, should focus on bridging any gaps between the government's mid-July proposals for an interim administration and the position adopted in the forthcoming LTTE counter-proposal.[52] On 31 October the LTTE document went public when Norwegian ambassador Hans Brattskar handed over the 'Proposals for an Agreement to Establish an Interim Self-Governing Authority for the Northeast' (ISGA) to G.L. Peiris in Colombo, some hours after receiving them from Tamilselvan.[53] Formally presenting the ISGA proposal the following day at a press conference in Kilinochchi, Tamilselvan stressed that finding a lasting solution to the conflict would require the government to look 'beyond the constitution'.[54]

Even a cursory glance at the proposals reveal why this point was emphasised: it was envisaged that the ISGA, consisting of an 'absolute majority' of LTTE appointees alongside government and Muslim representatives, would preside over an autonomous set of institutions—judicial, legal, fiscal and law and order-related—with powers of governance 'including all powers and functions in relation to regional administration exercised by the government in and for the North-East'. Formulations, in other words, that did not obviously square with the country's existing unitary constitution.

The government's initial response was cautious. While noting that the LTTE's vision differed from the government's in 'fundamental respects', it nevertheless underlined the government's conviction that the 'way forward' lay in 'direct discussion of the issues arising from both sets of proposals', and stated that the government would be asking the facilitators to set up a meeting to pave the way for the resumption of talks.[55] Tamilselvan, defending the new document as something that was 'definitely not a step towards separation', seemed to recognise that the next stage would involve a return to negotiations, noting that the government and LTTE 'may have to discuss the proposals before we agree on something'.[56]

President Kumaratunga, on the other hand, stated that she accepted the principle of devolution but that the ISGA appeared to go significantly further than that, and that she would make her final position known once she had consulted constitutional experts within her People's Alliance coalition.[57] Others were more strongly opposed. Dayan Jayatilleka, for example, argued that the LTTE's proposal was not 'about federalism or autonomy or devolution or peace processes'. Instead it was a 'set of demands for the total and unconditional relinquishing of power'. Jehan Perera argued that the LTTE proposals sought 'complete autonomy [in] virtually every aspect of political and economic life', and contained no reference to the 'federal consensus ... reached at the Oslo peace talks'. With that said, Perera believed that the simple fact that the LTTE had 'invested so much time and effort in a political and non-violent endeavour' was in itself a 'paradigm shift' for the Tigers, which needed to be 'appreciated' by anyone seeking a 'peaceful solution to the ethnic conflict'.

Indicative of international reaction to these developments, the day before Ranil Wickremasinghe was due to arrive in Washington for talks with

President Bush,[58] the US Administration issued a statement welcoming the LTTE proposal and urging both parties to 'build on this step by resuming negotiations in a timely manner'. It also underscored the US Administration's belief that the two sides could 'reach agreement on an interim administration which, over time, must lead into a permanent peace settlement and governmental structure'.

Sri Lankan responses to the ISGA

V. Rudrakumaran[59]

> The government was submitting proposals and always complained that the LTTE did not come up with its own. So I mooted this suggestion: why don't we put up some ideas? We set up a constitutional affairs committee: there were four or five members, all from the diaspora. Prabhakaran recognised that these people were trained for work like this, and their knowledge should be tapped. We got a lot of help from NGOs. We had a meeting in Ireland with some of the professors who helped forge the Good Friday Agreement.[60, 61] We were introduced to Anthony Reagan, who was instrumental in [the peace process in] Bougainville.

> There were fifty-two drafts of the ISGA. We went back to the hierarchy, and they gave some suggestions for the Preamble. A lot of effort was put into the document ... The Tamil diaspora in particular had high hopes that we were going to produce something [useful]. Some foreign experts told us: you people are asking for an independent state, so don't go below that to some confederal arrangement.[62]

> We put in a lot of human rights provisions. This is a Tamil area, but the government was allowed to play a role. The Tamils would have the majority, but it was not a mono-ethnic structure. We recognised Muslim rights: there was more protection and recognition for their rights in the ISGA than in the Constitution. We included the provision that 'there is no religion that is first and foremost', whereas the Sri Lankan Constitution says 'Buddhism is the first and foremost religion'. We envisaged a more liberal, secular polity.

Milinda Moragoda

> The ISGA format was clearly a negotiating position, and to take it anywhere else we really had to get into details, engage. The way it was articulated the trajectory would virtually have overshot federalism. The problem with the LTTE was that they always played the zero-sum game. In the beginning they showed flexibility, but whenever it came to core issues they did not want to be pinned down. They would say 'we don't have the expertise, we need time, we are a military organisation'. The two different timelines were also an issue. The LTTE timeline may have been thirty years; ours was the next election.

STALEMATE

Jayaveda Uyangoda

The ISGA was a good development, but Sri Lankan politics were so fractured. It gave Chandrika a chance to attack the government. There was never any serious discussion [of the proposal]. The LTTE made a fairly significant effort to present a set of political proposals. But this further polarised the polity and intensified the contradictions within the southern Sinhalese political scene.

Saravanamuttu Paikiasothy

The ISGA came about because of the LTTE's frustration with the government's inability, or unwillingness, to sit down and talk politics. [During the peace talks] three sub-committees were established: the political one never met. Part of the reason was that at that point the government negotiators were not talking to each other: Hakeem and Morogoda were not talking to G.L. Peiris, it was all about rivalry and competition. The LTTE felt strongly that the government was not interested in a political settlement and was using the CFA almost as a ruse to avoid one. If you did not bring in the political mechanisms, the LTTE's fear was that their control on the ground would be subverted by the investment coming in as a result of the peace process. They suspected they would end up as hapless bystanders: all this largesse was going to come in and the government would take all the credit for it.

Bala[singham] was one of the participants in the process. The overall design, however, was very much left to Prabhakaran and Tamilselvan. Bala[singham] was losing his influence: the leadership was worried that he and Peiris would produce a federal 'solution' that was too anodyne from an LTTE perspective. Whereas Tamilselvan, of course, was getting his orders directly from the top. The actual wording and drafting came from people in the diaspora. Former Attorney General Shiva Pasupati and others—but on the basis of clear directions as to what was wanted.[63] To be fair to them, when it was put out there were clear statements that the ISGA was negotiable. But by that time the anti-peace process forces in the South had gathered strength, and [the idea] that the ISGA was negotiable was something they were not even willing to contemplate. As far as they were concerned, the ISGA was the LTTE coming out in its true colours, and they just couldn't accept it.

Tyrone Ferdinands

I think the LTTE was very serious, had put a lot of effort into it. It was an exemplary process. Maybe the final result was tinkered with a little bit at the last moment by the leadership, but ... I remember G.L. Peiris as chief negotiator shivering in his boots, wondering what would come before the document was actually delivered. Kumar Rupesinghe, Norbert Ropers and Jayaveda Uyangoda, from our 'Group of Five', went to talk to him.[64] G.L. [Peiris] wanted our group to come and help him, not knowing how to manage this situation. It was surreal—a bunch of NGO people writing articles, issuing statements, when it was the government who should have been reacting ... But the government felt very helpless and lost at that time. And of course Chandrika used that to perfection in her move to oust the UNP.

When the LTTE ended up sending a stronger document than originally intended, I think it was with the intention of undermining Ranil. By that time they thought his usefulness was over—beyond this point they felt they couldn't work with him.

Shimali Senanayake

We knew that Chandrika would definitely not agree to the ISGA—but Ranil might have done so. If the whole seizing the ministries thing had not taken place, and Ranil had continued in power, he would have been willing to give [the LTTE] a lot that was in the ISGA. That is what I got from people close to Ranil. If things had been different, the indication was that Ranil was willing to let the LTTE administer [the Northeast] independently for a good period of time. Whether it was the right thing to do I don't know.

The facilitators' view of the ISGA

Vidar Helgesen

We learnt from our sources that before the ISGA proposal went to Prabhakaran, the final version was somewhat less maximalist. But in the end Prabhakaran opted for a very tough opening position—apparently there were some 'moderate' proposals tabled that had then been weeded out ... I was a bit disappointed by their maximalist position. My main observation, however, was that it should be seen as significant that the LTTE had produced a position document themselves for the first time.

I remember the meeting we had with G.L. Peiris [after the ISGA was released]. He was visibly shattered, extremely disappointed—almost personally offended, it seemed, by the LTTE's maximalist position ... In the Colombo media there was outright rejection, and the very predictable reaction in the South was that the ISGA was tantamount to secession. The LTTE was disappointed. They had put a lot of effort into the proposal and felt it wasn't being taken seriously.

The problem was that Peiris rejected [the ISGA] more or less out of hand. ... It would have been much better to say 'We believe this is going too far, but we are nonetheless pleased that LTTE has come out with a proposal for the first time, so let's get down to negotiations.' There would have been strong reactions in the South anyway, but Peiris almost locked himself into a corner.

STALEMATE

Erik Solheim

It was peculiar with the LTTE that they had been fighting for twenty-five years with a very unclear political platform: no charter, no programme defining its specific political aims. So it was a huge step when they proposed [the ISGA]. It was [intended as] an opening bargain position for negotiations—albeit a very strong, hard-hitting one. The main weakness of the LTTE was that its political wing, its think-thank, was very weak. In reality the political wing was Balasingham. Tamilselvan never showed any signs of independent political thinking. For the ISGA they brought in a number of Tamil intellectuals from around the world—people like Rudrakumaran and Maheshwaran—as well as several academics.

Bala[singham] was not happy with the ISGA proposal. He did not feel personal ownership of it. He wanted full personal control, being the senior personality in the movement and believing that he knew things best.[65] Secondly, he felt that it would limit the LTTE's freedom of manoeuvre for negotiations. It was too rigid in his view, and he knew that it would create huge challenges for Ranil. But he did accept it as a kind of opening gambit. The problem we did not fully understand at the time was that several of these Tamil diaspora people were academics, somewhat theoretical, with no great understanding of politics. Bala[singham] was the only person who provided genuinely independent ideas to the big leader. And among the diaspora there was always a tendency to take maximalist positions, since they thought that this is what Prabhakaran wanted to hear.

We had been very strongly supporting the idea that the LTTE should present a document that could be the basis for the resumption for talks, but there was disappointment that this was a maximalist document. Balasingham's approach was that he wanted a wide-ranging federal structure with wide-ranging powers in the Northeast, with Prabhakaran at the helm. He was the person who suggested a federal structure. He understood that they could not have a separate state.

[The ISGA proposal] was definitely more maximalist that Bala[singham] wanted it to be. He held that it would weaken Ranil's position in the South. But that tactical understanding would have been of lesser importance in the mind of Prabhakaran. Bala[singham] was principled on the demand for self-determination. That term can be interpreted—but independence cannot be. Self-determination was never formally defined by the LTTE as full independence. The term self-determination is a very flexible one. Bala[singham] always argued that the Tamils had a right to self-determination and that this could take different forms: it did not necessarily have to be a separate state. He believed that the Tamils and Sinhalese were separate peoples and could live happily separately, though deep down he may have felt that Tamils were far superior to the Sinhalese. He knew for sure, however, that they could not get a separate state. So he would have settled for far-reaching autonomy, and who knows what comes later? In any case Bala[singham] was on the sidelines of the ISGA: he was not really involved on the discussions.

What worried me then—and still does today—is how few there were (and are) in the Tamil leadership with an understanding of the political context of the South, or India, or the world for that matter. If you had that understanding you wouldn't have killed Rajiv Gandhi, for example. It's striking how much more mature the Tamil diaspora is in economic, social and cultural contexts than they are in their political understanding.

The president intervenes

On 4 November Sri Lankans awoke to the news that in order to 'prevent further deterioration of the security situation in the country', President Kumaratunga had sacked the ministers of defence, interior and mass communications and taken over their portfolios herself.[66] Later the same day she announced a two-week suspension of parliament. The sense of political crisis was heightened when, at the president's orders, troops proceeded to surround key public buildings, including the national broadcasting house and government printing press. In a televised address the same evening, the president appealed for calm and stated that she remained willing to discuss a 'just and balanced solution of the national problem' with the LTTE—but within 'the parameters of the unity, territorial integrity and sovereignty of Sri Lanka'.[67]

Kumaratunga's intervention came as Wickremasinghe arrived in Washington in advance of a planned meeting with President Bush. His initial response was to criticise the move as 'irresponsible and precipitous', insisting that he would not allow the president to 'undermine the peace process and economic prosperity'.[68] Tensions further increased the following day when Kumaratunga imposed a state of emergency, giving the Army wide-ranging powers of detention and placing a ban on public meetings. In Washington, Wickremasinghe's meeting with President Bush went ahead with the Sri Lankan Prime Minister reportedly telling Bush that the current crisis was 'part of Sri Lankan politics'—'for twenty-five years we have had these ups and downs'. He would 'sort it out'.[69]

Twenty-four hours later Wickremasinghe returned home to a rapturous welcome, with crowds lining the streets from the airport to such an extent that it reportedly took him eight hours to get to the city centre.[70] Shortly after his arrival, government officials announced that the state of emergency was being lifted. The fast-moving political drama continued the following day when, in the course of a televised address to the nation, Kumaratunga called for a government of national unity with Wickremasinghe. In the same breath she accused the government of neglecting the armed forces, and pointed to the fact that the LTTE had brought 'numerous arms shipments' into the country over the preceding two years.[71]

A number of analysts suggested that Kumaratunga's underlying strategy had been to take over the ministries and then persuade MPs from the governing UNF alliance who were 'on the fence' to 'cross the floor of the House'.[72] Support for this view came from Foreign Minister Tyronne Fernando, who on his return from the US with Wickremasinghe confirmed that the president had first offered him the premiership more than five months ago, in return for crossing over to the PA side.[73] The president and her team were also taken to task for their negative response to the ISGA proposal. While the 'short shrift' they had given to the ISGA may have been 'intended to please the gallery of Sinhalese nationalists', Jehan Perera suggested, it failed the 'ABC of conflict resolution, which is to show respect for the opponent with whom a negotiated settlement is sought. The president's team', he continued, 'seems to think that negotiating with the LTTE is like taking a legal brief to the courts. It is not. There is no judge to hear the case, there is only a facilitator who has no power, except what the parties to the conflict give it.'[74]

In the meantime, a new arena of political confrontation opened up. On 9 November, Wickremasinghe informed Kumaratunga—via the Norwegian and US ambassadors—that since he was unable to take negotiations with the LTTE forward without having control of 'all aspects of the process', notably defence, the president should assume responsibility for the peace process.[75] Compounding the growing sense of brinkmanship, in a BBC interview Kumaratunga suggested that as she had not signed the 2002 CFA, it was technically 'illegal'. Given her commitment to peace, however, Kumaratunga emphasised that she would nevertheless 'permit' the accord to 'remain in force'.[76]

Amid mounting fears of a slide back towards broader conflict, on 11 November Norwegian facilitators Solheim and Helgesen arrived in the country to try and figure out where—and how—peace efforts should be directed.[77]

Views of President Kumaratunga's intervention

Erik Solheim

> Of course Chandrika's move was linked to the ISGA proposal. She portrayed [the ISGA] as a threat to national security ... Most likely she had planned seizing the ministries just days after the ISGA was tabled. She was waiting for an opportu-

nity, perhaps. It was a gamble, because if it had failed, she would probably have been impeached ... But it was all about political strength, and Chandrika was aware of that. Ranil's reaction was to kind of do nothing. His response was protracted legal discussions, which went nowhere. He is not that type of aggressive politician ... All in all there was a clear expectation that talks would resume on the basis of the ISGA. That could have happened but for Chandrika's move. There was even a proposal for Thailand as a permanent site for talks, to end the travelling circus. There was also some discontent on the Indian side. They felt that we should push on. But the Ranil-Chandrika dispute was so intense that whatever we might have done would have made no difference.

Hans Brattskar

Chandrika removed Ranil's ministers when he was in the US on a visit. It was another example of the peace process being used in the[ir] political game—it was clearly a political ploy. To the LTTE, it was also obviously a political game.

Milinda Moragoda

Chandrika was intending to undermine things. Maybe the weakness in the process was that we were trying to build it on quicksand. In my view, if this was not the excuse then it would have been something else. Look at it from her point of view: she held a general election [in 2001] because she was forced to do so [after] her government collapsed. She lost. She had tenure, so she waited out her one year before acting. I must say that in the case of Ranil, he did all this without an election agenda. If he had not had idealism, he would not have started this process. He had supreme confidence that he could get this done. Politically speaking, even today people in his party criticise him for this. But in Chandrika's case, if it was not the ISGA it would have been something else.

Frances Harrison, former BBC Correspondent

Chandrika called me for an interview. We spent a long time lounging about in her house, waiting for her to appear. She was very hostile, very aggressive with me during our TV interview. It was an unpleasant experience. She denied that there was a state of emergency, even though her own spokesperson had already announced it! But at that time a lot of the country rallied around her, blaming the foreign media—BBC, CNN and so on—instead of her.

Jayampathy Wickramaratne

Ranil underestimated Chandrika. He should have got her on board with the peace process. As president, she was the person who could declare war or peace.

And Chandrika was also bitter about Ranil—what he did in 2000[78]—so he should have expected her to engage in some tit for tat. Shiral Lakthilaka tells me how he went to meet Ranil on some matter and they were discussing something to do with the peace process,[79] and Ranil said: 'Don't worry, we'll do that when I become the president'. He was dreaming of becoming president, pushing Chandrika out: it was foolish to do that.

Kumaratunga on the Norwegians

Jon Westborg kept asking me when [the Norwegians] could come and do something. He was the person who started the thing. 'Salmon eating busy-bodies!'[80] I thought they were very committed. The team that came didn't have that much skill in negotiating, but they were learning, and they had other teams they didn't tell us about that were advising them … My complaint was that they were very secretive with us, the government, and that was very annoying: Jon Westborg, Erik Solheim, all of them who were involved. They were doing things in this country without telling us and then announcing them to us as an afterthought.

I think they were naïve to the extent that they did not understand me. This is my feeling, I may be wrong, but they didn't understand me well enough and seemed to think that if they told me everything I might sabotage the peace process. They didn't realise how committed to the process I was, more than them even. I was deeply committed: if not I wouldn't have got myself nearly killed knowing very well that [the] LTTE would [try to] do that, and reduced my presidential term by one year! That was only to get the people to give us the green light to go ahead with [the devolution package].

For example, they would report to the leader of the opposition without ever telling me, and then tell me 'we met Ranil and told him'. They should have had discussions with us. These were very sensitive issues and if they studied what Ranil was doing here [they would have seen that] he could have sabotaged the peace process by giving them wrong advice, or sneaking to the LTTE.

I found that they were [passing on] everything and Ranil was misusing the details by passing them onto the press who would then work up the extremists. Ranil was doing this, and I told them, but they would just smile at me and go on doing the same thing. What I really resented was that when Ranil's government came in they had all kinds of dealings with him, and didn't tell me.

Then Ranil insisted on getting the defence ministry, which I shouldn't have given him constitutionally speaking. It was wrong, somebody could have taken me to court, but just for peace's sake I said OK, but on one condition: that you keep telling me what you are doing. He said we are discussing with the LTTE. I said very good, and offered to help. They didn't ask me anything. And then Ranil said we are trying to make this agreement: I said can I see some of the major conditions? They never told me that they were going to sign it. Then Ranil came and threw this paper at me and said 'I have signed it'.[81] I checked with Jon Westborg and said, 'It was your duty to tell me [about this].'

And he got up and said sarcastically, 'You know Madam. They said [that] they are in power.' I said: 'Oh, then I can walk off.' I was fully in power, I was sharing it with [Ranil]. I could have sacked the government, which is what I did finally. I had 75 per cent of the power and they had 25 per cent—and only because I decided to give it to them. When my government was 100 per cent in power, [the Norwegians] thought it was appropriate to go and talk to them all the time.[82] I think this was a very bad strategy.

Overall I think they tried to do their best. They tried to persuade the LTTE as much as they could. I don't think anybody could have done more. The LTTE were decided, they were definitive that they didn't want peace. Diplomatically [the Norwegians] were lucky that they were dealing with a president like me, otherwise I could have just ordered them out, even during Ranil's government: but I was committed to peace. They were so desperate to get some successes that they were fooled by Ranil telling them 'we will do everything you want, but don't listen to Chandrika'. So that was a bit bad. Vis-à-vis the LTTE and [the] process, however, they were OK. I gave them protection, but I was also not in a mood to defend them publicly, for I would have lost votes on that. Whenever I was interviewed, however, I always said that they did their job well—both while I was President and after I retired.

Norwegian facilitation in doubt

During their various visits to Sri Lanka the Norwegian facilitation team held talks with all the key players—the president, prime minister, Muslim leader Rauff Haukeem and Prabhakaran. Media reports of the meeting with the LTTE leader gave pride of place to Prabhakaran's pledge to maintain the ceasefire and respect the peace process; President Kumaratunga had earlier given the Norwegians the same guarantee, along with a reaffirmation of the freedom of movement of LTTE political cadres in government-controlled areas.[83] Some reports indicated that the LTTE supremo had also stressed the need for the LTTE to have 'clarity' over who they could continue to hold peace talks with: a clear echo—if not tactical appropriation of—the Norwegians' own position at this point.[84]

With respect to meetings in Colombo with government leaders and others, the Norwegians were widely reported to have communicated a decision to 'suspend' their facilitation role until the current political crisis was resolved.[85] At the end of their visit, Helgesen stated at a press conference that 'peace talks could have started tomorrow, provided there were clarity about who is holding political authority and responsibility on behalf of the government ... Until last week there was such clarity. Today there is no such clarity. Until such clarity is re-established, there is no space for further efforts by the Norwegian government to assist the parties.' He went on: 'This is a very serious situation. Not because the peace process is fragile, but because it might be made fragile ... the ceasefire will be much more difficult to sustain in a political vacuum.'[86]

Recalling this episode, Helgesen states that the 'main purpose of our visit was to assess the implications for the peace process of the president's takeover'. He continues:

> We were there when it was unclear who was in charge of the peace process—hence the press conference I gave on 14 November. Erik and I had a disagreement about it. I realise[d] that it would make a splash, so I called my minister Jan Petersen to get his clearance. ... On the government side there was no clarity as to who was in charge, so I said that we would go home and wait. That was my call. I didn't say that we would be abandoning the process, I simply said we would go home to wait. The national and international media said that we were suspending our mediation. But I don't think I used that word.

Solheim is frank about the disagreement with Helgesen over their respective assessments of the ground situation, and in particular the appropriate response to it from the Norwegian facilitators. 'I felt that we should hang in there continuously,' he states. In addition, he says he was 'somewhat afraid of us being seen too much as part of "Team Ranil".'

Lisa Golden, another member of the facilitation team, offers a different perspective. 'Vidar gave a press conference saying that we had to freeze our facilitation unless there was a will to make progress among the parties. It was a little bit hard to swallow at the time, kind of scary, going beyond how we had behaved up until then—always being there at the disposal of the parties,' she recalls. 'But with the benefit of hindsight it was an important thing to have done.'

Patten meets Prabhakaran

In the midst of these domestic uncertainties and controversies, an event of broader international significance took place towards the end of November

2003: a visit to Sri Lanka by EU External Affairs Commissioner Chris Patten, which was scheduled to include a meeting with Prabhakaran—one of a small number of encounters between the reclusive LTTE leader and international politicians that were successfully engineered by the Norwegian facilitators.[87] For Patten, like others in the international sphere such as Richard Armitage, interest in Sri Lanka went back some time—he had made his first visit to the country in 1987, when he was UK Minister of Development. Regarding his next visit to Sri Lanka sixteen years later, Patten explicitly acknowledged that its primary purpose had been to 'give support to the Norwegian efforts to end the conflict'.[88]

Despite vociferous protests and effigy-burning outside his Colombo hotel, after a series of meetings with government officials Patten travelled up to the Vanni on 26 November for his encounter with Prabhakaran, which to the intense annoyance of Sinhala nationalists, took place on the LTTE leader's birthday.[89] The meeting produced little of substance, but at a press conference afterwards Patten reported that Prabhakaran had responded to the EU Commissioner's demand that the LTTE abandon violence 'once and for all' by repeatedly pledging not to resort to war.[90]

Meeting Prabhakaran

Chris Patten[91]

> I was flown off in a government helicopter to the LTTE's headquarters in a ramshackle village called Kilinochchi. It was the rainy season and clusters of children had been marshalled in the drizzle to wave Tamil Tiger flags at us—terrorist ticker tape—as we drove from the helipad to a bungalow where we were to meet Prabhakaran. Given his fearsome reputation as a terrorist killer, he made little impression. Young men in dark glasses surrounded him, trying to look like TV 'hoods'. A man with a weak handshake, Prabhakaran left most of the talking to his two associates, rarely looking directly at us. He seemed extremely unsure of himself. He is unquestionably ruthless, but lacks even the negative charisma that one might associate with someone who has sanctioned so much killing.

Vidar Helgesen

> We wanted to have more international people come to meet Prabhakaran. Patten was interested in Sri Lanka. Chandrika didn't understand who I was talking about, but she had committed to it. The visit was controversial within the EU. The French were definitely opposed—talking to a terrorist and so on. Patten's main brief was to communicate clearly to Prabhakaran what the world looks like: terrorism has no support. Prabhakaran reiterated the LTTE's support for the

peace process. Talking to me about their meeting afterwards, Patten said he was stunned by Prabhakaran's feeble handshake. I apologised for getting him into trouble. His response: 'You are talking of their burning my effigy. Actually I think they made me look younger, blonder and slimmer.' He was quite a sport.

The day after his meeting with Patten, Prabhakaran gave his annual Heroes Day speech. Commenting on the political situation in the South, he accused the president of having 'severely damaged' the peace process through her intervention. After repeating the assurances given to the EU Commissioner regarding the LTTE's desire 'to resolve our problems through peaceful means', Prabhakaran went on to talk about the ISGA proposal, which he stressed did not 'constitute a framework for a permanent, final settlement'. That said, for all its 'interim status', the proposal called for 'substantial self-governing authority, without which', Prabhakaran argued, 'resettlement and rehabilitation programmes [cannot] be undertaken'. In conclusion, he returned to the situation in the South: 'Whenever the party in power attempts to resolve the Tamil issue, the [Opposition] party opposes it and derails the efforts.' The current crisis, he said, was a 'Sinhala political drama with its typical historical pattern' that has been 'staged regularly for the last fifty years'.[92]

Jockeying for position

In the meantime, sparring over political leadership of the country continued apace in Colombo. In a seemingly conciliatory move, Kumaratunga proposed the setting up of a Joint Peace Council (JPC) co-chaired by both sides; the creation of a new position of 'Minister Assisting Defence' nominated by the prime minister; and the continuation of Wickremasinghe's role in leading the peace process.[93] While these proposals were welcomed in some quarters, notably by those who had long been clamouring for the involvement of a wider range of stakeholders in consultations,[94] they were rejected by Wickremasinghe.[95]

Despite several rounds of talks between Kumaratunga and Wickremasinghe, as well as the conciliatory efforts of a specially appointed committee of high-level representatives, by the close of 2003 the two sides were no closer to agreement as to how—or indeed whether—they could work together.[96] The main bone of contention remained the defence ministry, with the prime minister arguing that in order to further the peace process he needed to be in charge of the country's armed forces, while the president insisted that the Constitution prevented her from even contemplating such a move.[97]

In the background, another set of negotiations was in progress. With fresh parliamentary elections increasingly touted as a means of breaking the deadlock, the idea of an electoral alliance between the President's People's Alliance (PA) and the left-nationalist Janatha Vimukthi Peramuna (JVP) was embraced with growing enthusiasm by many JVP members and by certain members of Kumaratunga's own Sri Lanka Freedom Party (SLFP), the majority party within the PA coalition. Supporters of a pact argued that a joint SLFP-JVP electoral ticket would immeasurably strengthen their chances of defeating the ruling United National Front (UNF) at the polls. The biggest obstacle to such an arrangement was the parties' differing positions on the ethnic conflict. Where Kumaratunga had long put greater devolution of powers to the regions at the centre of her strategy, the JVP remained implacably opposed to this approach, arguing for the retention of a unitary constitution, limited administrative 'decentralisation' and a tough military approach to the LTTE.

It was thus hardly surprising that negotiations between the two parties were marked by difficulties from the start. Throughout December the Sri Lankan media was filled with reports of missed deadlines for agreement between the SLFP and the JVP, the latter fearful that the slow-moving negotiations might turn out to be little more than a trial balloon floated by the SLFP for the 'real' goal of securing agreement with the UNF to form a government of national unity.

Into the new year, a number of things appeared to become clearer. First, that despite tensions and disagreements, an SLFP-JVP electoral alliance would almost certainly happen. Second, that the president and prime minister were still unable to reach agreement over who should control the defence ministry. Third, that a snap parliamentary election was the most likely outcome of the continuing impasse.[98]

On a more hopeful note, in mid-January the LTTE—in the form of Tamilselvan in the Vanni, and Balasingham in a London meeting with Erik Solheim—confirmed that the Tigers would continue to observe the ceasefire and that they were prepared to enter into negotiations with a 'government that has a mandate for peace from the Sinhala masses and ... the necessary legislative and executive authority to implement decisions'. Negotiations could recommence 'when a stable government assumed power in Colombo'.[99]

The sealing of an SLFP-JVP alliance on 20 January, however, elicited a markedly less positive response from the LTTE. Describing it as an 'anti-peace political pact', Balasingham suggested that the newly formed United

People's Freedom Alliance (UPFA) might 'create objective conditions for the resumption of the ethnic war'. Both the SLFP and JVP, according to the LTTE chief negotiator, were opposed to the principle of sharing power with the Tamil people—a position that was 'totally unacceptable'.[100]

On a similar note, Jayaveda Uyandgoda ascribed the pact's chief significance to the fact that it 'marked the graduation of the once anti-systemic and radical nationalist JVP into a member of Sri Lanka's Sinhala ruling class', while also noting that it had the potential to become a 'stumbling block' to 'further progress' in the country's 'conflict transformation and peace process'. Overall, he argued, the new alliance was 'one formed by Sinhala majoritarian groups, with Sinhala majoritarian intentions'.[101]

Adding to the sense of political ferment, towards the end of January there were reports indicating that Balasingham had asked the Norwegian facilitators to convey to the Indian government the LTTE's 'concern' over the Indo-Sri Lankan defence pact then under discussion between the two countries. Such an agreement might upset the current balance of forces to the Tigers' disadvantage, Balasingham suggested, and this could in turn lead to 'the disturbance of the ceasefire agreement—the very foundation on which the Sri Lankan peace process stands'. Moreover, he argued, a military pact with India might 'encourage the Sinhala political leadership' to take a 'hardline, belligerent attitude towards the Tamils' and as a consequence, 'eventually destroy the mutual trust between the estranged communities, a crucial factor necessary for the consolidation and promotion of peace.'[102]

In late January came a sign that Norway remained a central actor in the Sri Lankan peace equation despite the current political impasse and Oslo's temporary withdrawal following Kumaratunga's ministerial takeover in mid-November. Tamilselvan, heading an LTTE seven-nation tour of Europe, used the group's visit to Oslo and a meeting with Foreign Minister Jan Petersen (along with Vidar Helgesen and Erik Solheim) to urge Norway to take a lead in providing direct financial assistance for development work in the North and East, thereby bypassing the government mechanism for rehabilitation projects which, he emphasised, was non-functional due to the continuing political crisis in the South.[103]

Snap elections called

At the stroke of midnight on 7 February, Kumaratunga announced what many had seen as the most likely resolution to her feud with the prime minister: the dissolution of parliament, thereby paving the way for elections on 2 April 2004. Nearly four years ahead of schedule, this would be the third poll in the space of just under four years.[104] A number of commentators were quick to point out that in opting for this course of action, Kumaratunga had failed to consult the prime minister, in the process also reneging on a written promise she had made the previous autumn not to dissolve parliament as long as the government retained majority support.

The ruling UNF reacted forcefully to the election announcement, describing Kumaratunga as 'dictatorial' and 'unpredictable', but simultaneously asserting that it was 'ready to face any election' on a platform based on its main policies in government—continuing the peace process and national economic revival.[105] The LTTE described the dissolution of parliament as a 'grave setback' to the peace process, but pledged to maintain the ceasefire. Elaborating on this response, Anton Balasingham argued that in the forthcoming elections, the 'majority Sinhala people has the final choice to co-exist with the Tamils in peace, harmony and prosperity, or compel them to seek the path of political independence on the basis of their right to self-determination.'[106]

In the following days, Kumaratunga asked Wickremasinghe to continue as caretaker prime minister and appointed two of her own party stalwarts as cabinet ministers, including former foreign minister Lakshman Kadirgamar. She then used her constitutional prerogative to dismiss nearly forty junior ministers. With the procedural formalities set in motion, the country geared up for another—and some feared, highly divisive, and potentially violent—election campaign.

6

ELECTIONS AND DEFECTIONS

As the election campaign began, the peace process quickly emerged as a key issue. One of the first public discussions of the subject, broadcast on Norwegian TV on 17 February, was an extensive interview with opposition leader Mahinda Rajapaksa. Criticising the UNP government for having made the peace process a 'political project' in its 'thirst for power', Rajapaksa indicated that a UPFA government would resume the peace process on a 'broader basis'. The current administration's failure to involve an opposition representative was a 'serious political mistake', he maintained, and one that an alliance government would not repeat.[1] On the very same day, by contrast, the leader of the LTTE's political wing, Tamilselvan, was calling for what amounted to an ethnically divided political order, urging Tamils to ensure that 'South-based Sinhala parties' did not 'strike roots in the Tamil homeland during the election'.

Meanwhile, the Co-Chairs Group,[2] having met in Washington, called for the 'earliest possible resumption of talks', arguing that this was essential to sustaining a peace process for the 'benefit of all ethnic communities in Sri Lanka'.[3] The following week Erik Solheim travelled to London to brief Balasingham on the Washington meeting. Solheim emphasised what he termed the 'constructive' attitude of US Under Secretary of State Richard Armitage—the final meeting statement was the first not to include criticism of the LTTE—and the fact that official US donors had indicated that they would be able to support organisations that co-operated with the LTTE. On the question of US de-proscribing the LTTE, however, indications were that it was too early to expect any change.[4]

The voting arrangements in the North and East were a crucial issue. During a meeting in Kilinochchi on 28 February, Tamilselvan asked the SLMM's Trond Furuhøvde to provide monitors to help ensure that voters living in areas under LTTE control—an estimated 200,000 people—would be able to participate on polling day. As things stood, these people would have to cross over to government-held territory in order to cast their votes—at the last parliamentary elections army personnel had prevented many Tamils from doing so, hence the LTTE's request for SLMM monitors. However, SLMM deputy head Hagrup Haukland indicated that the SLMM would not get involved in the election arrangements. A couple of days later, another LTTE proposal—for the installation of polling booths in LTTE-controlled territory under police rather than army protection—was rejected by Elections Commissioner D. Dissanayake.[5]

At the same time, in a wide-ranging interview President Kumaratunga emphasised what became a standard refrain of the UPFA electoral campaign: her overall commitment to the peace process and what she termed her 'clear strategy' for restarting talks with the LTTE.[6] As the campaign developed, it became evident that the government regarded the opposition's position on negotiations with the LTTE as a major weakness in their platform, with ministers such as G.L. Peiris repeatedly attacking them over contradictory statements and positions—hardly surprising given the major differences between the JVP and the other alliance members on the subject.[7]

Solheim on the April 2004 election campaign

Chandrika's political platform was supporting the peace process, but not giving any concessions ... Chandrika was always in favour of peace, but maintaining power in Colombo—and this time round, returning her party to government—was more important to her. When she brought in the JVP, she said that even they would follow her peace line. Her attitude was to never respect the JVP as a real political partner, just to tap into them for their support base.

The thing I remember most from the election campaign, however, is the conversation I had with Ranil [Wickremasinghe], Milinda Moragoda and G.L. Peiris at Temple Trees a couple of days before the election. It was surreal. They were not focused on the main issues of the campaign or the main means of communication like TV or radio. Their focus was on loudspeakers and other completely irrelevant issues. It seemed to me that they had no political strategy, no communications strategy. I went away from the meeting absolutely convinced they would lose.[8] When elections were called in early 2004, I think that Ranil and company knew they were in trouble.

Karuna: discord in the LTTE's ranks

As the election campaign gained speed, news of an astonishing development began to filter through from the East. On 3 March Vinayagamoorthy Muralitharan, more commonly known as Colonel Karuna, commander of LTTE forces in the Eastern province, announced that from now on the Eastern section of the movement was to be 'treated separately' by all parties: the LTTE leadership,[9] the Norwegian facilitators and the government, with whom Karuna requested a separate ceasefire agreement.

Karuna, through the mouthpiece of his closest advisor Varathan,[10] identified a number of factors as having prompted the move. As an immediate cause, he cited a request from the LTTE leadership in Kilinochchi for an extra 1,000 Eastern cadres to be deployed to the Vanni. Secondly, there was the recent assassination of two non-LTTE political activists—one a prospective election candidate for the ruling UNP who survived long enough to tell the police that he could identify his LTTE attackers[11]—in the Batticaloa district.[12]

In terms of 'deeper issues', Varathan highlighted various forms of discrimination against Eastern cadres allegedly practised by the movement's 'Northern' leadership; an unequal distribution of resources for rehabilitation and reconstruction between the two regions; and lack of Eastern representation in the LTTE's administrative structures. 'Our people are asking why, among the thirty top officials of the Tamil Eelam administration, is there none from the Batticaloa-Amparai district? Because of this our people doubt if they will get justice under the ISGA which the LTTE is to set up in the North Eastern Province', he was reported as saying.[13]

In addition, it was alleged that the substantial funds raised in the diaspora by the Tamil Rehabilitation Organisation (TRO) were not reaching the East. It was charged that the Northern leadership were all 'living in luxury' while the Eastern cadres were left 'manning the forward defence lines'. Finally, Karuna's spokesperson stated that the request for the redeployment of 1,000 cadres from the East to the Vanni had been rejected because, having sustained so many casualties in past battles with the Sri Lankan army, the Eastern leadership had assured the families of the most recent recruits that they would not be sent into combat. 'How do we answer the parents of these boys', he was quoted as saying, 'when the North asks us for additional cadres during a period of peace?'[14] The veracity of this claim was thrown into doubt, however, by the conflicting accounts offered by Karuna and Varathan in the days that followed the split. In a BBC interview, for example, Karuna suggested that his main reason for not wanting to send Eastern cadres north was that he had reasons to suspect that the LTTE was preparing to return to war[15]—a suggestion flatly rejected by LTTE spokesperson Daya Master later the same day.[16]

Unsurprisingly, the LTTE leadership's response to Karuna's announcement was swift. Three days later, following an emergency meeting of the movement's central committee, Tamilselvan announced that the erstwhile Eastern commander had been 'discharged' from the LTTE and 'relieved of his responsibilities'. In his place, Karuna's deputy, Ramesh, was named 'special commander' and Kousalyan was made political chief of the Batticaloa-Amparai district. Tamilselvan went on to deny all of Karuna's allegations. The leadership had 'acted firmly' over what he contended was a 'problem concerning a single individual'; moreover, the impact of Karuna's defection on the peace process and the LTTE's military strength would prove negligible, he stated.

On this final claim, others were less optimistic. Not only had Karuna been among the most senior figures in the organisation; he was the only person Prabhakaran had trusted with combined political and military leadership in a region under LTTE control. It was Karuna, for example, who together with the LTTE leader had reputedly masterminded the assault on the strategically located army garrison at Elephant Pass in April 2000.[17] Indeed, with an estimated 6,000 troops still at his disposal—including the Jayanthan Brigade, heroes of the Elephant Pass operation—at this stage Karuna looked to be far from finished.[18]

The slanging match between erstwhile comrades-in-arms continued in the weeks that followed. On the LTTE side, it was said that prior to breaking away, Karuna was potentially facing disciplinary action for alleged financial and personal misdemeanours.[19] Responding in kind, Karuna called for the LTTE to expel three senior figures—Pottu Amman, Tamilendhi and Nadesan, respectively the heads of the Intelligence, Finance and Police divisions—for 'misconduct' and 'incompetence'. While Amman was labelled a 'terrorist', the other two were dismissed as 'unfit to be in the LTTE' on the grounds that they had 'surrendered' to the Indian army during the IPKF's presence in the country.

By way of response, sources in Kilinochchi suggested that Karuna's targeting of these three leaders stemmed from the fact that they headed the LTTE sections directly involved in the investigation into his own transgressions. Then, on 9 March, Varathan alleged that Pottu Amman and an LTTE assassination squad had recently arrived in Batticaloa to dispose of Karuna.[20]

Meanwhile, a group of senior Batticaloa religious and civil society leaders travelled to the Vanni in a bid to persuade the LTTE leadership to settle the dispute peacefully. Karuna also underscored his desire to avoid bloodshed, while Varathan reported that Karuna had asked the Norwegians to assist him in concluding a separate ceasefire agreement with government forces.[21] The cause of conflict resolution was not assisted, however, by reports of a huge protest in Batticaloa at which an effigy of Prabhakaran had been burned—the first recorded instance of such open opposition to the LTTE leader.[22]

Summarising the military scenario at this point, one analyst suggested that there were three main options for the LTTE: to assassinate Karuna (a move that would be 'in accordance with the LTTE's common practice'); to initiate a military operation to 'wrest back the East';[23] or to 'negotiate with Karuna regarding the grievances he has articulated'.[24] Following his arrival in the country in mid-March, Erik Solheim affirmed that the Norwegian facilitators had no intention of 'interfering' in the dispute.[25] They were, however, concerned that any effort by the LTTE to damage or destroy Karuna militarily would effectively be a renunciation of the Ceasefire Agreement, a move certain to provoke the wrath of the international community and in all probability the Sri Lankan state as well.[26]

Karuna's revolt: causes and consequences

With time to ponder the matter, aided by information and intelligence emerging from the Vanni and the East, analysts began to piece together a clearer picture of the causes—and likely consequences—of the rift within the LTTE. D.B.S. Jeyaraj and Sivaram, alias Taraki, two Tamil journalists known for their excellent contacts within the LTTE and the North and East generally, substantially advanced the same thesis regarding the background to the Karuna rebellion.[27]

Following Karuna's military exploits in the North in the late 1990s, which culminated in the conquest of the Elephant Pass garrison, Prabhakaran placed his now favourite commander in near-total control of the LTTE-dominated East, effectively handing him autonomy in running the region's affairs. With the advent of the 2002 CFA, however, tensions between Northern and Eastern Tamils surfaced as the LTTE high command tried to extend its diktat over the administration of the whole region, particularly in the East. Central divisional commanders now reported directly to Prabhakaran, as a result of which 'LTTE courts, police stations, income tax offices, and the dreaded intelligence wing TOSIS [Tiger Organisation

Security Intelligence Service] ... all functioned in the East without being subject to any regional control'.[28] Thus Karuna increasingly found that his previous special position was now being systematically undermined by the actions of the centre.

Compounding this 'centre-periphery' dynamic was a pervasive sense among 'Batticaloa Tamils' of being 'discriminated against or dominated by Jaffna Tamils'.[29] And on a personal level, it was suggested that relations between Karuna and Pottu Amman, which had been marked by rivalry since they had served together in Batticaloa in 1987, had now blossomed into more or less open competition to secure the position of de facto second-in-command within the LTTE. In pursuit of this goal, Jeyaraj argues, both began spying on the other: Karuna through a separate intelligence outfit he set up to monitor the activities of Pottu Amman's agents in the East; and Pottu Amman through an investigation of Karuna's activities initiated by TOSIS in co-operation with the central LTTE finance and police divisions.

When he got wind of the fact that traders in Batticaloa were being questioned about his business activities, an enraged Karuna ordered them not to co-operate. Nonetheless a charge sheet against Karuna was reportedly compiled and presented to Prabhakaran. The allegations included large-scale misappropriation of LTTE funds, building a house with the proceeds, encouraging anti-Muslim agitation, and having an affair with a senior female cadre. In early 2003 Prabhakaran appears to have requested that Karuna come to the Vanni to answer the charges. Sensing that this might turn out to be a visit from which he would never return, Karuna refused to comply. The immediate result was that he was left out of a group of senior cadres scheduled to travel to Europe with Tamilselvan.

The beginning of the election campaign in February appears to be when things really started to unravel. Karuna was already deeply concerned by intelligence reports that TOSIS operatives were infiltrating the Batticaloa area. Their objective, he suspected, was to abduct him. When a local UNP candidate was murdered and a Tamil political activist was gunned down soon afterwards, Karuna is reported to have panicked, fearing that this was the signal for an imminent strike against him by Pottu Amman's forces.

Recognising the significance of developments in the East, in mid-March Erik Solheim travelled to the country to assess the situation for himself. During the visit he met, as usual, with both government officials—the President and Prime Minister included—as well as the LTTE's Tamilselvan up in Kilinochchi. Tamilselvan is reported to have told Solheim that Karuna was operating alone and without the support of the majority of Eastern cadres. At the same time the LTTE political chief underlined the fact that the Tigers regarded it as a purely internal matter and were keen that other forces did not intervene in their own attempts to 'resolve' the dispute.[30]

Perspectives on Karuna's breakaway

Erik Solheim

> In the past there had been splits within the LTTE. But Karuna was trusted, and his breakaway came as a complete surprise. We had earlier identified Karuna as a different type: he was more jovial. For Westerners he was a much more charismatic character than most others in the LTTE ... Bala[singham] told us that the split had more to do with women and money than any real political differences. But he saw the immediate problem for the LTTE, being weakened in the East. He would also say, 'remember that Prabhakaran is a puritan, strict on alcohol or women', and that it did not play out well when someone had difficulties with that approach. Bala[singham] also suggested that this was mainly about using money for personal purposes, channelling money from the movement for personal use. Karuna had moved his family to Malaysia and was in love with another woman in Batticaloa ... The general view in the LTTE was that Karuna was a degenerate character.

Vidar Helgesen

> I had met Karuna during the peace talks, but I didn't visit him in the East. He was very charming, but it was a bombshell when he split ... From a pure process perspective we maintained the principled position that we would be willing to talk to anyone interested in talking to us, which of course the LTTE didn't like. In the end, however, there was limited dialogue with the Karuna faction. And not too long after he became embedded with Sri Lankan Intelligence. We didn't have much contact with the government at the time, because of the elections. The impression, however, was that they were quite happy with Karuna's split. We saw that it was going to complicate the peace process. After the split Karuna was always the LTTE's main issue for discussion.

Hans Brattskar

> I got a phone call from Karuna's advisor. He said that from now on I should deal directly with Karuna. I thought this was for real. The advisor sounded nervous: he also contacted the head of the SLMM. This had actually happened: Karuna had broken away from LTTE. It was a big blow to the Tigers. Some observers in Colombo felt it was the ceasefire agreement that created the environment that

made it possible for Karuna to break away ... The news of Karuna's defection was greeted with astonishment in Colombo. That this could happen in an organisation like the LTTE that had such brutal discipline—amazing! And yes, it was certainly clear to us that this internal struggle, this infighting had weakened the LTTE.

Aaron Darrin (advisor to Karuna)

I didn't suspect the split would happen at the time. Karuna did some specific things because he wanted to break away. ... He designed different regimental flags and insignia for the Eastern Tigers. Maybe Prabhakaran suspected something. Once when Karuna and I met Prabhakaran, he said 'Karuna, it's good that you are designing flags. But the Tiger symbol should be on top' ...

Prior to the split the relationship between the two was good. Karuna had been his bodyguard, and they grew up together in the LTTE. Once Karuna became in some sense an autonomous actor, and was given the Eastern region during the war, he acquired greater power ... Finances were the determining factor. During peacetime Prabhakaran sent people to audit things. Karuna felt slighted being questioned on finances. He could not tolerate that. This sudden centralisation— what was the motivation for it? The LTTE may have wanted to do it all along but could not during the war. And perhaps there were indeed some financial complaints against Karuna.

I do not think East versus North was a factor. Maybe there were some slight differences but the struggle was predominant. One can ask, why did Karuna take up these issues only at the time [of the split]? After all, he had been with the LTTE for a very long time. Karuna was acting instrumentally. And remember, it was Karuna who broke away, not the other prominent Eastern LTTE leaders. Thousands of junior cadres went with Karuna, but this does not mean they were diehard loyalists ... of the 5,000 or so cadres under his command, most of them simply went home after the split. ...

I think the Norwegians should have talked to Karuna. There was a possibility of turning the trajectory in a different direction. He thought he would be punished if he went to the Vanni. It all happened suddenly. He was summoned, he thought something bad would happen to him and then he didn't obey the order. All this created an unpleasant relationship between the Norwegians and LTTE. Maybe they did talk to the LTTE, and they told the Norwegians, 'you have to choose between Karuna and us'.

Shimali Senanayake

If Karuna hadn't split then things might not have ended the way they did for the Tigers. After I broke the story of Karuna's split, the LTTE never trusted me again. At the time, Tamilselvan's office in Kilinochchi summoned me ... When I arrived they all sat in a circle—Tamilselvan, two of the defectors from Karuna's camp. I never saw them after that: they just wanted to give their take. Tamilselvan walked us through all the cadres and told us that they were all armed to the teeth. The LTTE wanted to get across the message that this was purely the revolt of one person. ...

There wasn't one simple reason for the split: partly it was down to the fact that this guy had gone to all those rounds of peace talks, and he was young and smart. I asked him how his troops were going to survive after breaking away from the LTTE. He replied that he had already set up a network with the diaspora during the peace talks to send money directly to him. I thought Prabhakaran would have got wind of this. There were also accusations by the LTTE that he had misappropriated funds. These may not have been entirely untrue.

In the interview I did with Karuna at the time he said that the main reason [for the split] was that during all the major battles the Eastern cadres were put on the front lines, which was true. He said this must stop, and that he was committed to the peace process. I would give a lot of credit for this to the peace negotiations, which gave Karuna that turn of mind. At least one of the key actors was influenced to that degree by the peace process—a whole change of psyche in his case.

Susanne Ringgaard Pedersen

The Karuna split is misunderstood and misrepresented. The Norwegians didn't take on board what actually happened at the time. When it became known that there had been fighting across the [Verugal] river, for example, the head of the SLMM went to the government and said they should not take advantage of this, because it would have enormous consequences for the future of the peace process.

The government gave their assurances and this seemed to be the line toed in public by the Norwegians—that they kept that promise. Which is utterly untrue, of course. I had the evidence. I saw it with my own eyes. And it is also still unclear whether the government actually approached Karuna earlier—I have my suspicions. Certainly all of the killings I encountered [in the Batticaloa area] during the next six months were committed by the Karuna faction—which would only have been possible with the acquiescence and assistance of government forces. My successor, a Danish police officer, found the evidence. We were looking for this Karuna faction camp located within a Sri Lankan army camp from where they launched assassinations against LTTE political cadres. He found it. He took the evidence to Colombo and told me that he presented the findings. He was very disappointed when it was swept under the carpet. He said it was the beginning of the end: if the Norwegians and Americans did not take this on board, it would be the end. Because the LTTE never trusted the government after that. Already then they had started their journey [back towards war]. The government's reaction to the Karuna defection was seen as proof that it was not serious.

Regarding Karuna there was talk of embezzling money, a taste for the good life, that he had sent his kids abroad and had some expensive tastes. When he got wind that the noose was tightening, however, he recruited all these child soldiers. With just two months or less training he armed and prepared them. Then he took off, and there was real anger in the Tamil community: he was seen as a traitor.

The election campaign: the final stages

With tensions between the two factions simmering and the outcome of Karuna's revolt still unclear, the election campaign moved towards its concluding stages. In the hustings, with less than ten days to go until polling, President Kumaratunga and Prime Minister Wickremasinghe both made the peace process the centrepiece of their speeches. Kumaratunga put out something of a mixed message. On the one hand she emphasised her intention to find a solution to the ethnic conflict 'devoid of petty political gains' and to restart talks as soon as possible.[31] On the other, she appeared to suggest that in some respects the split within the LTTE's ranks might make it easier to deal with them—a view that led Tamilselvan to warn that the Tigers might be pushed back to war if a new government attempted to alter the peace process by imposing new conditions.[32] Moreover, she was not averse to drawing attention to warnings repeatedly voiced by sections of the military hierarchy as well as more hawkish, albeit well-informed, analysts, that the LTTE had used the ceasefire to triple the size of its forces while the Army had been systematically 'degraded and weakened'.[33, 34]

The prime minister, for his part, emphasised the government's superior 'peace' credentials—'only a UNF government can transform the ceasefire agreement into a political settlement assuring lasting peace for all communities'—while highlighting the fatal flaws in the opposition's strategy. He told one party election rally, 'Anton Balasingham has rejected the UPFA peace overture. I'm not surprised ... the SLFP and the JVP have two different views on devolution of power'.[35]

Coming to the end of what was widely considered a lacklustre campaign in which personalised attacks had taken precedence over serious political debate, the LTTE was agitating in support of candidates from the proxy Tamil National Alliance (TNA)—the first time the Tigers had engaged in electoral campaigning in the Northeast. Asked why she was prepared to vote for a party backed by rebels who abused the human rights of her fellow Tamils, one young woman in the Vanni responded with striking candour: 'Although they collect tax from us and recruit child soldiers, the Tigers are still the sole representatives of the Tamil people. They are fighting for us'.[36]

UPFA election victory

On the final day of electioneering Wickremasinghe reiterated his main campaign message, appealing to Sri Lankans to vote for the party best placed to take forward the peace process.[37] By 4 April, with all the votes counted, it was apparent that his plea had been in vain. Although it fell short of an absolute majority, Kumaratunga's UPFA emerged as the largest single party in the new 225-member parliament, with 105 seats—some way ahead of Wickremasinghe's UNP 82 seats.

The first issue to attend to was the nomination of a new prime minister. While early indications were that Kumaratunga's favoured candidate Lakhsman Kadirgamar would get the job, in the end it went to the man favoured by the rank and file of both the main parties in the UPFA coalition:[38] Mahinda Rajapaksa.

In the meantime, the result gave analysts plenty to chew over. A popular school of thought argued that the UNP's defeat was a sign of widespread disagreement over the way the peace process had been handled rather than an 'outright rejection of the process' itself.[39] In this context the UNP government's 'accommodating' attitude towards the LTTE—long viewed as tantamount to 'appeasement' by more hard-line elements within the Sinhalese polity—was usually contrasted with the approach to negotiations promised by the incoming Alliance administration.[40]

Less contentiously, many commentators identified the political extremes as the main election winners. At one end of the spectrum, Sinhala nationalist forces—as represented by the JVP and the recently formed Jathika Hela Urumaya (JHU)[41]—did particularly well, capturing forty and nine seats respectively.[42] For the JVP, this placed them in a position to assume ministerial positions for the first time—a major achievement for a party that only seventeen years earlier had launched its second armed uprising against the Sri Lankan state. For the JHU, formed only two months previously, the result was similarly spectacular. For the new administration, the parliamentary arithmetic pointed towards the JHU's group of Buddhist monk MPs as potential deal makers or breakers.

At the other end of the spectrum, the LTTE's decision to back the four-party TNA, and to boost its position by all but neutralising alternative political options for voters in areas under its control, resulted in a strong showing. The TNA effectively swept the board in the Northeast, winning twenty-two seats and thereby establishing itself as one of the major parties in the new parliament. As one commentator put it, 'The main beneficiaries of this election have been the political parties that espoused ethnic nationalism without compromise';[43] or as another expressed it more bluntly, 'It does not pay to make peace in Sri Lanka. This is the moral of the 2004 April general elections.'[44]

Shimali Senanayake on the rise of Mahinda Rajapaksa

I covered both of Mahinda's elections very closely. It was mainly a party thing. He was definitely the person within the SLFP who had the seniority to ascend to the post, first of Prime Minister, later of President. What was not exactly foreseen was how powerful he would later become. I for one didn't see it coming. Mahinda was definitely not on Chandrika's radar previously, but in the end she literally had no choice.

In his house after his swearing-in as prime minister, Mahinda told us journalists: 'You have no idea what I had to do to get to this position.' He felt he had earned it, that it was his due. Which may very well be true. Chandrika treated him like a nothing. He was not even allowed to stay the night at Temple Trees. He had the title of Prime Minister and not much else.

The only time he was really able do something was during the tsunami, because Chandrika was out of the country. He did a very effective job then. He is a born communicator and also a man of action. He is able to move things, make things happen. But later in 2005 she came back and took everything back from him.

Facilitators on the 2004 election result

Erik Solheim

When it came to choosing a prime minister, as a Tamil Kadirgamar could not really challenge in the long run. Foreign minister was probably the highest a Tamil could reach. Mangala Samaraweera, who is now one of Rajapaksa's fiercest enemies, was very close to Chandrika. He was really the architect of the SLFP-JVP alliance. When Rajapaksa became Prime Minister, Mangala became a government minister, but eventually they fell out.[45]

The JVP-SLFP alliance was a marriage of convenience, definitely not of love, but it energised the party rank and file. The JVP refused to speak to us ... Chandrika was our main interlocutor: everyone else was secondary. We kept Mahinda informed, and he was always friendly. He would ask us questions but was non-committal, didn't speak his mind. At that time, however, there was no signal that he was opposed to the peace process. But he didn't say anything on this count: he didn't see his political fortunes being served by making any statements—at this point. And that proved right for him in the end.

Vidar Helgesen

Chandrika wanted Kadirgamar [as prime minister], but Rajapaksa had worked himself upwards with a solid power base in the party. We had been nurturing contacts with Rajapaksa over the years. We were aware that he was a challenger to Chandrika. We used to meet him in his home. He volunteered subtle but fairly honest reflections on the president. When she formed the alliance with the JVP we looked at this as something potentially harmful to the peace process. We were intrigued that she was prepared to enter into an alliance with the party that killed her husband[46]—a testimony both to the utter pragmatism of Sri Lankan politics and the level of animosity between her and Wickremasinghe ...

There was a fight over whether to change the Constitution for the benefit of the sitting president.[47] Chandrika considered the entire peace process to be her own thing from before Ranil's time, and it was clear to us that now she was running the process with Kadirgamar, not Rajapaksa. We kept in touch with Rajapaksa because he was prime minister, but he was quite clear that on peace process issues we should talk to the president. I hadn't been dealing with Kadirgamar as foreign minister before. From what I had heard he was a difficult interlocutor. I had met him when he was the president's adviser. He was very diplomatic and skilful, and articulated the desire to get the process back on track. There was so much local politics going on, however, that these had to take precedence.

Karuna routed

As the political fallout from the election began to settle, on 9 April news emerged that heavy fighting between LTTE forces and cadres of the breakaway Karuna faction had broken out the previous night, north of Batticaloa. Already there were indications of a rapid advance towards the Karuna 'capital' of Batticaloa by an elite Tiger force, Karuna's troops having retreated rapidly from their initial positions along the Verugal river following heavy bombardment from the northern banks.[48]

Over the following forty-eight hours the LTTE advance morphed into a full-scale rout. With stronghold after stronghold falling to LTTE forces, the remaining Karuna faction cadres—and by this stage a number had already surrendered to the LTTE—retreated to a well-fortified base in the Thoppigala jungle, west of Batticaloa. On 13 April, a report on the situation was published under the title 'War ends', citing testimony from a '16-year old Tiger fighter' that the entire Karuna-controlled base west of Batticaloa had been 'dismantled'.[49]

It later transpired that a significant part of the LTTE force consisted of Eastern cadres who happened to be in the Vanni at the time of Karuna's initial breakaway, and were considered sufficiently trustworthy by

Prabhakaran to be sent into combat against him alongside crack LTTE commandos. Karuna's decision to abandon military opposition was perhaps influenced by the presence of these Eastern cadres on the LTTE side. With reportedly 'strong dissension' within his ranks regarding the rationale for 'a fratricidal fight', bolstered by 'strong pressure' from the parents of young conscripts, Karuna is said to have finally come to the conclusion that the best option would be to simply cut and run.[50]

Solheim on Karuna's defeat

Karuna's later role was just sad. Since there was no middle ground in Sri Lanka, he had few options but to become a puppet of the state. From then on Karuna had no independent operational role in the East. So later, whenever it was claimed that Karuna faction forces had killed this or that person, we were never in doubt that this could only have happened with the collaboration of the state. While they may not have controlled his every move, Karuna was an asset that could be turned on and off at will by the army and intelligence services.

New government initiatives

It soon became clear that two issues would dominate the incoming administration's political agenda: passing a new constitution and restarting the peace process.

Following discussions during the new government's first week in power, it was confirmed that, as detailed in the election manifesto, the key elements of the new constitution would be the abolition of the Executive Presidency and reform of the electoral system.[51] To bypass the requirement that any such reform must have a two-thirds majority in parliament (something that was clearly impossible), the government proposed to convene a constituent assembly made up of newly-elected MPs in order to push through a bill on the basis of a simple majority of votes secured there. Unsurprisingly, this specially-marshalled assembly was widely criticised as a partisan political device to provide President Kumaratunga with a means of retaining power. As things currently stood, she would have to stand down at the end of her second presidential term of office in 2005; under the new system, following abolition of the presidency, she could take over as prime minister.

With regard to the other key component of the government's programme—electoral reform—a number of voices were quick to speak out in defence of the existing proportional representation system, as opposed to the Westminster-style 'first past the post' method espoused by the new government, which Sri Lanka had inherited from its former colonial masters and duly dispensed with in the 1970s. With electoral inclusivity a key prerequisite of stable government in a divided society such as Sri Lanka's, it was argued, the last thing the country needed was a return to an electoral system with a proven tendency to exacerbate existing political divisions.[52]

Jayaveda Uyangoda

> Constitutional reform in a deeply divided society like ours should be an exercise in bringing the fractured polity together in a spirit of peace and reconciliation. It should not lead to greater polarisation, conflict and instability. The Alliance's reform initiative does not seem to have been guided by any of these objectives. It is primarily motivated by [its] political self-interest and ... adversarial power dynamics with the UNP.[53]

In the event, the Rajapaksa government's room for manoeuvre on its constitutional project was greatly reduced by its first significant political defeat, over the election of a new Speaker. Following a rowdy debate on the opening day of parliament (22 April) and two inconclusive initial rounds of voting, in the third round the opposition candidate W.J.M. Lokubandara squeezed ahead of the Alliance's D.E.W. Gunasekera by the narrowest of margins—109 votes to 108.[54]

Peace process in focus

Less than a week after the elections, Kumaratunga pledged her commitment to resuming talks with the LTTE, and called on all parties to support the incoming government in its efforts to find a lasting solution to the ethnic conflict.[55]

The first real test of the new government's stance towards the LTTE, however, came not over the negotiating table but on the ground—in the shape of the Karuna rebellion. Here, as some noted at the time, from a conflict resolution perspective the new government performed quite well.

Its official stance of non-interference in the LTTE schism was more or less exactly the one the (much-criticised) previous administration would have adopted. Indeed, diplomacy had the upper hand to the extent that there was no attempt to raise the issue of the Ceasefire Agreement, even when—in blatant violation of the accord—the LTTE launched a military assault on the Karuna faction.[56]

Early indications signalled a potentially new approach to the situation. Following Rajapaksa's swearing-in, the first person to receive a visit from the new prime minister was Indian High Commissioner Nirupan Sen. Prior to this, moreover, Rajapaksa had reportedly stated that he looked forward to India's 'active involvement' in the peace process[57]—a suggestion the High Commissioner politely but firmly discounted in the course of a return visit.[58] As Jehan Perera noted, India was not in a position to play a role in Sri Lanka similar to Norway's, on account of the 'heavy baggage of its past', having been both 'clearly partisan' to one side [the LTTE] at an early stage of the conflict and having subsequently tried—and failed—to mediate (1987–90).[59] Moreover, it was unlikely that India would prove to be an 'acceptable mediator' to the LTTE at this point in the peace process.[60]

As a measure of what was to come from the LTTE's negotiating strategy, a week after the elections the new TNA parliamentary caucus indicated that the demands outlined in the ISGA proposal would constitute the basis of the Tigers' position in any renewed negotiations.[61] Their position appeared to be significantly strengthened by election results in the Northeast—a vindication, it was argued, of the LTTE's arguments in support of Tamil self-determination.[62]

In mid-April SLMM representatives indicated that they would be holding a series of meetings with army and LTTE representatives in the East.[63] In addition, both sides indicated that they planned to hold regular bilateral talks in future—further confirmation that they were trying to consolidate their relationship.[64]

From a Norwegian perspective, the most important post-electoral development came in late April. The day after the government's unexpected defeat over the election of the parliamentary speaker, President Kumaratunga called Prime Minister Kjell Magne Bondevik to request that Norway resume its facilitation role.[65] Bondevik's response was immediate: 'I said that Norway was willing to comply, on condition that the LTTE also ask us to play that role.'[66] Two days later it was announced that at Kumaratunga's invitation, the Norwegian team led by Vidar Helgesen and Erik Solheim would be returning to Sri Lanka in early May. After a long hiatus, it appeared as if the Norwegians might finally be resuming their role as the mutually-accepted facilitators of efforts to end the Sri Lankan conflict.

To headlines proclaiming 'The Norwegians are back in town!',[67] the facilitators arrived on 1 May. As usual, a series of meetings in Colombo with Kumaratunga and others was followed by the journey up to Kilinochchi—by Solheim alone in this instance—for talks with the LTTE leadership. As widely anticipated, the LTTE position outlined by Tamilselvan rested on a series of demands: the ISGA as the basis for fresh negotiations with the government;[68] recognition of the LTTE as the sole representative of the Tamil people, and as such the government's only negotiating partners; and an undertaking from Colombo not to provide military or any other form of support to the Karuna faction.

Seemingly to dampen expectations (voiced by Kumaratunga) that talks with the LTTE would resume shortly, before leaving the country Helgesen stressed that it could well 'take some time' before the parties were 'in a position to return to the negotiation table'.[69] On a more upbeat note, on his return to Colombo from the Vanni, Solheim informed Kumaratunga that the LTTE was 'fully prepared' to recommence talks at any point 'convenient' to them. Solheim's talks in Kilinochchi were not, however, the end of Norwegian efforts at this point. Following Solheim's departure from Colombo on 4 May, it was announced that Foreign Minister Jan Petersen would be visiting Sri Lanka the following week. In advance of Petersen's visit, Anton Balasingham would be travelling to the Vanni for meetings with Prabhakaran and the rest of the Tiger leadership in order to 'map out a strategy' for talks with the new government.[70]

Champika Liyanaarachchi

The move against giving a separate delegation to the predominant community in the East when the most decisive issue of interim administration is taken up, is sure to spell doom for the peace talks. It is very unlikely that the Muslims in the Northern and the Eastern Provinces would tolerate such blatant exclusion. The tension in the East, especially the June 2002 Valachchenai riots, have proved that just as much as the Tamils do not want to be ruled by the Sinhalese, the Muslims in the East detest the idea of being dominated by the Tamils or the LTTE.[71]

New conditions?

The Norwegian foreign minister, accompanied by Vidar Helgesen, arrived on 9 May, and the following day they held talks with Kumaratunga, with the LTTE's ISGA proposal a key item of discussion.[72] When the Norwegians left for Kilinochchi the following day, they took a message from the president, proposing that discussions of a 'final settlement' of the conflict should be initiated in tandem with a focus on the ISGA.[73]

Petersen and Helgesen conveyed the message to Prabhakaran and Balasingham. At a press conference following the meeting, Balasingham expressed polite dissatisfaction. Concerning a 'final settlement', he noted: 'We have said that [it] required serious changes to the constitution. But we want first of all to have this interim administrative structure established.'[74] More bluntly, in an interview with the Tamil newspaper *Sudar Oli*, he stated, 'Talks can be held in the first place on matters connected with [Tamil] problems by implementing the ISGA proposals. There is no point in talking with a minority government in a hung parliament on other issues.'[75]

Putting a brave face on what looked to be another impasse, a Norwegian statement following the talks confined itself to noting that while both sides had expressed a 'clear commitment' to resuming negotiations, there remained issues that needed 'further discussion' before they could recommence.[76] Underlining the Norwegian facilitators' determination to keep things moving, in late May Solheim was back in the country—the third high-level visit from Oslo that month. Solheim's visit coincided with the appointment of former UN Under-Secretary General Jayantha Dhanapala as the head of the government's Peace Secretariat. Along with Kadirgamar and the new Foreign Secretary Palihakkara, Dhanapala participated in a meeting with Solheim and colleagues Brattskar, Tromsdal and Knappskog.[77] Ominously, immediately following Solheim's arrival, a report from the SLMM in Batticaloa indicated that yet another killing had taken place, this time of a local LTTE cadre. As was becoming the established pattern, while the SLMM did not identify the culprits, the LTTE pinned responsibility on the Karuna faction. This time, moreover, local LTTE political head Kausalyan took the step of denouncing the army for complicity in the murder—the second time the LTTE had levelled this charge since the Karuna faction's breakaway in March.[78]

Solheim's subsequent talks with Tamilselvan failed to make any headway. The LTTE position remained that the ISGA proposal constituted the starting point of negotiations, while the call for parallel discussions of 'core issues' was again firmly rejected.[79] By the end of his visit, Solheim admitted that there were no imminent prospects for the resumption of talks.[80]

Co-Chairs communiqué

Solheim left Colombo for Delhi, where he briefed Indian counterparts on his latest visit to Sri Lanka, before heading on to Brussels for a meeting of the Co-Chairs Group, whose high-level participants included Armitage, Akashi and Patten. While welcoming the commitment to renewed peace talks, the final statement following the Brussels meeting expressed concern over the recent spate of killings in the East. Most significantly, the Co-Chairs remarked that 'with so many other demands on donors, donor attention and funding might go elsewhere unless the peace process makes progress'.[81]

Back in Sri Lanka, the LTTE continued to accuse the army of complicity in Karuna faction killings, while the government denied any involvement with equal vehemence.[82] In the meantime, the LTTE was allegedly restoring military control over the Batticaloa area and rooting out the remaining Karuna cadres in the process.[83]

Following the Co-Chairs meeting, Solheim travelled to London for discussions with Balasingham. Referring to his recent visit to Sri Lanka, Solheim reported that the government were ready to have the ISGA as the 'only item on the agenda'. Their concern, however, was that the LTTE would present 'new conditions' as soon as they had officially 'given in' on the ISGA stipulation. A promise from the LTTE not to raise new conditions would put Kumaratunga in a position to convince sceptics in both the JVP and SLFP to accept negotiations solely on the basis of the ISGA.[84] While there is no official report of Balasingham's reply, it was unlikely that he viewed this as a sufficiently hard guarantee to elicit his consent.

In what appeared to be a significant presidential policy shift, during a mid-June meeting with Tamil MPs, Kumaratunga announced that she was ready to begin talks with the LTTE on the basis of the ISGA proposals. She followed this up with a national TV broadcast in which she emphasised that any 'interim measures' would have to be 'within the contours' of the 'sovereignty and territorial integrity of the country'.[85]

Where some saw this as a positive change in the government's approach to negotiations with the LTTE, others were quick to suggest that Kumaratunga's move was motivated chiefly by a desire to 'neutralise' the TNA vote in parliament and thus save her government from collapse.[86] Most importantly, the LTTE quickly rejected the president's offer as a 'devious plan' to begin talks as a means of releasing international aid, while allowing negotiations on an interim administration for the Northeast to drag on.[87] The LTTE's dismissal of Kumaratunga's offer stemmed from the fact that in her TV address, in addition to references to the ISGA's role as the starting point of negotiations, she had also underlined the need to 'engage in discussions on a permanent solution to the conflict'—a proviso absent in earlier discussions with TNA parliamentarians.

In the midst of these developments, Norwegian Foreign Minister Jan Petersen called President Kumaratunga on 15 June, reportedly to share the Norwegian facilitators' dismay at the prevailing lack of trust between the two sides. He suggested that the government share its statements with the LTTE in advance of making them public. Further, he underlined the LTTE's concerns about the JVP's lack of support for an 'interim solution'. Petersen told Kumaratunga that he planned to have a 'thorough discussion' of these and other related issues when he visited the country later that month.[88]

An indication of the complexities of the situation was provided by Tamilselvan's announcement that a meeting of the LTTE team of legal and constitutional experts scheduled for 20 June was being postponed 'purely because of the political situation in South'.[89] In a separate Tamil newspaper interview, however, he pointed to other factors as having determined the decision, notably 'violations of the ceasefire and other obstacles'—presumably a reference to the conflict with the Karuna faction in the East. There was no government reaction to this latest LTTE broadside, perhaps because Sri Lankan officials had taken note of the Norwegians advice that it was best to seek the other side's views directly instead of responding to media reports.

The Norwegians maintained their behind-the-scenes efforts to keep the lines of communication open. On 17 June, Solheim and Helgesen arrived in London for discussions with Balasingham and later with Kumaratunga, before flying to Delhi to brief Indian National Security Advisor J.N. Dixit.[90] 'The continuing role being played by the Norwegians can be seen', Jehan Perera wrote, 'by their unique placement as the sole source of trusted communication between the government and LTTE'.[91]

Peace strategy in the spotlight

A US intelligence report published in 2011 by *Wikileaks* provides insight into the Norwegian attempts to foster agreement on restarting peace talks. Briefing Colombo-based ambassadorial colleagues in early June on the current state of play, Hans Brattskar reported that the Norwegian facilitators were trying to 'put together a statement' that would allow talks to resume. While Oslo was in constant touch with both sides, the impression at this point was that they were 'moving farther apart'. In particular, he suggested, the government's insistence on holding 'parallel' talks on 'final settlement' issues was simply 'a non-starter'.[92]

At this point, evidence of the whereabouts of Karuna and key associates began to emerge. On 21 June, Nilavini, former LTTE women's commander for the Batticaloa-Amparai district and a Karuna supporter,[93] gave an impromptu press briefing at which she claimed that, following their departure from Batticaloa, she and other Karuna supporters had stayed in a house in a Colombo suburb provided by the Sri Lanka Army, having been taken to Colombo by opposition MP Ali Zahir Moulana. Nilavini went on to say that on 13 June, Karuna had informed the group that he was travelling abroad with his family, and had left the following day in an army vehicle. Subsequently, she and other members of the group had managed to 'escape' from the safe house, after which she and a number of others made their way back to Batticaloa and—in her case—back into the LTTE.[94] Moulana, a key advisor to UNP leader Ranil Wickremasinghe, resigned upon publication of the revelations. After admitting that he had transported Karuna to Colombo, he claimed that the rebel LTTE leader was a 'longstanding family friend', and that his action had been on purely 'humanitarian grounds'.[95]

At the end of June, Solheim returned to Sri Lanka, and immediately went to Kilinochchi for meetings with the LTTE leadership. The outcome, communicated to Colombo the following day, was the demand that the government should stop backing Karuna's forces in the East.[96] From Colombo, Solheim continued on to London for a meeting with Balasingham, who reiterated that the 'Karuna issue' had to be resolved before anything else could be discussed. In this context, the LTTE was pointing to the Ceasefire Agreement, specifically the section that stipulated the disarming of 'Tamil paramilitary groups'.[97]

Solheim on the impasse

Throughout this time there was a feeling that the peace process would resume in the near future. But in fact it just went on and on like that. Petersen visited Sri Lanka in May 2004. Chandrika told him that she had

no problem negotiating over an interim administration: she was convinced that the LTTE were serious about this. In July, we presented a
suggested agenda for talks to both parties. The main problem was that
both sides were ready to resume talks in principle, but both also had other
priorities. It was very difficult for us to do anything but carry on. You
never knew when the point would come where they were ready to resume
the peace process. So at any particular moment there could be a feeling of
despair, but in the long run you knew you just had to go on.
Internationally there was a clear belief that both parties did not want to
go back to war. But there was also a fear that all this postponing and
making excuses could lead to a slide back into war.

Violence continues

Tensions in the East came to a head on 3 July when the LTTE's annual
Black Tiger Day celebrations were marred by a series of attacks on Eastern
cadres that seriously injured Senathirajah, head of the Batticaloa political
wing, and killed one other. In a sign of official concern over the situation,
a top military team was reportedly despatched to the region as Kumaratunga promised a 'full scale probe' to identify the perpetrators, commonly
assumed to have been Karuna supporters.[98]

Further inflaming an already delicate situation, four days later a group of
fourteen suspected Karuna faction youths carrying automatic weapons
were arrested at a Buddhist temple run by a JHU-supporting monk. The
LTTE were quick to allege that this was a hit squad backed by an Army
Special Forces unit—a claim strongly denied by a military spokesperson. At
the same time, a JHU official denied any link between Karuna and his
party—an intriguing rebuttal, in view of the fact that the JHU had previously called on the government to support Karuna's forces.[99]

The following day an incident occurred that sent shockwaves through the
country. A suicide bomber blew herself up in a Colombo police station,
killing four policemen and injuring ten more, having failed to reach the
intended target, government minister Douglas Devananda. Devananda was
not only the leader of the anti-LTTE Eelam People's Democratic Party
(EPDP); he had also recently been in contact with Karuna, whom he was
reportedly urging to form a new political party—something Karuna had
intended to do.[100]

This first major incident of violence in the capital since the signing of the
Ceasefire Agreement was especially alarming to the government because it
occurred inside the high security zone surrounding the president's residence

and nearby US, UK and Indian diplomatic complexes.[101] The LTTE promptly issued a statement denying responsibility (something they had never done with earlier suicide attacks) and decrying it as the act of forces bent on 'destabilising' the peace process. Officially there was no reaction to this denial, although it was clear that police interrogation of the bomber's suspected accomplice had effectively established that the Tigers were to blame.

The sense that the LTTE were wreaking revenge for the Black Tiger Day attacks was compounded when two Karuna cadres were killed a couple of days later in mid-July, followed by a grenade attack on the Buddhist temple where a group of Karuna supporters had been arrested a few days previously. Worse was to follow later that month: in the early hours of the morning of 25 July, eight people—seven Karuna supporters and one Sinhalese civilian—were shot dead in their beds in an army safe house in a Colombo suburb.[102] Denying responsibility for the massacre, the LTTE claimed it was the work of Karuna faction dissidents who proceeded to 'surrender' to the LTTE later the same day.[103] Then, less than a week later, 'Plote' Mohan, a veteran Tamil militant turned army informant, was gunned down in Colombo. Having played a critical role in assisting covert army operations in the LTTE-controlled Northeast, Mohan had long been considered a prime target.

This spate of killings almost drowned out Kumaratunga's official public apology for the anti-Tamil pogrom of July 1983, issued on the anniversary of its inception.[104] Meanwhile Vidar Helgesen concluded his latest five-day visit with a press conference at which he stated that he saw no signs of an early resumption of peace talks. Specifically, Helgesen registered 'little scope for optimism' regarding the possibility of reduced tensions in the East—a situation that constituted a bigger impediment to talks between the two sides, he suggested, than their much-publicised disagreements regarding the agenda.[105]

Karuna and the 'Hidden Hands' of the East

In mid-August the Bangkok-based *Asian Tribune* published a four-part interview with Karuna,[106] who after an earlier spell in 'protective custody' in an army safe house in Colombo was now said to be outside the country—most probably in India—with his wife and children. In the course of outlining his version of events leading up to and following his break with the LTTE, the former Tiger commander made a number of extraordinary claims.

First, he suggested that in organising his forces to repel the LTTE advance expected in the wake of his defection from the Tigers, Karuna had received assurances of practical support from the Sri Lankan military. This claim was subsequently denied by official sources. Second, he said that the way in which LTTE forces had advanced in large numbers by both land and sea—and in clear contravention of the Ceasefire Agreement—was an 'intriguing development' which is still not clear'. The 'suspicion', he continued, was that this 'could not have happened without the assistance of the government'. He continued: 'We suspect that a large amount of money would have changed hands [with the LTTE] as far as the Sri Lankan Navy is concerned'. Deciphering these potentially explosive claims, Iqbal Athas suggested that Karuna was giving a 'two-fold warning' to Tamils as a whole: 'Do not trust the LTTE in the North, and the government in the South'.[107]

Killings on the increase

A spate of tit-for-tat killings between the LTTE and the Karuna faction was now in full swing, nor were they confined to the East: the LTTE in particular went after its victims wherever they could find them, including on the streets of Colombo. The LTTE's victims, moreover, were not only former Tiger cadres turned Karuna supporters. Spurred on by continuing allegations of official complicity in the activities of the Karuna faction, suspected army informers were targeted too—a notable example being Suresh, killed on 28 August at a house in a southern Colombo suburb to which he had fled following an LTTE manhunt for him in Batticaloa.[108] On the other side, one particularly serious incident occurred in early September when Karuna faction cadres conducted a night-time attack on an LTTE checkpoint at Pullumalai near Batticaloa, killing eight Tiger soldiers. Initially, the LTTE denied that any of their cadres had been killed and accused Army commandos of having carried out the attack.[109]

Continuing the Norwegian peace effort, Solheim returned in mid-September for five days; it was now two years since the first round of talks between the two sides had opened in Thailand. The visit followed the established pattern: a series of consultations in Colombo with both the government and opposition (but not with the JVP and JHU, which had refused to meet with him), followed by a trip to Kilinochchi for talks with the

LTTE. In advance of Solheim's arrival, Tamilselvan stressed in an interview that the ISGA proposals were neither 'rigid' nor 'non-negotiable'. With that said, he emphasised that counter-proposals from the government were 'unhelpful' at this point, as from the LTTE's viewpoint the ISGA was the sole basis for the resumption of talks. Tamilselvan also called for the government and the South as a whole to 'speak in one voice'. Otherwise, he suggested, 'we cannot take forward the peace process'.[110]

Any hopes for progress sparked by this interview, however, proved unfounded. Reports of Solheim's discussions with Tamilselvan and his colleagues indicated that no new ground had been broken. An LTTE statement suggested that the Norwegian facilitators 'did not bring any constructive message from the Sri Lankan government'.[111] A classified report of Solheim's subsequent meeting with US Ambassador Jeffrey Lunstead indicates the facilitators' frustrations over the current stalemate. Solheim told Lunstead that in his judgement what was needed now were 'bold steps' to restart the talks—a view he had communicated strongly to both sides during his recent meetings. Specifically, Solheim expressed guarded optimism that a resolution of issues over the wording of the 'agenda regarding the interim authority' could lead to a resumption of negotiations.

The killings in the East continued, however. A few days after Solheim's departure, Karuna's brother, Colonel Reggie, was killed in an ambush on the night of 22 September—the day after two unsuccessful landmine attacks on LTTE cadres by suspected Karuna loyalists.[112]

Unrest in the East

SLLM monitor Susanne Ringgaard Pedersen, based in Batticaloa for most of 2004, gives a first-hand perspective on developments in the East in the aftermath of the Karuna faction's split from the LTTE.

During the summer of 2004, the LTTE gave me photos of five men with names on the backs of them, and they told me that these were the key people involved [in the Karuna faction]. Not a lot of people, in other words. But it did require help from the army to do what they did: it was professional. The killings probably started in May, by which time Karuna was long gone from the area. These five guys, however, were said to be located in an army camp. These were the people he had deputed to run things. A number of LTTE political wing people I liaised with were killed during this period.

> Karuna became the errand boy for the government. It was their policy. They got something important out of it. I spoke to a former Lankan army officer who knew senior generals. He denied that any of his soldiers were involved in killings. This officer was close to Sarath Fonseka. Some of the senior army officers were not clear about what was going on, but some must surely have been helping the Karuna faction. The question we didn't ask at the time was whether there were other parts of the system involved: like the Special Forces,[113] for example.
>
> In 2004, several delegations from different countries came to visit us in Batticaloa. I remember military attaches coming, and us providing them with all the local information. But their judgements were all totally coloured by counterterrorism rhetoric. The military attaches from the various embassies were speaking a very different language from the political people. It was telling during this time that there was a double game going on: external support for the peace process and internal support for the army and special forces.

'A return to the Oslo Declaration?'

An indication that the government was having some success in bolstering their standing abroad came following an early October visit to Washington by Foreign Minister Kadirgamar, when the US State Department issued a statement urging the LTTE to end violence against its 'political opponents' and to cease recruiting child soldiers. The Americans also called on both sides to seek a negotiated settlement along the lines of the Oslo Declaration,[114] and during the course of a visit to Switzerland the following week by an LTTE delegation headed by Tamilselvan, Swiss Foreign Minister Micheline Calmy-Rey conveyed an almost identical message.[115] An approach based on the Oslo Declaration seemed to be gaining traction internationally. Confirmation that this was the new official line was provided by President Kumaratunga, who used the launch of the new National Advisory Council for Peace and Reconciliation (NACPR)[116] to spell out her requirement that the LTTE provide a commitment that an 'Interim Administration as well as the final solution' to the conflict would be 'based on the Oslo Declaration', specifically its stipulation that a 'Federal solution' be sought 'within the framework of a united Sri Lanka'.[117]

A week later, concluding their tour of European countries, the LTTE delegation travelled to Oslo for meetings with Petersen and Solheim. While Petersen stressed the need for the facilitators to meet Prabhakaran to discuss ways to move the peace process forward, Solheim briefed Tamilselvan on his recent visit to the USA and Canada, passing on the message that while the Tigers remained a proscribed organisation, the US would nonetheless support any peace settlement in which the LTTE was a partner.[118]

The Norwegians return

The meeting with Prabhakaran sought by the Norwegian foreign minister took place in mid-November in Kilinochchi. In a sign of the importance the LTTE attached to the visit, Balasingham flew in from London to participate in the meeting with the facilitation team. Beyond Petersen's reported emphasis on the flexibility that Kumaratunga was felt to be showing over restarting talks, the Norwegians brought no significant new message from the government side. In response, Prabhakaran said that the LTTE felt that what was needed now was a statement expressing the government's willingness (backed by a 'southern consensus')[119] to move to negotiations based on a discussion of 'an interim self-rule authority in the North and East'.[120]

In a press conference held after the talks, Balasingham addressed a number of issues, including the suggestion that the 2002 Oslo Declaration should form the basis for talks. 'There is no such declaration', he stated. 'After every round of negotiation, a statement was issued by the facilitators with the concurrence of the parties. In one such statement it was mentioned that the parties would explore finding a solution based on a federal principle. It is therefore not a declaration per se, as is being interpreted widely.' In an effort to paint the LTTE position in the best possible light, Balasingham stressed that the LTTE leader had told the Norwegians that he was not insisting on every word of the ISGA proposal, but was ready and willing to make changes if needed.[121]

The LTTE's request for a public statement in support of talks backed by all sections of the ruling coalition was duly passed on to Kumaratunga by the Norwegians, seemingly to little reaction. An indication that the Norwegians' efforts were having some impact came the following week when it was reported that in the course of a phone conversation with Richard Armitage, Kumaratunga had complained that the Norwegians were 'unduly pressuring' her for being 'inflexible', while not subjecting the LTTE to the same treatment.[122]

All eyes turned north towards the end of November, as the LTTE prepared for its annual Heroes Day celebrations, which this year coincided with Prabhakaran's fiftieth birthday. In a widely anticipated speech, the LTTE leader began by appealing to all political parties to declare publicly their 'official policy on the fundamentals of the Tamil national question, particularly on [our] core demands concerning homeland, nationality and the right to self-determination'. Describing the current stalemate as a 'political void', Prabhakaran intimated that there were 'limits to patience and expectations', hence his 'urgent appeal' to the government to resume 'unconditional talks without delay' on the basis of the ISGA proposal. In what many saw as a veiled threat, he went on to say that if the government 'adopts delaying tactics, perpetuating the suffering of our people, we [will] have no alternative other than to advance the freedom struggle of our nation.'

Criticising the JVP as 'an anti-Tamil political party steeped in a muddled ideology of racism, religious fanaticism and orthodox communism', the LTTE went on to contend that the April 2004 elections had 'paved the way for hegemonic dominance of Sinhala-Buddhist forces'. The president had 'embraced' a 'racist political party ... as the most important ally and partner in her coalition government'—a government made up of an 'unholy alliance of incompatible parties articulating antagonistic and mutually contradictory views and policies on the Tamil national question'.[123]

In a sign that it appeared to take Prabhakaran's speech seriously, the government reacted—the first time it had issued an official response to a speech by the LTTE leader—describing it as a 'call, couched in threatening language, for a resumption of negotiations without conditions' which none the less insisted 'unilaterally on a single agenda item'—an approach 'scarcely conducive to good faith negotiations'.[124]

In the background, the Norwegians felt growing unease over the JVP's vociferous campaign against their role in the peace process. Equally worrying, it appears, was the government's 'lukewarm' reaction to the JVP's anti-Norwegian tub-thumping. Responding to Hans Brattskar's concerns, US Ambassador Jeffrey Lunstead pointedly noted that the 'unknown' in the current political equation was whether the president was 'willing to bring the JVP to heel' given the party's 'crucial' role in 'ongoing machinations regarding her [own] political future'—an issue which Lunstead implied was currently 'a higher priority than the peace process' for Kumaratunga.[125]

Following an unofficial policy of visiting the country every six weeks to monitor the situation, in mid-December Solheim returned to Sri Lanka. During his initial meeting with the president, Solheim updated her on his conversations with Balasingham at the beginning of the month, during which the LTTE chief negotiator had reportedly stressed the Tigers' continued commitment to the ceasefire. On the government side, Jayantha Dhanapala requested that the LTTE publicly recommit itself to what were called the 'Oslo decisions'.[126]

Solheim duly took this message to Kilinochchi the next day. During his discussions with Tamilselvan, however, it was evident that the LTTE's priorities for talks lay elsewhere. Speaking to the press after their meeting, Tamilselvan reported that they had focused on 'issues that are endangering the peace process', and that the Norwegians were 'unable to give assurance that the ... government will take any constructive steps to take the peace process forward'. All of which gave a certain steel to Solheim's subsequent public expression of concern that instead of attempting to build mutual confidence, both parties were simply making 'statements that irritate each other'.[127]

Returning to Colombo before flying on to Delhi, Solheim was sombre. 'The peace process has reached its lowest ebb since the signing of the Ceasefire Agreement', he stated. 'As long as the two parties find it useful', however, the Norwegians would 'continue our facilitator role'.[128] It was hardly an encouraging note on which to sign off on his efforts to secure agreement on a new round of talks. Following a visit to London the following week for a meeting with Balasingham, it transpired that Solheim had brought with him a new set of proposals drafted by Dhanapal regarding 'interim arrangements' for the Northeast. The LTTE negotiator's immediate reaction to the proposals was that he would discuss them with Prabhakaran, pending a formal response from the Tigers.[129]

The response did not take long to materialise. On Christmas Eve—the third anniversary of the continuing military truce between the two sides—the LTTE issued a press release stating that, 'having carefully scrutinised the current version of the agenda as presented by the government', the LTTE leadership was 'displeased with its structure and contents'. 'As the JVP continues to declare its vehement opposition to peace talks ... based on the ISGA proposed by our organisation', it argued, 'the LTTE leadership insists on a clear, coherent, well-defined version of the agenda, without ambiguity or abstruseness.'[130]

V. Sambandan on 2004: year of stalemate?

In many respects, the main players in Sri Lanka's conflict resolution process painted themselves into a corner during 2004 ... For the SLFP, its initial condemnation of the LTTE's [ISGA] proposal and subsequent alliance with the JVP are turning out to be hurdles on the way to peace and devolution ... Politically [the LTTE] sidestepped the basic issue that Karuna raised—discrimination by the LTTE leadership against the Tamils

> of Eastern Sri Lanka—and instead used the rebellion to avoid the negotiating table. ... 30 months after the Ceasefire Agreement, there is a clear hardening of stance by an increasingly impatient and frustrated LTTE.[131]

With movement towards fresh talks still stalled, at the end of 2004 it appeared that the stage was set for renewed efforts—or as some viewed it, just more of the same—in the new year. That, however, was to reckon without the influence of other factors: in this case, a wholly unexpected and devastating force of nature.

7

THE TSUNAMI AND AFTER

The tsunami devoured the Sri Lankan coastline from Mullaitivu in the Northeast down to the Colombo area in the southwest. As a result of the failure of the country's early-warning system, it caught people in coastal areas completely by surprise. At 9.30am on the 26 December 2004, the beach at Peraliya—75km south of Colombo, where the railway line runs less than 200 metres from the shore—was struck by the first of a series of huge waves. The early Colombo-Galle train, which had left for the South packed with holidaymakers, was travelling through Peraliya just as the first wave hit, bringing it to a standstill. Soon after, a second and much larger wave descended, hurling the train's eight carriages into the buildings and trees lining the track. An estimated 1,700 people—possibly closer to 2,000—were killed, either crushed by the train, drowned inside the carriages, or swept out to sea.

This is just one story of the human and physical destruction wrought by the tsunami. As the days went by, tales of both terrible destruction and extraordinary courage emerged from across the country. At the same time, the full extent of the devastation became clear: between 35,000 and 39,000 people had been killed and up to 500,000 displaced. After Indonesia, Sri Lanka had the highest casualty figures in the region.

Four days after the disaster, President Kumaratunga extended an invitation to the LTTE's Tamilselvan to participate in an all-party Special Task Force for Disaster Management.[1] Any hopes of a new spirit of bipartisan co-operation that this move may have raised, however, were soon dampened when, prior to a mid-January visit by UN Secretary-General Kofi

Annan to tour tsunami-affected regions of the country, it emerged that the government was blocking Annan's access to the LTTE-controlled Northeast.[2] Needless to say, the LTTE leadership was furious over the implied slight, which was compounded, Tamilselvan protested, by the 'unfair distribution' of tsunami relief assistance at the expense of the Tamil people.[3] For its part, the LTTE was insisting that all relief destined for Tiger-controlled areas be channelled through its NGO wing, the Tamil Relief Organisation (TRO).[4] Politics trumped humanitarian concerns.

Meanwhile, a stream of international leaders visited Sri Lanka to observe the damage and show support for the rehabilitation and reconstruction effort. Among them was a Norwegian delegation headed by Foreign Minister Jan Petersen, which arrived in Colombo on 19 January.

In advance of the Norwegian visit, Prabhakaran appeared in public for the first time since the tsunami, thereby scotching rumours that he and other members of the LTTE leadership had perished in the disaster. The Norwegian delegation's tour of tsunami-affected areas included the Northeast: they visited Mullaitivu, which had been completely destroyed, and then held talks with Prabhakaran. Media reports suggested that a key item on the agenda was an effort by the Norwegians to develop a mechanism 'to get aid to people in the North'.[5] While humanitarian goals were paramount, an indication of the implicit connection with broader concerns was provided by Jan Petersen, who—following talks with Prabhakaran and Kumaratunga—emphasised that a co-ordinated relief effort could be 'conducive to a positive outcome' for the peace process.[6]

The aftermath of the tsunami

Erik Solheim

> Soon after the tsunami a delegation from Oslo went to Thailand, where many Norwegians had been killed, and then on to Sri Lanka ... We met Prabhakaran, and he was visibly disturbed ... The message was that reconstruction was the most important thing. The LTTE really showed it was interested in the people. On the government side, however, the impression was that they were interested in how the whole thing could be used for political purposes ... Chandrika responded to the tsunami like a true state leader, focusing on getting things going.

Vidar Helgesen

> We went up to Kilinochchi and met the Tamil Relief Organisation [TRO]. They were talking about the psychological trauma of people—something we

> heard very little of in Colombo. We met Prabhakaran and it was clear that
> he was personally very affected by the disaster. For all his brutality,
> Prabhakaran also had a strong loyalty to his people and cadres. The entire
> LTTE apparatus was affected. They had quickly shifted into the mode of
> doing something for the people, took the initiative, gave into government
> demands and changes as discussions on the P-TOMS [Post-Tsunami
> Operational Management System] evolved. It was quite clear that the LTTE
> was the party most eager to get something co-operative started. Chandrika
> was positive in principle but wanted national consultations. ...
>
> To be fair, she had the JVP and JHU attacking the whole joint mechanism
> concept.[7] I tried very strongly to argue that the P-TOMS would be the first
> time that the LTTE had explicitly agreed to take part in a national-level
> administrative structure, and that this could have positive political effects.
> She understood that. But at the same time, she never missed an opportunity
> to miss an opportunity, because Colombo politics always took precedence.

From Colombo, Helgesen and Solheim flew to Brussels for a meeting of
the Co-Chairs, also attended by Richard Armitage and Yasushi Akashi. In
the outcome statement, the Co-Chairs stressed their support for the 'efforts
of donors to ensure that the implementation of tsunami assistance is sensitive to and strengthens the peace process'.[8]

With a second round of talks on the proposed joint Northeast relief mechanism scheduled for the final week of January, first indications of its actual
content and likely political ramifications were beginning to emerge. At the
top, the proposed apex structure would have three chief co-ordinators, one
each for the Tamil, Sinhalese and Muslim communities—but headed, the
LTTE insisted, by their representative. At the next level would be an eleven
person co-ordinating council representing the six tsunami-affected districts,
consisting of six Tamils (appointed by the LTTE), three Muslims (chosen by
a majority of the northeastern Muslim MPs) and two Sinhalese (chosen by
the government), with respective ethnic ratios in the North and East also
taken into account (six Eastern, five Northern members).[9]

Reacting to this scheme, even long-standing LTTE critics like D.B.S.
Jeyaraj suggested that the 'prima facie flexibility displayed by the Tigers
seems truly remarkable'. Whereas only a year before the Tigers were not
'prepared to compromise or even accommodate power-sharing options'
with respect to the ISGA proposal, refusing to accept Muslims as an 'equal
third party', they now appeared to be 'more than generous to Muslim interests'. In addition, the LTTE seemed willing to put the 'ISGA or nothing'
demand into 'cold storage', opting instead for a 'task force structure with

limited and lesser power'. By way of explanation for this seeming transformation, Jeyaraj suggested that the LTTE had learned 'the hard way that it cannot lay hands on the big [assistance] bucks unless and until it enters into a strategic partnership with Colombo ... The Tigers know that the main opposition to [their] being given control of the North-Eastern structure will come from the Muslim and Sinhala communities. So it is bending over backwards to accommodate them.'[10]

Shimali Senanayake

If ever there was a time where both the communities pulled together it was the tsunami. It was wonderful to see. There was no differentiation at all. In LTTE-controlled areas the administration was still financed by the government and you had government agents and the ordinary people running the show.

Offering his perspective on the development of a joint aid distribution mechanism, Foreign Minister Lakshman Kadirgamar emphasised the government's commitment to ensuring that 'equal distribution of funds takes place'—a clear reference to what was already a persistent LTTE complaint that the Northeast was being unfairly marginalised in the post-tsunami relief effort. In addition to underscoring the 'non-political' nature of the 'working arrangement' envisaged, Kadirgamar reiterated the official position that funds could not be given directly to the LTTE, 'for the reason that it is not a state entity'.[11]

Sanjana Hattotuwa

If the LTTE states that relief efforts take precedence over political differences that existed prior to the tsunami, it is up to political forces in the South to take up this position and lock the LTTE into a national dialogue that uses long-term relief efforts as a springboard to re-energise a dormant peace process, and lock them into frameworks that are democratic, accountable and transparent.[12]

From Solheim's perspective the key people in the initial development of the P-TOMS document were Brattskar and the Australian-based Tamil Jay Maheswaran. 'Jay was very instrumental in the process', he says. 'From our perspective the benefit of the document was that it gave something to both sides. To the LTTE it gave a vehicle to receive large-scale aid. For the government it provided a structure under which the LTTE and others agreed to work with them. And in the beginning, the document was accepted by everyone'.

Tiger leader assassinated

In early February it was confirmed that former US President Bill Clinton had accepted the role of UN special envoy for tsunami relief. In a further demonstration of the politicisation of the tsunami relief effort in Sri Lanka, domestic reaction to the appointment focused as much on whether it signalled a new UN initiative to revive the peace process as its potential impact on the tsunami's victims.[13]

Work on finalising the joint mechanism document that had been tabled by the Norwegians received a jolt on 7 February, with the news that the LTTE Eastern Political Chief Kaushalyan had died in an ambush while crossing government-controlled territory west of Batticaloa. Appointed by Prabhakaran to oversee the Eastern Province following Karuna's defection in March 2004, Kaushalyan was the most senior LTTE figure to be killed since the 2002 Ceasefire Agreement had come into effect.[14] The Tamil National Force (TNF), a paramilitary group reportedly operating under Karuna's command, claimed responsibility for the attack. Alive to its potential impact on relations between the two sides, the government was quick to issue a condemnation of the killing. In an unexpected move, UN Secretary-General Kofi Annan followed soon after, expressing the hope that it would not herald a return to violence.[15] In the aftermath of the failure to gain access to the Northeast during his visit to Sri Lanka the previous month, Annan's statement was widely viewed as an important gesture from the UN to the Tigers.

Outrage aside, the LTTE's reaction focused on allegations that the assault had been carried out in cooperation with government forces—a pattern evident in the majority of Karuna faction attacks on LTTE cadres over recent months, it claimed. Needless to say, allegations of complicity were rebutted by government officials, even if few knowledgeable observers believed that Karuna's group could be operating independently.[16] Wherever the responsibility lay, however, what was certain was that the number of killings was steadily escalating—sixty-six since Karuna's defection the previous March, according to a statement from Japanese envoy Yasushi Akashi.[17]

Despite this setback, on the day prior to the third anniversary of the 2002 Ceasefire Agreement, Erik Solheim arrived in Colombo for talks on matters relating both to the proposed joint mechanism and the broader peace process. In Kilinochchi, Solheim complimented all parties for their shared success in maintaining the CFA, and stressed that the two sides were close to agreeing a joint mechanism for tsunami relief. At a press conference held after their meeting, however, Tamilselvan was decidedly less upbeat, warning that the Ceasefire Agreement was near 'breaking point' following the killing of Kaushalyan, and accused the government of conducting a 'clandestine war' against the LTTE.[18]

In his meeting with Kumaratunga two days later, Solheim stressed the importance of settling on a joint mechanism as soon as possible, and underlined a widely-held perception that the peace process would be badly damaged by a failure to agree on this issue. With regard to the ceasefire, he noted the lack of LTTE revenge attacks since Kaushalyan's death and suggested this was indicative of a desire to maintain and respect the existing agreement.

Two other critical issues, not reflected in these accounts of the talks, were very much present in the background. First, the government had been holding discussions on the proposed joint mechanism with the LTTE while simultaneously facing sustained pressure from the JVP, whose bottom-line remained that any joint mechanism agreed with the LTTE would lead to their pulling out of the ruling coalition. In a bid to appease the JVP, the government side insisted that the North and East should have separate relief mechanisms. The LTTE, though, was sticking to the position that here, as in all other matters, the North and East should be covered by a single mechanism.[19]

Second, on the day that Solheim was in Kilinochchi, Dhanapala made a speech in which he reiterated the government's commitment to reopening talks with the LTTE on the setting up of an interim authority in the Northeast. A bemused LTTE leadership wondered why at the precise point when talks with Solheim had focused on the immediate issues of establishing the joint mechanism and maintaining the ceasefire, the government had instead elected to raise the ISGA proposal. The JVP reacted to Dhanapala's speech with predictable fury, with Propaganda Secretary Wimal Weerawansa announcing in parliament that the party would leave the government were it to follow through on the proposal.[20]

Reflecting on the political climate at this point, Solheim confirms that the post-tsunami relief effort exacerbated political tensions in Sri Lanka. 'This could be seen most clearly in the North East', he says. 'In particular—as people there saw it—the unfair and biased approach of the international community in distributing relief, as the South got more international aid than they did.' Moreover, when 'nothing was happening on P-TOMS, the LTTE's frustration became apparent ... Money came in much smaller volumes than expected, and not in an organised way. But what the LTTE would not understand', he adds, 'is that many of those giving aid did not understand Sri Lanka; and secondly, that thanks to the LTTE's own acts, there was no support for a terrorist organisation.'

Norwegian efforts continue

Continuing efforts to take the joint mechanism forward, in early March Brattskar travelled to Kilinochchi for discussions with the LTTE. In the course of a meeting with Tamilselvan, Pulidevan and Tiger Police Chief Nadesan, Brattskar encouraged the LTTE to continue demonstrating 'flexibility' in negotiations with the government and 'restraint' with respect to the security situation. After briefing the Tigers on a recent visit to Delhi by Vidar Helgesen, he also informed them that in the context of an upcoming visit to Sri Lanka, EU External Affairs Commissioner Benita Ferrero-Waldner had expressed a wish to 'visit Kilinochchi and meet Prabhakaran'.[21]

A mounting sense of stalemate was illustrated, however, when a government-appointed commission assembled to investigate Kaushalyan's murder began hearing evidence towards the end of March. In their testimony, senior army officers denied that the Sri Lankan military were either assisting Karuna's forces or harbouring them in government-held territory.[22] The following day, however, SLMM Batticaloa Head Steen Jørgensen stated that he could 'confirm the presence of Karuna forces' in government-controlled areas. In the meantime, confirmation that Karuna faction forces were operational in government territory was provided by reports that a section had begun demanding taxes from (mostly) Sinhalese villagers in the Polonnaruwa area.[23]

Efforts to move the joint tsunami relief mechanism forward continued apace. Meeting President Kumaratunga at the end of March, Hans Brattskar informed her that the LTTE had now accepted the Norwegians' draft text.[24] But Kumaratunga, as Iqbal Athas noted, was in a double bind: 'If she does [sign the joint mechanism] aid will flow but her government faces a break in the middle. If she does not the aid will not come and the government may be forced into international isolation.'[25]

In mid-April, Solheim returned to Sri Lanka. As the exchange of killings between the LTTE and Karuna faction cadres continued, on the day before

Solheim's arrival, Acting Defence Secretary Vidura Wickremenayake declared that the government would be making the international community aware of the LTTE's violations of the Ceasefire Agreement—over 3,000 breaches to date, he asserted.[26] At the same time, LTTE Peace Secretariat Head Pulidevan suggested that the government were 'buying time and preparing themselves for a referendum on constitutional change.[27] [They are] not paying attention to tsunami victims.'

Taraki, Tamil journalist

The natural disaster has actually had a negative effect on the stalled peace process. It has aggravated many latent problem[s] rather than opening a window of opportunity ... The unitary system is so rigid that no one can bend the rules to acquire land or disburse money to help tsunami-affected people to restart their lives. In short, the tsunami has expanded the potential for conflict rather than creating the ideal humanitarian grounds for assuaging it.[28]

Seemingly on cue, at the beginning of her second visit to the country in mid-April, US Assistant Secretary of State for South Asia Christina Rocca urged the government to 'speak with one voice on the peace process' and to reach rapid agreement on a joint tsunami relief mechanism with the Tigers in order to ensure that 'assistance finds its way to people who need it—wherever they are in Sri Lanka.' Asked to give her view of internal struggles within the government, Rocca urged all parties to keep the post-tsunami reconstruction and wider peace process in focus—a clear if indirect warning to the JVP in particular.[29]

With President Kumaratunga absent on holiday, Solheim now focused his efforts on the Vanni and the East. In the East he paid particular attention to the Muslim community. During a meeting with Sri Lankan Muslim Congress (SLMC) leader Rauff Hakeem, frustration over the community's lack of representation in discussions of the joint mechanism was forcefully expressed. The 'whole purpose of setting up a joint mechanism' would be 'lost', Hakeem argued, if the Muslims who make up 'almost half of the tsunami IDP population' proceed to reject it. Commenting on the argument that the facilitators were constrained by the views of the parties on the Ceasefire Agreement (the government and the LTTE), Hakeem responded that while the Norwegians clearly felt they 'cannot do anything beyond the wishes of the principal parties', in his view they were not using the powers of their mandate 'to the full'.[30]

There was further evidence of mounting Muslim dissatisfaction during Solheim's visit to Batticaloa, where local leaders handed over proposals for a separate joint tsunami relief mechanism for the Muslim community. But while local TNA MP Joseph Parajasingham expressed 'concern' over the community's grievances, he also underlined the *realpolitik* of the present position. 'The government and LTTE are [the] principal parties involved. Therefore, they should work together jointly to solve problems. Muslims should understand this ground reality and cope with situation.'[31]

A few days after Solheim and Rocca's departure, Colombo was rocked by news of another high-profile murder. This time the victim was Taraki, an ardent Tamil nationalist and widely read journalist,[32] whose body was found on the edge of the lake surrounding parliament. Ten days after the killing, an unknown Sinhalese group claimed responsibility, accusing Taraki of 'defacing and darkening the international face of Sri Lanka'.[33] While many were persuaded that the government had a hand in the assassination, fellow Tamil journalist D.B.S. Jeyaraj suggested that a more likely perpetrator was his fellow Easterner and former friend Karuna. Although Taraki had encouraged Karuna to work for greater autonomy for Eastern Tamils within the LTTE, he had become a consistent critic of the renegade LTTE commander, much to Karuna's reported fury. And with Karuna still in hiding, Jeyaraj argued, the killing of Taraki must have been carried out with the connivance of the rebel LTTE leader's security service guardians: a chilling suggestion, and a premonition of things to come.[34]

Focus on the challenges of post-tsunami reconstruction returned in mid-May with an international Development Forum held in Kandy, attended by all the key national and multilateral donors. The outcome was up to $3 million pledged in reconstruction assistance:[35] this despite an intervention immediately following Kumaratunga's opening speech by the Buddhist monk heading the JHU, in which he lambasted the joint mechanism as a concession to an irredeemably terrorist LTTE.[36]

Immediately following the Kandy Forum, Solheim travelled to London to brief Anton Balasingham both on the forum and on a recent visit to Delhi, during which the Indians had said that they were hesitant to give public support for the joint mechanism because the LTTE were the only designated partners on the Tamil side.[37] Reportedly, Balasingham's response was to urge the Norwegians to ensure that an agreement on the joint mechanism was concluded without delay.[38]

A more ominous perspective, however, was provided by Tamilselvan towards the end of May. In an interview with a Tamil newspaper, the LTTE political wing leader described the joint mechanism as 'not a big subject', emphasising that it was not a 'programme to find [a] solution to the ethnic issue'. On that count, he argued, the Tamil people had little faith in the government: 'if the Sri Lankan government and its forces continue to behave in this manner', he argued, 'it cannot be said that our people will be patient or accept it. We have come to the end of our patience.'[39]

June proved to be a critical month for the joint mechanism, by now increasingly referred to by its acronym, P-TOMS.[40] Following a mid-month visit to Delhi by President Kumaratunga to try to secure Indian support, it became apparent that despite criticism from some ministers within her own party, as well as implacable opposition from the JVP, Kumaratunga had decided to press ahead with finalising the agreement.[41] True to their word, the JVP pulled out of the governing coalition on 15 June, as all eight of their ministers quit.[42]

With the finalisation of the agreement now in sight, Helgesen arrived in Colombo on 19 June. As with earlier negotiations between the government and the LTTE, a key point of contention remained the position of the Muslim community. In the course of their meeting, Helgesen reportedly informed SLMC leader Rauff Hakeem that Muslims would be adequately represented in the P-TOMS committee structure, though it was not a tri-partite document.[43] During his subsequent talks with President Kumaratunga, other Muslim leaders and the LTTE, Helgesen underscored the importance of recognising the tsunami's disproportionate impact on the Muslim community, and the fact that donors would be likely to insist on Muslim participation in the structure. In response, Kumaratunga emphasised her desire not to revisit the P-TOMS text, instead proposing a 'symbolic gesture' that would acknowledge their importance in the process. Tamilselvan, by contrast, simply insisted there should be only two parties to the agreement,[44] and was seemingly more concerned with focussing on how to 'salvage' a peace process he described as 'threatened seriously by ceasefire violations'.[45]

Agreement signed jointly

Finally, on 24 June—almost exactly six months since the tsunami had struck—the government and LTTE signed the Memorandum of Understanding underpinning the P-TOMS,[46] while the police grappled with a crowd of JVP-led protestors intent on halting the proceedings.[47] News of the signing was widely and warmly greeted internationally, notably by Kofi Annan.

Jehan Perera

> A comparison of the joint mechanism with the ISGA proposal would show a vast difference ... in the attitude of the LTTE. They [say they] have been prepared to be flexible because the joint mechanism deals with humanitarian issues arising out of the tsunami tragedy [and they have] been drawing a distinction between the joint mechanism and their yet unmet demand for an interim administration. Nevertheless, the LTTE's willingness to adopt a step-by-step approach to power sharing rather than a maximalist solution needs to be appreciated.[48]

After all the drama surrounding finalisation of the agreement, expectations that the focus of attention would finally move to the immense tasks of reconstruction and rehabilitation throughout the North and East were soon dashed. In a meeting with Dhanapala immediately before heading north for talks with Tamilselvan, Norwegian Embassy Deputy Head Laegreid heard the Government Peace Secretariat Head express the view that implementation of P-TOMS was 'doubtful'—less than a week after the signing of the agreement.[49] A couple of days later, Tamilselvan publicly disputed the president's suggestion—voiced in a widely circulated Sinhalese TV interview—that in signing the P-TOMS the LTTE had accepted Sri Lankan sovereignty.

Then, in early July, the JVP challenged the agreement's legality in the Supreme Court, which on 14 July suspended the operation of four key clauses of the P-TOMS agreement, pending a final determination—scheduled for 12 September—on their conformity with the Constitution.[50] Was Solheim surprised by this development? 'By then, no, not anymore', he responds. 'Most of the steam had run out of it.' And on the LTTE's reaction to this development, he suggests, 'they had largely given up on it by then. [The court judgement] was just a final nail in the coffin.'

Solheim's analysis chimes with a press briefing given by Tamilselvan following a meeting with TNA parliamentarians in Kilinochchi convened three days after the Supreme Court judgement. Describing the verdict as 'an unfortunate turn of events', Tamilselvan said that the LTTE now had 'no confidence that Sinhala leaders are capable of implementing anything they have agreed to'. His prognosis was gloomy: 'hopes of achieving a solution through negotiations have been shattered'.[51]

D.B.S. Jeyaraj

The humanitarian needs of North-eastern tsunami victims cannot be relegated to the backburner simply because Sinhala chauvinists have gone berserk ... Sinhala hawks as usual would have done Tigers a great favour then. Including LTTE in a joint mechanism certainly has its share of danger. Excluding it could turn out to be worse.[52]

Responding to the broader political situation, and in particular escalating violence on the ground, on 19 July the Co-Chairs issued a statement expressing 'alarm' over the 'deteriorating security situation' in the country. In particular, they called for the LTTE to 'stop all killings by their forces' and for the government to 'ensure' that 'all paramilitary groups are disarmed' and to 'guarantee the safety of unarmed LTTE cadres in government controlled areas'. Finally, they reminded both sides that 'maintenance of the Ceasefire Agreement is the responsibility of the two parties alone'.[53]

Perspectives on the P-TOMS negotiations

Hans Brattskar

I was the facilitator for the [P-TOMS] process, with very good help from colleagues both in Oslo and Colombo. The issues were challenging. I went to see Chandrika and told her that I was worried that if all this took too long then it was not going to be possible to carry it out. She said that with the Ceasefire Agreement, the big mistake was that we hadn't prepared the nation politically for it. I told her, 'my concern is that the JHU and others will mobilise against you instead of you pulling them with you'. This is not simply something we can say with the wisdom of hindsight: the danger was *very* clear at the time. But Chandrika was convinced of her own political ability to convince others and pull people along with her.

From day one we were worried that the nationalists would use that time to mobilise against us. With the P-TOMS finally you had the supreme court decision, which I saw as a straight political move, influenced by people who were thinking of what was good for the next election and not for the country after the tsunami or for the peace process as a whole. Nationalist forces were against the joint mechanism anyway, but there was also an (unconfirmed) rumour that Rajapaksa supporters wanted the Chief Justice to make certain that the P-TOMS would not succeed because a success for Chandrika would not play out well for Rajapaksa. In other words, elections were always on people's mind—an endless political cycle.

Vidar Helgesen

What we hoped to conclude with the P-TOMS document in February or March dragged on until it was effectively struck down in July. In the process there was also the international element, where the government blocked international aid and visits to the North and East on the argument that it would give legitimacy to the LTTE. They wanted all the relief to go through government structures, with all the attendant corruption.

There was plenty of discussion of all this with Chandrika, Kadirgamar and international actors. We encouraged the international community to be more proactive in insisting on going to *all* the tsunami-affected areas and trying to meet the LTTE. We saw this as an opportunity at that time, and later as the last and lost opportunity to do so. When we met Prabhakaran after the tsunami he was visibly shaken by the situation. But then, experiencing the fact that even in this situation the government couldn't care less about the Tamil people from his perspective, and that—again from his perspective—the international community also let down the Tamil people: I think that is where we really lost him.

The principle of impartiality in humanitarian assistance was blatantly impeded by the Sri Lankan government. The international community tried to get access, tried to have high-level visits to the North and East, tried to see the LTTE, but all this was simply rejected outright by the government. And the international community just remained silent ... National sovereignty is clearly there to be respected, but we didn't see much mobilisation by the international community to engage with the LTTE and put real pressure on the Sri Lankan government to obtain access to them.

The big issue was Chandrika's inability to say 'we will go for it'. Period. She could have done that by February. She was authoritative. She would have had bad media for a week and we could then have moved on. But she was obsessed with Colombo political considerations, wanting broad-based consultations. Again, it was her amazing characteristic to have grand vision and political courage and then to lose it whenever she had the opportunity, over some bickering. The political fact was that the more she allowed [the P-TOMS] to linger, the more opposition to it was building.

My own guess was that since he was eyeing the Presidency, Rajapaksa was trying to undermine the entire endeavour. Kadirgamar was very mindful of national sovereignty, and not at all helpful over allowing international figures to visit the North and East. On P-TOMS as well, he was not a progressive force. Eventually he took the same line as Chandrika—the need for more consultation. Dhanapala, then heading the Peace Secretariat, agreed with us that it was a disastrous lost opportunity on Chandrika's side.

Erik Solheim

The international community should have made it clear that we did not want to take a stand between the Tamils and Sinhalese; that we just wanted to make sure that the aid was given to everyone. A number of foreign ministers did make an attempt to visit the Northeast, but it wasn't forceful enough. No one really forced the issue with the government.

Chandrika Kumaratunga

In the end things were sabotaged by Mahinda Rajapaksa, together with the chief justice, because Mahinda wanted to come to power and realised that if the P-TOMS were successful, I would remain in power for a long time. But the JVP, which was always against everything, persuaded my two main lieutenants to oppose it,[54] saying they were going to leave my government, which would again lose [the presidential elections] and Ranil would come back: and then they would have to suffer out in the cold without their positions of power.

But they persuaded the Indian High Commissioner:[55] she was fooled and kept briefing the Indian Foreign Ministry in Delhi that they shouldn't agree [to the P-TOMS], my government would fall and Ranil—who is close to the BJP[56]—would come back. So I went to India, I knew a few important people around Prime Minister Manmohan Singh myself, whom I canvassed first, and I took a team there with me. And we came back from India with a statement saying they supported us. Both Lakshman [Kadirgamar] and Mangala Samaraweera were surprised: they thought I couldn't do it. Earlier they kept saying, 'what if India doesn't agree'? But I went to Delhi and managed to persuade them.

Although some people urged me to there was no way of moving faster on the P-TOMS, because we didn't have a two-thirds majority. If I had used my executive power I would have had to become an undemocratic leader. That is something I still agonise about. I could have been a dictator for a little while, used presidential power, become a temporary dictator and done it. But it was just not in me ... I was an effective democratic leader—at least I thought so—and I thought I could push it through by democratic means, using charm, persuasion. And we almost did it. If I could have pushed it through by myself then I wouldn't have needed the Norwegians. When the Norwegians tried, Prabhakaran didn't agree to anything. Finally he agreed to the ISGA because it gave him so many powers. He could have taken Tamil Eelam after that.

Paikiasothy Saravanamuttu

The tragedy of the post-tsunami period was that the unity born out of tragedy never translated into a political package of any kind. And that was because in order to defeat the Ceasefire Agreement, Chandrika had made a pact with the devil, bringing the JVP into government. They were all out to wreck P-TOMS,

arguing that if you gave [the LTTE] a mechanism to deal with tsunami reconstruction it would acquire a political significance.

A mechanism recognising the LTTE's role within the reconstruction effort was
something the government was willing to consider as long as they accepted the
government's edict. But as far as the LTTE was concerned, this was a 'no way'. The
tsunami provided an opportunity to build on, a bridge for a political settlement.
When the P-TOMS agreement finally came out it was contested in court, and the
whole thing collapsed. The idea that we are still a unitary state prevailed.

Chandrika herself was isolated on the issue. She said she would resign if she
didn't get P-TOMS, and she kicked the JVP out of government to get her way. But
by that time it was too late. She had put all her political capital on the line. To
start with any peace process you need the total commitment of the administration. It is difficult enough as it is to deal with a non-state actor like the LTTE that
is armed to the teeth. And when you have such a divergence of views within the
administration that holds the clout, it is very, very difficult.

Mounting tensions

On 27 July, two weeks after the court decision, Solheim met Balasingham in
London to review developments. In response to mounting evidence of escalating tensions on the ground, the government had recently proposed face-
to-face talks with the LTTE. Tamilselvan had refused, insisting that the
government must first show goodwill by disarming paramilitary groups—a
reference to the Karuna faction—and honouring the ceasefire.[57] Solheim thus
strongly urged Balasingham to persuade the LTTE leadership to agree to a
meeting to 'review CFA implementation', arguing that failure to do so at this
point would be 'incomprehensible' to the international community.[58]

A government proposal to 'renegotiate' the Ceasefire Agreement to
eliminate some 'deficiencies' was rejected outright by the LTTE. In an
interview explaining the Tigers' position, Balasingham argued that there
was 'essentially nothing wrong' with the agreement's structure, and that
the current escalation of violence 'could only be attributed' to the government's 'failure' to 'fulfil its obligations' under the existing agreement. The
solution to 'present problems', he argued, would come from 'implementing
the existing ceasefire agreement in letter and spirit'.[59]

In a sign that domestic politics—in particular upcoming presidential elections—remained firmly in Kumaratunga's sights, following an SLFP central
committee meeting in late July it was announced that Mahinda Rajapaksa
had been selected as the party's presidential candidate. Though he was
regarded as a moderate on issues relating to the ethnic conflict, some were

troubled by the lukewarm support he had given Kumaratunga over the P-TOMS negotiations. Moreover, indications of a growing understanding between Rajapaksa and the JVP provided ample reason to be concerned over what his leadership might presage. While the date of presidential elections remained unclear, the result of Kumaratunga's increasingly desperate efforts to push the poll forward to December 2006, the main contours of the electoral contest, which would be between Rajapaksa and UNP leader Ranil Wickremasinghe, were becoming clear.

Hans Brattskar

> After the tsunami I was in the North, and I met the opposition leader, Ranil Wickremasinghe, at Jaffna airport. I said that nearly 39,000 people had lost their lives and the devastation was unbelievable. So I asked him: do you think this will now be used an opportunity for peace? And he said no, he did not believe it would happen.

In early August Helgesen visited Sri Lanka for a round of talks with all parties and a visit to Norwegian-funded tsunami relief projects in the East. At a meeting with Kumaratunga and other government officials on 4 August, Dhanapala reportedly described the P-TOMS Supreme Court decision as 'by and large positive', since it clarified the fact that an agreement with the LTTE was legal. In addition, he expressed optimism that by the time of the final hearing in September, the Court could be persuaded to accept the P-TOMS *in toto*. In response, Helgesen conveyed the LTTE's disappointment over the decision, a reaction by all accounts fully shared by Kumaratunga.[60]

With respect to the Ceasefire Agreement, Kumaratunga signalled that the government was willing to conduct a joint review. Helgesen duly conveyed the message to the LTTE during a meeting with Tamilselvan in Kilinochchi the following day. The LTTE political chief's response was reportedly curt. What the Tigers wanted, he responded, was not a review of the CFA but strict adherence to it by all sides.[61]

The situation, however, was thrown wide open by an event that returned Sri Lanka to the centre of world attention: the assassination, on 12 August, of Foreign Minister Lakshman Kadirgamar.

8

ASSASSINATIONS AND ELECTIONS

Lakshman Kadirgamar was a hard-working government minister. The Tamil septuagenarian was usually at his desk until late into the evening, inside the guarded fortress that was his private residence in Colombo. On the night of Friday 12 August, Kadirgamar emerged from the house for his daily swim in his private pool. At around 11pm, after getting out of the water, he was hit by three sniper's bullets, one of which pierced his heart. He was rushed to a nearby hospital where an hour later he was pronounced dead.

The police commandos who descended on Kadirgamar's house in the wake of the shooting soon established the likely chain of events leading to his assassination. After breaking into an empty house less than one hundred metres away, they discovered that a first-floor bathroom had been purpose-fitted to give a sniper a clear view of Kadirgamar's pool.[1] The tripod that had been used to steady the killer's rifle remained in the bathroom, while downstairs several bags containing food and other provisions were found, suggesting that the assassin had been hiding in the building for some time, waiting for the moment to strike.[2]

With local media awash with reports of lapses by the security forces,[3] President Kumaratunga declared a state of emergency the morning after the murder. By then Tamilselvan had already issued a statement denying the LTTE's culpability, instead blaming 'forces opposed to the Ceasefire Agreement in the South'. Cabinet spokesperson Nimal Sripala de Silva announced that the government found it 'difficult to accept the [LTTE] denial',[4] and in a televised address the following day Kumaratunga went a step further, pointing the finger of blame directly at the Tigers.[5]

In a demonstration of the slain foreign minister's international standing, Kadirgamar's funeral on 15 August was attended by a large group of foreign dignitaries with official delegations from twelve countries, Vidar Helgesen and Norwegian Foreign Minister Jan Petersen included. Petersen's subsequent call 'for both parties' to 'do their utmost to fulfil their obligations according to the Ceasefire Agreement' appeared to capture the mood of many in the international community. Briefing representatives of the Co-Chairs on 16 August, Helgesen indicated that at a meeting with Balasingham in London scheduled for the following day, he would be presenting the LTTE with five 'areas of opportunity' in which to demonstrate that it was still a 'serious interlocutor'.[6] Most important among these was a proposal that the LTTE agree to meet with the government and SLMM to 'discuss CFA implementation'.[7]

Thereafter the pace of events quickened. The next day Petersen and Helgesen duly met with Balasingham in London. Stressing the seriousness of the situation in the wake of Kadirgamar's assassination, Petersen emphasised the need for the LTTE to take 'concrete actions' to keep the peace process alive.[8] Helgesen recalls that 'Balasingham didn't say the LTTE was behind the murder, but he didn't say it wasn't either.' The Norwegians handed over a letter outlining their suggested 'areas of opportunity' and asked Balasingham to forward it to the LTTE leader, which he agreed to do.[9]

On 18 August, following up on discussions with Helgesen and Solheim, President Kumaratunga wrote to Norwegian Prime Minister Kjell Bondevik requesting a meeting between the government and the LTTE to review CFA implementation.[10] A little over twenty-four hours later it was clear that both sides had agreed to the proposed meeting.[11] Wrangling over the venue then impeded further progress. After rejecting the idea of holding the discussions in Oslo, the government then spurned an LTTE proposal to meet at its headquarters in Kilinochchi. The Tigers followed suit by turning down the government's suggestion of Colombo, purportedly on the grounds of 'security concerns'.

In the search for a compromise, Hans Brattskar suggested holding the meeting in the 'no-mans land' between government and LTTE-controlled territory, such as at Omanthai in Vavuniya district. The deadlock, however, continued. The Norwegians suggested meeting at Colombo airport, but this was turned down by the LTTE. In the end, as Solheim observes, the whole initiative 'disappeared', and the focus of attention turned elsewhere—towards impending elections.

ASSASSINATIONS AND ELECTIONS

The facilitators on Kadirgamar's assassination

Erik Solheim

> Kadirgamar's assassination was a disaster for the peace process. It speaks volumes about Prabhakaran's mistaken belief that all problems have a military solution. The Tigers saw Kadirgamar as the ultimate traitor: as long as the peace process was continuing successfully they knew they could not hit him. So this act was a clear signal that the process was not working for them.[12]

> Many Tamils, and the LTTE generally, put forward the argument that the government had killed some LTTE commanders of the same rank that year. Vidar and I repeatedly told them—and Bala[singham] as well—that they would not be able to convince the world on this issue: and that if they didn't understand that, they would be in deep shit.

Vidar Helgesen

> Kadirgamar was always on the Tigers' target list. They hated him, and he was also the person who had been putting pressure on other countries to ban the LTTE. His funeral was a big outdoor event. Mahinda Rajapaksa was one of those who spoke, and he gave a fiery speech against terrorism. I stayed on a bit longer after the funeral and had a discussion with Mahinda, asking him for his views on the peace process, should he become President.

> This is when he told me that he would offer the LTTE a federal solution, and very quickly so. He said he wanted to move rapidly and strike a deal with the LTTE within six months, and wanted me to convey that message to Bala[singham] in London. Which I did. In the aftermath, it is possible to read that as part of the scheme that many claim was in place, whereby he struck a deal with Prabhakaran to have the LTTE boycott the presidential elections.[13] But it's very difficult to assess this issue.

Elections in focus: Sri Lanka

Towards the end of August, the Supreme Court issued a ruling on a question that had dogged Lankan political life over the preceding eighteen months: the date of the next presidential elections.[14] On the basis that she had called the previous elections a year earlier than stipulated in the constitution,[15] Kumaratunga had lobbied hard for her current term to be extended by a year, meaning that elections would be postponed from 2005 to December 2006. Ruling on the issue, the five-member Supreme Court bench delivered the unanimous verdict that Kumaratunga's term of office should end in December 2005.[16]

The stage was set for the beginning of the election campaign, something for which the political parties were already gearing up. An early indication of this came from Ranil Wickremasinghe's UNP, which organised a march to Colombo in July to demand that presidential elections be held in 2005. Next out of the blocks was Kumaratunga's own SLFP. Having been chosen—not without controversy[17]—as the SLFP's presidential candidate, Mahinda Rajapaksa swiftly proceeded to conclude a series of pacts with parties whose support was deemed vital to his election prospects. First came the leftist JVP, with whom an electoral agreement was signed on 8 September. Five days later, a similar deal was sealed with the Buddhist-nationalist JHU.

The agreements appeared to show that Rajapaksa intended to reverse Kumaratunga's approach to the ethnic conflict. Whereas Kumaratunga had emphasised a federal solution, these newly completed alliances clearly pointed to a preference for the country's existing political structure. The JVP advocated a unitary state based on what it called 'administrative decentralisation', whereas the JHU were opposed to granting self-determination in any form.[18] In terms of pursuing a peace agreement, the JVP's agenda insisted on a thorough revision of the 2002 Ceasefire Agreement to ensure that it left 'no room for terrorist activities', a 'serious reconsideration' of Norway's role as facilitator in view of the 'unprecedented bias and partiality' it had demonstrated towards the LTTE, and cancellation of the P-TOMS initiative.

What Rajapaksa told the Americans

A candid insight into Mahinda Rajapaksa's thinking at the time comes in a US Embassy Colombo cable dispatched on 12 September. Soon after his nomination as SLFP presidential candidate, Rajapaksa received a courtesy call from US Ambassador Jeffrey Lunstead. Lunstead began by noting that the accord recently signed with the 'Marxist JVP' had 'caught the attention' of the international community, and underscored the fact that, 'taken at face value', the agreement appeared to be a 'complete renunciation of the on-going peace process'—a process that had 'long enjoyed international support'.

In reply, Rajapaksa suggested that there was 'no cause for concern' as the agreement with the JVP was, as he put it, 'just words'. In order to win the election, Rajapaksa argued, JVP support was 'essential', and from experience he knew that 'the way to handle the JVP' was 'to agree to whatever they want in order to get their support.'[19]

Lunstead asked Rajapaksa if the agreement with the JVP was a signal that he wanted to 'replace' the Norwegian facilitators. 'No,' he replied. 'Nobody else could do the job.' Lunstead suggested that in that case it would be useful if the prime minister could make a public statement to that effect. 'If I say that, I will lose the elections,' Rajapaksa retorted, because, as he put it, '98 per cent' of voters in the South think that 'the Norwegians are biased in favour of the LTTE'.[20]

Elections in focus: Norway

The Norwegian facilitators' focus on the Sri Lankan elections was temporarily distracted by parallel electioneering in Norway. With polling day for parliamentary elections scheduled for 12 September,[21] ex-Left Party leader Solheim took a six week leave of absence from the Sri Lanka facilitation effort to assist with his party's campaign.

The election produced a significant swing to the left in the form of a victory for the opposition 'Red-Green' coalition,[22] which received 48 per cent of the vote, the biggest share going to the Labour Party (32.7 per cent). Solheim relates what happened next: 'The overall result of the elections was that a new [Labour-led] coalition government was formed. I was asked to become a minister. I asked to be minister of development, the main reason being so that I could combine it with continued engagement in the Sri Lankan and Sudanese peace processes. I took over from Vidar with respect to the peace process, and a little later, Jon Hanssen-Bauer replaced me as Sri Lanka Special Envoy. Jon had never had any specific party affiliation: he came from the trade unions and was working on the Middle East. He had no prior knowledge of Sri Lanka.'

'The co-operation with [outgoing Foreign Minister] Jan Petersen went very well', Solheim recalls. 'Petersen trusted Vidar completely. He had sound judgement, a common touch and not the slightest tendency towards arrogance. But he did not involve himself deeply in Sri Lankan affairs. His successor Jonas Gahr Støre was a different kind of character: a more brilliant intellectual with a strong personality and a much deeper desire to make personal decisions', Solheim notes. 'He showed an interest in Sri Lanka but always stuck to my handling things directly.'

For Helgesen, the centre-right government's defeat at the polls spelled his departure from the position of State Secretary, which he had held for four years. This did not, however, entail his exit from the facilitation effort in Sri Lanka.

EU moves

With the Sri Lankan election campaign in full swing, on 19 September the Co-Chairs—with Norway now represented by Vidar Helgesen—met in New York to review recent developments. Underscoring the fact that the peace process was currently facing its 'most serious challenges' since the 2002 ceasefire agreement, the meeting's outcome statement strongly condemned Kadirgamar's assassination, commended the government for the 'restraint' it had demonstrated afterwards, and called on the LTTE to take 'immediate public steps to demonstrate their commitment to the peace process and ... willingness to change'. After expressing 'disappointment' that agreement had not yet been reached over a venue for new talks, the statement went on to insist that a peaceful resolution to the conflict could only be achieved based on a 'federal model' of governance 'within a united Sri Lanka'.[23]

Ten days later, the EU announced that it was imposing a travel ban on the LTTE, and would forbid any EU delegations from meeting them—a move generally interpreted as a response to Kadirgamar's assassination. In addition, local media reports suggested that the Commission was also considering formally listing the LTTE as a terrorist organisation.[24] Reacting to the EU's decision, LTTE political wing leader Tamilselvan claimed that the declaration had caused 'irreparable damage' to the prospects for peace and 'ruined the Tamil people's trust in the international community'. He ended his statement by urging the EU to 'desist from being partial to one party' and to 'rescind' the declaration.[25]

On 6 October, Tamilselvan met Norwegian Ambassador Hans Brattskar in Kilinochchi. According to Tamilselvan, the discussion focused exclusively on his criticism of the EU decision and warnings about its negative impact on the ground—which included, he claimed, an increase in paramilitary activity.[26] By contrast, Brattskar later informed his Co-Chair colleagues that the crux of the meeting had been his own strongly-worded rebuke regarding the Tigers' recent conduct.

The election campaign heats up

Meanwhile, President Kumaratunga was trying persuade the party leadership to pressurise Rajapaksa to reverse his decision to retain a unitary state structure and abolish the P-TOMS. Her efforts were fruitless, as his campaign manifesto demonstrated.[27]

Further emphasising the difference in their approaches to the peace process, Rajapaksa's manifesto, publicly released in mid-October but widely flagged in advance, also contained an undertaking to open up 'direct talks' with the LTTE—including a suggested one-on-one meeting with Prabhakaran—based on a 'national consensus', to be reached through three months of 'broad-based consultations' following his election. Critical elements of the 'consensus', however, were already clear: recognition of the country's 'territorial integrity' and 'national identity', and a 'peaceful political solution' not 'tied up in the concept of traditional homeland [and] self-determination'. Finally, the Ceasefire Agreement (CFA) would be 'readjusted' to ensure that 'terrorist activities have no place', and 'remedial action' would be taken following a 'review' of the 'CFA monitoring process'.[28]

Peter Bowling

Chandrika had a profound sense of her significance for the future of Sri Lanka. [It was] a sense of self, mixed with doubts about whether she had the capacity, desire or commitment to be in that position. She had resisted political engagement for quite a while. When she came to power there was a need to change 'who' she was. But behind that there was a very decent person and a serious commitment to the peace process. There is deep chauvinism embedded in Sri Lankan Sinhala politicians, but that wasn't the case with her: and that was indeed rare. But it was also part of her failing in that she did not really understand how this impacted on the majority Sinhalese population.

Highlighting the tensions that a shift towards the Sinhala majoritarian approach would be likely to exacerbate in the Northeast, on 30 September the annual LTTE-orchestrated *Pongu Thamil* (Tamil Resurgence) campaign culminated in a Jaffna rally which by partisan estimates attracted over 200,000 people. Alongside the customary demands that the Sri Lanka Army vacate the 'Tamil homeland', speaker after speaker stressed that the time had come for Tamils to 'break away from a unitary setup' and 'commence our journey towards self-determination'.[29]

Developments on the Sinhala political scene also proceeded apace. In early October, key political parties representing the country's largest minorities, notably the Ceylon Workers' Congress (CWC),[30] Rauff Hakeem's Sri Lanka Muslim Congress (SLMC) and the Upcountry People's Front (UPF)—representing in total some 10 per cent of the country's 13.3 million registered voters—came out in support of Wickremasinghe's candidacy.[31]

At his first public rally, held in Kandy the day after presidential nomina-tions closed on 7 October, Wickremasinghe got straight to the point. Rajapaksa's pacts with the JVP and JHU, he argued, were preparing the ground for the division of the country, and only people who wanted a 'return to war' would vote for him.[32]

Significantly, criticism of Rajapaksa's decision to ally himself with the JVP and JHU was not confined to the ranks of the opposition. One well-informed commentary, for example, cited a 'senior SLFP minister-cum-lawyer' as stating angrily that while 'the monks [the JHU] insist on the unitary character of the state ... we have come a long way from that posi-tion. Has India disintegrated because it is a federal state?' he wondered. Another senior party member went even further, suggesting that the alli-ance with the JHU meant that the SLFP would 'never be able to rise' from the 'mud hole of communal politics', and that the country's 'festering ethnic wounds would never heal'.[33]

With the campaign by now in full swing, a stinging reminder of the frag-ile situation in the East was provided when an LTTE convoy was ambushed at a checkpoint on 10 October, leaving four Tiger cadres dead and seven wounded. All indicators pointed towards the Karuna faction as perpetrator of the attack—and everyone knew that Karuna could not take such an ini-tiative without the Army's blessing. At the same time, reports from Jaffna suggested that the shadow war between the LTTE and government forces was escalating in the North. In particular, the mid-October killing of two popular Jaffna school principals, one of whom was known to be openly critical of the LTTE on some issues, was thought to highlight the fact that government security personnel, reportedly assisted by anti-LTTE Tamil groups such as the EPDP and guided by military intelligence, were now operating in the LTTE-controlled North.[34]

Encounters with the Rajapaksas

Speaking of his meetings with Mahinda Rajapaksa—the first of which occurred in 2002, when the latter was a junior government minister—Solheim states that he 'came across as a people's man. It was a gradual development that he became the prime minister. When Chandrika was around there was no number two or three. In such a scenario, seeing the capacity of others was not easy. In the end Mahinda proved that you could be President of Sri Lanka with just the Sinhala vote.'

In terms of his approach to the peace process, Solheim emphasises that at this point Mahinda was 'ready for any option. His priority was not any particular solution to the Sri Lankan crisis, but establishing his own power. In fact during our conversations in January 2006, right after his election victory, he told me that he was ready to hand over the North to Prabhakaran, without elections, in a kind of backroom deal—and with few caveats, except that there would be no separate state.'

'What Mahinda was truly opposed to', he says, 'was protracted negotiations of the type preferred by the LTTE. Because he knew that would bring down his own all-Sinhala political constellation. And he would also certainly have preferred a dirty backroom deal to any well-organised process leading towards federalism.'

'Overall, our feeling was that this was the first time that an outsider family—and from the Deep South—had gained such importance: and one seen as having a much more common touch. This was a fresh development. I felt Mahinda was a party man: he had spent a lot of time in the SLFP. He was popular with the party cadre. This is one of the biggest paradoxes of the Rajapaksas. I mean here comes a man from outside "the families",[35] basically a self made man, definitely not from Colombo 7. And before long he establishes a family dynasty of which the Bandaranaikes or the UNP could never even dream!'

In pointing to Mahinda's long-standing SLFP associations—he was first elected as an MP on the party ticket in 1970—Solheim highlights a broader point concerning the Rajapaksa family. While historically neither as powerful nor as well known as President Kumaratunga's Bandaranaike clan, the Rajapaksas none the less occupy a significant place in SLFP party history. Mahinda's father, D.A. Rajapaksa, was a prominent independence activist, MP and later cabinet minister, while his uncle, D.M. Rajapaksa, was active in national politics as early as the 1930s, and wore a brick-red *kurakkan* shawl to symbolise the red earth of the home village—a garment that Mahinda subsequently made his own trademark.

Nor is this simply about family sentimentality. Combined with the family's rural landowning roots in the vicinity of the southern town of Hambantota, in office Mahinda consistently deployed this and other symbolic trappings of village life in the country's Buddhist heartlands to underscore a carefully cultivated image as a 'man of the people'.[36] Nether was the Rajapaksa political ascendancy confined to one member of the family. In 1989 Mahinda's brother Chamal became the second MP for the Hambantota district. Twenty years on, they had been joined in parliament by three further members of the family—Nirupama, Basil and Namal—and in government by another of Mahinda's brothers, Defence Minister Gotabhaya Rajapaksa.

International missions

In the midst of the election campaign two international figures with significant former roles in the peace process visited the country: Ian Martin, the human rights adviser; and Trond Furuhøvde, former SLMM Head.

Martin's mission was to follow up on the human rights component of the peace process, in particular the joint memorandum he had drafted prior to the sixth rounds of talks held in Hakone in April 2003. Summarising the outcome of his meetings to Colombo-based diplomatic representatives, Martin reported that he had found the government side 'very enthusiastic' about the notion of reviving the draft memorandum, and 'receptive' to the idea of strengthening the human rights component of CFA monitoring, but that Tamilselvan had stated that nothing could happen in this area before the talks on improving CFA implementation had been held. Martin's attempts to raise the broader issue of political killings reportedly 'got nowhere', and he also noted Tamilselvan's 'palpable anger' over the recently imposed EU travel ban.

Furuhøvde, for his part, reported that on the government side Peace Secretariat Head Jayantha Dhanapala had emphasised that Colombo wanted to add a policing element to the CFA, thereby moving away from the existing setup, where responsibility for enforcement rested entirely with the parties to the agreement. The LTTE, by contrast, expressed a clear preference for sticking with the current concept of CFA 'self-enforcement'. From his discussions in Kilinochchi, Furuhøvde gained the impression that the LTTE Central Committee had discussed the current situation and agreed on a strategy, its first element being to wait for the outcome of the election before taking any major decisions.[37]

Ranil and Mahinda: peace approaches under the spotlight

In the run-up to the presidential elections, a US Embassy cable analysed the two main candidates' likely approaches to the peace process. With respect to Rajapaksa, it argued that if applied in practice, the 'nationalist line' adopted during the election campaign threatened to 'polarise ethnic communities', encourage even greater violence in the 'chaotic East', and provide the LTTE with a 'convenient pretext for spurning negotiations'.

Despite this, the cable went on to note that 'recent discussions' with informed sources, including Rajapaksa campaign advisors, suggested that contrary to the 'unitary' state approach of the SLFP campaign manifesto, Rajapaksa himself was 'not opposed to federalism' and/or a 'significant devolution' of 'provincial-level power' to the North and East.[38] The suggested 'best-guess' conclusion was that Rajapaksa had 'well-intentioned, if somewhat naïve, thoughts on the peace process'.

In particular, the cable suggested, a Rajapaksa presidency would be severely handicapped in attempting to realise any 'good intentions' in this area by his lack of experience in dealings with the LTTE and by the JVP's certain rejection of any perceived softening of the hardline nationalist stance. With that said, the cable concluded that Rajapaksa might have a 'better appreciation of Tiger *realpolitik*' than his public comments to date had indicated.

Turning to Ranil Wickremasinghe's campaign, neatly dubbed the 'Time in a Bottle' strategy for peace, the cable suggested that Wickremasinghe appeared to think that if elected he would be able to 'simply pick up with the LTTE where he left off', without any prior need to weigh the 'complicating factors' that had emerged in the meantime. These factors, it was suggested, included 'apparent' government support to the Karuna faction; 'degradation' of the CFA on a 'near-daily basis'; heightened LTTE suspicion of 'southern sincerity' in the aftermath of the 'tsunami aid mechanism (aka P-TOMS) fiasco'; and the assassination of Kadirgamar and subsequent EU travel ban on the Tigers.

Overall, the cable argued that Wickremasinghe might well be counting 'too heavily' on his past dealings with the Tigers to 'compensate' for the 'greater distrust of the South spawned by the Karuna split'. As it pithily concluded, 'Wickremasinghe will be unable to pick up where he left off with the Tigers simply because the Tigers are not there anymore; they have moved back (along with CBK's government) from a point where negotiations still seemed possible to a more entrenched, less flexible position.'[39]

Elections: the initial LTTE take

LTTE spokesman Daya Master eventually broke the Tigers' silence on the subject of the elections in mid-October. In an interview with a leading Sunday newspaper he announced that the Tigers had 'gone through' both candidate's manifestos and on this basis decided to adopt a 'noncommittal' position. The inhabitants of Tiger-controlled areas would be permitted to cast their votes for whoever they chose, he said. 'The people will not be discouraged or forced to refrain from voting for any reason', was the clear—if highly questionable—conclusion.[40]

Indications that this might not be the LTTE's last word on the subject surfaced a week later. Reacting to reports that an organisation representing higher education institutions in the Jaffna district—generally believed to be an LTTE front—had issued a call for voters in the North to boycott the presidential election, Master argued that this was not the official LTTE line.[41] When the boycott call was echoed a week later by a second front organisation, the *Makkal Padai* (People's Force) via leaflets distributed in the Jaffna peninsula, uncertainty over the LTTE's position only increased.[42]

Compounding the sense of uncertainty—one reflected in media reports of pervasive reluctance among Jaffna inhabitants to talk about their voting intentions until the LTTE had 'pronounced' on the subject—at the last moment a meeting of the twenty-three Tamil National Alliance (TNA) MPs called by the LTTE to 'discuss the situation' was postponed to 10 November, only a week before polling day.[43]

Irrespective of these manoeuvrings, official preparations for voters in LTTE-controlled territory—a little over 700,000 of them in the Jaffna peninsula and nearly 100,00 in the Kilinochchi and Pachchilapalai districts—continued apace, with voting booths set up at strategic locations in 'cleared'—that is government-controlled—territory, close to the no-man's land separating the two sides.[44]

Campaign final stages

An intriguing and to many observers surprising side effect of Rajapaksa's electoral alliance with the JVP and JHU was the rapprochement between President Kumaratunga and Wickremasinghe that was increasingly in evidence as the campaign progressed. The source of the growing understanding between the erstwhile foes lay in the threat that Rajapaksa's election would pose to any federal solution to the conflict with the LTTE.

It appears that moves towards formulating a bipartisan SLFP-UNP position on the peace process had begun some months earlier. Soon after the July debacle over the P-TOMS agreement, Wickremasinghe had reportedly informed Indian Prime Minister Manhoman Singh of his intention to work with the SLFP on a 'national agenda' in advance of the forthcoming elections, a move Singh welcomed 'wholeheartedly'.[45] Following this, the UNP leader included a provision for a bipartisan initiative in his election manifesto, and for good measure reportedly sent Kumaratunga a personal copy of the document.[46]

In October, Kumaratunga and Wickremasinghe met to discuss, among other things, a common approach to the peace process.[47] In the event, their main conclusion was that a bipartisan agenda would be best developed after the elections, with SLFP nominees included in Wickremasinghe's cabinet in the event of his victory.

The significance of this development was not lost on Rajapaksa. Having also received the results of opinion polls that showed him trailing Wickremasinghe by 6 per cent, Rajapaksa's conviction that, as one commentator put it, 'the only option available to him was to project Wickremasinghe as a candidate who stands for the division of the country', was further strengthened. He deployed this argument consistently and effectively throughout the rest of the campaign.[48]

Erik Solheim

Ranil is a reserved person. A great intellectual, he was—and is—a visionary in many ways. In particular he wanted to reform the Sri Lankan economy, to make Sri Lanka the Singapore or Taiwan of the Indian Ocean. But we had the feeling he had difficulties in stirring the emotions of the masses ... He has the right ideas, great knowledge, knows the history and culture of Sri Lanka as hardly anyone else does: but he needs advice on how to be a better street fighter.

LTTE manoeuvrings

Concerned by the mounting sense of uncertainty in the Vanni, TNA MPs met to review the situation two days before a meeting with the LTTE. After a long discussion of the implications of issuing a call to boycott the election, the MPs came down firmly against a boycott. The decisive factor seems to have been the damage it was felt such a call would inflict on the

LTTE's international standing. The decision was communicated to Balasingham in London, who undertook to forward it to Prabhakaran.[49]

The TNA meeting with Tamilselvan and other leading LTTE figures took place in Kilinochchi on 10 November. Interpretations of the outcome varied widely. Under the heading 'Loud and clear message', for example, one report suggested that the decisive note had been struck by Tamilselvan, who was reported as saying that while the LTTE was not calling for a boycott, it none the less believed that Tamils living in LTTE-controlled areas would 'not be interested in the election'.[50] In contrast, another report focused on the viewpoint of the majority of the TNA MPs, and the fact that the 'final'—as opposed to 'official'[51]—communiqué gave the impression that, at least in a technical sense, their view had prevailed.[52] The report carried on *TamilNet* conveyed yet another interpretation. TNA parliamentary leader R. Sampanthan was quoted as saying that 'Nothing worthwhile would be achieved by supporting either of the two leading candidates', and that the Tamil people were 'not at all interested in the forthcoming Presidential election'.[53]

Another well-informed Tamil commentator—D.B.S. Jeyaraj—had doubts about the key electoral message from the LTTE. 'Despite the assertion that the LTTE-TNA are simply being supportive, the reality is that the Tigers want a boycott of the election.' Following an impassioned plea to Tamils to 'stand together' with other 'racial and religious minorities' against the 'Sinhala-Buddhist juggernaut threatening to crush them', Jeyaraj went on to argue that, viewed in this context, the 'LTTE-TNA call for a boycott' was 'nothing but a betrayal'. In the light of later developments, Jeyaraj's main conclusion bears repetition. 'The Tamil people and all right thinking Sri Lankans must realise that despite Wickremasinghe's shortcomings, the chances of war under his presidency are less than that of Rajapaksa. It is the Tamils who bear the brunt of [any] war. Let them not be indirectly responsible for inviting war upon themselves through boycotting the polls.'[54]

Those who were encouraging Tamils in LTTE-controlled territories to vote in the election were further undermined when, on the day before the LTTE-TNA meeting, the Sri Lankan Supreme Court ruled that polling stations originally due to be located close to official checkpoints between 'uncleared' and 'cleared' areas would have to be moved at least 500 metres away, and that any voter whose identity was questioned could be detained in police custody. This significantly reduced the incentives for the 250,000 prospective Tamil voters living in 'uncleared' areas to vote. Taken together with the fact that many of the approximately 700,000 Tamil voters living in the Jaffna peninsula would abstain if the LTTE directed them not to vote, the court's decision represented what seemed certain to prove a decisive factor in the election's outcome.

UNP own goals?

During the final stages of the campaign, two UNP MPs made public statements that provoked heated controversy. The first came from N. Dissanayake, son of murdered ex-party leader Gamini Dissanayake, who was widely reported to have stated that it would not be necessary for Sri Lankan forces to take on the LTTE as 'American and Indian forces' would fight them if 'Prabhakaran opts for war'. In addition he was quoted as saying that Karuna had Wickremasinghe's 'full backing' before he 'set out on his diversion'. The fallout from these reports spread rapidly: within days, posters quoting Dissanayake's remarks and calling for an election boycott were in evidence in Kilinochchi.[55]

At the same time, former official peace negotiator Milinda Moragoda gave interviews in which he made the same claims, albeit in a more sophisticated manner, describing Karuna as a 'product of the peace process for which the UNP made the bulk of the contribution'. In addition, he pointed out that during the UNP government's ceasefire with the LTTE, 'with the help of international intelligence ... our navy managed to intercept several armed LTTE vessels', and argued that the UNP had 'enmeshed' the LTTE's forces in an 'international safety net' and thereby prevented a return to war.[56]

The impact of these interventions was undoubtedly to heighten LTTE suspicions of Wickremasinghe's true intentions. One commentary, for example, suggested that the LTTE viewed this as a 'synchronised' attempt to 'win back' Sinhala voters tempted to opt for Rajapaksa's hard-line position on the peace process. It went on to suggest that this played into a debate raging within the LTTE between its political and military wings, the former arguing that the main southern parties had reached agreement on a federal solution to the conflict, and that the Tigers should capitalise on this fact, while the latter contended that a Rajapaksa victory would create a climate in which the armed hostilities necessary for achieving Tamil Eelam could resume.[57]

Tyrone Ferdinands

The LTTE was very good at complaining that the South was playing its own politics in saying 'we don't want to talk to the Tigers'. And the LTTE would remain silent throughout. But in every election, eventually they would intervene decisively. Three elections: first Chandrika comes in

---

because Dissanayake was bumped off by the LTTE in 1994; then she is re-elected in 1999 because there is an assassination attempt on her: and finally, Mahinda comes to power in 2005 because of the election boycott.

In November 2005 I came back from Kilinochchi: Mahinda met me and took my message [regarding the LTTE boycott] in stony silence. There were very few occasions when he didn't respond. But this time he didn't say a word, which was strange. Ranil didn't want to hear, refused to meet me: he thought he would be president. So I took the message to the UNP chairman, Ranil's confidante and an independent-minded person. I told him, and he panicked. Ranil was so convinced that he would pull it off at this election.

Election outcome

Polls opened on 17 November, and by the close of the day an estimated 75 per cent of the country's nearly 13.5 million voters had voted. In the Northeast, however, the percentages were radically different. In the LTTE-controlled Vanni, the figure was under 30 per cent. Most drastically, in Kilinochchi only one person voted, while more significantly in terms of numbers, in the Jaffna district the turnout was a little over 1 per cent.[58] The Tigers continued to maintain that the Tamil boycott of the election was a decision freely taken by the people themselves.[59]

The following afternoon, Election Commissioner Dayananda Dissanayake announced the result: a victory for Rajapaksa with 50.2 per cent of the vote, against 48.3 per cent for Wickremasinghe. By any standards, the margin of victory—around 180,000 votes—was extremely narrow, and in the midst of the Rajapaksa camp's victory celebrations there were plenty who noted the Tamil boycott's critical contribution to the result. Noted commentator Sonia Samarasinghe went so far as to say that the South had been 'outmanoeuvred by master strategist Vellupillai Pirapaharan [Prabhakaran]', who had 'once again proved to be the hand that guides the destiny of this nation'.[60] As Samarasinghe noted, for the first time ever a candidate who had campaigned without the support of any of the country's key minority groups had been voted into power, thanks as much to mass Tamil electoral abstention as to collective Sinhalese political assertion. It was widely believed that the LTTE had 'wished for a Rajapaksa victory' and ensured that result by 'exploding bombs' and 'flinging grenades' the night before the polls in Batticaloa and Jaffna. The question now was: why?[61]

A number of explanations were put forward for the seemingly strange decision that the Tigers had taken: the LTTE's wish to see the weaker candidate elected; their preference for the choice offered by a Rajapaksa presidency—peace, or war if necessary—as opposed to Wickremasinghe's single offer of what was 'possibly a peace trap';[62] their anticipation that Rajapaksa would be 'sufficiently extremist' to add international credibility to the LTTE when 'making a bid for a separate state';[63] antipathy to the statements made by Dissanayake and Moragoda during the election campaign; and suspicion of Wickremasinghe's perceived failure to take a clear pro-Tamil stand during the campaign. All these ideas, and more, were suggested at various points. Missing from most accounts at the time, however, was consideration of something that may well have played a decisive role in determining the Tigers' call for an election boycott: the possibility that there were secret negotiations, and ultimately a pre-election deal, between the Rajapaksa camp and the LTTE leadership.

D.B.S. Jeyaraj

> The Tamil people wanted a president [Wickremasinghe] to talk peace with the Tigers and prevent war, while the Tigers wanted a president [Rajapaksa] who could disrupt peace and bring about war. In such a situation, the franchise of the people became a casualty. This was the crux of the matter.[64]

Behind the LTTE election boycott

Prior to the election there appears to have been some indication of the existence of secret contact between Rajapaksa and the LTTE leadership. In a cable sent a week before the election, US Ambassador Jeffrey Lunstead noted:

> a local NGO official in contact with both the prime minister and the LTTE, told us on November 7 that Rajapaksa has been in back-channel communication with the Tigers since July and has proposed an interim authority, in the form of a provincial council with a five-year term for elected members, with expanded authority over police, land titles and the judiciary. The LTTE reputedly has not responded to this proposal, but described Rajapaksa's approach as 'practical'.[65]

Commenting on the 'back channel' issue, Erik Solheim says,

> I think it's very likely such a channel existed, but less likely that it went into anything close to negotiations. But it is highly likely that Mahinda would have floated suggestions he thought would reduce Tamil support for Ranil. How seriously it was taken is hard to tell. A word is not a word for Mahinda.

Similarly, Vidar Helgesen's view is that a back channel was 'probably in place'. He goes on to say that 'Mahinda was abundantly clear to me about [his desire for] a fast move to a federal deal'—a recollection that tallies with the Lunstead cable.

There is another element to the story which—if true—takes the 'back channel' allegation a good deal further. Not only was there covert communication, it is also suggested that there was a firm deal between the two sides regarding the presidential election.

Initial public suggestions of the existence of such a deal surfaced soon after the result had been announced. Writing in late November 2005, D.B.S. Jeyaraj alluded to 'speculation' that the new president and the LTTE had earlier come to an agreement to secure Rajapaksa's election 'through an enforced boycott of the Tamil majority regions of the Northeast'. The deal had been sealed, it was alleged, following a series of secret meetings in Kilinochchi between Tamilselvan and a 'special representative' of Rajapaksa. Allegedly the special representative was Tiran Alles, a close friend of Mangala Samaraweera, Rajapaksa's election campaign manager, who had asked Alles—with Mahinda's expressed approval—to establish contact with senior LTTE figures such as Tamilselvan, Pulidevan and Nadesan.[66]

This Alles had duly done. While the substance of the consequent deal—securing a Tamil election boycott—was supposedly clear from early on, the means by which it was to be implemented proved more problematic. Rajapaksa's electoral alliances with the fervently anti-LTTE JVP and JHU meant that an open deal with the Tigers was out of the question. Thus the talks honed in on the possibility of the Tigers offering 'indirect support' to Rajapaksa's campaign. This is what they in fact did, with the boycott campaign only really moving towards violence and open intimidation in the final 48 hours of the campaign—the result, allegedly, of a last-minute Alles visit to Kilinochchi to persuade the Tigers to step up their activities.

It is suggested that 'political and diplomatic circles in Colombo' were first alerted to Alles' role after reports of the particularly warm embrace and 'profuse thanks' he had received from Mahinda at a post-election victory gathering.[67] Concerning further details of the deal, Jeyaraj confined himself to off-the-record speculation that 'a financial arrangement was more likely than a political arrangement', noting that it was as yet unclear whether Prabhakaran was aware of the deal or if Tamilselvan had in fact 'gone behind his leaders back'.[68] How seriously this version of events was taken at the time by others, however, remains unclear.

Curiously, allegations of a Mahinda-LTTE deal went quiet for some time after the election, only returning to the spotlight in early 2007 in the aftermath of Tiran Alles' arrest—ironically on charges of contacts with the LTTE[69]—and a campaign in his support subsequently launched by Samaraweera, recently sacked as foreign minister after a series of policy disagreements with Rajapaksa. Following his arrest, Alles made a police statement in which he alleged that prior to the 2005 presidential election he, along with others—namely Presidential Advisor Basil Rajapaksa, Presidential Secretary Lalith Weeratunga and Finance Ministry Secretary Jayasundara—had held meetings with the LTTE. Based on agreements reached at these meetings, he alleged, the government had disbursed funds to the LTTE, with Alles ensuring their transfer to the Tigers.

After Alles' release on bail in June 2007, Ranil Wickremasinghe went on the offensive, demanding to know why Alles' alleged co-partners in a deal with the LTTE—the president's brother Basil Rajapaksa included—had not been arrested as well.[70] A mid-June cable from US Ambassador Robert Blake fills out the picture. A UNP source informed embassy staff that the key LTTE link-person was Emil Kanthan, 'a prominent Tamil businessman and suspected LTTE intelligence officer'. Reportedly, Alles had recorded 'at least one' of the meetings between Kanthan and 'Rajapaksa's election team (Basil Rajapaksa, Jayasundera and Weeratunga)' with his mobile phone's video camera, and several 'Embassy contacts' were reported to have already seen 'at least parts' of the video. The cable went on to note that Basil Rajapaksa 'had conceded to Ambassador [Blake] that the pre-election contacts with the LTTE had taken place. It is not yet established that money changed hands in these meetings.'[71]

The story continued to rumble on through the following months, fuelled by a further Alles statement, this time to the Terrorism Investigation Division (TID), following his release on bail and the disclosure of a number of official documents relating to the affair. Based on this information, in early July a media report alleged that a deal between Rajapaksa and the LTTE to secure an election boycott in November 2005 had involved two stages: an initial cash settlement handed over by Basil Rajapaksa directly to Emil Kanthan (subsequent reports put this sum at 180 million rupees; approximately USD $1.3 million); and, in the event of an election victory for Rajapaksa, a second and larger package involving an LTTE housing project, disarming the Karuna group, appointing 'LTTE nominees' to 'various political offices' and resuming talks in Thailand.[72]

A follow-up analysis of the larger 'package' by the same investigative journalist pointed to a complex operation.[73] It was alleged that initially, some three months after the election, Rajapaksa made a series of unsolicited multi-million rupee grants to bogus housing projects in the North in order to facilitate the agreed transfer of funds to the Tigers. By the time Rajapaksa produced a cabinet paper on these projects in August 2006, allegedly some 150 million rupees (USD $1.1 million) had already been paid out to a bogus company set up by Emil Kanthan—the mastermind behind the operation and by now identified by the TID as an LTTE intelligence officer. The cabinet paper foresaw the eventual release of 800 million rupees to the non-existent housing schemes.[74]

In retrospect, circumstantial confirmation of the allegations was provided by the fact that shortly after his election victory, Rajapaksa established a new apex body—the Reconstruction and Development Agency (RDA)—to front his effort to promote an alternative mechanism to the now abolished P-TOMS. The chairman of the new agency was to be Tiran Alles.[75]

With the scandal moving inexorably into the political limelight, on 21 September Parliament passed a motion calling for the appointment of a Select Committee to probe the affair.[76] In the course of a parliamentary debate, Basil Rajapaksa firmly denied that he had had any contact or dealings with the LTTE. Thereafter, the issue seems to all but disappeared from public view, only to resurface after the end of the war.

Following a grenade attack on his home in late January 2010, Tiran Alles repeated his original allegations at an impromptu press conference, focusing on the claim that Basil Rajapaksa had personally handed over 180 million rupees to Emil Kanthan—now described as the LTTE's 'financial controller'—to ensure an election boycott, and that the deal had taken place at Mahinda Rajapaksa's explicit request.[77] As before, a serious attempt to conduct an independent investigation into the allegations was conspicuous by its absence.[78]

Views on the LTTE boycott and the 'deal' with Rajapaksa

Erik Solheim

> We were surprised. We asked Bala[singham] and he said he was not in agreement, but that Prabhakaran was afraid of Ranil's scheme of an 'international safety net', which he feared would be an impediment to the LTTE ... Bala[singham] also said very clearly that he was opposed to the decision because he wanted Ranil elected: he had respect for Ranil, had trust in him.

> The reasons given [for the boycott] were vague, so it's hard to judge. A lot of credible people felt there was a deal. I am still a little hesitant [to accept this], however. First, Bala[singham] never indicated a deal to us. Secondly, whatever I think of Prabhakaran, he was not corrupt. The only reason could be [to get] money for purchasing weapons. He had no bank accounts abroad and was not

leading the high life. For sure, [the Rajapaksa brothers] were capable of [bribing the LTTE]. If that could bring them power they would have done it. ...

The LTTE must have believed that there were advantages with Mahinda as president: less experience, less contact abroad. But they did not understand that Ranil and Chandrika had liberal values, while Mahinda was a very different character, with no moral compass ... While Ranil, of course, was the banner carrier of the peace effort. And he would definitely have won the election if the LTTE had not boycotted it. So the boycott was a historic, astronomical blunder. And there was a real escalation of killings afterwards.

Tore Hattrem, Norwegian ambassador to Sri Lanka

Before the 2005 election there were many indications that there was an effort to cut a deal. Most likely money changed hands, and this is probably one of several reasons why the LTTE underestimated Rajapaksa. The LTTE boycotted the polls and Wickremasinghe lost, so they got Rajapaksa as president. As many have bluntly stated, the LTTE made the rope that hanged them. And Rajapaksa outsmarted Prabhakaran from that day onwards until the end of the war.

Tyrone Ferdinands

I think there must have been something going on. In any case, the LTTE thought Ranil was not going to be useful to them ... They thought that Mahinda would be weaker: politically that was their calculation. But there was something or other else that happened [as well]. I was talking to three LTTE leaders five weeks before the elections and I was told clearly, 'You know both sides. Tell their leaders that we will enforce a boycott. But only tell the two leaders.'

With the LTTE there was in any case a financial consideration involved whenever a deal was made with anybody—either a bank transfer or a project that was funded. It started with the Indians who trained them in this, gave them a taste of it. The Indians would always have bags of money: and here we are talking about the Indian state.

Arne Fjørtoft

Did they bribe the LTTE to boycott the elections? Definitely. The man who handed over the money told me so directly.

Shimali Senanayake

In his house at his swearing-in, Mahinda told us: you have no idea what I have had to do to get to this position. He felt he earned it and this was his due. Which may very well be true. Chandrika treated him like nothing. He was not even allowed to stay the night at Temple Trees when she was president! He had the title prime minister and not much else. The only time he was really able to do something as prime minister was during the tsunami, because Chandrika was out of the country at the time. He did a very effective job. He is a born communicator and also a man of action. He is able to move things, make things happen. But then she returned and took everything back from him.

After the election

Following his election victory, President Rajapaksa set about putting together a new cabinet. From the perspective of the peace process, the most important appointments were those of the JVP-friendly Mangala Samaraweera as Foreign Minister and seventy-three-year-old Ratnasiri Wickremanayake—a man known for his hard-line Sinhala nationalist views—as prime minister.[79] In his first public speech after the election, Rajapaksa underlined that he was willing to 'engage in direct talks' with the LTTE, but stressed that the 'current bi-lateral approach to peace' would be replaced by a 'multi-party approach', and that the ceasefire agreement would be revised in order 'overcome its defects'.[80]

Norwegians on the new Sri Lankan political landscape

Erik Solheim

After Mahinda won the presidential election, in his first speech to parliament he said that the government was ready for direct talks with the LTTE. But he also questioned federalism, minority self-government and the P-TOMS agreement, and he did not even mention the Ceasefire Agreement.

At the same time it's hard to tell whether Prabhakaran had made a decision to go back to war at this stage, or if it remained just a contingency plan. But it's certainly true that he was not making any steps for peace. Mahinda's public stand was that everything had been done in the wrong way in the past, and that now a new peace process would be started with a unilateral approach. Behind closed doors he told us that he would undermine his support in the South if he went for a long peace process, so he wanted to try and get an immediate deal with Prabhakaran—and everything except a separate state was thinkable in that context. He was not a man of principles but of pragmatic politics, serving his own interests.

Mahinda's preferred option was a rapid, 'big bang' deal. And he may have been somewhat right about this, because a 'big bang' deal would have made many people happy. He knew that this was contrary to the LTTE's view; he knew that their attitude was cautious. But at this point Mahinda had no plan to go to war—although Gotabhaya would probably have wanted that.

I don't recall Prabhakaran's speech that year exactly, but we got the same message it put across from other Tamil sources. People in the diaspora told us there was strong pressure to contribute money for a final assault. And there were few positive signals from Bala[singham] at this stage as well, And don't forget, they had recently killed Kadirgamar, which was an enormous provocation. So a number of things suggested they were moving in that direction.

Hans Brattskar

After the election I received instructions to go and meet the president-elect and ask him if he wanted us to continue with the job of facilitation. He was clearly very reluctant, but he said yes, he wanted us to continue. I told him, OK, but you have to say that publicly ... We had a good meeting, and in the end a press statement was put out saying that Norway would continue to act as facilitator. In Parliament, however, earlier on he had been very negative about Norway.

The point was that we didn't want to continue as facilitators unless the parties made it clear that they wanted us to. So it needed to be said that we were wanted, and Rajapaksa did that. We therefore had to deliver the same message to the LTTE, and they issued a statement expressing their support for our facilitation role again. To get that we went to Kilinochchi and met Tamilselvan.

Concerning the Ceasefire Agreement, in Colombo I was always hearing that it was dangerous in the sense that the LTTE got a chance to re-arm. I really heard that all the time. My sense was always that it also gave the government an opportunity to re-arm. It gave the government political legitimacy and opened doors that had previously been closed to them in capitals around the world. The Ceasefire Agreement gave the government a unique opportunity to gain an upper hand both militarily and politically, and the LTTE could sense that if it did not lead to anything permanent, it would certainly not strengthen their hand.

The first post-election test of the interaction between Rajapaksa and the LTTE came in the shape of the annual Heroes Day speech (27 November). No Prabhakaran speech has ever been more closely scrutinised. As in previous years, Prabhakaran put heavy emphasis on the many reasons why Tamils could and should not trust the Sinhala polity, but this time there was perhaps a stronger than usual appeal to the international community for 'greater understanding of the LTTE's position'.[81]

The most significant new element concerned Rajapaksa. Despite the contention that 'the new leader of the Sinhala nation' demonstrated no understanding of the 'Tamil question', Prabhakaran none the less described him as 'a realist committed to pragmatic politics'. And since Rajapaksa claimed to have a 'new approach' to the peace process, the LTTE leader noted, the Tigers would wait and 'observe, for some time, his political manoeuvres and actions'.[82] However, if the new government did not 'come forward soon with a reasonable political framework that will satisfy the aspirations of the Tamil people', the Tigers would 'intensify' the 'struggle for self-determination ... for national liberation to establish self-government in our homeland.' The message to Rajapaksa seemed clear: we will give you some time—but not much.

Balasingham's Heroes Day Speech

Mahinda Rajapaksa is a pure Sinhala Buddhist. He was chosen by Sinhala Buddhist votes, voted by the majority to elect him. Ranil got up-country, Muslim and Sinhala votes but if our people voted, he would have won. But a Sinhala Buddhist has been elected; he has twenty-seven parties with him, yellow robes and red shirts are all with him, and a Buddhist hierarchy has established itself. What happened in Tamil Eelam? Here, the cry for statehood has arisen.[83]

For all this talk of a 'wait and see' approach, developments on the ground in the week following Heroes Day suggested something different. Rising low-intensity violence in the Northeast, in particular a seemingly coordinated series of attacks on Army checkpoints, culminated with a claymore mine attack on an Army truck in Jaffna on 4 December. Seven soldiers were killed—the largest number of military fatalities in a single attack in what became the bloodiest week since the 2002 Ceasefire Agreement. Violence was increasing in the East too, although there, as often, it took the form of clashes between the Muslim and Tamil communities in the Trincomalee, Batticaloa and Amparai districts. While the instigators of the trouble in the East remained unclear, the LTTE's responsibility for the Jaffna attacks was unquestioned.[84]

Reviving the peace process returned to centre stage following President Rajapaksa's 8 December announcement that he would be asking Norway to continue to act as facilitator—one of a number of issues on which the Indians had expressed themselves emphatically a few days previously to visiting Foreign Minister Samaraweera.[85]

The immediate response from Oslo—specifically from Erik Solheim—took Rajapaksa by surprise. Norway, he stated, would be happy to continue in the facilitator's role, provided that certain conditions were met: first, that there was a public expression of the government's confidence in their role as impartial facilitators; second, that the Colombo authorities clarified their own thinking over how to move the peace process forward. But the Norwegians had conditions for the Tigers too: they explained to the LTTE that they would be seeking firm 'commitments' that the Tigers would honour 'all agreements reached', and would grant 'greater access' to Prabhakaran himself. Only when Norway had received responses to these stipulations from both parties would it make a decision on its role as facilitator.[86]

On the LTTE side, all the indications were that the emphasis would, as in the past, remain on full implementation of the 2002 Ceasefire Agreement as opposed to its review—something that Rajapaksa had pledged in his election manifesto and for which his allies in the JVP and JHU were pushing hard. For the Tigers, moreover, 'full implementation' remained more or less synonymous with army vacation of the High Security Zones (HSZs) in and around the Jaffna peninsula and the disbanding of paramilitary groups.

On the last of these issues, on 8 December the LTTE announced they would be holding a press conference with two Karuna faction cadres who had reportedly surrendered to the Tigers following a recent fire fight in Amparai, and had admitted that their group were operating out of a Special Task Force (STF) camp in the area. In addition to providing de facto corroboration of army complicity in Karuna faction operations, the two cadres also alleged that the same forces were behind the recent post-election attacks on Muslim worshippers that had inflamed inter-communal tensions in the East.

As well as attempting to distance themselves from attacks on Muslims, the LTTE, it was suggested, were developing the case against paramilitaries in order to bolster their call for implementation rather than review of the CFA.[87] Nothing Hans Brattskar heard from Tamilselvan on the subject during a bilateral meeting in Kilinochchi on 9 December appeared to dispel this impression.

The sense that each side was reverting to entrenched positions was compounded when President Rajapaksa informed a meeting of local Co-Chairs representatives that his government would be initiating negotiations with the LTTE with a view to agreeing a 'framework for a final solution' to the conflict, rather than the sort of interim arrangement that the LTTE had previously insisted upon as a first step. Rajapaksa also appears to have decided that the best way of meeting the Norwegians' conditions while placating the hardliners in the JVP and JHU was to call for Erik Solheim's removal as head of the facilitation team. The pretext for this was Solheim's public response to the president's announcement regarding Norway's facilitation role—a response which had, as one commentator put it, 'effectively turned the tables' on the government by asking it to 'appeal for assistance [to Norway] as an impartial facilitator'.

Rajapaksa's move against Solheim misfired badly. At a discussion between the two countries' foreign ministers held on the margins of a World Trade Organisation (WTO) meeting in Hong Kong in mid-December, Jonas Gahr Støre informed his counterpart that Solheim was Norway's chief envoy to Sri Lanka and as such would remain the leading figure in any continued facilitation effort. In addition, Støre reiterated the request first voiced by Solheim for the Sri Lankan government to make a public statement of confidence in Norway's role.

The Norwegians got what they wanted. First, the joint statement issued after the meeting reiterated Colombo's commitment to Norway's involvement. Second, it confirmed that Solheim—now installed as Development Minister—would play the lead role in a renewed Norwegian facilitation effort, and noted that Colombo was 'look[ing] forward' to an 'early visit' by Solheim to 'initiate the resumption of talks'.[88] Finally, the communiqué registered 'optimism' that talks on strengthening the 'implementation' and 'effective monitoring' of the ceasefire could commence 'early next year'—an emphasis that was pointedly different from the CFA 'review' advocated by Rajapaksa.[89]

In short, Oslo had got what it wanted, but in retrospect, this was the high point of Norway's influence over the Rajapaksa administration.

Co-Chairs meeting

A few days after the joint statement from Hong Kong, Solheim flew to Brussels for the 19 December meeting of the Co-Chairs. The importance attached to the group at this stage was manifested in the high-level attendance: US Assistant Secretary of State Christina Rocca, EU Commissioner Ferero Waldner and Japanese Special Envoy Yasushi Akashi, alongside

Solheim. As well as welcoming both the government's and the LTTE's recent 'confirmation' of their 'confidence' in Norwegian facilitation, the Co-Chairs expressed 'full and unequivocal support' for Oslo's efforts, while stressing that a new round of negotiations would 'build on progress made in peace talks held since the Ceasefire Agreement'.[90] Improving CFA implementation rather than reviewing the agreement itself was the goal; a statement unlikely to go down well among the Rajapaksa government's hardline supporters.

In the meantime, following a government announcement that they were prepared to consider another Asian country as the venue for talks, all eyes were on the LTTE to see what their response would be. Initial signals were not encouraging: two days before the Co-Chairs meeting, Tamilselvan announced that the Tigers would be insisting on Oslo.[91] Directly after the Brussels meeting, Solheim flew to London for talks with Balasingham, which resulted in an LTTE declaration that there would be 'no peace talks' if the government did not agree to holding them either in Oslo or another European capital.[92]

This impasse was paralleled by a steady escalation of violence in the Northeast. Between 20 and 22 December, there were no fewer than nine attacks on army personnel, killing two and wounding six.[93] Nor were the attacks confined to land. On 22 December the Sea Tigers ambushed two navy dinghies off Mannar. Three sailors were killed and another wounded in the ensuing exchanges.[94] Two days before Christmas, the government requested the local Co-Chairs representatives to visit Kilinochchi immediately to deliver a 'hard message' to the LTTE,[95] which—without the US Ambassador—they did the following day.

The Tigers' response to the Co-Chair's message was uncompromising. Though still committed to the ceasefire and willing to hold talks on it, Tamilselvan emphasised that the venue remained a problem for the Tigers, and again 'insisted' on Oslo. And while giving assurances that the LTTE would 'try' to curb the rising violence, the LTTE political wing leader argued that this was the spontaneous result of the 'people's anger' over recent events such as the army firing on protesting Jaffna university students, and the rape and killing of a Tamil woman, allegedly by Sri Lanka Army soldiers.[96]

Capping what proved to be a grim end to 2005, on Christmas Day veteran Tamil MP Joseph Pararajahsingham, an avowedly pro-LTTE politician who had been in parliament since 1990, was gunned down while attending Mass at St. Mary's Cathedral in Batticaloa.[97] A new low point had been reached.

As Solheim put it: 'Joseph was a friend. He had visited Norway and been a staunch supporter of the peace process. Many years earlier he escaped death in Batticaloa by millimetres. Now his time had come. His killing mirrors the worst of the LTTE's killings. Look, a government responsible for killing one of its own parliamentarians before hundreds of believers in church celebrating the birthday of Jesus Christ: it could hardly have been more ugly.'[98]

9

EELAM WAR IV

BEGINNINGS

Surveying the situation in Sri Lanka on the cusp of the New Year, US Ambassador Jeffrey Lunstead remarked that as 'a return to some sort of war becomes an increasing (but certainly not inevitable) possibility, the ... international community need to consider how best to help maintain some semblance of progress on the peace front.'[1] This semblance, he went on, boiled down to 'providing enough incentives (negative and positive) so that the Tigers feel they cannot go back to open hostilities, even if that is their aim.'[2]

Developments on the ground, however, suggested that war was coming. Jaffna, the focus of confrontation in December, remained relatively quiet through early January, but violence was increasing in the East. Following the deaths on 2 January of a group of Tamil students in Trincomalee, almost certainly at the hands of police Special Task Force (STF) commandos,[3] on 7 January a suicide attack off the coast of Trincomalee resulted in the sinking of a Sri Lanka Navy fast attack craft and the deaths of twelve sailors, two officers included. Subsequent LTTE denials of responsibility cut little ice with most observers.[4] Then, following the explosion of a car bomb in front of the SLMM's Batticaloa office and an LTTE attack on an army bus in Trincomalee, on 19 January the SLMM announced it was suspending activities in the area until further notice.

It was against this backdrop that Erik Solheim returned to Sri Lanka in his first visit since taking office as Development Minister. At this juncture,

Solheim's main objective was to try to get the government and LTTE to agree on a venue for a new round of negotiations, an issue that resolved itself remarkably quickly. During talks in Kilinochchi on 25 January, Solheim informed Prabhakaran and Balasingham—recently arrived in the Vanni from London—that Colombo had now suggested Geneva as an 'acceptable' European venue.[5] Prabhakaran responded positively.[6]

News of the agreement travelled rapidly: in the local media, for once Solheim was the hero. As one report put it, 'This time Buddhist monks were not burning [Solheim's] effigy, but bestowing merit on him. He was now Solheim the Saviour. The sinner had become a saint.'[7]

Solheim on the pre-Geneva negotiations

I remember I had a one-on-one discussion with Mahinda—at his initiative—and that is when he told me he would be happy to do a backroom deal with Prabhakaran that sorted everything out in one big bang. Mahinda was not concerned with democracy in the Northeast, but it was clear what he had in mind. For sure Prabhakaran could be first minister of the North and East, and the LTTE could arrange elections in such a way that that happened: the government would have no problem with that. Mahinda was not concerned with the fine details of a solution for the Tamils as long as it did not lead to a separate state. His focus was elsewhere. Above all, Mahinda did not want a protracted peace process—which was logical because a long process could easily have undermined his political base in the Sinhala nationalist alliance ... After this discussion I went up to the Vanni and met Prabhakaran. The offer of a backroom deal was a non-starter: Prabhakaran was not going to pick up on that. It was also discussed with Bala[singham] who was also completely opposed to it.

The sense of relief that greeted the announcement of renewed peace talks soon gave way to a focus on the issues, and it became evident that 'paramilitary forces' remained a major fault line between the two parties. On the LTTE side, the demand was simple. As the Tigers' Batticaloa military commander expressed it: 'Disarming the paramilitaries, their expulsion and the creation of normalcy ... are the essential prerequisites for the continuation of peace talks.'[8] The government's main counter-argument was that the Karuna group—with which the LTTE was most concerned—were formed after the CFA came into force, and thus disarming the group was not covered by the agreement.[9] With no compromise on this issue in sight, the two delegations travelled to Geneva for the opening of talks on 22 February.

Geneva

After a hiatus of nearly three years, it was to be expected that finding common ground between the two sides would prove challenging for the Norwegian facilitators. First on the list of difficult items to be addressed was the status of the Ceasefire Agreement itself.

The LTTE's position remained unchanged: the CFA was the foundation for peace in Sri Lanka, and accordingly the objective was to ensure the full implementation of the agreement. In his opening statement, the head of the government delegation, Nimal Siripala de Silva, argued that the government considered the CFA 'illegal', as it had been signed by the prime minister rather than president of the time.[10] Moreover, he maintained that some of its provisions were 'contrary to our constitution and law', and thus some amendments were necessary.[11] At the same time, the government 'acknowledged' that 'certain benefits' had flowed to the people from 'observance of the ceasefire', and they were accordingly 'determined' to uphold it. In addition, the CFA offered what de Silva termed a 'first step' towards achieving a 'negotiated settlement to the conflict'.[12] The contradictions inherent in the government position were all too apparent: it dismissed the CFA as an illegal and unconstitutional document, but at the same time was determined to uphold it.

With no obvious agreement in sight, formal consensus on the CFA's status was confined to general endorsements from both sides, with de Silva's emphasis on the government's 'strong determination and desire to preserve the ceasefire agreement' paralleled by Balasingham's assertion that 'the most constructive achievement of the Norwegian-facilitated peace process has been the signing of the Ceasefire Agreement'.[13]

On other critical issues, LTTE efforts to move paramilitaries up the agenda eventually led to an undertaking from de Silva that 'armed groups' would not be allowed to operate within government-controlled territory.[14] But given its insistence that the Karuna faction was not covered by the CFA because it came into existence after the agreement, in committing itself to taking 'all necessary measures in accordance with the CFA' to stop armed groups operating, the government side was in fact effectively leaving the door wide open for the Karuna faction to continue operating with relative impunity.[15] On the LTTE side, however, their commitment to ensuring that 'there will be no acts of violence against the security forces and police' was viewed by some as a significant departure, as it implied Tiger recognition of their responsibility for such attacks in the past—something they had generally avoided until this point.[16]

As a result of some determined pushing from the government, and with the support of the facilitators, the subject of child soldiers was discussed extensively. There were no practical recommendations or proposals on this issue, but de Siva and his colleagues emphasised their intention to make the LTTE's recruitment of children a high-priority issue at the next round of talks, scheduled for 19–21 April in Geneva. It was also agreed to ask the SLMM to report on both sides' CFA implementation record in the intervening period.

Recollections of the Geneva talks

Erik Solheim

> It was a different type of meeting from past [rounds of negotiations]. There was very little preparation. You got the strong feeling from Colombo that this was not very serious in their view ... A big government delegation came representing all shades of Sinhalese opinion. It was a town hall meeting not a negotiating team—there was no cohesion.

> For example, there was one professor in the delegation: he was the worst kind of Sinhala nationalist who spent his whole time abusing and provoking the LTTE, which made discussion, a real dialogue, completely impossible. However, the delegation head, Nirupal de Silva, was definitely serious. He had always been one of the most decent Lankan political leaders. He had been involved in earlier attempts to negotiate with the LTTE in the early 1990s. He was attacked by the Tigers in 1999 and nearly killed, but always favoured a negotiated settlement. He is a good man and would have been a good choice as a leader—if there had been anything to lead. The LTTE delegation included Balasingham and Tamilselvan. There were issues of harassment for them on the way to Geneva.

> Basil Rajapaksa came to Geneva. At first most of the government delegation had no idea he was in town. I went back and forth between the venue of talks and his hotel for discussions. When Basil was in Geneva he was directing everything.[17] For us, the main issue in this round of talks was to stop the killings and keep it that way. I think at this point Mahinda had not made up his mind which way to go—he was still keeping his options open. On the government side, he brought everyone to the table in Geneva, which meant a cacophony. Nirupal de Silva definitely tried to inject some sense into it, but when you bring every single voice to the table it's very difficult to get anything done.

> One of the Sri Lankan negotiators gave the best explanation of Mahinda's style of operation. He is the village chief, he argued, and the chief sits in the middle of

the room and everyone comes to him and he agrees to sort out this matter with you, that matter with someone else. There is no overall strategy: he may make a deal with you today that is contrary to the one he makes with me tomorrow. The village will be happy, they will have a great leader. And he will be kind to everyone, do his best for them. That is how the Geneva delegation was put together.

By the end of the talks it was clear that the government team were very pleased to have Karuna there and even happier to work with him. End of story.

Vidar Helgesen

The government had no real agenda because the[ir] delegation was such a mixed bunch. The LTTE had one point on their agenda: to rein in Karuna. I guess that must have been the motivation for them to participate in the talks—to see if Mahinda was prepared to bring Karuna under control ... The mood in the room was sombre, but with a few lighter moments. During the discussion on reining in paramilitary groups, the government's main response was that it didn't just want this, it also wanted to strengthen the rule of law generally, reducing crime and dealing with the criminal underworld. Balasingham responded that the LTTE didn't mind about the criminal underworld. 'We know all about them, we co-operate with them!' he retorted. The LTTE was concerned with Tamil paramilitaries, not common criminals.

Palitha Kohona, head of SCOPP

The first Geneva round of talks was significant in one respect. Balasingham said he would walk out if we insisted on any references to child combatants [in the final statement]. We had an agonising discussion in our delegation late into the night. Largely at my behest, Siripala De Silva agreed to make a statement in the morning telling Bala[singham]: 'You are free to walk out, but we are still going to be here'. Bala[singham] then pulled back very smartly and kept on talking. [As a result], for the first time we had a reference to child solider recruitment. And we agreed to meet again in two months time. My own assessment was that because of the perception that had been created around the LTTE at the time, if they had been constructive they could have got what they wanted at the negotiating table, instead of following this weird dream that they had to win on the battlefield. I thought Bala[singham] wanted to produce a result—that he had a picture in his mind that he wanted to realise before he died. I was quite hopeful because of that.

Shimali Senanayake

I went to the first round of talks and covered the second from Colombo. At the first round the Norwegians paid a lot of attention to the dynamics [and] the personal connections. [The government sent] a much bigger delegation with advisers—people who did not believe in the process, had no personal conviction that this was the way we should go. That made a huge difference. The expectation was that if they could come out and say there's a date [for another round of talks] that would be a mark of success. That's how low the expectations were. The LTTE used the talks a lot to meet their people, make connections. Meanwhile, the government delegation was doing its own thing. It took them both *so* long to agree on the joint statement. And the bottom line was that they were going to hold the next round. That's all that really came out of the first round in Geneva.

Tamilselvan on child soldiers

The government is not concerned about Tamil children as they treat children only as political commodities. If they were really concerned, they would not have bombed schools or places of refuge ... Thousands more were made orphans because their parents were killed in bombings ... Child soldiers is only a figment of imagination created by a group of people who call themselves politicians and who want to discredit the LTTE in front of the international community.[18]

After the talks

Controversy surfaced soon after the Geneva talks, when delegation member H.L. de Silva—best known in Sri Lanka for having equated federalism to a 'beguiling serpent'—stated publicly that the commitments tabled in the final statement amounted to an amendment of the CFA. Needless to say, this elicited a fierce response from the Tigers, with Balasingham describing de Silva's comments as 'ridiculous ... preposterous and totally unacceptable'.[19] Over the following weeks, other government figures appeared to distance themselves from de Silva's outburst, albeit without much obvious enthusiasm. On a more positive note, in mid-March the LTTE informed the government, via the SLMM, of their intention (as provided for in the CFA) of reopening their political offices in government-held territory, which had been closed down in late 2005 following the upsurge in violence.[20]

In the midst of these deliberations, the situation on the ground—particularly in the East—remained tense. Batticaloa was a case in point where, doubtless emboldened by the virtual free rein they continued to enjoy, the Karuna faction opened up a series of offices of their own under the logo of the newly-formed political party, the TMVP.[21] In response, the LTTE called a *hartal* (strike), which the Karuna faction answered by ordering shop owners to ignore it. As a result, local SLMM staff reported, shop owners could be seen standing in their doorways opening or closing up depending on which group—the LTTE or Karuna faction—they suspected was approaching them at any particular moment.[22]

On 29 March, with less than a month to go before the second round of talks, Erik Solheim and the newly-appointed Norwegian Special Envoy to Sri Lanka, Jon Hanssen-Bauer, travelled to London to meet with Balasingham. Predictably, the LTTE chief negotiator focused on the issue of paramilitaries, stating that unless armed groups were disarmed before the talks began, negotiations would be confined purely to practical modalities for their disarmament. In addition to issuing a categorical denial of LTTE responsibility for a recent attack in which eight Sri Lanka Navy and five Sea Tiger personnel had died, Balasingham took the opportunity to emphasise that LTTE participation in the talks was dependent on the government guaranteeing their safe passage to, and through, Colombo.[23] But most importantly, Balasingham emphasised the LTTE's willingness to continue talking. That same evening, Solheim and Hanssen-Bauer met Basil Rajapaksa, reportedly at the Conservative Club in London, for 'get to know' talks.

A week later Jon Hanssen-Bauer and then Solheim flew to Sri Lanka—the former's first trip to the island. Preparations for the next round of talks proved a challenge. Debriefing the Co-C31
hairs Ambassadors on 6 April following their return from Kilinochchi, Solheim and Hanssen-Bauer reported that the Tigers were not yet 'fully committed' to returning to Geneva. Moreover, after meeting with President Rajapaksa, Hanssen-Bauer noted that while the government side showed a strong desire to move the talks beyond CFA implementation to more 'substantive' issues of 'democracy, pluralism and human rights', what was lacking was a clear sense of how they proposed to get there.[24]

Immediately following the Norwegians' departure, a new spate of tit-for-tat killings began. In the wake of the assassination of pro-LTTE politician and prospective TNA MP V. Vigneswaran, gunned down in Trincomalee in broad daylight on 7 April, the Tigers launched a series of assaults on government forces that killed thirty in the space of just five days.

In the background, government officials were engaged in a combative series of exchanges with soon-to-depart SLMM Head Hagrup Haukland over the Mission's recent reports on ceasefire violations. Defence Secretary Gotabhaya Rajapaksa in particular took Haukland to task for claiming that

Karuna faction cadres had been sighted and contacted in the East: these reports, he said, were simply 'fabrications'.[25] Spurred by this latest surge of violence and ill will, a week before talks were due to open Solheim wrote to both sides expressing the facilitators' concern that, as he put it: 'Both parties are continually taking steps that are undermining the confidence of the other party, while expecting Norway to find solutions to problems that only the parties themselves can resolve.' He concluded: 'Unless the parties are quick to seize the opportunities that have arisen both during my visit in January and in the positive outcome of the talks in February, there will be very little Norway can do to bring the peace process forward at this stage.'

But Solheim's efforts were of little effect. Persistent violence continued, bringing the death toll for the ten days leading up to 17 April to seventy. Chillingly, a bomb attack on a vegetable market in Trincomalee on 12 April appeared to have been deliberately targeted at civilians—the first time either side had carried out such an attack since the CFA came into effect. In a somewhat fanciful move, *TamilNet* carried reports claiming that this and other recent attacks blamed on the LTTE were in fact the work of 'The People's Force', a spontaneous popular grouping supposedly unconnected to the Tigers.[26]

Taking things right down to the wire, on 16 April Tamilselvan announced in a letter to Hans Brattskar that the Tigers would not be present at the Geneva talks (already postponed by a week) due to the absence of travel security guarantees.[27] On the government side, refusal to provide transport in a military helicopter for the Eastern Tiger leaders was demonstrative of an approach to negotiations that was less accommodating of LTTE demands than had been the case in the past.[28]

The SLMM, now under the leadership of Ulf Henricsson, were non-plussed. 'What is it going to take for the parties to get their act together?' asked SLMM spokesperson Helen Olofsdottir. 'They have lost sight of the real issue and they are not acting ... in the best interest of the people.'[29] In an attempt to rescue the talks, Hanssen-Bauer returned to Sri Lanka 19 April for talks with both sides, to no effect.

Following the continued barrage of small-scale violent incidents, mostly involving LTTE claymore assaults on Sri Lankan security forces, towards the end of April the Tigers attempted their most daring sortie for some time: a suicide attack—said to have been carried out by a pregnant woman—on General Sarath Fonseka, inside the heavily-guarded Army Headquarters in Colombo. The attack on Fonseka's motorcade badly injured him, and killed nine bystanders.[30]

Ulf Henricsson on dealing with Gotabhaya Rajapaksa

Why were there no talks in April? Gotabhaya [Rajapaksa] definitely didn't want talks. He was furious. He would start shouting—in an uncontrolled way, and often in the wrong situations. For example, one time [the SLMM] made a statement saying the government was responsible for extra-judicial killings. He called me to his house and said straight away, 'You have to withdraw that'. I responded that I would not do that, as it was my firm opinion. And then he shouted at the top of his voice, 'Get out of my house'! His aides managed to calm him down after a while. Then Gotabhaya sat down in a corner, more or less playing with his mobile phone, while the rest of us continued with serious talks. For me, he was the main reason for the failure to have talks.

The fallout from the assault on the ex-Jaffna Commander, someone the Tigers had long viewed as one of their most implacable military enemies,[31] was immediate. Within hours, Sri Lanka Air Force jets bombed LTTE fortifications overlooking Trincomalee harbour, in what were officially described as 'deterrent' strikes—with inevitable consequences for civilian population.[32]

Hanssen-Bauer, still in Sri Lanka, joined the chorus of international condemnation both of the assassination attempt and the government response.[33] Some went further, with one noted commentator suggesting that 'the government action of targeting innocent civilians ... deserves strong condemnation. Even if the LTTE provoked the state, the wilful targeting of civilians by the security forces cannot be condoned.'[34]

Murali Reddy on the attack on Fonseka

[Rajapaksa] had an army chief who was three times more nationalist than him: [in fact], Fonseka was probably a racist, which perhaps got accentuated after the attempt on his life ... Think how that suits a setup and a military like that. When you can say that these [people] go to the extent of deploying an expectant mother to target one of our chiefs. Myself, I think it was a myth,[35] but it was a defining moment because I can't recall any instance even in LTTE records of a pregnant woman being used. Once you create that kind of an atmosphere, [think] how much easier it becomes for the government to poison minds. Until 2006, the rate of desertions in the Sri Lankan armed forces was very high. Zero morale, nobody had the guts to take on the LTTE. But afterwards ...

Increasing violence

On 30 April an LTTE attack on three Karuna faction camps located near Polonnaruwa left ten Karuna cadres dead. The situation seemed to be disintegrating rapidly. Ten days later, SCOPP Head Palitha Kohona and Jon Hanssen-Bauer travelled to Barcelona for notionally secret consultations on a long-term strategy for rescuing the peace process.[36] 'Erik stopped being the special representative and Jon came in', Kohona recalls. 'He created good links with the Sri Lankan establishment and became very friendly with me.' But Hanssen-Bauer has a somewhat different perspective.

> We got along very well together. Both of us ended up going to Barcelona, where we drew up a roadmap on how to get back to negotiations. [But] back home he gradually changed into more of a hardliner. This was confusing, as I no longer felt that we were working in confidence and towards the same goal as I had felt with him in Barcelona. For instance, he went to the media directly after our meetings to divulge messages he had sent with me to the LTTE. I felt my mission was undermined.

US Ambassador on Mahinda Rajapaksa

At this point US Ambassador Lunstead offered a succinct analysis of President Rajapaksa's approach to the peace process. '[He] seems sincere in wanting peace but unsure about how to go about achieving it. [He] does not seem to understand the depth of Tamil grievances and thus underestimates the profound changes that will be needed to address them.'

In another cable Lunstead argued:

> Many political commentators ... have observed that with his affable, good-ole-boy persona, Rajapaksa is the only Sinhalese who could sell a politically unpalatable settlement ... to the chauvinist South. [He] also knows that the peace process foundered on his predecessors' failure to build a southern consensus for a settlement. But broad consensus doesn't have to mean complete consensus, and the president's efforts to get the ... JVP on board so far have proven futile.[37]

There was to be no let-up in the violence. Just as the meeting in Barcelona was concluding, on the evening of 11 May news broke of a failed LTTE attack on a troop carrier that was transporting more than 700 military personnel back to base after home leave. According to eyewitness accounts, north of Jaffna a 'flotilla' of Sea Tiger suicide vessels laden with explosives attempted to ram the troop carrier,[38] but were eventually repelled by the accompanying fast attack craft in a battle that lasted several hours. In retaliation, Air Force jets bombed what the government described as the LTTE's 'illegal aviation facility'—a runway under construction at Iranamadu, in northern Tiger-held territory.[39]

Ominously, the troop carrier was flying under the SLMM flag and had a monitor on board—seemingly a signal that the Tigers were abandoning their past observance of the mission's neutral status under the terms of the CFA. In response, the SLMM described the LTTE attack as a 'gross viola-tion' of the CFA, and pointed out that as a 'non-state actor', the LTTE had 'no rights at sea'.[40] Unsurprisingly, the SLMM statement drew a furious response from the LTTE, with Tamilselvan asserting that the CFA was an agreement not between the 'LTTE as a non-state actor and the government as a state actor' but between 'two parties'. While the word 'equal' was absent from the statement, it was clearly present in intent.[41]

D.B.S. Jeyaraj, 'No other way than Norway'

Solheim said in Oslo that he no longer had time to work as both a minister and as peace envoy. But he would still be very much involved in the peace process. 'I will continue to work on Sri Lanka from day to day, but not from hour to hour.' ...

Many Sinhala politicians and opinion makers rant and rail against Solheim, but for most Tamils he is a great man who has accomplished a humane task well. The beleaguered Tamils are sorely in need of saviours and Solheim is seen as one. Had [he] taken the trouble to meet with ordi-nary Tamil people instead of the LTTE, EPDP and other Tamil 'represen-tatives', [Solheim] would have been gratified and even overwhelmed by the regard and affection they have for him. Many [see] him as the man who would deliver a just peace to the Tamils.[42]

The EU bans the Tigers

The latest upsurge in violence, and the Tigers' responsibility for much of it, strengthened the long-standing rumour that the European Union was about to proscribe the LTTE. On May 26, amid strong indications that an announcement from Brussels was imminent, Jon Hanssen-Bauer returned to Sri Lanka for discussions with both parties. In both cases, the impact of an LTTE ban on the SLMM's ability to function on the ground was high on the agenda. With this in mind, the Norwegian facilitators invited both parties to a high-level meeting scheduled for 8–9 June in Oslo, with the purpose of reviewing the implementation of the Ceasefire Agreement. Initially at least, neither side responded definitively.[43]

Three days later Brussels delivered the message everyone was expecting: a ban on the LTTE in EU countries, implying (among other things) a freeze on all Tiger financial assets and a prohibition on travel into or within the Union.[44] The following day (30 May) a Co-Chairs meeting in Tokyo, attended by Solheim and Hanssen-Bauer, produced a statement that called for the LTTE to return to negotiations, renounce 'terrorism and violence' and demonstrate willingness to 'make the ... compromises needed for a political solution within a united Sri Lanka'. But the statement also detailed a range of things expected of the government, including willingness to address the 'legitimate grievances of the Tamils'; 'immediate prevention' of 'groups based in its territory' from 'carrying out violence and acts of terrorism'; protection of the 'rights and security' of Tamils 'throughout the country'; and readiness to make 'dramatic political changes' to bring about a 'new system' that will 'enhance the rights of all Sri Lankans, including the Muslims'.[45]

Jon Hanssen-Bauer argues

> An important message came out from the Tokyo meeting. It was a very clear warning from the international community, and it was public. There was an intention behind it: to counter the effect of the EU listing, and to apply pressure that gave the government the possibility to take a step forward. The same thing with the LTTE; they were prepared to accept some of the things mentioned.

More broadly, Hanssen-Bauer notes that following the Tokyo meeting, the facilitators 'started using the Co-Chairs systematically to [try and] slow down the slide back to war. Through a series of meetings during the rest of 2006, we tried to nudge the parties back to talks. This was in full accord with India', he notes.

Perspectives on the EU's decision

Erik Solheim

> We had told Prabhakaran many times that if he wanted to stop moves to list them, the LTTE would have to stop things such as the killing of Kadirgamar. And that while they would argue that this was on a par with killing an LTTE com-

mander in the East, no one outside Sri Lanka would see it that way ... Remember the post-9/11 context, the total preoccupation with terrorism: everything had to refer to it. The feeling was that if others had been listed then the LTTE should also be included. The development with the SLMM was another negative step, although not as decisive as some people think. If [the parties] had wanted a strong mission then other members could have been found.

Jon Hanssen-Bauer

I discussed the issue of the EU listing several times with representatives of the EU on various levels. The timing was not elegant, and seemed unlinked to anything else happening, only coming out of a long internal EU process that happened to be concluded at this time. I said many times that just as much as the threat of listing could have a positive effect, the fact of firing that single bullet revolver would have nothing but negative consequences. Why should the Tigers behave better after being listed? Everybody knows that listing can be used only once and that it is one-way—it is practically impossible to be de-listed.

Ulf Henricsson

It was a silly decision. Very unprofessionally carried out, and under pressure from USA, and perhaps others ... Of course the ban gave the government carte blanche to fight the LTTE, because now they were officially 'terrorists'. I used to say that if you ban one you should ban the other, because they both used the same methods. For me, [the] government is mostly to blame. You can—and should—require more from a democratically elected government than an organisation like the LTTE.

Kristine Höglund

Proscription was not done in a sophisticated way. People in Colombo were against it. I think the decisions came from Washington and Brussels and not from people who knew what kind of implications it would have for the peace process in Sri Lanka. The Norwegians were trying their best to convince the others that it was not a good idea. The options left for the LTTE were fewer and fewer. Did they want terrorist listing? I was surprised by how forceful and ruthless the government was, first in the East and then onwards. The problem was also that the interest of the international community had waned. They had given up on Sri Lanka.

Abortive Oslo talks

Despite earlier threats to withdraw from the peace process in the event of an EU 'ban', the LTTE announced their willingness to attend the talks scheduled for 8–9 June in Oslo. At the same time, in an interview with the *Sunday Times*, Balasingham railed against the EU's decision, asserting that 'humiliated and globally isolated by world governments, the LTTE leadership may stiffen its attitude and adopt a singular, individualist approach, as if it is freed from the constraints of international norms and pressures.'[46]

The events that followed were almost comical. On 8 June the delegations assembled in Oslo. The following morning, just before talks were due to begin, Tamilselvan informed Solheim that the LTTE would not sit at the table with the government because there were no ministers in the delegation. They would, however, be prepared to negotiate by proxy, via the Norwegians. Faced with an LTTE no-show, the head of the government delegation, Palitha Kohona, called Rajapaksa to ask for instructions. The president's response was to tell Kohana and his team to pack their bags immediately—a move that prompted Tamilselvan to remark that the government delegation had 'given up too quickly'.[47] The same evening, before departing the country, the LTTE issued what it called the 'Oslo Communiqué'. Formulated in the style of a grand legal document, the communiqué laid out the Tigers' current positions on a range of issues, culminating in a reiteration of the determination to 'find a solution' to the 'Tamil national question' based on 'the realisation of its right to self-determination'.[48]

The situation was not improved by the release of the SLMM report on CFA implementation on 10 June, which had been shelved on account of the collapse of the talks that had been scheduled for April. Unsurprisingly, the report was critical of both sides. The government was taken to task for failing to meet its commitment to prevent armed groups from operating in government-controlled territory, and the security forces were accused of continuing to co-operate with the Karuna faction. Indeed, the report noted that the government 'denied even the mere presence of armed groups'. The LTTE, for its part, was charged with increased child recruitment and a series of blatant ceasefire violations.

A lengthy government response issued the same day rejected many of the report's allegations, and concluded by underlining its 'serious concerns' over the 'timing and content of the SLMM report', which it claimed in turn raised 'serious questions' regarding the SLMM's 'impartiality'.[49]

Norwegian facilitators on the Oslo impasse

Vidar Helgesen

> In the end the meeting did not even take place because the two sides arrived with completely different perceptions of why they were there. To me, this left the

impression that the Norwegian team had been so eager to get the parties together that the question of [an] agenda had been left out. It was all very bizarre. My reading was certainly that it was the LTTE that had destroyed this initiative. We were quite angry with the Tigers.

Erik Solheim

It should be pointed out that the LTTE delegation's composition changed on account of receiving new instructions from Prabhakaran at the last moment, as a result of which Bala[singham] didn't come and Tamilselvan headed the delegation. On the checking issue—the security hassles at Colombo airport that was one of the reasons the LTTE gave for pulling out of the talks—to the government we would say: why on earth do you waste your time on this? To the LTTE, we argued this was normal procedure for all officials, the US included. For the LTTE, it was very much an issue of diplomatic immunity, of status.

Jon Hanssen-Bauer

The Tigers were upset that the government delegation was not headed by a bureaucrat, not a minister, so they felt an imbalance ...They said they had accepted to come to Oslo but had never accepted to sit in the same room. The government side was also very suspicious of the whole thing. I think Prabhakaran agreed to send a delegation because he thought that by accepting to go to Oslo, the EU ban could be turned around ... The Tigers wanted us to pull out SLMM members from EU countries and replace them. The government wanted to keep the SLMM. We wanted to gain time and retain security guarantees. We asked both of them to issue a public statement that they would guarantee the security of the SLMM in the current set-up until it is changed. That was the practical outcome of the meeting in Oslo. We got that statement later. We formulated it in Oslo.

Palitha Kohona on the SLMM

We had a problem with the SLMM after General Henricsson took over [in 2006]. For one thing, he became an activist. We also had our reservations over the role of the SLMM: it recorded over 5,000 [CFA] breaches by the LTTE but never recommended any remedial action. They recorded 300-odd violations by the Sri Lankan forces, and again [there were no recommendations for] remedial action. I thought this was a very big gap in the peace architecture. You had two sides that did not trust each other and were jockeying for power. But when there was a violation, there was no mechanism to deal with it.

More attacks

A week after the breakdown of talks in Oslo, the country was shaken by news of an attack on a crowded bus some 50km northwest of Anuradhapura: sixty-four were killed and eighty wounded in what was the worst single act of violence perpetrated since the 2002 Ceasefire Agreement.[50] It was the second time in the space of two months that the Tigers had bombed a civilian target, and the Sri Lankan military's response was swift: it launched a series of 'limited' strikes on LTTE targets in the Trincomalee area, around the Sea Tigers' northern command base in Mullaitivu and on the claimed LTTE airstrip near Iramanadu.[51]

Skirmishes continued into the following week. Foiled attempts by Sea Tiger frogmen to blow up a ship in Colombo harbour were followed on June 17 by a Sea Tiger assault on the SLN base at Pesalai near Mannar, in which eleven sailors died.[52] Hours later, navy personnel were seen lobbing hand grenades into a church in the nearby village of Vankalaipadu, where several thousand Tamil civilians had reportedly taken refuge from the fighting. One person died and dozens were injured.[53]

Adding to the litany of woes, towards the end of the month Norwegian Ambassador Hans Brattskar reported to his fellow local Co-Chair representatives that the LTTE were now insisting on a thirty-day deadline for the withdrawal of SLMM EU member-state personnel. Despite strenuous efforts to persuade Tamilselvan that the Tigers would be best served by continuing with the present structure of the Mission, the Tigers' political wing chief stated bluntly that the 'leadership had decided'. An indication of the mood of the moment is provided by US Ambassador Jeffrey Lunstead's observation that the Norwegians 'have no plans for future peace initiatives at this point ...They are more depressed than we have ever seen them.'[54]

Compounding the sense that the Ceasefire Agreement was now in free fall, on 26 June, just outside Colombo, two LTTE suicide bombers on motorbikes killed Major General Parami Kulathunga, Deputy Chief of Staff and the third-highest ranking officer in the Sri Lanka Army. At the same time, reports emerged of an attempt by President Rajapaksa to bypass the Norwegian facilitators and strike a deal directly with the Tigers by proposing a two-week ceasefire as a prelude to renewed talks.[55] The proposal was quickly dismissed by the Tigers.[56] And for all the talk of new peace initiatives, the view among many observers was clearly articulated by an Indian media report of the time: 'despite the ceasefire ... and the so-called process for conflict resolution, an undeclared war has been [going] on in the country for almost six months'.[57]

In early July, a visit by Indian Foreign Secretary Shyam Saran underscored his government's unease over recent developments. Reportedly high on the list of Indian concerns was the president's failure to get the UNP engaged in developing a consensus proposal for devolution,[58] accompanied by a perception that elements within the Sri Lankan military and government were 'itching for a fight to the finish'.[59] Echoing this view in a 4 July address prior to his departure from Sri Lanka, US Ambassador Lunstead stated his belief that a solution to the ethnic conflict would require 'radical changes in the way the entire nation is governed'.[60]

Chandrika Kumaratunga on 'missed opportunities'[61]

After I retired [from politics] I was away in London for nine months, then came back to Sri Lanka for good. Ranil [Wickremasinghe] made a courtesy call and we were chatting for two hours. Then when he was about to go he said, 'Can I ask you a question, just for the record. Now that you realise how dangerous [things have] got, what do you think should have happened instead?'

I replied: 'The executive presidency was not abolished; I told you it would be OK if somebody democratic like me was there, but if a dictator comes it would get dangerous. And now you see what is happening ... If you had taken up my offer of voting for the constitution,[62] the war would have been over by now, probably in a peaceful manner', I said. 'We wouldn't have had an executive presidency and a dictator, and you would have been the president of this country.'

Earlier I had said to him the day you vote [for the devolution package], the next day I shall invite the UNP into a national government, but I can't invite you in until you vote. He looked at me, slightly askance, and said: 'I should have listened to you then'. I got up and said 'It's a bit late in the day, but at least you have realised it now'. And I escorted him to the car.

I was told by some friends in the UK Tamil diaspora who used to collect money and do things for the people in the Vanni—people who wouldn't have minded either Eelam or devolution: one told me that when a group of them had met Prabhakaran, roughly at the same time as Ranil had said this to me, they said to him: 'So now you realise how dangerous it was to have supported Mahinda in coming to power and not to have listened to Chandrika?' And Prabhakaran replied the same thing: 'I should have taken up her offer'.

War over water

In the third week of July the SLMM's Trincomalee office began receiving reports that villagers in the Verugal area had blocked the sluice gates at Mavil Aru, which controlled the flow of water from a nearby reservoir. While the reservoir itself was located inside LTTE-controlled territory, the lattice of connecting streams and canals provided a vital source of irrigation for some 15,000 families living in nearby government-controlled areas.[63] As had become standard practice, the LTTE initially denied involvement, arguing that the cut-off was instead initiated by Tamils in protest at the local authorities' failure to construct a water tank supposedly promised to them, and at the priority given to providing water access to Sinhalese villages.

The account of what happened next is hotly disputed. In the official version, consultations with SLMM monitors left government officials with a clear impression that the LTTE was more interested in finding a pretext to ramp up confrontation with Colombo than solving local problems. Faced with a clear challenge to its authority, and having an equally clear responsibility to provide water access to all citizens, the government decided to engage in what Foreign Minister Mangala Samaraweera described as a 'judicious use of force' to secure the reopening of the sluices.[64]

Needless to say, the LTTE's account differed radically. The Tigers maintained that the government ignored their openly-declared intention, following discussions with the SLMM, to reopen the sluice gates, and instead opted to attack LTTE positions. This the government undoubtedly did, in the form of SLAF strikes on the Mavil Aru area on 26 July. Equally undisputed, too, is the fact that from this point onwards armed hostilities escalated to a level not seen since before the 2002 Ceasefire Agreement.

A sustained campaign of bombing and shelling marked the first stage in what rapidly became a full-blown military offensive, codenamed 'Mission Watershed'.[65] With casualties mounting steadily on both sides, over the following days the fighting spread to the Trincomalee area. On 1 August, the China Bay naval base was attacked from the LTTE base at Sampur, located south of the bay, while at sea a Sea Tiger assault on the *Jetliner*, a ferry transporting more than 850 military personnel, was repelled by Navy Fast Attack Craft (FACs). There were also reports of airstrikes hitting areas southwest of Batticaloa—territory far removed from Mavil Aru.[66]

As government forces inched towards Mavil Aru in the face of LTTE resistance, the clashes spread to nearby Muttur. Following a surprise Tiger assault that briefly handed them control of the town on 1 August, government forces later announced they had driven the Tigers out after three days of fierce fighting. A critical aspect of army strategy here was the sustained use of multi-barrel rocket launchers (MBRLs). While MBRLs were not new to the Sri Lankan conflict, from this point onwards they assumed a new significance in the fighting. Together with a strengthened all-round artillery capability, these massively destructive weapons provided the army with a critical edge over the LTTE.

On the civilian front too, the fighting in Muttur signalled a significant escalation of the conflict. While the 25 April air strikes on Muttur, carried out in response to the failed LTTE assassination attempt on Sarath Fonseka, certainly resulted in some displacement of the town's predominantly Muslim inhabitants, the numbers involved were nowhere near the stream of refugees desperately seeking to escape the fighting in early August.[67]

Meanwhile, following the arrival of Jon Hanssen-Bauer in Sri Lanka at that time, the Norwegians attempted to cobble together an agreement to reopen the Mavil Aru waterways. With encouragement from Palitha Kohona and following a request from Erik Solheim to the LTTE leadership to reopen the sluice gates on 'humanitarian' grounds, on 6 August Hanssen-Bauer and Ambassador Brattskar travelled to Kilinochchi for talks. Hanssen-Bauer recalls:

> I urged the Tigers to reopen the water gates. I made the request directly and Prabhakaran said yes ... I managed to inform the Foreign Minister [Mangala Samaraweera] that the Tigers had said that they would reopen the gates. I also told him that Henricsson would be with them when they did this, and asked for the government to agree to a cessation of hostilities. The government pretended that they never got that message, and the shooting continued.

SLMM Head General Henricsson's version of events is more dramatic: 'When we were approaching the dam I had a phone call from Kohona. He said, "You can't go there, there will be an artillery barrage soon." I replied, "Yes we can. If you want to restart the war you can. But you know where we are and what we are going to do." [The Army] launched an artillery barrage when we were about 1km from the dam.'

Henricsson's main allegation—that the army shelled the Mavil Aru area knowing that he and some LTTE officials were making their way to the sluice gates—appears to have been accepted by most observers.[68] More controversial, though perfectly plausible, was his contention that the government side was bent on resolving the Mavil Aru stalemate by force.[69] This is what eventually happened. Two days after the shelling, the LTTE announced that they, together with local 'civilian representatives', had reopened the sluice gates.[70] Undeterred, the army pressed on with its advance.

As might be expected, Government Peace Secretariat Head Palitha Kohona's recollection of the Mavil Aru dispute paints a rather different picture:

> I remember General Henricsson driving to the fighting zone and reporting from there. 'He was an activist, not just a military observer. He kept on phoning, asking me to "tell your people to stop firing". I said that once the LTTE leaves, they will stop firing. Then there was a massive attack to the south of Trincomalee, and another in the Jaffna peninsula. The LTTE occupied Muttur and expelled all the Muslims there. They attacked three camps to the south with artillery, but we held our ground. It was the first time for many years that the Sri Lankan Army had successfully fended off an attack of that nature. A few days later the army re-occupied Muttur. This gave rise to the need to be in touch with Jon Hanssen-Bauer.

In a meeting with Gotabhaya Rajapaksa on 8 August, Hanssen-Bauer was informed that the facilitators' services were 'no longer required' over the Mavil Aru water dispute, as the security forces had been ordered to 'secure' the area.[71] Then, following the Army's recapture of Muttur, on 4 August, grim news emerged of an atrocity uncovered at the local compound of the French NGO *Action Contre La Faim* (Action Against Hunger—ACF): seventeen of the organisation's employees—sixteen ethnic Tamils, one Muslim and all of them aged under thirty-five—were discovered lying face down on the ground, having been shot in the head at close range. All were wearing white T-shirts clearly displaying the NGO's logo.

The security forces refused to allow SLMM staff and forensic experts access to the ACF compound on grounds of 'security concerns'—yet brought journalists into Muttur on escorted tours. General Henricsson's conclusion was inevitable: in an official SLMM 'ruling' on the massacre, he stated that there were 'very strong indications of the involvement of the security forces', and concluded that it constituted 'one of the most serious recent crimes against humanitarian workers worldwide'.[72]

Unsurprisingly, the government Peace Secretariat (SCOPP) immediately rejected the SLMM's ruling,[73] and official denials of responsibility for the crime continue to this day, contrary to carefully documented evidence and an ACF-led 'Justice For Muttur' campaign.

General Ulf Henricsson

> I have experienced this in the Balkans before. When you are not let in it's a sign that there is something they want to hide ... If there was clear evidence for the LTTE to have done it, why not let us in and see it?[74]

A few observations are warranted. First, in what was to become a familiar refrain, the government described the 'Watershed' campaign as a 'humanitarian operation' whose objectives were essentially defensive. In the words of G.H. Peiris, its 'principal objective' was 'the rescue of the civilian population entrapped under harshly repressive LTTE rule'. Soon the LTTE began to mimic this official rhetoric. Commenting on LTTE operations in the Trincomalee area in early August, Tiger military spokesperson Irasalah Ilanthirayan argued that 'urgent humanitarian need' had motivated what he termed 'defensive actions' against the Sri Lankan armed forces.[75] Second, it became apparent that in the quest for military victory, basic principals of human rights and international humanitarian law were going to be ignored wherever it was deemed necessary or convenient. The murder of seventeen ACF staff was more a grim harbinger of the future course of the war than a singular atrocity. Third, it is hard to discern the rationale for the Tigers' initial move on Mavil Aru, unless the objective was, as one commentator put it, to 'draw the security forces into battle using water as a weapon of war'.[76] What is certain, however, is that it handed the government the perfect alibi—one that some argued they were seeking—for launching an all-out attack on the Tigers. And fourth, the LTTE's determined and sometimes threatening attempts to prevent Muttur's civilian population from fleeing the town during the brief period they held it prefigured one of their most reprehensible later tactics: the use of civilians as hostages, negotiating pawns or, worst of all, human shields in their confrontations with Lankan military.

Views on the Mavil Avru dispute

Erik Solheim

The LTTE acted in a way that made it very hard—if not impossible—for the government not to react. If Gotabhaya wanted an excuse for all-out war, he got it.

At this stage no one thought that the government could win militarily. Also we expected them to continue by and large with the same tactics as before—generally with respect for human rights and globally accepted rules of war. In addition, no one expected that they would be able to break down the LTTE's strike capacity in the South, which they did I think largely through the use of white vans, torture and so on—methods that had generally not been used heavily in Sri Lanka for ten years or so. At best, the expectation was that the government could achieve a new military advantage and use that as the basis for restarting talks with the LTTE.

Also, with new weapons: no one thought they would be able to get funds voted through parliament for new arms purchases, as it would mean putting other key investments in the civilian sector on hold and the capacity to keep the number of soldiers dying on the battlefield outside of public view. In the past, casualties had not been reported in the media, but for sure there were funerals. And as to the Army's new, more brutal tactics: Gotabhaya and Fonseka may have had them in mind, but by and large we didn't think this could happen: and nor did most people.

One person who did understand that the water tank dispute was indicative of a bigger shift in the conflict was Bala[singham]. In the last few months of his life he said that the LTTE could easily loose the East, and maybe even the North. During summer 2006 he gave an interview [to Indian media] where he tried to reach out to the Indians and put the issue of Rajiv Gandhi's murder on the back burner. It wasn't a direct apology, but it was very close to that.[77] He was reprimanded for this, not directly by Prabhakaran but in a phone call from Tamilselvan. The fact that it came from a 'young boy' rather than the LTTE leader particularly annoyed Bala[singham]. I don't think he and Prabhakaran ever spoke again after that.

Ranil Wickremasinghe

By this point the peace process was dead, even for the Norwegians. Why they stayed on is a mystery to me. I told them that: after Mavil Aru, there was no reason [for them to be there] ... Because by this point the Prabhakaran-Rajapaksa relationship was under strain. The agreement was that they spoke to each other: I don't know in exactly which way, but they did. By this stage, however, the LTTE was anxious to move out of the facilitator-SLMM framework that we had set up. They were sending messages to this effect. The Tigers didn't want to deal with the international community any more.

Gotabhaya Rajapaksa's view

If one looks at the sequence of events in July/August 2006, the LTTE's grand plan seems to have been to sink the *Jetliner*, killing 1200 troops in one go. With bodies going to every district in the country, demoralisation would set in, which [the LTTE] would use to capture the Muttur jetty and consolidate their power south of the harbour mouth in Trincomalee. Thereafter they would blockade the harbour and stop all troop movements and supplies to Jaffna. Then they would attack Jaffna and take over the peninsula. If this grand plan had worked, the LTTE would have had their separate state. The LTTE had launched a major operation after a long time, and it had been successfully repelled.[78]

The war widens

After the bloodshed in Muttur there was little let-up in the fighting. On 11 August the LTTE initiated an attack from the Forward Defence Line (FDL) at Muhamalai, one of two crossing points between the Vanni and government-controlled Jaffna agreed under the terms of the CFA. The assault's objective was clear to all: Jaffna. Within a few days, however, Tiger forces were forced to retreat.[79] A simultaneous Sea Tiger assault on Kayts island, west of Jaffna, was also repelled, while LTTE shelling of the Navy base at China Bay, Trincomalee increased in intensity.

Responding to the fighting near Jaffna, following a hastily-convened meeting in Washington the Co-Chairs issued a statement underlining their concern over the 'continued violence'. Their call for both parties to 'cease hostilities immediately and return to the negotiation table' fell on deaf ears.[80] The government in particular did not take kindly to the Co-Chairs' statement, which Defence Spokesperson Keheliya Rambukwella criticised as 'unfair' for comparing the government with a terrorist organisation.[81]

On 14 August, news of a claymore attack in Colombo on the Pakistani High Commissioner's car that killed seven and injured ten was followed by reports that on the same morning SLAF jets had bombed a school compound in the LTTE-controlled Mullaitivu district,[82] leaving 61 girls and young women dead and more than 250 injured. Unsurprisingly, controversy erupted regarding the purpose of the bombing.

The LTTE maintained that it was a long-established orphanage for the children of Tamil war dead, and that the victims were all innocent participants in ten-day student leadership development workshop.[83] Against this, Rambukwella asserted that the Air Force attack had been preceded by months of intelligence gathering that had established that the school was 'an LTTE training camp'.[84] In the maelstrom of argument over the following weeks, one fact was largely forgotten: whether Tiger orphanage or training ground, all those killed or injured had been young girls.[85]

The failure of the LTTE attack on the Jaffna peninsula had some important consequences for the Tigers. First, it gave the army an opportunity to push the LTTE's forward positions back some distance, and to seize virtually all the Tiger infrastructure at Muhamalai. Second, it led to an army decision to close the Muhamalai crossing point, a move that effectively stopped all travel to and from Jaffna along the A9 road. The reopening of the A9 had arguably been the CFA's most visible achievement. Now it had been closed down, and it seemed to many that the LTTE were to blame. The economic impact also struck the LTTE. The Muhamalai crossing had grown into one of the Tigers' main sources of income, generating large amounts in taxes and 'import duties' on goods and vehicles moving in and out of LTTE controlled territory.[86] Finally, as become apparent over the following weeks, the road had been the principal transport route to Jaffna for food and other basic supplies, so its closure spelled a humanitarian disaster in the making for the Jaffna peninsula.

CFA in question

In the wake of the army's recapture of Muttur, government forces fixed their sights on the next critical target: the well-entrenched LTTE artillery emplacements at Sampur, across the Koddiyar Bay from Trincomalee, a town whose status was not defined by the 2002 Ceasefire Agreement, but over which the Tigers had subsequently seized control. Following the fighting at Mavil Aru and Muttur, in mid-August the LTTE stepped up their artillery attacks on the Trincomalee naval base—the SLN's largest—and with it the vital sea route to Jaffna. In a 21 August speech, President Rajapaksa reportedly gave an advance signal of the government's intention to 'neutralise' the LTTE threat from Sampur.[87]

True to their word, on 27 August the army began their attack.[88] A week later, President Rajapaksa announced the news of Sampur's capture to his SLFP party's fifty-fifth anniversary congress held in Colombo. Following initial celebration of the victory, however, he was quick to add that the attack on Sampur had been launched 'as a defensive mechanism … to protect vital national interests'.[89] For all the talk of 'defensive operations', it was difficult to resist the conclusion that the capture of Sampur was fundamentally an offensive operation, and as such in contravention of the 2002 Ceasefire Agreement.[90] Though some officials presented the assault as a 'humanitarian' operation aimed at facilitating the resettlement of displaced Muslims, General Fonseka was forthright in admitting that the military's objective was straightforward: to take Sampur.[91]

As if to underline the marginalisation of the CFA and those tasked with monitoring its observance, General Henricsson vacated the position of SLMM Head in time to meet the LTTE's 31 August deadline for the departure of EU-member monitors. He was followed by more than thirty Danes, Swedes and Finns, leaving twenty Norwegians and Icelanders to carry on. In the context of the escalating conflict, the announcement that Norway and Iceland would be sending an additional ten monitors did little to dispel the sense that the SLMM was fast becoming irrelevant. In the meantime,

Norway announced the appointment of Major General Lars Johan Sølvberg to the challenging position of SLMM Head of Mission.[92]

Rajapaksa meets Blair

In early September reports came to light of a recent meeting between President Rajapaksa and British Prime Minister Tony Blair. Among the details that emerged later was the fact that Sinn Féin deputy party leader Martin McGuinness had been instrumental in setting up the meeting, at Rajapaksa's direct request. On the face of it, nothing could be more bizarre—or ironic—than a former IRA leader facilitating a meeting between two heads of state who were fervently committed to combatting terrorism. How had this come about?

During his 2004–5 tenure as prime minister Rajapaksa had visited Northern Ireland, where he had met McGuinness. Rajapaksa duly invited McGuinness to visit Sri Lanka, which he did in early January 2006 following his presidential election victory. In the course of discussions, McGuinness expressed the conviction that there could be no military victory for either party. What was needed was a political settlement, which would in turn require both sides to display 'wisdom' and 'courage'.[93] Recalling the visit, McGuinness notes that from the outset he and Sinn Féin colleague Aidan McAteer were acutely aware of the 'number of soldiers on the streets and the checkpoints'—things all too familiar from their experiences back home in Belfast.

McGuinness also recalls a 'very clear impression' that the government was 'open to peace negotiations' with the Tigers. He was given the opportunity to provide an account of the Northern Ireland experience to 'people I assumed were going to be negotiators on behalf of the Sri Lankan government'. The most disappointing aspect of the visit, however, was the fact that despite initial assurances to the contrary, he was strongly discouraged from visiting the Northeast in order to meet with the LTTE leadership.

In spring 2006 McGuinness received a quiet visit from presidential advisor Sachin Vaas Gunawardena, who sounded out his willingness to establish links with the LTTE with a view to a potential new peace initiative. Once it was clarified that he would be allowed to travel up to the Vanni, McGuinness consented and returned to the country in early July. In doing so, he stressed that he was 'very conscious that the Norwegians were very much involved' and accordingly determined 'not to interfere in anything they were doing'.

In Kilinochchi, McGuinness and McAteer met for several hours with Tamilselvan and other senior LTTE figures.[94] He recalls: 'I relayed our experiences, how the British assessed they could not militarily defeat the IRA, and the IRA could not defeat the British army. So they had to come to the negotiating table.' In response, the Tiger leadership expressed their 'total distrust of the intentions of the Rajapaksa government. They ... appeared to be totally unconvinced that the government was interested in meaningful negotiations.'

After a debriefing with President Rajapaksa, the Sinn Féin deputy leader issued a statement calling on both sides to take 'decisive initiatives to build the peace process', though he was already convinced that, as he later put it, 'neither side was ready to accept meaningful peace negotiations.' He and McAteer also strongly suspected that 'the Sri Lankan government was gearing up for a military resolution to the conflict, not a peaceful one,' but nevertheless acceded when Gunawardena, returning to Northern Ireland, asked for McGuinness's help in setting up a meeting between Rajapaksa and the British Prime Minister.[95]

While the purpose of this meeting was never officially explained, Sri Lankan media sources alleged that it revolved around two issues: the appointment of a UK Special Envoy to Sri Lanka, and, more tentatively, a potential role for Blair himself in the peace process. Both suggestions, however, are discounted by both Martin McGuinness and Tony Blair's Chief of Staff Jonathan Powell, who was also present. 'Rajapaksa asked us if we could share information and so on from Northern Ireland. So we said yes, of course, and sent [former Northern Ireland Secretary of State] Paul Murphy to Sri Lanka. We had no idea of muscling in on anyone else's peace process—we had more than enough of our own to deal with over Northern Ireland.'

Martin McGuinness

My message to both sides was very clear: people can kill until kingdom come, or they can make a genuine attempt to resolve the conflict by going to the negotiation table. Given the history of Sri Lanka and the way the Tigers operated, one disappointment for me was that I did not get to meet Prabhakaran. He shut himself off from the outside world. That was a monumental blunder on his part. They were not listening to people who were well disposed to them.

Obviously the Rajapaksa administration believed they had gained a victory over Tamils, but they haven't resolved the conflict. They still have a situation whereby something like a million people living in the Northeast feel they are being treated like second-class citizens. Anger, bitterness, bad feelings, resentment: this could all explode at some future time.

> One last thought. I did meet Mahinda again, at Nelson Mandela's funeral. And I was so angry I couldn't even speak to him. Given what happened to the Tamils, all the slaughter, I couldn't bring myself to speak to him again.

Two months later it was announced that Paul Murphy would be visiting Sri Lanka for exploratory talks, which he duly did in mid-November, meeting government officials in Colombo and Tamilselvan in Kilinochchi.[96]

Martin McGuinness in Sri Lanka

Tyrone Ferdinands

McGuiness came back in early July. This time he went to Kilinochchi, and on the morning of his departure from the country the president said 'take him to Basil' ... Basil had only one thing he wanted to say to McGuinness, which was 'please try and create a direct line to the LTTE. We want to talk to them directly, without a facilitator'. McGuinness asked, 'What about the Norwegians?' And Basil answered, 'They can continue as the line to official talks. I am not proposing this to undermine [the Norwegians]. But there are things we need to discuss directly'.

At the meeting with Basil McGuinness's initial point was simple: when trust has broken down completely the facilitator can't help rebuild it. 'What are you going to talk to the LTTE about? You have such an extreme position, you are not willing to concede anything under the sun, you have gone back ten years.' Basil replied: 'You think we haven't talked to them already? We have, and extremely successfully. We have had direct talks, we have been very professional. We sent signals through envoys claiming to represent the other side, just to see if they really did represent them, we asked for public signals that were reciprocated: we are not kids, we can handle it, so please just set it up!'

Martin McGuinness

The Sri Lankans wanted a direct line to the LTTE leader, but he was not inclined to meet anybody. After my second visit, I became very sceptical over the prospect of anything of that nature happening. When I met Basil I got a sense that I was meeting a military figure—the military end of the Sri Lankan offensive against the Tamil Tigers. I also had a very clear sense that he was trying to convince me that [the government] were genuinely interested in a dialogue. The Tigers, of course, were not interested. So I told Basil that the likelihood of direct contact was remote.

Jon Hanssen-Bauer

I was informed that Blair was looking for a role for himself in Sri Lanka. I was vaguely briefed about the Sinn Féin connection, but I cannot remember that

Murphy was appointed as a special envoy—not on a permanent basis that was a threat to us at least—but he was sent to Sri Lanka. He visited the country. It was not a great success. He continued with some contacts, though, and I was kept informed.

The information about a potential role for other politicians was always disturbing. We struggled to keep focus on the [facilitation] work, not least to keep the president focused on it, and we were not happy about the prospects of an excuse for diverting his attention. I travelled to London to meet with Jonathan Powell, Blair's Chief of Staff, at No. 10. We spent some time discussing the situation in Sri Lanka. In the process I told him frankly that war was more likely than a continued peace process. He concluded that there was nothing that Blair could do—or gain—in Sri Lanka in the short term ...

The president was tireless in his efforts to find channels of communication to the LTTE outside the Norwegians. This annoyed Kilinochchi. The LTTE, they would meet anybody, but not accept a replacement of Norway, or another channel [of negotiation] ...My own view is that Rajapaksa saw in Northern Ireland a model in which the insurgent party had laid down arms and surrendered ... He wanted to use this case to impress upon the LTTE that they should give up the armed struggle. This was not a message they were particularly fond of hearing.

Erik Solheim

There was always a fascination with the Northern Ireland peace process in Sri Lanka because it took place just before theirs—although the argument was often put that Prabhakaran was no Gerry Adams. And the political elite is strongly pro-British, of course ...

As long as Bala[singham] was around, there was no big interest in Northern Ireland on the LTTE's part. Bala[singham] thought he knew what was needed. He was happy for LTTE leaders to go around looking at other countries in order to learn about federalism and so on. But he wanted to control it, and for Norway to be the one and only channel for contacts. And as long as the peace process was going well, arguably there was no need to bring others in.

The story of how Martin McGuinness got involved fits very well with my picture of Mahinda as the village chief. He wanted to open up as many avenues of contact as possible in order to give himself the greatest variety of options: that's why the delegations to the Geneva talks included both pro- and anti-peace people. It also fits with his opposition to a protracted peace process. Giving an opportunity to someone other than the Norwegians is in accordance with everything else we know. Looking for a shortcut would be absolutely logical from his point of view. But while he didn't want a protracted affair, I also think that initially, at least, he had no clear idea of how to pursue the peace process: this developed later.

Jonathan Powell

> One of the Wikileaks cables speaks of me trying to steal the Norwegian's role from them. This was a *complete* misunderstanding. We were simply trying to be nice by agreeing to see President Rajapaksa. Martin McGuinness came to us and said that it was really important that we got involved. It was at a crucial point in the Northern Ireland negotiations, and we wanted to do anything we could to be helpful. [A meeting] sounded like a very reasonable request, so we simply said 'yes'. Martin had worked in the Basque country, sent a number of [Sinn Féin] colleagues to Burma. I think he liked doing that sort of thing: sharing the lessons of Northern Ireland, supporting attempts to bring peace between insurgents and governments.

The road to Geneva

Efforts to resuscitate the peace process were at last rewarded when Tamilselvan informed the Norwegians in September that the LTTE were ready to hold 'unconditional' talks with the government. After some hesitation, Colombo gave the proposal the green light and, following a Co-Chairs meeting in Brussels on 12 September, it was announced that talks would be going ahead, possibly as soon as October.[97]

In addition to welcoming this new willingness to resume talks, the Co-Chairs statement urged both sides to 'cease all violence immediately', and to show a commitment to achieving a 'political solution' based on 'the previous rounds of negotiations'.[98] The statement's overall tone, combined with its extensive lists of demands on both sides, suggested that the Co-Chairs were moving towards a central role in international engagement with the Sri Lankan conflict.

Sri Lanka: the Cost of Conflict[99]

'Sri Lanka is the most militarised country in South Asia. In 2006–2010 it will continue to hold this dubious position ... Its defence expenditure as a percentage of GDP is the largest not only in the South Asian region but is also higher than among other comparable conflict-ridden countries such as Colombia, Myanmar, Sierra Leone, Sudan, the Philippines and Uganda, to name but a few.'

The weeks immediately following the Brussels meeting saw a marked decrease in the level of violence across the lines of confrontation.

Simultaneously, however, there were mounting international calls for independent investigation of alleged human rights abuses in Sri Lanka. Addressing the UN Human Rights Council, OHCHR's Louise Arbour issued a strong call for the establishment of a UN-sponsored human rights mission,[100] while directly criticising the government and the LTTE for the killings and forced disappearances they had perpetrated.[101] Similarly, the ICRC Deputy Head, Peter Krakolinig, accused the government and LTTE of 'contravening the obligations under international humanitarian law' by 'continuing to impede supply lines to the Northeast'.[102] The reality to which he was referring was the deepening shortage of foodstuffs and other basic items caused by the A9's closure: to date the LTTE had refused to guarantee the safety of sea-bound vessels making their way to Jaffna, thereby stalling UN efforts to move emergency supplies into the region for its estimated 500,000 inhabitants.

Karuna speaks out

A month before talks reopened in Geneva, an interview with Karuna by defence expert Iqbal Athas provided some revealing insights into the former LTTE's leader's thinking.

> The LTTE knows that it is very weak and the only way out is to buy more time ... to ask for unconditional talks reflects the desperate [situation] they are in at present. With my departure Prabhakaran is facing serious drawbacks. He has lost good calibre recruits and committed leadership which obtained major victories for the LTTE ...
>
> The LTTE has lost its credibility on all fronts. Prabhakaran is hiding in a bunker and is commanding a disabled bunch of commanders: they have become a spent force. The future is very bleak for the LTTE. It is not only in the Vanni: the LTTE is loosing grounds in the Tamil diaspora and even international opinion has turned against it. My departure ... was the starting point for its decline and it has lost [a] large chunk of real estate it controlled in the East. Very soon it will have to face our cadres in Vanni and Jaffna. [The LTTE] will go to extremes under Pottu Amman's direction and engage in suicide attacks. If the situation becomes life-threatening for Prabhakaran you could expect nasty things to happen.[103]

In October the LTTE and the government confirmed their readiness to participate in talks, now scheduled for 28–29 October in Geneva. At the same time, analysts and Colombo-based Co-Chairs ambassadors noted with concern the government's insistence that it reserved the right to take 'countermeasures' in the 'interests of national security'—which, as General Fonseka explained to Jon Hanssen-Bauer following his return to the country on 1 October, implied the intention to continue with 'pre-emptive' measures to curb LTTE terrorism.[104]

Military offensives

On 6 October, a little over three weeks after the announcement of the forthcoming talks, there were reports that fighting had erupted in earnest in Mankerni, a small coastal town located on what had become the only access road to Tiger-held territory further north, with significant casualties on both sides.[105] In a significant development, the LTTE subsequently claimed that Karuna faction forces had fought alongside government troops.[106]

Impressions of the Tigers from Lars Johan Sølvberg

The initial impression of the LTTE was very striking. They had been able to set up a seemingly well-functioning state system of a totalitarian, old-fashioned communist kind. My first reflection was that in a way this was a frozen 1970s liberation movement. The world has moved on, but you are still here as a semi-Maoist, communist, uniformed, brainwashed movement stuck with your values. But, I also thought, you can't survive as a state entity with that posturing today. The influence of Prabhakaran was overwhelming. The loss of Balasingham as moderator was the loss of a sense of reality.

Worse was to follow. On the morning of 11 October, government forces launched a major ground offensive across the forward defence line (FDL) at Muhamalai, south of Jaffna. But it soon became apparent that they had walked into a carefully prepared LTTE trap: in the space of a little more than two hours, around 130 soldiers were killed and a further 500 injured by sniper fire, artillery barrages and landmines.[107] Increasing the sense of debacle in Colombo, there were indications that at least one army tank had fallen into the LTTE's hands and that the decision to launch the Muhamalai assault had been taken without the government's knowledge—a sign, as one commentator put it, of the 'wide gulf between the political and military leadership'.[108]

Less than a week after the Muhamalai encounter, the LTTE struck back. The target was a parking lot at a major road junction close to Habarana, where buses transporting military personnel halted on their way to and from the naval base at Trincomalee. On 16 October a lorry packed with explosives rammed straight into one of the waiting buses. More than 130 sailors were killed in the resulting carnage and a further 130 were injured, many severely.[109]

With Colombo still reeling from the impact of two major LTTE assaults, on 18 October a group of five LTTE vessels attempted an attack on the navy's base in Galle harbour, known to be the location of the main naval arsenal, to which ever-growing arms supplies from Pakistan were brought directly by sea.[110] The daring raid, on a target at the heart of country's main tourist region, served as a potent statement of the LTTE's capacity to strike seemingly at will and across the country.[111]

On the domestic political front, in a landmark decision delivered on 16 October the Supreme Court ruled that the North-East province, created following the 1987 Indo-Lankan Accord, was unconstitutional and that the two provinces should accordingly be separated. The jubilation of the JVP, which had initiated the legal challenge, was matched by the despondency of many in the international community, not least that of the measure's original sponsor, India. A unified Northeast remained a cornerstone of India's approach to a political solution to the conflict, and some commentators viewed the decision to untie the two as likely to provoke a declaration of independence by Prabhakaran in his forthcoming annual Heroes Day speech.[112]

On an ostensibly more positive note, on 23 October the country's largest political parties, Rajapaksa's SLFP and the opposition UNP, signed a Memorandum of Understanding on what were termed 'national policies'— the first time in Sri Lankan history that a formal bipartisan agreement had been concluded. The MoU, which was welcomed by the Co-Chairs and India, would, it was hoped, pave the way for a hitherto elusive 'southern consensus' with regard to a 'final settlement' of the ethnic conflict.[113]

With military activity seemingly suspended at the time and following a procession of visits by US Assistant Secretary of State Richard Boucher, Yasusi Akashi and Jon Hanssen-Bauer, attention turned towards the impending meeting in Geneva. Jon Hanssen-Bauer informed Richard Boucher that Tamilselvan had suggested that in view of the worsening humanitarian situation in Jaffna, the LTTE delegation would be focusing on its demand that the government reopen the A9 road. In addition,

Hansen-Bauer indicated that the facilitators' modest objective for Geneva was agreement to hold two further rounds of talks, with 'agreed dates, venue and objectives'.[114]

Geneva II

The talks opened in an unorthodox fashion, without a formal agenda. Despite the Norwegian facilitators' best efforts in the lead-up to the meeting, the gulf between the two sides was such that it proved impossible to secure agreement on what should be discussed.

Matching the mood of the moment, Erik Solheim opened proceedings by stating that failure to implement the agreements reached during previous rounds of negotiations had led to a situation in which there were now over 200,000 internally displaced civilians, while the number of war casualties since the beginning of the year—nearly 3,000 in total—was even higher than that resulting from Israel's recent attack on Lebanon.[115] Stressing that there could be no 'support whatsoever' from the international community for a military solution to the conflict, Solheim emphasised the importance of achieving real progress for continued international economic and political support for the country.[116] He made it clear that three sets of issues would be on the table: the humanitarian crisis, military de-escalation and a political solution—and that priority would be given to the first.[117]

International Crisis Group (ICG)

Both sides are cynically exploiting the [humanitarian crisis]. The LTTE uses civilians as a fundamental part of its guerrilla strategy; the government seems to be using humanitarian aid to limit supplies to the LTTE and persuade people to move [away] from LTTE positions.[118]

Undeterred by the facilitators' words of guidance, the heads of both delegations launched into their prepared opening statements. Nimal Sirpala de Silva from the government side began with a long speech, described by one commentator as a 'reconstruction of events since the last talks' combined with an 'explanation of the government's agenda for engagement with the LTTE'.[119] Tamilselvan's response was similarly lengthy and, as a rehearsal of the LTTE's version of the conflict to date, was only tangentially related to the 'political issues' prioritised by the other side.[120]

On the second day, the LTTE delegation began by insisting that they only wanted to talk about issues relating to the closure of the A9. The government team rejected this suggestion, and the LTTE refused to continue. The Norwegian facilitators managed to bring both sides back to the table, but the rest of the morning was reportedly given over to an exchange of accusations, chiefly relating to the A9, which was described by Tamilselvan as a new 'Berlin Wall'.[121] In reply to Tamilselvan's insistence on the reopening of the A9 as the starting point for any further discussion, the government repeated its offer to organise sea transport of essential supplies to the Jaffna peninsula, which the LTTE again rejected. No doubt sensing that further progress was unlikely, the facilitators proposed a new round of talks in December, to be followed by another round in February. Tamilselvan reiterated that the LTTE would only attend further talks once the A9 had been reopened. Faced with this stalemate, talks were adjourned with no agreement reached on a further round.[122]

Speaking to the media, Erik Solheim made an effort to be optimistic. While admitting that a new meeting date had not been agreed, he noted that both parties had 'reiterated their commitment to the ceasefire agreement' and also promised 'not to launch any military offensives'.[123] While this was technically true, there was no disguising the despondency that was now enveloping the peace process.

Perspectives on Geneva II

Jon Hanssen-Bauer

The talks themselves were a problem from the first minute. We met on the first morning in a hall provided by the Swiss government. The two delegations sat behind desks. The LTTE sat on the right side, and the government delegation claimed the facilitators were giving them greater importance. The opening statement by Erik: I think he mentioned the LTTE first and that didn't go down well. The government delegation was angry. My impression is that they felt they had been forced into the negotiations ...

Nirupama De Silva led a large government delegation including people fully opposed to talks. Foreign Minister Bogollagama was part of the team, even if he preferred to stay in a five star Geneva hotel rather than at the somewhat spartan conference venue. We started to address content issues and it simply did not work. The LTTE were not ready to agree to a further meeting until they got a reopening of the A9. The government side's response was simply that this was unacceptable for security reasons. They said the LTTE really wanted it reopened for military reasons, and so this [was] a kind of trap laid by the Tigers. The

LTTE, however, said it was a humanitarian issue. It was unsolvable. The LTTE wanted to have something, and the government side had nothing to give.

Overall, I felt [the government side] didn't want to call off the negotiations, but they were not mandated to contribute. The government wanted to set new dates without giving anything away. We went to the media afterwards. There, both parties were polite, claiming that they were willing to talk—even though nothing came out of the meeting at all. The parties were not even willing to have a general dialogue. They wanted to fight.

Erik Solheim

For me, the fact that Bala[singham] wasn't present was the strongest indication that nothing of real substance would come out of [these talks]: at that point we didn't know that he was seriously ill. There were some discussions on minor military issues with Tamilselvan, but nothing substantial. Jon Hanssen-Bauer was pushing. He did his best but it was difficult, and he didn't have our background knowledge of the situation. He came in at the most difficult point, as things were sliding downwards. At this point the government wanted to keep every option open—very consistent with the Mahinda 'Village Chief' approach. Only late in 2008 could they feel quite certain that they would win the war.

Palitha Kohona

There was a degree of hope in Colombo that the Norwegians were capable of pushing the LTTE to the negotiating table. The first day's talks were very good. We went through a range of issues, and they were responding on how to deal with land, access issues. We came to a point where we were agreeing on certain things. There was a certain optimism on our side but after lunch on the second day, the entire LTTE delegation refused to come to the table. They said that unless the A9 was re-opened, they would walk out, which they did ... I was very depressed. I thought this is not going to work out. I don't think the LTTE delegation was convinced that the talks were going to go anywhere.

Vidar Helgesen

After the breakdown of the Geneva talks I felt that things were heading back to military confrontation, with extremely limited scope for any mediation efforts ... The argument that Norway kept going because everyone—the Americans, the Indians, the Co-Chairs—encouraged us to is probably correct ... I certainly feel that a high level of [facilitation] activity went on for too long. I hasten to add, however, that I was out of the system at this point so was not privy to all [the] considerations involved. The Sri Lankan government never formalised the fact that they didn't want us involved any longer. They sent out various people who lambasted Norway left, right and centre, but there was never a formal request for us to stop our activities.

Fighting resumes

Within days of the breakdown of talks, fighting resumed. A Co-Chairs statement condemning the violence and calling on both sides to 'refrain from military action' noted that an Air Force bombing raid on the Kilinochchi area on 2 November had killed five civilians and damaged the hospital, causing patients to flee the area—a violation of international humanitarian law.[124]

On 1 November artillery fire was exchanged on the Jaffna peninsula, prompting D.B.S. Jeyaraj to observe that both sides were simply 'taking off from where they were forced to stop due to Geneva'. The stage was being set, he continued, for 'resumption of hostilities on a major scale', the result of which would be 'no victors' but instead 'suffering, hardship and misery for the people of Sri Lanka in general and the Tamils in particular'.[125] Seemingly confirming Jeyaraj's prediction, on 8 November reports emerged of a Sri Lanka Army artillery attack on an IDP camp inside LTTE-controlled territory at the coastal village of Kathiraveli, that left nearly 50 people dead and over 135 injured.[126] An initial SLMM investigation found no evidence of LTTE artillery in the camp, and subsequent government claims that the Tigers had been using civilians as a 'human shield' were discredited.[127]

The Island *on the Vakarai shelling incident*

> The army cannot trot out any excuses in extenuation of the civilian deaths on Wednesday. The LTTE never hesitates to achieve its military objectives at the expense of civilians, be they Tamils, Sinhalese or Muslims. A professional military must be different from a group of terrorists, if it is to be worthy of its name ... The army must always be mindful of its mission; it has been deployed to protect citizenry and defend the country. A hunt for terrorists must end where the safety of civilians begins. Even if a hundred terrorists were to escape, the army must hold its fire if there is the slightest doubt that it will harm civilians. There is no alternative![128]

On the same day a dramatic incident at Pooneryn, a short distance across the lagoon south east of Jaffna, saw SLMM Head Lars Sølvberg narrowly escape an army shelling attack. Following an officially sanctioned visit to Kilinochchi to discuss a government proposal for an alternative land route to Jaffna involving the disused ferry jetty at Pooneryn, and having duly informed the Sri Lanka Army of his intended movements, Sølvberg and a fellow monitor had driven to Pooneryn to check the state of the infrastructure. As they approached, artillery shells began falling nearby. Solberg and colleague took shelter in a bunker, before eventually being spirited out of the area by accompanying LTTE cadres.[129]

After receiving a full briefing on the incident, Erik Solheim declared that there was 'no doubt' that the shells were intended 'to kill those who were there'. The only mitigating circumstance, he suggested, was the fact that those doing the shelling were 'probably' unaware that they were targeting Norwegian monitors.[130] The government, as Sølvberg recalls, were 'very sorry, gave all sorts of excuses and promised this would not happen again'. Whatever the truth regarding official knowledge of Sølvberg's presence, the SLMM's Jon Oskar Solnes viewed the Pooneryn 'event' as symptomatic of a deterioration in the monitors' relations with the government Peace Secretariat in general and its Head, Palitha Kohona, in particular. In addition, Solnes traces the SLMM's plummeting popularity in the Sinhalese media to late 2006, when details of bilateral SLMM-Peace Secretariat discussions began to be 'splashed in the state newspapers the day afterwards' whenever Kohona had been present at a meeting.[131]

Parallel developments on the political front were equally depressing. On the morning of 10 November TNA MP Nadarajah Naviraj was gunned down in his car, along with a bodyguard.[132] The second TNA MP to be assassinated since Rajapaksa had assumed the presidency, Naviraj was unusual among Tamil MPs in his fluent command of both Tamil and Sinhalese, and had been considered as someone who might have bridged the country's ethnic gulf. His killing was a setback for the voices of moderation; it was also interpreted by some as evidence of a government campaign to silence all such voices, regardless of ethnicity.[133] President Rajapaksa's reaction—a request to the UK's Scotland Yard for assistance in the murder investigation—prompted questions about what this presaged for the credibility of a recently-announced Independent Commission of Inquiry into human rights violations.[134] The underlying message seemed to be that the authorities were unable to conduct judicial investigations without outside help.[135]

Amid reports of fighting on a number of fronts in the North and East, including a fierce sea battle off the coast at Mannar,[136] on 19 November the government announced its intention to re-open the A9 road at Muhamalai checkpoint on a 'trial' basis. The proposal was rejected by the LTTE, who saw it chiefly as a move intended to coincide with the Co-Chairs meeting on humanitarian issues scheduled for 21 November in Washington.[137] In the meantime, it did not go unnoticed that the government's new budget, presented to parliament on 16 November, included a 45 per cent increase in defence expenditure.[138] Coupled with the creation of a new arms procurement company under direct Ministry of Defence control, the budget appeared to give a clear signal of the government's strategic intentions.[139]

Further stirring the pot, at the end of a ten-day visit Special Adviser to the UN Secretary-General Allan Rock confirmed that, along with reports of continuing LTTE child soldier recruitment, he had also received eyewitness accounts that government soldiers were assisting the Karuna faction in recruiting under-age cadres. The same charge had been levelled in an earlier SLMM report, but coming from a UN Adviser who was due to present his findings to the UN Security Council in January, its impact was now considerably greater.[140] Increasing the international pressure on the government, the Washington Co-Chairs meeting concluded with a statement that 'reminded' the parties of their 'responsibility to respect all rulings by the SLMM and to implement the Ceasefire Agreement fully, including re-opening the A9 highway'.[141]

Heroes Day Speech

On 27 November Prabhakaran gave his much-awaited annual Heroes Day speech. A year earlier, the LTTE leader had described President Rajapaksa as a 'realist', and appealed to him to 'find a solution to the Tamil National question with urgency'. This year, Prabhakaran argued, the government had 'unleashed a two-pronged war, military and economic' on the Tamil people. The 'uncompromising stance of Sinhala chauvinism' had left the Tigers 'no other option' than the pursuit of an 'independent state for the people of Tamil Eelam', said Prabhakaran, before concluding with a rousing appeal for international recognition of the Tamil people's 'freedom struggle'.[142] One analysis noted that while the speech had declared the CFA 'defunct', the LTTE leader had nonetheless avoided calling for all-out war. At the same time, it was suggested, the speech made it clear that the 'armed struggle' would now have clear priority on the LTTE agenda. It would thus be critical for the international community to press the government to react to the speech by redoubling its efforts to 'draft a viable settlement proposal'.[143]

In early December the Indian Prime Minister, Manmohan Singh, pressed President Rajapaksa on the need for a political solution to the conflict. Reportedly, Rajapaksa's response was that the government would present an interim devolution proposal 'by the middle of the month'.[144] But just four days after the LTTE leader's speech, Defence Secretary Gotabhaya Rajapaksa narrowly survived an assassination attempt. His motorcade was on its way to Temple Trees for a cabinet meeting when a three-wheeler driven by an LTTE suicide bomber attempted to ram his armoured car. The blast killed three members of his escort and wounded more than fifteen people, both military personnel and civilians. A dazed Rajapaksa was bundled into another vehicle and whisked off to Temple Trees, where—following a much-photographed reunion with his brother, the president—he attended a meeting of the national security council.

The immediate consequence of the attack was to push the government into introducing a new raft of anti-terrorism legislation. The former Prevention of Terrorism Act (PTA) had been effectively nullified by the 2002 Ceasefire Agreement, but the new measures, some suggested, appeared to be every bit as draconian, not least because they could be used as much to stifle protest in the South as to combat the LTTE in the North.[145] For those looking to put a brighter spin on things, there was the consolation that the government had stopped short of the outright ban on the LTTE urged by some ministers.[146]

An assessment of the Rajapaksa brothers from a senior Western diplomat

Basil Rajapaksa is political, smart, friendly: easy to talk to, but also very tactical and strategic. He was able to handle daily politics and look into long-term needs. He was fairly emotional but also quite open. Gotabhaya is stern, rigid, less willing to change or engage in debates on issues. Once he had made his mind up on something he simply went into explanatory mode. He did not open up in the sense that he would always talk more than listen. In that particular context, however, this was probably an effective approach—in the sense that it was about achieving victory, conducting the campaign to its end.

Mahinda is super-political: charming, cunning, funny, smart, but a complex personality in many ways. It is difficult to imagine Mahinda, the eldest, being successful without his brothers. But one should never, ever underestimate him. If he is insulted, if someone tries to kill his brothers, for example, then that's personal. And he means it. And that's what led him to the conclusion 'I reached out my hand to Prabhakaran in 2005, then he tried to kill my brother. So OK, now I will show him'. That was basically the line he pursued.

In the meantime, Jon Hanssen-Bauer returned to Sri Lanka, though the prospects of reviving the peace process appeared bleak. Not only were both parties locked into positions that left little room for negotiation, it also appeared that the government was more interested in mobilising a pro-war constituency than in exploring new peace initiatives. It seemed hardly coincidental, for example, that a few days before Hanssen-Bauer's arrival the government-controlled *Daily News* published an extensive interview with Karuna in which the former LTTE commander alleged that Erik Solheim had given Prabhakaran a huge TV set, handed over 16 million Norwegian crowns in cash to Balasingham, and received 'help' from the LTTE in buying his Oslo house.[147] Needless to say, the Norwegians dismissed these claims as arrant nonsense, but the intended damage had been done.[148]

After several days of talks in Colombo, Hanssen-Bauer eventually held discussions with the LTTE on 8 December.[149] Tamilselvan reportedly refused all the initiatives proposed by the government, including reopening the A9 for a 'one-time' humanitarian convoy and a proposal to hold fresh peace talks as soon as possible. In addition, the LTTE were said to have underlined their overall lack of faith in the international community, the Norwegian facilitators and the SLMM, since none of them appeared to be able to hold the government to its commitments. Hanssen-Bauer left Kilinochchi having told the Tigers that there was 'no point' in his making future visits if they didn't yield any results.

Jon Hanssen-Bauer on Norway's changing role

In 2006 we thought a lot about what was best, whether we should continue, or play down our role. We tried to adjust as things evolved. I understood very early that things were going back to full-fledged war. Up until the Geneva II talks, we kept on pushing for the resumption of talks. Before the November Co-Chairs meeting we decided to lower the Norwegian profile, both in the context of the Co-Chairs and in public, and to rather focus on holding the parties accountable for their own decisions. We saw a high Norwegian profile as counterproductive at this stage.

It contributed chiefly only to triggering increased attacks on Norway and had little effect on the war's conduct. Therefore, we preferred that the Co-Chair countries step up their involvement. We contributed to such a role by organising local meetings and sharing our information with the Co-Chair capitals. Locally, we focused on our specific role as the channel for communications with Kilinochchi.

In this context, we also wanted to lower the SLMM's profile. It was difficult to withdraw the monitors completely without being seen as the party to

---

abrogate the CFA. Both the government and the LTTE hesitated to take that step. We had real security concerns, however, and looked for ways to lower the monitor's exposure to battle-related risks. We also feared that the increased criticism of Norway could lead to the SLMM being targeted.

I went to Colombo in early December and that is when I confronted Basil, asked him if they had decided not only to secure Trincomalee harbour but also to take the whole of the Eastern province, then try to wipe out the LTTE completely. And he said: 'Yes. I would rather be open with you. We have taken the decision.'[150] Later, some children were killed in heavy firing on a school and I told Basil: 'You just can't do that.' And he was very angry, telling me: 'Why can't you Norwegians and others force the Tigers to come to open territory so we can take them on, and avoid civilian casualties?' By the end of the four-hour meeting Basil said: 'We are in war.'

I said in that case there's nothing we can help you with. I asked him, do you want us to remove the SLMM, pack up and declare the Norwegian role here is over? He said, 'No, I may need you, I am not certain we have the military strength to succeed. If we don't we know we will have to go back to negotiations.' He said he wanted the SLMM to be there as long as it could, even in its reduced format. His reasoning was that he would like to have an independent eye on the ground. And finally, he said that they needed a channel open to the Tigers in Kilinochchi.

Balasingham dies

Earlier in the autumn, Anton Balasingham, the 68-year-old chief LTTE negotiator, was diagnosed with a rare bile duct cancer and given only a few weeks to live by his doctors. In late November, he was quoted as saying: 'I am deeply sad that I am crippled by this illness, unable to contribute any-thing substantial towards the alleviation of the immense suffering and oppression of my people.'[151] A few weeks later, on 14 December, he died at his home in London. Prabhakaran issued a special statement, conferring on Balasingham the title 'Voice of the Nation'. 'In the great family that is our movement, he was its eldest son, and its guiding star for three decades', he stated. 'The strength of his soul was inspirational. I grieve for him'.[152]

Reflections on Balasingham

Erik Solheim

Soon after the October Geneva talks, Adele called and told me that Bala[singham] was seriously ill with cancer. I came to visit soon thereafter, just a couple of weeks before he died. He was completely lucid—the only difference from before was that he stayed in bed. He was still very well informed. He was very disillusioned with Prabhakaran and what he saw as the very negative way things were developing. He did not speak to Prabhakaran during the last months, I think.

He understood the importance of India for the Tamil struggle and was dissatisfied with Prabhakaran's strategy. By then Bala[singham] may have come to the conclusion that he [Prabhakaran] was part of the problem. Bala[singham] told me that he thought they might lose the East and the North now. He saw clearly what could happen—and indeed later did happen ...

[In retrospect] the main issue [was] the two sides' overall strategy ... The most important issue in this respect is the death of Balasingham in December 2006. After that, there was no new initiative from the LTTE side. That all came down to the fact that Bala[singham] had died. His power was always his ability to reach out to Prabhakaran. With him went the LTTE's ability to come up with meaningful political proposals as well as a moderating influence on the military campaigns.

Narayan Swamy, Indian journalist

At some point Balasingham probably thought he knew more about the LTTE and the Tamil struggle than Prabhakaran. Which is why a statement Erik made when Balasingham died became controversial. Erik said he was one of the most honest men he ever met: that is because Balasingham disagreed with Prabhakaran, but could not speak openly about it. He told the truth to Erik, but the rest of the world did not know *that* Balasingham. The world knew a different Balasingham who could justify or at least not criticise every [LTTE] killing.

I won't say he had no influence, just that he did not have a determining influence. The one time the truth was spoken by Prabhakaran about Balasingham was in 1985, when India made three Lankan Tamils *persona non grata*, including Balasingham. An angry Prabhakaran told Rajiv Gandhi, 'You are blaming him for influencing me. I do listen to him, but I don't get influenced by him. I take the decisions that I think are best for [the] LTTE.'

N. Ram, Editor-in-Chief, *The Hindu*

Balasingham was a diplomat and had a special relationship with Prabhakaran. He was like his external affairs minister. Prabhakaran called him his elder brother. But everybody knew he was not a fighter, or in the command. He was treated with respect but did not deal with strategy, only external affairs. In my first interview with Prabhakaran, Bala[singham] translated, and [afterwards] we found it was highly embroidered. I don't know whether Prabhakaran fully got the English, but it was understood that Balasingham would put across what was suitable for the external world, for the record. There was a gap between what was actually said by Prabhakaran and what was presented, and I think that was part of the diplomacy. But he was very loyal. He probably saw the wrong turns taken by the LTTE.

Civilians under fire—and the SLMM pulls back to Colombo

With Christmas approaching, government forces stepped up their offensive on Tiger-held territory south of Trincomalee, focused around the coastal town of Vakarai. As all too often, it was civilians of all ethnicities—Tamil, Muslim and Sinhalese—who bore the brunt of the fighting. While figures for non-combatants killed in the crossfire were contested, there was little disputing the fact that around 40,000 civilians had been displaced by the fighting around Vakarai, swelling the total number of IDPs in the Northeast to over 200,000.

Just as LTTE tactics were focused on preventing civilians from leaving the area, the Army seemed intent on de-populating Vakarai and its surroundings prior to proclaiming it as 'cleared' territory.[153] Taken together with the increasing deprivations suffered by the population of the Jaffna peninsula, still cut off from land contact with the rest of the country and thus deprived of regular supplies of food and other essentials, Sri Lanka at the end of 2006 presented a sorry picture.

Immediately after Christmas, the SLMM announced that it would be changing its operations due to 'increasing military activity'.[154] In reality, what was involved was a major downscaling of the monitoring operation. Lars Johan Sølvberg explains: 'In early December I was summoned back to Oslo. I was very anxious due to the fact that Norwegian security police had discovered that there was a concrete threat to kill SLMM monitors. Three individuals were named as targets. When I came back to Colombo I was collected at the airport by the Norwegian ambassador's armoured car. That kind of protection was totally new. And this was when I started bringing everybody back ... First we pulled everybody back to close to Colombo. We established new headquarters and worked on what to do, because the only sensible approach to adopt at that time was to say this is a war, and we should not be out there at the moment.'

Jon Hanssen-Bauer on the Co-Chairs in 2006

During 2006 we had five capital-level meetings of the Co-Chairs. We also increased the level of consultation and co-operation between ambassadors locally. We agreed on pursuing slightly different roles. When we were not received as a group, the US Ambassador was often charged with meeting the government on our behalf. We focused on humanitarian issues, in particular the protection of civilians during war. We all raised these issues in conversations with civilian and military leaders—repeatedly, and particularly after events where we felt government forces were in breach of international humanitarian law. We [the Norwegians] also took similar messages to the LTTE.

I was a bit surprised that Colombo accepted this expanded role for the Co-Chairs, but they did interact with the group. In my view the presence of Japan in addition to the US was important. Colombo also understood and felt we had backing from India. Hans Brattskar and myself went to visit the different force commanders, and we were received politely. We presented our task and role as a facilitator, and raised the issue of international humanitarian law. We also raised this several times with Basil and Gotabhaya. All in all, after some very bad incidents initially, the war was conducted with relatively low battlefield civilian casualties. The high civilian death toll occurred outside the battlefield—until autumn 2008 that is.

The SLMM would, however, have been heartened by the assessment of US Ambassador Blake in the aftermath of their withdrawal from the North. The monitoring mission, he commented, 'continues to play an indispensable role in sorting out fact from fiction on the ground. There is no other authority we trust for impartial assessments of the realities regarding the numerous acts of violence'.[155]

10

EELAM WAR IV

THE DENOUEMENT

2007 started as 2006 had ended, with a low-level war of attrition that left little room for mediation. The re-emergence of LTTE bomb attacks on civilian targets and public transport, however, added another grim feature to an already bleak conflict. A bus bombing on 5 January at Nittambuwa, some 20km east of Colombo, was followed by another just twenty-four hours later near the southern tourist resort of Hikkaduwa. In both cases the impact of the killings was heightened by the fear and uncertainty generated by the Tigers' ability to strike whenever—and seemingly, wherever—they wanted.[1]

On the military front, in mid-January the government announced that its forces had captured the coastal town of Vakarai, a key Eastern Tiger stronghold. Absent from the messages of congratulations to the armed forces, however, was any official recognition of the humanitarian crisis that the conflict continued to fuel. In early February, UN agencies estimated that the previous ten months of fighting had created over 210,000 internally displaced persons (IDPs). Taken together with those that had been languishing in camps since the 2004 tsunami, the country now had a total refugee population estimated at over 500,000.[2]

Equally disturbing were intelligence reports of the LTTE's conduct before it finally abandoned Vakarai. It was alleged that the Tigers had forcibly detained civilians as a 'human shield' around the hospital in order to 'ensure speedy medical care for wounded cadres', and that the LTTE had stopped a large number from fleeing the area.[3] Moreover, it was now apparent that LTTE artillery had been located 'in the middle of a large civilian population concentration near Vakarai hospital'.[4] In the context of their escalating military confrontation with government forces, in other words, the Tigers' concern for the welfare of the Tamil population—the very people in whose name they were fighting—appeared to feature low on their list of priorities.[5]

General Sarath Fonseka, New Year 2007 address to the Sri Lankan army

> We have come forward in order to annihilate the common enemy and protect the territorial integrity of our Sri Lankan Motherland and her nation. Our sole intention is to create a peaceful and conducive environment where everybody could live in peace and harmony after granting every citisen his/her human rights. This is possible after rooting out terrorism.

Government strategy

In what was described by US Ambassador Robert Blake as a 'hard-hitting' presentation to donor ambassadors in advance of a 'Development Forum' held late January in Galle, Centre for Policy Alternatives (CPA) Director Dr Paikiasothy Saravanamuttu argued that the government was more interested in consolidating its legislative majority than developing a credible devolution proposal—a view strengthened by the 28 January announcement that eighteen UNP and six SLMC MPs had crossed over to the government side.[6]

By contrast, Saravanamuttu argued, the LTTE had been 'significantly weakened' by recent fighting, and since the Tigers had never previously been willing to engage in peace negotiations from a position of weakness—and weakening them was now clearly the government's main aim—a period of 'protracted conflict' was likely. In this context, he castigated the donor community for allowing the government to 'take [them] for a ride' by 'promising peace and respect for human rights' while pursuing a military strategy and what was described as 'creeping authoritarianism'.

Overall, he depicted the government's attitude to the international community as one of 'let's see what we can get away with'. In particular, critical 'statements and snubs' were not taken too seriously because donors had not been willing to initiate 'more punitive action' to back them up. Moreover, even if Western countries were willing to take such action, Saravanamuttu argued, the government had 'other options'—notably the Chinese, Pakistanis and Israelis—who were willing to provide weapons and other military equipment 'with no conditions attached'.

Chiming with his analysis, after the Galle Development Forum Hans Brattskar shared with Robert Blake his view that the government would 'do what they want to do anyway', because they felt that the military campaign was going well. As an illustration of the government's attitude towards the international community, he pointed to a recent media interview in which Gotabhaya had stated that the security forces would 'chase the Tigers out' of the North. A few days later, however, speaking at the Galle Forum, Gotabhaya had said that the government was 'pursuing a peaceful settlement'—'because they know that's what we want to hear,' Brattskar commented.

Brattskar also informed Blake that during a private conversation in Galle, Basil Rajapaksa had asked him to inform the LTTE that if the Tigers '[got] out of the East', the government security forces would not 'go for the North'. Brattskar intimated that the government believed it had received a 'back-channel message' from the LTTE that it would be prepared to accept this arrangement. He himself, however, thought the LTTE leadership would 'not even entertain' the proposal.[7]

In early February, Brattskar travelled to Kilinochchi for talks with the LTTE, his first visit for some months. After complaining that government forces were occupying territory defined by the 2002 Ceasefire Agreement as LTTE-controlled, Tamilselvan called on the international community to insist that the government halt what he described as its 'war-like' activities. Asked how he envisaged the possibility of restarting the peace process, Tamilselvan proposed a 'return' to the original starting point—the CFA. Pushed on what that would mean in terms of the new territorial configuration of the East, Tamilselvan's reply was characterised by what Brattskar termed 'constructive uncertainty' as to whether the Tigers would call for government withdrawals from Sampur, Vakarai and the rest of its recently captured territory in the East.[8]

Whatever the LTTE might or might not call for by way of territorial reconfigurations, at this point the consensus among international observers was that, following the capture of Vakarai, it was only a matter of time before the Sri Lankan military seized control of the East in its entirety.

Moreover, to underline the point that military advances were creating new 'facts on the ground', in the wake of a judgement issued by the Supreme Court in late October 2006, the government announced its intention to annul the merger of the Northern and Eastern Provinces established by the 1987 Indo-Lanka Accord.

In the meantime, commentators were registering the implications of developments in the East for overall prospects for peace. As one argued, it would now be 'politically impossible' for the government to give up any of the territory recently taken in the East—and at such a high cost—on the basis of the CFA. Yet if Tamilselvan's recent remarks to Brattskar were any guide, the CFA was precisely the basis on which the LTTE appeared to be prepared to consider talks. And without the CFA, what other basis was there on which the Norwegians could try to broker talks between the two sides?

Opposing Sri Lankan views

Gotabhaya Rajapaksa

> We must show perseverance, We must not be stopped by obstacles, by internal and external pressures over human rights or humanitarian crises ... All measures are fair to defeat terrorists.[9]

Mangala Samaraweera

> President Rajapaksa is creating a quasi-police state where racism is now the official policy ... pushing Tamils into the lap of the LTTE. And in the guise of fighting terrorism, Gotabhaya and his cronies [have] initiated a witch-hunt against all democratic opposition to the Rajapaksa brotherhood.[10]

Air attack

Towards the end of March government forces received a huge shock: during the night of 26 March, the LTTE's nascent air wing carried out its first ever attack, on the Katunayake Air Force base opposite the international airport due north of Colombo. While the destruction was relatively minimal—only two of the three bombs aimed at grounded fighter jets exploded, and those that did missed their target, killing three and injuring another sixteen[11]—psychologically the raid's impact on the southern population was enormous.

Predictably, the raid gave rise to all manner of conclusions, of which some of the clearest—and the most hawkish—came from Dayan Jayatilleka:

> The fundamental lessons ... are quite the opposite of those that will be drawn by the appeasers and their patrons in the West. ... These elements will say that the raid proves that a military victory over the LTTE is impossible and that only a peaceful negotiated settlement is feasible. I would argue the exact opposite. The air raid demonstrates the utter impossibility of peaceful coexistence between a militarised, Tiger-controlled territory and the Sri Lankan state. The Tiger air force was the product of the Ranil Wickremasinghe–Erik Solheim CFA. It is the same CFA that Britain's Tony Blair wants us to go back to. Such a restoration ... would only enable the LTTE to build up its fledgling air arm into an even more dangerous parallel air force. It would be suicidal for SL to re-enter such a trap.[12]

A month later, two further Tiger air strikes came in rapid succession. First in the early morning of 24 April Tiger planes attempted—and according to official accounts, failed[13]—to bomb a section of the Palaly air base on the Jaffna peninsula.[14] Five days later, on 29 April a pair of Tiger aircraft struck again, this time targeting the Colombo fuel depots used by the Sri Lanka Air Force. For the purposes of publicity, they could not have timed things better: most of the city's population was awake, watching Sri Lanka play Australia in the Cricket World Cup Final, and so were treated to the spectacle of sirens, power cuts and anti-aircraft fire lighting up the Colombo skyline. Out of the ensuing chaos came a government announcement that Colombo airport would be closed to night flights. With some 40 per cent of civilian flights out of the country's only international airport needing to be rescheduled or cancelled as a result, this was an extremely costly move.[15]

Views on developments in early 2007

Lars Johan Sølvberg

> Slowly, we [the SLMM] tried to expand our operations again in 2007, and eventually we were back in some—but not all—of the outlying districts. We went back to Jaffna, Trincomalee and Vavuniya ...

> Then you had the question of the extent to which the monitoring mission should be connected, or even subordinated to the peace process, or the Norwegians. Because according to the CFA, the SLMM was an independent international entity, unconnected to the facilitators. This gave the Head of Mission real authority, which was stimulating, but also very stressful: deciding whom to talk to, drawing your own conclusions and taking responsibility for them. And all the time making sure that we were not the source of the peace process's collapse.

Jon Hanssen-Bauer

During the first months of 2007 the war's progress was very unclear. It took some time to see that the government offensive had been successful. The Tigers regrouped and retreated. We used SLMM information a lot and relayed it to the other Co-Chairs. We kept discussions with the LTTE going on the phone and through other means. We maintained contact with both the parties. The Co-Chairs would go directly to the government when we thought they were not behaving correctly with respect to the civilian population. We conveyed our concerns to the LTTE about its use of civilian shields. In the beginning of 2007 Basil [Rajapaksa] told me that because of our work, the war would take *much* longer. We also focused on IDPs. We started organising support and coordinating between the different organisations.

I travelled to the US for meetings at the UN in order to try and step up the humanitarian work. We tried our best to limit casualties among civilians. Information was shared regularly between the Co-Chairs ambassadors. In my view the Co-Chairs now became *the* instrument for Norway and the rest of the international community to follow up on the conflict, try to influence the parties to reduce casualties and to come back to talks—which, of course, did not happen.

For me, the SLMM setup was very rational. You had a monitoring device that was light-footed, able to be more an eye on the ground than a helping hand, and you left the responsibility with the parties. Many said it was too weak and had no influence. But it wasn't set up to stop the parties going back to war but to help them make peace—quite different things. If you had a peacekeeping force you would have needed 25,000 men. India tried to do it with many more but they couldn't manage it. So, that was the alternative.

The criticism [of Norway as mediator and monitor] is tainted by the misunderstanding that we could judge between the parties. That was not the intention, [which] was to assist the parties with implementation in the field and trying to solve the conflict at its lowest level. That's why the SLMM was unarmed: originally they envisaged having very few people travelling around on the ground. But that situation changed. The SLMM began to issue judgements on what happened and who was to blame in different situations. And one could argue that it was a bad idea to make public statements in this way ... They did not realise that by going public they were becoming targets ...

When I went to Kilinochchi, the LTTE said they wanted civilians to be protected as much as possible. The Tigers wanted the SLMM to be there, they wanted the channel with the government. So I told Oslo that while Norway has no real role now, we will [try to] keep channels of communication open. We wanted to avoid a major clash between the civilian populations. At that point more killings occurred outside the battlefield than on it. The situation between the Tamil and Sinhalese populations was tense. By having someone in the field to calm things down, we thought the negative effects [of the conflict] on civilians could be reduced.

EELAM WAR IV: THE DENOUEMENT

Murali Reddy

The Rajapaksas represent the majority Sinhala mindset. Whether they took this route out of total conviction or simply as an electoral strategy is hard to say. I think there's a mix. Mahinda pretty much spelt out his formula, his solution for the whole 'problem'. And of course, the definition of the 'problem' was different from both sides. He had defined it, advocated it in such black and white terms that from his perspective it had to be a military solution. There was zero thought or space given to a simultaneous political process like engaging the stakeholders, or trying to promote a sense that there is a link between the two processes [military and political]. That was entirely missing.

Gotabhaya invited foreign journalists to come and talk to him in 2007. It was a pretty heated discussion. He was brazen. The man had arrived with a clearly thought-out plan. When I interacted with Mahinda in [early] 2007, the conflict in the East was tilting decisively in the government's favour, and he went to the extent of saying, 'Let them keep the North, we are content with the East'. Of course I couldn't write this at the time, because this was the president talking on an informal, off-the-record basis. If I had reported it, next time we met he would not have said a word. So in mid-2007, the president himself did not anticipate that they would go anywhere into the North.

New proposals

In early May 2007 the ruling SLFP finally unveiled its 'devolution package'.[16] The main point of contention was the unit of devolved power it proposed. Whereas most proposals, both recent and old, envisaged the provinces as the unit of devolution, the SLFP instead wanted devolution to the local district level. This idea met with instant criticism, from all sides. While the JVP denounced it as contrary to the SLFP's unitary, anti-federalist platform at the 2005 presidential elections, non-LTTE Tamils dismissed it on the grounds that district-level autonomy had been tried twice previously, and proved to be unsatisfactory. Others maintained that district as opposed to provincial devolution was mainly a scheme to ensure that Colombo remained the centre of power. All in all, as one analysis suggested, the key problem was that even if—as minister and peace negotiator Nimal De Silva reportedly emphasised—the proposal was not necessarily the government's last word on the subject, it nonetheless had 'little in common with the other [proposals on the table].'[17]

Paramilitaries: splits and official uses

In mid-May 2007, evidence began to emerge of serious dissension within the ranks of the Tamil People's Liberation Tigers (TMVP),[18] as the Karuna

Group now designated themselves. The cause was ostensibly an argument between Karuna and his deputy Pillayan over the group's finances, but other factors were at play, including rivalry over the leadership and opposition to Karuna's reported efforts to transform a ruthless paramilitary formation into a new political force.[19] In this context, one analyst provided a candid assessment of the current role and function of government-supported Tamil paramilitary groups.

Paramilitary formations such as the Karuna group and Devanda's Eelam People's Democratic Party (EPDP) had, it was argued in a US Embassy Cable at the time, helped the government to fight the LTTE, kidnap suspected Tiger collaborators and frighten critics into silence, while giving the government a measure of 'deniability'. There were confidential reports that some [Army] commanders in Jaffna wanted to clamp down on paramilitaries but had orders from Gotabhaya not to interfere with them, on the grounds that they were doing 'work' that the military could not do, owing to international scrutiny.

The government had a history of funding paramilitary groups. [A well-informed source] pointed out that under President Kumaratunga it had begun the practice of paying paramilitaries to refrain from engaging in criminal pursuits. However, the current cash-strapped government had ended this arrangement. Instead, Gotabhaya authorised the EPDP and Karuna Group to collect money from Tamil businessmen. This might have accounted for the sharp rise in lawlessness, especially extortion and kidnapping, that many had documented in Vavuniya and Colombo.

[A Tamil MP] had confided that even MPs feared that the government would use Karuna to assassinate them. A number of other MPs, Muslims as well as Tamils, had privately admitted that they feared for their lives. [The Tamil MP] said he believed Karuna set up the assassination of MP J. Pararajasingham on Christmas Day [in] 2005 with the help of EPDP leader Devananda. He was also positive that Karuna cadres were employed in the killing in Colombo of Tamil MP N. Raviraj on 10 November 2006.[20]

Ultimately, the government's objective was to turn Karuna and Devananda into pro-government political leaders in the East and North. The hope was that this would ensure long-term control over these areas, even if some form of devolution were instituted.

Solheim and Rajapaksa

In mid-June Erik Solheim, accompanied by Jon Hanssen-Bauer, met President Rajapaksa in Geneva—their first direct contact for over a year.

The main items on the Norwegian agenda were straightforward: what were the government's intentions with respect to the LTTE, and what was their expectation of Norway as a facilitator? Rajapaksa's reply carried a familiar mix of threat and promise.

On the one hand, the military campaign would continue: the only thing that could halt it, Rajapaksa stated, would be if Prabhakaran publicly pledged to cease violence and enter into negotiations. On the other, the president was quoted as saying that he '[did] not want to pursue a military solution. I want to talk with the LTTE without any pre-conditions.' Rajapaksa urged Norway to continue with its efforts to bring the LTTE to the negotiation table. But at the same time he pronounced himself 'not in favour' of a follow-up visit to Sri Lanka by the Norwegian Special Envoy, suggesting instead that contact with the LTTE leadership be established from Oslo.[21]

A number of analysts ascribed Rajapaksa's opposition to a Norwegian visit to the fact that the battlefront was gradually shifting towards the North. A visit to Kilinochchi by Hanssen-Bauer at this point would probably have necessitated a temporary halt to military operations in the area—something to which both military commanders and seemingly the president himself were opposed, even if this might have revived prospects for talks. Reviewing the Solheim-Rajapaksa meeting, one analyst suggested that Norway was now left with what he termed 'remote control diplomacy'.[22]

Reporting to the Co-Chairs meeting held ten days later in Oslo, Solheim emphasised that the Norwegian facilitators were dealing with 'two entities not interested in diplomatic niceties'. Describing Rajapaksa as a man 'focused on his Sinhalese electorate', Solheim said he sensed that the president had 'no plan or strategy to solve the Tamil issue', while on the LTTE side, he argued, Prabhakaran was now fully preoccupied with 'waging war'.

While communication with the government side remained more or less open, it had become more difficult for Norway to assess the Tigers' position, Solheim noted, owing to the combination of its lack of regular contact with the leadership inside the country and the absence of a senior Tiger leader outside the country able to fill Balasingham's shoes. Accordingly, Solheim emphasised that a high priority was to keep lines of communication with the Tigers open, particularly through renewed access to Kilinochchi.[23]

The All-Party Representative Committee (APRC)

The APRC was set up by President Rajapaksa in 2006 as a mechanism for the development of proposals for a political solution to the conflict endorsed by all parties. The UNP and JVP both withdrew at an early stage, but in December 2006 an expert panel produced a majority report (so-called because four of the panel's fifteen members rejected it) that proposed 'maximum possible devolution', with the province as the unit of devolved power. Seemingly careful to keep its distance from the report's conclusions, after months of speculation the government finally presented the ruling SLFP's own 'devolution package' to the APRC in May 2007—to near universal criticism.

True to the expectations of many, for the rest of 2007 the APRC process trundled forward slowly. By December, the government were still saying that a final proposal would be tabled shortly, a situation that led one analyst to remark that 'far from its original goal of forging a consensus for a solution to the ethnic divide, the biggest challenge before the APRC currently is to stay afloat as a credible entity'.[24] In this context, the conclusions of an International Crisis Group (ICG) report published in late 2007 are apposite: 'The failure of the [SLFP-UNP] MoU and the president's lack of enthusiasm for the APRC suggest the government is not serious about a political solution. Instead of working for a compromise the UNP could endorse, it has coerced most of the political establishment to support its military strategy, which has been accompanied by serious human rights abuses. Yet that strategy, especially if it remains unattached to serious political proposals, is unlikely to succeed.'[25]

Two weeks after the Co-Chairs meeting, Brattskar was able to travel to Kilinochchi for discussions with Tamilselvan, their first encounter since March, most probably due to the government's assessment of the—from their perspective—improved security situation resulting from their strengthening military hold over the East.[26] Briefing Co-Chairs Ambassadors afterwards, Brattskar described the mood on the LTTE side as 'serious, sombre and determined'. After expressing his belief that Rajapaksa was using the APRC process simply as a vehicle to 'buy time', Tamilselvan had reportedly criticised the international community for not pressing the government over adherence to the 2002 Ceasefire Agreement.

'It is difficult to imagine the government and LTTE resuming negotiations any time soon', the US Embassy concluded. 'If the prospect of a political settlement emerges from the APRC process, it will be despite the LTTE, which almost surely will reject any proposal.'[27]

New thoughts on peace strategy from the US Embassy Colombo

To counter southern scepticism that the LTTE will string out negotiations to give itself time to rearm, the Co-Chairs should give thought to how the negotiating process itself can be invigorated and expedited. One model is to encourage the parties to engage continuously ... such as was done in the Northern Ireland process. The Co-Chairs also should consider whether Norway, or possibly some other mediator, should go beyond the current Norwegian facilitation role and take on a more direct mediation that could accelerate the overall process.[28]

'Clearing' the East

In July the focus shifted sharply towards the military campaign in the East. On 11 July the government announced that the region had been 'liberated' from the LTTE. The final campaign had focused around the last remaining Tiger position in Thoppigala, a remote forested area northeast of Batticaloa that had been transformed during Karuna's time as Eastern Commander into an LTTE stronghold that nobody—the Indian peacekeeping force of the late 1980s included—had hitherto been able or willing to wrest from them.[29] The region's highest point, a rocky outcrop known as 'Baron's Cap' since the British colonial era, was the scene of victory celebrations that were duly splashed across the front pages of southern newspapers.

The president soon announced that 19 July would be a national day of celebration for what was officially dubbed the *Neganahira Navodaya*—'New Dawn in the East'. While few denied that the capture of Thoppigala constituted a major success, opinion was more divided over its broader strategic implications. It was clear, for example, that the majority of LTTE cadres had withdrawn from the area sometime before the assault, most reportedly heading for the North to reinforce Tiger encampments in the Vanni. Moreover, it appeared that LTTE troops had taken most of their military hardware with them, perhaps in preparation for a return to the guerrilla tactics that had served the Tigers well in their earlier days.[30]

The assassination of a senior government administrator in Trincomalee five days after Rajapaksa's declaration of victory in the East served as a forceful reminder that the Tigers had far from disappeared from the region.[31] Nonetheless, the officially orchestrated celebrations went ahead. For outside observers, perhaps the most notable feature of the president's speech was his dismissal of the 2002 Ceasefire Agreement. 'There is no country other than Sri Lanka where the criminal act of conceding a legal act of control to terrorists has been implemented through an agreement', he maintained. 'Today the demonic forces of terror who for several decades robbed the freedom of the Sinhala, Tamil and Muslim people ... in the fertile lands of the East ... have been completely driven away.'[32]

Tamilselvan

As far as the LTTE is concerned, we were never defeated. We adopted military strategies to suit the place, the environment and the time ... No people will accept the occupation of their land by a foreign force ... Very soon the Sinhala forces will understand the trap they have set themselves.[33]

The UN in Sri Lanka

In the aftermath of the Sri Lankan military's victory in the East, relations between the government and UN bodies, hitherto characterised by a stance of reluctant mutual accommodation, took a significant blow. An early August visit by Under Secretary-General for Humanitarian Affairs John Holmes—Jan Egeland's successor—sparked a bitter public exchange. Making the first high-level UN visit to the country in over a year, Holmes was given full access to government officials, but his team were prevented from meeting NGO representatives and a request for permission to visit Kilinochchi was summarily turned down. In an interview with Reuters, released after his departure, Holmes called on the government in Colombo to consider setting up an international human rights monitoring mission, and described Sri Lanka as one of the 'most dangerous places in the world' for humanitarian workers.

The comment caused uproar. Prime Minister Wickremanayake expressed his 'utter rejection' of what he called Holmes' 'uncivilised' assertion regarding the lack of safety for humanitarian workers.[34] Rising to the realms of fantasy, Chief Government Whip Jeyaraj Fernandopulle described Holmes as a 'terrorist' intent on harming the country's international reputation, who had most probably been bribed by the LTTE.[35]

The government soon had another major military success: at a specially-convened press conference on 12 September, Navy Commander Wasantha Karannagoda announced that three large LTTE weapons supply ships had been sunk over the previous forty-eight hours. In the process, the Navy claimed to have destroyed three light aircraft, a bulletproof vehicle—purportedly for Prabhakaran's personal use—and a large quantity of weapons and ammunition.[36] And yet, two months after the victory in the East, it was clear that the 'stabilisation' process would prove rather more challenging than the government had anticipated. In an exchange with US Ambassador Robert Blake, Basil Rajapaksa—who was responsible for co-ordinating the reconstruction and stabilisation programme in the East—conceded that Karuna's TMVP forces were undermining government credibility by continuing to rob and harass the local civilian population, but said that he was stepping up the appointment of civilian-military liaison officers in the area. After comparing notes with a 'respected Sri Lankan NGO official' who had recently attended an official presentation of the government's plans for developing the East, Blake concluded that Rajapaksa had 'good intentions, but neither he or any of his assistants are experienced in development work, and have not hired people that may be able to help'.[37]

In mid-October, political attention shifted to the five-day visit by UN High Commissioner for Human Rights Louise Arbour. From the outset, the government appeared to be doing its best to stir controversy. First, Arbour's request to visit Kilinochchi was flatly turned down on the grounds of the potential propagandistic uses of such a visit by the Tigers, along with unspecified 'security concerns'.[38] Next, Colombo made clear its firm rejection of proposals, favoured by the UN and others, to establish an international monitoring presence in Sri Lanka, which arose in response to the mounting evidence of disappearances and other human rights abuses across the country. The stark dichotomy between the two sides' positions was made painfully apparent at the press conference held at the end of the visit. While Arbour underlined her belief that relations between the government and her office needed to move beyond technical co-operation to a direct field presence,[39] Human Rights Minister Mahinda Samarasinghe reiterated that the government was 'not willing in any way [to accept] a UN presence in Sri Lanka for monitoring purposes'.[40]

A week later, a well-organised LTTE attack, spearheaded by the nascent Air Tigers, hit the Air Force base at Anuradhapura. All the indications were that the damage inflicted by the attack was considerably higher than suggested in official statements. According to one estimate, for example, fourteen military helicopters (75 per cent of the SLAF airborne surveillance capacity) were destroyed by the LTTE ground forces that occupied the base following the air raid. Another estimate, from Iqbal Athas, maintains that twenty-four of the twenty-seven craft in the base were either damaged or destroyed.[41] More important that any destruction, however, was the signal it sent: despite recent government victories in the East, the Tigers were far from finished. With that said, the Anuradhpura attack was, in the words of one commentator, 'arguably the last spectacular military feat in the history of the LTTE'.[42]

Tamilselvan killed

Ten days later it was the government that scored a direct hit. In the early morning of 2 November, SLAF bombers targeted a LTTE bunker situated on the outskirts of Kilinochchi. Reportedly, a single US-built MK-84 'Hammer' bomb completely obliterated the bunker, killing six of its seven sleeping occupants. As the LTTE announced later that morning, one of those killed was S. P. Tamilselvan.[43] Whether the government had intended to kill Tamilselvan was hotly debated. The view favoured by many in the international community was that security forces had received information that a senior LTTE member was at the location, and had accordingly decided to bomb it. What they had not known was that the person in question was Tamilselvan.[44]

The LTTE were quick to announce Tamilselvan's successor: the new political commissar was Nadesan, previously the Tigers' police chief. A number of commentators noted that Nadesan, whose wife was Sinhalese, spoke Tamil, English and Sinhala and had participated in the two rounds of peace talks held in Geneva in 2006. However, international opinion regarding his suitability for the job was divided. At a meeting of the Co-Chairs Ambassadors held in Colombo on 6 November, for example, the Japanese and EU representatives reportedly concurred that selection of the relatively inexperienced Nadesan was a signal from Prabhakaran that he wanted to 'draw back from the international community'. By contrast, a senior Norwegian Embassy official who knew Nadesan well offered a more upbeat assessment, emphasising the Tiger police chief's linguistic skills, intellectual capacity and 'ideological flexibility'.[45]

Nicholas Burns on the US position

The government's claim to defend their actions in the name of the 'War on Terror' increasingly became a contradictory claim for us. We did not support the Tigers, but we certainly felt that the Tamil population in the North deserved protection. I met with President Rajapaksa and raised our strong concern over human rights issues in 2006. Then I met him again in the fall of 2007 at the UN and raised the same issue again very strongly: our sense [was] that he was heading in the wrong direction, that the government was not overseeing the military carefully enough, that the military was using force carelessly, and that innocent people had died.

I also met Sarath Fonseka in Washington. I told him that we would be curtailing some of our military assistance because we could not be party to what they were doing, and wanted to protest it. So our relationship turned in a very difficult direction in 2006 and 2007 over this issue. Overall, my reading was that the civil war was coming to a close, but in a disastrous way for the people of the North. We were very concerned about the excessive and unchecked use of force. Our relationship with the government really frayed and we separated from them on this issue.[46]

Within Sri Lanka, reactions to Tamilselvan's death were predictably diverse. At the Sinhala nationalist end of the spectrum, the JHU described his death as having been 'in accordance with the laws of natural justice', while the JVP called it a 'victory for the nation'. On the other hand, the UNP surprised many by failing to condemn Tamilselvan's killing,[47] and during the course of a parliamentary debate the following day SLMC leader Rauff Hakeem offered a message of condolence to the LTTE. For Tamils, the Ceylon Worker's Congress' (CWC) R. Yogaran, a government deputy minister, probably spoke for many when he said: 'All the Tamil people feel sympathy. The Sinhalese people seem to be happy about it. We have sympathy because we consider him a political leader of the Tamil people, and he has been an activist of the peace process.'[48]

Focusing more on the consequences of Tamilselvan's death, the US Embassy's assessment was that it made it 'likely' that 'LTTE hardliners will become even more dominant'.[49]

At another meeting of the Co-Chairs Ambassadors, held the previous day to Tamilselvan's killing, Tomas Stangeland sounded an ominous note of warning regarding the SLMM. Recognising that the monitors had long since abandoned counting or ruling on CFA violations and were accordingly struggling to find a new niche, Stangeland emphasised the Norwegians' desire to retain the mission as a conflict resolution mechanism 'should the opportunity arise'. Overall, two things stand out from the record of this and other meetings between international actors in Sri Lanka: a sense that moderate voices were becoming increasingly marginalised as military action intensified; and as a consequence, the seemingly diminishing influence of the established peace facilitator, Norway, in favour of both 'hard' and collective power—the USA and the Co-Chairs respectively.[50]

Perspectives on the SLMM

Lars Johan Sølvberg

The last time the Norwegian Special Envoy was in Sri Lanka was in December 2006, so all through 2007 I was almost the only official third-party person going up to Kilinochchi. At this stage it was business as usual: when we reported back to [both] parties on violations of the agreement it wasn't making very much of an impression. At a certain stage in 2007 we decided to stop the whole thing of providing accounts of breaches of the CFA, because the magnitude of the violations was almost impossible to keep track of.

Bernard Goonetilleke

The SLMM was like giving a chunk of meat to a toothless person. There was no way they could get a grip because it [had] a limited mandate, a difficult situation. When a violation took place, all they could do was to show a red flag, but the player could not be sent off the field.

Paikiasothy Saravanamuttu

We had a great [many] dealings with SLMM. In terms of performance, some individuals were good, others did not quite understand the politics of this country and how to communicate and navigate those waters. There was insufficient popular understanding of what the SLMM was supposed to do. Most people in the South in particular ran away with the impression that [the] SLMM was pro-LTTE.

Vidar Helgesen

The role and mandate of the monitoring mission came back to haunt us. What we did was right in that we didn't want it to be an enforcement mission: that in any case wouldn't have been possible ... We tried to communicate that the SLMM would never be in charge of ensuring respect for the ceasefire agreement. But over time it was impossible to stop the impression that this was a big part of the failure of the Ceasefire Agreement. If you look at the mission's size, its unarmed nature and limited mandate, there was no way it could have saved the CFA. In principle, placing responsibilities with the parties was very important. The SLMM took on more of a preventive role, which was useful but only when there were low-intensity issues and conflicts. And the preventive role was unavoidable. I call it constructive mission creep. If you can defuse tension by sending a car to the venue, then fine.

Karuna's arrest

At the beginning of November, news of a completely unexpected development arrived from the UK: the arrest of Karuna at a house on the outskirts
of London. The fact that the former LTTE Eastern Commander was in the
UK was news enough in itself, but even more extraordinary were indications that Karuna had entered the country under a false name and on a
false diplomatic passport that had been secured for him, along with a UK
visa, by 'high-level' manoeuvrings in Colombo.

The reason for Karuna's departure from Sri Lanka was thought to be the
friction between himself and his former deputy Pillaiyan, now leader of
the TMVP. The government, it appeared, had chosen Pillaiyan as its proxy
leader in the East and wanted Karuna out of the way, at least for a while.
As one analyst pointed out, the revelation of Colombo's involvement
in Karuna's illegal entry to the UK cleared up any lingering doubts
regarding the relationship between government security forces and the
Karuna group.[51]

As November drew to a close, all ears were directed towards Prabhakaran's Heroes Day speech, broadcast as usual on 27 November, the LTTE
leader's birthday. On this occasion, however, the speech nearly didn't make
it onto the airwaves. Ninety minutes before the scheduled broadcast, an
SLAF bombing raid flattened the 'Voice of Tigers' building in Kilinochchi—
further proof that President Rajapaksa was, as one analyst put it, 'determined to take the fight right into the heartland of the LTTE'.[52] Thanks to a
backup transmitter, the speech went out as planned, and for anyone outside
the community of diehard Tiger supporters it did not make for appetising
listening. Beyond the customary broadsides against Sinhala chauvinism
and racism, the LTTE leader's most strident criticisms were reserved for
the international community, in particular what he termed its military,
economic, political and moral support for the Sri Lankan government. Most
pointedly of all, Prabhakaran castigated all the key actors—Norway, the
SLMM, the Co-Chairs and India—for their failure to secure a negotiated
end to the conflict. With respect to the Co-Chairs, Prabhakaran asked
scathingly: 'What exactly is [the] purpose of their meeting from time to
time in different places? Is it their intent to assist [the] Sinhala regime to
wipe out Tamils?'[53] Taken as a whole, the speech was widely interpreted as
indicative of the siege mentality that was increasingly taking hold among
the LTTE leadership.

In the final month of 2007 fighting between the two sides continued, with
clashes focused around the northwest coastal district of Mannar. The clear-

est indication that war, not negotiations, was the government's strategy for dealing with the LTTE was provided in an interview given by Gotabhaya Rajapaksa on 29 December. After describing the CFA as having 'become a joke', he went on to suggest that 'the most sensible thing' would be simply to declare that it had now come to an end. For good measure, he added that it was also high time that the LTTE were formally banned.[54]

In even starker terms, the following day army chief Sarath Fonseka told the media that over the next six months the SLAF planned to 'attack all LTTE bases. Our daily target is to kill at least ten terrorists'. He went on: 'We have weakened the LTTE by 50 per cent or more and we are confident that we can go the extra mile in the coming year'.[55]

Tore Hattrem, new ambassador

Following Hans Brattskar, I became Norwegian ambassador in late summer 2007. Trying to engage with the president took some time: but after a while I didn't have any problem with accessing all sections of Sinhalese society. ... When I arrived in Sri Lanka there was a certain suspicion of Norway and our actions. I tried to widen the Embassy's network, talk to Sinhalese leaders, military leaders, civil society, explain where we were coming from. I tried to re-balance an incorrect impression that we were pro-Tamil; we were just pro-peace, pro-negotiations. Additionally, at this stage there were no negotiations and there was military success, so official tension vis-à-vis Norway lowered.

Norwegian perspectives on the military build-up

Erik Solheim

The government purchased military hardware in large quantities [in 2007]. They were really building up their capabilities, and we were expecting that they would move away from trench warfare. The government's successful reduction of the LTTE's presence in the South was a factor: overall, they significantly reduced the LTTE network's impact there. Even so, we expected that the Tigers would come out with surprise retaliation moves in the South. Army kidnapping of a large number of people was also an important factor. Even if the LTTE had been able to advance militarily, at no point did the government reject the option of talks. That was always kept open.

Even though we were well aware that the Sri Lanka Army was on a shopping spree in 2007—Milinda [Moragoda] went to Iran during that period, for example—we didn't see any possibility that these moves would shift the strategic balance so completely. How Prabhakaran could be so foolish is also hard to understand. The government destroyed the LTTE apparatus in the South, built a global alliance for weapons supplies, and were also able to blank out all negative news such as the extent of army losses.

Hilde Haraldstad

There were a lot of rumours about the military build up. In late 2007 the press officer at the Embassy went to a local press conference in Colombo at which Fonseka and Gotabhaya said 'we will win against the LTTE within two to three years'. I think that it was one of the first times they said so explicitly that they were prepared for war—and a fully-fledged one.[56] There was this period of 'no peace no war'—but gradually it became clear that a war would take place. The last [Norwegian] visit to LTTE-controlled areas was in mid 2007. Hans [Brattskar] went there. The earlier visit was in September 2006—we went there and met with Tamilselvan and his team. It become more and more difficult to get the government's support to go there, and in mid 2007 we didn't get permission to travel to Kilinochchi any more. We kept in contact with Pulidevan and the peace secretariat via phone and email. There were several LTTE attacks in 2007. As the war escalated the LTTE continued to express an optimism about their own military capacity. They seemed not to understand the direction in which it was all going. Having said that, the LTTE also wanted a ceasefire: for example, they did ask for or declare that unilaterally for the SARC summit in 2008.

Talking to the LTTE: a government perspective and a Norwegian response

Palitha Kohona

I would constantly hear statements from the Norwegians that the LTTE would negotiate only when they felt they were equal in strength to the Sri Lankan government. Having come from the UN where sovereignty is sacrosanct, I thought this was an outrageous position to take. Here you had a terrorist organisation that was proscribed in almost every single democracy in the world, and then you have the Sri Lankan government—a sovereign state—and the Norwegians telling us how you have to let the LTTE become a little stronger before they will negotiate with you. You were literally creating a state from a terrorist group so that peace could be created between the two sides.

I knew the Norwegians were providing funding for training to the LTTE police force, for their TV and radio stations. They were the main source of funding for the LTTE peace secretariat, which was playing a major role in international propaganda. The Sri Lankan government may have conceded all this in 2002, but to me, coming from the outside, I found this a little more than curious. I did raise it with Hanssen-Bauer. He would listen, go away and two weeks later he would call and say: the problem is, they feel they are still not your equals.

Jon Hanssen-Bauer

I do not remember such conversations, but certainly there is a relationship between military strength and willingness to talk. The LTTE was reluctant to talk from a relatively weaker position. But from there to argue that the government should first strengthen the LTTE to prepare for talks—that was not my way at all. I may well have explained why the LTTE was not ready for talks: Kohona often asked us to 'deliver' the LTTE at the table, but I never took this as a serious attempt at starting talks.

It is correct that we continued to finance the LTTE peace secretariat, but with the understanding of both the Sri Lankan government in general and Kohona in particular. We were careful not to finance the LTTE as such. Increasingly, there was an acute humanitarian crisis to deal with for the Tamil population and the displaced. We were very worried by the way the Tamil population was treated: they suffered tremendously. Gradually, Norwegian humanitarian assistance was stepped up.

Ceasefire terminated

On the morning of New Year's Day, opposition UNP MP T. Maheswaran was gunned down while attending prayers with his family at a Hindu temple. The latest in a line of assassinated senior Tamil MPs, Maheswaran was a former government minister who in recent years had made a small fortune through business dealings, some of questionable legality, centred on the import and sale of goods in the Jaffna peninsula, an area starved of many essential supplies since the A9 road was closed in August 2006.

A widely quoted *TamilNet* report argued that Douglas Devananda's EPDP was behind the killing. Devananda had decided to silence Maheswaran, it suggested, because on TV the previous evening Maheswaran had announced that he would shortly be revealing details of how the 'terror campaign' underway on the Jaffna peninsula was being directed by the government using the EPDP as its executor.[57]

The next day the government announced that, following a majority Cabinet vote, it was withdrawing from the 2002 Ceasefire Agreement, a document which Foreign Minister Rohitha Bogollagama contended had been formulated 'without proper consultation' with key stakeholders, and had alienated 'Tamil democratic forces'.[58] For all Bogollagama's assurances that the CFA's abrogation would in no way impede the pursuit of a negotiated political settlement—a process in which Norway would also continue to play the role of facilitator, he insisted—few non-partisan observers were convinced.

The UNP argued that the government had chosen to annul the CFA chiefly as an expedient to secure support from the fiercely nationalist JVP and JHU for a budget that it had, after a good deal of controversy, recently managed to guide through parliament.[59] The UNP also offered a spirited defence of the agreement, pointing out that it had been initiated at a 'critical time' when the country was suffering from 'severe military setbacks' and the economy was 'in a shambles'.[60] The CFA's main objectives had, it argued, been both to 'find a negotiated settlement to the conflict' and to 'safeguard the territorial integrity of the country'. A joint statement issued shortly afterwards by Nordic foreign ministers reinforced this positive evaluation of the CFA's impact, noting in particular that during its first three years, casualties had 'dropped to almost zero'.[61] Erik Solheim issued a stark warning of the consequences of the decision to tear up the CFA: 'I am deeply concerned that the violence and hostilities will now escalate even further.'[62]

As anticipated, the LTTE's official reaction, issued a week later in connection with a meeting between Nadesan and departing SLMM Head Lars Johan Sølvberg, expressed 'shock' and 'disappointment' over Colombo's 'unilateral abrogation' of the CFA. In an illustration of the Tigers' propensity for sticking to positions irrespective of real-world developments, the statement also called for 'full implementation' of all CFA provisions and the continuation of Norway's role as official peace facilitator.[63]

A Norwegian perspective on CFA termination

Jon Hanssen-Bauer

> We reduced the size of the SLMM after the EU ban in 2006: it was reshaped. In autumn 2006 we appointed a new head of mission and gave him orders to lower [his] media profile and get out of the field. The Tamils were very upset by this. We reduced the monitoring gradually in 2007 owing to the escalating fighting. The parties had no use for the SLMM by this point. Neither of them tried to hide the fact that they had gone to war, and neither did we.
>
> After the ceasefire was abrogated, my time was spent cleaning up: taking care of employees, sorting out what to do with the archives. This should

not be seen as a purely bureaucratic issue either. There was an enormous security risk involved, as the archives contained interviews with people. The main thing was to protect people on the files, protect their identity. We had to negotiate with the government over this, and it took a couple of months to get everything out.

Tore Hattrem

There had been numerous violations of the ceasefire and the LTTE was responsible for the large majority of them. Given the fact that there was an on-going war, I guess it was just a question of time before one or the other party decided to formally abrogate the ceasefire ... It wasn't a withdrawal of Norway as the formal peace mediator: we continued our dialogue.

On 5 January, an Army LRRP squad assassinated LTTE military intelligence head Colonel Charles in a claymore mine attack on his vehicle as it was travelling on the Mannar–Pooneryn road. Inducted as a child soldier, Charles had become a protégé of Tiger intelligence chief Pottu Amman and over the years was reputed to have masterminded a string of major attacks in the South, notably the July 2001 assault on Katunayake airport. He was also credited with having helped to establish a clandestine LTTE presence in Colombo in the early 1990s.[64]

Three days later, the Tigers assassinated government minister D.M. Dissanayake in a claymore attack as his car was on its way from Colombo to the airport. Intelligence intercepts suggested the assailants were not aware of the specific identity of their target—it sufficed that he was in an official motorcade. Less likely to have been circulated widely at the time was an Indian diplomat's reported view that the murdered Minister was a 'known thug' who was widely considered to be highly corrupt, with a charge sheet of allegations against him that included human trafficking, widespread assault against supporters of his political opponents in Puttalam and the murder of his main opponent in the 2004 parliamentary elections.[65]

Jayaveda Uyangoda

What is scary in [the] post-CFA scenario is that both adversaries are preparing for what each of them may see in its own terms as the 'final' war ... Alarmingly, [it] is not likely to generate much international attention unless it produces a massive humanitarian emergency. At a time when the world is pretty much preoccupied with West Asia and Africa,

> Sri Lanka's conflicting parties will continue to enjoy a great deal of autonomy from international pressure to take their war forward. There are no regional actors seriously committed to preventing [the country] from moving fast on the path to the abyss.[66]

Some days later, following intense consultations between its members, the Co-Chairs issued a statement expressing their 'strong concerns' over the government's decision to terminate the CFA and the human rights situation in the country. They also called on Colombo to reopen access to the LTTE leadership in Kilinochchi for the Norwegian facilitators and Co-Chairs representatives.[67] But those present concurred that all the indications were that the government would not be looking to reopen negotiations with the LTTE until they had 'pushed a military solution as far as possible'. At the same time, Colombo had a strong interest, it was suggested, in keeping the Norwegian facilitators and Co-Chairs in place so that it can 'tell the international community that it remains committed to a negotiated settlement'. It was thus critical, US Ambassador Robert Blake argued, that the Co-Chairs should not allow themselves to become 'a smokescreen for the government's military agenda'.[68]

Views on the conclusion of the SLMM operation

Lars Johan Sølvberg

> The final report from the operation is this. The SLMM is absolutely convinced that this complex conflict cannot be solved by military means ... Future heroes in Sri Lanka will be those who recognise the complexity of the situation, and prove able to manage this complexity in a way that reduces rather than increases human pain, fear and hopelessness—those capable of respecting people with different perceptions and bringing them together. The SLMM will close its operation at 1900hrs today. To the people of Sri Lanka; thank you and farewell.[69]

Jayaveda Uyangoda

> The SLMM's role in defusing tension and resolving and managing conflicts between the government and the LTTE during these years is hardly recognised in Sri Lanka. The SLMM got a rough deal from the LTTE as well as its counterparts in the Sinhalese polity.[70]

Towards the end of January, the APRC submitted its long-awaited devolution proposal to President Rajapaksa. In formulating it, the committee dutifully followed a presidential instruction to base it on 'full implementation' of the 13th Constitutional Amendment and its devolutionary provisions, in turn derived from the 1987 Indo-Lanka accord that led to the setting up of provincial councils. Government interference in the drafting process did not stop there, however. A senior Tamil committee member confided to local diplomats that the final document had been 'virtually dictated by a few close Presidential advisers', with few inputs allowed from the APRC members themselves.

Of the specifics that survived the presidential diktat, the most significant were a proposal, now that conditions there were considered 'conducive', to hold immediate elections for the Eastern Provincial Council, and a recommendation to set up an Interim Council for the Northern Province, much of which remained under LTTE control. One analyst characterised the document as 'woefully inadequate', while the TNA parliamentary caucus described it simply as a 'fraud'.[71]

In the meantime, reports from the North—which, as defence correspondent Iqbal Athas bemoaned, were subject to increasingly heavy-handed military censorship—indicated that government forces were steadily advancing in the Mannar area. The focus of LTTE defensive manoeuvres was on securing its remaining naval bases on the northwest coast, the existence of which was vital to maintaining the Tigers' seaborne supply lines from neighbouring Tamil Nadu.[72]

Erik Solheim

If we had really banged the alarm bells during 2007–8, the only interpretation would have been that we were out to try and save the LTTE in a war that most people saw as being of their own making. We knew that there was no one who was going to come in and stop the war ... No one apart from the Indians had Sri Lanka near the top of their agenda. There was sympathy for the Tamil cause, though not for the LTTE.

Violence intensifies

Reports from the UK indicated that Karuna had been sentenced to nine months in prison for 'identity fraud'—the diplomatic passport he had used to enter the country having been issued under a false name. Testifying in court, Karuna stated that the passport had been issued after he had made a direct request to Defence Secretary Gotabhaya Rajapaksa. At home, at least, Gotabhaya was able to shrug off any political fallout from the revelation that he had personally assisted Karuna in securing fake diplomatic credentials. Internationally, however, Gotabhaya's perfunctory dismissals of the whole affair were not so well received.[73] Furthermore, there was strong pressure on the British authorities to try Karuna for alleged war crimes, although human rights groups acknowledged the difficulties of persuading witnesses to come forward to testify against him.[74]

February saw a marked increase in the level of violence. LTTE bomb attacks on mostly civilian targets—including several suicide bombings—resulted in substantial casualties, while the death-toll in the Mannar area was increasing daily. Informed sources indicated that the Sri Lanka Army was losing around twenty-five men each day, chiefly the result of LTTE booby traps, landmines and mortar fire rather than direct combat, of which there appears to have been little at this stage.[75]

Despite upbeat official military news bulletins, all indications were that the government advance in the North was progressing much slower than anticipated, principally due to a dogged resistance by LTTE forces, whose numbers had been significantly boosted in recent months by a campaign of forced conscription that had reportedly swelled their ranks by 12–15,000 cadres.[76] Indeed, one analyst described government forces as being 'bogged down' in the North, and suggested that their success depended on sustained deployment of 'superior firepower', in particular a combination of incessant airstrikes and artillery bombardments. How long Tiger forces would be able to maintain their resistance in the face of such a sustained assault indeed remained an open question.[77]

Another high-level assassination occurred on 6 March, the victim this time being the senior TNA Jaffna district MP K. Sivanesan, a firm LTTE supporter who was reputedly nominated for his Jaffna seat by former Tiger political chief Tamilselvan.[78] The assassination occurred in the LTTE-controlled territory of the Vanni, but there were strong suspicions that an Army LRRP unit had carried out the attack.

In a sign that international opinion—or at least a section of it—was beginning to lose patience with the government, on the day of Sivanesan's murder the International Independent Group of Eminent Persons (IIGEP) announced that they were quitting. Established in February 2007 by the president to monitor the work of a Commission of Inquiry that had been tasked with investigating alleged incidents of serious human rights abuse since August 2005, the IIGEP now cited the government's 'lack of political will' to conduct serious investigations as the main reason for its resignation.

In a response that spoke volumes about the habitual official attitude to outside criticism, the Attorney General responded with the accusation that the Group had timed its action to coincide with the opening of the annual meetings of the UN Human Rights Council in Geneva and in this way to 'ensure an international condemnation of Sri Lanka'.[79]

The New York Times

> Foreign Secretary Palitha Kohona put it plainly when he said that Sri Lanka's 'traditional donors', namely the United States, Canada and the European Union had 'receded into a very distant corner', to be replaced by countries in the East. He gave three reasons: the new donors are neighbours; they are rich; and they conduct themselves differently. 'Asians don't go around teaching each other how to behave', he said. 'There are ways we deal with each other—perhaps a quiet chat, but not wagging the finger.'[80]

A week later the authorities invited Colombo-based diplomats and journalists for a briefing on the outcome of the elections that had just been concluded in Batticaloa—the first to be held in the East since the government had seized the region. The TMVP's resounding victory, winning control of eight of the nine local bodies, came as little surprise to many observers, as virtually all the other major parties had pulled out, with the UNP and TNA citing the failure to disarm the TMVP and the prevalence of intimidation as the main reasons for their boycott.[81] Foreign Minister Bogollagama nonetheless described the elections as an 'important milestone' in its policy of 'restoring democratic rights to the people in areas that were previously dominated by the LTTE', and in the TMVP's 'transition ... into the democratic political mainstream'.

US Embassy Colombo

> Given the physical violence and intimidation that preceded the [Batticaloa] elections for months, and the resulting climate of fear in which they took place, it would be difficult to assess them as free and fair. [And] the

> danger is that if armed groups gain power through a flawed process and remain armed, the elections will perpetuate an undemocratic system that is at the root of the 25-year conflict.[82]

By early April, reports from the northern battlefields were indicating that government forces had advanced to within two or three kilometres of Madhu church, whose Our Lady of Madhu statue was widely venerated by Tamil Catholics. Under pressure from the LTTE leadership, the local Catholic hierarchy decided to remove the statue, thereby denying government forces the propaganda victory its capture would have entailed—and, as one commentator noted, adding Our Lady to the swelling ranks of the displaced in the region.[83]

Political killings continue

The spate of high-level assassinations continued on 6 April when Tamil government minister Jeyaraj Fernandopulle was killed, and more than ninety others injured, by a suicide bomb detonated as he was flagging the start of a New Year's Day marathon in Gampaha, some 25km northeast of Colombo. A controversial and outspoken anti-LTTE politician, at the time of his death Fernandopulle was preparing the government's campaign for the Eastern provincial council elections scheduled for 10 May.

On 20 April Father Karunaratnam, a well-known human rights activist and long-standing friend of Anton Balasingham who had co-founded the pro-LTTE North East Secretariat on Human Rights (NESOHR), was killed in a claymore mine attack. Reportedly, Father Karunaratnam's espousal of NESOHR's uncritically pro-Tiger stance (the Secretariat only reported on government-perpetrated human rights abuses, opting to gloss over the LTTE's) was leavened by persistent efforts to persuade the leadership to avoid violations, in particular the recruitment of child conscripts, an issue on which he and others enjoyed limited success.[84]

Erik Solheim

> The situation would have been completely different if Balasingham had been there. He would have been focused on how to get out of the mess. Instead, during this period we called Nadesan and Pulidevan, and they told us that everything was fine, there was nothing we needed to do. Bala[singham] was of course important for our communication with the

LTTE, but the main point is that he was a vital moderating factor, bringing some sense and international perspective into the discussion. Once earlier he had said to us, 'Don't forget that Prabhakaran is a warlord. And never underestimate the capacity for violence.' Both warnings proved to be extremely accurate.

Failed offensive

Early on the morning of 23 April government forces unleashed a concerted offensive on and around the forward defence line at Muhamalai and the narrow isthmus linking the Sri Lankan mainland to the Jaffna peninsula.[85] The military was quick to label this a 'defensive' action undertaken in response to an LTTE attack. It did not take defence analysts long, however, to figure out why army officials had advanced this curious-sounding claim. It transpired that as many as 5,000 soldiers, having driven the LTTE back by hundreds of metres, had suddenly been subjected to a surprise onslaught of artillery, mortar and sniper fire.[86] After sustaining heavy losses, army forces retreated in some disarray to their original positions, leaving Tiger cadres to seize a large quantity of weapons and ammunition. It seemed, as one military analyst put it, that the SLA had been guilty of catastrophic 'over confidence'.[87]

Any political advantage the LTTE might have gained from the encounter at Muhamalai, however, was cancelled out when the Tigers detonated a bomb at a bus station in a southern suburb of Colombo a few days later, killing twenty-six and injuring thirty-eight civilians—an act of terrorism that served only to strengthen the hand of those urging a military 'solution' to the conflict. 'Each time the LTTE engages in an act of terrorism, the hardliners get reinvigorated', D.B.S. Jeyaraj argued. 'The underlying justice of the Tamil cause gets undermined. The terrible situation of the Tamil people is overlooked. The Tamil problem is easily distorted into a terrorist problem'.[88]

Eastern Provincial Council elections

In May, official focus moved briefly away from the war in the North to the Eastern Provincial Council (EPC) elections scheduled for 10 May—the first to be held in the region for twenty years. Whether by fair means or foul, the government coalition triumphed by a narrow margin: the UPFA-TMVP ticket won twenty seats on the EPC,[89] the UNP-SLMC fifteen seats, and other parties—the JVP included—one seat each. The UNP rejected the results, citing allegations of ballot box stuffing at nearly 100 voting centres throughout the region.[90] Bolstering the UNP view, moreover, none of the three main civil society groups monitoring the elections described them as 'free and fair'.

But fair or not, the lack of public outcry suggested that, however grudgingly, most of the Eastern province's population appeared to accept the result. Now attention shifted rapidly to the tussle over who would be appointed as the region's Chief Minister. The two main candidates were the TMVP's Pillaiyan and UPFA Muslim leader M. Hisbullah—a choice that encapsulated the divisions between the Tamil and Muslim communities. Reportedly, a decisive factor in the government's decision over whom to nominate for the post was Defence Secretary Gotabhaya's view, expressed at a National Security Council meeting, that the support of Pillaiyan's TMVP cadres was needed to prevent 'the re-infiltration of LTTE operatives in the East', since this would leave the Army 'free to pursue the government's offensive in the North'.[91] Pillaiyan secured the government's support and on 16 May he was sworn in by President Rajapaksa as Eastern Chief Minister.[92]

Two days before the elections, former LTTE leader Karuna Amman was released from prison in the UK, after serving half of his nine-month sentence for entering the country on a false diplomatic passport. Exactly when he would return to Sri Lanka, and whether he would be formally deported, remained unclear. Given the unresolved tensions between the two, however, it seemed certain that TMVP leader Pillaiyan preferred his return to be delayed until after the EPC poll.[93]

The latter half of May saw the Colombo political world exercised by the country's bid for a second term on the UN Human Rights Council, a high-profile body whose critical comments on Sri Lanka's human rights situation in recent years the government hoped to be able to temper by securing renewed membership. In the event its attempt failed, a development widely interpreted as stemming from the international response to continuing serial rights abuses in the country.[94]

Archbishop Desmond Tutu

Government security forces summarily remove their own citizens from their homes and families in the middle of the night, never to be heard from again. Torture and extrajudicial killings are widespread. When the

317

human rights council was established, UN members required that states elected must themselves 'uphold the highest standards' of human rights. On that count, Sri Lanka is clearly disqualified.[95]

On 20 May, Brigadier Balraj, one of the LTTE's most experienced and capable commanders, and one who had played a key role in the Tigers' seizure of Elephant Pass in May 2000, passed away.[96] In the years before, he had been dogged by ill-health and ultimately died not in battle but from a heart attack, aged only 43.[97] It was a loss that the Tigers could ill afford at this critical stage, with government forces advancing inexorably through the Vanni.

Media intimidation

Media reporting of the war, a long-standing point of contention with the government, came to the forefront of attention on 22 May, when Keith Noyahr, associate editor of *The Nation* and the paper's defence analyst, was abducted from outside his house in suburban Colombo and severely beaten by unidentified assailants, who dumped him near his home seven hours later. Speculation was rife that Noyahr had been attacked as a result of a recent article in which he strongly criticised Army Commander Sarath Fonseka[98]—Noyahr's abductors had apparently been keen to find out who his military sources were.[99] Local commentators were quick to point out that, coming only twenty-four hours after the country had been voted off the UN Human Rights Council, the assault offered a graphic demonstration of one of the main reasons for Sri Lanka's exclusion: the escalating suppression of the media.[100]

As if to prove the point, two senior staff at Lake House, the government-owned publishing house, were summoned to a meeting with Gotabhaya Rajapaksa a few days later to be sternly rebuked for taking part in a rally protesting Noyahr's abduction. They were told that as government employees they had no right to participate in protests, and that if they continued with their critical stance 'people who know how to do it will finish you off'.[101]

Gotabhaya Rajapaksa on the Noyahr abduction

There will be no investigation ... Human rights mean nothing. We do not want to be bothered about it while we're fighting a war. Because of the international campaign we can't arrest anyone. But I don't care; I will do what I want.[102]

Sign inside the army media briefings room, spring 2009

> It's the soldier, not the reporter, who has given us the freedom of the press. It's the soldier, not the poet, who has given us freedom of speech.

Two weeks later it was the president's turn to read the riot act to the media. At a 6 June meeting attended by senior editors and publishers, Rajapaksa reportedly informed them that stories critical of the government's military campaign would no longer be tolerated, and that failure to comply with this instruction would lead to the introduction of strict censorship and anti-defamation measures. Commenting on the meeting—on which all present were instructed not to report—one analyst noted: 'The government knows ... that an overt move to legislate press censorship would attract worldwide criticism. The Rajapaksas have therefore reverted to tried-and-tested tactics of "friendly persuasion" to try to hold [the] independent press in check.'[103]

UTHR-J Special Report

Life in Jaffna has become a dizzy mixture of the barbarous, anarchic and grotesque. Killings by state forces have taken a viciously sadistic form ... victims questioned by the army and told that they are cleared ... have soon after been targeted and killed—often before their wives and families—by state killers on a routine shooting safari on motorbikes. In about 75 per cent of cases [of disappearance] nothing more is heard ... we estimate that the government ... are responsible for murdering in cold blood upwards of 700 unarmed civilians in Jaffna during 2006 and 2007.

The absence of political engagement has left the army looking barbaric, ridiculous and stupid, chasing after schoolboys, peeping into school attendance registers, beating up boys, wives and mothers, shooting unarmed women on the street ... Scores of people neither charged with any offence, nor told what they are guilty of, fearing the state's safari killers, voluntarily enter remand prison ... In an ironic reversal of roles, civilians innocent in law seek official protective custody—from official defenders of the law freely indulging in manslaughter.[104]

Indian concerns

Towards the end of June a high-level Indian delegation, headed by Defence Secretary Vijay Singh, made a two-day visit to Colombo. Reports from the talks indicated that the Indians put strong emphasis on the need to pursue a political solution to the conflict, and in particular to table a viable devolution proposal as soon as possible. Another year of bloodshed, they reportedly argued, was neither sustainable nor acceptable. The government's response was that it needed another year to achieve military victory, and that a political solution was impossible as long as Prabhakaran was still alive.[105]

After the now ritual Indian injunction to Colombo to implement the 13th Amendment in full, the Indians then encouraged the government to demonstrate its commitment to devolution by allowing the new Eastern Chief Minister Pillaiyan to exercise his full powers.[106] The Indian Defence Secretary also raised concerns about some of the weapons Colombo had recently received from China and Pakistan, such as anti-tank missiles, which seemed incompatible with the threat posed by the LTTE. It was clear, however, that Gotabhaya was not going to back down on weapons procurements any more than on the pursuit of a military 'solution' to the conflict.[107]

Karuna returns

In early July, Karuna returned to Sri Lanka from the UK after the Crown Prosecution Service announced that it possessed insufficient evidence for him to be charged with gross human rights violations, as urged by a range of human rights groups. Following his return, Karuna indicated that he had declined Pillaiyan's proposal that the TMVP's founder should again take up the movement's leadership and, if desired, take over as Eastern Chief Minister. Instead, he stated that he intended to stand at forthcoming national elections.

The two met in Colombo on 12 July for several hours of talks—a meeting also attended by Gotabhaya, it later turned out. Subsequent media reports indicated that the important issues, both personal and political, had not been resolved.[108] Further evidence of a standoff surfaced two days later, with reports that Karuna had returned to Batticaloa without informing Pillaiyan, and with army tank protection. Karuna had then asked Pillaiyan to come and meet him at the TMVP offices in Batticaloa (Karuna's power base), an invitation that the Chief Minister had declined. From the tone of the comments coming from the Pillaiyan camp, it seemed that the Eastern Chief Minister and his supporters were alarmed by Karuna's reappearance and deeply suspicious of his intentions.[109]

A few days earlier, Rajiva Wijesinha was quoted as suggesting that a new peace initiative was in the pipeline.[110] In particular, the initiative involved telling the LTTE that its disarmament was a precondition of future talks, and insisting that all Tamil political parties, the TMVP included, would need to be represented in any negotiations. Unsurprisingly the Tigers rejected both conditions, with military spokesperson Ilanthirayan emphasising that the Norwegians would need to be allowed to meet the LTTE leadership before they would even consider participating in new talks.[111]

Speaking to US Ambassador Robert Blake, his Norwegian counterpart Tore Hattrem suggested that these media reports were probably a reflection more of Wijesinha's personal views than of any new government policy. Hattrem also noted he was 'not optimistic' that he would be able to meet the LTTE leaders in the foreseeable future: since taking up his post in Colombo more than six months previously, he had not once been given official permission to travel to Kilinochchi.[112]

Fighting escalates

In mid-July, the army announced it had succeeded in capturing Vidattal-thivu, a coastal village northeast of Mannar, whose naval base, along with a number of other bases further north, had helped the Tigers to maintain vital supply lines across the Gulf of Mannar from Tamil Nadu. And while there were reports that after abandoning Vidattalthivu the Tigers had moved northwards to another installation at Nachchikuda, analysts pointed out that this none the less rendered their sea-bound supply lines far more exposed to interdiction by the Sri Lanka Navy.[113]

On 21 July the Tigers announced they would observe a ten-day 'unilateral ceasefire' ahead of the South Asian Association for Regional Cooperation (SAARC) summit due to open on 4 August in Colombo.[114] The government summarily rejected the offer to reciprocate.[115] Opinion may have been divided on the genuineness of the LTTE's proposal, but there were many in Colombo who agreed with the Indian defence analyst who commented that even a ten-day ceasefire would have broken the momentum of the Sri Lankan advance and given 'a vital breathing space for the LTTE forces'.[116]

US Embassy Colombo

> Until recently the government had said that its strategy was to weaken the Tigers first, then force them to the negotiating table. Perhaps due to the military's recent advances, [their] stance on this seems to have tough-ened considerably over the last several months, with all other priorities now taking a back seat to the pursuit of a military victory over the Tigers.

> This emphasis on a military solution also underpins domestic political strategy, which depends on maintaining widespread public perception in the Sinhalese South that the government is on track to win the war. However, [it] appears unable to hear voices calling for a viable power-sharing plan as [a] political counterpart to its military strategy. We and most other observers remain convinced that this would be best way to undermine the Tigers' support both within Sri Lanka and among the Tamil Diaspora.[117]

The following month saw a significant surge in fighting. On 2 August, Vellankulam, the last LTTE-held fortified location in the Mannar district, fell to government forces, ending the SLA campaign to recapture the area. With the fighting rapidly increasing in intensity, international concern was focusing on the humanitarian consequences of the conflict as much as on the troop movements.

At the end of August, UNDP Resident Representative Neil Buhne was allowed by the government to visit the Vanni, where he found the humanitarian situation to be 'worse than expected'. He had, for example, met Tamil families who had already been forced to move as many as twenty times.[118] It was now estimated that there were some 160,000 internally displaced persons (IDPs) in the Vanni, and Buhne conveyed an urgent demand to the LTTE that they allow these people freedom to leave Tiger-controlled areas should they so wish. In response, Nadesan stated that IDPs would not be allowed freedom of movement since to do so would be to invite their mistreatment in government-controlled areas. Reportedly, however, he did at least express agreement with Buhne's insistence on the importance of keeping civilians away from combat areas.[119]

Buhne also reported that an IDP camp he had visited on 26 August had been shelled the following day, killing five people. The army's denial of responsibility was not credible, he said, going on to note that government forces 'typically' drop shells close to villages 'in an effort to clear them of civilians before fighting begins'.[120]

On 2 September, following weeks of heavy fighting, the army announced they had taken Mallavi, another important Tiger garrison that had served as the de facto LTTE command centre until the Tigers' capture of Kilinochchi in November 1998.[121] With government forces now battling the Tigers on three fronts—the western Vanni, north of Weli Oya, and southwards along Elephant's Pass—the stage appeared set for a coordinated attempt to advance on Kilinochchi itself.[122]

US-Sri Lankan military co-operation

Devinda Subasinghe

> Military [co-operation] was focused on trying to track arms shipments, upgrading the Sri Lanka Navy's firepower, radar systems, intelligence sharing. All of this was over a period of time, and much of it kicked in during 2007–2008 ... The US had a lot of eyes and ears in Southeast Asia that helped us tremendously.
>
> ... All in all I would say that the war could not have been won without US help, their strategic inputs. The arming was done by the Chinese, Pakistan and the Israelis to some extent: but the strategic inputs came from [the] US. From the Israelis we got cannons, radars, UAVs.[123] All of that was in the space that the CFA provided, and because of the forward-leaning leadership that the US took, thanks to [Richard] Armitage. By 2009 we had benefitted from everything that Washington was doing. I think those were critical interventions, without which we would not have got to where we ended up.

Richard Armitage

> At one time the US military provided support to Sri Lanka, mostly as a way of easing our Indian Ocean deployments laterally. The Chinese were spurred on by our Indian friends, who at every opportunity saw a string of pearls [developing], of which Sri Lanka was one. So it was more of a denial strategy, a way to at least keep our foot in the door. The engagement was initially for positive reasons, and later military involvement was to try to stop China from making Sri Lanka a complete subsidiary. The military was more forward-leaning on involvement with Sri Lanka than the State Department felt was warranted.

Internationals evacuate the Vanni

On 8 September, in the midst of military developments, the government made a game-changing announcement. All international humanitarian agencies and their expatriate staff operating in the LTTE-controlled Kilinochchi and Mullaitivu districts were ordered to evacuate immediately, and to relocate to Vavuniya, where a new logistics hub would be built. The only exception was the ICRC, due to the government's Geneva Convention-related obligations. Henceforth, it was indicated, the government would be assuming the lead for distributing relief supplies to IDPs in the Vanni.

Explaining the decision, Human Rights Minister Samarasinghe argued that it had been taken chiefly to ensure the security of UN and INGO foreign staff, something that could no longer be guaranteed in the conflict zone.[124]

However, one of the staff on the ground at the time—ex-UN Sri Lanka spokesperson Gordon Weiss—has a rather different view of the government's motives. 'The government regarded the UN as [an] impediment to their conquest of the Tamil Tigers', he argues. 'By removing those organisations there were no longer international witnesses to what was coming. I think they intended to remove independent witnesses to what was coming'.[125] Benjamin Dix, another UN staffer, says of the moment of departure: 'For me that was the worst moment of my life. It seemed like it was their greatest hour of need where you had an army sitting on the doorstep, wanting to take the town, and we drove out. There was a real sense of abandonment of these people.'[126]

With the UN preparing to leave Kilinochchi on 15 September, it had become apparent that the LTTE were refusing to allow Tamil staff and their dependents to join the exodus. As a result, over 500 Tamil employees of the UN and other international organisations were forced to watch their international colleagues depart.[127]

Palitha Kohona

In September [2008] there was an effort to broker a ceasefire via the UN. The UN, I think, was simply conveying messages. The government response was that the LTTE must surrender. It was only after this that the LTTE started dragging the entire civilian population with it. It was the biggest blunder in guerrilla history. I can't recall the Norwegians ever playing any role in trying to broker a ceasefire. In early 2009 there were calls being made by the Brits and others to try and stop the military advance, but the Norwegians were not prominent in that. Maybe by now they had realised that their influence level had diminished.

Indian pressure

With the Army's 57th Division said to be within 2 kilometres of Kilinochchi by early October, reports indicated that the LTTE had evacuated the town's population and emptied most of its buildings in anticipation of the town's fall.[128] Aerial footage taken after one of the frequent air raids showed what one analyst described as a 'ghost town with crumbled buildings and burnt-out vegetation'.[129]

In Kilinochchi, as throughout the remaining Tiger-held territory, a notable feature of LTTE defences were earthwork walls fronted by ditches, sometimes several kilometres in length. Known as *bunds*, these earthworks were built at strategic locations to halt the Army's advance, and they had become the scenes of some of the bloodiest battles. Another factor contributing to the slowdown in the government army's advance was the weather. Following the onset of the monsoon season in early October, heavy rains made it far more difficult for the SLA to break through the network of fortified bunkers surrounding Kilinochchi.

General Sarath Fonseka

I strongly believe that this country belongs to the Sinhalese, but there are minority communities and we treat them like our people. We being the majority of the country, 75 per cent, we will never give in and we have the right to protect this country ... They can live in this country with us. But they must not try to, under the pretext of being a minority, demand undue things.[130]

Reacting to political pressure from Tamil Nadu, in early October the Indian National Security Adviser M.K. Narayanan summoned the Sri Lankan Deputy High Commissioner to express Delhi's 'grave concern and unhappiness' over the latest military developments, in particular the growing number of Tamil civilian casualties. An official statement issued after the meeting spoke of the need for the Sri Lankan government to act with 'greater restraint' and to 'revive the political process'.[131]

The following day President Rajapaksa met Indian High Commissioner Alok Prasad, and reportedly assured him that Colombo was doing everything possible to address Indian concerns. He followed this up by calling a meeting of the APRC on 11 October to underscore the official Colombo line that the government was still looking for a 'political solution' to the ethnic conflict.[132]

In the meantime, Tamil Nadu was putting more pressure on Delhi to act decisively in response to developments in Sri Lanka. First, a fast was held in support of Lankan Tamils—participants included the Dravida Munntetra Kazhgam (DMK), a regional party that was also part of the country's Congress-led ruling coalition. In the meantime, Tamil Nadu Chief Minister

Karunanidhi organised a telegram campaign and an all-party conference calling for an immediate ceasefire in Sri Lanka. Spurred into action, the DMK organised a series of protests, including a state-wide human chain.[133]

As D.B.S. Jeyaraj was at pains to emphasise, however, the political ferment in Tamil Nadu was not to be interpreted as a show of support for the LTTE. Rather, he argued, ordinary Tamils in Tamil Nadu wanted to see their 'co-ethnic kinfolk' in Sri Lanka 'live in peace with full rights in a united, but not necessarily a unitary Sri Lanka'.[134] Moreover, speaking to US Ambassador Robert Blake towards the end of the month, President Rajapaksa indicated he had 'received word' from Karunanidhi that as long as Colombo 'took care of the civilians' and 'spoke of a political solution', the Tamil Nadu Chief Minister would be 'satisified'.[135]

The 'smoke and mirrors' aspect of Indo-Sri Lankan relations regarding the conflict was further emphasised when Basil Rajapaksa was dispatched to Delhi on 26 October to provide reassurances regarding the situation of the Vanni's Tamils. A final communiqué noted that the two sides had discussed the need to move towards 'a peacefully negotiated settlement', while also agreeing that 'terrorism should be countered with resolve'.[136]

Just what that 'resolve' entailed had been highlighted two weeks earlier by Basil Rajapaksa, when he noted in a media interview that Colombo received 'maximum support' from India in its efforts to 'crush the LTTE'. Militarily speaking, this meant everything from equipment such as radar systems and anti-aircraft guns to Air Force training and military intelligence. By this stage of the conflict, moreover, shared Indian naval intelligence was proving critical to the Sri Lankan Navy's increasingly successful efforts to intercept and destroy LTTE vessels bringing arms and other supplies into the Vanni.[137]

D.B.S. Jeyaraj

'Re-unification' in essence is the rationale for [this] war. The manner in which [it] is conducted suggests otherwise. It is as if war is being waged in a hostile country against an alien people. When military plans are formulated practically no concern is displayed for the fate of civilians. Recently Gotabhaya boasted that the SLAF had conducted more than 6,000 air raids, as opposed to six by the LTTE. The tragic irony of an air force bombing its own people on its own soil 6,000 times seemed to be lost on the defence secretary. The Tamil people are constantly reminded that the war is against the LTTE and not them; but the way in which it is conducted makes [them] feel differently.[138]

Underscoring the Sri Lankan military's relentless advance, on 18 November the Army captured the town of Pooneryn, which with the concurrent fall of the Tiger naval base at Nachchikuda gave it effective control of the entire northwest coast. In strategic terms the impact of these losses was highly significant. First, they made the vital sea-bound supply routes to Tamil Nadu a much more difficult proposition for the Tigers.[139] Second, they removed the threat to government military installations in the Jaffna area that had been posed by LTTE heavy artillery in Pooneryn, which was reportedly dismantled and moved eastwards by Tiger forces in advance of abandoning the town. Consequently, the Army could move as much as half of its Jaffna garrison's 40,000 troops up to the front in preparation for the impending assault on Kilinochchi.[140]

University Teachers for Human Rights-Jaffna (UTHR-J)

By October 2008 the LTTE had once again become very aggressive in conscription. They visited families with lists: for a family with three or four children they demanded two fighters; one for a family with two; and none for a family with one. The general attitude now is not to quarrel with the LTTE. [People] figure that many of those who objected to conscription had been placed on the front line and are dead. But many of those who joined without resistance have been placed in safer areas and have survived. Since early September, sources from the Vanni say that the LTTE has conscripted 9,000 'very young' persons who are now under training.

The relationship with the LTTE is complex. The general mood among the people of the Vanni was strongly anti-LTTE four months ago, and resistance continues. Resistance however to the LTTE is either passive or tragically fatalistic. With increased aerial bombing and shelling and stories of increasingly repressive treatment of minorities coming from other parts of the country, the mood is changing.[141]

Prabhakaran's Heroes Day speech

Seemingly unshaken by the Tigers' recent territorial losses, on 27 November Prabhakaran delivered his annual Heroes Day speech in markedly defiant tone. Underlining what he termed the LTTE's continued commitment to a peaceful resolution to the conflict, the Tiger leader went on to describe the government's pursuit of a military solution as racist, genocidal and bound to fail. The authorities in Colombo, he maintained, were 'living in a dreamland of military victory. It is a dream from which they will awake. That is certain.'[142] Without directly naming the US, EU and others, Prabhakaran went on to criticise the 'so-called Peace Sponsors' who had, he maintained, 'impaired' the negotiations process by proscribing the LTTE and obstructing their humanitarian activities.

In a carefully calculated political play, the LTTE supremo minimised past tensions with Delhi, highlighting the (highly questionable) contention that the Tigers had never viewed India as a hostile force, and thanked Indians in general and the people of Tamil Nadu in particular for their support, while urging them to stop the Sri Lankan military onslaught.[143] As one analyst pointed out, while the appeal to Delhi doubtless reflected the fact that by this stage the Tigers saw Indian pressure as the best—if not only—means of bringing the government back to the negotiating table, the fact that it was launched on the same day as major terrorist attacks in Mumbai made an Indian intervention 'even less likely' than had already been the case.[144]

Bård Thorheim, First Secretary at the Norwegian Embassy, on government military strategy

Famously, the CIA put out a report in 2006 arguing that the LTTE would not be defeated in the foreseeable future. Some high-level generals also had the same analysis in 2007. In the late summer of 2008 no strategic locations had been taken, but the Sri Lankan military was continuously making advances, the area controlled by the LTTE was shrinking, and everyone was still expecting the Tigers to hit back. In this respect everyone had the IPKF experience in mind.

I looked at the military tactics in use ... The Sri Lankan military had two advantages: first, the Army and Air Force started to co-operate closely. Airstrikes were coordinated with the movement of ground forces, which meant they became much more effective against LTTE defence positions. The Navy was also proving effective against the Sea Tigers. Secondly, the Army started using reconnaissance units instead of first putting infantry platoons into the battle. Twelve men would go into Tiger-held territory, engage the LTTE in combat, then withdraw and report back on how the LTTE defences were organised and provide co-ordinates to the Air Force. This allowed the main assault to become much more effective and targeted.

The Sri Lankan Army constantly adapted their tactics based on what worked and what didn't. On the LTTE side there was seemingly little reinvention of tactics. Several military attachés were puzzled as to why the LTTE stuck to conventional warfare defending territorial borders, whereas they might have been much better off militarily if they had switched to guerrilla warfare and given up territorial control in large parts of the Vanni. As observers, in the critical situation they were in, militarily and strategically speaking asymmetrical warfare seemed to us to be a much better option for the LTTE.

The Rajapaksa government put a lot of emphasis on the military, on how to build a military that could win the war. They got rid of a lot of the corruption which had previously allowed the LTTE to buy off army officers in order to help them plan and conduct attacks on government targets. Recruitment procedures got much better. Importantly, they also used the intelligence provided by Karuna. Karuna provided the SLA with ex-LTTE cadres trained in espionage and they went into Tiger held territory, mapping what—and where—the Tiger defences were. Perhaps the most significant development, however, was that the Sri Lankan government started receiving more intelligence on ships arriving in the North supplying the LTTE with weapons, ammunition and other equipment. As a result the LTTE became weak on logistics.

At the Embassy, from early on we analysed and took into account the effectiveness of government forces. Despite the LTTE's claim to the contrary, we doubted that they were going to hit back hard. It was clear that Jon Westborg and Erik [Solheim] were more inclined to believe the LTTE version, or at least their claims. The Mumbai attack of 26 November 2008 changed the mood in India, I believe. Earlier there was immense pressure on the Indian government from Tamil Nadu to do something ... the Mumbai attack took attention in India away from the LTTE at that critical time.

The Embassy maintained sporadic contact via Skype and phone with some LTTE cadres in the political wing, and on various levels. It struck me that they seemed to firmly believe that India would somehow come to their rescue if the LTTE came to the point where it was existentially threatened. This was surprising. Our reading of the Indian position, as it developed in late 2008, was very different. We always tried to provide the LTTE with a realistic and honest reading of the international situation, but there were some messages that they were simply not prepared to acknowledge.

The fall of Kilinochchi

By early December the battle lines were edging ever closer to Kilinochchi town. 'Edging', however, remained the best description of the SLA's advance. Faced with the prospect of losing their de facto capital, the LTTE had pulled many of their toughest, most experienced cadres into its defence, and with the monsoon season by now in full swing the government forces were finding it hard to push past the elaborate network of *bund* defensive earthworks thrown up by the Tigers.[145]

By mid December over 7,000 troops were said to be engaged in the offensive on Kilinochchi, which by this stage was being conducted by four Army Task Forces on as many fronts around the town.[146] Combat was fierce and the terrain was treacherous, much of it knee-deep in mud. Though the casualty figures put out by both sides were no doubt inflated, the toll in dead and injured was certainly very high.[147]

Erik Solheim

In 2008, we started thinking that there could be a government victory—the Indians told us that for the first time in August 2008. I always took the view that the Indians were the best informed. When [M.K.] Narayanan expressed this view to me[148]—and he had been saying the opposite for many years previously—I took the view that, well, indeed this was what might happen now. When the fighting came close to Kilinochchi it became clear that a negotiated settlement was not going to happen.

Erik Solheim recalls talking to Pulidevan the day before Kilinochchi fell, and being told that 'everything was fine'. At the Norwegian embassy, however, they knew better. In the words of Bård Ludvig Thorheim: 'Increasingly we reported back that we thought that the LTTE was really in trouble. Even then, Oslo—Erik and others—took the position that yes, the LTTE was in a bit of trouble, but they couldn't come to any final conclusion; and the LTTE might always bounce back. But we in Colombo said that it's a matter of when, not whether.'

The decisive moments came over the New Year. Following weeks of failed LTTE counter-attacks to try to prevent government troops from taking the crossroads town of Paranathan immediately north of Kilinochchi, on New Year's Eve 2008 the Tigers withdrew towards Mullaitivu on the Eastern coast, leaving behind a shattered ghost town. On the morning of 2 January, Sri Lankan troops entered Kilinochchi. President Rajapaksa publically announced the victory over the Tigers, and within a short space of time a firework display as extravagant as the New Year celebrations filled the Colombo skies.[149]

EELAM WAR IV: THE DENOUEMENT

Why did Mahinda Rajapaksa succeed against the LTTE where all previous governments had failed?

Erik Solheim argues that Rajapaksa's war strategy had a number of distinctive elements:

- A new acceptance of military losses combined with vigorous efforts to keep the southern public unaware of how many soldiers were being killed. There was little press coverage of Army casualties, and military funerals were kept as far away from public view as possible.
- The Sri Lankan military began fighting the war using what Solheim calls 'LTTE methods' and those deployed against the JVP during the 1971–72 and 1987–90 uprisings: torture, kidnappings, liquidations and the widespread use of 'white vans' to abduct people. The immediate effect, Solheim argues, was the disruption of LTTE networks in the South. 'Eventually it brought Tiger activities in the South almost to a halt, which made more troops available for the war in the North.'
- Insulating the country from international interference by both India and the West. Here the principal means deployed, Solheim argues, were 'playing to the competition with China' and acquiring weapons from China, Pakistan, Iran and Israel—countries that to varying degrees were happy to sell armaments to Colombo without human rights or other ethical conditionalities.
- Improving the Army's military quality by significantly reducing direct political involvement in senior appointments and all-round decision-making, and hefty increases in the budget allotted to defence expenditure.
- Access to higher-quality intelligence provided by the US and India, particularly following the outbreak of renewed hostilities in autumn 2006. Perhaps the most important effect of the Sri Lankan military's access to higher-quality intelligence, Solheim suggests, was the impact it had on LTTE arms smuggling. Simply put, Navy strikes became far more effective, squeezing the Tigers' capacity to respond at precisely the time when Army advances into LTTE-held territory were making this capacity increasingly critical. What motivated the US and Indian change of heart? 'Basically, the feeling that the Tigers had had a huge opportunity to go for peace but just hadn't taken it,' says Solheim.
- Brutal military tactics. 'Now it was a case of going back to the way Stalin, Hitler and Genghis Khan fought, with hardly any concern for losses,' Solheim maintains. 'I don't think Mahinda came into power with this clear strategy in mind. But he was certainly provoked by LTTE assas-

sination attempts on Gotabhaya [Rajapaksa] and Sarath Fonseka, and its intransigence over the Mavil Aru incident.'

- Curbing critical voices in the South through a combination of corruption, intimidation and, as in the case of newspaper editor Lansantha Wickrematunga, assassination. 'In fact they used assassinations against anyone—the media included—who opposed them. White vans, no court proceedings,' comments Solheim. 'And while there had been brutal combat and heavy losses in the past, previous Sri Lankan governments had fought the war with much more thought for international implications—how their actions would play out with the media and public opinion, both in the country and internationally. Media censorship was far lower in the past, and there were also more decent individuals in charge: leaders who fought more in line with the norms of the 21st century, with some concern, for example, for what the USA and others would think.'

- Effective insulation from international pressure. 'This was important, but not as important as domestic factors: hiding funerals of soldiers, hiding killings of opponents from the Sinhalese public,' says Solheim. 'I tend to believe domestic factors are always more important than international ones.' At the same time, Solheim recognises that,

> if the true scale of what happened had been made public then it would have been difficult—for example for India—not to intervene. But there are very few theatres of operation today where you can isolate yourself from world public opinion in the way the Rajapaksa government did. And in that sense, despite what some argue these days regarding a new 'Sri Lankan option', I don't think it actually provides much of a role model for dealing with conflicts in other countries. For example, if the so-called 'Sri Lankan model' had been applied in Gaza in 2008–2009 there were would have been 50,000 casualties, not 2,000.

Erik Solheim on critical blunders and failings in LTTE strategy

Military misjudgements

> Why do you waste millions on an air force of no military value, for instance? It was an amazing effort: getting thousands of Tamils all over the world to collect the money, importing the spare parts, constructing some runways, getting the aircraft up in the air: no other non-state actor has ever done this. Why do you continue to pursue conventional warfare against a far stronger adversary? And why do you ensure the withdrawal of international monitors precisely when you really need them?

> Around Prabhakaran there was a group of young, talented people who were simply not free to tell him what they wanted. Most of them had

never even been to Colombo, and had definitely not seen the outside world. Following Prabhakaran, there was a belief that every question has a military answer: if you don't like someone, kill him and so on. Military means are helpful. 'But in the end they have to be subordinated to political strategy—they are no substitute for a political approach.

Strategic weakness

Many people considered Prabhakaran to be a genius. Even beyond the LTTE—far into Indian, American ranks—there was a lot of respect for his military capabilities. After 2006 the LTTE was pushed to the wall, but they were not able to respond with any meaningful military initiative. Now we know that before 2006 it was Balasingham who fronted or sparked all political initiatives. Absent him and there was no one else with the ability to do that. Remember, too, that the LTTE generals were youngsters recruited by Prabhakaran, with a limited world-view. At the end they didn't understand the rest of the world, the thinking in Delhi, New York or Beijing.

Narrow vision

They miscalculated the big picture, in particular the character of the Sri Lankan leadership. KP told us the LTTE leadership was living in a dream world. They didn't understand foreign forces: they believed in a BJP election victory in India, that street demos in Europe would put so much pressure on European politicians that they would intervene. None of it came true. But most importantly it *couldn't* have come true: it was complete nonsense. A clear understanding of the politics would have told them this.

11

ENDGAME

Hard on the heels of the Army's capture of Kilinochchi, President Rajapaksa—having issued an ultimatum to the Tigers demanding that they release all civilians trapped in the war zone by the New Year—now followed up by issuing a ban on the LTTE on 7 January.[1] Some, noting that the Tigers were already proscribed in thirty other countries, argued that the ban was long overdue. Others, however, suggested that the move was chiefly a means of distracting attention from the increasingly urgent humanitarian crisis enveloping at least 300,000 Tamil civilians who were now boxed into a shrinking corner of the Northeast, increasingly exposed to the fighting and without access to adequate medical and food supplies.[2]

General Sarath Fonseka's motto for SLA troops

Go for the kill, maximum casualties and destruction of infrastructure of the enemy with minimum possible damage to the troops.

As the US embassy in Colombo noted, one thing was incontrovertible: the ban marked the 'final end of the already moribund peace process'. Perhaps the only glimmer of hope for a peaceful settlement was provided by Foreign Minister Bogollagama's assurances to the US Ambassador that Norway's facilitation role and the Co-Chairs' efforts were both 'independent' of the 'now-defunct peace process', and as such could continue as before.[3]

High-profile assassination

The following day the country was rocked by the news that Lasantha Wickrematunge, the widely-respected editor of *The Sunday Leader*, had been assassinated in his car in downtown Colombo.[4] The murder was widely ascribed to the reports on official corruption that he had been running over the preceding months, many of them focusing on deals involving Defence Secretary Gotabhaya Rajapaksa.[5]

The murder of Wickrematunge was unparalleled, even in Sri Lanka: he had been a member of the country's elite, a former secretary to Srimavao Bandaranaike when she was prime minister, and a journalist known to everyone in Colombo's political circles. As Erik Solheim put it:

> It was as if the editor of *The New York Times* had been murdered in Times Square in broad daylight and the NYPD had made no effort whatsoever to catch the murderer. The government could hardly have sent a stronger signal to the media on the need to 'behave'. An investigation has not, and will not happen. At that stage no one could have committed such a crime without support at the highest levels.

But Wickrematunge's murder was by no means the only high-profile assault on the Sri Lankan media at this time. Two days earlier, an armed gang had invaded the main studios of the independent MTV network, holding the staff at gunpoint before proceeding to wreck much of the building. The attack came only days after state media had criticised MTV for its 'unpatriotic' coverage of the fall of Kilinochchi.[6]

Nor did things stop there. Towards the end of the month there were reports that at least nine journalists had fled the country due to threats and intimidation, with a further five reportedly considering leaving for the same reasons. As a US Embassy cable noted in characteristically deadpan style, 'a concerted effort appears to be underway to intimidate and silence independent voices in Sri Lankan society as the military makes a final push against the LTTE's last stronghold in Mullaitivu prior to National Day celebrations [4 February].' By way of conclusion, it noted that Reporters without Borders' 2008 Press Freedom Index ranked Sri Lanka 165 out of 173 countries—the worst-ranking of any formally democratic country and below those of Belarus, Zimbabwe and Uzbekistan.[7]

And Then They Came For Me

Below are excerpts from Lasantha Wickrematunge's last editorial, addressed to Mahinda Rajapaksa and published posthumously on

11 January 2009. The title is taken from Martin Niemöller's poem 'First they came ...', lambasting the cowardice of German intellectuals in the wake of Hitler's rise to power. As Wickrematunge notes in the editorial, he and Mahinda Rajapaksa had been friends for over twenty years.

> A military occupation of the country's North and East will require the Tamil people of those regions to live eternally as second-class citizens, deprived of all self-respect. Do not imagine that you can placate them by showering 'development' and 'reconstruction' on them in the post-war era. The wounds of war will scar them forever, and you will also have an even more bitter and hateful Diaspora to contend with. A problem amenable to a political solution will thus become a festering wound that will yield strife for all eternity. If I seem angry and frustrated, it is only because most of my countrymen—and all of the government—cannot see this writing so plainly on the wall.
>
> It is well known that I was on two occasions brutally assaulted, while on another my house was sprayed with machine-gun fire. Despite the government's sanctimonious assurances, there was never a serious police inquiry into the perpetrators of these attacks, and the attackers were never apprehended. In all these cases, I have reason to believe the attacks were inspired by the government. When finally I am killed, it will be the government that kills me.
>
> In the wake of my death I know you will make all the usual sanctimonious noises and call upon the police to hold a swift and thorough inquiry. But like all the inquiries you have ordered in the past, nothing will come of this one, too. For truth be told, we both know who will be behind my death, but dare not call his name.

Simultaneously, the army's advance continued with the capture of LTTE front-line positions at Muhamalai on the Jaffna peninsula and, soon after, of the Tiger base at Elephant Pass. With the taking of Elephant Pass, government troops now controlled the entire stretch of the A9 road from Jaffna to Kandy for first time since the Indian Peace Keeping Force's departure in 1990.[8] The army's latest victory, however, was not announced by President Rajapaksa until the following day—a fact many put down to fears that, in the understated words of a US Embassy cable, the day on which Wickrematunge had been murdered 'might not be propitious for announcing a major military victory'.[9]

Amidst international outrage over Wickrematunge's death and calls for an independent enquiry into his killing,[10] on 9 January opposition leader

Ranil Wickremasinghe made an impromptu statement in Parliament. Alleging that 'elements of the state intelligence apparatus' were behind both this murder and the attack on the MTV studios, Wickremasinghe pointed the finger firmly at Fonseka and Gotabhaya.[11]

D.B.S. Jeyaraj

Like a compulsive gambler Prabhakaran has risked the entire existence of the Tamil people ... for the elusive goal of Tamil Eelam. It is an all or nothing gamble for him. He is like an invading military general who burns his boats so that his soldiers have no choice other than to fight on for victory or face death. There is no turning back. If the soldiers win the war, the general will be praised for his steely determination. If they lose, there won't be anyone left to tell the tale.[12]

The allegation appeared to have hit its mark when, in an address to the nation broadcast later the same day, President Rajapaksa supplemented his homily to the army's capture of Elephant Pass with a warning that efforts to 'belittle [this victory], to turn the attention of the people in other directions' were underway. A 'conspiracy' was in operation, said the president— one involving 'certain international forces' and instigated by 'those who have been driven to fear due to the successes of our armed forces'.[13]

University Teachers For Human Rights-Jaffna

For both Prabhakaran's war of national liberation and Rajapaksa's war for national sovereignty, one unstated motive assumed the greatest significance—the entrenchment of unchallenged personal power. Rajapaksa followed Prabhakaran in calling his political enemies 'traitors'. Both used the cover of war to kill their enemies ... for both the expression of critical independent opinion was anathema [and] both ran regimes that killed exponents of independent opinion.

[Wickrematunge's] assassination, along with intimidation of journalists and exclusion of the foreign media, was meant to regulate the truth about how the war was waged, to check criticism and to hide the truth about the world's greatest 'hostage rescue' operation. It was becoming a phenomenal cover up operation, as the rescuers showed little compunction about killing the hostages. The role of the government's 'political wing' was almost a leaf out of Prabhakharan's book: Not to question, but to justify to the world, the actions of the 'military wing'.[14]

Mounting crisis in the Vanni

The humanitarian crisis in the Vanni was deepening. On 17 January, a UN World Food Programme (WPF) convoy—the eleventh to have been dispatched to the Vanni since the UN and other international organisations had been ordered out of the area the previous September—was due to return to Vavuniya, having delivered its load of more than 800 tonnes of food to Tamil civilians. The convoy was prevented from leaving the town of Puthukkudiyiruppu (PTK) by heavy shelling from the army, and three days later was still waiting for official permission to leave. It was later alleged that the army was using the convoy's presence as a cover for advancing their frontlines. Further complications arose when the convoy was finally given the green light on 23 January. At gunpoint, the LTTE refused to allow the eighty accompanying dependents of local UN workers permission to leave the Tiger-controlled zone, with the result that the convoy finally departed without half of its trucks and most of its members.[15]

> The UN team was allowed into the war zone in January 2009 only to deliver food to displaced people, but as their convoy moved past the Forward Defence Line into the LTTE areas they noticed Sri Lankan soldiers walking alongside their lorries, using them as cover to advance their forward positions. At that point they had no idea this would turn out to be the last delivery of food by road to hundreds of thousands of hungry destitute people trapped in the war zone for the next four months.[16]

Covering events that took elsewhere in the Vanni during this period, UN Colombo spokesperson Gordon Weiss provides searing testimony to the consequences of the sort of shelling that had delayed the WFP workers:

On the night of 22 January, inside the Vanni triangle, the SLA relentlessly shelled a convoy that included 132 children, women and men under the protection of two international UN officers. All were huddled in hastily built log and earthen bunkers at the edge of [the] 'no fire zone' ... Civilian campfires surrounded the bunkers—people who had been drawn to this supposed sanctuary by government broadcasts claiming that it would be safe from artillery fire. As the shelling continued throughout the night, the UN officers frantically transmitted the coordinates of their position to senior Sri Lankan army commanders, as well as descriptions of the carnage being inflicted.

They could do little more than listen to the screams of people dying beside their campfires as artillery blasted them. In the morning ... the senior UN security officer on the ground, a former infantry colonel, surveyed a scene he described as 'nothing short of the intentional murder of civilians'. The bodies of entire families with whom he had been idly chatting the night before lay scattered about him. Blood and shrapnel had spattered UN vehicles, body parts were underfoot, the corpse of a baby hung from a tree. The government denied any responsibility.[17]

Evidence of this sort was precisely what the government's ejection of the UN from the Vanni, alongside its refusal to allow almost all international media access to the combat zone, was designed to prevent from reaching the outside world. In many senses, the final stages of the conflict took place out of sight—if not mind—of the international community.

The 'safe zone'

In the meantime, as a sign that the government had not completely eliminated Norway from its facilitation role, indications emerged that at Colombo's request, Norwegian Ambassador Tore Hattrem had forwarded an offer of amnesty to the LTTE for all cadres except Prabhakaran and Security Head Pottu Amman. However, noting that Rajapaksa had not mentioned such an offer to Indian Foreign Secretary Menon during his recent visit, Hattrem informed his US counterpart that he questioned the proposal's seriousness.[18]

Bård Ludvig Thorheim

In early January Tore Hattrem received a text message from a high-ranking official close to the president outlining an amnesty proposal to the LTTE, and including an offer to continue their struggle by political means, forming a political party.

Tore Hattrem probably understood the situation better than me. I was very optimistic that this might be our moment to make a difference, that we could potentially help saving lives in the last phase of the war. We were asked to convey [its contents] to the LTTE, which we did. But they never got back to us ... I raised the issue with some LTTE contacts and their response was, 'No, we are going to succeed in stopping government forces militarily'. That was all I got, after several attempts at engaging with them on this. Then there was National Day. Just days before, Tore wanted to discuss an idea with the political team at the Embassy that, given the situation, someone ought to state publicly what we all saw so clearly: that the LTTE was going to lose, and that in order to save lives in this last phase of the war they should, under certain conditions, agree to lay down their arms.

Of course we did wonder whether the official had consulted Mahinda about sending the message offering amnesty and some sort of political way out for parts of the LTTE. Perhaps I put more emphasis on it than some of the others in our team because to me it showed that even while the government were bashing us in the media, at the same time they were also eager to meet us on a regular basis, and to make use of the contact we had with the LTTE. They encouraged this. If things went really wrong for the government, they maintained the option of communicating with the Tigers through Norway. And it was worthwhile tolerating some public Norway-bashing by the government for the sake of maintaining a channel of communication between the warring parties.

On 21 January, in belated recognition of the ground situation, the army unilaterally declared the creation of a civilian 'safe zone' (or 'No Fire Zone'—NFZ) northwest of PTK, in territory that was still under nominal Tiger control, and thus accessible by the Tamil civilian population. The unilateral basis on which it had been set up meant that it hardly qualified as a safe zone in the formal, bilateral sense of the term. Indeed, according to one eyewitness report, the zone's creation 'only made matters worse': between 21 and 29 January, the zone experienced 'intense shelling by the army, resulting in astounding levels of civilian casualties. Civilians who had experienced intense shelling on 20 January said that it became even worse once the area was declared a safe zone'.[19]

Four days later, Mullaitivu, a coastal town that had been under LTTE control since 1996, fell to the army. In a live TV broadcast the following day, Army Commander Fonseka announced the capture of Mullaitivu, virtually the last town of significance still under Tiger control. As had happened at Kilinochchi, the retreating Tigers appeared to have withdrawn all their major military assets before vacating the town. The same went for the civilian population, who—along with the rest of the inhabitants of the Vanni—were now squeezed into thirty-five square kilometres of the government's self-declared 'safe zone'. In an indication of the political forces at play, a US Embassy cable noted that government forces were under pressure to conclude the job of defeating the LTTE in time for 4 February National Day celebrations, thereby paving the way for Rajapaksa to announce 'final victory' over the LTTE.[20]

Jayaveda Uyangoda

'Endgame for the LTTE.' That is how the media described [the] Army's entry into Mullaithivu. It is clear that the LTTE's military backbone has been broken decisively ... at the time of writing the remaining LTTE cadres, trapped in a small area in the Mullaithivu jungles, seem to be fighting a losing battle. Many thousands of civilians are also trapped with [them]. There does not seem to be any respite ... all of them obviously struggling in absolute fear and in extremely precarious and terrifyingly harsh conditions. The warring sides have been playing politics out of [their] fate. The international actors, other than making pious statements, are waiting and watching how the 'endgame' will end a civil war they have come to view as an unwanted and unending headache.[21]

It did not take long for the credibility of the 'safe zone' to be sorely tested. Only four days after the announcement of its creation, UN Resident Coordinator Neil Buhne informed US Ambassador Robert Blake that government forces had repeatedly violated the zone, also noting that the LTTE were firing on army positions from within the area and that the SLA were returning fire.[22] An ICRC representative provided similar information. According to reports from a government medical officer inside the area, at least 300 civilians had been killed there recently. As a result, both the UN and ICRC ordered their staff to evacuate the zone, and both sides allowed the ICRC to evacuate more 200 patients and hospital staff from PTK to Vavuniya.[23]

On 28 January, however, Defence Spokesperson Brigadier Udaya Nanayakkara issued one of a string of denials that the armed forces were harming civilians: 'We are targeting the LTTE. We are not targeting any civilians so there can't be any civilians killed.'[24] In a similar vein, and despite clear evidence that they were returning fire from the vicinity of the PTK hospital, the LTTE resolutely denied they were shooting either from this location or from inside the NFZ.[25]

Murali Reddy

There is no denying that the government's war strategy did not really factor in the interests of civilians trapped in the rapidly shrinking LTTE territory. But the LTTE, too, cannot deny responsibility for confining such a large number of citizens to an increasingly hostile battle zone that is slipping out of its control. The LTTE leadership perhaps considered the presence of such a large number of civilians as the best insurance against advancing forces.[26]

International pressure and the Co-Chairs' statement

In a further indication of growing international anxiety over the direction in which the ground situation was moving, on 26 January UN Secretary General Ban Ki-Moon met Basil Rajapaksa in New York and urged both parties to 'respect' no-fire zones and safe areas. In addition, Ban Ki-Moon expressed 'deep concern' over the humanitarian situation in the Vanni and called on both parties to facilitate civilian movement out of the war zone.[27] Continuing Indian unease was underscored by a lightning visit to Colombo the following evening by Indian External Affairs Minister Pranab Mukherjee. Rajapaksa reportedly assured Mukherjee that his government was 'receptive' to humanitarian concerns but, while acknowledging that the army was shelling LTTE artillery positions in part of the 'safe zone', resolutely denied that 300 civilians had been killed over the preceding few days.[28]

Irrespective of Presidential denials, the news from the northern battlefront suggested that in reality, following the end of a 48-hour ceasefire declared by Rajapaksa during which the LTTE were asked to—and by all accounts did—let civilians move into the 'no fire zone', the army was exercising little, if any, restraint. On the afternoon of 1 February and night of 2 February, PTK hospital was hit by shells, forcing medical staff to remove around 300 of its more than 500 patients to a community centre at Puttamatalan. ICRC staff working in the hospital reported that nine people were killed and twenty injured.[29] In a 2 February media interview, however, Gotabhaya was adamant that none of the alleged incidents had taken place. The Defence Secretary was then asked whether a hospital was considered a 'legitimate target' if it was located outside of the 'safe zone'. He responded: 'Yes ... That is why we clearly gave these no fire zones ... everything beyond these zones is a legitimate target.'[30] The Defence Secretary's position was in flagrant contradiction of international humanitarian law, under which attacks on any humanitarian site are illegal, irrespective of location.[31]

On the day of Gotabhaya's interview, the Co-Chairs were meeting. It had become evident to many in the international community that the LTTE had been defeated and the endgame was now under way. By the end of January, the Norwegian team had come to the conclusion that the Co-Chairs needed to make an appeal to the LTTE to put an end to the war—to save what could be saved, so to speak, via a negotiated surrender. The Americans were supportive of the Norwegian position, and on 2 February a Co-Chairs meeting drafted a common statement that appealed for an end to shelling into and out of the no-fire zone, and called on the LTTE to initiate discussions on 'the modalities for ending hostilities, including the laying down of arms, renunciation of violence, acceptance of the [government's] offer of amnesty, and participating as a political party in a process to achieve a just and lasting political solution'.

The statement had a major impact, not least among the Tamil diaspora, many of whom were shocked by the international community's announcement that the LTTE had lost the war; in fact, many did not appear to believe what the statement said. As for the government, Basil Rajapaksa welcomed the 'spirit and essence' of the Co-Chairs' statement, and the foreign minister even privately praised it to the US Ambassador during the 4 February Independence Day celebrations in Colombo. Gotabhaya, on the other hand, was quoted in a 5 February front-page media article as calling the statement 'ridiculous'.[32] Stating that 'nothing short of unconditional surrender' could bring the army's campaign to an end, the Defence Secretary lambasted the Co-Chairs' statement as 'nothing but a transparent attempt to save the Tigers'. In addition, he openly scorned the proposal for a 'pause' in the fighting to allow sick and wounded civilians to be evacuated from the war zone, which he characterised as 'detrimental to Sri Lanka's efforts to wipe out terrorism'.[33]

The Co-Chairs' statement also marked a shift in the Norwegian role in the final stages of the conflict. In essence, the main goal was no longer to get the parties talking—it was to reduce the amount of suffering, and to save as many civilians as possible. Accordingly, in practical terms the focus shifted to issues of humanitarian access in order to provide food and medicines to civilians trapped in the war zone, while also attempting to convince the LTTE to lay down their weapons.

At the beginning of the week in which the Co-Chairs' statement was issued, the Defence Ministry came out with a statement indicating that the territory still held by the LTTE was down to around 200km[2]—less than 5 per cent of the area it controlled in July 2006, at the start of Eelam War IV.[34]

At the same time, Tore Hattrem received a phone call informing him that there were 'strong voices' within the LTTE calling for a face-saving mechanism that would allow civilians to leave the war zone. Following consultations with the Americans, a proposal was tabled to use the ICRC to register people's names: if LTTE cadres wanted to surrender they could simply discard their weapons, it was suggested. The Americans added the suggestion of having evacuation ships docked on the Vanni coastline. The government was hesitant, but the Norwegians were confident that pressure from the US, India and others would bring about a change of mind in the event that the LTTE accepted an 'organised end to the war'.

That confidence appeared to be short-lived, however: in a note to Basil Rajapaksa sent on 16 February, the Norwegian Ambassador indicated that there had been 'no response' to a proposal sent to the LTTE 'through several channels' regarding modalities for the 'release [of] the civilian population'—nor, he suggested, was it likely that the Tigers would 'agree with this in the near future'.[35]

UN Special Envoy Tamrat Samuel, who made a three-day visit to Colombo in February, was struck by two things: a general feeling of 'helplessness' among the ambassadors he talked to, and the government's confidence that the end was near. Of his meeting with Basil Rajapaksa, Samuel says: 'My message to the government was basically that you need to understand your responsibility for the lives of the trapped civilians, and every effort should be made to discuss an end to the conflict in a definitive way.' It appeared that the government was ready to talk, and that 'basically they were looking for a surrender agreement'. As for the LTTE, 'my message to them was: agree to sit with the government to discuss how to end the conflict. We did not use the word "surrender", but by this stage the options for the LTTE were very limited. And this continued until April: they kept talking about lowering their demand from full independence to something else. They were so removed from reality.'

Erik Solheim

The situation for the civilians trapped in the war zone was desperate. It was clear that the LTTE was forcing Tamil civilians to remain with them. It was also clear that the government was pursuing the war with increasing brutality. I knew that the government would not stop the war when they were so close to finally wiping out the LTTE: few victorious powers would do that and certainly not one as brutal as the Rajapaksa government. So I took the line that the one and only way of saving tens of thousands of lives was to point to the fact that the LTTE had lost the war at this point, and so should accept an ending with as little bloodshed as possible and in such a way that the Tamils could continue their struggle effectively in new and peaceful forms.

... A plan for an 'organised end to war' was the description we agreed upon among the Co-Chairs. The broad approach in the international community, however, was no support for the Tigers and no tears over their destiny. There was concern for Tamil civilians, but not to the extent that people were ready to do something substantial.

I suggested the language of the Co-Chair statement and pushed it with the support of the US. It was an appeal to both sides and was not what either of them wanted to hear. The focus was on the need for the LTTE to accept that the war had come to an end. The government wanted to push on with the war while the LTTE was demanding a ceasefire. There was a negative reaction [to the statement] from the LTTE and Tamils, who said that by calling on them to give up we were making demands on the weaker party. There was no positive reaction from the government either, but of course they were in a much stronger position than the LTTE. Had the LTTE accepted our proposal, they would today have been in a position to continue their struggle by other means, like say the Kurds in Turkey.

Civilian attacks

On 5 February SLAF jets twice bombed the hospital at Ponnambalan, a short distance northeast of PTK, killing seventy-five people, most of them patients. Announcing the attack the following day, a Defence Ministry press release stated that the Air Force had successfully destroyed a 'hideout of senior LTTE leader Soosai', and included a video clip of the raid. However, close examination of the video revealed that the destroyed building was not a luxury house belonging to the Tiger leadership, as was claimed; it was Ponnambalan Memorial Hospital. While subsequent testimony established that the medical facilities had been used by the LTTE for treatment of their cadres—mostly against the staff's expressed wishes—the fact that it had something of the character of a military hospital made no difference in terms of its status as a protected site under international humanitarian law.[36]

By early February it was becoming increasingly obvious that the onslaught was weakening the LTTE's control over the civilian population. According to one report, in the week of 6–11 February an estimated 22,000 civilians managed to escape into government-held territory. Escapees painted a grim picture of the Tigers' efforts to halt the refugees. Sister Mary Colostica, a 74-year-old Catholic nun, told Reuters: 'at least ten to fifteen people die a day and no one is there to bury them.' Others described how the LTTE fired at civilians moving towards army lines waving white flags,[37] and diplomatic sources in Colombo stated that the LTTE killed sixty civilians attempting to flee by boat during the night of 13 February.

In addition, the LTTE was using suicide bombers for the same intimidatory purposes. On 9 February, a Black Tiger blew herself up at a checkpoint in the Visuamadu area of Mullaitivu, often used by civilians fleeing the combat zone. Twenty-eight people were killed, the majority of them soldiers, with scores of others wounded.[38] Three days later, the army announced the creation of a new 12 kilometre-long 'no fire zone' (NFZ) stretching along the coast east of PTK, and called on civilians to move into it for their own safety. From the start, the new zone's location—extremely close to the front lines—was a source of concern.[39]

Provincial elections

In the meantime, the domestic political cycle continued apace. On 14 February, elections for the Northwest and Central provincial councils resulted, as anticipated, in thumping victories for President Rajapaksa's ruling coalition. The voting was indicative of the Sinhalese electorate's support for the war, but the Tamil and Muslim communities' strong backing for opposition candidates signalled an altogether more sceptical attitude—a *TamilNet* commentary concluded that the elections pointed to the need to partition the island.[40]

The following week brought little respite from the gloomy news emanating from the war zone. On 16 February, UN Resident Coordinator Neil Buhne noted recent reports of firefights within the new NFZ and called on both sides to desist from fighting 'in areas of civilian concentration'.[41] The following day UNICEF issued a statement pointing to 'clear indications' that the LTTE had 'intensified forcible recruitment of civilians' and described it as 'intolerable' that 'children as young as 14' were now being targeted.[42]

In a bid to reassure the international community, on 20 February Gotabhaya informed US Ambassador Blake that once it had successfully surrounded the 'safe zone', as it shortly expected to, the army would revert to what he called 'passive mode', withholding fire from the designated area.[43] That same evening the LTTE air wing conducted what proved to be its final mission. Clearly intent on a suicide attack, two light aircraft were brought down by artillery fire, one crashing close to the Air Force headquarters in central Colombo and the other coming down near the main SLAF base opposite Colombo international airport.[44]

The following day, UN Under-Secretary General John Holmes wound up a 72-hour stopover that included a visit to the official refugee camps set up in Vavuniya and a meeting with President Rajapaksa. At a widely publicised press conference, after calling on both parties to avoid a 'final bloodbath', Holmes urged them to ensure the safety of civilians still inside LTTE-controlled areas, while also noting that non-combatant 'deaths and more injuries' were occurring on a daily basis in the war zone.[45] Holmes' neutral-sounding account of the ground situation—one he relayed to the

UN Security Council a week later—infuriated some commentators, in particular those sympathetic to the LTTE, who felt that in view of the prevailing ground situation, any attempt to present a 'balanced' account was tantamount to being pro-government. Holmes' Security Council briefing, 'largely endorsing and trusting Colombo's agenda and assurances for civilians', was in effect giving a 'knowing wink' to the government.[46]

John Holmes

> The government assured me at every level that they have virtually stopped using heavy weapons because of their recognition of the need to spare the civilian population, who are of course their own citizens. It remains unclear how far this is the case in reality.[47]

Last-gasp Norwegian peace efforts

Now the LTTE addressed an appeal directly to the outside world. On 22 February Tiger Political Chief Nadesan asked the international community to help to secure a ceasefire and then to work towards a 'political solution' rather than being deflected by demands that the LTTE lay down arms as a precondition for a settlement.[48] While Nadesan's eloquently argued appeal was addressed to the widest possible audience, it was not clear what actual response it elicited.

Towards the end of February reports began to emerge of a Co-Chairs initiative to move civilians trapped in the war zone via the deployment to the northeast coast of US military assets, principally Navy and Air Force craft. Foreign Minister Bogollagama pronounced himself 'aware' of the initiative while also underlining the fact the government was talking to 'several other friendly countries'—in particular India—about the options for evacuating civilians. There were few illusions regarding the difficulties to be overcome, not least among them the fact that the LTTE had so far 'flatly rejected' any such plans.[49]

Critical to continued Norwegian efforts to achieve a peaceful ending to the conflict was a secret meeting in Kuala Lumpur between Ambassador Tore Hattem and chief LTTE international representative Kumaran Pathmanathan, commonly known as 'KP'. Organised with the support of Basil Rajapaksa, the meeting was also attended by Jon Westborg and Tomas Stangeland on the Norwegian side, and V. Rudrakumaran and Jay Maheswaran on the LTTE side.

Tore Hattrem picks up the story. 'Before the meeting with KP there was a lot of conversation, particularly between the US and Norway. I had intelligence that there were strong forces within the LTTE that would like to find some honourable way out of the bloodshed. I knew that this was not coming from Prabhakaran himself. But we thought the sensible thing to do would be to work with these forces and through them try to convince Prabhakaran to come to the same conclusion', Hattrem recalls. 'Then we came up with a face-saving mechanism: to offer the LTTE a situation where the ICRC moves into the borderline areas and the civilians leave the area and go over to the ICRC. The LTTE cadre could decide what to do: whether to take off their uniforms, come out without arms, escape or continue fighting. They could do whatever they wanted themselves, but they had to let the civilians out,' he continues. Unfortunately, says Hattrem, KP 'understood that the LTTE had lost, but spoke of his inability to convince Prabhakaran of this ... He simply felt he could not deliver Prabhakaran. He also had a couple of advisers with him who tried to buy time.[50] All in all, I was disappointed by the whole thing.'

Tore Hattrem debriefed Basil Rajapaksa on the meeting, stressing his doubts that KP would be able to secure Prabhakaran's support for what the Norwegians were proposing. Basil Rajapaksa was reportedly 'disappointed' to hear this news. Subsequently, the local media ran stories insinuating that Norway was now attempting to save the LTTE—Hattrem suggests that these 'probably' originated from sources within the government who now saw the real possibility of a military victory. However, media attention soon faded, which Bård Ludvig Thorheim attributes to the government's realisation that if the Norwegians received too much criticism for having assisted the LTTE, they could cover themselves by revealing that the government had been fully informed about all contacts with the LTTE, and had even passed on messages to the Tigers via Norway not long beforehand.[51]

Erik Solheim on early contacts with KP

I had a secret meeting with KP in Bangkok around 2004, at the time when it was planned that he would retire as the LTTE's weapons procurement officer. Already at that point there was the suggestion that he would eventually become the future Balasingham. I met him to discuss how he would move from weapon procurements into a political role, based in a European capital. But no European nation was willing to allow him in unless the Sri Lankan government supported it, and at that point there was the CBK-Ranil political division, so getting their agreement would have been difficult.

Then, after the fall of Kilinochchi, Prabhakaran announced that KP had been appointed as the LTTE's international focal point, picking up the role Balasingham had played. I still have quite a lot of respect for KP. He is one of the few people who has been taken on board by the government since the war who has not made ridiculous statements about the past—like Karuna—or blamed each and everyone else.[52]

Army operations

In March the Army launched a fresh set of operations aimed at seizing the last bit of Tiger territory via an offensive from its western flank. An immediate result was that on 3 March government forces reached the major road junction at PTK, the last remaining LTTE-controlled town in the Vanni, although it took nearly four weeks before the entire town was pronounced to be under their control. Two days later the Co-Chairs met to review the latest developments.

Concerning the supply of food and other basic requirements, there was a consensus that the government was 'making an effort' to address 'most' of the concerns voiced by the international community. Robert Blake noted, for example, that Basil Rajapaksa had recently promised to immediately dispatch more food to the safe zone, in response to the first 'credible reports' of starvation. Presented with persistent reports of Army shelling in the zone, however, Hattrem reported that Basil Rajapaksa was 'not comfortable discussing the subject', although he did at least acknowledge that it was occurring.

Saravanamuttu Pakiasothoy

Whilst it is necessary, correct and safer and non-controversial to slam the LTTE for its barbaric excesses, the government has yet to convincingly rebut the charges that its artillery has hit medical facilities, civilians within and outside the no fire zone and that its strategy in the face of the humanitarian catastrophe in the Wanni is driven by military considerations to the point that it is better described as one of elimination of LTTE and its support base, rather than one of containment which accords civilian protection the priority it deserves and demands in these and all other circumstances.[53]

In a sign that the LTTE were not yet finished as a fighting force, on 7–8 March there were reports of heavy fighting and high casualties on both sides in the aftermath of a Tiger counterattack in and around PTK and Chalai, the last of their naval bases to fall. In a dry commentary on the LTTE fight-back, a US Embassy cable notes that it 'appears to undermine' official claims that 'only about 500 LTTE cadres remain. It is not clear how such a small force would be capable of keeping government forces in the area numbering about 50,000 at bay while simultaneously preventing 100–200,000 civilians in the "safe zone" from fleeing.'[54]

A further indication that Tiger cadre were still operative across the country came when a Black Tiger targeted a 9 March parade in the southern town of Akuressa, held in honour of the Prophet Mohammed's birthday. Fifteen people were killed and more than thirty injured, including a number of government ministers and local government officials. In the midst of the fighting in the Vanni, on 10 March it was announced that after months of tension between Karuna and his erstwhile deputy Pillaiyan, the former LTTE commander plus an estimated 2,000 ex-Tiger cadres loyal to him had joined the ruling SLFP at Temple Trees, the official presidential residence in Colombo. In customary fashion, President Rajapaksa proceeded to add Karuna to the list of government Ministers—which now stretched to 105.[55] The irony in appointing the man who had been responsible for dividing the LTTE as Minister of Reconciliation did not go unnoticed.

Anti-conscription protests in the 'Safe Zone'

Drawing on eyewitness testimony, a University Teachers for Human Rights report suggests that in the wake of a let-up in army shelling of the 'safe zone' in early March, acts of open rebellion against LTTE conscription gangs broke out with increasing frequency. On one occasion, for example, when a gang attempted to abduct an eighteen-year-old boy he allegedly seized the leader's gun, shot him and ran away, firing at and injuring three other gang members as he did so. There was a grim price to be paid for such defiance. Tiger cadres reportedly returned the next day, seized the boy's fifty-five-year-old father and executed him. In another instance, several Tigers were said to have opened fire on the Church of Our Lady of the Rosary at Valaignarmadam before driving off with a number of young people who had been trying to avoid conscription by seeking sanctuary there.

> Just why people were so desperate to escape the Tiger-controlled area and avoid conscription is summarised as follows: 'Many decided that whatever the risk, escape was preferable to what seemed slow and certain death in the NFZ … Persons conscripted and forcibly taken to the battlefront died by the hundreds. There was among the Tigers not an iota of remorse for these deaths. They roamed as drunken men abducting persons without number, showing no trace of civilization or humanity. A Tiger media man himself admitted that with their end so near, they no longer needed the people's support.'[56]

UN Commissioner's statement

Back on the Vanni battlefront and despite government pledges to stop the use of artillery, on 10 March state TV news included footage of the army shelling LTTE positions near PTK. One medical worker inside the 'safe zone' described it as the 'worst day' to date because of the army's repeated use of air burst, incendiary (white phosphorous) and high explosive shells.[57] The same source also begged the UN for more medical supplies with which to treat the spiralling number of civilian injuries. By this stage of the fighting, medical installations within the zone were forced to perform major operations without anaesthetics because the government had refused to provide such medicines on the grounds that they could end up in LTTE hands.[58] Confirmation of the appalling consequences of intensive shelling inside the 'safe zone' was provided by the (unofficial) casualty figures for 10 March alone: 124 people killed and 180 injured, with 59 of the victims children.[59]

Controversy regarding the way in which war was being conducted in the Vanni was further heightened on 13 March by the release of a statement from UN Human Rights Commissioner Navi Pillay, expressing growing alarm at the number of civilian casualties and the evidence of all-round disregard for their safety inside the war zone. 'Certain actions' by both sides, she argued, 'may constitute violations of international human rights and humanitarian law'. Pillay's statement noted that a 'broad range of credible sources' indicated that since 20 January more than 2,800 civilians had been killed and more than 7,000 injured, over two-thirds of them inside the no-fire zones, and that the majority of casualties had been caused by artillery and other heavy weapons. Since the 24 February announcement that government forces would no longer fire into the no-fire zones, the statement contended, more than 500 people had been killed and 1,000 injured in precisely those areas.

Casualty figures: controversy within the UN

Throughout the final stages of the conflict, the government unswervingly maintained that the civilian casualty count resulting from the army's 'humanitarian mission' to destroy terrorism and rescue civilians trapped in the Vanni was zero. On the UN side, Navi Pillay's 13 March statement might lead one to conclude that the organisation took a similarly resolute, albeit opposing, position on this issue. In reality, nothing could be further from the truth.

The majority of those in senior UN positions dealing directly with the Sri Lankan conflict maintained that the figures for dead and injured civilians released by Pillay, as well as subsequent casualty statistics generated from within the UN, were factually unreliable, or politically undesirable (or both), and accordingly should not be officially released by the UN mission in Colombo. Such views consistently prevailed, to the organisation's ultimate embarrassment and shame.

In an email sent to Pillay the day before her statement was released, for example, Ban Ki-Moon's Chef de Cabinet Vijay Nambiar argued that 'the severity of the draft statement you propose to make is likely to have very serious political and legal repercussions for the rest of us, and I hope you can consider carefully this fact while finalising your statement.' Pointing out that UN Resident Coordinator Neil Buhne and Under-Secretary General John Holmes had also stated that 'the accuracy of figures remains still quite questionable', he argued that 'it would have been better to be a little more general or tentative about the figures.'[60] Holmes himself argued against 'being too specific about the casualty figures' because of what he called 'the difficulty of being able to defend them with confidence', and went on to suggest that the statement's reference to war crimes would also be 'controversial'. To their credit, High Commissioner Navi Pillay's office went ahead and published the UN casualty statistics anyway.

With respect to the LTTE, Pillay accused the Tigers of continuing to use civilians as human shields and of firing at civilians attempting to escape. Highlighting allegations of the continued forcible recruitment of civilians—including children—it suggested that this 'brutal and inhuman treatment of civilians ... should be examined to see if it constitutes war crimes'. All in all, the UN High Commissioner stated, 'the current level of civilian casualties is truly shocking, and there are legitimate fears that the loss of life may reach catastrophic levels, if the fighting continues in this way,' and she issued an appeal to both sides to suspend hostilities immediately in order to allow for the civilian population's evacuation by land or sea. In conclusion, Pillay urged the government to give the UN and other independent agencies 'full access' to the conflict zone in order to permit an accurate assessment of human rights and humanitarian conditions there.[61]

Predictably, the government response to Pillay's statement was fiercely critical, with Human Rights Minister Mahinda Samarasinghe pronouncing himself both 'disappointed' and 'dismayed' at the publication of casualty figures that, as he claimed at a press conference, 'tally closely' with those put out by '*TamilNet* and other pro-LTTE organisations'. Foreign Minister Bogollagama contended that it was 'unfair in terms of [its] conclusions and quite contrary to the factual position'.[62]

Humanitarian rescue mission

At the same time, the Co-Chairs' suggestion of a sea-directed civilian rescue mission to the Vanni, first mooted toward the end of February, again came to the fore. The seriousness with which the US in particular had been treating the idea was underlined by reports that a high-level team from the United States Pacific Command (PACOM) headquarters in Hawaii had visited the country in late February to evaluate the logistics of such an exercise.[63] After initially seeming to give the initiative the nod, by mid-March Foreign Minister Bogollagama was pouring cold water on it, suggesting that the government had neither 'permitted any international forces to evacuate civilians from the Vanni' nor received 'any proposal from any country in that regard'.[64]

One issue this affair served to clarify was the fact that while Norway remained the primary point of contact for discussions with the LTTE—a position it retained until the end of the fighting—by this stage the USA had become the de facto frontline for Co-Chair dealings with the government, and diplomatic discussions in general, a fact reflected in the increasingly bluntness of its dealings with the government in Colombo. A US Embassy cable from late March makes the point clearly. During a meeting between Blake and Bogollagama to discuss a scheduled UN Security Council briefing on the fighting in the Vanni—something that Colombo strongly opposed—the foreign minister reportedly repeated claims that government forces were 'not shelling into the safe zone', to which Blake is said to have replied this was 'simply not true'.[65]

An illustration of the way the LTTE were treating the civilian population under its control is provided by reports of what happened towards the end of March when hundreds of civilians trapped in the NFZ reportedly attempted an escape across the lagoon separating them from army-controlled territory north of Puttumatalan. LTTE cadres got wind of the attempt and set up sentry points near the edge of the lagoon. When civilians began to cross, they were surrounded by Tiger cadres. Men were separated from the women and children and a number of the unmarried males, including children, were forcibly recruited, while the others were ordered to help build bunkers for LTTE cadres. Protesting family members were beaten.[66]

On 30 March, following unofficial reports from inside the 'safe zone' that heavy shelling and aerial bombardment were continuing, and with high civilian casualty levels, Bogollagama announced that government forces would be 'suspending' fighting for a brief period in order to 'provide humanitarian relief aid to civilians in the safe area', although he did not specify when exactly this would occur.[67] Defence spokesperson Keheliya Rambukwella added that an additional goal of the government's 'humanitarian pause'—a move he described as one 'suggested by the UN Security Council'—was to 'pave the way to rescue civilians used as human shields by the LTTE'.[68]

Robert Blake on the US-led rescue plan

At a certain point we probably became more of a target than Norway because we were seen to be pushing hard on human rights. I worked extremely closely with Tore [Hattrem] and Hans [Brattskar]. At the end of the war there were basically four of us: myself, Tore, Neil Buhne and the head of the ICRC. We often made sort of quadripartite demarches. We would all go in together and talk to Gotabhaya or Basil. We made our point, mostly about civilian casualties. We were always trying to be even-handed, and were very careful to say that a lot of the responsibility fell on the LTTE.

We could have said that all of this should come to a halt, there should be no military action whatsoever, but we made the judgement that that was not correct; it was perfectly reasonable for the government to prosecute a war against the LTTE, provided they were careful about civilian casualties. Until January 2009 or so their record was pretty good.

[Earlier] we had realised that UN withdrawal was quite an ominous development. A lot of NGOs did not want to put people in harm's way, but many had Tamil staff who did not want to be separated from their families. We had a regular meeting with the government. We all got together: Gotabhaya, Basil, army officers were there. The Norwegians still had contact with the LTTE and that remained an important role. The other big effort we made was to see if we could use American ships to go

---

in and pull a large percentage of the IDPs off the beach. Erik [Solheim] and I were prepared to go in and try to negotiate that. I brought the Pacific Command in to send a whole team out to look at it. They had detailed conversations with the Sri Lankan military.

The idea was that we would send a landing craft, and the ICRC would have supervised some sort of screening procedure on the beach itself to make sure that none of [the IDPs] were armed. Then we would take them to a Sri Lankan ship somewhere off the coast. From there they would go to the normal IDP screening procedure further south. It was a relatively simple idea. There were several thousands of people at risk. Many of them were injured. Since the government had conceded that the ICRC could come in and provide food to these people [we argued], why shouldn't we take as many as possible out of there?

Where the idea finally ran aground was that in the end Gotabhaya was worried that Erik and I would be taken hostage. That was his stated reason. What he was really worried about was that we might actually succeed and that that would lead to a renewed Norwegian peace effort, and he didn't want that. He wanted to put an end to the whole thing militarily. Right till the end we were trying to negotiate a diplomatic solution. We were not going to allow the LTTE to leave but we were hoping that most of the cadres would be allowed to leave of their own volition. Some sort of deal whereby they would not be prosecuted, although obviously the senior leadership would have to be.

There was a lot of talk of how Prabhakaran and others had these submarines and probably could have escaped, and to this day I don't know why he didn't try to escape and live to fight another day. He didn't choose that, and I'm still not clear why.

UN–LTTE contacts

The revelation that UN Under-Secretary General John Holmes had recently been in phone contact with KP unleashed a frenzy of local media commentary, with the nationalist JVP MP Wimal Weerawamsa arguing that the government should break diplomatic ties with Norway because of its alleged role in facilitating contact between the UN and the LTTE. Ambassador Tore Hattrem was duly summoned to hear an expression of the Foreign Ministry's 'displeasure', but formally the matter didn't go any further than this. In addition Robert Blake took the step of posting a comment on a 'widely-read newspaper website' pointing out that the purpose of the conversation with KP was to persuade the LTTE 'to allow citizens to leave and observe international humanitarian law.'[69]

Despite the wave of hostile sentiment generated by this affair, the Norwegians diligently continued with their attempts to persuade the LTTE leadership to accept an 'organised end' to the conflict. On 2 April, for example, *TamilNet* ran a report on a phone conversation between Solheim and Nadesan regarding the 'plight of the civilians in Vanni'. The report also noted that Nadesan had reiterated the standard LTTE position emphasising the call for an 'immediate ceasefire' and resumption of negotiations, with no mention of Tigers disarmament.[70]

D.B.S. Jeyaraj

As Mao Ze Dong said, guerillas are the fish who swim in an ocean of people. If the ocean dries up the fish flounder. Likewise, if the conflict zone is drained of civilians the Tigers become sitting ducks. It is not in the interests of LTTE to give up the civilians and become more vulnerable. One may rant and rail at LTTE for this inhuman attitude but the Tigers faced with extinction are not likely to listen. That's the reality.

When LTTE and pro-Tiger lobby calls for a ceasefire the international community counters it by saying—let's have a temporary one to get the people out. To this the LTTE won't agree. If there's a permanent ceasefire there is no need to evacuate the civilians is the counter argument. The government too is wary about a truce as it sees itself on the verge of winning the conventional war. Colombo does not want the LTTE to wriggle out through a ceasefire ... If one were to dispense with the 'concern' displayed for entrapped civilians and appraise the situation realistically, what Colombo and the international community are asking the Tigers to do is to commit politico-military *hara-kiri*. Given the LTTE track record it is impossible that the organisation would do so. For that matter no entity in the world is likely to let itself be led to the slaughter willingly.

If necessary the LTTE will go down fighting to the very end and also take down a large number of civilians with them. But they won't let people go. In a worst-case scenario around 15,000 civilians at least could die during the military push. I fervently hope and pray that such a situation will not come to pass. Despite all agony and anxiety, one feels utterly helpless in this climate of impending doom.[71]

LTTE leadership massacre

Giving voice to mounting international concern over developments in the Vanni, on 3 April Ban Ki-Moon issued a statement deploring the LTTE's refusal to allow people to leave the conflict area and their 'forced recruitment of civilians, particularly children', while reminding the government of its 'responsibility to protect civilians', and specifically to 'avoid the use of heavy weapons' in areas where they were congregated.[72] At the same time, a large LTTE contingent under Commander Theepan were preparing a major counter-attack, the result of Prabhakaran's reported decision to make Aanandapuram, where he and many cadres were holed up, the Tigers' 'Stalingrad'.[73] Army battalions advancing on the Tiger-controlled zone caught wind of this and responded rapidly, and soon the Tiger cadres—penned inside a small area close to PTK—were facing the prospect of encirclement by a much larger group of Army Special Forces and Commando formations.[74]

For more than two days the Tiger cadres put up a determined resistance. Eventually, however, the inevitable occurred: completely cut off from reinforcements as well as food, water and medical supplies, they were wiped out.[75] To finish off the job government forces enlisted the assistance of fighter jets, artillery and multiple-barrel rocket launchers. There were subsequent allegations, staunchly denied by the army, that white phosphorus had been used in the assault.[76]

LTTE casualty counts varied but one credible source suggested that more than 625 bodies were recovered the following day, many of them from the elite 'Charles Anthony' brigade that had played a major role in numerous critical military encounters.[77] What made the losses especially crippling was that more than twenty senior commanders had been killed, including the top four women—the biggest leadership loss sustained by the Tigers to date. Among the dead was Theepan, overall commander of LTTE Northern Front fighting formations, a popular and brave leader who during the CFA era had held regular meetings with his Sri Lankan counterpart Sarath Fonseka. Also killed were Keerthi and Nagesh, commanders of the Eastern Jeyanthan brigade, and 'Gaddafi', a former Prabhakaran bodyguard who was one of a ten-member squad trained in anti-aircraft missile operations by the Indians in the 1980s.[78] In the view of KP, this was 'the defining moment of the war'.

Two days after the LTTE rout, UN Under-Secretary General John Holmes published an article in *The Guardian* calling for 'decisive action' by all parties 'before it is too late'. Stressing that 'a bloodbath on the beaches of Northern Sri Lanka' seemed an 'increasingly real possibility', he urged both sides to agree to a 'temporary humanitarian lull' to allow aid workers and relief supplies to reach the '150,000 to 190,000 civilians trapped in the [conflict] zone'. In an illustration of the murderous reality underlying Holmes's appeal, on the same day it was reported that health facility compounds in the northeast section of the NFZ had been repeatedly hit by shells on 8 April, including one where a large group of people—mostly women and children—were queuing to collect milk powder. The shelling was alleged to have come from an army-controlled area. Moreover, security force aerial surveillance vehicles had been seen flying over the area prior to the attack, and the timing and location of the milk powder distribution had been communicated to the army in advance.[79] At least sixty civilians died in the attacks.

On the weekend of 11–12 April, immediately prior to the Sri Lankan New Year, President Rajapaksa announced a 48-hour ceasefire. Observers reported that Army shelling of the NFZ diminished, while firing from inside the zone itself stopped entirely. In conversations with the US Ambassador, Basil Rajapaksa indicated that the ceasefire could be extended, particularly if the LTTE began releasing civilians.[80] UN Secretary General Ban Ki-Moon welcomed the move, noting that while it was 'less than the full humanitarian pause of several days' he had requested, it was nonetheless a 'useful first step' as well as an 'opportunity to move towards the peaceful and orderly end to the fighting'.[81]

Renewed attempts at diplomacy

A 13 April US Embassy cable reported that during a meeting between US Ambassador Blake and Foreign Minister Bogollagama, Blake had asked Bogollagama whether he had 'shared' the 'Norwegian information' that 'some LTTE leaders favour talks to work out a surrender'. Bogollagama responded that he had, but that Norway had 'lost credibility'. In response, Blake told the foreign minister he was 'forced to conclude' that Colombo had decided that the military would 'go into the "safe zone" and settle this', which would, he contended, be 'disastrous' both for 'trapped civilians' and the government itself. In conclusion, Blake stated that the government was missing a 'big opportunity to negotiate an LTTE surrender and save many lives'. Bogollagama hesitated at first, then responded, 'let's wait to see how the 48-hour period goes'.[82]

A *TamilNet* report cited in a Sri Lankan newspaper the same day stated that following the end of the military's two-day ceasefire, which concluded at midnight 12 April, the army recommenced operations and the two sides were soon exchanging 'rocket and gunfire'.[83] Reacting to this development, John Holmes told reporters at the UN's New York headquarters that it was evident that 48 hours had 'not been long enough to allow us to get in significant amounts of aid, or to allow visits by humanitarian workers to the area', and repeated his earlier warning of the possibility of a 'blood bath'.[84]

Dismissing the temporary pause in the fighting as 'political drama' aimed at 'deceiving the international community and the Tamil people', the LTTE reiterated its call for an 'unconditional and permanent ceasefire conducive for peaceful negotiations'.[85] A senior Defence Ministry official responded that the 'question of permanent ceasefire will arise only after the LTTE lays down arms',[86] a sentiment echoed in comments made by Gotabhaya Rajapaksa in the course of a meeting with the US Ambassador in which the Defence Secretary reiterated the government's willingness to offer an amnesty to all LTTE cadres except Prabhakaran and Pottu Amman following a surrender.[87]

During a low-key 16–17 April visit to Sri Lanka, the UN Secretary-General's Chief of Staff Vijay Nambiar held talks with President Rajapaksa and other government figures that focused on the issue of releasing civilians from the war zone. Briefing the Co-Chairs Ambassadors on the outcome of these discussions, Nambiar indicated that the president, Gotabhaya and Bogollagama had all expressed firm opposition to the idea of an extended 'humanitarian pause', arguing that it would only give the Tigers an opportunity to re-group and forcibly recruit more civilians.[88]

By the end of Nambiar's visit a compromise of sorts appeared to have been reached, which centred on a proposal for a joint ICRC-UN 'working-level' visit to the NFZ to explore options for civilian evacuation. During a lunch for Nambiar hosted by Bogollagama, the US Ambassador took the opportunity to tell the host that if the government elected to pursue a military solution without first allowing a 'high-level UN diplomatic effort' to secure the rescue of civilians from the no-fire zone, it would be seen around the world as the 'aggressor' and would be held responsible for the 'high number of civilian casualties that would certainly occur.'

Underlining the fact that the USA and 'many other countries' were 'seriously concerned' about the 'already high number of civilian casualties', Blake told the Sri Lankan foreign minister bluntly that comparisons were 'already being made to what transpired in Rwanda', where the international community had 'not done enough to prevent a catastrophe'. If Sri Lanka elected to 'pursue the military option', Blake continued, the country could expect 'escalating international criticism' along with 'actions to demonstrate international concern', which may include 'suspension of aid, closer scrutiny of IMF lending to the country, possible war crimes investigations and other actions'.[89]

Erik Solheim

> From January onwards we continued to try to impress upon the LTTE the need for an organised end to the war, to save the lives of civilians as well as LTTE cadres. We had two main lines of communications for this message. By phone directly with Nadesan and Pulidevan in the rapidly shrinking LTTE enclave, and more importantly, through KP.
>
> Conversations with the Wanni were surreal and we would never know whether our messages had actually been conveyed to Prabhakaran. They insisted on a ceasefire and invited us to come, but only to talk to Nadesan, not Prabhakaran. KP told us that the LTTE leadership was living in a surreal world: no real contact with the world, believing in miracles. There was a belief in a BJP electoral victory in the May Indian elections to the Lok Sabha, and the LTTE thought they would pull something off. A BJP victory was not unrealistic, but the idea that a new Indian government would suddenly turn Indian policy around certainly was.
>
> Second, they believed in the miracle of the Tamil diaspora pressurising for a much stronger response from the West. Again, as anyone and everyone could have told them, we knew it would not happen. KP agreed with our line. He told us that he would try to convince Prabhakaran. Whether that message ever reached him is difficult to know. KP was constantly agreeing with the 'organised end to the war' proposal. He said he would do his utmost to convince Prabhakaran about it but that there would be severe difficulties in doing so.

Oslo in the spotlight

Norway's facilitation role in the conflict was placed firmly in the spotlight after a spate of highly critical media reports focusing on Hattrem's late February meeting with KP, described as a 'known terrorist wanted by Interpol', as well as accusations that in recent months Oslo had been brokering 'secret negotiations' to try and secure 'safe passage/security for the LTTE leadership'.[90] The latter charge was described by Tore Hattrem as 'pure and simple rubbish', who emphasised that in reality recent Norwegian efforts had been 'solely focused on the humanitarian situation for the IDPs'.[91]

Concerning the charge of secret negotiations, in public Hattrem confined himself to noting that he had met President Rajapaksa in advance of the meeting with KP to explain the reasons. As if on cue, brandishing placards showing the Norwegian Ambassador in LTTE fatigues and sporting slogans such as 'Throw Out Viking Terrorists', a demonstration organised by Wimal

Weerawamsa's National Freedom Front and the Buddhist JHU party outside the Norwegian Embassy in Colombo called for Hattrem's expulsion from the country for trying to help the LTTE leadership escape.[92] And as Solheim points out, the government's double game—encouraging Norway in private to keep all lines of communication to the LTTE open, while condemning the same in public—continued throughout the final weeks of the war.

Nor was this the end of the story. Like its counterparts in several other countries such as the UK and Canada, the Norwegian Tamil diaspora was by now holding regular demonstrations to protest the situation in the Vanni. Following one such demonstration, a group of protestors stormed and ransacked part of the Sri Lankan Embassy in Oslo.[93] An embarrassed Norwegian government offered its profuse apologies and undertook to cover the costs of refurbishing the building. The political damage, however, had already been done. A formal note handed to Jon Hanssen-Bauer in Oslo and Tore Hattrem in Colombo stated that the Sri Lankan government 'perceive[d]' that there was 'no room for Norway to act as a facilitator in its engagement with Sri Lanka in the current context'.[94] Reacting to the demarche from Colombo, Hanssen-Bauer stated, 'we cannot be facilitators in a peace process which has in effect been suspended since 2006'.[95]

Civilian exodus

Seizing the military initiative, on the night of 19 April a large army force breached the LTTE's defences and advanced into the NFZ. The immediate impact of this manoeuvre was to unleash a flood of Tamil civilians attempting, and in most cases succeeding, to escape into government-held territory.

Three days later, Foreign Minister Bogollagama briefed Colombo diplomats that nearly 103,000 civilians had been 'evacuated' from the NFZ over the preceding 72 hours. In belated recognition of the extreme inaccuracy of previous official estimates of the numbers of people trapped inside the zone, in notes accompanying his speech (though not in the speech itself) Bogollagama acknowledged that previous government estimates of 50–60,000 were flatly discredited by the number who had fled in recent days.[96]

Colombo's spirits were boosted, however, by the news that Daya Master, the LTTE media spokesperson, had been among the refugees and had surrendered to the military, as had George, Tamilselvan's former translator.[97] Asked why they had given themselves up, the pair cited the fact that the Tigers had been shooting at civilians to prevent them from escaping, and had been conscripting children.[98]

Conspicuous by its absence from Colombo-based media coverage of the civilian exodus, however, was any reference to the terrible human costs of what Colombo insisted on continuing to refer to as the army's 'humanitarian rescue' operation. Even allowing for the exaggeration applied to such figures by LTTE sources, the government appeared to be oblivious to the fact that the military onslaught had resulted in high civilian casualties. Information obtained independently from two of the makeshift hospitals operating in the area, for example, indicated 121 civilians dead and 765 injured during 19–20 April,[99] many as a result of aerial bombardment and artillery shelling.[100] When recalling the night of 19 April, one eyewitness described the actions of the army as 'indifferen[t] to any number of civilians being killed, as long as the army could parade the number who made it out as a major success'.[101] While celebrating the release of such a vast mass of people, many were apprehensive about the fate of the estimated 40–50,000 still stuck inside the war zone.[102]

D.B.S. Jeyaraj

Since it is demonstrated beyond doubt that the LTTE is restraining civilians from leaving, [Colombo] can always claim to be mounting a humanitarian operation. The human costs will be depicted as collateral damage. A massive bloodbath seems very likely and the world at large seems unable or unwilling to prevent it.[103]

Seemingly responding to continuing international expressions of concern—most recently articulated by visiting Indian Security Adviser M.K. Narayanan and Foreign Secretary Shiv Shankar Menon[104]—on 27 April Colombo announced that it was ending 'combat operations'.[105] Army spokesperson Udaya Nanayakkara was at pains to explain that this did not amount to a 'ceasefire' declaration. Since the government had decided that combat operations had 'reached their conclusion', he stated, the security forces had been instructed to 'end the use of heavy calibre guns, combat aircraft and aerial weapons which could cause civilian casualties'.[106] Irrespective of this statement, however, eyewitnesses that very afternoon reported 'a rain of army shells' falling among civilians encamped two miles south of the fighting at Mullivaikal.[107]

> *Leaflet addressed to Tamil civilians dropped over the combat zone,*
> *late April 2009*
>
> I am aware of tremendous difficulties faced by civilians who are unfortu-
> nately still being held hostage by LTTE in NFZ. Your suffering is pro-
> longed by this action of LTTE who are holding you as a human shield for
> their own safety and security. I appeal to every one of you to come over
> to the cleared areas. My government will continue to give utmost priority
> to ensur[ing] the safety and welfare of each and every one of you.[108]

Colombo moves to exclude Norway

On 24 April, Foreign Minister Bogollagama summoned the Co-Chair
Colombo diplomatic representatives, excluding the Norwegians, for a discussion of the group's proposal for a mediated surrender by the
LTTE. When asked why the Norwegian Ambassador had not been invited,
Bogollagama replied, 'we no longer recognise Norway as a member of the
Co-Chairs'. The Co-Chair representatives responded that this was unacceptable and broke off the meeting. In a subsequent US Embassy cable it
was suggested that since a mediated surrender could 'probably not occur
without Norwegian facilitation', Colombo's action indicated that it was
'unlikely' to 'pursue the option of a mediated surrender'.[109]

At the same time, the UN's John Holmes returned to the island on
24 April. Speaking to Colombo diplomats in the course of his visit, Holmes
informed them that his primary objectives were to secure a 'humanitarian
pause' in the fighting and to determine if there were any openings for a
'negotiated surrender' by the LTTE.[110] Regarding the first objective, government officials soon made it clear that they still rejected the idea. Regarding
the second, as Holmes doubtless learned in Colombo, against all the odds
the Norwegians were continuing to pursue the possibility of an 'organised
end' to the war.[111]

The following day, reports emerged of a series of shell attacks on another
hospital inside the 'safe zone' at Mullivaikal, resulting in multiple civilian
deaths, including ten people unloading supplies from an ICRC ship at a
nearby dock. As on a number of previous occasions, defence spokesperson
Keheliya Rambukwella denied that government forces were firing into the
NFZ, contrary to eyewitness accounts.[112]

In a sign that international attention was increasingly focused on the
fighting in the Vanni, on 29 April British and French Foreign Ministers

David Miliband and Bernard Kouchner paid a twenty-four-hour visit to Sri Lanka.[113] Erik Solheim recalls that he briefed Miliband by phone before he and Kouchner left Europe, but himself declined to take part in the mission in order, as he puts it, 'not to make it possible for the Sri Lankan government to deflect attention from the pressure exerted by the British and French ministers by attacking Norway'. Yet again, the president and Gotabhaya firmly rejected any suggestion of a ceasefire.[114] As one analyst concluded, despite exhibiting an increasing awareness of the 'possible costs of its actions', the government was not shifting from 'its resolve to continue military operations in the NFZ until the remaining territory comes under its control and the last LTTE leaders still there are captured or killed'.[115]

KP and the ceasefire plan

The Co-Chair's Norwegian-led efforts to obtain the LTTE's agreement to a ceasefire plan continued. According to Erik Solheim, the primary focus was on rescuing civilians trapped in the war zone and facilitating the surrender of LTTE cadres who wished to do so. This would be achieved by sending a large ship under international supervision to the Vanni coast. Civilians would be taken to Colombo and set free; LTTE cadres would hand in their weapons, be registered and have their photos taken to ensure that their identities were known in order to protect them from government harm. A general amnesty would apply for everyone other than Prabhakaran and Pottu Amman.

In discussions with the LTTE, KP served as the principal interlocutor. Although KP, according to Solheim, thought that the Tiger leaders were 'living in a dream world', it seemed that he must have received 'some kind of positive response' to the Norwegians' ideas, because he agreed to a meeting was in Oslo, in April.

Interviewed in 2012 by D.B.S. Jeyaraj, KP's account differed from Solheim's on certain details of what was being proposed. In KP's version, the focus was on an organised surrender of LTTE cadres, to include: cessation of hostilities; handover of weapons to UN representatives; negotiations between Colombo and the LTTE with Norwegian facilitation; prospective evacuation of '25–50 top leaders with their families'[116] to a foreign country 'if necessary'; general amnesty for 'low level junior cadres'; and detention and 'relatively minor sentences' for middle-level leaders and cadres. KP also stated that he had personally secured 'Western' support for this plan, as well as agreement from three countries to 'accommodate' high-level LTTE leaders and American agreement to 'send their naval fleet in to do evacuation if necessary'.[117] Solheim suggests that KP may have expanded upon the Norwegian ideas with the aim of getting the go-ahead from Prabhakaran.

The scheduled meeting in Oslo was called off at the last minute. Reportedly Norwegian security police had already arrived in Kuala Lumpur to escort KP to Oslo by the time news of its cancellation came through. In a 2012 interview, KP stated that he had faxed a '16-page memorandum' to the LTTE leadership in advance of the meeting. In response, KP says, '[Prabhakaran] rejected the 16 pages in just three words: *Ithai* Etrukolla Mudiyathu' (This is unacceptable). So I had to drop it'. Whatever disagreements Solheim and KP may have had on the proposal's contents, they agreed over who rejected it—the LTTE leader himself.

Civilians under fire

In an interview with Al-Jazeera on 1 May, Foreign Secretary Palitha Kohona—responding to UN satellite imagery showing evidence of air attacks carried out between mid-February and mid-April—conceded that the Air Force had indeed been carrying out raids over the NFZ. At the same time, Kohona maintained that the raids had only targeted Tiger artillery—a justification that contradicted his own categorical denials that the army had launched attacks on the 'safe zone', made only twelve days previously. Likewise, President Rajapaksa had recently stated, 'If you are not willing to accept the fact that we are not using heavy weapons I really can't help it. We are not using heavy weapons. When we say no, it means no.'[118]

Evidence of the government forces' continuing assault arrived on 2 May when sources within the NFZ reported that a makeshift hospital at Mullivaikal had been shelled twice that morning. As the main medical centre within the zone, the hospital was overflowing with patients. The first shelling reportedly hit the outpatients department, killing twenty-three civilians and injuring thirty-four, including two medical staff. Based on testimony from one of the hospital doctors, a Human Rights Watch report later claimed that the second attack resulted in a further forty-five deaths and over fifty injuries.[119] Army spokesperson Nanayakkara denied that the attacks had taken place.[120]

On 5 May, at a meeting with the Co-Chair Ambassadors called by President Rajapaksa, the US Chargé d'Affaires showed the president and Kohona satellite images for the period 27 April–3 May, which had been provided by the State Department for the express purpose of the meeting. The images clearly showed shelling damage in the 'no fire zone' from after 27 April, the date on which Rajapaksa had declared an end to army operations. While not denying outright that shelling had occurred, Rajapaksa maintained there was no hospital in the zone and that government forces would not shell civilian areas. Kohona responded that before declaring it a 'safe zone' the Air Force had indeed bombed the area due to the presence of 'Sea Tiger bases' along the adjoining coastal strip.

Putting a positive spin on the situation, a US Embassy cable suggested it was 'possible' that 'individual field commanders or the army command' might have 'resorted to the use of heavy weapons while protecting the Commander-in-Chief from this information'. And while the government had 'conceded nothing' with respect to the satellite images, it was possible that the president might now conduct his own inquiries and bring about a 'change of the [army's] conduct'. In conclusion, the cable noted that Rajapaksa had 'remarked before this meeting that India had satellites and was monitoring the ground situation in Sri Lanka. It will now be equally clear that we are watching too.'[121]

The government followed up this meeting with a diplomatic briefing that focused on what it was now starting to describe as the conflict's 'conclusion', along with its development plans for the North. With the LTTE now confined to an area of less than six square kilometres, President Rajapaksa repeated claims that government forces were following a 'zero civilian casualties' policy and that the use of heavy weapons and aerial attacks had been halted. Arguing that the Tigers' failure to release civilians during previous pauses in the fighting rendered ceasefire proposals 'redundant', he described the Sri Lankan armed forces' current advances as one of the 'greatest rescue operations in history'.[122]

Meantime, reports from the combat zone indicated that progress was being made despite determined resistance. Army units were being subjected to increasingly frequent suicide attacks by Black Tiger cadres, which made every advance a hazardous business.

Report to US Congress, 2009

On or around 8 May, an eyewitness inside the NFZ saw an army drone conduct a reconnaissance mission over the hospital at Valayanmadam. Shortly after the hospital was attacked, killing 4–5 people including a doctor and wounding more than 30. Several witnesses subsequently informed Human Rights Watch that each time a hospital was established in a new location, the facility's GPS coordinates were transmitted to the government to ensure that the facility would be protected from military attack. The same witnesses stated that on several occasions, artillery attacks on the hospitals took place the day after the coordinates had been transmitted.[123]

On 8 May the government announced a redefinition of the 'no fire zone', reducing it to an area smaller than three square kilometres between the coast and Nanthikadal lagoon, north of Mullaitivu. Over the following forty-eight hours there were reports of sustained and heavy shelling within the zone, resulting in the deaths of more than 300 civilians and more than 1,000 injuries. A doctor working at a temporary hospital located at Mullivaikal stated that the facility was struggling to cope with the latest surge in casualties, noting that the civilian population in the 'safe zone' had been 'shocked by the ferocity and intensity' of the artillery shelling, and, on 10 May, by reports of two air strikes just south of the zone.[124]

Government sources denied these reports, arguing that the LTTE had 'blindsided' international media. They advanced the bizarre claim that any shelling that had taken place within the zone was the responsibility of the Tigers, not the army. Gotabhaya was cited in local media as calling the accusations 'ridiculous', and, in reference to recent controversies over external aerial intelligence, suggested that the army 'couldn't have mounted a large scale artillery assault without the international community knowing it.'[125] Army spokesman Nanayakkara was similarly dismissive. 'The military conducted rescue operations,' he said. 'We used only small arms. There was no shelling of those areas.'[126]

'Credible allegations'

The text below is excerpted from the Executive Summary of the March 2011 UN Secretary-General Panel of Experts Report, and summarises allegations of war crimes and other atrocities that the panel found to be 'credible':

> Between September 2008 and 19 May 2009, the Sri Lanka Army advanced its military campaign into the Vanni using large-scale and widespread shelling, causing large numbers of civilian deaths. This campaign constituted persecution of the population of the Vanni. Around 330,000 civilians

were trapped into an ever-decreasing area, fleeing the shelling but kept hostage by the LTTE. The government sought to intimidate and silence the media and other critics of the war through a variety of threats and actions, including the use of white vans to abduct and to make people disappear.

The government shelled on a large scale in three consecutive No Fire Zones, where it had encouraged the civilian population to concentrate, even after indicating that it would cease the use of heavy weapons. It shelled the UN hub, food distribution lines and near the ICRC ships that were coming to pick up the wounded and their relatives from the beaches. It shelled in spite of its knowledge of the impact, provided by its own intelligence systems and through notification by the UN, the ICRC and others. Most civilian casualties in the final phases of the war were caused by government shelling.

The government systematically shelled hospitals on the frontlines. All hospitals in the Vanni were hit by mortars and artillery, some of them repeatedly, despite the fact that their locations were well-known to the government. The government also systematically deprived people in the conflict zone of humanitarian aid, in the form of food and medical supplies, particularly surgical supplies, adding to their suffering. To this end, it purposefully underestimated the number of civilians who remained in the conflict zone. Tens of thousands lost their lives from January to May 2009, many of whom died anonymously in the carnage of the final few days. ...

Despite grave danger in the conflict zone, the LTTE refused civilians permission to leave, using them as hostages, at times even using their presence as a strategic human buffer between themselves and the advancing Army. It implemented a policy of forced recruitment throughout the war, but in the final stages greatly intensified its recruitment of people of all ages, including children as young as 14. The LTTE forced civilians to dig trenches and other emplacements for its own defences, thereby contributing to blurring the distinction between combatants and civilians and exposing civilians to additional harm. All of this was done in a quest to pursue a war that was clearly lost ...

From February 2009 onwards the LTTE started point-blank shooting of civilians who attempted to escape the conflict zone, significantly adding to the death toll in the final stages of the war. It also fired artillery in proximity to large groups of IDPs and fired from, or stored military equipment near, IDPs or civilian installations such as hospitals. Throughout the final stages of the war, the LTTE continued its policy of suicide attacks outside the conflict zone. Even though its ability to perpetrate such attacks was diminished compared to previous phases of the conflict, it perpetrated a number of attacks against civilians outside the conflict zone.

In the meantime, news on the civilian front was grim. On 13 May the ICRC ship *Green Ocean* attempted to deliver another vital food shipment and evacuate injured civilians. Later the same afternoon the ship was heading back to Trincomalee having achieved neither objective, the result of what ICRC head Paul Castella described as 'chaotic conditions' at the landing site, as well as nearby firing. Castella also confirmed reports that the improvised hospital at Mullivaikal had been hit by artillery fire for the third time.[127] The following day, ICRC headquarters in Geneva issued a statement noting that ICRC staff on the ground were witnessing 'an unimaginable humanitarian catastrophe'. Under such circumstances, the Red Cross was 'unable' to help civilians.

President Obama, 13 May 2009

Tens of thousands of innocent civilians are trapped between the warring government forces and the Tamil Tigers with no means of escape, little access to food, water, shelter and medicine. This has led to widespread suffering and the loss of hundreds if not thousands of lives. Without urgent action, this humanitarian crisis could turn into a catastrophe ... I urge the Tamil Tigers to lay down their arms and let civilians go. Their forced recruitment of civilians and use of civilians as human shields is deplorable. These tactics will only serve to alienate all those who carry them out.

The government should stop the indiscriminate shelling that has taken hundreds of innocent lives, including several hospitals, and [it] should live up to its commitment to not use heavy weapons in the conflict zone. [It] should give UN humanitarian teams access to the civilians who are trapped between the warring parties so that they can receive the immediate assistance necessary to save lives. [It] should also allow the UN and the ICRC access to nearly 190,000 displaced people within Sri Lanka so that they can receive additional support that they need. The USA stands ready to work with the international community to support the people of Sri Lanka in this time of suffering. I don't believe that we can delay.[128]

Mopping up operations

With the Tigers and the trapped civilians pushed back into an ever-shrinking patch of territory, reports of LTTE cadres firing on those attempting to escape continued to emerge. In several instances the Tigers resorted to shelling, resulting in heavy casualties. Further reports from the combat zone indicated that the Tigers were continuing to direct mortar and gunfire at government forces from among the mass of civilians, provoking murderous retaliation. Chillingly, reports also surfaced of LTTE cadres going to bunkers where civilians were sheltering, and asking 'So you want to run away to the army do you?', before opening fire.[129]

In turn, the army proved itself more than capable of equal brutality. Eyewitness reports indicate that from 13 May onwards, advancing soldiers regularly fired or threw grenades into civilian bunkers as a 'precaution' against the possibility of the LTTE using them to launch attacks. The frequency with which this occurred, it was suggested, was directly related to the number of casualties sustained by government forces. In all probability it was also related to their experiences during the earlier battle for PTK, during which wounded Black Tiger cadres allegedly hid themselves in bunkers until an army unit passed by, whereupon they simply blew themselves up. Eyewitnesses reported seeing heavy army vehicles flattening bunkers that contained civilians.[130]

On 14 May a rumour that Sea Tiger leader Soosai had announced that the LTTE would soon put down their arms spread rapidly among Tamil civilians. Following news that the Tigers had discharged all female cadres that day, there were also reports of their having announced that civilians who wanted to leave would now be able to do so. But the behaviour of Tiger cadres was unpredictable: some seemed to believe that a ceasefire deal had been worked out with the army; others did not, and were often murderous. While the Sea Tigers were said to have allowed a group of over 1,000 civilians to cross to the government side on the evening of the 14th, earlier that day a large group attempting the crossing were fired on by LTTE cadres, killing approximately 500.[131]

UTHR-J Report

Sivalingam and family had to keep moving trying to choose every time a new place that seemed safer. In front of his tent were a father, mother and three children who were all killed when a shell fell on them. There had also been a business family, who were in a tent next to his. A shell fell killing all 16 of them. He said that at this time the LTTE was killing escapees mercilessly. There were many instances when the Tigers waited for the escaping family to get into the water and fired bursts at the children, watching them writhe and die, in convulsions of hands and legs.[132]

On the morning of 15 May, and again the following day, groups of civilians repeatedly attempted escape south towards Mullaitivu. Each time Tiger cadres would reportedly block their exit. If the crowd pushed forward they would shoot at their legs and even kill a few people, in a bid to deter the rest. By the end of the day, however, army advances left the LTTE in control of just one of the three defensive *bunds* they had thrown up in the southern section of the combat zone, and little remaining territory.[133]

Final ceasefire deal attempt

In the meantime it emerged that a deal to end the fighting was being negotiated between the leaderships of both sides, and that three TNA MPs were among those involved. Reports indicated that the government would accept the surrender of surviving LTTE cadres and leaders, and permit a limited section of the leadership to leave the country. The stipulated conditions were rumoured to be: surrender of all weapons and equipment; release of all civilians; and release of all Sri Lanka Army prisoners held by the LTTE.[134] Reportedly, LTTE moves to honour the deal were already in evidence on 15 May. Huge clouds of smoke could be seen billowing across the combat zone, thought by some to be signs that the Tigers were destroying their weapons.[135]

On 16 May the Sri Lanka Army captured the last remaining section of coastline held by the Tigers. Attending a G-11 summit meeting in Jordan, President Rajapaksa issued what amounted to a declaration of victory, announcing that in an 'unprecedented humanitarian operation', the government had 'finally defeated the LTTE militarily' and that as a result he would be returning to Sri Lanka as 'a leader of a nation that vanquished terrorism'.[136] At the same time, while official army reports suggested that Prabhakaran and his comrades were planning mass suicide, there was increasing speculation in some quarters that the LTTE leader and as many as 300 senior cadres might already have taken their own lives.[137]

President Rajapaksa's speech at the 16 May G-11 meeting

History has taught us that solutions externally prescribed, with little understanding of the complexity of the problem on the ground, are prone to failure. My government is, therefore, firmly committed to seeking a home-grown solution acceptable to all communities.[138]

Late on 16 May, Tore Hattrem called his American counterpart Robert Blake to inform him that KP had communicated that the LTTE were now prepared to surrender unconditionally to a third party. ICRC Head Paul Castella also reported that Gotabhaya was amenable to the proposal, so long as the Tigers provided a list of the names of leaders who wished to surrender.[139] Talking to Blake the following morning, however, Gotabhaya appeared to change tack, responding to suggestions that the ICRC should enter the conflict zone to mediate surrender by stating 'we're beyond that now'. More than 50,000 civilians had escaped from Tiger control over the last twenty-four hours, he pointed out, and 'very few' non-combatants now remained in the war zone. With respect to an LTTE surrender, Gotabhaya informed the US Ambassador that the army had issued instructions to all commanders to 'accept surrenderees'[140]—a claim that some argue may have been the exact opposite of the actual instructions.

Despite being confined within an area no more than 400 by 600 metres, the remaining LTTE cadres resumed fighting on the morning of 17 May. Army sources put the number of civilians left inside the conflict zone in the hundreds, although there are reasons—not least the large number of civilians who continued to pour out of the area—to think that the real figure was in fact far higher. For example Ponnambalan, TNP MP for Jaffna, called the US Embassy on 17 May to report a phone conversation the previous night in which KP had told him that an estimated 3,000 civilians had been killed and 15,000 wounded that day, also suggesting—somewhat improbably—that as many as 100,000 were still stranded inside the conflict zone.[141]

Later the same day Robert Blake urged the UN Emissary Vijay Nambiar—in Colombo, in advance of a visit by the UN secretary-general—to reinforce 'messages' communicated earlier to Foreign Minister Bogollagama regarding the likely size of the civilian population remaining in the conflict zone, and the corresponding need for government forces to 'do everything possible' to protect them.[142] There were reports that some elements of the government were in favour of restraint, but whatever the veracity of these rumours, on the evening of 17 May a 'final operation' was launched involving elite special forces and commando units, who entered the combat zone with a view to finishing off the LTTE.[143]

Selvarasa Pathmanathan ('KP')

Know that the Tamils are a people deeply rooted in culture and history. No force can prevent the attainment of justice for our people. Our sons and daughters have taken up this call without question and without hesitation or fear of death. None have hesitated to make the supreme sacrifice for the cause of liberating their motherland. We have not forgotten that it is for our people that we fight.[144]

The final stages

The story of what happened during the army's final assault remains murky. One well-informed source states that sections of the LTTE leadership focused on a last-minute attempt to obtain a ceasefire. In tandem with this, there is alleged to have been a diplomatic attempt to persuade the government to accept the Tigers' proposal and to declare a temporary ceasefire in order to allow for the evacuation of injured civilians.[145]

It is suggested that, following a rebuff from army command, groups of the Tiger leadership attempted to flee across the Nanthikadal lagoon and were soon cut down. The only exception may have been a group including Prabhakaran, and possibly the rest of his family, which, initially at least, may have managed to move northwards, beyond army lines. Hopes of a real escape, however, proved short-lived. On the following morning (19 May), an army infantry regiment claimed to have discovered the LTTE leader's body, along with those of four of his bodyguards, lying on the banks of the Nanthikadal lagoon. Prabhakaran had been shot at close range, blowing off the top of his head.

Prabhakaran's son

In early 2013 photos emerged of Prabhakaran's 12-year-old son Balachandran, alive and well in the custody of the Sri Lanka Army on the morning of 19 May 2009—along with further photos taken less than two hours later of the boy lying dead, with five bullet wounds through his chest. Military officials vigorously denied allegations that the army was responsible for the summary execution of a child, but publication of these photos added to the evidence of war crimes and increased the pressure on the government to allow an international investigation.[146]

The corpses of more than 350 Tiger leaders and commanders were later displayed by the army, signalling a virtual eradication of the organisation. It transpired that a significant group of these, led by Nadesan and Pulidevan, had tried to surrender under terms that a number of international and domestic actors—Erik Solheim and Norwegian Embassy personnel included—had negotiated with Foreign Secretary Palitha Kohona. Nadesan reportedly asked for the presence of Vijay Nambiar to witness the surrender, but was informed (via American journalist Marie Colvin) that President Rajapaksa had guaranteed the safety of surrendering LTTE leaders. Early on the morning of May 18 Nadesan and Pulidevan duly led a group of a dozen men and women out towards the SLA troops, holding a white flag, as agreed. Exactly what happened thereafter remains fiercely contested. According to one Tamil witness who later escaped the area, the SLA responded with a stream of gunfire. Eyewitness accounts further state that when the army began firing at the group, Nadesan's Sinhalese wife shouted at them: 'He is trying to surrender to you and you are shooting him!' She herself was then gunned down.[147]

Although many are alleged to have died as a result of this incident, not all those who surrendered to the army appear to have been executed in this way. In Pulidevan and Nadesan's case, for example, other eyewitness testimony points to their having been initially received and even offered tea by government forces. Their close-range execution took place at some point in the hours that followed, as was confirmed by the photos of their bullet-riddled corpses that later surfaced, and as may well have happened to a number of other 'White Flag' surrenderees.[148] Needless to say, the evidential difficulties of establishing exactly what happened are further confounded by the Colombo authorities' blanket refusal to date to acknowledge that anything resembling predetermined executions by army personnel occurred.

Government sources offered conflicting accounts of what happened. Foreign Secretary Kohona, for example, both denied that there had been any prior surrender deal with the LTTE—despite the fact that there is clear evidence that he himself had been involved in the negotiations—and also claimed Tiger cadres had shot their own leaders in the back for daring to surrender to government forces.[149]

'White Flag' incidents

A recently-produced report, '5 years On: The White Flag Incident 2009—2014',[150] provides the most detailed and damning account to date of events surrounding the 'white flag' incident. As well as demonstrating that more than 100 LTTE leaders and people associated with them 'disappeared' following their surrender to the army on 18 May, the report argues that the available evidence points to an 'organised government plan not to accept the surrender of the top ... leadership of the LTTE—but to execute them'. It further alleges, as others have also done, that this plan was approved 'at the highest level'. Finally, the report notes that Pulidevan and Nadesan's surrender plan was implemented in full consultation and with the explicit approval of Mahinda, Basil and Gotabhaya Rajapaksa, as well as Foreign Secretary Palitha Kohona.

If and when allegations of war crimes become the subject of serious official investigation—national or international—in Sri Lanka, it seems clear that this incident will receive much closer scrutiny.

In a bitterly ironic episode, it was left to Karuna and Daya Master, Prabhakaran's former deputy and spokesperson, to confirm the identity of the body found lying on the banks of the Nanthikadal lagoon. The official announcement of the LTTE leader's death was made later on 19 May, putting an end to days of feverish speculation. The only group that appeared to be unmoved by the physical evidence of Prabhakaran's demise was a section of the Tamil diaspora that maintained the LTTE leader was still alive. To this day, a few continue to indulge in this extraordinary piece of denial.[151]

On 19 May President Rajapaksa delivered his official victory speech in parliament. Sri Lanka 'did not need others' to advise on 'how to care for its own people', he contended, nor would it be subject to foreign 'experiments' to solve internal political problems. There were no longer any ethnic or other minorities in Sri Lanka, he stated, only 'patriots and a few others who do not love their country'. The army's victory, he concluded, was for those who 'rally around the national flag'.[152] In celebration, a national holiday was called for the following day.[153]

UTHR-J

While carrying some good sentiments in a nebulous way, [the speech] left little room for optimism. [The president] again spoke of a home grown solution to the country's ethnic impasse [but] said nothing about how he understood the problem and how he would approach it, except to play to the xenophobic gallery by repudiating 'imported solutions'. One cannot begin without acknowledging that the home grown idea of Sinhalese-Buddhist hegemony has always stood in the way of any solution, was the principal cause of the bloody anarchy we faced and needs to be explicitly repudiated. The need for reconciliation was [also] missing from his speech.

All peoples and nations share a common fund of experience and a common history. 'Home grown' has in the tenure of this government served as populist rhetoric to mask what is really just evasion of responsibility, arrogance and a refusal to understand. Except for those blinded by their narrow vision, all that we have seen of 'home grown' ideas in the last six decades is homicidal ignorance, communal violence rooted in majoritarian ideology, based in turn on third rate history, and a total erosion of standards.

The president thought it a brilliant stroke to abolish the word 'minority' and make everyone equal, as if all it took were a royal proclamation. Along with this he recognized only two kinds of people, those who love their motherland and those who do not, the latter being the lesser ... Thousands of Tamil youth fought and willingly gave their lives, not because they did not love their country fervently, but because they believed their country was Tamil Eelam ...

The only way Tamil families and communities that have lost loved ones can find meaning in their loss and begin to think about a future as part of Lanka is if they as a people are granted equality and dignity through a just political process. Making them feel Lankan will be hard work, and the president seems to lack that sensitivity.[154]

Further recollections of the final stages

Tore Hattrem, Norwegian ambassador to Sri Lanka

In the last month everybody was saying 'we hope the LTTE gives up', because there was enormous suffering. For us diplomats, however, it was about humanitarian law, food, medicine; a bigger assessment was almost unnecessary ...

There was a lot of work, back and forth about food, medicine, provisions for civilians in the conflict zone involving communication from the ICRC, Norway, US, EU to Basil, government institutions. Our appeal was always to uphold international humanitarian law with regard to the 'safe zones', especially over artillery shelling in them ... I assume that the LTTE hoped that government forces would stop in the end because the collateral damage would be off the scale of what the international community were prepared to accept. The government's precaution was to bar the media from the combat areas.

Erik Solheim

Prabhakaran was making all the decisions. There was no strategic vision, no understanding of the need to reach out to the Sinhalese and the US, no compassion for the suffering of the people, while also claiming to speak on their behalf. And then believing in miracles ... The UNHCR was in touch with Tore [Hattrem], but at the political level no one thought Norway could really have any influence at this point, persuade the government to refrain from horrendous acts—the only ones who could perhaps have done that were the US. Our main role was to convince the LTTE to give up ... If the LTTE leader had accepted our proposal it would have been impossible for the government to say no.

It's quite striking how little we know of what Prabhakaran was thinking in the final period. It's all qualified guesswork: the key people who would know are all dead. The main surviving person qualified [to know] is KP. There may also be a few of the second-level people—Yogi, Balakumar and so on—who are still alive in government internment camps. But I doubt it. Right up to the end the LTTE's behaviour was so surreal. The government's was simply brutal ... So many died, for what? No purpose, no achievement. We had hoped that the president would use this opportunity of the war's end to reach out. But no ... Strong media pressure should have been there, international leaders should have told the Rajapaksas that there are international courts, and you will be judged after the war. But that didn't happen. The Americans, for example, only spoke up afterwards.

Bård Ludvig Thorheim

After having declined several times to discuss options involving some kind of surrender, the LTTE finally came around to this at a very late stage when they were basically rounded up ... The government did react to KP's statement: they said it was out of the question, but that the LTTE could surrender to government forces instead. We spoke to KP and suggested UN observers could be involved along with government forces, but the LTTE responded saying they did not trust the government. I think KP did raise this issue with Prabhakaran. We didn't hear anything back. Then right in the final few days of the war KP said that the LTTE would be willing to surrender to the government. By this time there was little time to arrange anything, and KP was in any case very unspecific. He did not present any plan for an LTTE surrender, which you would have expected if they were very serious about it.

UTHR-J

Human Rights Minister Mahinda Samarasinghe claimed without batting an eyelid (on 17 May) that 'soldiers saved all Tamil civilians trapped inside the war zone without shedding a drop of blood'. The war was over and the

---

> LTTE [were] militarily shattered at Anandapuram in early April. The 'No Fire Zone' being subsequently turned into a massacre zone in the name of hostage rescue is a monstrosity that cannot humanly be accepted.[155]

The 'White Flag' Killings

Erik Solheim

There can no doubt that the Army did not want to capture the LTTE leadership alive ... Concerning the deaths of Nadesan and Pulidevan in particular there are only two possible interpretations: either they were killed as the result of a specific order, or a general command to kill everyone in this category was in operation. The army maintained its morale and disciple right up to the end of the war, so no general would have dared to take such decisions by himself: clearly, they would have been taken at the highest level of command. We felt a personal loss with Pulidevan. He was not responsible for atrocities. In fact he was the first person who received us in the Vanni in 2000.

Tore Hattrem

I got a call from Tomas Stangeland [on the night of 17 May] saying he had spoken to Pulidevan. I got in touch; I could hear the gunshots in the background. Pulidevan said they were confined to a very small area: he was there with Nadesan. He said he didn't know where Prabhakaran was. I said surrender was the only possibility: use a white flag ... I called Basil [Rajapaksa], didn't get through and then sent text messages to a bunch of people—Gotabhaya and others. I reported my conversation with Pulidevan and said they would show a white flag. The same morning we met early with Blake and others for a Co-Chairs breakfast—Nambiar was also there. Pulidevan had been ringing others as well. Then we received the information that Pulidevan and the others had been killed.

Bård Ludvig Thorheim

During the night of 17–18 May Pulidevan was making call after call to people saying 'we want to surrender, please convey this to the government'. Then he contacted a TNA MP. In the middle of the night this MP called me, the political counsellor at the US Embassy, and Dominic Williams at the British High Commission. The TNA MP said he had already been in contact with Basil Rajapaksa. He had even spoken to the president, who had said yes, these people's surrender will be respected and accommodated. The MP then asked for instructions on how to surrender to government forces. Robert Blake and Tore Hattrem texted Gotabhaya about it, Blake called him up. The next day it became clear that the LTTE cadres who had called in had all been killed. The government said either they were killed by their own cadres, or they didn't show up as instructed, or they turned up with weapons. Even Fonseka later questioned this narrative.

Human Rights, War Crimes and Accountability

Erik Solheim

What is normal in wars is an unbelievable use of violence. Unless there are clear directions from the top over maintaining human rights there will be mayhem. I don't think Mahinda involved himself in details, military decisions: he left that to more competent people, so they had a free hand. Basil had the role of keeping the political coalition behind him, everyone happy—and keeping us at bay. He was the main liaison person. As things turned out there were no limits to the killing. There were wildly differing estimates of the number of people trapped in the conflict zone. The truth of course is at the high end, perhaps even more. The government was deliberately lying in saying there were less than 100,000 or so civilians when in fact there must have been more like 300–400,000.

Vidar Helgesen

There were some media reports [at the time], but the magnitude of the human rights violations became evident only towards the end, when it became clear that a huge number of people were encircled in a steadily narrowing piece of land. The limited investigations conducted to date point strongly to the fact that war crimes did take place—certainly they are more than enough to provide the basis for a fully-fledged international investigation, although the international community has fallen short of that to date. The fact that both parties had failed to protect civilians was evident from very early on, and that in itself was a breach of international law. The more targeted shelling of hospitals and so on became clear through the initial UN Expert Report and the Channel 4 Documentary 'Sri Lanka's Killing Fields'.[156]

Robert Blake

I'm sorry that the Sri Lankan military has put out a report saying that they were not responsible for civilian casualties. That is not true. The question is, to what extent they were actually targeting civilians. My guess is they were probably not targeting them. There were many instances where the LTTE intentionally put its armed fighters among civilians precisely in order to draw fire from the Army and then be able to say, 'look at the terrible war crimes that are happening'. The LTTE was pursuing a very cynical policy and putting its own people at risk ...

My strong supposition is that the government did not exercise sufficient caution with respect to civilian casualties and frequently responded with untargeted munitions. The proof of that was that among the wounded that were evacuated a huge number had injuries from shell fragments. And many were civilians ... Where we also faulted the government was that while they did allow food in, they did not allow medicine into the combat zone as frequently. So many people died who probably could have been saved, if the government had allowed more evacuations by the ICRC, or at least allowed it to deliver more medicines and surgical equipment.

The UN report faulted them for using food as a weapon.[157] I don't think that's a fair accusation. We spent a lot of time negotiating with the government and the LTTE to allow World Food Programme shipments to the North. And a lot of them did go: there were no mass starvations. People didn't die of starvation, they died because they were killed, they were shelled.

Anonymous

We knew what was happening with the civilians [during the final stages], that the LTTE was taking them along with them. We also knew the army was advancing. The real bloodshed happened during the last week or so. We tried to report, but in order to do so you had to be with the government. They had these organised tours. It was an eye-opener. After Kilinochchi had been taken we went to the edge of Chundikkulam lagoon east of the town.

You could say that civilians were on one side and the military on the other. We heard shelling, but we could never tell exactly where it came from. As we were leaving there were civilians just beginning to coming out over a land pass: they were almost dead, nearly collapsing. Soldiers were giving them crackers to eat. Lunch was organised at a house being used as a camp. There were civilians under trees, simply collapsed on the ground. A military commander asked me what I thought about it. I said I felt really sorry for them. He was very upset, and said 'but they chose to stay there!' That was the way the commanders were conditioned.

Travelling back, our chopper took off but had to land because of some technical problem. Then we were shifted to another chopper with missiles under it, and it was full of wounded soldiers. I had one soldier's head on my knee, and we had to keep him stable. I was holding his hand and stroking his hair. The last thing he told me as I was getting out at Vavuniya was 'Don't tell my family'. He was worried they would be in shock. He didn't even know I didn't know him. I saw two sides that day: there was no one side.

Later I went to a village. A mother was howling, her 16-year-old boy had lied about his age, joined the military, and been killed. Forty boys from the village had died in the last few months. Their graves were still fresh. The level of death in those last few weeks was enormous. One thing the international community did not understand was that, one way or another, the government were going to end it. They had gone too far, lost too many people. 'Enough of the LTTE'—it was clear to us. My problem was that they trapped people in the 'No-Fire Zones'. There were not enough efforts to get those civilians out. I didn't see [their being bombed], but from circumstantial evidence it's pretty obvious that's what happened.

Accountability has to be on both sides. The LTTE also played a major role in getting those people trapped: the No-Fire Zones worked for them as well. The more you talk of one-sided accountability in this country, the more people will support their government. The LTTE leadership are all dead but there are others, people who were with the Tigers, and there is not even lip service being paid to that fact. If it is civilians you are talking about, there were civilians on both sides. You will not find mass support among the Sinhalese for a war crimes tribunal.

India and the Final Stages

Murali Reddy

The government had given the Military Attaché in the Indian High Commission in Colombo access to the operations room. However, from my interactions with officials in the mission I came to the conclusion that Indian access—military or otherwise—was limited. I was also convinced at the end of the war that the Indian government had little clue as to what exactly was happening on the ground. At the fag end of the military campaign, for example, I was shocked to hear from one of the very senior officials that Prabhakaran had fled from the battle zone.

Narayan Swamy

The tragedy in the understanding of India vis-à-vis Sri Lanka is that few realised that several arms of the government were working at the same time—at times at cross purposes, and some in complete secrecy. What happens unless one has a larger and a more comprehensive view is that the views of one unit or department are construed as the Indian stand, which may or may not be true. I disagree, however, that Indians didn't know what was happening on the ground.

Of course they knew: but that does not mean they knew every inch of the ground. Remember, the Indian military set up field hospitals in the Northeast during the end stages of the war, and the doctors [who were] furiously performing surgery after surgery surely knew what was going on.[158] Indians were also monitoring LTTE communications from Chennai, and they knew pretty well what was going on ...

Overall, India was always very clear: we will never allow Tamil Eelam to emerge. This was what Erik was told as well. We will be happy if the LTTE goes down, but if it can be submerged in a democratic process that would be fine. But remember India is not a single entity. There is a Congress-led India and a BJP-led India. Even during the last phase of the war and the army's rapid progress there was a fear among Lankans as to what would happen if the BJP came to power. So there was a definite effort to finish off the LTTE before the Lok Sabha[159] election results were announced on 16 May 2009. Because Lanka feared that if the

BJP came to power, there could be pressure on it to come to an agreement with the LTTE. Even the super-nationalist Tamil Nadu politician Vaiko had told Prabhakaran that.

Norway's Actions in the Final Stages

Erik Solheim

Of course you can debate whether we should have banged the drum harder during the final stages, involved CNN, the BBC and so on in a call for international intervention. But the government would have dismissed this as LTTE propaganda, and in any case I doubt whether it would have had any real impact ... Look at Syria today: you can see things would not have changed with more drum banging. You might have had more high-profile international visits *à la* Kouchner and Miliband if there had been more of an international outcry, but nothing to change the course of events on the ground. By this point the government was dead serious about wiping out the LTTE, they knew they were close to it, and there was nothing that was going to stop them, except if the LTTE had come forward and accepted an organised end to the war. Look at Turkey: Ocalan is now the prime partner of Erdogan in talks on how to settle the Kurdish issue. Even after ten years in prison he is still a primary authority for Kurds in Turkey. And I have no doubt that even from prison, Prabhakaran would have still have enjoyed immense authority over Sri Lankan Tamils.

Vidar Helgesen

After 2007 I don't see there was much that Norway could have done differently to change the scenario. Any changes it could have made would more have been directed at safeguarding our international reputation as mediators. But that wasn't directly to do with the Sri Lankan conflict. Even if the brutal nature of the endgame to the Sri Lanka conflict had been understood by the international community at the time, there would not have been a military intervention or anything of that sort as a result. Sri Lanka is not in that league. What might perhaps have changed things was if there had been more of an outcry in Tamil Nadu.

Jon Hanssen-Bauer

I don't feel responsible for the ending. It was not Norway that failed: it was the whole international community that did nothing. In any case our role was insignificant in the big picture. India started supplying the government with ammunition in the last phase, and China did it all the way through. I'm quite certain the US provided intelligence. None of them was able to slow down the massacre in May ...

The UN was toothless. I had two rounds of secret meetings with UN on what they could do, and the answer was nothing. We managed to get the Sri Lanka issue up to the Security Council but India did not want it discussed. It was brought in informally but Ban Ki-Moon did not follow it up. That happened in 2008. Part of my job was to push the UN but it was impossible. If the US had really wanted to stop [the end game] they would have used other means that they didn't deploy. India had no intention of stopping it. I feel we were very clear from December 2006 onwards that we were no longer negotiating peace in Sri Lanka. We were keeping contact because it was worth the effort.

Bård Ludvig Thorheim

During some twenty-five years of conflict between the government and the LTTE you can count about four or five peace efforts, depending slightly on what you define as a peace effort. The one in which Norway was involved was by far the most promising and best carried out. In peace efforts you can't talk about complete success or complete failure. If it is a serious attempt, and the parties show a genuine interest, it is worth trying. Peace negotiations generate knowledge among the parties regarding the option of solving the conflict politically. That may at a later stage lead to a settlement when certain parameters have changed. On the other hand, negotiations may lead to the conclusion that the parties are still very far from a political agreement, which will lead to them reverting to settling the conflict militarily.

12

LESSONS LEARNED

History has taught us that solutions externally prescribed, with little understanding of the complexity of the problem on the ground, are prone to failure. My government is, therefore, firmly committed to seeking a homegrown solution acceptable to all communities living in Sri Lanka.

President Rajapaksa announcing victory over the LTTE at a G-11 Summit in Jordan, 16 May 2009

A 'homegrown solution acceptable to all communities'. In the aftermath of the government's declaration of victory over the LTTE in mid-May 2009, what exactly did that solution look like to the outside world? To some it was abundantly clear. Over the following months, governments from Thailand, Bangladesh and Burma to Pakistan and the Philippines were all reported to be considering the merits of the 'Sri Lanka option' as a means of addressing their own internal conflicts. And the influence of Colombo spread far beyond South and Southeast Asia.[1]

In the summer of 2014, for example, following the visit of a Sri Lankan delegation, the Nigerian Chief of Defence Staff issued a statement noting that it was 'seriously considering the counter-insurgency experience of the Sri Lankan military' in its fight against the militant Islamist movement Boko Haram, who had launched their bloody insurgency only two months after the LTTE were crushed. For Sri Lankan military commanders the key concept was 'total security', defined as the 'translation of all the nation's assets into military power to counter the scourge of terrorism'.[2]

For all the self-confidence implied by the Sri Lankan leadership's promotion of their 'homegrown' model for winning the war, however, it is far from clear that they have succeeded in the equally critical enterprise of securing the peace. Indeed, in the words of a noted civil society activist interviewed in this book, Sri Lanka remains mired in post-war, rather than post-conflict conditions. And in this context, a fundamental factor—reiterated by many interviewees—is that an effective resolution of the Sri Lankan conflict ultimately requires a political rather than a military approach.

In the aftermath of the war, stung by widespread criticism of its performance and perceived failure to take effective action, the United Nations set up an internal review panel that conducted one of the organisation's most thorough-going 'lessons learned' exercises to date. The outcome was a report presented to UN Secretary General Ban Ki-Moon by its chief author, Charles Petrie, in November 2012.[3] The report, which received widespread media publicity, offered a vigorous critique of the UN's response to the Sri Lankan conflict, both at ground level and inside the Secretariat in New York. Speaking about the report for the first time, Ban Ki-Moon emphasised its 'profound implications for [the UN's] work across the world'.

He went on: 'I am determined that the United Nations draws the appropriate lessons and does its utmost to earn the confidence of the world's people, especially those caught in conflict who look to the organisation for help'.[4] But in the light of conflicts such as the Syrian civil war and the international community's muddled response to the bloodshed there, can it truly be said that the institutional lessons from Sri Lanka have been 'learned' by the UN? Indeed, have those lessons been any more effectively learned than those derived from the Rwandan genocide? Rwanda showed the importance of keeping UN personnel on the ground as an insurance against massacres, for example—but was that lesson in any sense used or otherwise applied in Sri Lanka?

The Petrie Report[5]

While internal UN disagreements over casualty figures were well known to insiders in the diplomatic community, they didn't get a public airing until the November 2012 release of the Petrie Report. Even here, however, the issue was dogged by controversy. The version of the report released for public consumption included a number of sections that were either blacked out—or in the case of the

Executive Summary, left out entirely. At least one media outlet managed to get hold and publish the missing summary,[6] however. The following excerpts are taken from the Executive Summary:

> For the UN, the last phase of the conflict in Sri Lanka presented a major challenge. The UN struggled to exert influence on the government (GoSL), which, with the effective acquiescence of a post-9/11 world order, was determined to defeat militarily an organisation designated as terrorist. Some have argued that many deaths could have been averted had the Security Council and the Secretariat, backed by the UN country team (UNCT), spoken out loudly early on, notably by publicizing the casualty numbers. Others say that the question is less whether the UN should assume responsibility for the tragedy, but more whether it did everything it could to assist the victims.
>
> The Panel's conclusion is that events in Sri Lanka mark a grave failure of the UN to adequately respond to early warning and the evolving events during the final stages of the conflict and its aftermath, to the detriment of hundreds of thousands of civilians and in contradiction with [its] principles and responsibilities.
>
> Decision-making across the UN was dominated by a culture of trade-offs. Options for action were seen less as responsibilities and more in terms of dilemmas. Choosing not to speak up about GoSL and LTTE broken commitments and violations of international law was seen as the only way to increase UN humanitarian access. Choosing to focus Security Council briefings on the humanitarian situation rather than the causes of the crisis and the obligations of the parties ... was seen as essential to facilitate Secretariat engagement with Member States. There was a sustained and institutionalized reluctance to stand up for the rights of the people they were mandated to assist.
>
> In Colombo, many senior UN staff simply did not perceive the prevention of killing of civilians as their responsibility; and agency and department heads at UNHQ were not instructing their staff in Sri Lanka otherwise. The UN's failure to adequately counter the GoSL's under-estimation of population numbers in the Wanni, the failure to adequately confront the GoSL on its obstructions to humanitarian assistance, the unwillingness to address GoSL responsibility for attacks that were killing civilians, and the tone and content of UN communications with the GoSL and Member States on these issues, contributed to the unfolding of dramatic events.
>
> Most crucially, the UN did not use all the political and advocacy tools at its disposal. In particular, it did not keep Member States or the public fully informed. Nor did it warn the GoSL or the LTTE of the consequences of their actions, including their responsibility for possible war crimes and crimes against humanity.

Despite these caveats there are, of course, important things to be learned from the Sri Lankan experience. What follows is a compilation of the wide-ranging set of lessons from the conflict identified by those interviewed for this book. In line with the book's overall focus, the emphasis is on lessons derived from or otherwise relating to the Norwegian role in peace-making efforts in Sri Lanka. Most, but not all interviewees were willing to have their names attached to the contributions below. Regardless of whether their authorship is hidden or revealed, it is hoped that the combined insights and recommendations detailed here will prove useful both to followers of, and actors in Sri Lankan affairs, as well as those more broadly concerned with strengthening and improving international conflict resolution and peace-building strategies and practices.

The need for bipartisan political support

Erik Solheim

> From the very beginning we had defined the lack of bipartisanship in Sri Lankan politics as one of the biggest obstacles to any peace process. We took the view that Norway could not resolve that issue, and that only India would have been strong enough to bring real pressure to bear on the two key political parties and their leaders. It was a main weakness that the 2002 Ceasefire Agreement (CFA) was basically between Ranil [Wickremasinghe] and the LTTE. But Ranil was in a position of political dominance at this point, and we thought that the huge force of peace opinion at the time could resolve [the bipartisanship] problem further down the road ... To this day there has never, ever been bipartisanship in Sri Lanka. At the time of the CFA people thought, 'we must assist Ranil in creating a peace opinion that is so strong that it limits others' ability to undermine it'. And for a while, things certainly looked like that. But sustaining the momentum was another matter. It was not a bottom-up process.

Oyvind Fuglerud

> You can say that if he [Ranil] was for something, she [Chandrika Kumaratunga] would be against it ... Without some kind of understanding between the two parties in the South, [a peace agreement] was, and is, impossible. So without this it is simply not worth engaging in a process. To Erik I would have said at the time: you will have to go through this discussion with the parties on both sides. And you will also have to find some sort of solution to the tension between the LTTE and the Muslims. Otherwise, you should know that this is not going to work.

LESSONS LEARNED

Building international support for the process

Erik Solheim

The international community could have been better organised: there should have been more high-level political engagement with the Sri Lankan conflict. There is only so much ambassadors can do: you needed ministers to come in and take it on as a priority. At this point, however, Iraq was dominating the global agenda, and heads of state hardly engaged in Sri Lanka.

Vidar Helgesen

It is vital to involve and build the commitment of the international community more systematically. Initially there was a strong international interest in the Sri Lankan process. Many governments wanted to be supportive—Canada, Switzerland, the UK, for example. And we could—and should—have designed a real international safety net with more depth, more strategic intent. When you look at how it all derailed later, how the international community wasn't able to deal with the LTTE because of its terrorist status: maybe we could have mitigated this by weaving them more strategically into the fabric of the peace talks. It's hard to know if we could have done that in practice, because there was strong Indian resistance to bringing more international heavyweights into the picture. To some extent there was also reluctance towards this on the LTTE's part. And there was also the unilateral streak in Norwegian peace diplomacy to contend with ...

In my view that encapsulates the major failure in Norway's approach to peace processes in general: insufficient attention to the design of an international support structure. When a Norwegian peace process fails, there is a tendency to focus on Norway as having failed, not understanding the broader parameters ... Post 9/11, while we were basically aware that negotiating with terrorists was a difficult thing, we didn't do enough to 'massage' the international community's attitudes on the subject ...

9/11's impact on our efforts in Sri Lanka was that it created a number of blunt instruments, like the terrorist listing used by the EU. It didn't impact on the couple of years of direct negotiations because there was willingness, including even from the Americans, to support the process to see if it might lead to something substantial. But when the process began to unravel and the LTTE started to use terrorist means again, the bluntness of the instruments meant that once you put them on a list—just like with Al Qaeda—the situation gets blocked.

Tomas Stangeland

The international community should have acted more rapidly on generating economic development during the CFA period. We tried: maybe it is nobody's fault ultimately. The international system works that way, it takes time. But the LTTE was not used to that: it was used to things happening immediately. They thought it was all Ranil's fault. Had we all gone in faster with real money, it would definitely have helped. And if the government had encouraged international contact with the LTTE it would certainly have been easier.

Nicholas Burns, US Under-Secretary of State

The Security Council, the Permanent Five, in hindsight might have taken a more proactive role. China, of course, began to work very closely with the Sri Lankan government and China and the US were sending completely different signals to them. We were operating at cross-purposes. My 'take away' was that China and the US should have done more to coalesce in our efforts and not be divisive. I think we were in the right place, to defend human rights. China going its own way was very disruptive for this process.

Andrea Nicolaj

One of the major challenges was getting India on board. India was not part of the Co-Chairs structure, but it was still playing a very important role. India did not really want to get involved, but can you really aspire to change things without the big superpower in the region being actively involved? They were briefed, but remained outside the process.

Prabhakaran

Erik Solheim

A very important lesson is that contact with the LTTE should not have been restricted. More high-level visits, more encounters with Prabhakaran would have helped. [The restrictions] were mainly due to the government and because of domestic politics, narrow-minded thinking: they were afraid of being attacked by the opposition, the media. But it was a big mistake. There should have been more visits: they would have had a very positive effect. We took LTTE delegations outside Sri Lanka, but with the exception of Bala or Tamilselvan they were not decision-takers in the main. At the end of the day it was about Prabhakaran.

Raymond Johansen, Deputy Foreign Minister for Norway

The main challenge was dealing with the leader of the LTTE. He was not directly part of the whole [negotiation process] yet was responsible for it. He was there in the sense of his contact with Balasingham. But we should not have agreed to be so heavily involved without the LTTE leader sitting at the table. Having the person responsible for the whole thing not there—it's like having negotiations with the PLO with Yasser Arafat just sitting in a cave.

LESSONS LEARNED

Vinya Ariyaratne

From the very beginning you [should] make it clear that on certain fundamental principles you don't compromise, or you don't agree to facilitate. Like the issue of child soldiers. The Norwegians were in a good position to tell it to the Tigers here. I was convinced that it would be very difficult to convince Prabhakaran of the need for a negotiated settlement. When the IRA's McGuinness went to meet him he told the LTTE that our lesson is that the military wing of the IRA was controlled by the political wing. During the ceasefire period the LTTE could have made the [same] transition. But Prabhakaran was a fanatic: he believed in the military.

Narayan Swamy

Prabhakaran genuinely wanted a separate state and thought for a long time that he could achieve it ... The ideology of killings was, he thought, the way to go forward. Thinking I will keep on bumping my enemies off until not many are left behind—but not realising that the reverse will happen. He just created more enemies. In the political science sense, the LTTE had no ideology. Balasingham had a left-wing background. He may have been a genuine Marxist at heart, but that Marxism never permeated as an ideology into the LTTE at any point. Basically the LTTE was a one-man show and that man had no ideology. And because Marxist thinking never permeated the LTTE, the fascist streak always dominated. The LTTE never believed in moderate punishment. It just killed ... The problem that arose for the Norwegians was that a lot of people in Sri Lanka thought: why are you being friendly with this bastard? ...

Indian foreign affairs minister Jaswant Singh told Erik: 'You will have to stay the course for a long time.' This was born out of a realisation that Prabhakaran was not going to listen. It came out of the hard realities that the Indians had gone through. The fact that he would not compromise was known to many people ... The maximum that can be related to Prabhakaran was that he had a Tamil ideology—albeit a very narrow one. It was not even that the Tamils should live: Tamils who disagreed should die. Eventually, in the end, he was almost a loner ...

Look at the growth in his support—from less than forty people and twenty weapons in 1983 to 1986, when he was in a position to destroy the most other powerful rival Tamil group, and was controlling parts of Jaffna; and the years that go by when he is ruling parts of the Northern Province. By 2002 he is lord and master of all that he surveys in the North and East. Look at this from his point of view: 'My path, my methods have paid off. You may criticise me for no democracy, but do you think I would have got it following your methods?' That made him think that it was an invincible path. When the Norwegian intervention came he thought the world was beginning to understand him. 'If Kosovo could become independent, why not I?' He thought everything was hunky-dory.

Tamrat Samuel

We knew that [the LTTE's] level of tolerance and ability to involve the Tamil population in wider politics and the peace process was limited. And eventually that is what undermined the LTTE in the whole Tamil cause. Because it was Prabhakaran, one single person deciding what to do and leading the whole cause down the drain ... if peace were to be sustainable and succeed there should have been a broader involvement of Tamils in a more open and inclusive process. As part of the process there should have been an effort to get the LTTE to accept other Tamil voices. Again, it was back to the problem of one man deciding for the entire Tamil community that led to this. There's a big lesson to be learned from that.

Nirupama Subramanian

Prabhakaran, by all accounts, was not prepared to play second fiddle. He wanted to be 'the leader'. He did not want some kind of compromise deal with the Sinhalese ... He perhaps thought that nations are built on blood. I think he was probably into all that heroic figure stuff.

Norway's role

Vidar Helgesen

We did well, I think, in dealing with the immediate stakeholder picture internationally. With India, there was complete openness and transparency. Similarly with the US, though that was down to a stroke of luck based on Richard Armitage's interest in Sri Lanka. Our dealings with India were based on an early reading of the regional context—that we would get nowhere unless we chose to be completely open with Delhi ... With the CFA we saw the need for international support and money, so we reached out, in particular to the EU, which set the stage for the Co-Chairs Group. Bringing Japan in was more complicated. We had actually reached out to them much earlier than the Tokyo donor conference: they had signalled an interest, and also appointed Akashi as Special Envoy. It was very important to provide non-Western balance and the Sinhala Buddhist affinity for Japan was helpful.

Shimali Senanayake

In terms of positives, the fact that the Norwegians were able to stay in there for the long haul, and the fact that they had the backing of the international community both weighed well. Sri Lanka is a very tricky place, they did the best that they could and a lot of people appreciate that in hindsight.

LESSONS LEARNED

Nirupama Subramanian

[The Norwegian Evaluation][7] contains an interesting conclusion, namely, that peace initiatives from outside a geographical region are not that viable anymore, especially in this part of the world, with China and India as the big players whose interests you have to take into account.

Richard Armitage

I don't think [the Norwegians] could have done anything differently. I have nothing but the highest regard for the country, the nation and their individual efforts ... but there are times you have to hold 'em and fold 'em. You can always deal another hand. There were times when the shock bag of disengagement by Norway might have been a good thing. Not a full disengagement. 'Now, you guys aren't ready for us, here's our telephone number. We've got other efforts internationally.'

Gopalkrishna Gandhi

Norwegian facilitation was an important initiative and one that the Indian government looked at with a combination of interest and support. The support was not in the sense of being a part of the process, but it was one of saying that we would like this to work. Because anything that was done to enhance the prospects of peace and end violence was something we valued. We have tried it many, many times but with various degrees of success, not with anything like abiding success. We had our reservations and doubts. Serious misgivings as to whether it would work. But we wanted it to work.

We never participated in the process directly, because that was neither the intention of the government of India, nor part of the scheme of facilitation—and certainly not part of the Sri Lankan government's scheme either. But we held discussions on a regular basis and kept our principals in headquarters informed. It was the Norwegians' call from the start. They showed extraordinary patience. There were occasions where they were disappointed with both sides, and also encouraged them. It was a mixed bag of experiences. They persevered, which is a remarkable thing. We certainly would have had difficulty in doing what [the] Norwegians did. After all, in the region we are neighbours; the Norwegians' distance was both their strength and disadvantage.

Narayan Swamy

The fact that for a long time guns were not fired—it was a great credit to the Norwegians. They tried, did their level best. Lack of knowledge [of the context]—no crime. Lack of understanding of the LTTE—absolutely no crime. The Norwegian effort was worth it. It fell off the tracks for many reasons. Even if you were to call Norway a part culprit, theirs is a very small part of the culpability.

Iqbal Athas

The Norwegians were caught in the crossfire. They had a mission as peacemakers. It was possible for the Chandrika government to exploit this. The Norwegians had a greater responsibility: they brought these two warring factions together, they spent a lot of money. In doing that, it would have been better on their part if they had asked the government to say: 'Work out a strategy, get the peace message across to the rural population.' So there was a lack of communication. They never understood the grey areas they need to deal with in order to make their mission successful. The monitors behaved like colonial rulers of the past. They were abrasive in their conduct and dismissive of the local vernacular media. Their dissemination of information in most instances was confined to the Colombo-based foreign media. As a result, they created a divergence and that contributed to the widening of the chasm between the Sinhalese and the Tamils.

When SLMM head Tellefsen proposed that the LTTE Sea Tigers be recognised officially it created a huge uproar in the defence establishment. Chandrika called the Norwegian government to get him withdrawn. That proves my point: whatever the Norwegian intentions—which were very good, I don't doubt that one bit—their lack of understanding of the psyche, the nuances of our people, the grey areas, created a problem. When you venture into an area like this you have to make an effort to understand how much of the message is reaching into the countryside: how are the Sri Lankans viewing what we are doing? Erik did his best, he was quite genuine. He had a passion for this, was devoted. He spent sleepless nights concentrating and was very well informed. He knew. Unfortunately, he was just one large cog in a bigger wheel.

Shimali Senanayake

It was such a difficult task: sometimes I feel sorry for them. There would be so many barricades, effigies being burnt ... Certain members of the team were not considered to be neutral. Erik for example. But he was in such a difficult spot. No matter what he did he was considered pro-LTTE ... [but] if he had not had that connection with Bala[singham] he would probably not have got the leeway to push for things, negotiating, facilitating meetings—something Erik worked very hard on from the start. In terms of engagement the Norwegians could have been better strategically ... But just the fact that they were still able to meet face to face, you have to give a lot of credit to them. Despite all the flak they were getting, one of their achievements was that they were able to stay true to their mission of hanging in there.

Julian Wilson

[The Norwegians] were scrupulously treading a fine line and they never strayed away from being facilitators ... The basic thing that decides whether a facilitator will be successful or not is the commitment of the two parties involved. And that changed on both sides: because of elections and then because of things happening within the LTTE—and if they were in the beginning, I don't they were honest towards the end. The process failed because the needed level of commitment was not there.

Norwegian unilateralism

Vidar Helgesen

[We] should have been more strategic in designing and orchestrating input from different international actors that wanted to be helpful. And there was a range of them who wanted to be helpful—Canada, Switzerland, the UK, Germany, the Nordic countries for example.

It's not that we were against doing this, more that we never allocated the resources and strategic thinking to deciding what the different actors could do. We encouraged some to receive delegations, and that worked well. But in Sri Lanka itself: what could the different countries have done, how could we have woven more of them into the peace process? Because when things got difficult there were not enough countries sufficiently deep into the process to stand up for the right things: whether that was on the EU terror listing or after the tsunami, to really insist that high-level visitors needed to visit Tamil areas.

Erik Solheim

A problem here was that while we could always speak candidly to the Indians and Americans without any fear that this would leak to the media or the parties to the conflict, with some other countries you could never be sure—and if things leaked they would end up with people who used the information to harm the peace process. If we had started earlier on the issue it wouldn't have been so sensitive. The focus could have been on the kind of projects other internationals could have been supporting—peace education, building constituencies for change, which is also one of the more domestic lessons learned. A challenge here was that India was reluctant to see too broad and deep an international involvement in Sri Lanka. But enticing more of the significant donors to allocate more of their aid budgets to supporting the peace process in Sri Lanka is an area that would have benefited from more strategic thinking on our side.

Jon Westborg

Part of Norwegian foreign policy for the past 4–5 years has been: don't go it alone, the best thing is to work with others. But if you look at our successes in terms of being a facilitator, you would find that we are best when we are alone. When it came to the crunch in Sri Lanka, for example, we didn't sit with India on our back, or go about doing the things that it very politely told us to do.

Aid and the peace process

Vidar Helgesen

> A general lesson from peace processes is that there is still too little strategic think-
> ing about the role of the economy, including aid, in building peace. The political
> issues are more exciting, action-orientated, and as a politician you are naturally
> drawn to them. But in the end the ground situation—in particular the economy—
> means more to ordinary people ... Norwegian aid was quite well attuned to the Sri
> Lankan peace process. But the bigger picture issue is what we could have done to
> ensure that other donor's assistance programs were better strategised and orches-
> trated with us towards supporting the Sri Lankan peace process.

Erik Solheim

> We didn't focus much on aid at all: our basic analysis was that politics was the
> core element, and that this could not be replaced by aid. This was correct in my
> view. But we could—and probably should—have thought more about the aid
> dimensions, taken them up in another way, thought about how aid could be used
> more strategically. As it was we focused on the politics. There were a number of
> small projects and programmes intended to support peace, but the rest of the aid
> budget was left to the technical expertise of different nations, who kept on fol-
> lowing a 'business as usual' approach. There was never any real overall discus-
> sion among the donors of how their combined assistance efforts could be used
> more strategically.

The challenge of communication

Shimali Senanayake

> The Norwegians probably thought the onus was on the government to take on
> communication with the domestic audience. That's a lesson learned. There
> should be a communication strategy even before you come into a country. Even
> covering little things like where is Norway situated, what it is they have been
> doing so far, their goodness of heart. The political parties in Sri Lanka were able
> to play on the insecurities generated by the uncertainties, and there was a lot of
> anger as a result.

> I know colleagues in the vernacular press who would try to get a comment, but
> there would be a problem in their not understanding what was said. There's this
> colonial thing of being embarrassed about not knowing English, so they would
> end up writing something completely different [to what was said]. So you really
> should have had local resources to tell your story in Sinhalese or Tamil. You had
> a clear divide between the English and vernacular press. And you also had more
> Tamil journalists who could speak English better: so more quotes from
> Norwegians in the Tamil press as a result, and the undercurrent that the
> Norwegians were pro-LTTE. That also built up over time.

LESSONS LEARNED

Erik Solheim

[The government] always thought that we should keep a low profile, not respond to critiques, that it was their job to present the peace process exactly as they wanted to. If we had communicated more forcefully in the English, Sinhala and Tamil media, they thought it would never be accepted in the same way as if the government did it. The LTTE would have had no problem. But at every occasion the Sri Lankan government advised us not to communicate or respond publicly.

It would also have been difficult for us to adopt a higher profile. It would have created controversy. Maybe we should have had a rapid response mechanism to answer lies and accusations against us. But quite often we took the view that it was best to remain silent, because if you refuted something it would only lead to more controversies. We should have had a clear media strategy. Many Sri Lankan politicians were also too elitist to be able to communicate well with the rank and file. There was no overall government strategy for presenting the peace process. G.L. Peiris rushed to the media without a strategy, although he did give the peace message. Ranil was a megastar at the time. Initially the peace process was enormously popular. It may have been a problem that it was pursued at the same time as some unpopular economic reforms initiated by Ranil's government.

Shimali's point about Tamil and Sinhalese communicators is a very fair one. We did discuss it, but in that sense did not have sufficient contact with Sri Lankans. We had some listening posts, but far too few. We should have given press briefings in local languages: but we had the impression that there was a major opposition to that from the government.

Vidar Helgesen

Our softly-softly approach would have been OK if the government had had an inclusive approach towards civil society. But they didn't ... We should have had an overall media strategy. We tended to think that it was better not to respond. And while we couldn't—and shouldn't—have got into a position where we were having arguments with individual Sri Lankan politicians or journalists, we should have reinforced our message and corrected mistakes and misrepresentations. You have two choices. Either you ignore the mistakes—which is what we did—or you have to correct and respond to them consistently. Which also means you need a strong media monitoring capacity. The Sinhalese media: that is somewhere we should have invested more resources.

Tomas Stangeland

The parties were not able to sell or market what they had achieved between the rounds of talks. [In] the Colombo press, yes, but out in the country nobody had heard of the Oslo Declaration. People didn't have a clue. The negative parts were well known because the JVP was out in the countryside. The positive parts, the progress as a result of the peace process, that was not widely known.

Maybe they miscalculated, thought that as long as they catered to the press in Colombo all was fine. But they needed to deal better with grassroots feelings. Like telling people that the reason fruit is cheaper now is because of peace, the reason tourists are coming back is because of peace. Talk about the link: I really see it now in retrospect. It was difficult for us to market this. We hoped that the parties would have done this. The government may have not liked to talk much about it, because they thought they had made concessions to the LTTE. And perhaps the LTTE simply felt that not much was happening on the ground. The peace dividend was certainly much more obvious in the South.

Frances Harrison, former BBC correspondent

The Norwegians should have hired a PR company for the government, or just done a lot more to sell the peace process to the Sinhalese. Things moved too fast for the LTTE to engage with the international community. You can't expect people to change overnight. There should have been more media from Jaffna, more stories on how Tamils had suffered, what the benefits of the peace process were. The Norwegians should have set up a peace correspondent based in Vavuniya and Jaffna. There were loads of stories to cover.

Palitha Kohona

The Norwegians probably made a mistake that many Western missions continue to make, of thinking that Sri Lanka is the English-speaking Colombo elite. I immediately sensed it when I came back from New York in 2006—that the Western diplomatic community was totally isolated from the mainstream of Sri Lankan thinking. Their sources of information were English-speaking NGOs, LTTE sympathisers and the English language media, all of which were extremely critical of mainstream thinking. Unfortunately the Norwegians thought that by reflecting this view they were also helping the peace process. That is why they were so enthusiastic about P-TOMS. They didn't seem to realise that the vast majority of people did not subscribe to those views.

Was there a Norwegian pro-LTTE bias?

Erik Solheim

It's fascinating to see that there is still that perception among the Sinhalese. I'm attacked by extremist Tamils as well. They claim I am responsible for the death of Prabhakaran. In the diaspora the perception is that the international community let them down. We were the main contact point with the LTTE, so this perception [of pro-LTTE bias] had to come sooner or later. I met Balasingham all the time, although actually we met the government far more. But I was the person with the most contact with the LTTE, so the perception came easily. I supported the core Tamil demand, for a separate entity: not a separate state but self-government in the Tamil-dominated North and East; self-rule within Sri Lanka. That is in accordance with globally accepted norms regarding federal governance structures. I still believe that [self-rule] is a fair demand. [During the peace process] I had to explain the LTTE position and so was targeted in an environment where Sinhala supremacy was ingrained ... Since no one else was presenting the LTTE view to international actors I had to do it. It is a perception one has to live with—though I did not always get credit from Tamils for speaking on their behalf.

Shimali Senanayake

Sometimes, even the perception of people like Erik could have been easily countered if the government had just come forward and said: 'Yes, we completely trust him'. But that never came from Chandrika, Ranil or Mahinda: a *clear* statement of support. That Erik has some background, has certain advantages, and we are fully confident of him.

Palitha Kohona

There was a feeling that the Norwegians were championing the LTTE too much. I know that Erik and Jon [Hansen-Bauer] repeatedly deny it, but this was a perception. They needed to have done something to get rid of that perception. Whenever an LTTE delegation was taken overseas, it was under the auspices of the Norwegians. The impression created amongst the majority Sinhalese population was not very helpful. It was not as if the LTTE was going there on its own because it wanted to negotiate peace: it was if they were guests of the Norwegians.

Lalit Mansingh, Foreign Secretary for India

Part of the problem was that the Norwegians at some stage lost the confidence of the Sri Lankan government, and were seen to be partisan. Once you lose the confidence of one of the parties, it is impossible to carry out facilitation or mediation. I don't know how they reached that point, but the impression in Colombo was that they were actually tilting towards the LTTE. In Colombo they saw the West as being sympathetic towards the LTTE cause. I'm surprised the Norwegians did not detect this: it was clear to us that the Lankans were losing confidence in the Norwegians. The fact that they had such a direct line to Balasingham—there was a suspicion of intimacy with one side that made their task difficult.

Narayan Swamy

Many Tamils who were ranged against LTTE thought that [Erik] was always articulating the LTTE viewpoint. Erik may have articulated it simply out of the fact that 'I have met Prabhakaran, you never have, so this is what he feels'. But they claimed Erik was enamoured of the Tigers. In reality, the kind of criticism heaped on Norway came down to the fact that some people had a vested interest, and most people did not know.

N. Ram, Editor-in-Chief, *The Hindu*

Norway came in with good credentials, sought after by both the Tamils and the Chandrika government. Ranil pounced on it. They were always in touch with India: there was nothing to fault them on that score ... But even we were surprised that they tended to equate the two sides, the state and LTTE. The Norwegians also got mixed up between the role of facilitator and mediator. Evidence of this is provided by the Oslo Declaration: they tried to craft something and the LTTE really didn't stand by it. And we knew they wouldn't: it was clear there was no way the LTTE would accept a solution, federal or otherwise. They only said that they would talk about it. The Norwegians took themselves too seriously, the way the Indians did earlier. Their role in the SLMM got them into a controversy. They were blamed for everything.

Nirupama Subramanian

I always felt they had a soft corner for the LTTE. My assessment was purely based on media reports. I also felt that the LTTE was comfortable with Norway, as if they understood the struggle and had no strategic interests. The LTTE were very comfortable with Norway. They did not trust Japan, they thought it had interests.

Facilitation: ambiguities and challenges

Jon Westborg

We should have stayed clearly in our facilitation role, leaving it to the parties and not ending up in a situation where we gradually started feeling that this was the Norwegian peace process. To some extent we were pushed into that and we should have let it go. The only one who dared to do something differently was Vidar, who said: 'Thank you very much: we've done our best, now you had better decide whether you want to continue or not.' ...

There you have a difference of opinion within the Norwegian team, because Erik felt we should continue. So Norway continued. In this case, since Erik took over the responsibility that is what he would have to defend. Our Indian friends would say, stay in there, because as long as you are there they will pick on you, not on us. The Americans would say the same thing. And the Sri Lankans asked us to stay on because it was also good for them to have somebody to pick on. And that's why I think Vidar was right.

Shimali Senanayake

[There] was never clear demarcation on whether they were a mediator or a facilitator—that was very ambiguous. In the minds of Sri Lankans these guys were expected to bring peace. The Sri Lankan on the street did not understand these dynamics, because there was lack of clarity. The political administration was able to play on all the fears, because they wanted them out. The Norwegians should have got more commitment. As a facilitator, it's a very loose role. They were more or less expected in various quarters to provide the function of a mediator. That was the difficulty because maybe in the larger scale, they wouldn't have even got in if they were mediators: the government only wanted facilitators. So both the parties were very easily able to put the blame on the Norwegians because of the lack of clarity over their role. They have to take some blame for that.

Bård Ludvig Thorheim

I think the Norwegian team started treating the parties equally at an early stage. This is the natural instinct and of course both parties are equally important in order to reach an agreement. But at some occasions I believe it should have been made more explicit that the parties were not equal in status. A democratically elected government on one hand and the LTTE on the other: those are two quite different entities, which cannot always be treated as equal opposites.

Another lesson to me is that, given that the political dynamics in the Sri Lankan conflict were determined to a large extent by developments on the battlefield, the Norwegian team ought to have included an expert on military affairs right from when they started working on the ceasefire agreement. It has been pointed out by others that the Sri Lanka Army was not properly included in the discussions about the CFA. Moreover, the Norwegian team would have benefited from greater military expertise even in the period when the SLMM was there and beyond.

Either you need a big communication apparatus or you need to keep a lower profile. [The facilitator] should have had a lower profile and forced the parties to be at the centre. There is not even a word for facilitation in Sinhalese. That was a disconnect.

Lalit Mansingh

This kind of facilitation is better when done through a group of countries and not one country, and especially if that one country is small and does not have hard power. It is easy to ignore a small country, as the Sri Lankans have done. If it were a group of countries—say the EU decides to have a mediatory role—they would have been taken more seriously. See the Israeli-Palestinian issue: the Americans and Europeans bring in that weight and even then it's so difficult. That's the principal lesson. You are dealing with real politics. A solo effort is like a missionary effort. If you want to bring weight to what you are doing you need a larger group.

Erik Solheim

The reason Norway was selected in the first place was that no one wanted the US, or anyone with a big stick, to be involved. Secondly, no one with a big stick wanted to be involved. The Indians had tried once. It was a war between the two parties in Sri Lanka, they wanted someone lightweight: they wanted a way to communicate between themselves, not someone who could punish or carry a big stick. We had to think throughout about the way in which we could mobilise other forces. Even for big powers there were clear limitations on what kind of stick they could really use. It's the same in most conflicts.

Lisa Golden, senior Norwegian official in the SLMM

Maybe we could have been a bit more creative about leverage, though we tried. Getting Kumaratunga and Wickremasinghe on the same page was necessary to seal any deal. We could not facilitate between them, but we kept her well informed. I think it might have been worth making even more of an issue out of this structural problem, seeing if we and others could get Wickremasinghe to include Kumaratunga more in the talks. The divide in southern politics was very deep. We always said the three main challenges were transforming the LTTE, transforming southern politics and reaching an agreement that addressed the interests of both sides and Sri Lankan society. These were large issues for the peace process to resolve.

Kristine Höglund

The mediator becomes really weak when there is no outside mandate, nothing to base it in the UN or some other system. Maybe a stronger group of friends that has set down some kind of parameters for engagement would have made a difference.

Norway did not have much leverage and they were afraid that if they over-stepped their mandate, they would be forced to withdraw, and they didn't want that. Partly because of their own investment but also because they thought it was important that we stay, because as long as there is a chance of the peace process succeeding it is the right thing to do. But it also made them really weak. It's a kind of almost request-driven mediation; as if this is the type of intervention the parties wanted and could accept ...

You could think of creative ways of trying to strengthen that. In the early days, the government was open to those kind of options. Norway could have done much more in terms of having its own agenda vis à vis the media, public relations. They were trying to counter-balance their image and purpose for being there. They could have been more proactive. There are ways of strengthening the monitoring mechanism. Its Nordic composition was a good idea, but they were so dependent on the EU countries. But it was a compromise solution. There was a mismatch between the negotiation process and the broader peace-building activities in which civil society organisations were trying to engage. They had these elaborate proposals for the type of institutional reforms that were required, whereas the things on the negotiation table had to do with confidence building, not institutional reforms.

Judith Large

The very qualities that gained the Norwegians access were their downfall. In these complex situations, and with Sri Lanka's ruthless history, to come in as a small, perceived soft, non-threatening facilitator: there has to be a backup in old-fashioned power terms.

Should Norway have continued its engagement?

Ranil Wickremasinghe

[The Norwegians] should have known by 2005–2006 that it was time to roll it up. They might still have been called up at this stage, but trying to push it further had antagonised Sinhalese Buddhists. Having a third party and a framework is good, as they did, but [the third party] should not get involved in domestic politics. You have to deal with everyone: you can't pick your favourites and then decide and then pit them against each other. The Norwegians had to decide what was their role in Sri Lanka. They are not even clear about that now. You can't get people together today by talking to a few MPs or Ministers: you have to be willing to talk directly to the heads of the parties.

Kristine Höglund

What is unique about the Norwegian experience in Sri Lanka is that it was an engagement that was not really discontinued at any point, compared to how mediators in other countries have approached things ... The problem with the Norwegian mediation effort was that they always seemed to want to be there, which made the tactic less effective because the parties knew the Norwegians wanted a solution and would stay until the very end.

If they had withdrawn much more forcefully, that could have changed dynamics. They would say that they did not have the mandate to withdraw; but I think they could have tried either to withdraw much more forcefully or to engage much more. That was the weakness of their approach, because they did not do more than they were mandated to do. On paper they were only facilitators, but actually they did more.

Dharisha Bastians, Sri Lankan journalist

There were only two primary parties in [the] negotiations, and this was criticised by many as exclud[ing] larger segments of Sri Lankan society. Important stakeholders such as the Muslim minority, non-LTTE Tamil groups and civil society were left out. ... the exclusive nature of the peace negotiations [meant that] it was possible to achieve a ceasefire in a relatively short time, but simultaneously the two-party model ultimately led to reduced legitimacy for the peace process. Mandated by two primary parties, Norway lacked the power to open up negotiations to include other stakeholders. In this situation ... the Norwegian mediation goal of local ownership proved to be awkward and deleterious towards the [overall] peace process.[8]

A top-down peace process?

Vidar Helgesen

[A] strong government-civil society relationship ... was clearly lacking. It is not something that outsiders can and should interfere in. So we could have mitigated some of the negative consequences but we could not have changed the basic design of Sri Lankan politics, which is deeply elitist.

When we asked Ranil's team he didn't want us to do anything on that front. Ditto Chandrika's team. We did do some outreach. Some of the Buddhist clergy we met, however, were somehow discredited by their association with foreigners, because the clergy are the biggest carriers of nationalism. So I think it is the government that should have done more on this score. The best way to have tried to change those sentiments would probably have been to initiate a relationship with senior Buddhist clergy much earlier.

Erik Solheim

In terms of reaching out our biggest failing was probably with the Buddhist clergy. Reaching out to Buddhists would have meant reaching out to those who didn't agree with us—regular visits to Kandy to talk to senior monks to pay our respects, listen politely. Which might also have given them a platform from which to attack the peace process—which in turn may be part of the reason Ranil and Chandrika did not want us to reach out to them.

Tore Hattrem

One needs to use time and resources to understand the context of the country you are working in and speak to absolutely everyone, without prejudice. I think we did that, but we should have better understood the deeply rooted Buddhist concerns early in the peace process. But we were not alone in this. Many Sri Lankan political leaders also overlooked the need to reach out to the Buddhist *Sangha* early in the peace process.

You have to act based on a deep political understanding of what's going on. As an external actor and facilitator one should also be cautious in trying to support or invest in civil society with a view to shaping the country's views on a particular issue, or the peace process in general. That is the responsibility of the parties themselves.

The negative fallout of adopting such an approach might be large. One must accept that national political discourse is chiefly shaped by the citizens and domestic institutions. It must be the parties themselves that shape the national dialogue on peace, and they must have the determination to achieve peace. In Sri Lanka, organisations that received external support for peace-related work were not very important in the national debate, and questions were raised about their constituency and legitimacy. Those organisations that were useful in the peace process were not NGOs with a high public profile but knowledgeable, specialised organisations that kept a very low profile. They provided us with analyses that were correct.

Paikiasothy Saravanamuttu

[The peace process] wasn't about a political settlement or deal between the government and the LTTE. In effect it was about an architecture for a new Sri Lanka. It had to be talked about in those terms for the population at large. Because one of the arguments levelled against the whole thing was that it is a new Sri Lanka rather than the old Sri Lanka, and it is happening by stealth, because they are selling out the country. The facilitators may well take the view that this is not their role: but if you are facilitating a peace process that is a huge lacuna in the way you are approaching things. You also need to be aware of what the shortcomings are. You need to have a holistic perspective as to what the peace process requires. [Because] if what you are leaving out is what is eventually going to undermine the whole thing, then you are investing time and energy in a process that is fundamentally flawed and thus unlikely to succeed. And if it succeeds in the short term, it is unlikely to sustain itself: so you have to understand the internal dynamics.

Jayaveda Uyangoda, Sinhalese political analyst

The mistake the Norwegians and others made was that they reduced the conflict to the government versus the LTTE. There are so many actors, and levels. Bringing a protracted civil war to an end is much more complex and difficult than this liberal peace-building approach through negotiations and economic development envisages. Restoring peace in the context of an ethnic civil war is easier imagined than actually implemented. It requires fundamentally reforming the state. It's about sharing state power: that's the question to be addressed.

Peace process ownership

Vidar Helgesen

We had no choice. And even if we had had a choice, a highly nationalist country like Sri Lanka would not have been welcoming of an approach where the international party was more directive. And it would have to have been someone else—most likely India. And they tried that once previously. We could and should have tried to be more forceful facilitators when it came to the modalities for the negotiations. But what would be the alternative to emphasizing that ownership of the peace process rests with the parties—and the same with implementation? 10,000 international peacekeepers? That is not realistic.

Time and trust

Erik Solheim

You must be patient—there are no shortcuts. You must be prepared to spend years, as the Indians told us. You must have an understanding and knowledge of the country, you must get to know the personalities: all this we did well. We established a high degree of trust with the key actors. The facilitation team was structured equally, Norwegian style. A flat structure is positive: it gives you more ability to learn. And you need completely dedicated people.

The SLMM

Erik Solheim

Overall the SLMM was successful. Very few, if any, of the major problems in the peace process can be attributed to it. It was a small mission based on the assumption that the two parties wanted the ceasefire to work and that it could assist them in that. One of the flaws was the lack of ability. It was assumed that the monitors would make a judgement as to what did or did not constitute a ceasefire violation. The problem with that was that there was a counting of violations rather than qualification of violations. How can you compare a murder with an unacceptable hoisting of a flag? With obvious and serious violations such as assassinations there was a lack of ability to handle those in a way that really told the parties a lesson. But the SLMM leaders were very good. Trond Furuhøvde, for example, was the incarnation of an intellectual general.

You needed a military component, the military spine, of the mission. Other people brought other qualifications and abilities. It may be the case that we could have had more military people to speak more clearly to the parties on serious violations. The people who came in knew little of the context. But the key people in the SLMM remained for a long period of time ... They did a very good job of working with the military leaders on the ground, finding compromise solutions. Overall, it is difficult to know whether they ideally should have taken a more high profile role. Clearly the parties did not want that, neither did India.

Kristine Höglund

I visited the SLMM offices throughout Sri Lanka on several occasions. I think the first batch were really experienced people. It was a mixed bunch. But even with little resources, and poorly staffed, they achieved quite a lot in establishing their presence in those first years [of the SLMM].

Different countries had different recruiting strategies. The Finns pretty much only recruited military people, Iceland had only a few people. The Swedes were quite mixed—there were quite a number of police who had experience of international missions, and quite a number of military people. There were not many people in the SLMM from a purely civilian background. The Norwegians had a mix, both military and police. The Danes had former diplomats. It was clearly male dominated. I didn't see any kind of scepticism against the SLMM when I was travelling with them. There were lots of misperceptions as to what they were actually doing, could do and what their link was to the mediation effort. People came to them about their missing family members. In general, since they were in the areas of conflict, they were viewed as some kind of protection for some civilians.

Overall the SLMM had a weak mandate: they had no investigative powers. Given the mission's small size it was unreasonable to expect a more robust mandate and demands on them. In the beginning the SLMM could manage many of the incidents of violation that were reported, but when the conflict began to escalate it became impossible for them to do anything but just monitor ...

The problem with such missions is that they are completely dependent on the will of the parties. More people would have helped a little, but in terms of establishing presence, fifty or so people would not have changed things very much the way the conflict was developing. They become toothless tools quite early on. When you talk to the monitors, they would still say it was important for them to remain as some kind of international witness. But I don't know if the people on the ground perceived the SLMM as such.

Lars Johan Sølvberg, SLMM Head of Mission

Very simply, there was no professional component in the civilian operational support to the peace process. That I see as a huge gap and a possibility to develop in the future. We had this basically traditional military headquarters conceptual approach—all the familiar functions you will find in any military mission. This is fine in a way, but when you put together something with a non-military component, it should be something other than military personnel in civilian clothes.

As military people we tended to be very practical, very geographical: we took out maps, divided up sectors and so on. But you have other sectors of the operation that were less tangible like monitoring political sentiments, religious movements and all the other intangibles: the economy, the arts, trade, behind-the-scenes development and so on. Coming with experience from typical military observer missions is fine. But this is only one dimension of the mission at hand, because you have to take care of more things.

Susanne Ringgaard Pedersen, SLMM monitor

One of the things the SLLM could have done differently was to have had a human rights approach to monitoring: to have recruited experienced human rights officers, for example. I also think it was a very military-run organisation, not very transparent. For example, it was very difficult for us to know whether our recommendations to headquarters would be used the way we intended, although we had monthly meetings with the mission. We did not know very much about the peace process. I only knew what Erik did through the news and through colleagues, obviously.

So communication was a problem. It's kind of ironic. It was a little bit like it was in 2009 in the UN. There were lots of people on the ground that were reporting on what was happening, and yet inconvenient facts were not being transmitted, and it was too uncomfortable to report on them. There were a lot of things which never really went anywhere in the SLMM. We did not have a mechanism for high-level advocacy. Also things like the disbanding of paramilitaries—a key CFA provision and we kept asking: so what are you doing about it? The facilitators really didn't have the courage. Their hands may have been seriously tied by the terms of CFA. Then again this is what the Sri Lankan government do to everyone, every organisation that's ever operated in Sri Lanka. I just think the Norwegians erred on the side of caution. They got bullied too quickly. I don't think they were tough enough—or experienced enough in some ways, perhaps.

Shimali Senanayake

The SLMM should have had a more robust mandate. Maybe because of the IPKF experience, the parties didn't want to give them any powers. It's good they had Nordic monitors but I don't know how culturally immersed they were. Some were quite oblivious to the local context. With Asians a lot depends on bonding. Hagrup [Haukland] was quite disillusioned by the end. What was sad also was the lack of communication. It's really important to try and take the people with you.

Parity of status?

V. Rudrakumaran, US-based LTTE advisor

The Norwegians should have taken a principled position, or walked away if both parties were not playing by the rules. I wouldn't fault the Norwegians because the whole system is state-centred: that's international relations. Our position was that we were a de facto state and wanted parity and equality in each and every thing. So the banner of the first peace talks read: Sri Lankan Peace Talks. And I told Bala[singham] it should have been: Sri Lanka-Tamil Peace Talks.

Judith Large

Concerning the question of legitimacy and equality in terms of the process, the government felt the Tigers had been given a parity that they did not deserve. That it came too fast and was based on an emotional and sentimental acceptance of them as freedom fighters. Whereas the government had experienced the Colombo side of that, the bombing side. Basically they felt it wasn't fair.

Gopalkrishna Ghandi

The Norwegians had the great difficulty that they were dealing with a sovereign state that perhaps had policy corrections to make, and on the other side a non-state entity that was hugely effective on the ground. I once had a discussion with Vidar and I asked him, how is it that you are able to reconcile the situation of giving parity to a state and a non-state entity? He said: We are not treating state and non-state parties as equals, but around the discussion table there is no difference between the discussants.

That was a very interesting response. It also said something of the Norwegians' methodology. To sum up: on one side a state with a policy that by its own admission needed modifications in order to move forward; and on the other, a non-state entity with a cause overlaid by a method that was anathema to all civilised nations. Then we had the Norwegian facilitators, who were also constantly modifying, evolving, refining a procedure to deal with policy on the one hand and method on the other.

Palitha Kohona

This is an impression that I developed: I would constantly hear statements from the Norwegians that the LTTE would negotiate only when they felt that they were equal in strength to the Sri Lankan government. Having come from the UN where sovereignty is sacrosanct, I thought this was an outrageous position to take. Here you had a terrorist organisation that was proscribed in almost every single democracy in the world and then you have a sovereign state, and the

Norwegians telling us that you have to let the LTTE become a little stronger before they will negotiate with you. I found that an outrageous position to adopt. You are literally creating a state from a terrorist group so that peace could be created between the two sides.

Accountability

Lalit Mansingh

The Sri Lankans must go through this stage as the South Africans did, come clean and then the process of healing will begin. Because if they don't do this the suspicions will remain there forever. It will be a big factor in reviving Tamil hostility within Sri Lanka. Personally, I think they are being very short-sighted in ignoring the long-term consequences of suppressing the facts and not making any progress on that issue.

The impression I got was that the president [Rajapaksa was] surrounded by people who [were] telling him: 'You do not need to do anything on this issue. We had an enemy, we've defeated it, the Tamil problem is over and now let's go ahead with our own agenda.'[9] Second, I think President Rajapaksa believed that all you [needed was] economic progress: that if all Lankans are beneficiaries the Tamil problem will go away. Third, there's a feeling that Tamils have not been good citizens and it's time they started to look at themselves as such. Tamil demands are not taken very seriously. There's a feeling that if you give something only to the Tamils, you are being unfair to the other provinces. There are also right-wing extremists who say that Tamils have to take life as it is: if you want to stay in Sri Lanka, it's a Buddhist majority country and you must accept Sinhala as the main language.

Jayaveda Uyangoda

The importance you accord to accountability depends on where you come from. From the perspective of international humanitarian law, yes; from the perspective of Sinhalese nationalism, no; from the perspective of Tamil nationalism, yes. As with the question of reconciliation, there is a particular Western—liberal, Christian, humanistic—notion and attitude ... Let us forget and move on: that is what Rajapaksa was, and is articulating. Reconciliation is a contested concept in Sri Lanka, and accountability and reconciliation are linked in this debate. That reconciliation presupposes accountability: that is how the debate is framed in Western terms. But things are not so straightforward in Sri Lanka.

Judith Large

Adam Roberts has said that Sri Lanka sacrificed its legitimacy internationally by breaking every rule in the book in pursuing victory. By doing this they emerged victorious but illegitimate, and that's what they are still up against in the world.

They used the terrorist card to wipe out human beings ruthlessly, with not a shred of remorse or regret.

Anonymous[10]

A lesson we haven't learnt is to integrate. We fought this massive war, killed many people, and became a dehumanised government as a result. We fought for some land whose people were rejecting us. The government feel we have captured this territory, it's ours, but let's just leave those people behind. Let's just keep them as farmers, fishermen. [Tell them] 'Don't go any further, don't try to study, just be under our control forever and we will tolerate you.' ...

I can't get over the fact that the government are celebrating death in this country. I can't accept what they are doing after the war: it's bizarre. You have to apologise. You cannot move forward in Sri Lanka without apologising. Get up and say: 'look, we did this, we are sorry'. Stop living the lie ... Instead they hire buses and people glorify the fact that this is the place where Prabhakaran or this or that person died. They shut out the fact that there are kids who lost their parents, who saw shells fall. I have kids showing me their injuries, telling me and smiling: that's where my grandmother died. That's not normal.

India's role

Lalit Mansingh[11]

We were somehow scarred by the 1987 experience. That influenced our later policy in the sense we clearly knew what we did not want to do. But we kept an open mind: after all Sri Lanka as a neighbour is important for us. It was quite clear that some of the things they wanted us to do, like arms supplies, were out of the question, and they also understood the political sensitivities about this. But the basic line that we stood for was the territorial integrity of Sri Lanka. Short of supplying [an] army, we helped them in every possible way ... We were, however, a bit disappointed that when we held back, Sri Lanka allowed other elements to come in. It became an active arms bazaar: the Pakistanis, Chinese, Israelis, British were all rushing in.

Even now, however, the Sri Lankans acknowledge that without our tacit support they could not have defeated the LTTE. Subsequent misunderstandings have been about subsequent events. The basic issue of how to deal with the Tamils, and give them the dignity they deserve as Sri Lankans: that unfortunately has not been resolved. While we don't criticise Sri Lanka in public, messages have been conveyed unofficially. We are watching and communicating. I personally am very disappointed that the Rajapaksa government, being in such a strong political situation, has proved unable and is perhaps unwilling to deal with the problem. If they continue on this road another similar problem will emerge. And the signs of that are not very difficult to see.

Fortunately for Sri Lanka, Tamil Nadu remained quiet until the LTTE was crushed. If it had been politically active it would have been difficult for the central government in India to maintain a cooperative attitude. What is happening now is that it is becoming a political issue in Tamil Nadu and if this were to get out of hand, it would be impossible to continue the current co-operation with Sri Lanka.

I find it interesting that Washington and Delhi, who exchange notes all the time on Sri Lanka and neighbouring countries, look at things in more or less the same way. The approach is this: we have strategic interests in the country. While what has happened is unfortunate, we need to protect those strategic interests and move forward. So there is this impatience with Sri Lanka, with the fact that they are not doing the minimum required for the issue to be put aside and to [allow us to] move ahead.

> When talks collapsed and violence resumed, siding with the Sri Lankan government was the logical default position [for India] ... Tore Hattrem described India as suffering from a 'Burma syndrome' in its Sri Lanka policy, meaning that it would not place a focus on democracy and human rights issues ... for fear of pushing the country into a closer relationship with China. India continued to express support for Norway's efforts, but with the resumption of war Delhi's support for the Sri Lankan government (whether open or tacit) amounted to pursuing peace through the military defeat of the LTTE.

N. Ram, Editor-in-Chief, *The Hindu*

The negative side is the past arming, training and financing [of the LTTE]. It contributed to the troubles in Sri Lanka, for the Tamils as well. The only saving grace was never supporting the idea of 'Eelam'. The plus point, too, is what emerged with the Indo-Lankan Agreement and the 13th Amendment, which is still the best thing in place and can be built upon. So the plus is really devolution within Sri Lanka. At that point [in 1987] it was called merger minus or a provisional merger. And President Jayawardene promised the Indians that if it goes well and LTTE stops fighting and lays down arms, gradually the merger between the North and the East could become permanent.

The other positive contribution is what came after the assassination [of Rajiv Gandhi]. Every Indian government has played it right: hands off. They banned the LTTE and helped various other governments in doing that, which made things difficult for them. When the endgame approached, India was as much with the Sri Lankan government as China or Pakistan. India did not demand a ceasefire, it only expressed concern over the fate of civilians. The Tamil Nadu government made a big noise but did not follow up on it. Nor was there any great feeling for the LTTE, barring some fringe groups. Nobody wanted the LTTE to be around at that point. I think the Indian government liked Ranil, had very good relations with him in the past, but preferred Rajapaksa at that point [2005] because he was not known to be pro-LTTE. The view was that too much leeway had been given to the LTTE during the CFA period.

Narayan Swamy

You could say that India was sympathetic to [the] LTTE. It trained them. You could say that to every country that allowed the LTTE to open offices, even after it was proved that they killed Rajiv Gandhi. Allowing the LTTE to function legitimately from Paris, provincial capitals, was the biggest mistake committed by anyone. There is a counter argument that by giving the LTTE space, we thought we could influence them. But the problem with the LTTE setup was that this was a façade. You could never influence Prabhakaran, and the people who ran his offices were minions. India was very clear: we will never allow Tamil Eelam to emerge. This was also said to Erik. We will be happy if LTTE goes down, but if it can be submerged in a democratic process that is fine.

In the last stage of the war there was rapid progress by the Sri Lankan military because there was a fear among Lankans of the BJP coming to power in India: there was a drive to finish off the LTTE before the Lok Sabha election results were announced on 16 May 2009. The Lankans feared that if the BJP came to power there could be pressure on the government. Even the Tamil super-nationalist Vaiko had told Prabhakaran that.

Nirupama Subramanian

What India has done on Sri Lanka in the UN Human Rights Council is a surprise. In 2012 they abstained on the resolution criticising Sri Lanka. In 2013, the draft resolution was revised, and India [still] voted against Sri Lanka. It went against my reading of the government. I don't know how much further they are willing to go, if India is secure enough to do that—secure as a nation, that is. Because we have problems of our own as well. If you back something like that—an accountability measure—you expose yourself: on Kashmir, on the Armed Forces Special Powers Act (AFSPA), for example.

Sri Lanka: Conflict Resolution the Post-American Way

Vidar Helgesen, 24 May 2009

The government of Sri Lanka (GoSL) has, with remarkable success, concluded its military strategy and defeated the LTTE. The political packaging of the strategy has been that of the War on Terror. Was it? At one level, yes. The LTTE had been ruthless in its use of terror and it can be claimed that its downfall was actually the first successful 'war against terrorism', as conceptualised by the former US administration.

At another level, no. Rather than reflecting a US style 'War on Terror', Sri Lanka can be seen as an example of conflict resolution the post-American way. The GoSL dealt a lethal blow to the LTTE, but also left the international community wounded. Sri Lankan politicians and media fiercely attacked the 'IC' [international community] as they dubbed it, but effectively they meant the West: Western governments, Western-based humanitarian and human rights NGOs, Western-funded UN agencies, foreign (Western) media. Access was denied, insistence on respect for humanitarian law was ignored, calls for a political process rejected, and Western political and diplomatic representatives were lambasted in the process. We have seen similar tendencies elsewhere—Sudan, Zimbabwe, Burma—but possibly nowhere as systematically and blatantly as in Sri Lanka. Its defiance is all the more striking given Sri Lanka's claim to democratic respectability.

How could Sri Lanka be so successful in this military strategy against the LTTE and political strategy against the West? A significant part of the answer lies in the fact that the international community is not-so-international and not-so-communal. The government of Sri Lanka had, in different ways, the backing of key powers in the so-called post-American world. On the military side, such powers provided material support, intelligence support, training. On the economic side, they provided some cushioning. On the political side they provided, with equal significance, encouragement—or silence.

As a result the GoSL stands not only victorious on the battlefield but also feels relatively comfortable on the international scene. It has got the backing it feels it needs. It does not feel it needs the West, as long as it has the rest. A telling image from a Sri Lankan daily was the presentation by the Chinese ambassador of a humanitarian contribution to President Rajapaksa for the government's use in its camps for displaced Tamils—camps that are a disgrace by established standards of humanitarian law and principles.

The lesson learned for governments waging internal conflicts? Count on post-American powers that don't meddle in your internal affairs: keep the international community out if they are not with you; and engage only those who come with open purses and closed eyes. The lessons learned for the outside world? Firstly, that the international community exists as such only in rare situations. As a consequence, the space for diplomatic pressure or third-party support for the peaceful settlement of conflict is severely limited, unless supported by the post-American powers.

Secondly, that the space for multilateral action is limited as long as a government has the support of parts of the international community to ignore the rest of it. This begs the question whether recent emerging international norms and architecture for human security, the responsibility to protect, peace mediation, peace building and so on are becoming obsolete before they really got started. Coordination of international efforts for peace and security is a noble objective— but of little help in situations where these are not shared international objectives in the first place. While the US may have returned to multilateral fora, post-American powers seem to have left through the back door. The collaborative leadership of Obama may mean the US is better at listening, but it is not necessarily listened to. The EU's post-modern pooling of sovereignty may work well for Europe, but does not necessarily carry much weight elsewhere.

At the heart of the matter lies state sovereignty. The concept was out of fashion in the post-Cold War worldview, which was for a time believed to be universal, but which was an essentially Western worldview. With other states now increasingly defining the global normative framework, state sovereignty is once again a comfortable concept from behind which a government can conduct its internal affairs as it sees fit. Westphalia may have left Europe, but only to emerge stronger elsewhere. Much as we are seeing a resurgence of economic nationalism triggered by the financial crisis, we are also seeing political nationalism promoted and protected by the new balance of power in the international system. Sri Lanka has taken full advantage of this. Who's next?[12]

APPENDIX

In 2010, the Norwegian Foreign Ministry commissioned an evaluation of the country's peace engagement in Sri Lanka. The resulting report, *Pawns of Peace: Evaluation of Norwegian peace efforts in Sri Lanka, 1997—2009,*[13] was published a year later by the National Agency for Development Co-operation (NORAD). Below is a summary of the report's key findings and conclusions with respect to Norway's 'peace performance' in Sri Lanka:

The Sri Lankan peace process is largely a story of failure in terms of bringing an end to the civil war. Norway, however, cannot be held solely or primarily responsible for this ultimate failure, and its involvement contributed to several intermediate achievements, including the Ceasefire Agreement, the Oslo meeting in which both sides expressed a commitment to explore a federal solution, and the signing of a joint mechanism for post-tsunami aid. The ceasefire in particular had positive impacts on the ground situation, but in the end these accomplishments proved to be ephemeral.

The peace process failed to induce fundamental changes in the disposition of the state and anti-state formations in Sri Lanka, and to some extent caused a further entrenchment of positions. The stalemate that led to the Ceasefire Agreement (CFA), initial peace talks and a period of 'no war-no peace', was followed by an escalating shadow war and finally open hostilities, ending in the defeat of the LTTE in May 2009.

Many factors contributed to this train of events, but the following were crucial.

First, both the government and the LTTE entered into the peace process while staying committed to their cause. That is not to say they were not genuine in exploring a political solution, but there was an incommensurable gap between what the South would countenance (a unitary state with limited devolution) and what the LTTE demanded (a separate state in all but name).

Second, peace efforts were constrained by structural features of the Sri Lankan state and politics. The conflict is understood here as being rooted in processes of incomplete state formation, which led to competing ethno-nationalist projects. Conflicts over territory are particularly resistant to negotiated settlements. Several features of Sri Lankan politics made the challenge even harder, including dynastic and inter-party rivalries, patronage politics and nationalist mobilisation that resisted state reform and foreign interference.

Third, the window of opportunity for a negotiated settlement was short, and was based upon a unique constellation of domestic and international factors—including a [mutually] hurting stalemate, leading to an acceptance by both sides of a measure of military and political parity, a Western-oriented government and multi-faceted international backing for negotiations. These factors were to change relatively quickly. Perhaps most importantly, the 2004 split in the LTTE shifted the military balance decisively in the government's favour. This decreased incentives for substantive concessions by both sides. Policies associated with the war on terror, rather than concerns for the specificities of the Sri Lankan case, undermined the potential for LTTE transformation and increased the isolation of Norway as the sole state conduit to the organisation.

Fourth, there were important changes in the international positioning of the Sri Lankan government. The effort led by the UNF government to internationalise the peace process through security guarantees, donor funding, and politically sensitive economic reforms sparked a Sinhala-nationalist backlash. This contributed to the emergence of a nationalist-oriented administration with a commitment to a more hard-line position towards the LTTE and greater resistance to Western involvement. The new administration constructed its own version of an international safety net by drawing on the financial support and diplomatic cover of Asian powers. This allowed the Rajapaksa government to pursue an ultimately successful military 'solution' to the conflict.

As a weak, soft-power mediator, Norway was not in a position to counter or transform these dynamics. In the absence of a strategic road map, or a robust network of international actors, the peace process failed to lock the parties into permanent concessions and commitments. To some extent this can be attributed to [the] limitations of Norway's 'ownership' model, which allowed both parties to avoid core political issues, while continuing to pursue incompatible goals.

Many of the constraints identified above were not amenable to external mediation and it should be recognised that all actors were operating in an environment of great turbulence and incomplete information. However, different courses of action by Norway might have mitigated some of these problems.

LESSONS LEARNED

First, a stronger understanding of the domestic context—particularly an apprecia-tion of the material and symbolic effects of external intervention—would have helped the team to predict many of the dynamics sparked off by the peace process. Second, the rather passive ownership-based model left Norway open to instrumen-talisation, and this could have been addressed by placing stronger parameters and minimal conditions on the Norwegian involvement from the beginning. Third, a careful monitoring of such parameters should probably have led to Norway with-drawing from its roles as mediator and monitor at an earlier stage.

Norway's experience in Sri Lanka yields some broader lessons for peace building elsewhere:

1. Peace processes produce unforeseen and unintended consequences. Mediators need to consider the potential costs of their actions. A consequentialist ethic and precautionary principles are required, including benefit/harm analysis and the careful and continuous weighing of possible scenarios and outcomes.

2. There is a need to think about the balance between hard and soft power. Norway's approach may be suitable to bring parties into negotiations, but harder forms of leverage may be required to reach and implement a settle-ment. Even so, as shown by the Sri Lankan experience, hard power deployed by external actors cannot override domestic political dynamics when the constituency for peace is weak or limited. Norway should avoid situations where it is a weak and isolated mediator, with limited and inconsistent inter-national backing. This means placing more attention on 'multilateralising' peace processes by building links to, and borrowing the leverage of other more powerful actors and coalitions.

3. There is a need for mediators to attach firm conditions to their involvement, including: the right to engage with all parties deemed to be relevant; the right to preserve public communication channels to speak out against malpractices or defend either the process or themselves; and the right to maintain or acquire leverage in relation to the parties.

4. Aid may play a supportive role in peace processes, but cannot be a substitute for politics. Moreover, poorly conceived aid has the potential to destabilise fragile political settlements. At one end of the spectrum in Sri Lanka, working 'on' conflict sometimes amounted to trying to 'buy peace'. At the other end, economic reforms were based on a simplistic understanding of the relation-ship between economic efficiency, growth and peace. It is in the middle ground between these two positions that aid is most likely to play a sup-portive role in the pursuit of peace. This necessarily involves a more modest but conflict-sensitive role for aid in the context of peace processes.

5. Norway played several roles in Sri Lanka, not all of them easily compatible: these included diplomatic broker, arbiter of the ceasefire, and humanitarian and development funder. Norway's experience in Sri Lanka underlines that when multiple roles are combined, there is a need to develop a robust strate-gic framework, which optimises synergies and complementarities between them. Otherwise tensions and trade-offs are more likely, particularly in the

context of an unconditional ownership approach and a flimsy international framework.

6. Norway has usually been a mediator in conflicts between a state and non-state actor, employing an approach of even-handedness. The Sri Lankan case highlights the difficulties of following such an approach in the context of the 'War on Terror'. This suggests a need for careful reflection on whether it is possible for Norway to square the circle of showing a united front with other international players on countering terrorism, whilst attempting to talk with 'terrorists' in order to bring peace.

7. The Sri Lankan peace process reflects broader global changes. It began as an experiment in liberal peace-building but was brought to an end by a very different 'Asian model' of 'conflict resolution'. Building on Westphalian notions of sovereignty and non-interference, a strong developmental state, the military crushing of 'terrorism', and the prevalence of order over dissent, this model may serve as an inspiration for other countries in the region. This global 'eastward' shift may have far-reaching implications for the possibilities of Norwegian-style mediation in the future.

EPILOGUE

The biggest challenge will be reconciliation with the minorities and resolving the Tamil national issue. The new government has signalled a willingness to reach out. They will investigate human rights abuses during the final stages of the civil war. The international community will continue to call for war criminals and human rights abusers to be held accountable. This is good, but the international community must give the [new] government enough time and space.

To bring [the conflict] to a close, the Sinhala majority must also be brought on board and understand what Sri Lanka looks like from a Tamil perspective. Accountability unfortunately takes time, as we saw in Chile and Serbia. But at the end it will come ... The new 'Sri Lanka model' could make many dictators lose their sleep. If the new democracy is able to deliver results; democratic reforms, inclusive development and Tamil and Muslim rights, it will become a true role model.

Erik Solheim, 'Shock and Joy in Sri Lanka', *Huffington Post*, 29 Jan. 2015[1]

With respect to the epilogue to this book, timing is more than usually of the essence. If it had been written before the end of 2014, as originally planned, it would have painted a significantly different picture of the situation five years after the end of the war from the one outlined below. The reason? Faced with evidence of his declining popularity, in November 2014 President Rajapaksa called a snap presidential election—'snap' because constitutionally speaking his term in office still had two years to run.[2]

With opinion polls and recent provincial election results both pointing to his government's plummeting popularity, Rajapaksa's calculation seems to have been relatively straightforward. Run a campaign marked by a tried-and-tested combination of tub-thumping populist rhetoric, scaremongering over the continuing threat of an LTTE 'resurgence', and resolute facing off against the international community over calls for an international enquiry into wartime abuses, and it would prove enough to secure a third term in office and the opportunity to consolidate what one analyst described as Rajapaksa's distinctive 'developmentalist-national security state'.[3] Many seasoned observers, moreover, were inclined to believe that he could, and would, pull it off.[4]

But there was an additional reason why Rajapaksa was convinced he would triumph at the polls: the election date—8 January—appears to have been chosen on the basis of his long-time personal astrologer's advice that this constituted an 'auspicious' day on which to hold an election. In terms of reading the omens, to some the anniversary of the January 2009 murder of prominent journalist and editor Lansana Wickrematunga—a murder in which many argue Rajapaksa's government was directly involved—seemed an odd choice for polling day. His astrologer's subsequent claim that all his prognoses included a standard 5 per cent 'margin of error' provided an amusing, if somewhat unconvincing, explanation for what proved to be a spectacular predictive failure.[5]

For in the event, a widely-anticipated Rajapaksa victory is not the way the portents played out. Within days of calling an election a wholly unexpected presidential challenger emerged in the form of Maithripala Sirisena, until then a minister in Mahinda's government and—even worse—chairman of his own Sri Lanka Freedom Party (SLFP). Not only was Rajapaksa's new opponent an insider in terms of party allegiances, but politically Sirisena's profile was that of a (moderate) Buddhist nationalist and provincial son of the soil (in his case from Polunnaruwa)—the core components of Rajapaksa's own appeal to the island's majority Buddhist Sinhalese population.

Standing as the 'Common Candidate' for an ad hoc opposition coalition comprising everyone from UNP leader and ex-prime minister Ranil Wickremasinghe, ex-president Chandrika Kumaratunga, to the fervently nationalist JHU and JVP,[6] the self-effacing Sirisena, a devout Buddhist with a reputation for clean, simple living, soon began his campaign. His emphasis on the brazen official corruption plaguing all aspects of public life, the Rajapaksa family's seemingly inexorable capture of the political sphere—brothers as ministers, relatives of all descriptions as high public officials, diplomats, company bosses—and the declining living standards of all but the wealthy few instantly struck a popular chord.

In the run up to polling day, indications of the way voter preferences were moving began to emerge. Nonetheless, as Sri Lankans awoke on 9 January most were unprepared for the news that greeted them: a Sirisena triumph at the polls by just over 51 per cent to Rajapaksa's 47.5 per cent—a margin of some 450,000 votes. Although he still commanded the majority of his core traditional ethnic Sinhalese vote, reports indicated that Rajapakasa's share of that vote had nonetheless declined. Additionally, it became clear that the minorities—Tamils and Muslims in particular—had voted overwhelmingly for Sirisena. In spite of strenuous efforts by some elements of the Tamil community, there was to be no repeat of the electoral boycott in the Northeast called by the LTTE that had handed a narrow victory to Rajapaksa over his opponent, Ranil Wickremasinghe, in the December 2005 presidential elections.

Whatever their take on the election returns, commentators expressed varying degrees of astonishment over the final outcome. In particular, why, they wondered, hadn't Rajapaksa simply fixed the final result, as many predicted he would do in the event of the polls going against him? If allegations are to be believed, however, that is precisely what the outgoing president had attempted to do. While the details remain unconfirmed, an official complaint lodged by incoming Foreign Minister Mangala Samaraweera—an office he had first taken up ten years previously under Rajapaksa—stated that on the morning of 9 January there had been a brief, desperate attempt by the outgoing president, aided and abetted by members of his inner circle, to cling onto power. Predictably, the chosen means depended critically on security support from the military leadership.

Summoned to an emergency early morning meeting at Temple Trees also attended by, among others, Gotabhaya Rajapaksa and Chief Justice Mohan Peiris, Attorney General Y. Wijethilake, Police Chief N. Illangakoon and Army Commander Dayan Ratnayake were asked to give their views on the legal grounds for and military possibilities of suspending or annulling the election result. In reply, all reportedly stood their ground against what Samaraweera described as plans to make 'an illegal attempt to stay in power using military force'—a cause of incredulity to some on account of the military command's previously symbiotic relationship with the Rajapaksa brothers.[7]

At any rate, following this decisive check, any plans to alter the electoral facts on the ground appear to have been abandoned. Sometime after four o'clock in the morning, Rajapaksa is reported to have made a call to opposition leader Ranil Wickremasinghe, and at around five, the prime minister-in-waiting arrived at Temple Trees for further talks. The end came rapidly: by half-past-six, the first media reports appeared—complete with camera footage—of a sombre-looking Rajapaksa departing quietly—or as some suggested, slinking away—to his hometown of Tangalle in the southern Hambantota area.[8]

Thereafter a victorious Sirisena moved quickly to announce a new government,[9] headed by UNP leader Wickremasinghe as prime minister and comprising ministers drawn from the eight-party coalition that had backed him as 'Common Candidate'. Immediately after putting together a new administration, Sirisena proceeded to make a number of moves—under the banner slogan of *yahapalanaya* ('good governance')—that were significant as much for their political symbolism as their practical impact.

First he removed the Northern Province governor, a prickly major general appointed by Rajapaksa soon after the war's end, known for his obstructive attitude to the TNA-led provincial council.[10] Soon afterwards, as Sirisena had promised, his civilian replacement—a senior former diplomat—was announced.[11] Next, the lifting of restrictions on foreigners travelling to the North and media access was either promised or directly enacted. Additionally, an end to wiretapping, police intimidation and the notorious 'white van' abductions and disappearances that had been a regular feature of the Rajapaksa era was promised.

An undertaking to return land seized from civilians by the military in the Northeast was accompanied by the announcement of moves to establish the number of Tamils detained under the Prevention of Terrorism Act (PTA) with a view to releasing them, the latter gesture in particular eliciting both domestic and international praise.[12]

In the international arena, Prime Minister Wickremasinghe and Foreign Minister Samaraweera started to address the human rights-related concerns by underscoring the government's willingness to engage with the United Nations Human Rights Council, where a March 2014 resolution had set in motion an international investigation into the war crimes allegedly committed by both sides during the Sri Lankan conflict. In addition, the new administration announced its intention to establish what it described as a 'credible domestic process' to address past rights violations, while also extending invitations to the UN Human Rights High Commissioner and its Working Group on Enforced and Involuntary Disappearances to visit the country in the near future.[13]

From the perspective of promoting reconciliation—an issue with which Rajapaksa's failure to engage was widely criticised—perhaps the most significant initiative to date was the decision that in tandem with National Day (4 Feb) celebrations, the new administration would act on one of the recommendations of the 2012 'Lessons Learnt And Reconciliation

Commission (LLRC)'s Final Report,[14] namely: to hold a 'separate event ... to express solidarity and empathy with all victims of the tragic conflict and pledge our collective commitment to ensure that there should never be such bloodletting in the country again.'[15]

This it did in the form of issuing an official statement, read out on the day by President Sirisena, paying respects to 'all' Sri Lankan citizens 'of all ethnicities and religions, who lost their lives due to the tragic conflict that affected this land for over three decades'.[16] In another sign of the changes taking hold in the wake of the new administration, two senior TNA MPs participated in official Independence Day celebrations held in Colombo—something no representative of a Tamil political party had done in decades.[17]

In international terms, the key issue requiring immediate attention was the investigative report due to be presented at annual meetings of the UN Human Rights Council in Geneva in March 2015.[18] In mid-February, and in the wake of successful visits to key allies by Foreign Minister Samaraweera and President Sirisena,[19] the government got what it wanted: a six-month deferral of the UN war crimes report, until September 2015.

The 'one time only' deferral requested by UN Human Rights Commissioner Zeid Ra'ad Al Hussein and agreed to by the Council would, the government argued, give it time to put in place a 'credible' domestic accountability mechanism, to be established in consultation and with support from the UN.[20] Explaining the apparent turnaround by international actors that had hitherto pushed for the UN report's presentation in March 2015, one analyst suggested that the key factor was a widespread perception that the incoming administration needed time to 'settle in' and wanted to avoid a 'politically explosive report coming out just before elections'.[21]

Unsurprisingly, the decision to delay the UN report was criticised by many. Tamil groups held sizeable demonstrations in the North and East, and in advance of Al Hussein's announcement on 10 February the Northern Provincial Council passed a resolution calling for a UN investigation into the 'genocide' against Tamils allegedly perpetrated by the Sri Lankan authorities: a move that proved controversial, not least among those sections of the Tamil community—the diaspora included—keen to seize the opportunity to promote a prospective resolution of 'the national question' opened by Sirisena's assumption of power.

Several months into the new government's mandate, then, what do future prospects for genuine progress on the critical issues of reconciliation, accountability and political accommodation between the majority and minority communities look like? At this point, informed opinion falls into two categories: those buoyed with optimism on the one hand, and those who remain pessimistic about the prospect of genuine political change on the other. As well as pointing to the positive developments noted above, proponents of the first view underline the fundamental fact that, as one local commentator put it, 'the fear has gone'. After the fear and repression of the Rajapaksa era, in other words, this is a genuine case of regime change—and for the better.

But those who take a more pessimistic view are not without evidence to support their intepretation. An open letter from late February 2015 to President Sirisena from Human Rights Watch, for example, provides an overview of key outstanding areas of human rights-related concern: the well-entrenched police culture of both routine torture and ill-treatment of suspects, including for the purpose of pursuing 'personal vendettas' or extort[ing] funds'; the actions of Buddhist ultra-nationalist groups, notably the Bodhu Bala Sena (BSS), responsible for inciting violence against minorities and Muslims in particular; the continuing presence of unofficial detention centres in which torture is routinely practiced; and concern that the 'domestic mechanism' proposed to address critical issues of accountability both appears to exclude international actors from anything more than an advisory role and runs the risk of heading down the well-trodden path to public oblivion taken by numerous previous official Sri Lankan investigations and commissions of inquiry.[22]

Whichever of these views one favours, it is important to keep in mind the fact that after a decade of Rajapaksa rule, the new government is engaged in a delicate balancing act. On one side are ranged a series of pressing, and thoroughly justified, demands—those of civilians, for example, predominantly Tamils in the North and East, for the return of lands taken from them during the war and in its aftermath by the military, and the release of those detained under the PTA, many of them held for a number of years. On the other side, it has to contend with suspicion among sizeable sections of the majority Sinhalese community over any measures that might be construed as 'appeasing' the Tamil community, not least when the prime minister overseeing those changes—Ranil Wickremasinghe—is the very man charged by the Rajapaksa regime with having 'sold out' to the LTTE during the Ceasefire Agreement (CFA) era.[23]

Erik Solheim, for one, is crystal clear in his view of the country's new political landscape: 'While there are any number of reasons for scepticism, it is hard to believe that Sri Lanka will in any foreseeable future have a more enlightened, experienced and moderate leadership', he contends.

'Many more Tamils are ready for painful compromises now than during the last couple of decades. There is minimal appetite for more bloodshed and futile sacrifices. In short, the time to finally resolve the Tamil national question in Sri Lanka is now. The glass is half full.'

Overall, the approach to President Sirisena adopted by important sections of the international community appears to be to give the new government leeway in which to begin getting its house in order, while retaining concrete, time-bound benchmarks of progress, a thoroughly sensible attitude under existing circumstances.[24]

Looking to the future, many, as Indian Prime Minister Modi did during his landmark March 2015 visit to Sri Lanka,[25] will focus on the politics of change—not least the need for a genuine devolution of powers to the regions as envisaged in the 13th Amendment to the Constitution. But I want to end on a different note. In the course of one of many interviews with Erik Solheim, I asked him whether he thought ethnic nationalism remained a major issue in Sri Lanka.

'Very much so', Solheim replied. 'Sri Lanka needs to look into overlapping identities. If you are an Indian Tamil from Tamil Nadu then you become first an Indian, second from Tamil Nadu, third maybe a Hindu and fourth, perhaps something else as well. Sinhalese nationalism has a very limited view with respect to treating all Tamils as equals and respecting Tamil nationalism. The example of India is important: there is an enormous potential for communal violence, there are many, many languages, but it has been able to forge a national identity.' And in this context, he emphasised, 'acceptance of overlapping identities is absolutely essential'.

Indian political scientist turned politician Yagendra Yadev once argued cogently that in a democracy, minority rights are at least—if not more—important than majority rights as a test of quality. Since achieving independence from Britain, he suggested, the Sri Lankan state has consistently argued that undue concessions to minorities—in this case, primarily the Tamil population—lead to secessionism. This in turn is why it has always opposed a federal structure and instead opted to maintain a unitary state. However, as he pointed out, the reality is that Sri Lanka's approach to minorities ultimately resulted in a destructive, decades-long civil war— something that it could probably have avoided, Yadev argued, if it had opted for the federal approach adopted by the Indian state after independence, achieved only six months before Sri Lanka.

There is a striking parallel here. Both countries entered the independence era with significant Tamil populations, and while Sri Lankan Tamils initially couched their demands in moderate, non-secessionist terms, initially the Tamil political elite of Madras State (today's Tamil Nadu) were strongly inclined to seek their own independence. With the combination of a devolved federal governance structure,[26] full recognition of Tamil as an official state language and other accommodating gestures initiated by the Indian government, however, over time demands for independence waned, and today, Tamil Nadu is an integral part of the Indian polity.

In Sri Lanka, the precise opposite occurred. Decades of structural discrimination against Tamils, a pervasive majoritarian political culture combined with official intransigence in the face of moderate demands for cultural-linguistic recognition, and backed by a form of regional administrative autonomy, succeeded in radicalising Tamil opinion, thereby creating the conditions for the emergence of the LTTE, and from 1983 onwards, a bloody and hugely destructive civil war.[27]

The comparison of trajectories underscores the fact that state policies with respect to minorities have the potential to either make or break the contours of a democratic polity—for minority and majority populations alike. Or as a Nepalese analyst once put it, 'Indian experience shows that if you allow prevailing diversities to enter through the front door of democracy and give them a legitimate place in politics, their creative energies can be harnessed'. And much though they tend to dislike examples, less still lessons, from their powerful neighbour across the water, here is something that genuinely bears reflection on both by the new government in Colombo as well as Sri Lankans of all stripes.

Finally, since this is a book about the Norwegian engagement in the Sri Lankan conflict, I end with a question I put to Erik Solheim regarding the key lessons from that engagement, and how those have impacted on the way in which Norwegian peace diplomacy has operated since.

'The experience in Sri Lanka has not reduced our resolve to continue to engage in peace diplomacy, that is very clear', Solheim responded. 'A general lesson learnt was that we should have been a bigger team, with more resources available—although it is still not clear that will happen in future peace efforts.' The key specific lesson he identifies from Norway's experience in Sri Lanka, however, is this: 'Engage with everyone; speak to everyone.'

POSTSCRIPT

If the public mood in Sri Lanka was significantly lifted by the January 2015 presidential elections, the very opposite is true of developments that took place just as this book goes to press. Further to Sirisena's late June announcement of a date for scheduled parliamentary elections—17 August— the President followed up on this with news that surprised just about everyone. In early July Sirisena announced that ex-president Mahinda Rajapaksa, the very man he had defeated at the polls six months earlier in what has come to be known as the 'Silent Revolution', thereby heralding in a new, and seemingly more hopeful political era in Sri Lanka, was being nominated to contest the elections on a UPFA ticket.

The shock waves from this announcement coursed rapidly through the Colombo political establishment. While Sirisena subsequently lapsed into silence,[1] his erstwhile allies in the coalition that had earlier defeated Rajapaksa moved quickly to establish a new coalition, dubbed the 'United Front For Good Governance' (UNFGG) and led by the UNP's Prime Minister Ranil Wickremasinghe, in order to contest parliamentary elections. Following a brief interval, then, as prospective prime minister-in-waiting Mahinda Rajapaksa is once again in the political limelight. Whatever else remains uncertain at this point—not least the election result—his return to the Sri Lankan political stage has certainly ensured a lively, closely-fought, and hopefully not overly violent, electoral campaign.

ANNEX

INTERVIEWEES

Below is an alphabetical list of all those interviewed for the book, grouped by country of origin or, in some cases, organisation. Unless specifically indicated, all citations in the book derive from these interviews. Not all those interviewed inside Sri Lanka wished to be identified by name—and in a few cases those previously based there for professional reasons have also felt the need to remain anonymous. Their wishes have been respected in every instance. Additionally, in instances where Sri Lankan interviewees are not currently based in the country, I have indicated this fact in brackets.

Principal interviewees

Erik Solheim, Special Envoy to the Sri Lankan peace process (1998–2005). Minister of Environment and International Development, overseeing Norwegian peace involvement in Sri Lanka (2005–2009).
Vidar Helgesen State Secretary for Foreign Affairs (2001–2005).

Norwegian Ambassadors to Sri Lanka

Jon Westborg, Ambassador to Sri Lanka (1996–2003).
Hans Brattskar, Ambassador to Sri Lanka (2004–2007).
Tore Hattrem, Ambassador to Sri Lanka (2007–2010).
Hilde Haraldstad, Deputy Chief of Mission (2008–2010) Ambassador to Sri Lanka (2010–2012).

Senior Norwegian Ministry of Foreign Affairs (MFA) officials

Jon Hanssen-Bauer, Sri Lanka Special Envoy (2006–2009).

Jan Egeland, State Secretary for Foreign Affairs (1995–1999).

Wegger Christian Strømmen, State Secretary for Foreign Affairs (1999–2000).

Raymond Johansen, State Secretary for Foreign Affairs (2005–2009).

Colombo Embassy staff, Oslo-based Sri Lanka facilitation team members and advisors

Tone Allers, Deputy Head, Peace & Reconciliation Section (2010–2014), Head of Section (2014–).

Sondre Bjotveit, Sri Lanka advisor, Peace & Reconciliation Section (2005–2008).

Lisa Golden, Advisor, (2002–2007), acting Special Envoy (summer/fall 2005), Senior Advisor (2009).

Tomas Stangeland, First Secretary, Colombo Embassy (2000–2004), Head, Peace & Reconciliation Section (2010–2014).

Bård Thorheim, First Secretary, Colombo Embassy (2008–2010), Peace & Reconciliation Section staff member (2012–).

Kjersti Tromsdal, Advisor, Sri Lankan affairs (1998–2003), First Secretary, Colombo Embassy (2003–2005).

Academia

Øyvind Fuglerud, Professor of Cultural Anthropology, Oslo University.

Sri Lanka Monitoring Mission (SLMM)

Major Ulf Henricsson, Head of Mission (April–Sept. 2006).
Major-General Lars Johan Sølvberg, Head of Mission (Sept. 2006–Jan. 2008).
Hagrup Haukland, Deputy Head of Mission (2002), Acting Head of Mission (2003–2004), Head of Mission (2005–March 2006).
Anne Sender, Monitor (Sept. 2002–Dec. 2003, 2007).
Susanne Ringgaard Pedersen, Monitor (Dec. 2003–Dec. 2004).

India

Gopalkrishna Gandhi, High Commissioner to Sri Lanka (2000), Ambassador to Norway (2000–2003).

Lalit Mansingh, Foreign Secretary (1999–2001), Member, Non-Official Group of Friends (NGF) of Sri Lanka.

N. Ram, Editor-in-Chief, *The Hindu/Frontline.*

Nirupama Subramanian, former Colombo correspondent, *The Hindu/ Frontline.*

Muralithan Reddy, former Colombo correspondent, *The Hindu/Frontline*

M.R. Narayan Swamy, journalist specializing in Sri Lankan affairs.

Sri Lanka

Iqbal Athas, Defence Correspondent & Senior Analyst, *The Sunday Times.*

Vinya Ariyaratne, General Secretary, Sarvodaya Foundation (Sarvodaya Shramadana Movement).

Aron Dannrin, former deputy to Karuna (in Europe).

Tyrone Ferdinands, Director, Initiative for Political and Conflict Transformation (INPACT).

Austin Fernando, Defence Secretary (2001–2004), advisor to President Siresena, (Jan. 2015–).

Arne Fjørtoft, Founder, Worldview International Foundation.

Bernard Goonetilleke, Secretary-General, Government Secretariat for Co-ordinating the Peace Process (SCOPP) (2002–2004).

Frederica Jansz, former Editor, *The Sunday Leader* (in exile).

Dayan Jayatilleka, Ambassador to the United Nations, Geneva (2000–2009).

Palitha Kohona, Secretary-General, Government Secretariat for Co-ordinating the Peace Process (SCOPP) (2006–2007), Foreign Secretary (2006–2009) (in New York).

Chandrika Kumaratunga, President of Sri Lanka (1994–2005).

Milinda Morogoda, Minister of Economic Reform and principal government negotiator (2001–2004); Senior Adviser to President Rajapaksa (2011–2015).

Suthaharan Nadarajah, journalist, academic, former advisor to Anton Balasingham (in London).

Saravanamuttu (Sara) Paikiasothy, Director, Centre for Policy Alternatives (CPA).

Jehan Perera, Executive Director, National Peace Council (NPC).

Visvanathan Rudrakumaran, Chair, Provisional Transnational Government of Tamil Eelam (in New York).

Shimali Senanayake, former Colombo correspondent, *The New York Times* (in New York).

Sonali Samarasinghe, former columnist, *The Sunday Leader*, widow of Lasantha Wickrematunga (in exile).

Devinda Subasinghe, Ambassador to the USA (2002–2005) (in Washington DC).

Jeevan Thiagarajah, Executive Director, Consortium of Humanitarian Agencies (CHA) .

Jayadeva Uyangoda, Professor of Political Science and Public Policy, Colombo University.

Bradman Weerakoon, Private Secretary to the Prime Minister (2000–2004).

Jayampathy Wickramaratne, Counsel to the President, Senior Advisor, Ministry of Constitutional Affairs (1994–2001), appointed advisor to President Siresena (Jan. 2015–).

Ranil Wickremesinghe, Prime Minister of Sri Lanka (1993–1994, 2001–2004), appointed Prime Minister for the third time (Jan. 2015–).

USA

Richard Armitage, Deputy Secretary of State (2001–2005).

Robert Blake, Ambassador to Sri Lanka (2006–2009), Assistant Secretary of State for South and Central Asian Affairs (2009–2013).

Nicholas Burns, Under-Secretary of State for Political Affairs (2005–2008).

Teresita Schaffer, Ambassador to Sri Lanka (1992–1995).

Ashley Wills, Ambassador to Sri Lanka (2000–2003).

UK

Dominic Williams, First Secretary, Colombo Embassy (2008–2011).

European Union (EU)

Helen Campbell, Head of South Asia Unit, External Relations Directorate (2006–2008).

Andrea Nicolaj, Sri Lanka Desk Officer, South Asia Unit, External Relations Directorate (2006–2008).

Julian Wilson, Head of South Asia Unit, External Relations Directorate (2003–2005); Head of Delegation to Sri Lanka and the Maldives (2005–2008).

ANNEX

United Nations

Tamrat Samuel, Special Envoy to Sri Lanka, Dept. of Political Affairs (DPA), (2008–2009).

Other

Peter Bowling, Executive Director, International Working Group on Sri Lanka.

Frances Harrison, BBC Sri Lanka Correspondent (2000–2004).

Kristine Höglund, Associate Professor, Peace & Conflict Department, Uppsala University.

Judith Large, Secretary, Non-Official Group of Friends (NGF) of Sri Lanka.

Ian Martin, Human Rights Adviser to the Sri Lankan peace process (2003–2005).

Martin McGuinness, Deputy First Minister, Northern Ireland (2007–).

Jonathan Powell, Downing Street Chief of Staff, UK (1997–2007).

Norbert Ropers, Director, Berghof Centre Sri Lanka (2001–2008).

NOTES

INTRODUCTION

1. Romesh Gunesekara, 'A long, slow descent into hell', *Sunday Leader*, 10 May 2009.
2. In response to a militant ambush on Sri Lankan army forces in late July 1983 that left thirteen soldiers dead, widespread anti-Tamil rioting broke out in Colombo and rapidly spread across the country. Estimates of the resulting death toll range from 400 to over 3,000. The riots led to a mass exodus of Tamils from the country and among those who stayed, thousands of mostly young Tamils joined militant groups, notably the LTTE.
3. In Oct. 2014 the Sri Lanka Army announced they were re-imposing earlier restrictions on foreigners visiting the northern war zone. In the interests of 'national security' all foreign nationals would now be required to submit a request for permission to the Defence Ministry in advance of a visit—a 'request' that was also to include a 'clear indication' of the visit's aims and purposes. Explaining the move, a senior official claimed that the Army had 'information' that 'some foreigners [were] trying to cause discord among ethnic communities' in the region. Media commentaries suggested that the Army's move may have had more to do with preventing those involved in the investigation of alleged war crimes due to present a report to the UN Human Rights Council in spring 2015 from visiting the area. See M. Srinivasan, 'Sri Lanka Imposes New Curbs on Travel to North', *The Hindu*, 16 Oct. 2014. In early 2015, less than ten days after Mathripala Sirisena's electoral defeat of Mahinda Rajapaksa, the Ministry of Defence announced that these restrictions were being lifted with immediate effect, on the grounds that 'there is no war situation in the country'. See 'Sri Lanka lifts restrictions for foreigners visiting North, no troops reduction', *The Colombo Page*, 16 Jan. 2015.
4. Quoted in J. Hyndman & A. Amarasingham, 'Touring "Terrorism": Landscapes of Memory in Post-war Sri Lanka'. *Geography Compass*, 8, 2014, pp. 560–575. James Stewart's recent work on 'war tourism' in Sri Lanka is also worth consulting in this context. See James Stewart, 'War Tourism in the North of Sri Lanka', *Overland*, 18 June 2013, at http://overland.org.au/2013/06/war-tourism-in-the-north-of-sri-lanka; and James Stewart, 'After the Slaughter: War Tourism in Modern Sri Lanka',

E-International Relations, 28 Feb. 2014, at http://www.e-ir.info/2014/02/28/
after-the-slaughter-war-tourism-in-modern-sri-lanka/
5. 'Sri Lanka Velupillai Prabhakaran's Bunker is Destroyed', *BBC News*, 4 Oct. 2013.
6. In Sept. 2013—conceivably around the same time as Prabhakaran's bunker at
   Viswamadu was blown up—media reports indicated that the military had decided
   to demolish the Farah III to sell it off for scrap metal, and that visitors were now
   being kept away from the area. 'MV Farah sold as scrap', *Daily Mirror*, 10 Sept.
   2013. Despite this, more recent photographic evidence suggests that the vessel's
   hulk remains in the water, at the same spot on the Mullivaikal beach as before.
7. When I set out to write this book I also successfully applied, in partnership with
   Uppsala University, for financial support from the Norwegian MFA. Since Erik
   and Vidar have both held/are holding public office, it is important to underline
   that when the initiative to write this book was taken, neither of the two held
   public office in Norway, nor have they received any financial benefit from its
   production or publication.

1. BEGINNINGS

1. Interview with Jon Westborg.
2. In reality, the New Year speech amounted to little more than public confirmation of something that was already an open secret on the Colombo grapevine.
3. According to official Norwegian Agency For Development Co-operation
   (NORAD) figures, bilateral assistance to Sri Lanka for the period 1977–2013
   totalled 4.2 billion kroner ($700 million).
4. The essentials of the following account have been verified by a former Norwegian
   MFA official with a long-standing involvement in Sri Lanka.
5. The Norwegian Agency for Development Co-operation, the official Norwegian
   development agency.
6. A major town on the south coast of the country: also home and power base of
   former President Rajapaksa.
7. Approximately $9 million.
8. Velupillai Prabhakaran, leader of the LTTE—one of a number of militant Tamil
   groups formed in northern Sri Lanka during the 1970s. Following a series of
   moves aimed at the often ruthless elimination of opponents and rival groups
   during the course of the 1980s, the LTTE established themselves as the dominant proponents of the call for an independent Tamil homeland.
9. At this point in the development of Norway's assistance programme in Sri Lanka,
   programme delivery was entirely through local and international NGOs.
10. The largest Tamil political party, formed in the early 1970s, which advocated an
    independent Tamil state created on the basis of non-violent, parliamentary, dem-
    ocratic politics. TULF leader A. Amirthalingham was later assassinated in 1989
    on Prabhakaran's direct orders. See Narayan Swamy, *Inside An Elusive Mind:
    Prabhakaran*, Colombo: Vijitha Yapa, 2003, pp. 208–210.
11. Literally 'Tamil homeland'. The term was used by the LTTE from early in its

existence, and in the eyes of many—not least the Sinhalese—became synonymous with the organisation and in particular, its core objectives.

12. As with all casualty figures from the Sri Lankan conflict, estimates of deaths as a result of the July 1983 pogroms vary widely. Tamil sources, for example, often cite a figure of over 3,000 deaths.

13. Useful accounts of the Thimpu talks are provided in Anton Balasingham, *War And Peace: Armed Struggle And Peace Efforts Of Liberation Tigers* Mitcham: Fairmax, 2004, pp. 77–85 and Swamy, *Inside an Elusive Mind*, pp. 126–128.

14. See the 'Indian Peacekeeping Force (IPKF)' section below for more on this subject.

15. See Balasingham *War and Peace*, p. 76.

16. The naval wing of the LTTE, founded in 1984. Initially the Sea Tigers' main task was smuggling personnel and equipment between LTTE bases in Tamil Nadu and Sri Lanka, in particular Jaffna. Over time the Sea Tigers grew in both experience and confidence. As a result, by the mid 1990s they were carrying out offensive operations against the Sri Lankan Navy. The Sea Tiger fleet included a small but highly effective group of suicide bomber vessels. To date the LTTE is the first and only rebel group in history to establish its own 'air force' and probably also the only such entity to establish a naval wing—a testimony to the organisation's enduring military sophistication.

17. Army commanders leading the operation later claimed that they would have inflicted a crushing, perhaps even fatal defeat on the LTTE if they had been allowed to continue the military offensive.

18. A dedicated LTTE squadron whose mission was to carry out suicide attacks on military and civilian targets, both on land and at sea. Between the squadron's formation in 1987 and the end of the war in 2009, the Black Tigers are estimated to have carried out over 330 suicide attacks.

19. For an analysis of the differences in the ways in which post-colonial India and Sri Lanka dealt with minority issues in general, and their own Tamil minorities in particular, see Mark Salter, 'Democracy for All? Minority Rights and Minorities' Participation and Representation in Democratic Politics', International IDEA, 2011, pp. 19–20.

20. A prime interview source for this book. Later sections of this chapter (and 'Interviewee Annex') provide biographical details on Solheim.

21. In his autobiography Gen. Gerry de Silva, Jaffna Security Forces Commander at the time, states that he received the following order: 'Stop the advance and consolidate the line you are holding, or the Indians will come'. Quoted in S. Ferdinando, 'A catastrophic hell-born raid on Jaffna campus', *The Island*, 15 Jan. 2003.

22. The original rallying point for the JVP insurgency was outrage over the referendum called by President Jayawardene to cancel the holding of elections in 1983 and thereby allow the parliament elected in 1977—in which the UNP enjoyed a substantial majority—to continue until 1989.

23. The Janathā Vimukthi Peramuṇa was founded in the mid-1960s with the goal of promoting socialist revolution in Sri Lanka. The JVP spearheaded two armed

uprisings. The first in 1971, against Mrs. Bandaranaike's ruling Sri Lanka Freedom Party (SLFP), claimed an estimated 15,000 victims, most of them young. Following the second failed uprising in 1987–9 against Jayawardene's UNP administration the JVP entered into democratic politics, and eventually into government coalition in the 2000s.

24. Michael Ondaatje's novel *Anil's Ghost* provides a chillingly atmospheric insight into life in Sri Lanka during this period.

25. US journalist William McGowan's *Only Man Is Vile* provides a vivid and compelling account of the escalating clashes between the LTTE and the IPKF in and around Jaffna during the months following the Indian Army's arrival in the country. Following the 10 Oct. launch of its first major offensive against the Tigers—codenamed 'Operation Pawan'—IPKF forces took control of the Jaffna peninsula, something the Sri Lankan Army had tried (and failed) to achieve for three years.

26. 'Premadasa threatened to commit suicide, says former Indian envoy in new book', *Sunday Times*, 15 May 2011; S. Narayan, 'When Premadasa threatened to go to war and kill himself...', *The Island*, 4 Aug. 2012. Premadasa's desperation to get the IPKF out appears to have stemmed largely from the extent to which their presence provided a rationale for both the JVP insurgency in the South and continued LTTE guerrilla operations in the North. In addition there is evidence to suggest that right from the start Jayawardene's government had been highly sceptical of the idea of an Indian peace-keeping force. Immediately prior to the signing of the 1987 Indo-Lanka Accord, for example, Jayawardene had famously declared that he would 'fight the Indians to the last bullet'.

27. Adele Balasingham gives an account of the discussions of covert arms transfers between Anton Balasingham, Foreign Minister Abdul Hameed and Defence Secretary General Attygalle that is also quoted in Bradman Weerakoon, *Rendering Unto Caesar: A fascinating story of one man's tenure under nine Prime Ministers and Presidents of Sri Lanka*, Elgin, IL: New Dawn Press, 2004, p. 287.

28. See Bradman Weerakoon's account of the talks from his 'front row' perspective as foreign secretary to the president. Weerakoon, *Rendering Unto Caesar: A fascinating story of one man's tenure under nine Prime Ministers and Presidents of Sri Lanka*, pp. 273–290.

29. A new party, named the People's Front of Liberation Tigers (PFLT) was duly established in spring 1989 with Mahattaya, LTTE Deputy Leader as its President, and a copy of its constitution was handed over to the Sri Lankan Election Commissioner in order to register the new entity. See Balasingham, *War and Peace*, pp. 177–79.

30. S. Ferdinando, 'The Gujral factor', *The Island*, 29 Jan. 2013. According to another analyst's assessment, the government weapons transfers to the LTTE 'prolonged the conflict for another 20 years'. See Rajan Hoole, *Palmyra Fallen: From Rajani To War's End*, Jaffna: UTHR-J, 2015, p. 150. The same author also suggests that government-LTTE collaboration went beyond arms transfers at this point: LTTE units, he alleges, were even 'involved in search parties in the South to hunt JVP rebels'. (Ibid., p. 165)

31. See *Pawns of Peace: Evaluation of Norwegian Peace Efforts in Sri Lanka*, NORAD, 2011, p. 83, citing M. Palihapitiya, 'Of a 'Norwegian Summer and a Viking Intervention in Sri Lanka', *Asian Journal of Public Affairs*, Vol. 1, 2007, pp. 39–53.

32. See Ch. 2.

33. Council elections held in Nov. 1998 were blatantly rigged by the IPKF. The LTTE argued that the Council was illegitimate, should be dissolved and fresh elections for a new Council be held—elections that the LTTE would have been almost certain to dominate through its recently formed political party the PFLT. See Adele Balasingham, Ch. 3 in Balasingham, *War and Peace*, pp. 137–193, for an LTTE perspective on the talks.

34. The Amendment, enacted by President Jayawardene in the wake of the July 1983 riots, affirms the unitary structure of the Sri Lankan state and outlaws secession and its promotion. The Amendment was viewed by the LTTE as an attempt both to placate what it called 'Sinhala-Buddhist extremists', and to prevent the organisation from engaging in the political process. See Adele Balasingham in Balasingham, *War and Peace*, p. 185.

35. Among other things the massacre highlighted the serious risks inherent in Premadasa's strategy of arming the LTTE. A Presidential Commission Report later alleged that the LTTE used weapons obtained from the SLA to kill the surrendered police. Awareness of the massacre, including allegations of former Tiger Commander Karuna Amman's direct involvement in the killings, resurfaced in early 2011 following the testimony of retired Senior Police Superintendent T. Saviratne before the Lessons Learnt and Reconciliation Commission (LLRC). See S. Ferdinando, 'President's shocking complicity in massacre of policemen', *The Island*, 19 Feb. 2013.

36. See Weerakoon, *Rendering Unto Caesar*, p. 290, and S. Ferdinando, 'ICRC push for Jaffna demilitarised zone angers Ranjan W', *The Island*, 22 Aug. 2013.

37. Bondevik himself indicates that, in the aftermath of the ceasefire's breakdown in June, he received a direct phone request for Norwegian 'support' for the faltering peace process from Hameed in July. See Bondevik's keynote address (excerpts) at the ACS Hameed commemoration lecture, Colombo, 17 Aug. 2000. www.sundaytimes.lk/000827/plus5.html

38. At the funeral of a veteran LTTE intelligence cadre killed by an Army claymore attack in early 2008, LTTE intelligence chief Pottu Amman alleged that during the 1990 peace talks the Tigers had received 'credible intelligence reports' suggesting that Wijeratne and the Sri Lankan military were planning to assassinate LTTE leader Prabhakaran in Jaffna. 'Col. Charles laid to rest in Kilinochchi', *TamilNet*, 9 Jan. 2008.

39. For another well-informed account of Norwegian involvement in peace efforts at this stage, see 'Norway's role has no way?', *Daily Mirror*, 22 April 2009.

40. Again, in many respects the term 'ethnic cleansing' seems more appropriate.

41. Hardly any of these Muslims have returned to Jaffna. This act of ethnic cleansing created a lasting wound between the Tamil and Muslim communities and also served to strengthen perceptions of the LTTE as an intolerant, chauvinist Tamil entity.

42. See K.M. De Silva, 'Politics of East and the rise of SLMC', *Sunday Times*, 1 Dec. 2002, excerpted from K.M. De Silva, *Reaping The Whirlwind: Ethnic Conflict, Ethnic Politics in Sri Lanka* New Delhi: Penguin, 2000, pp. 251–271.

43. S. Ferdinando, 'Exodus of Muslims and a war-time "relationship"', *The Island*, 28 Feb. 2013.

44. For a detailed account of the assassination see Swamy, *Inside an Elusive Mind*, pp. 223–230.

45. S. Ferdinando reports that starting on 9 Dec. 1992, UNHCR held a 'series of talks' with the LTTE aimed at finding a means of reopening the Pooneryn-Sangupiddy route across the Jaffna peninsula. Despite several rounds of talks, Ferdinando states that the negotiations broke down over Prabhakaran's insistence on the withdrawal of Army forces from Pooneryn and Nagathevanthurai. Following the advice of his military commander, President Premadasa rejected the LTTE leader's demands. See S. Ferdinando, 'Chaos leading to CBK-P'karan pact of Jan. 5, 1995', *The Island*, 21 Oct. 2014.

46. The one confirmed meeting seems to have taken place shortly before President Premadasa's assassination by the LTTE on 1 May 1993. S. Ferdinando, 'Tigers' two-track policy: talks and assassinations', *The Island*, 11 Nov. 2012.

47. In his detailed account of talks between the LTTE and Kumaratunga's govern-ment, Balasingham states that within two weeks of her swearing in as prime minister (19 Aug. 1994), Kumaratunga ordered the relaxation of some aspects of the economic embargo in force on Jaffna. See Balasingham, *War and Peace*, p. 203. The move certainly appeared to demonstrate a high degree of self-confidence. Under the terms of the country's 1978 Constitution the prime minister enjoys distinctly limited powers—the president, who is elected separately, heads the government. As things turned out, however, Kumaratunga's seeming self-con-fidence was vindicated by the results of the Nov. 1994 Presidential elections (see below).

48. This exchange and the voluminous correspondence between Kumaratunga and Prabhakaran as well several other government officials and LTTE representa-tives during the following months is reproduced in Balasingham, *War and Peace*, pp. 204–332.

49. Balasingham, *War and Peace*, p. 224, notes that 'Tamil circles' put Dissanayake's assassination down to the prominent role he played in the 1981 destruction of the Jaffna Public Library. Veteran Lankan journalist Shamindra Ferdinando is a good deal more categorical on the subject. Realising that a UNP-led government under Dissanayake would never give in to one of the LTTE's key demands, namely the lifting of the armed forces' siege on the Jaffna peninsula, he argues, Prabhakaran ordered the UNP leader's assassination—one of a series of high-profile interventions in Sri Lankan elections by the LTTE leader over time—thereby greatly strengthening Kumaratunga's presidential prospects. Ferdinando clearly considers Kumaratunga's espousal of a 'peace' electoral platform to have been based on a thoroughly naïve reading of the 'diabolical nature of the LTTE' and as such, to have been a potential danger to the country. As evidence

Ferdinando points, among other things, to the government's failure to raise the issue of responsibility for Dissanayake's murder in its exchanges with the LTTE leadership in late 1994. See 'An assassination in the run-up to the presidential election', *The Island*, 14 Oct. 2014; 'Chaos leading to CBK-P'karan pact of Jan. 5, 1995', *The Island*, 21 Oct. 2014; 'Post-CBK victory in Nov 1995 presidential poll: Pooneryn factor', *The Island*, 28 Oct. 2014; 'Rev. Dr. Emmanuel on collapse of CBK-P'karan talks', *The Island*, 4 Nov. 2014.

50. See S. Ferdinando, 'An assassination in the run-up to the presidential election', *The Island*, 14 Oct. 2014.

51. See Ferdinando, 'Chaos leading to CBK-P'karan pact of Jan. 5, 1995'.

52. The text of the joint Declaration, which was jointly signed by Prabhakaran and Kumaratunga, is in Balasingham, *War and Peace*, pp. 254–256. Interestingly, in important respects the Declaration reads very much like a draft version of the 2002 Ceasefire Agreement (CFA).

53. Specifically in Jaffna, Mannar, Vavuniya, Mullaitivu, Trincomalee and Batticaloa-Amparai.

54. Two Norwegians (Audun Holm and Johan Gabrielson), one Canadian (Maj-Gen. C Miller) and a Dutchman (Lt. Col. Paul Henry Hosting). One media report suggests that as part of the mission, Holm and Gabrielson later met Prabhakaran in Jaffna in early April. Bizarrely, the same report criticises the Norwegians for 'remaining silent' when the LTTE 'resumed hostilities' on 19 April following the lapse of their self-proclaimed ceasefire. S. Ferdinando, 'Focus on costly propaganda blitz', *The Island*, 21 Jan. 2014.

55. See Ferdinando, 'Chaos leading to CBK-P'karan pact of Jan. 5, 1995'.

56. See Ferdinando, 'An assassination in the run-up to the presidential election'.

57. Balasingham, *War and Peace*, p. 276.

58. For the full text of the letter see Balasingham, *War and Peace*, pp. 284–286.

59. Balasingham later told Solheim that the LTTE always believed that a third party should be a government, since no individual would have the capacity to sustain protracted talks. The LTTE was also very suspicious of France. None of the top LTTE leaders spoke French, and they further believed that France would favour President Kumaratunga since she had studied there and spoke the language fluently. See also Ferdinando, 'Rev. Dr. Emmanuel on collapse of CBK-P'karan talks'.

60. The exchange is reproduced in full in Balasingham. *War and Peace*, pp. 204–332. At some points, the correspondence on the government side is under the signature of Col. Anurudda Ranwatte, Deputy Minister of Defence.

61. Pointing to the devolution package, notably for the North and East, touted by Kumaratunga's government since its parliamentary tabling in Aug. 1995, Subramanian (note 63 below) notes that at the time, she and other journalists described Kumaratunga's policy as a 'two-pronged strategy—a military plan against the Tigers, and a political plan for the Tamils'. Attempts to separate the LTTE from its popular base among the Tamils of the North and East remained a leitmotif of Sri Lankan politics in the following years.

62. Some estimates suggest the figure was considerably higher—up to 500,000—mak-

ing it 'one of the largest displacements of human beings in a single day anywhere in the world'. This quotation comes from Indian journalist and former
Colombo correspondent Nirupama Subramanian's 'The Exodus', a graphic
account of the enforced evacuation of Jaffna reproduced in *Sri Lanka: Voices
From a War Zone*, New Delhi: Penguin India, 2005, a hard-hitting set of journal-
istic essays from her time spent based in Sri Lanka that pays particular attention to the human costs of the conflict on all sides.

63. University Teachers of Human Rights-Jaffna (UTHR-J), 'The Exodus From Jaffna',
Special Report No. 6, Dec. 1995. http://www.uthr.org/SpecialReports/spreport6.
htm

64. Veteran defence correspondent Iqbal Athas notes that according to well-placed
sources within the Ministry of Defence, the day after the LTTE's capture of
Mullaitivu a young SLA officer in LTTE custody threw a grenade killing at least
six Tiger cadres. Enraged LTTE cadres responded by 'summarily executing' him
and over 200 fellow government soldiers who had been taken prisoners.
'Censorship out: then events unfurled', *Sunday Times*, 13 Oct. 1996.

65. As a result of the 'Operation Unceasing Waves II' offensive launched in Sept.
1998, the LTTE retook Kilinochchi and forced the SLA to abandon its plans to
wrest control of the A9 from the Tigers. The town became the LTTE's administrative capital, a position it retained up until Dec. 2008, when Kilinochchi again
fell to government forces following some of the most intense, and bloody, fighting of the entire conflict. See Ch. 10.

66. Official estimates put LTTE casualties at over 2,000.

67. Public transport—buses in particular—was a favoured target for LTTE bomb
attacks and remained so until the end of the conflict.

68. The Temple, one of the holiest Buddhist shrines in the world and a centre of religious veneration and pilgrimage for Sri Lankan Buddhists, is located within the
Kandyan Royal Palace complex. The relic, supposedly of the Buddha's tooth,
has long played an important role in local politics since it is commonly believed
that whoever holds the relic also controls governance of the country.

69. Norway established diplomatic relations with Ceylon in 1952. From the time
Norway established an embassy in New Delhi in 1960, this ambassador was also
accredited to Sri Lanka. Sri Lanka and Norway signed a bilateral development
co-operation agreement in 1976. This agreement envisaged NORAD (the official
development agency) establishing a representation in Sri Lanka. The Resident
Representative arrived in late 1977, but overall diplomatic ties were still handled from New Delhi. The NORAD representation in Colombo was upgraded to
a full embassy with a resident Ambassador in Oct. 1996.

70. *Redd Barna* in Norwegian.

71. The National Peace Council worked separately on the issue, although they were
also funded by the Norwegians. Interview with Jon Westborg, Oslo, Nov. 2012.

72. Ranil Wickremasinghe, Leader of the United National Party (UNP).

73. Following elections and a change of government in Oct. 1997.

74. Interview with Peter Bowling, London, April 2013.

75. *Sosialistisk Venstreparti* (Norwegian). A democratic socialist party founded in

the early 1970s. The party formed part of the Labour Party-led coalition government that ruled the country 2005–2013.

76. Titled *Nærmere* ('Closer'), a reference to the book's attempt to bring readers closer to the inner workings of Norwegian politics.

77. Tiruchelvan was a noted moderate Tamil thinker and politician whose party, the Tamil United Liberation Front (TULF), advocated a negotiated settlement to the ethnic conflict in Sri Lanka. At times a vocal critic of the LTTE, he was killed in July 1999 by an LTTE suicide bomber.

78. The LTTE—almost certainly among those Solheim met on this occasion was Veerakathi Manoharan, head of the Tigers' Paris-based International Secretariat.

79. There were already two Deputy Foreign Ministers at the time.

80. 'Deputy/Vice Minister' and 'State Secretary' can be used interchangeably as translations of *Statssekretær*, the position's Norwegian title.

81. Adele Balasingham, *The Will To Freedom: An Inside View of Tamil Resistance* London: Fairfax, 2001. Although Balasingham's version of events has not been corroborated by government sources, in the author's view there is no particular reason to doubt its veracity. It also concurs substantially with Solheim's account.

82. Ibid., pp. 350–351.

83. It is worth noting that in his obituary for the LTTE's chief political advisor, D.B.S. Jeyaraj suggests that after receiving information regarding Balasingham's perilous medical condition, Prabhakaran 'enlisted the services of the ICRC, sections of the Catholic clergy and Norway' to 'make a direct appeal to ... Kumaratunga on humanitarian grounds. She was requested to grant permission for Balasingham to travel abroad through Colombo for medical treatment'. 'Bala Anai was the voice of the Tamil Eelam nation', *The Sunday Leader*, 17 Dec. 2006.

84. At some point towards the end of Nov. 1998.

85. Reportedly 'significant reciprocal humanitarian gestures' was the official formulation. See Balasingham, *The Will to Freedom*, p. 352.

86. It should be noted that other official Norwegian sources are a good deal more sceptical about the latter part of Solheim's analysis.

87. Balasingham indicates that the list of government demands included the following: guarantees that the LTTE would not disrupt government administration in the Northeast province, attack sea/air supply vessels to the region, or target public buildings anywhere in the country; and finally that it would release all prisoners held in its custody. See Balasingham, *The Will to Power*, p. 352. Jeyaraj suggests that 'it was clear that Kumaratunga was seeking to exploit Balasingham's vulnerability and trying to extract major concessions in return'. He also suggests that Anton and Adele both told Prabhakaran to 'reject the demands outright' and that Anton stated he was 'prepared to die with honour and self-respect rather than acceding to these humiliating demands'. See Jeyaraj, 'Bala Anai was the voice'.

88. Goonetilleke was appointed head of the government peace secretariat (SCOPP) by incoming Prime Minister Ranil Wickremasinghe at the time of the Ceasefire Agreement (CFA) in Feb. 2002.

89. See Balasingham, *The Will to Freedom*, p. 358.

90. The geographical term used by the LTTE at this stage to describe their preferred sea routes at the time. In fact Balasingham was taken to Phuket, Thailand, in an operation that, according to Jeyaraj, involved the pair being ferried out in a vessel captained by Sea Tiger Chief Soosai, to link up with another LTTE vessel in the ocean off the coast of Sri Lanka. See Jeyaraj, 'Bala Anai was the voice'.

91. According to Jeyaraj the couple moved from Bangkok to Singapore before leaving for London. See Jeyaraj, 'Bala Anai was the voice'.

92. The emergency treatment included the removal of one of his kidneys. See Balasingham, *The Will to Power*, p. 361.

93. The meeting took place on 10 June 1999. A three person Norwegian delegation participated.

94. Adele Balasingham states (p. 363) that the operation took place in 'the early part of 2000', which suggests that it may have been slightly earlier.

95. Interestingly, Adele Balasingham suggests that in an interview published soon after her husband received his kidney transplant in Oslo, Kumaratunga claimed that she had given the Norwegians 'permission' to treat him. Reportedly, a statement rebutting this claim was issued at the time by the Norwegian Foreign Ministry.

96. Backed by less than a third of the MPs in Norway's 165-member parliament (*Stortinget*), the new administration drew its parliamentary support from three of the country's centrist parties. What Strømmen describes as the 'small parties' government' came into being chiefly as a consequence of PM Thorbjørn Jagland's pre-1997 election declaration that the Labour Party would not continue in government if it received less than 36.9 per cent of the vote—the percentage his predecessor Gro Harlem Brundtland had achieved in 1993. In the event the party scored 35 per cent. Infighting between the much larger Labour and Conservative parties allowed the minority coalition government to remain in power 1997—2000.

97. In an interview, a senior Norwegian official suggested—off the record—that he was convinced that at some point in the past Balasingham had worked for British Intelligence.

98. This, it appears, is what he was prepared to concede in private discussions with Solheim. Publicly Balasingham expressed regret over the murder, but stopped short of outright acceptance of the LTTE's responsibility for it.

99. By which he means lawyers.

100. See below.

101. As a result of the LTTE's ruthless opposition to any alternative militant voices, many Tamil splinter groups ended up either working with the Sri Lankan government as paramilitaries or denouncing violence and subsequently joining mainstream politics. Some legitimate Tamil-oriented political parties remain, all of which have now officially distanced themselves from the LTTE's vision of an independent Tamil Eelam. For a detailed and arresting description of the

struggles between the LTTE and other militant Tamil factions, see the early sections of Swamy, *Inside an Elusive Mind*.

102. A negotiating framework that the LTTE also sought to apply to the peace talks initiated in the aftermath of the landmark 2002 Ceasefire Agreement.

103. Without the two ever meeting, however, the Norwegian's aim here was simply to explore possibilities.

104. Balasingham gives an account of a failed 1995 initiative to involve a French intermediary (with the support of the French government) as well as an exchange of letters between Kumaratunga and Prabhakaran on the subject. Among other things, according to Balasingham, the LTTE reaction to the proposal for a French intermediary focused on the suspicion that he was a personal friend or contact of the president's stemming from her student years in Paris, and more generally that her choice of a French intermediary was dictated by her perceived Francophile sympathies. Balasingham, *War and Peace*, pp. 292–297.

105. The discussion of UK involvement stemmed from the 1997 agreement brokered by Conservative government minister Liam Fox between the main Colombo political party leaders Wickremasinghe (UNP) and Kumaratunga (UPFA). Under the terms of the agreement, both leaders undertook to promote a bipartisan consensus over efforts to end the national conflict, and to abstain from attacking each other on this subject.

106. Reportedly this was communicated by Kadirgamar during a meeting with the Norwegians in early June 1999. At the same meeting it also became apparent that the government's interest in a UK peace facilitation role was waning as a consequence of what was felt to be London's increasingly high-handed approach, including agitating for a role in determining how contacts with Balasingham should be handled. According to the same source, the possibility that discussions of a peace facilitation role were also initiated with India during this period should also not be ruled out.

107. The Oslo Process was a Norwegian-instigated attempt to achieve direct agreement between the Israeli government and the Palestinian Liberation Organisation (PLO), involving the first ever face-to-face negotiations between the two sides. Initiated in 1991, it continued in the form of a series of secret meetings held in Oslo at the Fafo Institute. The secret meetings were completed in Aug. 1993, and the resulting Accords were officially signed at a televised ceremony held in Washington, D.C., on 13 Sept. 1993 in the presence of PLO chairman Yasser Arafat, Israeli Prime minister Yitzhak Rabin and US President Bill Clinton.

108. The April 1992 'National Pact'. See Kåre Lode, 'Mali's peace process: context, analysis and evaluation', *Accord 13*, 2002. http://www.c-r.org/accord-article/mali%E2%80%99s-peace-process-context-analysis-and-evaluation

109. Previous LTTE operations with the 'Unceasing Waves' code name—both of which resulted in military victories—took place (I) around Mullaitivu, 18–25 July 1996 and (II) Kilinochchi, 27–29 Sept. 1998.

110. S. Ferdinando, 'Suicide attack on CBK as Tigers peak on Vanni front', *The Island*, 18 Oct. 2012.

111. Leader of the United National Party (UNP), the largest opposition party at the time.

112. On the face of it, at least, the personal animosity detected by Solheim makes the close co-operation between the two evident in the successful campaign to defeat Mahinda Rajapaksa in the Dec. 2014 presidential elections all the more surprising. As many Sri Lankans would doubtless point out, however, there are other factors at work here, not least the dynastic proclivities that have, as in many of Sri Lanka's South Asian neighbours, dominated the country's political life since independence.

113. V. Sambandan, 'Living through the bombs', *Frontline*, Vol. 16, Issue 27, Jan. 2000.

114. Interview, Colombo, Nov. 2013.

2. 2000

1. Immediately prior to this Vollebaek and Solheim travelled to London (Feb. 12) for preparatory talks with Balasingham in what was the Norwegian foreign minister's first encounter with the LTTE representative. According to Solheim, Balasingham emphasised the fact that the LTTE were 'serious' about talks, although he also stated that he could not offer any guarantees at this stage.

2. Despite being formally speaking a parliamentary democracy.

3. For a useful account of the talks see D.B.S. Jeyaraj, 'A Norwegian Initiative', *Frontline*, 4–17 March 2000.

4. The Bharatiya Janata Party (BJP), together with the Indian National Congress (INC) one of the country's two biggest political parties. From 1998 to 2004 it led a national coalition government.

5. *Oyatha Alaigal* in Tamil.

6. Contemporary media reports suggest that at almost the same time as the LTTE attack on Elephant Pass, the SLA were planning a major advance aimed at recapturing LTTE-held territory on both the Jaffna peninsula and the mainland. One source suggests that the LTTE offensive pre-empted the planned government attack by no more than forty-eight hours.

7. S. Ferdinando, 'Oslo-CBK peace initiative amidst war', *The Island*, 21 Oct. 2012.

8. D.B.S. Jeyaraj points to a number of factors that help explain the LTTE's failure to advance into Jaffna town. These include: extended supply lines leading to significant delays in getting the weapons—in particular artillery—needed to carry out an assault on the town centre to LTTE front lines; and as the town's self-proclaimed liberators, the wish to avoid (Tamil) civilian casualties in high-density population areas such as Jaffna town and nearby Chavakachcheri. See 'The Battle of Jaffna', *Frontline*, 27 May–9 June 2000; 'A Deceptive Calm', *Frontline*, 10–23 June 2000. Erik Solheim notes that during their discussions at this time, Balasingham argued that 'a lot of Tamils would be killed, so the LTTE stalled the march in Jaffna.' Solheim considered this an 'unlikely argument'.

9. From internal reports of these discussions it is evident that the LTTE's interest

in pursuing negotiations was now more or less on hold pending the outcome of the military offensive on the Jaffna Peninsula.

10. Late in the month (29 May) Pickering made his first visit to Sri Lanka and issued a strong statement of support for the government. In particular, Pickering memorably described the idea of an independent Tamil Eelam as a 'dead planet'. See N. Subramanian, 'The Sri Lankan Standoff', *Frontline*, 10–23 June 2000.

11. For a report on both the latter sets of talks, see J. Cherian, 'Of Arms And Assistance', *Frontline*, 27 May–9 June 2000.

12. In late May an additional 24 billion rupees (USD $320 million) was added to the 54.2 billion rupees (USD $729 million) in defence expenditure already allocated for the year—a 35 per cent increase. See Subramanian, 'Of Terror and Hope'.

13. The purchase of fighter aircraft from Israel necessitated re-establishing diplomatic links between the two countries, which had been severed for decades. Arms purchases from Pakistan were also reportedly the first time the government had acquired weapons from this source.

14. Most probably during the talks with Jaswant Singh and Lalit Mansingh held on 11 May. See above.

15. *Maaveerar Naal* (in Tamil). An annual ceremonial day initiated in 1989 by Prabhakaran to promote Tamil remembrance of all LTTE cadres killed in combat. Its place in the calendar, 27 Nov., marks the date on which the first LTTE member, Lt. Shankar, is supposed to have died in combat with the Sri Lankan security forces in 1982.

16. 'The entire world rushed to help Sri Lanka with emergency military assistance when Chandrika raised the alarm of an impending military disaster, claiming that 30,000 lives were in danger.' Quoted in V. Suryanarayan, 'Propaganda Blitzkrieg', *Frontline*, 6–19 Jan. 2001.

17. The Delhi-based Research and Analysis Wing (RAW), the country's elite external intelligence agency, founded in 1968.

18. Deputy Head of the LTTE; Prabhakaran's 'Number 2' at that time.

19. Mathaya and a number of other LTTE members were alleged to have been part of an Indian-backed plot to assassinate Prabhakaran and top LTTE commanders loyal to him and take over leadership of the organisation. They were all found 'guilty' and summarily executed on 28 Dec. 1994. For a fuller LTTE 'insider' account of the circumstances surrounding Mathaya's execution, see Balasingham, *The Will To Freedom*, pp. 296–298.

20. With this as with all earlier versions of the devolution package, the objective was to provide a constitutional framework for the devolution of power to the majority-Tamil North and East.

21. By the end of the consultation process the two sides had reportedly met more than thirty times to discuss the devolution package. See N. Subramanian, 'Back to the Freezer', *Frontline*, 19. Aug.–1 Sept. 2000.

22. The Tamil United Liberation Front (TULF), the Eelam People's Democratic Party (EPDP), the People's Liberation Organisation of Tamil Eelam (PLOTE) and the Tamil Eelam Liberation Organisation (TELO).

23. As outlined in the original version of the devolution package put forward by

Kumaratunga in Aug. 1995. For the text of the 1995 proposal, see S.I. Keetha-poncalan, *Conflict and Peace in Sri Lanka: Major Documents*, Chennai: Kumaran Book House, 2009, pp. 190–205.

24. For the full text of the proposed new constitution see Keethaponcalan, *Conflict and Peace in Sri Lanka*, pp. 206–402.

25. Unhappiness with the bill was seemingly not confined to the ranks of the opposition. During the course of the second day of debate, a certain Mahinda Rajapaksa, an SLFP member and at that point Minister of Fisheries, reportedly got up and walked out of Parliament in order to greet the Buddhist monks protesting outside. 'Everything will be alright' he told them, to loud cheers. See Subaramanian, 'Back to the Freezer'.

26. In Jan. 2015 Wickremaratne was appointed a senior advisor to incoming President Maithripala Sirisena.

27. Dissanayake. See Ch. 1, p. 24.

28. Following the Jan. 2015 presidential elections, Wickremasinghe was appointed prime minister—the third time he had held the position.

29. If the proposal to move to a prime ministerial governance system following the next parliamentary elections (Oct. 2000) had been retained untouched, then constitutionally speaking, Kumaratunga would presumably have had to step down as president. In all probability this explains the amendments discussed above.

30. N. Subramanian, 'Rough Ride Ahead', *Frontline*, 28 Oct.–10 Nov. 2000. Following a visit to Oslo made immediately after the elections, Kadirgamar appeared to soften his stance somewhat, stating that while the Norwegian initiative appeared to have reached an 'impasse' on account of what he termed the LTTE's 'lack of interest' in dialogue, the government nonetheless urged Oslo to continue exploring the possibilities for dialogue with the Tigers. N. Subramanian, 'Norwegian Envoy Meets LTTE Chief', *The Hindu*, 2 Nov. 2000.

31. Anton Balasingham states that the meeting took place at Mallavi, which is located c. 15km southwest of Kilinochchi. See Balasingham, *War and Peace*, p. 341.

32. Colonel Shankar, a relative of Prabhakaran's, was founder of the air wing and marine divisions of the LTTE. He was killed by an army claymore mine attack on 26 Sept. 2001.

33. Tamilselvan was founder and leader of the political wing of the LTTE, and a member of the Tigers' delegation to all rounds of the Norwegian-brokered peace talks. He was killed, along with five other high-ranking LTTE officers, by a precision Air Force strike on Kilinochchi on 2 Nov. 2007.

34. The kind of practical issues noted in Solheim's account.

35. Both the quotations here are taken from Balasingham's account of the talks. Balasingham, *War and Peace*, p. 341.

36. N. Subramanian, 'Prabhakaran keen on settlement: Solheim', *The Hindu*, 2 Nov. 2000.

37. Ratnasiri Wickremanayake, appointed Prime Minister by Kumaratunga in Aug. 2000 to replace her aging mother and veteran former leader Sirimavo Bandaranaike, who stepped down from office at the age of eighty-four.

38. As detailed in an internal Norwegian MFA document.
39. The text of the draft MoU, formally titled 'Agreement Following An Understanding on Humanitarian Issues', is reproduced in John Gooneratne, *Negotiating With The Tigers (2002–2005): A View From The Second Row*, Colombo: Stamford Lake, 2007, pp. 135–139. Anton Balasingham gives a fairly detailed account of the document as well as the LTTE's evaluation of, and response to it at the time. See Balasingham, *War and Peace*, pp. 342–243.
40. MoU, ibid., Article 1c.
41. MoU, ibid., Article 3.
42. V. Surayanarayan, 'Propaganda Blitzkrieg', *Frontline*, 6–19 Jan. 2001.
43. For the text of the LTTE ceasefire offer see Balasingham, *War and Peace*, pp. 343–344.
44. See N. Subaramaniam, 'War over Truce', *Frontline*, 6–19 Jan. 2001.

3. ELECTIONS AND CEASEFIRES

1. Later reports suggest that during the first month of the ceasefire government troops advanced unopposed through a large portion of the territory they had lost to the LTTE a year previously, and established a new forward defence line 15km north of Elephant Pass. See N. Subramanian, 'Starting all over again', *Frontline*, 12–25 May 2001. A well-informed source suggests that 97km^2 of territory was taken from the LTTE during the ceasefire period. See D.B.S. Jeyaraj, 'Peace prospects, again', *Frontline*, 26 May–8 June 2001.
2. As cited in J. Cherian, 'A significant neighbourly call', *Frontline*, 3–16 March 2001. In a lengthy interview conducted during her Feb. visit to India and published in the same edition of *Frontline*, Kumaratunga also refers to what 'seems to be the best window of opportunity that has been offered to any government since the war began'.
3. Statement reproduced in Balasingham, *War and Peace*, pp. 347–348.
4. Interestingly, noted Tamil journalist Taraki later argued that with hindsight it was clear that as a result of the Dec. 2000 ceasefire declared by the LTTE with Oslo's encouragement as a gesture of goodwill, 'wittingly or unwittingly' the Norwegians had provided the Sri Lankan military with a 'singular window of opportunity ... for planning the offensive and for achieving a concentration of forces in Jaffna'.
5. Earlier in his account Balasingham states that during the ceasefire period, the LTTE had prepared a detailed plan to 'lure' SLA troops 'to locations targeted for artillery and mortar fire and to entrap them in camouflaged minefields'. Balasingham, *War and Peace*, p. 349.
6. Balasingham, *War and Peace*, p. 349. It is worth pointing out that the LTTE strategist's account of the fighting is corroborated in its essentials in D.B.S. Jeyaraj's longer, more detailed and doubtless well-sourced report from the time. See Jeyaraj, 'Peace prospects, again'.
7. Officially the LTTE claimed that seventy-five cadres were killed during the four days of fighting. Unsurprisingly, government sources put the LTTE casualty

figures a good deal higher at 300 killed and approximately 500 wounded. See Jeyaraj, 'Peace prospects, again'.

8. According to an internal MFA memo, in his talks in Colombo the following day Solheim explained the absence of Prabhakaran as a way for the LTTE to avoid him having to communicate what Solheim called 'negative messages' to the Norwegians—principally meaning the LTTE's unwillingness to commit to a date for commencing negotiations and insistence on de-proscription as a precondition for talks.

9. See Iqbal Athas, 'Foiled assassination attempt and stalemate in peace talks', *The Sunday Times*, 20 May 2001. A pattern of landmine ambushes and other targeted assassination attempts on senior LTTE leaders continued throughout the following months, particularly in the East. The highest-placed victim was Col. Shankar, head of the LTTE's military intelligence division and one of Prabhakaran's closest confidants, who was killed in a 26 Sept. mine attack in the Mullaituvu area. See D.B.S. Jayaraj, 'Predators as prey', *Frontline*, 13–26 Oct. 2001. A Presidential Commission of Inquiry into the breakup of the Millennium City military 'safe house' in early 2002 revealed that the 2001 attempt to assassinate Tamilselvan was carried out by Long-Range Reconnaissance Patrols (LRRPs, commonly known as the 'Lone Rangers'), a clandestine military outfit specialising in deep penetration missions into LTTE-held territory, notably the assassination of high-level targets. J. Perera, 'An insight into the benefit of dual governance', *Daily Mirror*, 30 Dec. 2003.

10. For a more detailed account of the diplomatic situation, see Jeyaraj, 'Peace prospects, again'.

11. Interestingly, an internal MFA memo from the talks in Washington indicates that it became apparent to the Norwegians that there was a lively debate going on within the US Administration over whether the LTTE should continue to be officially classified as a terrorist organisation or, alternatively, as an 'armed rebel group'.

12. See D.B.S. Jeyaraj's 'The facilitator fracas', *Frontline*, 23 June–6 July 2001, which provides a highly detailed and well-sourced account of the circumstances surrounding Jagland's visit to Colombo, in particular the government's reported dissatisfaction with Solheim's facilitation efforts. Iqbal Athas suggests that with respect to the third item on the meeting's agenda, the government expressed unease over Solheim's high level of 'media exposure' over the Sri Lanka facilitation effort. Iqbal Athas, 'Lanka wants Oslo but not Solheim', *The Sunday Times*, 10 June 2001.

13. It is worth noting that a credible media source reports that when in Washington, Solheim allegedly encouraged US officials to put pressure on Colombo to deproscribe the LTTE. This, combined with Solheim's high media profile, was reportedly viewed as 'problematic' by Colombo. See Iqbal Athas, 'Lanka wants Oslo but not Solheim'.

14. D.B.S. Jeyaraj, 'The facilitator fracas'.

15. Solheim's recollection is not entirely accurate. MFA documents indicate that he

met once with Balasingham in London, on 30 June, before the rupture in communication became fully operational.

16. See N. Subramanian, 'Chandrika's challenge', *Frontline*, 7–20 July 2001.

17. See N. Subramanian, 'A presidential gambit', *Frontline*, 21 July–3 Aug. 2001.

18. In this context Balasingham uses a quotation from the 2001 Annual Report of the Central Bank of Sri Lanka underlining the importance of restoring peace to reviving the national economy. See Balasingham, *War and Peace*, p. 352. Coming as it does immediately after a detailed account of the destruction wrought by the 24 July attack, the quotation seems incongruous, to say the least.

19. Balasingham argues that in 'designing' the attack, the LTTE had two key strategic objectives. First, to 'neutralise the destructive potential of the air force' which 'under the guise of fighting "terrorism",' he claims, 'was increasingly utilised ... to attack civilian targets'. Second, to 'inflict a major economic blow ... by destroying the Sri Lankan state's assets.' Balasingham, *War and Peace*, p. 351.

20. This was not how everyone viewed things. For example, Helgesen notes that it was 'no secret' that the Foreign Ministry Secretary General 'would not have opposed Erik's exit from the ministry'. Solheim was perceived by some in the Ministry as 'a disturbance', not least because of a tendency to 'defy line management'.

21. According to Helgesen, reports from Petersen indicated that both Kadirgamar and Kumaratunga regarded Solheim as 'too much of a freelancer'. He also suggests that this was 'probably the line they were giving to Jagland when he met the two alone in Colombo in June'.

22. Solheim notes that he and Kadirgamar had 'very different personalities. He was much more formal, big on protocol. In that regard I got along much better with Chandrika because she was a typical politician, a street fighter, someone who loves mingling with people.'

23. See Ch. 1, p. 10 for more on the JVP.

24. The MoU underpinning the temporary pact states that 'the PA agree not to bring in ... proposals for devolution of power ... until such time as a broad consensus is arrived at'. Quoted in Iqbal Athas, 'Back to the battlefront', *The Sunday Times*, 9 Sept. 2001.

25. The cross-floor exodus to the UNP continued over the following weeks. Traditionally, swapping political allegiances has been very much part of Sri Lankan political culture. One of the ministers who did so in Oct. 2001 was GL Peiris, who soon became an important figure in the new UNP government, a position he maintained after crossing back to the SLFP in 2004.

26. The extent of the 9/11 attacks and resulting 'war on terror's influence on the conflict in Sri Lanka remains a contested issue. Interestingly, only two weeks after the attacks the US Embassy in Colombo's spokesperson stated that the US Administration 'had not changed its stand in calling upon the government to initiate peace talks with the LTTE. We are fighting against terrorists who are not asking anything; they are not demanding anything, and not coming for negotiations. ... There is a distinction between the LTTE and the terrorist in the

Middle East.' S. De Silva, 'US excludes LTTE from global war', *Sunday Times*, 23 Sept. 2011. This stance did not, however, prevent the US Administration from later reconfirming the LTTE's inclusion on its list of officially proscribed terrorist organisations.

27. Described by one commentator as tantamount to 'playing the communal card'. See 'Vote to solve ethnic conflict', *Sunday Times Political Column*, 2 Dec. 2001.

28. N. Subramanian, 'In quest of peace—somehow', *Frontline*, 22 Dec. 2001—4 Jan. 2002.

29. For example, Balasingham notes that in his post-election meeting with Westborg, Wickremasinghe also asked the Norwegian Ambassador to convey a message to the LTTE leadership that 'his government would soon implement measures to bring relief and redress to the Tamil people'. See Balasingham, *War and Peace*, p. 353.

30. India's strategic importance for Sri Lanka aside, Wickremasinghe was a familiar figure in Delhi, having developed a wide network of political friends and contacts over the years, and in the process acquired a sophisticated knowledge of Indian culture. See Weerakoon, *Rendering Unto Caesar*, pp. 346–349.

31. At this time the country's overall economy was estimated at $16 billion. See J. Cherian, 'For a durable peace', *Frontline*, 5–18 Jan. 2002.

32. On 23 Jan. 2002 both sides extended their temporary ceasefires by another month, pending the completion of a more permanent agreement.

33. Yasushi Akashi is a senior Japanese diplomat who has held numerous high-level positions within the UN, including the Secretary-General's Representative in former Yugoslavia, and supervisor of the Cambodia peace talks and subsequent elections in 1993.

34. To secure the signatures of the leaders on both sides, prior to the ceremony in Vavuniya Jon Westborg travelled up to the Vanni to receive Prabhakaran's signature, following which he brought the document to Wickremasinghe for the public ceremony on 22 Feb. 2002.

35. For details, see CFA, Annex A.

36. It is important to note that particularly on the government side, views on the dynamics of the CFA drafting process differ significantly. John Gooneratne, Deputy Head of SCOPP, for example, argues that the LTTE 'had the advantage' in the drafting process on account of the fact that 'the drafts shown to the government seemed to have been first shown to the LTTE'. Gooneratne, *Negotiating With the Tigers*, pp. 11–12. He further argues that while the Norwegians later 'provided more comprehensive drafts incorporating the views of both sides ... there were [government] suggestions that did not find a place in the final CFA'. (In fairness, Gooneratne also notes that some of their suggestions were incorporated). See also the views of Bernard Goonetilleke, Head of SCOPP (see below).

37. The text of the 2002 Ceasefire Agreement (CFA) is reproduced in a number of places, notably Gooneratne, *Negotiating With the Tigers*, pp. 123—134. All quotations are drawn from this version.

38. A demand pushed strongly by the LTTE at the time that remained controversial throughout the following years.

39. The numbers are defined as fifty as of D-Day +30, an additional 100 as of D-day +60, and finally 'all unarmed LTTE members' from 'D-day +90'. As we shall see later, this was another provision of the CFA that proved to be highly controversial on the government side.

40. This stipulation was inserted at the SLA's insistence. The Annex includes a detailed list of the specific amounts of each of these items allowed into LTTE-controlled territory. Suffice to say that from the SLA's perspective these restrictions were aimed at curtailing LTTE access to fuel and building materials. The fact that civilians were equally affected was seen as, at best, an unfortunate side effect.

41. A hugely important provision in both symbolic and practical terms. At this point the A9, the main artery of communication between the North and South, had been closed since 1984.

42. The six locations were Jaffna, Manar, Vavuniya, Trincomalee, Batticaloa and Amparai.

43. Helgesen recalls that 'the Danish State Secretary called me to say that his government considered it a 'hostile act' that they had not been included in the monitoring mission. Quite a strong statement in the circumstances.'

44. For the text of Petersen's statement at the Oslo press conference see Balasingham, *War and Peace*, pp. 360–361.

45. See N. Subramanian, 'A fragile peace', *Frontline*, 16–29 March 2002.

46. Ibid.

47. Following the change of government in Dec. 2001, Kadirgamar assumed the position of presidential advisor.

48. A reference to Clause 1.8 of the CFA whereby the government undertook to disarm 'Tamil paramilitary groups' by D-day +30 'at the latest'.

49. See Chapter 5.

50. Political movement founded in 1905 that later came to be closely identified with the Irish Republican Army (IRA).

51. South Africa's African National Congress, founded in 1923, and since the ending of apartheid in 1994 the country's ruling party.

52. The SLMM legacy website is a well-structured and highly informative source of information regarding all aspects of the Mission's operations during its nearly six years of existence. See www.slmm-history.info

53. See N. Subramanian, 'A Prime Minister in Jaffna', *Frontline*, 30 March–12 April 2002.

54. Ibid. Interestingly, at this point the US position appeared more outspoken than the government's. Reacting to the US Embassy statement, Defence Minister Tilak Marapana, for example, claimed that he had not heard any negative reports of the LTTE's behaviour since the CFA's signature. By way of explanation, one government official was quoted as saying 'We don't want to rock the boat at this stage. Our commitment is to get the peace talks started as soon as possible'. See Iqbal Athas, 'Govt. focuses on security forces changes as talks on talks loom', *Sunday Times*, 17 March 2002.

55. 'US spells out formula for Tiger deban', *Sunday Times*, 17 March 2002.

56. Solheim's own comments on the arrangements: 'We organised everything. Bala[singham] did not want to go through Colombo—he said the government could not guarantee his security. I went with him to Dubai, then Male. Norway provided a seaplane that could take him to Kilinochchi. They had to fit it [with] new fuel tanks. It was a project to get Bala[singham] into the country—it also had to take place outside Indian airspace.'

57. See D.B.S Jeyaraj, 'Now to Bangkok', *Frontline*, 13–26 April 2002 and Iqbal Athas, 'LTTE's formula for a "conducive climate" to peace talks', *Sunday Times*, 31 March 2002, which also examines the content of the Norwegian-LTTE discussions. Balasingham himself provides an account of the journey and surrounding circumstances—interestingly without referring to the Indian 'setback'—See Balasingham, *War and Peace*, pp. 363–365.

58. The last time had been in early April 1990, when reportedly he spoke to a small group of reporters in Jaffna following the IPKF pullout from the north of the country. See T.S. Subramanian, 'Prabhakaran in First Person', *Frontline*, 27 April–10 May 2002. The April 2002 press conference was attended by some 350 journalists.

59. For another lengthier account of the press conference from a well-informed Indian perspective, see N. Swamy, *Inside an Elusive Mind*.

60. Not just 'answer' in the sense of 'provide a straight, literal translation' of the LTTE leader's remarks. Reports from the press conference indicate that Balasingham both embroidered Prabhakaran's answers to journalists' questions and added longer statements of his own views on issues such as the definition of self-determination and an interim agreement for a Northeastern administration.

61. According to one account Balasingham's (as opposed to Prabhakaran's) response was 'This is a tragic incident that took place ten years ago. We don't want to comment further on it'. See. T.S. Subramanian 'Prabhakaran in First Person'. Another commentator suggests that the expression 'tragic incident' implied 'neither an admission nor a denial of the LTTE's role in the assassination'. In this sense, he suggests, the LTTE appeared to be appealing for 'a policy of letting bygones be bygones'. See V. Suryanaran, 'Singing the same tune', *Frontline*, 27 April–10 May 2002.

62. A reference, among other things, to the LTTE's brutal expulsion of up to 80,000 Muslims from the north of the country in Oct. 1990. See Chapter 1.

63. An issue at the top of Hakeem's agenda at this point on account of mounting reports of Muslims being subjected to financial extortion by LTTE cadres, notably in the East.

64. For the text of the MoU, see Gooneratne, *Negotiating With the Tigers*, pp. 54–55.

65. 'A timely and prudent step by the LTTE', interview with Rauff Hakeem, *Frontline*, 8–21 June 2002.

66. Helgesen mentions Indian journalist Anita Pratap's account of her meetings with Prabhakaran during a series of interviews with him conducted throughout the 1980s, both in India and Sri Lanka. See Anita Pratap, *Islands Of Blood*, New Delhi: Penguin India, 2001.

67. March 2002 *Peace Confidence Index* (PCI). PCI was produced bi-monthly by the Centre for Policy Alternatives (CPA) from 2001 until late 2008. See http://www.cpalanka.org/survey-research/
68. N. Subramanian, 'Govt. yet to implement truce agreement: LTTE', *The Hindu*, 19 June 2002.
69. While this was the first meeting between the prospective negotiators, government Peace Secretariat Head Bernard Goonetilleke had previously made two visits to Kilinochchi for talks with LTTE political chief S.P. Tamilselvan (21 May, 18 June). On both occasions the agenda for discussion comprised both immediate concerns, notably LTTE complaints over the army's failure to vacate public buildings as specified in the CFA, and broader issues including the agenda of forthcoming peace talks. See N. Subramanian, 'Kilinochchi talks focus on highway dispute', *The Hindu*, 21 May 2002; 'Govt. yet to implement true agreement: LTTE', *The Hindu*, 18 June 2002.
70. Helgesen further recalls, 'With the EU I broke the news about the CFA to [Commissioner] Chris Patten three days before it happened, because I was in Brussels and met him then. I asked him what the EU could contribute towards confidence-building measures. So we started engaging with the EU even prior to the CFA announcement, because it was important to mobilise other actors. Patten was extremely helpful: he also went to meet Prabhakaran later. When it came to financial assistance, the EU bureaucracy listed modalities. I said to Patten that since Norway wasn't a member state I wouldn't have an understanding of their internal budget processes. "Lucky you" was his reply.'
71. During the latter stages of the Vietnam War, Armitage served on a US Destroyer stationed off the coast of the country before volunteering for several combat tours with the South Vietnamese Navy's advisory forces, learning to speak fluent Vietnamese in the process.
72. Oslo in Nov. 2002. See Ch. 4.
73. Senior officials from the Research and Analysis Wing (RAW).

4. PEACE TALKS

1. The four person delegations on each side were: G.L. Peiris, M. Moragoda, R. Haukeem, B. Goonetilleke (Govt.); Anton Balasingham, Adele Balasingham, V. Rudrakumaran, J. Maheshwaran (LTTE).
2. See V.S. Sambandan, 'A start at Sattahip', *Frontline*, 28 Sept.—11 Oct. 2002.
3. Ibid.
4. For the text of Balasingham's opening speech and his detailed account of the first session of talks see Balasingham, *War and Peace*, pp. 375–386.
5. Balasingham, *War and Peace*, p. 380.
6. Gooneratne, *Negotiating With The Tigers*, p. 24.
7. Balasingham, *War and Peace*, pp. 382–83.
8. Ibid., p. 383.
9. Gooneratne, *Negotiating With The Tigers*, p. 24.
10. Alongside Peiris' assessment of the constitutional obstacles, it is important to

bear in mind the political difficulties the proposal would have encountered. In particular, Kumaratunga's opposition meant that in practice the government would have needed to pass a constitutional amendment removing her veto powers—something that in turn required a two-thirds majority in parliament, which it was highly unlikely to achieve. Even in the unlikely event of this obstacle being cleared, under the Constitution the proposal would still have had to be submitted to a referendum—potentially an even more challenging hurdle. See N. Ram 'The peace process—a reality check', *Frontline*, 4–16 Jan. 2003.

11. Balasingham, *War and Peace*, pp. 384–85.

12. In a revealing aside Balasingham states that 'though we reluctantly agreed to form committees, I expressed serious reservations over this typical problem-solving methodology of Sinhalese governments, which invariably created an ever-expanding corrupt bureaucracy while failing to resolve the problems'. Balasingham, *War and Peace*, p. 384. At the same time, within days of the talks the LTTE were claiming that they and the government would soon be embarking on a joint effort to raise funds for redevelopment of the North and East of the country—a clear indication that the Task Force proposal was taken seriously on the LTTE side.

13. For the Norwegian statement issued at the end of the talks, see Gooneratne, *Negotiating With the Tigers*, pp. 151–53.

14. 'Bala, G.L. clarify concepts', *Sunday Times*, 22 Sept. 2002.

15. Ibid.

16. 'PA brought into peace process', *Sunday Times*, 29 Sept. 2002.

17. Throughout this period Kumaratunga repeatedly maintained that she had no intention of dissolving parliament or calling fresh elections as long as the government maintained its majority.

18. The government would also have needed a two-thirds parliamentary majority to carry through the constitutional reforms needed in order to address a number of the 'core issues' of the peace process, for example, establishing an interim administrative council for the North and East. D.B.S. Jeyaraj, 'Colombo contradictions', *Frontline*, 26 Oct.–8 Nov. 2002.

19. The Supreme Court's ruling was based on the argument that the clause applied only to this specific bill; such a clause could only be introduced, it argued, if the conscience vote was applied to all future parliamentary bills or motions.

20. 'SC ruling shows a way out', *Sunday Times*, 13 Oct. 2002.

21. An elite police counterterrorist and counterinsurgency unit formed in 1983, most of which was stationed in the East.

22. In addition to continuing LTTE pressure to remove STF camps from the area, in Oct. there were several outbreaks of violence in the East relating to other issues, notably at Valachchenai, where protestors demanded the opening of the Batticaloa–Colombo road as envisaged in the CFA, and in Trincomalee and Akkaraipattu, where Tamil and Muslim mobs confronted each other and a number of people died in the resulting clashes.

23. Seemingly underscoring her dissatisfaction with the way things were proceed-

ing—in particular her own marginalisation from the peace process—Kumaratunga cancelled a meeting with the Norwegians scheduled for their return from the Vanni. The 'compromise' was a meeting with Kadirgamar, where among other things, the terms of reference for the JTF, drafted by the Norwegians, were discussed. 'SLMC rebels a threat to UNF', *Sunday Times*, 27 Oct. 2002.

24. Balasingham, *War and Peace*, pp. 385–86.

25. Also present as observers were John Gunaratne and Janaka Jeyasekara of the Government Peace Secretariat, and the LTTE's V. Rudrakumaran and J. Maheswaran, who had both been present at the Sattahip talks.

26. See Ch. 1 p. 28.

27. Gooneratne, *Negotiating With the* Tigers, p. 25. There are certainly strong indications that during Oct. 2002, supporters of the dissenting Athauallah faction within the SLMC were responsible for inciting violence against Tamils in places such as the southeastern coastal town of Akkaraipattu. By contrast, during the Rose Garden Resort discussions, Hakeem pointed to LTTE cadres as the instigators of Tamil-Muslim riots in areas such as Valaichenai and Muttur. See Balasingham, *War and Peace*, p. 387

28. Gooneratne, *Negotiating With the Tigers*, p. 25.

29. D.B.S. Jeyaraj, 'Perpetuating a peace process', *Frontline*, 23 Nov.–6 Dec. 2002.

30. I. Athas, 'LTTE "law courts" in the East from Friday', *Sunday Times*, 10 Nov. 2002.

31. Ibid.

32. Interestingly, a number of other countries that had also banned the LTTE—notably the USA, UK and Australia—opted to take part in the Oslo conference. Explaining this move, a US official noted that participation in the meeting would have 'no bearing' on US designation of the LTTE as a terrorist organisation. See 'India keeps out of Oslo show, but pledges support for peace', *Sunday Times*, 24 Nov. 2002.

33. See the summary outline of their speeches in Balasingham, *War and Peace*, pp. 391–92.

34. See Balasingham, *War and Peace*, p. 393.

35. Ibid.

36. For the text of his speech see Balasingham, *War and Peace*, pp. 393–98.

37. As a sign that issues of contention were not being ignored, during the discussion Wickremasinghe reportedly brought up the question of LTTE-run Courts in the East. Balasingham responded that these only functioned in areas under LTTE control, and had been in existence for four years. Nonetheless, at a meeting with newspaper editors held soon after his return to Colombo, Wickremasinghe stated that he had observed a 'marked shift' in the LTTE's approach as articulated by Balasingham during their discussions in Oslo. 'US urges LTTE to come clean', *Sunday Times Political Column*, 1 Dec. 2002.

38. Linking Prabhakaran's Heroes Day Speech and Balasingham's stance in the negotiations was doubtless helped by the fact that the LTTE leader's speeches were invariably drafted in full by Balasingham.

39. V.S. Sambandan, 'Sticking to his guns', *Frontline*, 7–20 Dec. 2002; and Balasingham, *War and Peace*, p. 401.

40. The argument is stated in full in Balasingham, *War and Peace*, pp. 399–400.
41. Balasingham notes that after meeting Japanese Special Envoy Yasushi Akashi at the Oslo Conference, Solheim informed him that the Japanese were planning to hold a major donor conference in May 2003. In the event it was held in June 2003—with neither LTTE nor official Norwegian participation. See pp. 154–156.
42. The Sub-Committee on De-Escalation and Normalization (SDN) met for the first time in Omanthai on 10 Nov. 2002. The next meeting took place as scheduled at the same location on 14 Dec. 2002. See Gooneratne, *Negotiating With the Tigers*, *pp. 175–77* for the (Norwegian Embassy issued) press releases from both these meetings and below (p. 23). The Sub-Committee on Immediate Humanitarian and Rehabilitation Needs in the North and East (SIHRN) held its first meeting in Kilinochchi on 18 Nov. 2002. See 'Secretariat formed to manage NE development', *TamilNet*, 18 Nov. 2002. At the next meeting, held in Kilinochchi on 16 Dec. 2002, the Sub-Committee Secretariat's offices were opened by Norwegian Ambassador Jon Westborg. 'Norwegian envoy encouraged by discussions in Kilinochchi', *TamilNet*, 17 Dec. 2002.
43. In the event, Rauff Hakeem rushed back to Colombo on the opening day of the talks to deal with another outbreak of political infighting between the various SLMC factions.
44. Taken as a whole the text makes it clear that the primary issue in focus here was the recruitment of child soldiers—a practice for which the LTTE had long been criticised.
45. There were also some smaller, security-related decisions, notably that the future transportation of [LTTE] area commanders would take place under SLMM supervision, and that the LTTE would accept the right of political groups to carry out political work, including in the Jaffna peninsula and the islands' provided they are unarmed, as stipulated by the Ceasefire Agreement'. C.f. Record of Decisions.
46. 'Declaration' is something of a misnomer: the document containing the 'federalism' statement is actually titled 'Working Outline for the discussion of political matters', and was intended to serve as background material for future deliberations in the Sub-Committee on Political Matters—the third of the subcommittees agreed at the Rose Garden talks. The key passage quoted above was also repeated in the Norwegian Statement at the end of the talks, which is where it was picked up on by a broader audience. The Statement text is reproduced in Balasingham, *War and Peace*, pp. 160–162.
47. Interestingly one experienced commentator notes that the formulation 'historical habitation of the Tamil peoples' is taken directly from the text of the 1987 Indo-Lanka Accord. Thus it was much more acceptable to the Indians than the phrase 'the Tamil homeland' commonly used in LTTE statements. c.f. N. Ram, 'The peace process—a reality check', *Frontline*, 4–16 Jan. 2003.
48. Balasingham, *War and Peace*, p. 404.
49. The FoF seminar was held 3–4 Dec. 2002 in Oslo, during the middle two days of the Oslo peace negotiations. FoF President Bob Rae and Dr. David Cameron, a

Professor of Political Science at Toronto University, provided inputs on the margins of all subsequent rounds of talks.

50. Balasingham, *War and Peace*, pp. 404–405.

51. D.B.S. Jeyaraj, 'A tactical shift', *Frontline*, 21 Dec. 2002–3 Jan. 2003. All quotations in the following paragraphs are from this source.

52. J. Perera, 'Looking Ahead', *Frontline*, 23 Dec. 2002–3 Jan 2003. Earlier he pointed out that some analysts' had previously believed that the LTTE 'would settle for nothing less than a confederation'.

53. Ibid.

54. A proposal that the statement further characterises as upholding the 'devolution of power along [the lines of] a federalist or Indian model within a united Sri Lanka'. See Perera, 'Looking Ahead'.

55. The first had been held at the same location—Omanthai, in the no-man's land between LTTE and SLA-controlled territory—on 15 Nov. 2002.

56. 'LTTE demands EPDP withdrawal', *Sunday Times*, 15 Dec. 2002. At the meeting Karuna reportedly indicated both that Prabhakaran wanted the HSZs vacated for the re-settlement of civilians 'without delay', and that if this failed to materialise, the LTTE would withdraw its participation in the sub-committee. See I. Athas, 'HSZ issue: who caused the blunder?', *Sunday Times*, 6 Jan. 2003.

57. Issues relating to the EPDP presence in and around the Jaffna peninsula were first addressed in the Oslo final statement, which includes a government commitment to achieve a solution—in consultation with all relevant parties—to the situation on the Delft Island. Delft Island had long been an EPDP stronghold and in the run up to Oslo there were increasingly vocal protests—clearly orchestrated by the LTTE—against their continued presence. In this context it is worth noting that the LTTE also undertook to accept the right of (unarmed) political groups to carry out political work 'including in the Jaffna peninsula and the islands'.

58. Fonseka's Plan contained a number of additional proposals that were more or less buried in the controversy surrounding the suggestion that an Army withdrawal from the HSZs should be 'matched' militarily by the LTTE in the terms outlined above. Among these was a set of guidelines for enhancing understanding between the SLA and LTTE commands, and an expansion of the SLMM mandate to cover 'neutral' supervision of the de-escalation process. 'Army chief rejects Army charges', *Sunday Times*, 29 Dec. 2002. The full text of the De-escalation Plan is reproduced in A. Fernando, *My Belly Is White*, Colombo: Vijitha Yapa, 2008, pp. 450–457.

59. Extracts of the LTTE statement are quoted in Balasingham, *War and Peace*, pp. 410–412.

60. Shelani Perera, 'SLMM stands by its HSZ view', *Sunday Times*, 29 Dec. 2002.

61. Balasingham, *War and Peace*, p. 414. The LTTE chief negotiator also indicates that at the forthcoming round of talks, Prabhakaran instructed him to announce that in the LTTE's view the HSZ controversy had rendered the sub-committee defunct.

62. Balasingham, *War and Peace*, p. 415.
63. Of these, the 9 Jan. 2003 Norwegian final talks statement, 'Accelerated Action on Resettlement and Humanitarian Action, Progress on Human Rights', is reproduced in Gooneratne, *Negotiating With the Tigers*, pp. 163–167.
64. Initially the government had wanted UNDP as the custodian. The LTTE, however, suggested the more market-oriented World Bank. In this context, Solheim suggests that the LTTE may have been acting on advice from diaspora Tamils who regarded the World Bank as the more effective institution of the two.
65. At Helgesen's recommendation, Dr. Astrid Heiberg, Professor of Psychiatry at Oslo University and a former President of the International Red Cross Federation, was subsequently appointed as resource person and facilitator. For the press statements from the two meetings the sub-committee held in Kilinochchi in March (5–6) and April (4–5) 2003, see Gooneratne, *Negotiating With the Tigers*, pp. 179–181.
66. Ibid., p. 31.
67. Estimates vary, but IDPs outside the HSZs probably numbered as many as 250,000 people, while those within the HSZs amounted to some 130,000.
68. With, it should be noted, the important rider: 'as and when they are released by the Security Forces for resettlement'.
69. Reportedly this reflects a last-minute compromise put forward at the talks by Milinda Morogoda. In all probability Morogoda also had a role in proposing Gen. Nambiar as author of the expert report.
70. In fact Nambiar's final report was not made public until several months later—May 2003—although sections of the initial draft were leaked to the Colombo press in Jan., giving rise to a spate of commentary from both sides on its recommendations. The full text of the final report is in Gooneratne, *Negotiating With the Tigers*, pp. 140–150.
71. Sri Lankan academic and wife of Ranil Wickremasinghe
72. Balasingham offers a different version of events. According to a message received directly form the Vanni, the SLN had 'impounded' an LTTE boat and the vessel was being 'towed to the Navy camp'. Balasingham, *War and Peace*, p. 419.
73. Reportedly, both delegations to the Berlin talks were 'kept informed of developments'. See Gooneratne, *Negotiating With the Tigers*, p. 31.
74. V.S. Sambandan, 'A shaky phase', *Frontline*, 15–28 Feb. 2003.
75. Well-informed sources reported the events as follows: against the navy's advice, SLMM monitors boarded the trawler on the morning of 7 Feb. Soon after they uncovered the weapons and ammunition concealed below deck and reported this fact, following which the three LTTE cadres set fire to the vessel. One, who was wearing a suicide jacket, then drew the other two closer to him and detonated it—on the direct instruction of Sea Tiger leader Soosai, according to Sri Lankan intelligence sources. 'Mission for weapons ends in suicide'; I. Athas, 'Leak foils bid to capture arms ship' *Sunday Times*, 9 Feb. 2003.
76. Sambandan, 'A shaky phase'.
77. See, for example, 'Child Conscription and Peace: A Tragedy of Contradictions', issued by the Jaffna-based University Teachers for Human Rights (Report 16,

18 March 2003). Focusing on the peace process' failure to address the LTTE's continuing, often forced recruitment of child soldiers, it concludes that 'trying to pursue peace negotiations without a serious attempt to hold the LTTE accountable plays into its [the LTTE's] hands ... Bringing in the international community is meaningful only if it enhances human rights ... sadly, the international community has largely failed [and] appeasement remains the dominant theme of peace activity ... After a year there is no monitoring mechanism effective in the LTTE-controlled area[s], where the people have been left entirely at [their] whims and fancies'. Section 15, p. 32.

78. All quotations in this paragraph are from the 8 Feb. 2003 Norwegian Embassy Berlin press release issued at the end of the talks. See Gooneratne, *Negotiating With the Tigers*, pp. 168–170.

79. 'UNICEF estimates that there are 900,000 children in the Northeast, all of whom have been seriously affected. Many of these children are faced with malnutrition, poor health care and education facilities, continued displacement, loss of parents and families, and landmines. The LTTE has agreed to work with UNICEF to draw up an action plan for children affected by armed conflict. Such an action plan will include an intensified effort by the LTTE to stop underage recruitment. The LTTE restated its pledge to bring the practice to an end.' Excerpt from Norwegian Embassy Berlin Press Release, 8 Feb. 2003. See Gooneratne, *Negotiating With the Tigers*, pp. 168–170.

80. Balasingham, *War and Peace*, p. 420.

81. Norwegian Embassy Berlin Press Release. See Gooneratne, *Negotiating With the Tigers*.

82. Gooneratne, *Negotiating With the Tigers*, p. 170.

83. 'LTTE mark truce day with hartals', *Sunday Times*, 23 Feb. 2003.

84. 'Revolt in the north: LTTE warns TULF', *Sunday Times*, 16 Feb. 2003.

85. V.S. Sambandan, 'The story of the Jaffna Public Library', *Frontline*, 15–28 March 2003.

86. Gooneratne, *Negotiating With the Tigers*, p. 41.

87. Balasingham, *War and Peace*, pp. 421–423.

88. See Gooneratne, *Negotiating With the Tigers*, pp. 45–47 for an overview of the sub-committee's activities. A second meeting of the SGI was held 4–5 April in Kilinochchi. As with all the sub-committees, after 21 April 2003 no further meetings took place on account of the LTTE's suspension of its participation in the negotiations.

89. D.B.S. Jeyaraj, 'A troubled course', *Frontline*, 29 March–11 April. 2003.

90. CFA, Article 1.3. See also 'Sinking of ship violated cease-fire: LTTE', *Sunday Times*, 16 March 2003.

91. Citations are from the 21 March 2003 Hakone Talks 'Record of Decisions', Sections 1 & 2. The relevant section is also contained in the 'Agreed Statement on behalf of the Parties' issued on 21 March 2003 and reproduced in Gooneratne, *Negotiating With the Tigers*, pp. 171–174.

92. Balasingham, *War and Peace*, pp. 426–427.

93. I. Martin, 'Human Rights Issues Relating To The Peace Process', 19 March 2002. The paper did not receive wider circulation.
94. See the 'Hakone Talks Record Final of Decisions', Annex 1, and 'Agreed Statement'.
95. Ibid.
96. See Ch. 3 on FoF.
97. See Jeyaraj, 'A troubled course'.
98. Ibid.
99. Balasingham, *War and Peace*, p. 429 summarises of Helgesen's report.
100. It is worth noting that as of Dec. 2013, nineteen countries—including Egypt, Mexico, North Korea, Iran, the USA and the UK—were continuing to recruit minors as young as sixteen into their armed forces. See *The CIA World Factbook, https://government.cia.gov/library/publications/the-world-factbook/fields/2024.html#139*
101. 'Hakone Talks Record of Final Decisions', Section 10. One of the meeting's stated purposes was to develop an agenda for the seventh round of talks.
102. The decision to 'explore' federally-based solutions to the conflict.
103. Following a 1920 League of Nations determination regarding a dispute between Sweden and Finland over possession of the Åland Islands—a small archipelago in the Baltic Sea—the islands became an autonomous Swedish-speaking region of Finland, a status they have retained ever since. Significantly, from an LTTE perspective, while the island population's initial demand for self-determination was not met, recognition of the island's autonomous status a year later (1921) provided the basis for what proved to be a broadly accepted—and sustainable—political settlement.
104. 'LTTE political team begins Nordic tour', *TamilNet*, 30 March 2003, 'LTTE delegation completes Norway, Sweden visits', *TamilNet*, 6 April 2003.
105. J. Cherian, 'A President's concerns', *Frontline*, 26 April—9 May 2003.
106. The initial seminar invitations went out under US Secretary of State Colin Powell's signature.
107. Gooneratne suggests that the option of 'persons not directly connected with the LTTE' attending the meeting 'on their behalf' was aired, but was rejected by the LTTE. Gooneratne, *Negotiating With the Tigers*, p. 43.
108. Both statements are reproduced in Balasingham, *War and Peace*, pp. 431–433.
109. R. Armitage, Opening Remarks, Washington Seminar on Sri Lanka, 14 April 2003. http://2001–2009.state.gov/s/d/former/armitage/remarks/19615.htm
110. M. Morogoda, Address to 'Pre-Tokyo Sri Lanka Seminar', Washington DC, 14 April 2002. http://government.slembassyusa.org/statements/2003/minister_moragoda_pre_tokyo_14apr03.html
111. Ibid.
112. D.B.S. Jeyaraj, 'The foreign aid factor', *Frontline*, 26 Apr—9 May 2003.
113. Ibid.
114. Following the Indian Peace Keeping Force (IPKF) intervention in Sri Lanka.
115. The Sri Lanka donors conference held in July 2003 (see below pp. 154–156).
116. 'Curfew in Muttur, three more killed', *Daily Mirror*, 18. April 2003. The clashes

began following a Muslim protest campaign started in response to a Muslim woman committing suicide after the abduction of her son and another youth, allegedly by the LTTE.

117. At his own admission, the lengthy 21 April 2003 statement announcing LTTE suspension of its participation in the talks was written by Balasingham. See Balasingham, *War and Peace*, pp. 434–439. Commentators were quick to seize upon the symbolic significance of the date of the announcement—exactly three years since the LTTE began its April 2000 offensive aimed at recapturing Elephant Pass.

118. Balasingham, *War and Peace*, p. 430.

119. Ibid., p. 430.

120. Ibid., p. 434.

121. Gooneratne, *Negotiating With the Tigers*, p. 42; Balasingham, *War and Peace*, pp. 440–441.

122. Balasingham, *War and Peace*, pp. 441–442.

123. Quoted in V.S. Sambandan, 'Peace process in trouble', *Frontline*, 10–23 May 2003.

124. Ibid.

125. US Embassy Colombo, 'In another negative signal, Tigers postpone meeting', 24 April 2003. Wikileaks Cable 03COLOMBO705.

126. US Embassy Colombo, 'Tigers announce they are suspending peace talks', 22 April 2003. Wikileaks Cable 03COLOMBO688.

127. Gooneratne, *Negotiating With the Tigers*, p. 75.

128. Balasingham, *War and Peace*, p. 442.

5. STALEMATE

1. See Ch 1. pp. 24–27.

2. 'Oslo envoys hold extensive talks with LTTE', *Daily Mirror*, 2 May 2003; 'Oslo takes PM's letter to LTTE', *Daily Mirror*, 30 April 2003.

3. S. Dias, 'Japan wants LTTE "yes" within a week', *Daily Mirror*, 10 May 2003.

4. 'Tigers seek more control of donor funds', *Sunday Times*, 11 May 2003.

5. Respectively the Sea Tigers Head, Senior Army Commader and Artillery Unit Leader.

6. See Ch. 4. Although the final version of the report incorporated some important modifications to the draft circulated at the beginning of the year, the LTTE's fundamental objection—the linking of Army withdrawal from the High Security Zones to simultaneous demilitarisation moves by the LTTE on the Jaffna peninsula—remained as strong as ever.

7. I. Athas, 'Tigers seek more control of donor funds', *Sunday Times*, 11 May 2003. The presence of both Tellefsen and the Sea Tiger Commander Soosai at the meeting may explain why the issue was raised here, but not with Akashi the previous day. Unsurprisingly, the proposals were met with outrage by the Sri Lankan military, notably the Navy command, which viewed them as potentially under

mining control over the coastline and thus as constituting a potential threat to the country's territorial integrity.

8. S. Dias, 'US tells UNF and PA to come together', *Daily Mirror*, 15 May 2003. At this point tensions between the two major parties were at a high following a recent move by President Kumaratunga to seize control of the Development Lotteries Board, a government department answering to Milinda Morogoda, Minister for Economic Reform.

9. Balasingham maintains that he was feeling 'very unwell and tired' as a result of the journey to Sri Lanka, combined with the 'intensity of the diplomatic work', and that 'a concerned Mr. Pirapharan [Prabhakaran] supported our decision to leave the Vanni'. Balasingham, *War and Peace*, p. 445.

10. As quoted in Gooneratne, *Negotiating With the Tigers*, p. 80. Balasingham describes Prabhakaran's request to the government as being for a 'set of ideas for an interim administrative mechanism'. Balasingham, *War and Peace*, p. 445.

11. 'Elements of a Strengthened and Expanded Mechanism for Reconstruction and Development of the North and East'.

12. See Gooneratne, *Negotiating With the Tigers*, p. 81.

13. Reporting on a 20 May meeting with the LTTE leadership, US Embassy Colombo contacts in the Tamil National Alliance (TNA) noted that Tamilselvan had told them that the LTTE was 'fed up' with the government and that—while 'basically well intentioned'—in their view it was 'not strong enough or would not carry through on its plans because it was too afraid of Sinhalese chauvinists'. Reportedly, Vidar Helgesen 'made this same point in vivid terms' when describing recent Norwegian interactions with the LTTE leadership to US Embassy contacts. US Embassy Colombo, 'Tigers issue hard-edged letter demanding interim structure in north/east', 21 May 2003. Wikileaks Cable 03COLOMBO851.

14. See Balasingham, *War and Peace*, pp. 446–453.

15. 'Norway, Japan work out compromise', *Daily Mirror*, 23 May 2003. These reports soon led President Kumaratunga to denounce both countries for becoming over-involved in efforts to persuade the LTTE to attend the Tokyo conference—in Norway's case she emphasised that it had been invited to serve as a facilitator of talks, not a mediator between the two sides.

16. Quotations are drawn from the text of both the government proposals and the LTTE response reproduced in Gooneratne, *Negotiating With the Tigers*, pp. 203–218.

17. 'LTTE rejects Govt. proposals', *Daily Mirror*, 30 May 2003.

18. Gooneratne, *Negotiating With the Tigers*, pp. 220–222.

19. Ibid., pp. 222–225.

20. 'LTTE wants new and refined agenda', *Sunday Times*, 8 June 2003.

21. D.B.S. Jeyaraj, 'In dread of democracy', *Frontline*, 7–20 June 2003. Writing a month later, Jeyaraj amplified the argument with the observation that in Tokyo, initially the donors were planning to require both the government and LTTE to sign up to a 'benchmark document', titled 'Basic Principles of Peace and Democracy', as a prerequisite for receiving aid—a move strongly resented by the LTTE which, he maintained, was not prepared to 'relax its grip' on Sri Lankan

Tamil society in the 'name of democracy or human rights'. 'Politics of brink-manship', *Frontline*, 21 June–4 July 2003.

22. J. Perera, 'Changing the win-win mind set for progress in the peace process', *Daily Mirror*, 10 June 2003.

23. Pledges made at the Tokyo conference included: Japan $1 billion, Asian Development Bank (ADB), $1 billion, EU $293 million, USA $54 million.

24. 'Tokyo Declaration on Reconstruction and Development of Sri Lanka', 10 June 2003. http://www.mofa.go.jp/region/asia-paci/srilanka/conf0306/declaration.html

25. 'Japan freely contributes, but notes LTTE's absence', *Daily Mirror*, 10 June 2003.

26. Statement on 'Meeting of Sri Lankan Donor Co-Chairs Group', Washington DC, 13 June 2005. http://2001–2009.state.gov/r/pa/prs/ps/2005/47891.htm

27. 'Foreign cash fails to lift Sri Lanka peace proposals', *Daily Mirror*, 14 June 2003.

28. Quoted in Balasingham, *War and Peace*, p. 460.

29. See Jeyaraj, 'In dread of democracy'.

30. US Embassy Colombo, 'Tensions notch up over sinking of Tamil Tiger ship and latest slaying of a Tiger opponent', 16 June, 2003. Wikileaks Cable 03COLOM BO1053. According to a BBC report, this was the thirtieth political killing by the LTTE since the CFA, while other local sources put the figure as high as fifty.

31. D.B.S. Jeyaraj, 'LTTE's killing spree', *Frontline*, 5–18 July, 2003. As another commentator put it at the time, 'After the signing of the CFA, the LTTE has access to the whole of the country. Therefore its opponents have nowhere to hide.' J. Perera, 'Peace can't wait for another three years', *Daily Mirror*, 17 June 2003. For an overview of recent LTTE political killings and a scathing indictment of government, Norwegian facilitators and SLMM monitors' perceived indifference to the Tigers' relentless campaign of assassinations against their Tamil opponents—real and imagined—see the University Teachers for Human Rights-Jaffna statement, 'The murder of T. Subathiran: Sri Lanka's end game', 15 June 2003. http://www.uthr.org/Statements/Subathiran.htm

32. V.S. Sambandan, 'Conflicting signals', *Frontline*, 5–18 July 2003.

33. S. Dias, 'LTTE agrees to resume talks', *Daily Mirror*, 25 June 2003.

34. 'Peace talks to resume soon—LTTE', *Tamilnet*, 25 June 2003.

35. 'Record crowds throng Jaffna *Pongu Thamil* rally', *Tamilnet*, 27 June 2003.

36. S. Perera, 'Fresh proposals go to LTTE: Govt. confident', *Daily Mirror*, 16 July 2003. The full text of the proposals was published in *The Sunday Times*, 20 July 2003 and is reproduced in Gooneratne, *Negotiating With the Tigers*, pp. 226–233.

37. Gooneratne, *Negotiating With the Tigers*, pp. 228–229.

38. Quoted in 'Counter proposals to be sent soon', *Daily Mirror*, 29 July 2003. See also 'Tamilchelvan says doors to peace wide open', *Tamilnet*, 28 July 2003. In a brief review of the exchange of letters regarding the government's proposals for an interim structure, Gooneratne argues that the failure to achieve agreement was partially due to the fact that Balasingham's responses were characterised by loose, inconsistent use of terms such as 'Interim Administrative structure'. Overall the LTTE's approach here, he argues, had 'all the marks of deliberately befuddling the issue'—an argument symptomatic of the mutual lack

of trust increasingly evident by this stage. See Gooneratne, *Negotiating With the Tigers*, pp. 82–83.

39. 'LTTE puts its best heads together', *Sunday Times*, 17 Aug. 2003

40. 'Service chiefs rush to Trinco', *Daily Mirror*, 8 July 2003. An indication of wider concerns over the camp is provided in US Embassy Colombo, 'Tigers still refusing request from monitors to vacate forward base', 15 July 2003. Wikileaks Cable 03COLOMBO1262.

41. V. Sambandan, 'Sri Lanka's troubled east', *Frontline*, 25 Oct.-7 Nov. 2003. The Indian correspondent also noted reports of a significant increase in LTTE abductions and conscriptions, as well as child soldier recruitment, in the East over the previous few months.

42. 'Solheim fails to get Kinniya camp shifted', *Daily Mirror*, 17. Aug 2003.

43. 'Paris meeting "Positive and Innovative"', *Tamilnet*, 30 Aug. 2003.

44. V. Sambandan, 'Charting a course', *Frontline*, 13–26 Sept. 2003.

45. Ibid.

46. Meeting Norwegian Foreign Minister Jan Petersen in Oslo a week later, Tamilselvan stated that in Ireland they had been able to 'gather input from intellectuals, members of the Irish Parliament, constitutional experts with particular backgrounds in conflict resolution in Bougainville and South Africa, including members of the African National Congress'. 'LTTE delegation meets Norwegian FM', *Tamilnet*, 16 Oct. 2003.

47. The prime source of these reports was the *Sunday Times* Senior Defence Correspondent Iqbal Athas, whose *Situation Report* column carried maps and other details of the construction of new LTTE camps—up to seventeen of them it was claimed—in the Trincomalee area. See 'Tiger trap for Trinco seige', *Sunday Times*, 3 Aug. 2003; 'The cover up of a Tiger build up in Trincomalee', *Sunday Times*, 14 Sept. 2003.

48. 'President's open letter to Premier', *Daily Mirror*, 8 Oct. 2003.

49. 'Remove SLMM chief, CBK tells Norway', *Daily Mirror*, 24 Oct. 2003; I. Athas, 'Don't take SLMM chief's advice: President tells armed services commanders', *Sunday Times*, 26 Oct. 2003.

50. 'LTTE ready to resume talks any time', *Daily Mirror*, 21 Oct. 2003. The LTTE's announcement of renewed willingness to engage in talks with the government was directly related to the imminent release of the ISGA proposal, which they appeared to regard both as a solid, practical basis on which to recommence negotiations.

51. S. Perera, 'Talks to resume early next year', *Daily Mirror*, 24 Oct. 2003.

52. 'Norwegian facilitators confident', *Daily Mirror*, 25 Oct. 2003.

53. 'Tigers release historic power-sharing plan', *Daily Mirror*, 1 Nov. 2003.

54. 'Look beyond the constitution, says Thamilselvan', *Sunday Times*, 2 Nov. 2003.

55. 'Statement by the Government of Sri Lanka', 1 Nov. 2003, reproduced in Gooneratne, *Negotiating With the Tigers*, pp. 85–87.

56. S. Perera, 'No more war, say Tigers', *Daily Mirror*, 3 Nov. 2003.

57. 'LTTE proposals go far beyond devolution—CBK', *The Island*, 3 Nov. 2003.

58. Their second meeting in just over a year, the first having been held in July 2002, also in Washington.
59. One of the diaspora experts asked to assist with the drafting of the ISGA. Rudrakumaran also participated in several rounds of peace talks as a member of the official LTTE delegation.
60. See above pp. 159–160.
61. Landmark 1998 Northern Ireland Peace Agreement.
62. It is worth pointing out that Rudrakumaran may be somewhat exaggerating his own role in the formulation of the ISGA proposal here.
63. Sri Lankan Attorney General (1975–1988).
64. Along with the individuals mentioned, the group—an informal gathering of leading civil society activists and thinkers—included Saravanamuttu Pakiosthoy (CPA). Not long after the ISGA proposal was released, the group published a joint discussion paper that proved influential at the time. 'The Sri Lankan Peace Process at a Crossroads: Lessons, Opportunities and Ideas for Principled Negotiations and Conflict Transformation'. http://www.cpalanka.org/the-sri-lankan-peace-process-at-a-crossroads-lessons-opportunities-and-ideas-for-principled-negotiations-and-conflict-transformation/
65. For reasons that were never completely clear, Balasingham was sidelined from the process of developing the ISGA proposal—a fact that opened up a flurry of intensive media speculation at the time. Accordingly, in his account of the period the proposal receives only the briefest of treatments—certainly far less than the attention given to his exchange of letters with Wickremasinghe. Balasingham's book does, however, provide the actual text of the proposal, in an Annex. See Balasingham, *War and Peace*, pp. 503–514.
66. 'Sri Lanka 'plunging into chaos', BBC News, 4 Nov. 2003.
67. 'I did it in the national interest, says President', *Daily Mirror*, 5 Nov. 2003.
68. 'Sri Lanka 'plunging into chaos', BBC News, 4 Nov. 2003.
69. 'Sri Lankan president condemned', BBC News, 6 Nov. 2003.
70. V. Sambandan, 'A crisis in Sri Lanka', *Frontline*, 22 Nov.–5 Dec. 2003.
71. 'Sri Lanka call for unity cabinet', BBC News, 7 Nov. 2003. In her address to the nation, Kumaratunga also argued that the Army had 'permitted' the LTTE to continue with the 'forcible recruitment' of children ... to the point that the LTTE's hardcore cadres' had increased 'from 6,000 to 18,000 during the Ceasefire period'. See 'My commitment to peace is total', *Daily Mirror*, 7 Nov. 2003.
72. Essentially the same point was made by Jehan Perera who suggests that Kumaratunga 'anticipated that members of the government would cross over to their side and provide ... a parliamentary majority. The president and her team believed that they could actually form a new government on their own.' See Perera, 'A three-point solution to the crisis in cohabitation', *Daily Mirror*, 11 Nov. 2003.
73. 'Takeover plot with PMship for Tyronne?', *Sunday Times*, 9 Nov. 2003. Fernando also stated that while he favoured the idea of a national government being touted by Kumaratunga, it should be under the leadership of Wickremasinghe.' 'At least

for the sake of the peace process and the dealings with the LTTE, the two sides must get together', he is also quoted as saying.

74. Perera, 'A three-point solution to the crisis in cohabitation'. In contrast, veteran defence commentator Iqbal Athas argued that 'even if one is viewed as being an apologist for President Kumaratunga ... her takeover ... has done the nation a great service—it has halted a rapidly deteriorating military balance after the ceasefire'. I. Athas, 'Why a Defence takeover', *Sunday Times*, 15 Nov. 2003.

75. K. Abeyewardene, 'PM asks CBK to handle peace', *Daily Mirror*, 10 Nov. 2003.

76. 'Ceasefire accord "illegal", but will stand says CBK', *Daily Mirror*, 10 Nov. 2003.

77. 'Peace envoys enter Sri Lanka fray', BBC News, 11 Nov. 2003.

78. A reference to the UNP's failure to support the constitutional reform 'package' Kumaratunga was planning to steer through parliament in summer 2000. As a result of their opposition, it was eventually withdrawn by Kumaratunga in Aug. 2000. See Ch. 2.

79. Lawyer who worked in the constitutional affairs ministry during the UNP government (2001–4).

80. Shortened version of an expression coined in May 2003 by Mangala Samaraweera, a party colleague of President Kumaratunga, later appointed foreign minister (Jan. 2015), in response to remarks attributed to Norwegian Prime Minister Kjell Bondevik. See 'Norwegians—salmon-eating busy-bodies', BBC News, 31 May 2003. http://news.bbc.co.uk/2/hi/south_asia/2950698.stm

81. The 2002 Ceasefire Agreement (CFA).

82. Ranil Wickremasinghe's UNP, in opposition from 1994 up until the Dec. 2001 parliamentary elections.

83. D. Perera, 'Prabha pledges to maintain ceasefire', *Daily Mirror*, 14. Nov. 2003.

84. 'Political stability necessary for talks—Pirapaharan', *Tamilnet*, 13 Nov. 2003. Mainly a report of Tamilselvan's press conference following the Norwegian visit, quoted in V. Sambandan, 'The LTTE's response', *Frontline*, 22 Nov.–5 Dec. 2003.

85. R. Sirilal, 'Oslo envoys suspend their peace role', *Daily Mirror*, 13 Nov. 2003.

86. K. Abeywardene, 'Norway suspends facilitation', *Daily Mirror*, 15 Nov. 2003; 'Peace talks on hold', BBC News, 14 Nov. 2003.

87. In fact, apart from the Norwegian Foreign Minister Jan Petersen and Japanese Special Envoy Akashi, Patten was the only senior international figure to meet the LTTE leader in Sri Lanka during the entire conflict.

88. Chris Patten, *What Next? Surviving The Twenty-First Century*, London: Penguin, 2009, p. 96.

89. 'Sri Lanka protests over EU envoy', BBC News, 25 Nov. 2003.

90. 'EU envoy supports Sri Lanka peace', BBC News, 26 Nov. 2003; 'Prabha assures Patten, no more war', *Daily Mirror*, 27 Nov. 2003.

91. Patten, *What Next? Surviving The Twenty-First Century*, pp. 96–97.

92. 'Pirapaharan's Heroes Day Address, *Tamilnet*, 27 Nov. 2003; V. Sambandan, 'The Tiger's refrain', *Frontline*, 6–19 Dec. 2003.

93. 'CBK offers compromise deal on defence job', *Daily Mirror*, 29 Nov. 2003. Here,

however, the devil was very much in the detail. With regard to the peace process, for example, Kumaratunga proposed that the current negotiating team
restart 'initial talks', after which a 'National Peace Negotiation Delegation'
would be set up to hold the 'main talks' with the LTTE. In this context the
overall negotiating framework as well as guidelines for the talks would need
to be approved by the JPC before negotiations began—a clear indication of
Kumaratunga's intention to have a far greater say over the conduct of the
peace process in future. See V. Sambandan, 'Changing equations', *Frontline*,
6–19 Dec. 2003.

94. See Jehan Perera, 'Unilateral actions are inappropriate when consensus is the
goal', *Daily Mirror*, 2 Dec. 2003. Alongside a Joint Peace Council, the
Kumaratunga proposals envisaged the establishment of an Advisory Council
on Peace (ACP) to assist its work, consisting of representatives of all the political parties, the clergy, professional and other national/civil society groups.

95. During the same period Wickremasinghe turned down a suggestion from
Kumaratunga to form a national government of unity with the President's
People's Alliance (PA).

96. The Committee consisted of UNP Chairman Malik Samarawickrema and
Presidential Advisor Mano Tittawela.

97. For a good example of the kind of arguments wheeled out by Kumaratunga
and her advisors in defence of this position, see P. Rodrigo, 'The President sticks
to her guns', *Daily Mirror*, 10 Dec. 2003. At the same time some commentators
suggested that historical precedent provided some backing for her position.
One, for example, argues that 'from 1978 onwards the president ... [and there
have been three prior to Kumaratunga] retained the defence portfolio'. The
main argument here, however, is for power sharing over the defence ministry,
for which historical precedents are also indicated. See J. Perera, 'Present political crisis: who should compromise more?', *Daily Mirror*, 16 Dec. 2003.

98. It is worth mentioning two other issues at this point. First, the vexed question
of the length of the president's term of office. Second, the prime minister's suggestion (first tabled in early Jan. 2004) that since the president now controlled
the defence ministry and thus the conduct of the peace process, she was free
to renegotiate or otherwise amend the 2002 Ceasefire Agreement with the
LTTE. Failing that, she should put her signature on the current document. See
R. Sirilal, 'PM insists: Defence or nothing', *Daily Mirror*, 9 Jan. 2004.

99. 'Tigers await Colombo outcome, vow to observe truce', *Daily Mirror*, 16. Jan
2004. Also present at Solheim's meeting with Balasingham in London was Trond
Furuhøvde, recently re-named as head of the SLMM following the enforced
departure of Tyggve Tellefsen from the post.

100. 'Alliance may lead to war, says LTTE', *Daily Mirror*, 22 Jan. 2004.

101. J. Uyangoda, 'The SLFP-JVP alliance, political realities and minority question',
Daily Mirror, 23 Jan. 2004.

102. 'LTTE expresses "serious concern" over Indo-Lankan defence pact', *Tamilnet*,
26 Jan. 2004. For a hard-hitting exposé of the importance of 'strategic parity'

to LTTE thinking by Sivaram, alias Taraki, the noted—and later assassinated—Tamil journalist who claimed to have formulated the concept of the 'balance of forces' as the basis for the 2002 Ceasefire Agreement, see 'The LTTE will negotiate only with parity of status', *Daily Mirror*, 29 Jan. 2004.

103. 'LTTE seeks direct aid', *Daily Mirror*, 1 Feb. 2004.
104. 'Sri Lanka leader sacks parliament', BBC News, 8 Feb. 2004.
105. V. Sambandan, 'Moving into election mode', *Frontline* 14–27 Feb. 2004; R. Sirilal, 'Decision dictatorial: UNP', *Daily Mirror*, 9 Feb. 2004.
106. 'LTTE sees grave threat in dissolution but pledges to maintain ceasefire', *Daily Mirror*, 10 Feb. 2004.

6. ELECTIONS AND DEFECTIONS

1. 'Peace talks on broad basis under Alliance: Mahinda', *Daily Mirror*, 17 Feb. 2004. The following night, the interview with Rajapaksa was re-broadcast on Sri Lankan state TV.
2. Formally known as 'The Co-Chairs of the June 2003 Tokyo Conference on Reconstruction and Development of Sri Lanka (USA, EU, Japan and Norway).
3. 'Sri Lanka Donor Co-Chairs Call for Early Return to Peace Talks', 17 Feb. 2004. http://2001–2009.state.gov/r/pa/prs/ps/2004/29522.htm
4. Norwegian MFA internal memo on the Solheim-Balasingham Feb. meeting in London.
5. S. Dias, 'No polling in LTTE-occupied areas', *Daily Mirror*, 1 March 2004.
6. Beyond the fact that the LTTE would be told 'quite openly and frankly' what 'we can offer them—at least a framework', the content of this 'clear strategy' remained unclear. See V. Sambandan, 'We will provide continuity with change: Chandrika', interview with President Kumaratunga in *The Hindu*, reprinted in *Daily Mirror*, 2 March 2004.
7. See, for example, 'If you want continued peace, the choice is simple: G.L.', *Daily Mirror*, 3 March 2003.
8. A perspective supported by the following media commentary: 'The second blunder the green camp is making is the total boycott of state media ... a strategic blunder that will cost the UNF heavily in the forthcoming elections. The UNP has not successfully even designed a PR campaign ... as yet a single poster is [still] to come out on [their] general elections platform.' H.R. Vidanage, 'Sangha politics could generate a new force', *Sunday Times*, 22 Feb. 2004.
9. While stressing that the East would function 'independently', Karuna at least initially held out for the notion of a continued link to the LTTE under the 'direct leadership' of Prabhakaran. See V. Sambandan, 'A rebellion in the east', *Frontline*, 13–26 March 2004.
10. A pseudonym. Karuna's advisor Aaron Danrin was interviewed for this book: portions of the interview appear later in this chapter.
11. After the initial attack, the UNP candidate was taken to hospital for treatment. Early the next morning, LTTE gunmen reportedly entered the hospital unchal-

lenged and gunned him down at close range. See V. Sambandan, 'A rebellion in the east'.

12. By all accounts Karuna had no principled objection to the killings. What seems to have concerned him was the fact that they had been carried out by cadres outside his military control—Pottu Amman's intelligence wing, in other words. Accordingly, Karuna argued that he could not be expected to take responsibility for disciplinary action against LTTE forces that were not directly answerable to him. The extent to which the fact that the victims were Eastern Tamils concerned Karuna is unclear, although at the time some commentators clearly considered it significant. See J. Perera, 'Root causes of LTTE split need to be addressed', *Daily Mirror*, 9 March 2004.

13. K. Noyahr, 'The explosive rift in the LTTE', *Daily Mirror*, 6 March 2004. At the same time there were suggestions that Karuna's nomination as a member of the LTTE negotiating team for the peace talks was a 'calculated move' to 'neutralise the Eastern factor' against any potential move to undermine negotiations—the concern apparently being that 'the East' had undermined peace efforts in the past. See D.B.S. Jeyaraj, 'The Eastern Warlord', *Frontline*, 27 March–9 April 2004.

14. 'LTTE Eastern leader talks tough in interview', *Daily Mirror*, 6 March 2004. It is worth noting here that since the 2002 ceasefire agreement the recruitment of child soldiers was particularly prevalent in the East. Karuna regularly urged every family to 'give one member' to the LTTE. Some reports suggest that the practice went back further to 2001. See University Teachers for Human Rights-Jaffna, Bulletins 26–28 (2001). http://www.uthr.org/Bulletin.htm

15. F. Harrison, 'Interview with breakaway Tamil Tiger', *BBC News*, 10 March 2004.

16. 'Tamil Tigers deny war plan claims', *BBC News*, 10 March 2004.

17. See Sambandan, 'A rebellion in the east', *Frontline*, 13–26 March 2004.

18. Ibid. At the same time there were serious questions regarding both the fighting capacity and ultimate loyalties of many of Karuna's troops. One well-informed analyst suggested that the figure included 2,000 'young and inexperienced' recruits (which most took to mean child soldiers), another 1,000 who had indicated their desire to remain 'neutral' in the LTTE internal struggle, 200 already departed for the Vanni to remain in the LTTE and 500 of the newest and young female recruits who had already been sent home by Karuna. Consequently, only 2,500–3,000 could reasonably be regarded as 'experienced fighter cadre ready, willing and able to fight and die for Karuna'. DBS Jeyaraj, 'Tiger vs. Tiger', *Frontline*, 27 March–9 April 2004.

19. A potentially important but less discussed aspect of the critique was that, like Karikalan whom he appointed to replace Kausalyan as Batticaloa political leader, Karuna's past actions suggested a fundamentally anti-Muslim attitude—something the LTTE was keen not to be seen to condone, still less espouse.

20. S. Perera, 'LTTE plot to kill Karuna?' *Daily Mirror*, 9 March 2004. An effigy of newly appointed LTTE Eastern commander Ramesh was reportedly burned as well, and the following day Karuna supporters organised a *hartal* (strike) in

Tamil-populated districts of Batticaloa and Amparai. US Embassy Colombo, 'Heightened tensions in East', 10 March 2004. Wikileaks Cable 04COLOMBO435.

21. 'Batticaloa peace team to resolve Karuna crisis', *Daily Mirror*, 8 March 2004.

22. See Jeyaraj, 'Tiger vs. Tiger', *Frontline*, 27 March–9 April 2004.

23. As the LTTE had done previously with rival Tamil military organisations in the mid-1980s.

24. See J. Perera, 'Root causes of LTTE split need to be addressed', *Daily Mirror*, 9 March 2004.

25. 'Oslo won't intervene in LTTE crisis', *Daily Mirror*, 11 March 2004.

26. In his obituary for Balasingham, who died in Dec. 2006, D.B.S. Jeyaraj states— without specific dates—that following the 'unforeseen development' of the Karuna revolt, Bala[singham] 'tried hard to patch up the split' since he clearly understood the 'long-term consequences of a N-E divide and an alignment of Karuna with the state'. A 'temporary truce' was agreed and reportedly, Karuna was 'prepared to quit the country'. Balasingham's efforts were supposedly undermined by the 'hard line' adopted by the 'mainstream LTTE', which ultimately had the effect of 'driving' Karuna 'into the arms of the state'. D.B.S. Jeyaraj, 'Bala Annai was the voice of the Tamil Eelam nation', *The Sunday Leader*, 17 Dec. 2006.

27. Taraki in particular was known to be a close acquaintance of Karuna. D.B.S. Jeyaraj, 'The conflicts within', *Frontline*, 27 March–9 April 2004; Taraki, 'Money, power and the rebellion in the LTTE', *Daily Mirror*, 17 March 2004. See also F. Harrison, 'Questions over renegade Tamil Tiger', BBC News, 9 May 2008.

28. See Jeyaraj, 'Tiger vs. Tiger', *Frontline*, 27 March–9 April 2004.

29. Ibid.

30. US Embassy Colombo, 'Norwegian Special Envoy reviews latest', 15 March 2004 detailing the outcomes of Solheim's visit as communicated in two meetings with US Ambassador Jeffrey Lunstead (13, 15 March). Wikileaks Cable 04COLOMBO456. In conclusion the cable states: 'The Norwegians still appear firmly engaged, which is a significant positive. Their mettle is clearly being tested in this confusing, volatile period, however.'

31. P. Rodrigo, 'President ready to welcome long-term solution to country's ethnic conflict', *Daily Mirror*, 24 March 2004.

32. 'LTTE warns of possible war', *Daily Mirror*, 25 March 2004.

33. Figures commonly cited during this period were an increase in LTTE cadre strength from approximately 6,000 in late 2001 to 18–19,000 by early 2004.

34. See, for example, P. Rodrigo, 'The country cannot face another war, says CBK', *Daily Mirror*, 26 March 2004.

35. S. Wijewardana, 'Ranil tells people the UNF only party able to carry forward peace process', *Daily Mirror*, 25 March 2004.

36. F. Harrison, 'Tamil Tigers seek voters' support', BBC News, 31 March 2004.

37. 'Ranil says "a vote for UNF is a vote for peace and development"', *Daily Mirror*, 1 April 2004.

38. The President's own Sri Lanka Freedom Party (SLFP) and the leftist Janatha Vimukthi Peramuna (JVP).

39. V. Sambandan, 'A victory and after', *Frontline*, 10–23 April 2004.

40. Exactly what this 'correct approach' consisted of remained unclear, not least because up until this point, the deep differences between President Kumaratunga and the JVP's approaches to the peace process made it all but impossible for the Alliance to adopt joint policy positions in this area.

41. Commonly translated as the 'National Sinhala Heritage' Party. All its elected candidates at the April 2004 parliamentary elections were monks: their decision to enter politics gave rise to considerable controversy within the Lankan Buddhist community.

42. As a result of their alliance with the SLFP and drawing on the 'national list' component of the electoral system, the JVP got considerably more seats than their actual voter support warranted.

43. J. Perera, 'Learning from the UNP govt's electoral defeat', *Daily Mirror*, 6 April 2004.

44. Taraki Sivaram, 'Tamils see rejection of Ranil as rejection of peace process', *Daily Mirror*, 7 April 2004.

45. Samaraweera, by now foreign minister, was sacked from the government by then President Rajapaksa in Feb. 2007. In Jan. 2015 he returned to the same position in the government formed by President Sirisena

46. Vijaya Kumaratunga, a legendary national film star and singer, was assassinated outside the family house in Colombo in Feb. 1988. The killer later confessed to having acted on the orders of the JVP, at that point in the throes of a bloody armed uprising against the Sri Lankan government.

47. See above.

48. 'Good Friday battle for control of East', *Daily Mirror*, 9 April 2004. At the same time an SLMM spokesperson indicated that a number of LTTE cadres involved in the advance had arrived by sea at Kathiraweli—a clear violation of the 2002 Ceasefire Agreement.

49. 'War ends: Karuna faction disperses', *Daily Mirror*, 13 April 2004. Taraki gives a graphic and well-informed account of the final showdown between the two sides. 'Why Karuna ran: story of showmanship and suckers', *Daily Mirror*, 16 April 2004. It also became apparent that much of Karuna's army consisted of young conscripts who were ill prepared to meet the force that engaged them. According to one report, for example,168 of the 269 cadres involved were 'less than 18 years old'. C.f. 'LTTE hands over 269 cadres to their parents in Batticaloa', *TamilNet*, 13 April 2004

50. D.B.S. Jeyaraj, 'The Fall of Karuna', *Frontline*, 24 April–7 May 2004, It is worth noting that an immediate impact of Karuna's military defeat was that the five TNA MPs recently elected in the Batticaloa-Amparai district on a pro-Karuna ticket indicated that they would be following the official TNA—meaning LTTE— line from now on.

51. Reflecting the new government's self-confidence, in his first media interview Rajapaksa stated boldly: 'We will change the Constitution and bring the president back to parliament', also indicating this would happen within four months.

K. Noyahr & K. Karunaratne, 'Executive Presidency out within 4 months: PM', *Daily Mirror*, 7 April 2004.

52. For a stalwart defence of the PR system, see 'Constitutional reforms', *Daily Mirror*, 16 April 2004.

53. J. Uyangoda, 'After General Elections: the political fire walking', *Daily Mirror*, 9 April 2004.

54. 'Lokubandara Speaker after sensational battle in House', *Daily Mirror*, 23 April 2004.

55. 'President seeks early talks with LTTE', *Daily Mirror*, 8 April 2004.

56. J. Perera, 'The difficulties in fulfilling election-time promises', *Daily Mirror*, 20 April 2004.

57. 'Mahinda pledges to pursue peace', *Daily Mirror*, 7 April 2004.

58. See K. Noyahr & K. Karunaratne, 'Executive Presidency out within 4 months: PM', *Daily Mirror*, 7 April 2004.

59. J. Perera, 'Arresting the slide towards breakdown', *Daily Mirror*, 13 April 2004.

60. Ibid.

61. 'All TNA MPs back Tigers and ISGA'. *Daily Mirror*, 9 April 2004.

62. Taraki, 'Tamils see rejection of Ranil as rejection of peace process', *Daily Mirror*, 7 April 2004.

63. S. Dias & N. Parameswaran, 'SLMM to talk to Govt., LTTE to re-establish contact in the East', *Daily Mirror*, 16 April 2004.

64. 'Tigers to hold regular talks with military'. *Daily Mirror*, 17 April 2004.

65. P. Rodrigo, 'President requests Norway to resume peace talks', *Daily Mirror*, 24 April 2004.

66. 'Immediate yes from Oslo', *Daily Mirror*, 24 April 2004.

67. Sathya, 'Norway role reassessed', *Daily Mirror*, 3 May 2004.

68. Elsewhere, this demand was justified by the LTTE on the grounds that it had been 'unanimously endorsed' by the Tamil-speaking people of the Northeast at the elections; that is as part of the TNA's electoral platform, and as dictated by the LTTE, some hastened to add. 'Moves to jump-start peace talks', *Sunday Times*, 2 May 2004. At the same time, internal Norwegian reports of the meeting with Kumaratunga indicate that she emphasised her 'openness' to negotiations on the basis of the ISGA.

69. 'Oslo pushes ahead despite protest', *Daily Mirror*, 4 May 2004. Also sounding a cautionary note at this stage, Iqbal Athas argued that the early resumption of talks expected by the government was in fact 'highly unlikely'. This he suggested was due not only to the conditions laid down by the LTTE but also the 'lack of a proper approach [to resuming negotiations] by the UPFA government'. 'Peace process bogged down in more questions', *Sunday Times*, 2 May 2004.

70. 'Bala, Petersen in the Vanni soon', *Daily Mirror*, 5 May 2004.

71. 'Pursuing peace sans the Muslim dimension', *Daily Mirror*, 12 May 2004.

72. Internal reports indicate Petersen stressed the importance of Norway serving as the 'sole channel' between the two parties as well as the need for its facilitation efforts to be presented 'more positively' in the Sri Lankan media.

73. Internal Norwegian MFA memo.

74. S. Dias, 'LTTE insists on ISGA first, CBK parallel talks move turned down', *Daily Mirror*, 12 May 2004.

75. Quoted in I. Athas, 'Progress on peace moves amid security concerns', *Sunday Times*, 16 May 2004. Athas' inside sources also produced the revelation that the Norwegians had reportedly conveyed 'certain assurances' to the LTTE regarding the role of the security forces with respect to the activities of Karuna faction cadres. A spate of recent killings, mostly of LTTE cadres and primarily in the East, had given rise to LTTE accusations of Karuna faction responsibility and suspected army complicity. In early June, the SLMM issued a warning that the killings constituted a 'serious threat' to the peace process.

76. See Dias, 'LTTE insists on ISGA first, CBK parallel talks move turned down', *Daily Mirror*, 12 May 2004.

77. 'Solheim back in quest for peace', *Daily Mirror*, 24 May 2004; and internal Norwegian MFA memo on the meeting.

78. S. Jayasiri, 'Monitoring Mission hands over items of evidence to police', *Daily Mirror*, 24 May 2004.

79. 'LTTE insists on ISGA first', *Daily Mirror*, 27 May 2004. Informally, the Norwegians indicated that the two sides remained 'poles apart' on items to be included in the talks agenda. Reportedly, there were also substantial differences on the proposed venue and level of media access to the talks.

80. M. Mustaq, 'No signs of early talks', *Daily Mirror*, 29 May 2004.

81. Co-Chairs Press Statement, 1 June 2004. http://www.mofa.go.jp/region/asia-paci/srilanka/joint0406.html

82. This pattern was exemplified in the case of A. Nadesan, a veteran Tamil journalist gunned down in Batticaloa on 3 July 2004, purportedly by the Karuna faction. See S. Jayasiri, '*Hartal* in North-East over killing of journalist', *Daily Mirror*, 3 June 2004.

83. I. Athas, 'Drifting away from peace?', *Sunday Times*, 4 June 2004.

84. Internal Norwegian MFA memo on the meeting.

85. 'ISGA, CBK may bypass Parliament', *Sunday Times*, 11 June 2004.

86. Sathya, 'Chandrika-TNA talks lead to cautious optimism', *Daily Mirror*, 14 June 2004.

87. 'LTTE accuses President of duplicity', *Daily Mirror*, 14 June 2004.

88. Internal Norwegian MFA memo on their phone discussion.

89. K. Noyahr, 'All eyes on the crisis-hit East', *Daily Mirror*, 19 June 2004.

90. I. Athas, 'Of city bombs and Batti clashes', *Sunday Times*, 20 June 2004.

91. 'Second turning point of peace process within reach', *Daily Mirror*, 22 June 2004.

92. US Embassy Colombo, 'Recent meetings show the way forward for the SL peace process is troubled', 9 June 2004. Wikileaks Cable 04COLOMBO953.

93. As well as being Karuna's lover, according to several sources.

94. 'Karuna stayed with SLA in Colombo—Nilavini', *Daily Mirror/TamilNet*, 23 June 2004.

95. 'UNP MP quits over Karuna link', *Daily Mirror*, 24 June 2004.

96. 'Settle Karuna issue first: L TTE', *Daily Mirror*, 1 July 2004. This is confirmed in a Norwegian MFA memo on Solheim and Brattskar's discussions with Tamilselvan

and senior LTTE members. The memo also reiterated the view that the key
issue remained the prevailing 'lack of trust' between the two sides.

97. I. Athas, 'CID tracks Tiger link in suicide attack', *Sunday Times*, 11 July 2004.
This view was reiterated more forcefully by Tamilselvan in an interview with
a Tamil newspaper. V. Sambandan, 'LTTE hardens stance on talks resumption',
The Hindu, 12 July 2004.

98. S. de Silva, 'Chief of Staff rushed to East', *Daily Mirror*, 5 July 2004.

99. S. de Silva, 'Suspected Karuna hit squad in JHU monk's temple', *Daily Mirror*,
7 July 2004.

100. V. Sambandan 'War clouds on the horizon', *Frontline*, 17–30 July 2004. The
attack was one of a series of LTTE assassination attempts that Devananda has
survived.

101. 'Attempt on Devananda's life fails', *Daily Mirror*, 8 July 2004.

102. V. Sambandan, 'Striking terror, again', *Frontline*, 14–27 Aug. 2004. Iqbal Athas
suggests that the only reason news of the killings became public was because
two undercover army informants who were part of the assassination squad
informed Colombo after the event. An immediate consequence was that the
activities of the Karuna faction were the first item on the agenda for the following day's talks in Kilinochchi between Tamilselvan and Helgesen, who had
arrived in the country the previous day. I. Athas 'Kill, kill, kill: Battle for east
hots up', *Sunday Times*, 1 Aug. 2004.

103. A press conference the 'dissidents' were allegedly to give in Kilinochchi was
later 'postponed indefinitely' by the LTTE. See Sambandan, 'LTTE hardens
stance on talks resumption', *The Hindu*, 12 July 2004.

104. V. Sambandan, 'An apology to Tamils', *Frontline*, 14–27 Aug. 2004.

105. See Sambandan, 'War clouds on the horizon', *Frontline*, 17–30 July 2004. At a
meeting in Kilinochchi on 26 July, Helgesen presented a new text formulated
by Norway as the suggested basis for resuming talks. The text was reportedly
'turned down' by Tamilselvan. The Norwegians left, indicating that the process of producing a 'mutually agreeable text' would continue. Developments
such as this may help to explain the pessimism underlying the overall assessment offered by Helgesen at the end of his visit.

106. http://www.asiantribune.com/

107. I. Athas, 'Angry Karuna attacks govt: Who blundered?', *Sunday Times*, 15. Aug.
2004.

108. I. Athas, 'Norway blame Govt., LTTE as killings continue', *Sunday Times*,
29 Aug. 2004. In Suresh's case, Athas subsequently revealed the cloak-and-dag-
ger story behind his assassination. See 'Suresh's outraged wife reveals LTTE
secrets', *Sunday Times*, 5 Sept. 2004.

109. Ibid.

110. 'LTTE says ISGA proposals not final, open to negotiation', *TamilNet*, 16 Sept.
2004.

111. 'No constructive message from Colombo—Tamilselvan', *TamilNet*, 17 Sept. 2004.

112. 'Eastern situation smoulders on', *Sunday Leader*, 10 Oct. 2004. There were strong
indications that LTTE attacks such as Reggie's murder relied on intelligence

from the 'moles' the Tigers had successfully planted within the Karuna faction.

113. One of two special operations units (along with the commando regiment). Also considered the most secretive—and one of the most deadly—combat units in the Sri Lankan armed forces.

114. 'End violence, stop child recruitment: US tells LTTE', *Sunday Times*, 3 Oct. 2004.

115. 'LTTE says won't budge on ISGA', *Sunday Times*, 10 Oct. 2004. During the visit to Switzerland the LTTE delegation met with Vidar Helgesen in Geneva, during which Helgesen underlined Norwegian concerns that continuing political assassinations represented a growing threat to the peace process. c.f. Norwegian MFA internal memo on the meeting. Reportedly the Swiss foreign minister also indicated that during her talks with the LTTE delegation they had emphasised that the ISGA proposals 'were not set in stone'. Suranimala, 'Alliance battle hots up', *Sunday Leader*, 17 Oct. 2004.

116. The forum for broad-based consultation earlier proposed by the government as a means of making the peace process more inclusive.

117. I. Athas, 'CBK shoots down Rs. 20b. tank deal', *Sunday Times*, 10 Oct. 2004.

118. Norwegian MFA internal memo on the meetings. Helgesen was not part of the meetings as he was in Delhi at this point briefing Indian officials on current developments in Sri Lanka. Two weeks later Helgesen met Richard Armitage, and informed him that the Indians had emphasised their view that any proposed change to the Sri Lankan constitution resulting from talks would have to be 'in accordance with the law'—and would be happy if the US saw fit to take the same position in the external communications.

119. From the context it was clear that Prabhakaran specifically had the JVP in mind when inserting this proviso.

120. 'Norwegians return empty-handed', *Sunday Times*, 14 Nov. 2004.

121. Ibid.

122. 'President complains of Norway's pressure', *Sunday Times*, 21 Nov. 2004. Her complaint was reflected in a parliamentary statement made by Information Minister Mangala Samaraweera during the same week, emphasising the Norwegians' role as a facilitator, not a mediator or arbitrator. 'The facilitator', it concluded, 'has no judgemental role to play in the process of negotiations'.

123. All quotations from the official version of the speech carried on *TamilNet*. 'Tamil Tigers will launch freedom struggle if peace talks are further delayed—LTTE leader', *TamilNet*, 27 Nov. 2004.

124. I. Athas, 'Raw intelligence sparks bogeys and canards', *Sunday Times*, 8 Dec. 2004.

125. US Embassy Colombo, 'Norwegians concerned by JVP orchestrated campaign against them', 29 Nov. 2004. Wikileaks Cable 04COLOMBO1919. In mid-Dec. 2004, the Colombo ambassadors of three out of the four members of the Co-Chairs consortium (USA, the EU and Japan) issued a press release expressing their concern over 'JVP-led actions' against the peace process in general and the Norwegians as facilitators in particular. 'Address the JVP problem—Tokyo co-chairs urge President', *TamilNet*, 15 Dec. 2004.

NOTES

126. Internal Norwegian MFA memo on the meeting.
127. 'GoSL entirely responsible for resuming talks—LTTE', *TamilNet*, 15 Dec. 2004.
128. I. Athas, 'No war, no peace—for how long?', *Sunday Times*, 19 Dec. 2004.
129. 'LTTE leadership studies fresh government agenda for talks', *TamilNet*, 21 Dec. 2004. As an indication of the almost complete lack of trust between the two sides at this point, Balasingham pointed out to Solheim that the proposal came 'not from the government or even from the president, but simply Dhanapala'. He also noted that it spoke of 'an interim arrangement' as opposed to the LTTE ISGA proposal specifically—doubtless a tactical ruse to get the government's counter-proposal on the table, he argued. Finally, Balasingham 'viewed with suspicion' the complete absence of reference to 'core issues', considering this 'yet another tactical ploy' to try and bring them up once talks resumed. A. Perera, *Sunday Leader*, 26 Dec. 2004.
130. 'LTTE calls for clear, well defined agenda for talks', *TamilNet*, 24 Dec. 2004.
131. 'The stalemate in Sri Lanka', *Frontline*, 18–31 Dec. 2004.

7. THE TSUNAMI AND AFTER

1. 'CBK invites Tamilselvan to join task force', *Daily Mirror*, 1 Jan. 2005. Not long after, the LTTE reportedly declined the invitation.
2. 'Annan's visit to LTTE areas blocked', *Sunday Times*, 9 Jan. 2005.
3. 'LTTE attacks Govt. on Annan visit and aid flow', *Daily Mirror*, 12 Jan. 2005.
4. J. Perera, 'LTTE must work jointly to rebuild', *Daily Mirror*, 4 Jan. 2005.
5. 'LTTE puts politics on hold', *Sunday Times*, 23 Jan. 2005.
6. 'Joint body for tsunami aid', *Daily Mirror*, 25 Jan. 2005.
7. An indication of this is provided by media reports that news of the proposed joint mechanism prompted Kumaratunga's JVP government coalition partners to decide to withdraw from the alliance—a decision they reportedly drew back from only at the last minute. 'Jan. 26: The day the JVP nearly quit', *Sunday Times*, 30 Jan. 2005.
8. Final Statement, Co-Chairs Meeting, Brussels, 25 Jan. 2005. http://www.mofa.go.jp/region/asia-paci/srilanka/press0501.html
9. D.B.S. Jeyaraj, 'Tigers playing for high post-tsunami stakes', *Sunday Leader*, 30 Jan. 2005.
10. See Jeyaraj, 'Tigers playing for high post-tsunami stakes'.
11. 'For equitable allocation of funds', interview with V. Samabandan, *Frontline*, 12–25 Feb. 2005.
12. 'A month after tsunami: opportunities and dangers ahead', *Daily Mirror*, 1 Feb. 2005.
13. See T. Deen, 'Clinton's job: tsunami chief, peacemaker or secretary general?', *Sunday Times*, 6 Feb. 2005. 'Whatever happened to the Norwegians?' wondered Deen—the paper's UN correspondent—in this context.
14. S. Jayasiri, 'Kaushalyan shot dead', *Daily Mirror*, 8 Feb. 2005. A TNA MP was among those killed in the early evening ambush.

15. V. Sambandan, 'Setback for Tigers', *Frontline*, 26 Feb.-11 March 2005. Needless to say, Annan's statement was roundly condemned by Sinhala nationalist forces.
16. As Solheim observes, 'throughout the war there were very few "freelancers". Virtually all killings were orchestrated by either the LTTE or Sri Lankan state forces.'
17. In a sign of their anger over Kaushalyan's killing, the LTTE leadership refused to schedule a meeting with Akashi to discuss their proposals for the tsunami relief joint mechanism.
18. S. Dias, 'Solheim hopeful after talks', *Daily Mirror*, 23 Feb. 2005.
19. Suranimala, 'A government at breaking point', *Sunday Leader*, 27 Feb. 2005
20. S. Wijewardena & G. De Chickera, 'UPFA Govt. on brink of split', *Daily Mirror*, 25 Feb. 2005. Following his return from Sri Lanka, Solheim held talks with Anton Balasingham in London. As well as briefing him on the state of discussions on the joint mechanism, Solheim also communicated government concerns over intelligence reports that the LTTE had recently completed building an airstrip close to Kilinochchi and also acquired at least one Czech-built light aircraft. I. Athas, 'Govt. losing control of east', *Sunday Times*, 13 March 2005.
21. Norwegian MFA internal memo. Reportedly, the LTTE informed the Norwegians that the LTTE leader was currently 'unwell' the same evening, and thus unable to receive a visit from the EU Commissioner.
22. The denials included one from Brigadier Herath, responsible for the area close to Batticaloa where the LTTE Commander had been ambushed. C. Kalamendran & A. Fuard, 'Killings yes, but no Karuna camps', *Sunday Times*, 10 April 2005.
23. 'Now Karuna group collecting taxes from Sinhalese', *Sunday Times*, 17 April 2005.
24. Norwegian MFA internal memo.
25. I. Athas, 'Grim Choice for President: Aid of UPFA?', *Sunday Times*, 24 April 2005.
26. S. Jayasiri, 'Int'l community to be made aware of LTTE killings and atrocities', *Daily Mirror*, 18 April 2005.
27. A reference to reports that President Kumaratunga was planning to hold a referendum during the autumn linked to her determined attempt to retain power beyond the expiry of her second term of office in Dec. 2005.
28. 'Can the Govt. shirk red tape to become a responsible state?', *Daily Mirror*, 16 Feb. 2005.
29. K. Noyahr, 'US tells Govt. to speak with one voice', *Daily Mirror*, 20 April 2005.
30. E. Bird, 'Joint mechanism a dead duck: Hakeem', *Daily Mirror*, 21 April 2005.
31. K. Bandara, 'Muslims want separate body for reconstruction work', *Daily Mirror*, 21 April 2005.
32. Quotations from a number of his columns are featured in this book, including in the present chapter.
33. V.Sambandan, 'The end of a dissenter', *Frontline*, 21 May–5 June 2005.
34. 'Did Karuna personally kill Taraki?', *Sunday Leader*, 8 May 2005. Jeyaraj also states that according to 'knowledgeable Eastern Tamil sources', Karuna had earlier called Taraki his mortal enemy and made a vow that he would kill him *endai kaiyaale* (by my own hand). The case has never been officially resolved. For a

fuller account of the background to Taraki's murder and his own complex rela-
tionship to the Tamil nationalist cause, see UTHR-Jaffna, Special Report No. 19,
'The Curse of Impunity Part II: Defiance, Hope and Betrayal—The Times of
Sivaram', 9. Sept. 2005. http://uthr.org/SpecialReports/spreport19ptII.htm

35. N. Cassim & L.B. Senanratne, '3 million dollar bumper package for Lanka', *Daily
Mirror*, 18 May 2005.

36. P. Rodrigo & L.B. Senanratne, 'JHU monk interrupts forum, slams LTTE', *Daily
Mirror*, 17 May 2005.

37. Internal Norwegian MFA memo on the meeting. In other Norwegian meetings
with Sri Lankan officials at this stage, the message communicated was somewhat stronger, suggesting that the Indians were inclined towards opposing the
whole idea of entering into a formal agreement with the LTTE.

38. 'JVP redder than red with rage', *Sunday Times*, 22 May 2005.

39. Quoted in 'Deception by Govt—LTTE', *Sunday Times*, 29 May 2005. Solheim also
recalls that by this stage the LTTE leadership was coming under 'increasing
pressure' over the continued 'lack of progress with finalising the P-TOMS'.

40. Post-Tsunami Operational Management Structure.

41. It is also worth noting that an opinion poll conducted by the Presidential
Secretariat in late May indicated that over 60 per cent of the population were
opposed to the P-TOMS, with only 22 per cent in favour and 17 per cent with
no particular view to offer on the question. 'Presidential survey shows over 60
percent against JM', *Sunday Times*, 12 June 2005.

42. V. Sambandan, 'A parting of ways', *Frontline*, 2–15 July 2005.

43. R. Ladduwahetty, 'P-TOMS deal finalised, Helgesen tells angry Hakeem', *Daily
Mirror*, 21 June 2005.

44. Norwegian MFA internal memos on the meetings.

45. 'No breakthrough in tsunami aid deal', *Daily Mirror*, 23 June 2005.

46. The final text of the P-TOMS agreement can be found in a number of places
including Gooneratne, *Negotiating With The Tigers (LTTE) 2002–2005*, Colombo:
Lake House, 2007, pp. 135–139; S.I. Keethaponcalan (ed.), *Conflict and Peace in
Sri Lanka: Major Documents*, Chennai: Kumaran, 2009, pp. 461–472; and *TamilNet*,
'GoSL, LTTE sign P-TOMS', 24 June 2005.

47. V. Sambandan, 'A deal for co-operation', *Frontline*, 2–15 July 2005.

48. 'Multiple achievements possible through joint mechanism', *Daily Mirror*, 21 June
2005.

49. Norwegian MFA internal memo on the meeting, 30 June 2005.

50. The clauses in question related to the proposed location of one of the regional
P-TOMS committees, in LTTE-controlled Kilinochchi, as well as the funding
process for relief activities under the joint mechanism. See S. Selvanayagam,
'Supreme Court blocks P-TOMS deal', *Daily Mirror*, 15 June 2005.

51. 'Colombo's political drama shatters hopes for peace—LTTE', *TamilNet*, 18 July
2005, quoted in V. Sambandan, 'A mechanism restrained', *Frontline*, 30 July—
12 Aug. 2005.

52. 'JM has provisions to check Tiger dominance', *Sunday Leader*, 12 June 2005.

53. 'Stop killings immediately, Co-chairs tell govt. and LTTE', *Daily Mirror*, 20 July 2005. *TamilNet* also carried the full text of the statement.
54. Media Minister Mangala Samaraweera and Finance Minister Sarath Amunugama.
55. Nirupama Rao, later Indian Foreign Secretary, first female ambassador to China and most recently Indian Ambassador to the United States.
56. The conservative Baratiya Janata Party (BJP), India's second largest political party.
57. 'Oslo acts to defuse tension', *Sunday Times*, 24 July 2005.
58. Norwegian MFA internal memo on the meeting.
59. 'LTTE rejects Govt. proposal to renegotiate truce pact', *Daily Mirror*, 28 July 2004; 'LTTE: "no need to renegotiate ceasefire"', *TamilNet*, 27 July 2005. The four areas of treaty non-compliance outlined by Balasingham were: (1) removal of the armed forces from populated Tamil areas; (2) disarming of Tamil paramilitaries working in collaboration with the army; (3) ensuring the security of unarmed LTTE political cadres working in government-controlled areas in the Northeast; and (4) provision of adequate military security for LTTE cadres moving between LTTE- and government-controlled areas.
60. Norwegian MFA internal memo on the meeting.
61. 'LTTE wants ceasefire agreement unchanged', *Sunday Times*, 6 Aug. 2005.

8. ASSASSINATIONS AND ELECTIONS

1. V. Sambandan, 'Assassination and after', *Frontline*, 27 Aug.–8 Sept. 2005.
2. Reportedly, the police also found six packs of 40mm grenades and a grenade launcher in the back garden, and the following morning, the sniper rifle in a bush near the house. 'How the sniper carried out the assassination', *The Sunday Leader*, 14 Aug. 2005.
3. Standout criticisms included: reports that the police had received intelligence reports of an imminent potential attack on Kadirgamar 72 hours beforehand, which they had failed to act on; questions about how the assassins had managed to enter a house located so close to the foreign minister's and remain there seemingly completely undetected for several days; and puzzlement as to how the assassins had managed to escape undetected following the shooting. See 'Security lapses led to Kadirgamar's murder', *The Sunday Leader*, 14 Aug. 2005.
4. Quoted in Sambandan, 'Assassination and after'.
5. As one media report opined at the time, 'According to the police the assassination had all the hallmarks of a well-planned and precisely executed LTTE operation'. See Sambandan, 'Assassination and after'.
6. US Embassy Colombo, 'Helgesen briefs Co-Chairs on Norwegian Intentions in the wake of Kadirgamar's assassination', 16 Aug. 2005. Wikileaks Cable 05COLOMBO1440.
7. See Wikileaks Cable, 'Helgesen briefs Co-Chairs on Norwegian Intentions in the wake of Kadirgamar's assassination'.
8. Norwegian MFA internal memo on the meeting with Balasingham.
9. For the text of Petersen's letter to Prabhakaran, see US Embassy Colombo,

'Norwegian facilitators send letter to LTTE leader Prabhakaran via London: GSL asks EU to list LTTE as terrorist organisation', 18 Aug. 2005. Wikileaks Cable 05COLOMBO1453.

10. Norwegian MFA internal memo.

11. Reportedly LTTE Peace Secretariat Chief Pulidevan called Norwegian Ambassador Hans Brattskar late on the evening of 18 Aug. to inform him that the LTTE had decided to meet the government to 'improve implementation of the CFA'. US Embassy Colombo Cable, 'LTTE agrees to meet with government', 19 Aug. 2005. Wikileaks Cable 05COLOMBO1460.

12. At this point Solheim had taken six weeks leave of absence from his role as Sri Lanka Special Envoy to assist his party in canvassing for the upcoming Norwegian parliamentary elections.

13. For a fuller discussion of this issue see pp. 241–246 below.

14. As one commentator puts it, 'To a large extent, this issue had been overtaken by other important matters such as the stalled peace talks and the post-tsunami reconstruction activities.' See V. Sambandan, 'Ending a controversy', *Frontline*, 10–23 Sept. 2005

15. In 1999 as opposed to 2000, having first been elected president in 1994.

16. See Sambandan, 'Ending a controversy'.

17. Not least between Rajapaksa and Kumaratunga. The president's suspicions about Rajapaksa's intentions, in particular with respect to the peace process, were heightened by the pacts with the JVP and JHU. Following the agreement with the JVP, Kumaratunga fired off a letter to Rajapaksa—sections of which were leaked to the media—strongly criticising him for the move. She stated, 'Our government has agreed that devolution of power is the solution to establish peace without dividing the country. There is no solution which has been reached in the world as suggested in your agreement where any devolution of power could be implemented based on a unitary state structure.' R. Abeynayake, 'Mahinda delays his response to CBK', *Sunday Times*, 11 Sept. 2005. A few days later, Rajapaksa reportedly told his supporters that his real battle in the election campaign was with Kumaratunga, not Wickremasinghe. 'CBK—Mahinda in battle of the blues', *Sunday Times*, 11 Sept. 2005.

18. It is also worth pointing out that in effect it amounted to reneging on the agreement between the government and LTTE to explore a solution 'based on a federal model' reached during the Oslo peace talks held in Dec. 2002.

19. Interestingly a cable from later the same month reports that at a meeting with the UNP's G.L. Peiris, the former leader of the government peace negotiations team argued that 'on economic issues, peace and foreign facilitators', publicly Rajapaksa would say 'whatever it takes to get elected'. Peiris went on to suggest that during the run up to the presidential nominations deadline (7 Oct.), the SLFP would need to be 'especially strident' in order to stop the JVP from 'running its own candidate' and thereby 'spoiling' Rajapaksa's chances of winning the election. US Embassy Colombo, 'SLFP Alliance with JVP may polarise election along ethnic lines', 21 Sept. 2005. Wikileaks Cable 05COLOMBO1672.

20. US Embassy Colombo, 'Prime Minister Rajapaksa assures Ambassador electoral

pact with JVP 'just words', commitment to peace process not in question', 12 Sept. 2005. Wikileaks Cable 05COLOMBO1605.

21. By law Norwegian parliamentary elections are held on the second Monday of the ninth month (Sept.) every fourth year.

22. The Labour, Socialist Left and Centre parties.

23. 'Statement of the Sri Lanka Co-Chairs', 19 Sept. 2005. www.regjeringen.no/en/archive/Bondeviks-2nd-Government/ministry-of-foreign-affairs

24. B. Jayasekara, 'EU imposes immediate travel ban on LTTE', *The Island*, 28 Sept. 2005.

25. 'Thamilchelvan urges EU to reconsider stand on LTTE', *TamilNet*, 28 Sept. 2005; 'LTTE shift after EU ban?' *Sunday Times*, 2 Oct. 2005.

26. 'Norwegian Ambassador meets LTTE Political Head', *TamilNet*, 6 Oct. 2005.

27. 'President's efforts come a cropper', 'Isolated CBK losing battle with Mahinda', *Sunday Times*, 2 Oct. 2005.

28. 'An Undivided Country, Consensus of the Majority and Peace with Dignity', [A summary of Rajapaksa's election manifesto], *Sunday Times*, 16 Oct. 2005.

29. 'Thousands attend Jaffna Pongu Thamil rally, seek Army withdrawal', *TamilNet*, 30 Sept. 2005.

30. Political party-cum-trade union originally founded in 1939 to represent and protect the interests of Tamil plantation workers of Indian origin.

31. A smaller, more radical party with pronounced LTTE sympathies also representing Indian Tamil plantation workers.

32. N. Nonis, 'For unity and prosperity, vote for me, says UNP leader', *Sunday Times*, 9 Oct. 2005.

33. D. Handunnetti, 'The journey back to 1956', *The Sunday Leader*, 2 Oct. 2005.

34. D.B.S. Jeyaraj, 'Principal for principal as shadow war moves to Jaffna', *The Sunday Leader*, 16 Oct. 2005. Jeyaraj also alleges that the EPDP may have been behind the first assassination, which was followed less than twenty-four hours later by the LTTE's murderous, tit-for-tat response. Interestingly, in a subsequent analysis of the killings Jeyaraj suggests that in killing the Central College Principal Kanapathy Rajadurai the LTTE had stirred up a potential hornet's nest for itself, as his murder was perceived as a direct attack on the Dalit caste to which both he and many Jaffna Tamils belonged. D.B.S. Jeyaraj, 'Tigers face community wrath over Rajadurai', *The Sunday Leader*, 23 Oct. 2005.

35. A reference to the select group of families that ever since independence had, until Mahinda Rajapaksa's advent, enjoyed unbroken rule over the country—a dynastic pattern that Sri Lanka shared in common with many of her South Asian neighbours. In Sri Lanka 'the families' refers specifically to three dynasties: the Senanayakes, comprising the country's first two post-independence Prime Ministers, D.S Senanayake and Sir John Kotelawala; the Bandaranaikes, of whom Chandrika Kumaratunga and her mother, onetime Prime Minister Srimavo Bandaranaike are politically speaking the most prominent members; and the Jayawardenes, whose ranks include former Prime Minister J.R. Jayawardene and the current incumbent, J.R.'s nephew Ranil Wickremasinghe.

36. The fact that this image is somewhat out of step with the reality of his relatively

privileged upbringing, in particular an English-language education, never appears to have caused Rajapaksa any significant political problems.

37. This section draws substantially on the report of diplomatic debriefing sessions with both men in Colombo in US Embassy Colombo, 'Envoys make little progress on Human Rights and CFA', 21 Oct. 2005. Wikileaks Cable 05COLOMBO1837.

38. A view indirectly supported, it should be noted, by Rajapaksa's comments on the subject to Vidar Helgesen after Kadirgamar's funeral. See pp. 246–251 below. In addition, during the election campaign itself Wickremasinghe noted on several occasions that only two years previously, Rajapaksa had argued publicly that an Indian-style federal system offered a potential solution to the ethnic conflict. Here, as on the issue of the CFA, which he had also previously supported but now criticised, the UNP leader claimed that Rajapaksa had changed position simply to placate the JVP. S.M. Silva, 'Mahinda dancing to JVP tune: Ranil', *Sunday Times*, 30 Oct. 2005.

39. US Embassy Colombo, 'Implications of election for US policy on peace process', 9 Nov. 2005. Wikileaks Cable 05COLOMBO1929.

40. 'Tigers remain non-committal', *The Sunday Leader*, 23 Oct. 2005. Daya Master's position was echoed some days later by LTTE Jaffna district head Ilampartithi, who stated that the Tigers had not taken a decision regarding the presidential elections and would 'not be exert[ing] any pressure over this issue'. 'Voting decision rests with the Tamil people—Ilamparithi', *TamilNet*, 4 Nov. 2005. '

41. 'LTTE disclaims poll-boycott call', *Sunday Times* 30 Oct. 2005.

42. 'Which way the vital Wanni vote?' *Sunday Times*, 6 Nov. 2005.

43. 'Will they won't they and the LTTE's role', *Sunday Times*, 6 Nov. 2005.

44. 'All go says G.A.', *Sunday Times*, 6 Nov. 2005.

45. Suranimala, 'Brutuses and the move towards UNP-SLFP consensus on peace', *The Sunday Leader*, 30 Oct. 2005.

46. Ibid.

47. 'CBK-Ranil in crucial meeting today', *Sunday Times*, 23 Oct. 2005.

48. See Suranimala, 'Brutuses and the move towards UNP-SLFP consensus on peace'.

49. Suranimala, 'PM's budget debate and the LTTE's electoral dilemma', *The Sunday Leader*, 13 Nov. 2005.

50. Ibid.

51. The same report notes that, uniquely, on this occasion there was no official LTTE statement or comment on the discussions with TNA MPs.

52. 'Nation in confusion over Tiger stance', *Sunday Times*, 13 Nov. 2005.

53. 'LTTE-TNA conference concludes: "Tamil people have no interest in SL Presidential elections"', *TamilNet*, 10 Nov. 2005.

54. D.B.S. Jeyaraj, 'Why the Tamils must vote', *The Sunday Leader*, 13 Nov. 2005. In another article published the same day, 'Why is the LTTE disappointed with Wickremasinghe?', Jeyaraj attempted to explain Tiger disenchantment with the UNP leader and hence—it could reasonably have been assumed—the reasons for their stance on the presidential election. While understandable in the circumstances, this approach ignored other critical factors that may have been at play—see below.

55. 'Why should LTTE back Mahinda?', *Sunday Times*, 13 Nov. 2005.
56. 'We trapped and split LTTE, sank their ships, says UNP', *LankaNewspapers*, 12. Nov. 2005.
57. See 'Nation in confusion over Tiger stance', *Sunday Times*, 13 Nov. 2005.
58. Evidence of LTTE intimidation of prospective voters was most pronounced in Jaffna itself, with reports of Tiger cadres conducting door-to-door visits the night before the election warning Tamils not to vote and—on polling day itself— complaints from local election monitors that the LTTE were conducting surveillance operations on all polling stations in order to intimidate would-be voters. See US Embassy Colombo, 'Polling peaceful; Tiger intimidation keeps numbers down in North and East', 17 Nov. 2005. Wikileaks Cable 05COLOMBO1971.
59. D.B.S. Jeyaraj, 'Tigers disenfranchise NE Tamils', *The Sunday Leader*, 20 Nov. 2005.
60. S. Samarasinghe, 'Challenges before Mahinda', *The Sunday Leader*, 20 Nov. 2005. A common estimate is that a 40 per cent voter turnout in the Northeast as a whole, a little above the actual figure for Batticaloa, would almost certainly have changed the election result.
61. See Jeyaraj, 'Tigers disenfranchise NE Tamils'.
62. Ibid.
63. D.B.S. Jeyaraj provided another even more incisive version of the same analysis as that found in US Embassy Colombo, 'Polling peaceful'. 'A hard-line government in Colombo was seen [by the LTTE] as more conducive to an outbreak of war. It was felt that international opinion would be firmly opposed to such a regime. This in turn was expected to be beneficial to the LTTE.' See Jeyaraj, 'Tigers disenfranchise NE Tamils'.
64. See Jeyaraj 'Tigers disenfranchise NE Tamils'.
65. See 'Nation in confusion over Tiger stance', *Sunday Times*, 13 Nov. 2005.
66. As former Chairman of the national Airport and Aviation Services, Alles had had plenty of opportunities to interact with LTTE leaders such as Tamilselvan when they passed through Colombo airport en route to rounds of peace talks, international visits and so on. In this context there were also suggestions that he had previously been used by President Kumaratunga to pass messages to and from the LTTE. 'Govt-LTTE go-between to head tsunami rehab body', *Sunday Times*, 27 Nov. 2005.
67. According to one report, Rajapaksa's words to Alles were simply 'You made it possible'. 'Meet Tiran Alles', *The Nation*, 11 March 2007.
68. All quotations in the preceding paragraphs are from D.B.S. Jeyaraj, 'Did LTTE have secret deal with Mahinda to enforce boycott?', *TamilWeek*, 27 Nov.–3 Dec. 2005.
69. The real reason for his arrest, according to Samaraweera at least, being *Maudima*, a newspaper financed by Alles, which had become increasingly critical of the president in recent months. See U. Kurukulasuriya, 'Rajapaksa-Tiger deal on Wikileaks and political analysis', *Colombo Telegraph*, 7 April 2012.
70. P. Dissanayake, 'Ranil queries why Tiran's co-partners in "deal with LTTE" not

arrested', *The Island*, 6 June 2007. Already in Feb. Wickremasinghe was publicly accusing Rajapaksa of having a secret deal with the Tigers in advance of the 2005 presidential election. 'Mahinda 'in pact' with LTTE', BBC Sinhala Service, 27 Feb. 2007.

71. US Embassy Colombo, 'Opposition leader calls for arrest of President's brother, Chief of Staff, and Treasury Secretary', 14 June 2007, Wikileaks Cable 07COLOMBO844. Following his Feb. arrest, Alles had reportedly placed a DVD copy of a film of at least one of the secret meetings in a secure location. On the same day he was released on bail (13 June), Alles' house was reportedly ransacked and the DVD stolen. See Kurukulasuriya, 'Rajapaksa-Tiger deal on Wikileaks and political analysis', *Colombo Telegraph*, 7 April 2012.

72. S. Samarasinghe, 'President's Tiger Deal Exposed, *The Sunday Leader*, 6 July 2007, reproduced in *Lanka eNews*, 10 July 2007.

73. The journalist in question was Sonali Somarasinghe, who married *Sunday Leader* Editor Lasantha Wickrematunga in 2009, shortly before he was assassinated. Following threats to her life, Somarasinghe fled the country to the USA and has not returned since.

74. S. Samarasinghe, 'Payment vouchers to Tiger companies for vote swindle surface', *The Sunday Leader*, 23 Sept. 2007.

75. Ibid.

76. 'Motion to appoint PSC to probe deals with LTTE passed', *The Island*, 21 Sept. 2007.

77. 'Mahinda gave Rs. 180 million to the LTTE through Basil, charges Tiran Alles', *TransCurrents*, 24 Jan. 2010.

78. G.H. Peiris provides a good example of this lack of attention to, less still critical analysis of, the evidence for an alleged electoral deal with the LTTE. After considering various theories regarding the LTTE's motivations for effectively ensuring Rajapaksa's victory in the presidential polls, Peiris concludes with a brief consideration of what he calls 'by far the most bizarre explanation' of the 'financial deal' allegation. Describing it as an accusation 'hawked by Wickremasinghe' in the aftermath of his defeat at the presidential polls, Peiris's summary conclusion is that the allegation 'carries the hallmark of churlishness impelled by the sheer frustration of ... the collapse of the grand strategy upon which Wickremasinghe had placed all his political hopes.' In other words, a wild claim lobbed at a victor by an enraged loser in the perennial bear-pit of Sri Lankan electoral politics. G.H. Peiris, *Twilight of the Tigers*, New Delhi: Oxford University Press, 2009, p. 210.

79. Reporting on an early Dec. meeting with Samaraweera, US Ambassador Jeffrey Lunstead noted that the new foreign minister came across as 'well-disposed to the U.S. and eager to work closely with us' as well as 'focused' on the peace process. 'Foreign Minister eager to maintain US ties, focused on peace process'. US Embassy Colombo Cable, 6 Dec. 2005. 05COLOMBO2042.

80. V. Sambandan, 'I am willing to hold direct talks with LTTE, says Rajapaksa', *The Hindu*, 20 Nov 2005.

81. 'Tiger Leader's Annual message gives new govt limited time for settlement', US Embassy Colombo Cable, 28 Nov 2005. 05COLOMBO2008.
82. D.B.S. Jeyaraj 'Tigers give Rajapaksa breathing space', *The Sunday Leader*, 27 Nov. 2005.
83. Quoted in Suranimala, 'President and LTTE get set to talk while preparing for war', *The Sunday Leader*, 4 Dec. 2005. Balasingham's speech was delivered in London.
84. US Embassy Colombo, 'Body count mounts in the North and East', 5 Dec. 2005. Wikileaks Cable 05COLOMBO2040.
85. Suranimala, 'President's final solution and the return to war, *The Sunday Leader*, 11 Dec. 2005. Others included the fact that Rajapaksa's government should aim at a solution to the conflict based on a 'united Sri Lanka as opposed to a unitary state'. Ibid.
86. 'Norway wants character certificate to continue as facilitator', *The Sunday Leader*, 4 Dec. 2004.
87. See Sambandan, 'I am willing to hold direct talks with LTTE, says Rajapaksa'.
88. Suranimala, 'President looks to UNP support as Norway makes govt. eat humble pie', *The Sunday Leader*, 18 Dec. 2005.
89. See 'Norway wants character certificate to continue as facilitator', *The Sunday Leader*, 4 Dec. 2004. In a sign of the level of political controversy involved here, other media reports of the talks in Hong Kong provided a more sympathetic interpretation of their outcome from the Sri Lankan government's perspective. See, for example, D. Samaranayake, 'Confusion over Oslo's conditions—Lanka wants Solheim sidelined', *Sunday Times*, 18 Dec. 2005.
90. Co-Chair Meeting—Final Statement Brussels, http://slembassyusa.org/embassy_press_releases/co-chair-meeting-final-statement-brussels/
91. 'LTTE rejects Asian venues, insists on Europe', *Sunday Times*, 18 Dec. 2005.
92. 'LTTE stands firm. Talks in Oslo or no talks', *The Sunday Leader*, 25 Dec. 2005.
93. US Embassy Colombo, 'Steady attacks pressure govt. while emergency regulations are renewed', 22 Dec. 2005. Wikileaks Cable 05COLOMBO2149.
94. 'Tigers ambush patrol off Mannar', *The Island*, 23 Dec. 2005.
95. US Embassy Colombo, 'Govt. asks Co-Chairs for action as violence escalates: Tigers stiff Co-Chair reps', 28 Dec. 2005. Wikileaks Cable 05COLOMBO2158.
96. Ibid.
97. Reportedly the 71-year-old Tamil MP was shot nine times as he returned from receiving communion. Both his wife and seven other churchgoers standing close to him at the time of the attack were injured before the two gunmen fled the scene. US Embassy Colombo, 'Murder in the Cathedral: Assassination of pro-Tiger MP in the East followed by mine attack on Army convoy in the North', 27 Dec. 2005. Wikileaks Cable 05COLOMBO2157.
98. Although officially the issue of responsibility for Pararajasingham's murder remained as cloudy as was generally the case with such assassinations, there was plenty of circumstantial evidence to suggest that in this instance, in all probability it was the work of local Karuna cadres aided and abetted by the security forces. A detailed statement issued in late 2006 by the Inter-Parliamentary Union

(IPU) noted that St Mary's, the church in which the Tamil MP had been gunned down, was located inside a High Security Zone, between two military checkpoints. At the time of the murder, moreover, the church was reportedly 'surrounded' by military personnel—inviting the obvious conclusion that the only way the perpetrators could only have escaped was with assistance from the security forces. The IPU statement also noted that the fact that one of the assassins was a member of the Karuna Group was 'public knowledge': nevertheless no action had been taken on the matter. See IPU, 'CASE No. SRI/49—JOSEPH PARARAJASINGHAM'. A UTHR-J Special Report Supplement, 'Before Time Obscures the Moul'dring Heap', 13 Dec. 2006 provides further circumstantial detail on this and other assassinations of Tamil politicians and leaders during the same period.

9. EELAM WAR IV: BEGINNINGS

1. US Embassy Colombo, 'Is Sri Lanka going back to war—and what we can do about it', 3 Jan. 2006. Wikileaks Cable 06COLOMBO4.
2. Ibid.
3. A claim later supported by the district SLMM Head, it should be noted.
4. 'Tiger Suicide attack on Navy draft kills 12', *Sunday Times*, 8 Jan. 2006.
5. In fact, the suggestion of Geneva as a venue originally came from the Norwegians. Additionally, and somewhat surprisingly, during Solheim's discussions with Rajapaksa the Sri Lankan president indicated that he would not be opposed to a second round of talks being held in Oslo. Suranimala, 'How LTTE trapped UPFA into CFA', *The Sunday Leader*, 29 Jan. 2006.
6. According to US Ambassador Jeffrey. Lunstead, following his return to Colombo Solheim noted that the LTTE leader had indicated his agreement with Geneva as venue for talks 'almost before [Solheim] had opened his mouth in Kilinochchi'. Solheim had further been told that the Tigers had agreed to Geneva first, in order to 'help out Norway', and second to demonstrate to the international community that the LTTE were 'serious about peace'. Glossing this explanation, Solheim suggested that key factors underpinning the acceptance of Geneva as a venue were the existence of a 10,000-strong Tamil expatriate community in the Geneva area, and its proximity to London, allowing an increasingly and visibly fragile Balasingham to travel there easily. US Embassy Colombo, 'Solheim on CFA talks', 26 Jan. 2006. Wikileaks Cable 06COLOMBO152.
7. 'Solheim: sinner becomes saint', *Sunday Times*, 29 Jan. 2006.
8. Suranimala, 'Govt. peace team gets tuition as SLFP and JVP part ways', *The Sunday Leader*, 12 Feb. 2006.
9. This was reportedly the thrust of the argument presented to US Ambassador Jeffrey Lunstead by Chief Negotiator De Silva in advance of the Geneva talks. The 'Karuna faction of the LTTE' did not fall under the CFA section (1.8) dealing with 'paramilitaries', he contended, also pointing to the fact that when Karuna first broke away from the LTTE in March 2004, the Tigers had described it as an 'internal matter' not requiring any government intervention. In reply, Lunstead

suggested that, legal formalities aside, the government nonetheless had an obligation to maintain law and order 'regardless of who the perpetrators of violence might be'. Reportedly De Silva 'took the point'. US Embassy Colombo, 'Govt. in serious preparations for CFA talks', 9 Feb. 2006. Wikileaks Cable 06COLOMBO213.

10. By Ranil Wickremasinghe rather than Chandrika Kumaratunga.

11. See Suranimala, 'Govt. peace team gets tuition as SLFP and JVP part ways', *The Sunday Leader*, 12 Feb. 2006.

12. 'Sri Lankan Government's opening statement at Geneva', *TamilNet*, 23. Feb. 2006.

13. From Balasingham's opening statement at the talks. See 'How Bala checkmated the government in Geneva', *The Sunday Leader*, 26 Feb. 2006. The Geneva Talks Final Statement simply noted that both sides were 'committed to respecting and upholding the CFA'. For the text of the (brief) final statement, see *Sunday Times*, 26 Feb. 2006.

14. 'Geneva talks: the inside story—Who foxed who at Chateau de Bossey', *Sunday Times*, 26 Feb. 2006.

15. In a sign of the spin the LTTE intended to put on the outcome, the pro-LTTE website *TamilNet* published the final statement released by the Norwegian government on behalf of the parties under the rubric 'GoSL to disarm armed groups'. As subsequent accounts of the talks make clear, however, the formulation 'armed groups' was used on account of the government side's dogged resistance to use of the term 'paramilitary', favoured by the LTTE delegation on account of its use in CFA Article 1.8. US Embassy Colombo, 'Govt. delegation member's perspectives on CFA talks with LTTE', 2 March 2006. Wikileaks Cable 06COLOMBO340.

16. The point is made clearly in US Embassy Colombo, 'Monday Morning Quarterbacking on Govt. Talks with the LTTE', 27 Feb. 2006. Wikileaks Cable 06COLOMBO308.

17. Following the talks, details of Basil Rajapaksa's backstage role in the negotiations began to surface in the Sri Lankan media. In particular it was suggested that it took a direct intervention by the presidential advisor—and brother—to persuade delegation leader Nimal Siripala de Silva to agree to the joint final talks statement. In response to de Silva's main concern, the statement's reception back home by the JVP and JHU on account of its express commitment to upholding the CFA, Rajapaksa reportedly responded: 'I will take care of the JVP and JHU once I get to Colombo. You don't have to worry about that. I will speak to Solheim and finalise the joint statement'. 'Mahinda's secret emissaries to Geneva', *The Sunday Leader*, 5 March 2006.

18. As quoted in an extensive interview with Tamilselvan, 'Govt. has reneged on Geneva agreement', *The Sunday Leader*, 19 March 2006.

19. 'Balasingham rejects Sri Lanka's "amendment" concept as absurd', *TamilNet*, 27 Feb. 2006.

20. 'LTTE moves to reopen political offices in the NE', *Sunday Times*, 12 March 2006. By the end of March, however, Norwegian Embassy officials were informing their US counterparts that these plans were being 'stymied' by a 'host of infor-

mational requirements'—twenty-eight of them, according to a 26 March *Sunday Times* report—imposed by the government. The government were refusing to provide LTTE cadres with helicopter transport when they were travelling from the North to the East—not a formal CFA provision, but something the Wickremasinghe government had provided on a regular basis. US Embassy Colombo, 'Norwegians concerned about prospects for the second round of talks', 24 March 2006. Wikileaks Cable 06COLOMBO467.

21. *Tamil Makkal Viduthalai Pulikal*, or 'Tamil Peoples Liberation Tigers'.

22. US Embassy Colombo, 'LTTE-Karuna tensions remain high in Batticaloa', 30 March 2006. Wikileaks Cable 06COLOMBO508.

23. Suranimala, 'Indo-Pak politics in Sri Lanka and peace talks after local polls', *The Sunday Leader*, 2 April 2006.

24. As US Ambassador Lunstead expressed it in a record of the debriefing session, [Hanssen-Bauer noted that] 'while the GSL has a picture of where it wants to go, it does not have a plan [for] how to get there'. US Embassy Colombo, 'Tigers not yet committed to second round of talks, govt. ready to broaden', 7 April 2006. Wikileaks Cable 06COLOMBO557.

25. US Embassy Colombo, 'Violence, verbiage threaten Geneva talks', 12 April 2006. Wikileaks Cable 06COLOMBO592.

26. US Embassy Colombo, 'Claymore mines and mob violence as LTTE all but jettisons Geneva', 17 April 2006. Wikileaks Cable 06COLOMBO620.

27. 'Talks possible only after hurdles are cleared—Thamilchelvan', *TamilNet*, 16 April 2006.

28. For a graphic account of the tense standoff over sea transport arrangements for senior LTTE leaders, see Jon Oskar Solnes, *A Powderkeg in Paradise*, New Delhi: Konark, 2010, pp. 130–131.

29. C. Kalendran & S. Senanayake, 'LTTE move puts talks in limbo', *Sunday Times*, 16 April 2006.

30. Subsequent reports indicated that the suicide bomb attack had been carried out by a pregnant LTTE Black Tiger operative, who infiltrated Army Headquarters by attending the regular maternity clinic provided for civilians at the military hospital located inside the complex. At the same time, questions were asked about how it had been possible for the LTTE to breach the high security procedures of a key military installation in central Colombo.

31. Interestingly, reporting on discussions with an Indian Embassy official following the attack on Fonseka, US Ambassador Jeffrey Lunstead notes the 'popular supposition' that Fonseka was 'the architect behind setting up Karuna'. He also notes the view of 'contacts' including some 'in the government', that 'the Indian government is behind Karuna'. US Embassy Colombo, 'Indians still hoping talks can resume under "broader agenda"', 3 May 2006.

32. V. Sambandan, 'Frayed Truce', *Frontline*, 6–19 May 2006.

33. 'Air raids violation of CFA: SLMM disputes Government's claim', *Sunday Times*, 30 April 2006.

34. D.B.S. Jeyaraj, 'International pressure forced government to suspend retaliatory attack', *The Sunday Leader*, 30 April 2006.

35. Reddy's view—on the pregnancy issue at least—is contradicted by other commentators. See, for example, 'D.B.S. Jeyaraj, 'Suicide bomber was five months pregnant', *The Sunday Leader*, 30 April 2006.

36. 'Notionally' because reports of the talks were carried the same week in Sri Lankan media. See S. Senanayake, 'EU mulls slapping ban on LTTE: Govt. Holds secret talks in Barcelona', *Sunday Times*, 14 May 2006.

37. US Embassy Colombo 'Norwegian Facilitators see slight hope for Geneva talks', 19 April 2006 Cable 06COLOMBO634; 'Sri Lankan Peace Process: What can we other do about it?', 21 April 2006. Wikileaks Cable 06COLOMBO654.

38. Navy sources were quoted as saying that twelve LTTE suicide boats and the same number of armed SLN vessels were involved in the confrontation at sea. One navy fast attack craft was destroyed, killing seventeen sailors. At least five Sea Tiger vessels were reported destroyed, resulting in an unknown—but in all probability substantial—number of LTTE casualties. A. Perera & J. Najmuddin, 'No war, no peace', *The Sunday Leader*, 14 May 2006.

39. I. Athas, 'Chalai attacks bear [sic] CFA charade', *Sunday Times*, 14 May 2006.

40. SLMM statement quoted in D.B.S. Jeyaraj, 'SLMM chief on urgent mission to Kilinochchi', *The Sunday Leader*, 14 May 2006.

41. V. Sambandan, 'Straining ceasefire', *Frontline*, 20 May–2 June 2006.

42. D.B.S. Jeyaraj, 'No other way than Norway', *The Sunday Leader*, 2 April 2006.

43. 'Govt, LTTE coy to talk in Oslo', *Sunday Times*, 28 May 2006.

44. A. Baruah, 'EU bans LTTE', *The Hindu*, 31 May 2006. For the text of the 'Declaration by the Presidency on behalf of the European Union concerning listing of the LTTE as a terrorist organisation', see http://www.statewatch.org/terrorlists/docs/89790.pdf

45. The text of the Co-Chairs Tokyo statement is contained in a US Embassy Tokyo Cable, 'Co-Chairs appeal to Sri Lanka to pull back from crisis', 31 May 2006. Wikileaks Cable 06TOKYO2987.

46. As cited in US Embassy Colombo, 'Tamil Tigers threaten withdrawal after EU ban announcement, but agree to attend Oslo talks on role of SLMM', 5 June 2006. Wikileaks Cable 06COLOMBO941.

47. US Embassy Colombo, 'LTTE refuses to meet Govt. Delegation in Oslo, Angry Govt reaction to report by CFA monitors', 12 June 2006. Wikileaks Cable 06COLOMBO990.

48. 'LTTE issues Communiqué in Oslo', *TamilNet*, 9 June 2006. One analyst suggested that the Communiqué's final sentence implied 'essentially a rejection of the political process—and perhaps a harbinger of a return to open conflict.' The same analyst also noted the Communiqué criticism of what it called 'the recent misguided attempt' to 'differentiate the Tamil nation from the LTTE, the sole interlocutor of the former in the negotiations' as 'injurious to the peace process'—most probably a reference to a 1 June public statement by US Assistant Secretary of State for South Asia Richard Boucher that differentiated between Tamil grievances' and the LTTE. See US Embassy Cable, 'Norwegians running out of steam, EU monitors to leave in 30 days', 23 June 2006. Wikileaks Cable 06COLOMBO1047.

49. As reported in US Embassy Colombo, 'LTTE refuses to meet Govt. Delegation'. The full text of the SLMM report and the government's response were published in *The Sunday Times'* 11 June 2006 edition. The official version of this and all other SLMM reports are available at www.slmm-history.info.

50. US Embassy Colombo, 'Worst LTTE attack on civilians since 2002 CFA prompts military response and localised ethnic backlash', 15 June 2006. Wikileaks Cable 06COLOMBO1018.

51. I. Athas, 'A full-scale war about to begin', *Sunday Times*, 18 June 2006.

52. A. Fuard & C. Kamalendran, 'Deadly plan to blast Colombo port', *Sunday Times*, 18 June 2006.

53. US Embassy Colombo, 'Growing evidence that naval personnel targeted Tamil civilians during weekend LTTE attack on Mannar', 21 June 2006. Wikileaks Cable 06COLOMBO1041. In an account of the incident based on local SLMM intelligence, Solnes states that 'unidentified men wearing blue clothes burst into the church and opened up with machine guns, wounding forty people'. Buildings and fishing boats were set on fire and four fishermen were shot 'at close range'. See Solnes, *A Powderkeg in Paradise*, pp. 114–117.

54. US Embassy Colombo, 'Norwegians running out of steam, EU monitors to leave in 30 days', 23 June 2006. Wikileaks Cable 06COLOMBO1047.

55. 'President moots secret deal with LTTE: seeks secret pact in the face of imminent war', *The Sunday Leader*, 25 June 2006.

56. 'Tamilselvan responds to President's secret deal offer', *The Sunday Leader*, 2 July 2006.

57. V. Sambandan & M. Reddy, 'Deepening crisis', *Frontline*, 1–14 July 2006. Responding to the deepening crisis in Sri Lanka, the Chennai-based *Frontline*, a sister magazine to *The Hindu* and long an informed source on Lankan affairs published an in-depth feature in its early July 2006 edition that included reports on the mounting exodus of Lankan Tamils to neighbouring Tamil Nadu. Relaying her reasons for fleeing to India, a Sri Lankan Tamil stated, 'There is no guarantee for our lives there. The Army keeps firing multi-barrel shells from its camp in Trincomalee town towards Sampur [an LTTE stronghold]. Forty shells can land at a time and destroy an entire locality. The noise of explosions forever fills the air. If you go to work you are not sure whether you will return home alive. And when you are at work, you are worried whether your family members are safe at home'. Another alleged that the Army increasingly 'took it out' on civilians in the aftermath of LTTE claymore attacks. 'If you are walking along the road the soldiers will seize the [mobile] phone from you. If you question them, they will shoot you'. T. Subramanian, 'Fleeing to safety', *Frontline*, 1–14 July 2006.

58. 'Saran tells Mahinda to get on with finding a political solution', *The Sunday Leader*, 9 July 2006.

59. M. Reddy, 'Mission to Colombo', *Frontline*, 15–28 July 2006.

60. Ibid.

61. The former president's comments on conditions in the country at this point are unrelated to the SLFP's decision—reportedly at President Rajapaksa's behest—

to divest Kumaratunga of leadership of the party, on her birthday (29 June). For more on this see 'The queen is dead, long live the king', *Sunday Times*, 2 July 2006; 'Mahinda's birthday gift to CBK', *The Sunday Leader*, 2 July 2006.

62. See Ch 2, pp. 159–161.

63. M. Reddy, 'Water war', *Frontline*, 12–25 Aug. 2006.

64. Ibid.

65. Interestingly, it appears that President Rajapaksa chaired a meeting of the National Security Council the same day (26 July) that airstrikes were initiated. Reportedly, the Mavil Aru water reservoir issue was one of the main items on the agenda. I. Athas, 'Eelam War IV: Trinco in danger', *Sunday Times*, 6 Aug. 2006.

66. US Embassy Colombo, 'Water-related military action continues for a fifth day', 1 Aug. 2006. Wikileaks Cable 06COLOMBO1262.

67. According to one estimate, by early Aug. some 15,000 Muttur inhabitants and 45–50,000 civilians in the Eastern province as a whole had been displaced by the fighting. D.B.S. Jeyaraj, 'Govt. unleashes 'humanitarian' war on Eastern Tamil civilians', *The Sunday Leader*, 13 Aug. 2006.

68. See, for example, Suranimala, 'Govt. shifts water policy midstream', 'JVP exposes war strategy of govt.', *The Sunday Leader*, 13 Aug. 2006.

69. An LTTE statement argued that the attacks proved that the government was paying 'scant regard' to Norway's peace efforts, while also asking the international community to 'consider' what they revealed about the government's real 'intentions'. Reportedly, soon after the 26 July attacks Henricsson told Colombo-based foreign correspondents that he wondered if water was the 'real issue' behind the escalation. See Reddy, 'Water war', *Frontline*, 12–25 Aug. 2006. Henricsson was not the only senior member of the SLMM to raise questions about the government's motivations for initiating a military offensive. SLMM Chief of Staff J.O. Solnes' account of the Mavil Aru dispute, for example, describes Army Commander Sarath Fonseka as 'jumping' on this 'unexpected opportunity' and 'perfect excuse' for 'teaching the Tigers a lesson'. See Solnes, *A Powderkeg in Paradise*, p. 136.

70. 'Maavilaru sluice gates opened by LTTE, civil representatives', *TamilNet*, 8 Aug. 2006.

71. See Suranimala, 'Govt. shifts water policy midstream', 'JVP exposes war strategy of govt.', *The Sunday Leader*, 13 Aug. 2006.

72. 'Assassination of 17 civilian aid workers in Muttur on the 4th August 2006', ruling addressed by Ulf Henricsson, Head of SLMM, to Sri Lankan Secretariat for Coordinating the Peace Process (SCOPP), 29 Aug. 2006. http://news.bbc.co.uk/2/hi/south_asia/5298748.stm. A week earlier the widely-respected University Teachers for Human Rights-Jaffna, (UTHR-J) issued a wide-ranging report that came to largely the same conclusions as the SLMM with regard to the ACF killings. *Hubris and Humanitarian Catastrophe*, UTHR-J Special Report No. 22, 23 Aug. 2006. www.uthr.org/SpecialReports. Somewhat surprisingly, the relevant sections of the report were reprinted in the pro-government newspaper *The Island*, 28 Aug. 2006.

73. SCOPP press release in response to the SLMM's ruling of 29 Aug. 2006, http://www.sundayobserver.lk/2006/09/03/news01.asp

74. Henricsson interview with Reuters quoted in Suranimala, 'India takes the lead role as UNP gets set to deal with MR', *The Sunday Leader*, 3 Sept. 2006.

75. As Ilanthirayan actually put it, 'There was an urgent humanitarian need to neutralise the Sri Lankan military's attacks on civilian targets'. 'LTTE says operations 'to defend civilians', *TamilNet*, 2 Aug. 2006.

76. See Suranimala, 'Govt. shifts water policy midstream', 'JVP exposes war strategy of govt.', *The Sunday Leader*, 13 Aug. 2006.

77. See, for example, 'Rajiv assassination "deeply regretted": LTTE', *The Hindu*, 28 June 2006; 'Rajiv Gandhi assassination "a monumental historical tragedy"—Balasingham', *TamilNet*, 27 June 2006. According to Rajan Hoole, a 'well-placed' source later informed UTHR-J that the interview was a conciliatory gesture on the LTTE's behalf agreed in advance by Balasingham and Indian National Security Advisor M.K. Narayanan, with whom the Tigers' Chief Advisor was allegedly in 'friendly contact', as a basis to 'enable India to rescue the expiring Oslo process'. Rajan Hoole, *Palmyra Fallen: From Rajani To War's End*, Colombo: UTHR-J, 2015, p. 140.

78. C.A. Chandraprema, *Gota's War*, Colombo: Ranjan Wijeratne Foundation, 2012, p. 329.

79. SLMM reports on the fighting suggested that army helicopter gunships had played a major role in beating back LTTE forces. See Solnes, *A Powderkeg in Paradise*, p. 149. I. Athas' 'Situation Reports', *Sunday Times*, 20, 27 Aug. 2006, provide more detail on the course of the fighting around Jaffna, although the heavy hand of military censorship is visible in his apologies for the fact that 'serious external constraints' prevent him from 'making a fuller appreciation of recent developments and what they portend' (27 Aug.).

80. 'Sri Lanka Co-Chairs call for immediate cessation of hostilities', Press Statement, 11 Aug. 2006. http://2001–2009.state.gov/r/pa/prs/ps/2006/70312.htm

81. M. Reddy, 'Sri Lanka co-chairs call for truce', *The Hindu*, 13 Aug. 2006.

82. According to Gotabhaya's biographer, the attack on the High Commissioner's motorcade was not, as many suspected at the time, a consequence of Pakistan's role as one of the country's principal arms suppliers. Rather it was a case of 'mistaken identity': earlier in the day a three-wheeler packed with explosives had reportedly missed its intended target—a government minister—when the remote detonator failed to work. Subsequently the LTTE cadre in charge of the operation had hit the Pakistani Commissioner's motorcade because its army escort led him to believe it was the returning minister. See Chandraprema, *Gota's War*, pp. 319–320.

83. D.B.S. Jeyaraj, 'Aerial terror and massacre of the innocents', *The Sunday Leader*, 20 Aug. 2006.

84. D. Handunnnetti, 'A country racing back to the past', *The Sunday Leader*, 20 Aug. 2006.

85. Surveying the available evidence, one media report noted that both the SLMM and UNICEF's 'tentative conclusions' on the incident 'fly in the face of govern-

ment assertions' that the compound was an LTTE training camp. Needless to say, the government contested these conclusions, arguing that it was indeed a Tiger 'transit camp', as verified by months of close observation of the site. M. Reddy, 'Massacre and dispute', *Frontline*, 26 Aug.-8 Sept. 2006. Intriguingly, a US Embassy Cable reports that President Rajapaksa had told a visiting US State Department official that in view of its role as a 'training ground for LTTE cadres' there was 'a real possibility' that LTTE Leader Prabhakaran 'might have been' at the facility when it was bombed. Reportedly, SLMM Head Henricsson 'concurred' with the official version of events, and also speculated that the attack 'may have been an attempt to kill Prabhakaran'. 'Pressing GSL for cessation of fighting', 22 Aug. 2006. Wikileaks Cable 06COLOMBO1366.

86. Assessing LTTE income accurately was a notoriously challenging task. At this point, for example, one report stated that the Tigers' annual income was 'anywhere between \$175–375 million'. M. Reddy, 'Conflicting signals', *Frontline*, 7–20 Oct. 2006.

87. M. Reddy, 'Sri Lankan army captures Sampur', *The Hindu*, 5 Sept. 2006.

88. Jon Hanssen-Bauer notes that with encouragement from the Norwegians, the LTTE offered to move their heavy weaponry south, out of reach of Trincomalee harbour. The offer was rejected by government forces.

89. M. Reddy, 'Uncertain gain', *Frontline*, 9–22 Sept. 2006.

90. See CFA Section 1.2. Government forces were not alone in having breached the CFA by this stage of the conflict. The (unsuccessful) LTTE attack at Muhamalai initiated on 12 July, for example, was equally in contravention of the Ceasefire Agreement.

91. D.B.S. Jeyaraj, 'Army advances as Sampur battle enters new phase', *The Sunday Leader*, 3 Sept. 2006. According to Gotabhaya Rajapaksa's biographer, the assault on Sampur began with the introduction of 'special infantry operational teams (SIOTs) into the area. Throughout the operation, forty small SIOT and 'Special Forces' teams were in the field, their objective being to target LTTE cadres, and restrict vehicle movement. After 'wearing down' (or killing) LTTE cadre, regular infantry forces then moved in. A pattern of military operation was thus developed, with Special Forces and SIOT teams 'dominating' advance areas with infantry following behind them—a pattern that was subsequently 'to be followed through the war'. See Chandraprema, *Gota's War*, p. 332.

92. A. Perera, 'Army eyes Sampur', *The Sunday Leader*, 3 Sept. 2006.

93. 'Breakfast with Percy Mahinda', *The Island*, 22 Jan. 2006; 'Ex-IRA negotiator sees N. Ireland parallels in Lanka', *Daily Mirror*, 19 Jan. 2006.

94. 'Martin McGuinness meets Tamil Tiger leadership in Sri Lanka', Sinn Féin website, 3 July 2006. http://www.sinnfein.ie/contents/7005

95. N. de Silva, 'Britain to send special peace envoy', *Daily Mirror*, 17 Sept. 2006.

96. M. Reddy, 'S. Lanka peace process needs to be inclusive: Paul Murphy', *The Hindu*, 17 Nov. 2006.

97. 'Unconditional talks next month', *Daily Mirror*, 13. Sept. 2006. Interestingly, during a meeting in Kilinochchi later that month (22 Sept), Hans Brattskar reported than Tamilselvan had informed him that he came with a message 'direct from

Prabhakaran', namely that the LTTE leader had listened to the Co-Chairs advice to resume talks and accordingly decided that to heed it. US Embassy Colombo, 'Co Chairs Ambassadors meeting: Readout of Kilinochchi meeting ...', 26 Sept. 2006. Wikileaks Cable 06COLOMBO1578.

98. 'Statement by the Co-Chairs of the Tokyo Donor Conference on Sri Lanka, Brussels 12 Sept. 2006', http://www.regjeringen.no/en/dep/ud/whats-new/news/2006/statement-by-the-co-chairs-of-the-tokyo-2.html?id=419664

99. Strategic Foresight Group (SFG), Mumbai, India (2006), Ch. 2, pp. 12–15, cited in S. Samarasinghe, 'Can Mahinda walks the diplomatic walk?', *The Sunday Leader*, 24 Sept. 2006, and extensively covered in Reddy, 'Massacre and dispute', *Frontline*, 26 Aug.-8 Sept. 2006. Reddy notes that the SFG report stated that Sri Lanka had c. 8,000 personnel per 1 million people—twice as many as Pakistan and six times as many as India. Military expenditure as a percentage of GDP was 4.1% as compared to Pakistan's 3.5% and India and Nepal's 2.5%. www.strategicforesight.com/publications.php?page=8#.U57lzqjbbss. Concerning government procurement, the practice of issuing calls for tenders was eliminated as this had effectively ensured that the LTTE 'knew exactly what was being purchased and in what quantities'. He also suggests that President Rajapaksa had to intervene personally to 'obtain the necessary arms shipments' from China [and Pakistan], as the Chinese Ambassador in Colombo was reportedly subject to 'tremendous pressure' by Western Ambassadors not to supply arms to the Sri Lankan Army. See Chandraprema, *Gota's War*, pp. 318–319.

100. UN Officer of the High Commissioner for Human Rights, www.ohchr.org

101. 'Calls for int. human rights mission intensify', *The Sunday Leader*, 24 Sept. 2006.

102. A. Perera, J. Najmuddin, 'Govt, LTTE accused of violating international humanitarian law', *The Sunday Leader*, 1 Oct. 2006. Not mincing its words, the International Security Network (ISN) accused the government in particular of using food as a 'weapon of war'. See 'Setting the stage for talks and Rajapaksa's human rights nightmare', *The Sunday Leader*, 1 Oct. 2006.

103. I. Athas, 'Special Report: LTTE planning big hits', *Sunday Times*, 1 Oct. 2006

104. 'Co-chairs Ambassadors to meet MR tomorrow', *The Sunday Leader*, 8 Oct. 2006.

105. A. Perera, J. Najmuddin, 'Heavy casualties in Makerni battle', *The Sunday Leader*, 8 Oct. 2006.

106. In response, Karuna faction (TVMP) officer Pradeep Master reportedly confirmed that their troops had participated in the attack, but denied direct cooperation with government troops. Responding, the Tigers insisted that Karuna forces had been used as guides, and wore green armbands to identify themselves. A captured TVMP cadre reportedly told essentially the same story to *TamilNet*, although his account was not independently verified. A. Perera, 'Battles dampen peace hopes', *The Sunday Leader*, 15. Oct 2006.

107. I. Athas, 'Muhamalai debacle: the shocking story', *The Sunday Times*, 15 Oct. 2006. Solnes, *A Powderkeg in Paradise*, pp. 159–160, mentions the 'unofficially acknowledged' figure of 300 deaths reportedly cited by Gen. Fonseka during a late Nov. meeting with US Undersecretary of State Nicholas Burns in Washington, as also confirmed by Chandraprema, *Gota's War*, p. 333. Solnes

also states that some months later, in the course of 'discreet talks in Jaffna', local Army commanders intimated that 'up to four hundred coffins had been transported to the South' in the wake of the operation.

108. See I. Athas, 'Muhamalai debacle: the shocking story', *Sunday Times*. Chandraprema notes that 'not a word' about the attack had been exchanged in the now weekly meetings of the national security council, held with President Rajapaksa in regular attendance. He also suggests that this was Gotabhaya Rajapaksa's 'worst moment in the entire war'. Apparently his biggest worry was that the 'incident' would turn 'opinion within the cabinet' against any plans to 'conduct offensive operations against the LTTE'—the CFA's express prohibition of such operations clearly counting for less in the Defence Secretary's own calculations. See Chandraprema, *Gota's War*, p. 334.

109. See Solnes, *A Powderkeg in Paradise*, pp. 161–162; I. Athas, 'Real heroes and mock heroics', *The Sunday Times*, 22 Oct. 2006.

110. D.B.S. Jeyaraj, 'Tigers pounce on navy in Habarana and Galle', *The Sunday Leader*, 22 Oct. 2006.

111. 'Navy foils Sea Tiger attack on Galle base', *Daily Mirror*, 19 Oct. 2006.

112. M. Reddy, 'Divisive decision', *Frontline*, 21 Oct.-3 Nov. 2006; Suranimala, 'Prabhakaran's de-merger and the road to Eelam', *The Sunday Leader*, 22 Oct. 2006.

113. 'Bravo, they did it', the title of *The Daily Mirror's* lead article on the agreement is indicative of the hopes placed in it by the country's southern political leadership. K. Bandara, *The Daily Mirror*, 24 Oct. 2006.

114. US Embassy Colombo, 'Tigers going to Geneva because of Co-Chair efforts', 25 Oct. 2006. Wikileaks Cable 06COLOMBO1759.

115. July–Aug. 2006.

116. L. Wickrematunge, 'Intl. Community puts Lanka on red notice', *The Sunday Leader*, 29 Oct. 2006; 'Solheim; Govt. LTTE failed to fully implement CFA', *The Island*, 30 Oct. 2006.

117. Suranimala, 'The Geneva show that backfired', *The Sunday Leader*, 5 Nov. 2006.

118. ICG Asia Report No. 124, *Sri Lanka: The Failure of the Peace Process* (28 Nov. 2006), p. 21.

119. M. Reddy, 'From bad to worse', *Frontline*, 4–17 Nov. 2006.

120. 'Peace process depends on ceasefire implementation—LTTE', *TamilNet*, 28 Oct. 2006.

121. 'Geneva talks break down on A9 highway', *Daily Mirror*, 30 Oct. 2006.

122. Ibid.

123. 'Statement by the Norwegian Facilitator, Geneva 29 October 2006', http://www.regjeringen.no/nb/dokumentarkiv/stoltenberg-ii/ud/Nyheter-og-pressemeldinger/nyheter/2006/statement_geneva.html?id=424212#

124. 'Govt. offers alternate land route to LTTE', *The Sunday Leader*, 5 Nov. 2006.

125. D.B.S. Jeyaraj, 'War clouds loom large on political horizon', *The Sunday Leader*, 5 Nov. 2006.

126. D.B.S. Jeyaraj, 'Massacre of innocent civilians at Kathiraveli', *The Sunday Leader*,

12 Nov. 2006. According to Jeyaraj artillery shells and MBRL missiles were fired 'indiscriminately' on the refugee camp.

127. M. Reddy, 'Rights and wrongs', *Frontline*, 18 Nov.—1 Dec. 2006. With that said, a statement issued by UN Under-Secretary General Jan Egeland, as well as condemning the shelling attack also noted that there were 'equally disturbing reports' that the LTTE had 'prevented over 2,000 people from fleeing to safety'. Jeyaraj suggests there was strong evidence supporting this claim. At the same time, he argues that government forces had their own equally compelling reasons for wanting the civilian population out of areas where they were engaging LTTE forces. As had been the case in Sampur, Jeyaraj suggests, the Army wanted these areas depopulated before they entered triumphantly: and duly 'invited'—or as some saw it, compelled—the 'liberated' civilian population to return.

128. 'Probe Vakarai tragedy', *The Island*, 10 Nov. 2006, quoted in Jeyaraj, 'Massacre of innocent civilians at Kathiraveli', *The Sunday Leader*.

129. Suranimala, 'HR noose strangulates govt', *The Sunday Leader*, 12 Nov. 2006. J.O. Solnes provides a vivid account of the shelling episode as witnessed from inside the SLMM Operations Centre in Colombo. See Solnes, *A Powderkeg in Paradise*, pp. 170–172.

130. Ibid.

131. See Solnes, *A Powderkeg in Paradise*, pp. 173–176. It was during this period, Solnes states, that the monitors were dubbed 'White Tigers' in the state media.

132. 'TNA MP assassinated', *The Island*, 11 Nov. 2006.

133. A US Embassy cable suggests that the 'most likely' culprits for Naviraj's assassination were Karuna faction cadres. Confirmation was provided by the fact that the hitherto unknown group that eventually claimed responsibility for the attack reportedly posted an 'explanation' of the killing on the Karuna faction's website. 'Tamil MP assassinated in Colombo: thousands protest', 13 Nov. 2006. Wikileaks Cable 06COLOMBO1896.

134. An illustration of the depths to which a 'culture of impunity' had taken root is provided by the fact since the beginning of 2006 alone, there had been a reported fifty cases of killing, abduction and extortion in Colombo alone. See Reddy, 'Rights and wrongs', *Frontline*.

135. Ibid.

136. US Embassy Colombo, 'Military engagements on five fronts', 20 Nov. 2006. Wikileaks Cable 06COLOMBO1947.

137. US Embassy Colombo, 'Govt. announces trial opening of A9 highway for humanitarian convoy to Jaffna', 20 Nov. 2006. Wikileaks Cable 06COLOMBO1946.

138. 'Sacrifices for brighter tomorrow', *Daily Mirror*, 17 Nov. 2006. Budget estimates projected that defence spending would jump from an estimated 96.21 billion rupees ($850 million) in 2006 to 139.55 billion rupees ($1.29 billion) by Dec. 2007. 'Rajapaksa renews call to LTTE', *The Hindu*, 17 Nov. 2006.

139. I. Athas, 'Rajapaksa: The grim realities', *Sunday Times*, 19 Nov. 2006.

140. A. Perera, 'Sri Lanka under the microscope'; 'LTTE and Karuna deny UN charges', *The Sunday Leader*, 19 Nov. 2006

141. 'Joint Statement by Co-Chairs of the Tokyo Donors Conference Regarding Violence in Sri Lanka', Washington, 21 Nov. 2006. http://2001–2009.state.gov/r/pa/prs/ps/2006/76478.htm
142. 'No option but Eelam: Prabha', *Daily Mirror*, 28 Nov. 2008.
143. US Embassy Colombo, 'Tiger leader Heroes Day speech just short of a declaration of war', 28 Nov. 2006. Wikileaks Cable 06COLOMBO1985.
144. J. Cherian, 'Neighbour's concern', *Frontline*, 2–15 Dec. 2006.
145. J. Uyangoda, 'That sinking feeling', *Frontline*, 30 Dec. 2006–12 Jan. 2007.
146. US Embassy Colombo, 'SL keeps peace process alive; reinstates parts of PTA', 6 Dec. 2006. Wikileaks Cable 06COLOMBO2021.
147. 'Norway gave money to the LTTE: Karuna', *Daily News*, 27 Nov. 2006.
148. One prominent commentator described Karuna's allegations against Solheim as 'without proof, highly comical and defamatory'. Like the Norwegians, no doubt, many must have wondered why the allegations had been published in a government-controlled paper when the government in question was 'the very state that … invited Norway to be the facilitator, in addition to time and again reposing confidence in them publicly'. Suranimala, 'India gives MR food for thought and the Rock evidence on child recruitment', *The Sunday Leader*, 3 Dec. 2006.
149. 'Bauer holds crisis talks with the Tigers', *Daily Mirror*, 8 Dec. 2006.
150. Rajapaksa's comments to Hanssen-Bauer were echoed in remarks he is reported to have made around the same time to Berghof Institute Director Norbert Ropers in Colombo. See Suranimala, 'President prepares for war and toys with general election option', *The Sunday Leader*, 24 Dec. 2006.
151. From a *TamilNet* report quoted in Jeyaraj, 'Massacre of innocent civilians at Kathiraveli', *The Sunday Leader*.
152. D.B.S. Jeyaraj, 'Bala Annai was the voice of the Tamil Eelam nation', *The Sunday Leader*, 17 Dec. 2006. Jeyaraj's article provides a useful, succinct biography of Balasingham.
153. D.B.S. Jeyaraj, 'Civilians suffer in battle over Vaharai', *The Sunday Leader*, 24 Dec. 2006.
154. J. Najmuddin, 'SLMM to effect changes', *The Sunday Leader*, 31 Dec. 2006.
155. US Embassy Colombo, 'SLMM adapting to resumed armed conflict', 9 Jan. 2007. Wikileaks Cable 07COLOMBO36. With that said, Blake went on to argue that it was 'hard to see how the mission will be able to operate effectively without having a forward base of operations closer to the main theatres of hostilities in the North and East'.

10. EELAM WAR IV: THE DENOUEMENT

1. I. Athas, 'Position pregnant with possibilities', *Sunday Times*, 7 Jan. 2007.
2. M. Reddy, 'No end in sight', *Frontline*, 10–23 Feb. 2007.
3. I. Athas, 'Vakarai: the reality behind the euphoria', *Sunday Times*, 21 Jan. 2007.
4. US Embassy Colombo, 'Sri Lankan Army takes Vakarai; Tigers attack supply ship off Jaffna', 22 Jan. 2007. Wikileaks Cable 07COLOMBO127.

5. Here, as with the conduct of the war from 2006 onwards in particular, *Gota's War*, an officially-sanctioned biography of Gotabhaya Rakjapaksa cum history of the conflict provides an informative, if highly partisan, account of developments. In the case of the siege of Vakarai, it notes with evident satisfaction that within a week of the deployment of Army 'Special Infantry Operation' (SIOT) teams in the Vakarai area, 'all LTTE vehicle movement in the jungle stopped'. Added to this, the SIOT teams 'saw to it' that LTTE cadres in the jungles 'were even deprived of cooked food by attacking [their] logistics bases and cook houses just as the food was to be taken for distribution'. Further 'ruses' to 'draw the LTTE out' are detailed. C. A. Chandraprema, *Gota's War*, pp. 347–348.

6. '104 portfolios for 113 Govt. members', *Daily Mirror*, 29 Jan. 2007. The major MP crossover also effectively spelt the end of the Memorandum of Understanding (MoU) between the UNP and ruling SLFP, reached to much fanfare,only six months previously. The fact that this took place a few weeks before the fifth anniversary of another major pact that was looking increasingly moribund— the 2002 Ceasefire Agreement—was noted by several commentators. See M. Reddy, 'Graveyard of pacts', *Frontline*, 10–23 March 2007.

7. US Embassy Colombo, 'Respected NGO analyst tells Donors to expect protracted conflict', 25 Jan. 2007; 'Norwegian Ambassador says Tigers will reject government bid to trade East for North', 31 Jan. 2007. Wikileaks Cables 07COLOMBO158, 07COLOMBO189.

8. US Embassy Colombo, 'Norwegian Ambassador's visit to "tense" Kilinochchi', 6 Feb 2007. Wikileaks Cable 07COLOMBO221.

9. As quoted in US Embassy Colombo, 'Defense Secretary candidly briefs foreign media', 21 March 2007. Wikileaks Cable 07COLOMBO464.

10. Speech at a public event announcing the creation of a new party, the SLFP–Mahajana Faction (SLFP-M). US Embassy Colombo, 'Two Ex-ministers join the opposition, form new party wing'. 20 June 2007. Wikileaks Cable 07COLOMBO883.

11. 'Midnight thunderball: government seeks unity', *Daily Mirror*, 27 March 2007. Significantly, the pair of fixed-wing light aircraft reported by the air control tower to have entered the air base area were able to return northwards unhindered by anti-aircraft fire. By the time fighter planes had been scrambled into the sky, the Tamil Eelam Airforce (TAF) planes had long since vanished into the Vanni.

12. As quoted in M. Reddy, 'State of shock', *Frontline*, 7–20 April 2007.

13. 'Military thwarts LTTE aerial attack on Palaly air base', *The Island*, 25 April 2007.

14. 'Flying Tigers miss target', *Daily Mirror*, 25 April 2007.

15. The Tiger Air Force went on to carry out at least nine air attacks before its final destruction by government forces in late Feb. 2009.

16. Formally speaking, the SLFP proposal constituted the party's submission to the All Party Representative Committee (APRC), a body set up by the government to try and develop a 'southern consensus' proposal for a 'political solution' to the conflict as the basis for future peace talks with the LTTE. The APRC produced a so-called majority report, endorsed by eleven of its seventeen expert members, in Dec. 2006. After months of prevarication—or at the very least, fail-

ing to take a position—on the report, the SLFP finally came up with its own draft proposal in May 2007.

17. US Embassy Colombo, 'Criticism of ruling party devolution proposal mounts', 4 May 2007. Wikileaks Cable 07COLOMBO661. See also M. Reddy, 'In attack mode', *Frontline*, 19 May–1 June 2007.

18. *Tamil Makkal Viduthalai Pulikal* in Tamil. Known in English as the 'Tamil People's Liberation Tigers'.

19. US Embassy Colombo, 'Karuna faction fractures; EPDP threatens Jaffna students', 16 May 2007. Wikileaks Cable 07COLOMBO709.

20. US Embassy Colombo, 'Sri Lankan Government complicity in paramilitary factions' human rights abuses', 18 May 2007. Wikileaks Cable 07COLOMBO728.

21. Reporting on the meeting to the Co-Chairs Ambassadors, Hans Brattskar suggested that Rajapaksa 'did not give a clear answer about whether GoSL [government of Sri Lanka] would lift its recent restrictions, but his body language did not suggest Sri Lanka is leaning in a positive direction'. Bizarrely, Human Rights Minister Samarasinghe, who was also present, suggested that Norway drum up 'Co-Chair and Indian support for its request to visit Kilinochchi'. See US Embassy Colombo, 'Scenesetting for June 25–26 Co-Chair meeting in Oslo', 21 June 2007. Wikileaks Cable 07COLOMBO890.

22. I. Athas, 'Heavy casualties as war intensified', *Sunday Times*, 24 June 2007.

23. 'WikiLeaks: GSL And LTTE Not Interested In Diplomatic Niceties—Solheim To Co-Chairs In 2007', *Colombo Telegraph*, 16 Oct. 2012.

24. M. Reddy, 'Resting on laurels', *Frontline*, 3–16 Nov. 2007.

25. 'Sri Lanka: Sinhala Nationalism and the Elusive Southern Consensus', International Crisis Group report, 7 Nov. 2007.

26. On two earlier occasions the government side had vetoed Brattskar's intended visits to Kilinochchi on the grounds that his security could not be guaranteed. US Embassy Colombo, 'LTTE sombre in latest talks with Norwegians', 13 July 2007. Wikileaks Cable 07COLOMBO978.

27. Ibid.

28. See US Embassy Colombo, 'Scenesetting for June 25–26 Co-Chair meeting in Oslo', 21 June 2007. Wikileaks Cable 07COLOMBO890. Unlike previous Co-Chairs events, the June 2007 Oslo meeting did not produce a final statement.

29. As D.B.S. Jeyaraj puts it, 'The region's remoteness made it virtually inaccessible ... During Karuna's time the Tigers always melted away into the forests if and when the security forces invaded. This was the situation even when the Indian army entered the region'. 'Will "Tamil Kudumbimalai" be turned into "Sinhala Thoppigala"?' *The Sunday Leader*, 15 July 2007.

30. I. Athas, 'Toppigala: a victory but bitter battles ahead', *Sunday Times*, 15 July 2007.

31. M. Reddy, 'Celebrating war', *Frontline*, 28 July–10 Aug. 2007.

32. See 'Rajapaksa slams International Community at 'Thoppigala' ceremony', *TamilNet*, 19 July 2007

33. 'Only CFA Can Save Sri Lanka—Tamilchelvan', *TamilNet*, 25 June 2007; 'Military, economic structures future targets', *Tamil Guardian*, 18 July 2007.

34. US Embassy Colombo, 'Prime Minister lashes out at UN Under Secretary Holmes', 14 Aug. 2007. Wikileaks Cable 07COLOMBO1123. Over dinner, Holmes reportedly told a US Embassy official that his visit to Jaffna had been of little use as he had been accompanied by military personnel 'the entire time'. According to information received afterwards, prior to Holmes' visit the military commander of Jaffna held a meeting at the Palaly airbase at which he instructed local NGOs not to brief the UN official on human rights issues.

35. 'Top Sri Lanka official calls U.N. aid chief "terrorist"', Reuters, 15. Aug. 2007. http://in.reuters.com/article/2007/08/15/idINIndia-28991720070815. The UN was sufficiently perturbed by Fernandopulle's remarks that Secretary-General Ban Ki-Moon issued an official complaint about them to the Sri Lankan government. See Solnes, *A Powderkeg In Paradise*, p. 213.

36. S. Jayasiri, 'SL Navy destroys Sea Tiger fleet', *Daily Mirror*, 12 Sept. 2007.

37. US Embassy Colombo, 'Discussion with Presidential Advisor on Stabilization and Reconstruction in Eastern Sri Lanka', 1 Oct. 2007. Wikileaks Cable 07COLOMBO1349. Indicative of the challenges confronting reconstruction efforts in the East were reports that development agencies were threatening to pull out of the Trincomalee area in protest at the extortionate rates local TMVP members were forcing them to pay for building materials via the 'Rural Development Association' operating under their control. 'Aid agencies in the East threatening to pull out', *Daily Mirror*, 11 Oct. 2007. Reports the same month from the SLMM and ICRC also points to continuing issues in the East with regard to disappearances and related human rights abuses, mostly carried out by TMVP cadres. 'TMVP kidnappers moving freely past checkpoints: SLMM', *Daily Mirror*, 12 Oct. 2007.

38. A. Perera, 'Arbour reiterates call for UN field presence', *Sunday Leader*, 14 Oct. 2007; M. Reddy, 'Denial as strategy', *Frontline*, 20 Oct.–2 Nov. 2007.

39. Office of the High Commissioner for Human Rights (OHCHR). www.ohchr.org

40. C. Kirinde, 'Showdown on key human rights issues', *Sunday Times*, 14 Oct. 2007.

41. US Embassy Colombo, 'Air Base attack results in heavy damage, new security procedures', 30 Oct. 2007. Wikileaks Cable 07COLOMBO1479. M. Reddy, 'Despair in the air', *Frontline*, 3–16 Nov. 2007.

42. Solnes, *A Powderkeg in Paradise*, p. 211–12. Symptomatic of the increasing brutality of the conflict, Solnes records that the bodies of the twenty-one Black Tigers killed in the attack were subsequently stripped naked, thrown onto a cart and pulled away from the base in clear public view.

43. D.B.S. Jeyaraj, 'Direct hit', *Frontline*, 24 Nov.–7 Dec. 2007.

44. US Embassy Colombo, 'Tamilchelvan's death: aftermath and reactions', 7 Nov. 2007. Wikileaks Cable 07COLOMBO1523. In an extraordinary flight of fancy, writing in 2008 noted Lankan academic G.H. Peiris alludes to the possibility that Prabhakaran may himself have arranged for Tamilselvan's killing, the context being a trend toward 'factional disintegration' in the LTTE leadership allegedly in evidence since Karuna's departure in spring 2004, and likely to intensify, in Peiris's view, if a rumoured weakening of the Tiger leader's grip over the organisation proved to be correct. It would be hard to find a better example of the

Lankan penchant for conspiracy theories with respect to the ethnic conflict—however outlandish they may be—as is undoubtedly the case here. See *Twilight of the Tigers*, New Delhi: Oxford University Press, 2009, pp. 276–278.

45. See US Embassy Colombo, 'Tamilchelvan's death: aftermath and reactions', 7 Nov. 2007. Wikileaks Cable 07COLOMBO1523.

46. US Under Secretary of State for Political Affairs (2005–2008).

47. A clue to their position is perhaps provided in the party national organiser S.B. Dissanayake's comment that Tamilselvan had been instrumental in arranging the LTTE's boycott of the 2005 Presidential elections, a move that proved decisive in securing Rajapaksa's victory over his UNP opponent Ranil Wickremasinghe.

48. US Embassy Colombo, 'Tamilchelvan's death: aftermath and reactions', 7 Nov. 2007. Wikileaks Cable 07COLOMBO1523.

49. Ibid.

50. US Embassy Colombo, 'Co-Chairs see little prospect of a near-term return to peace', 8 Nov. 2007. Wikileaks Cable 07COLOMBO1527.

51. N. de Silva, 'Karuna crowded by crooked shadows', *Sunday Times*, 4 Nov. 2007; US Embassy Colombo, 'Government of Sri Lanka helped Karuna enter UK on false passport', 8 Nov. 2007. Wikileaks Cable 07COLOMBO1526.

52. M. Reddy, 'Despair and distrust', *Frontline*, 8–21 Dec. 2007.

53. 'Propping up genocidal Sinhala State counterproductive, International Community should change approach—Pirapaharan', *TamilNet*, 27 Nov. 2007.

54. Gotabhaya's exact words on the subject were reported as follows: 'The Ceasefire Agreement exists only on paper. Obviously we can see that there is no ceasefire. It has become a joke ... I think the most sensible thing is that we must end this Ceasefire Agreement by officially declaring there is no Ceasefire Agreement.' R. Wijayapala, 'Ban LTTE, end truce', *Daily News*, 29 Dec. 2007.

55. US Embassy Colombo, 'Government ups war rhetoric, fighting continues', 31 Dec. 2007. Wikileaks Cable 07COLOMBO1708.

56. The press conference referred to is most probably one of the media events mentioned in R. Wijayapala, 'Ban LTTE, end truce', *Daily News*, 29 Dec. 2007.

57. For a detailed and well-informed analysis of Maheshwaran's killing against the background of his questionable business dealings and often fractious relationship with both the LTTE and Colombo-based political parties, see D.B.S. Jeyaraj, 'The Assassination of Thiagarajah Maheswaran', *LankaeNews*, 10 Jan 2008 http://www.lankaenews.com/English/news.php?id=5200; 'Maheswaran: Blend of Business Acumen and Political Savvy', 5 Jan. 2008. http://dbsjeyaraj.com/dbsj/archives/14476

58. Quoted in M. Reddy, 'All-out war', *Frontline*, 19 Jan.–1 Feb. 2008.

59. It is worth recalling that CFA abrogation was one of the JVP's key conditions for supporting Rajapaksa in the 2005 presidential elections. That it took over two years for him to act on the condition says much about the malleability of political promises under Rajapaksa.

60. See M. Reddy, 'All-out war', *Frontline*, 19 Jan.–1 Feb. 2008.

61. For the text of the statement see 'Nordic countries regret Colombo's decision to abrogate CFA', *TamilNet*, 4 Jan. 2008.

62. Suranimala, 'Violent beginnings in the new year and the abrogation of the CFA', *The Sunday Leader*, 6 Jan. 2008. For the text of Solheim's statement see 'Norway regrets Sri Lanka's decision to terminate CFA', *TamilNet*, 3 Jan. 2008.

63. 'LTTE requests Norway to continue facilitation, urges IC's support for Tamil rights', *TamilNet*, 10 Jan. 2008.

64. D.B.S. Jeyaraj, 'Mastermind behind LTTE attacks outside N-E killed', *TransCurrents*, 12 Jan. 2008. http://transcurrents.com/tamiliana/page/5?s=jeyaraj

65. US Embassy Colombo, 'Tiger attack kills Minister outside Colombo', 8 Jan. 2008. Wikileaks Cable 08COLOMBO34.

66. J. Uyangoda, 'Point of no return', *Frontline*, 19 Jan.–1 Feb. 2008.

67. 'Co-chairs request Colombo to provide diplomatic access to Kilinochchi', *LankaNewspapers.com*, 12 Jan. 2008.

68. US Embassy Colombo, 'Akashi readout of visit to Colombo', 16 Jan. 2008. Wikileaks Cable 08COLOMBO74.

69. SLMM Press Release, 16 Jan. 2008, reproduced at http://transcurrents.com/tamiliana/archives/date/2008/01/16

70. See J. Uyangoda, 'Point of no return', *Frontline*, 19 Jan.–1 Feb. 2008.

71. M. Reddy, 'Pressured to act', *Frontline*, 2–15 Feb. 2008; D.B.S. Jeyaraj, 'In the aftermath of the APRC debacle', *TransCurrents*, 9 Feb. 2008, at http://transcurrents.com/tamiliana/archives/530; US Embassy Colombo, 'Government unveils proposal for first steps on devolution', 24 Jan. 2008, Wikileaks Cable 08COLOMBO93.

72. I. Athas, 'Pressure mounts on LTTE: Tell the truth now', *Sunday Times*, 27 Jan. 2008.

73. R. Jayasundera, 'The Karuna case uplugged', *The Sunday Leader*, 3 Feb. 2008.

74. 'Renegade Tamil rebel leader jailed in UK', BBC News, 25 Jan. 2008.

75. US Embassy Colombo, 'Spike in deadly attacks continues to target civilians', 5. Feb 2008; 'Fighting intensifies in the North', 13 Feb. 2008. Wikileaks Cable 08COLOMBO135.

76. D.B.S. Jeyaraj, 'Tigers fight defensive war on N-W front', *TransCurrents*, 23 Feb. 2008. http://transcurrents.com/tamiliana/archives/551

77. S. Kumara, 'Sri Lankan military bogged down in Northern offensives against the LTTE', *TransCurrents*, 7 March 2008. http://transcurrents.com/tamiliana/archives/568

78. I. Athas, 'Troops make progress in North, but major battles ahead', *Sunday Times*, 9 March 2008.

79. M. Reddy, 'Mission failure', *Frontline*, 29 March–11 April 2008. The quotation from the IIGEP Statement is excerpted from the same source.

80. S. Sengupta, 'Take Aid From China and Take a Pass on Human Rights', *The New York Times*, 9 March 2008.

81. M. Reddy, 'Showcasing a success', *Frontline*, 29 March–11 April 2008.

82. 'Government-backed ex-Tigers sweep local elections in East', 11 March 2008. Wikileaks Cable 08COLOMBO246.

83. D.B.S. Jeyaraj, 'Madhu Church: Tragic casualty of politico-military crossfire',

The Nation, 4 April 2008; I. Athas, 'Bishop defends shifting of statue as Madhu war hots up', *Sunday Times*, 6 April 2008; 'Displaced Our Lady of Madhu Statue: Danger of Disappearance', *TransCurrents*, 11 April 2008. http://transcurrents. com/tamiliana/archives/date/2008/04/11

84. D.B.S. Jeyaraj, 'Claymore kills "Kili Father" M.X. Karunaratnam at Ambaikulam', *TransCurrents*, 22 April 2008. At http://transcurrents.com/tamiliana/archives/622

85. I. Athas, 'The aftermath of Muhamalai confrontation', *Sunday Times*, 27 April 2008.

86. D.B.S. Jeyaraj, 'Tigers demonstrate military prowess at Muhamalai Front', *The Nation*, 27 April 2008. http://www.nation.lk/2008/04/27/newsfe1.htm

87. B. Raman, 'Over-confident SLA walks into a deadly LTTE trap', *TransCurrents*, 25 April 2008. http://transcurrents.com/tamiliana/archives/date/2008/04/25

88. D.B.S. Jeyaraj, 'Tigers sustain three-pronged strategy', *The Nation*, 4 May 2008.

89. The UPFA-TMVP result included two 'bonus' seats that, under prevailing election rules, were awarded to the party that secured a majority in the Amparai district This the UPFA-TVMP combine did by a reportedly slim margin. See US Embassy Colombo, 'Government wins Eastern polls by a narrow margin: opposition cries foul', 12 May 2008. Wikileaks Cable 08COLOMBO463.

90. Ibid.

91. Ibid.

92. US Embassy, 'President names Pillaiyan Chief Minister of Eastern province', 20 May 2008. Wikileaks Cable 08COLOMBO483.

93. US Embassy Colombo, 'Karuna released from UK prison; may be deported', 12 May 2008. Wikileaks Cable 08COLOMBO462.

94. W. Gnandass, 'Sri Lanka loses at UNHRC due to perpetration of human rights violations', *The Nation*, 25 May 2008; D.B.S. Jeyaraj, 'An analysis of military operations', *TransCurrents*, 28 May 2008. http://transcurrents.com/tamiliana/ archives/date/2008/05/28

95. 'No right to be there', *The Guardian*, 15 May 2008.

96. Col. R Hariharan, 'Death of Balraj and the dearth of experience', *TransCurrents*, 23 May 2008, http://transcurrents.com/tamiliana/archives/650

97. D.B.S. Jeyaraj, 'Brigader Balraj led from the front', *The Nation*, 25 May 2008.

98. Senpathi, 'An Army is not its commander's private fiefdom', *The Nation*, 11 May 2008.

99. I. Athas, 'War on media takes ugly turn', *Sunday Times*, 25 May 2008.

100. 'Journalist in Sri Lanka kidnapped', BBC News, 23 May 2008. http://news.bbc. co.uk/2/hi/south_asia/7416485.stm; US Embassy Colombo, 'Defense journalist abducted, beaten and released', 27 May 2008.

101. US Embassy Colombo, 'Defense Ministry mobilises against media critics', 2 June 2008, Wikileaks Cable 08COLOMBO528. The cable is summarised in 'WikiLeaks: 'There Will Be No Investigation, No One Will Be Able To Find Out What Happened To Keith'—Gota', *Colombo Telegraph*, 27 June 2012. The cable offers an incisive analysis of the broader context of the assault on Noyahr.

102. Ibid.

103. US Embassy Colombo, 'President tells press to toe the line', 13 June 2008. Wikileaks Cable 08COLOMBO581.

104. University Teachers For Human Rights-Jaffna, 'Slow Strangulation of Jaffna: Trashing General Larry Wijeratne's Legacy and Enthroning Barbarism—A Bequest of Mahinda (Jathika) Chintana', Special Report No. 28 (Dec. 2007), quoted in M. Reddy, 'Reign of fear', *Frontline*, 10–23 May 2008.

105. US Embassy Colombo, 'High level Indian delegation urges political solution', 24 June 2008. Wikileaks Cable 08COLOMBO610; D.B.S. Jeyaraj, India seeks clarification about ongoing war in Sri Lanka', *The Nation*, 29 June 2008.

106. An argument to which Basil Rajapaksa was reportedly receptive, and his brother Mahinda decidedly more 'evasive'. Ibid.

107. Ibid.

108. See, for example, 'Pillaiyan mum on Karuna's right to overrule him', *The Sunday Leader*, 13 July 2008; 'Karuna and Pillaiyan in 5-hour talks', *Sunday Times*, 13 July 2008.

109. US Embassy Colombo, 'Tension in the TMVP; Karuna and Pillaiyan meet; Defense Secretary outlines shift of TMVP to Army, Police and Home Guards', 21 July 2008. Wikileaks Cable 08COLOMBO695.

110. At this point Wijesinha was head of the government peace secretariat (SCOPP).

111. US Embassy Colombo, 'GSL floats idea that peace talks must include TMVP', 9 July 2008. Wikileaks Cable 08COLOMBO660.

112. As the cable went on to point out, the standard government line that security conditions did not allow for such a visit was somewhat undermined by the fact that UN expatriate staff had been operating in the Vanni throughout the same period, without incident. Ibid.

113. I. Athas, 'The significance of the Vidathaltivu victory', *Sunday Times*, 20 July 2008. D.B.S. Jeyaraj argued that government forces had taken the naval base largely thanks to the use of new and 'superior' military tactics. These tactics, he suggested, essentially consisted in moving 'off the beaten track' and then 'striking unexpectedly behind enemy lines'—a pincer-cum-encircling movement strategy that was used with considerable success throughout the latter stages of the government's military campaign. 'Advantage Army: Tigers outmanoeuvred in the North', *The Nation*, 3 Aug. 2008.

114. J. Najmuddin, 'LTTE announces unilateral ceasefire', *Daily Mirror*, 22 July 2008.

115. I. Athas, 'SAARC safe, but heavy battles loom', *Sunday Times*, 3 Aug. 2008; B. Raman, 'LTTE's ceasefire: public relations or more?', *Rediff News*, 25 July 2008. Intriguingly, based on conversations with 'Western diplomats', veteran Indian journalist Narayan Swamy made the (unconfirmed) suggestion that the LTTE ceasefire offer was the result of behind-the-scenes pressure from the Norwegians not to carry out attacks during the SAARC meeting. Allegedly the Tigers' ceasefire proposal went well beyond the Norwegians expectations, and its dismissal by the government—and in particular the international community's silence on the subject—infuriated the Tiger leadership. 'Norway-LTTE ties sour over theft of NGO vehicles', IANS, 21 Aug. 2008. Reprinted in N. Swamy, *The Tiger Vanquished: LTTE's Story* New Delhi: Sage, 2010, pp. 136–137.

116. As quoted in A. Perera, 'Tigers will lose more land—Karuna', *The Sunday Leader*, 27 July 2008.

117. US Embassy Colombo, 'Boucher finds commitment to military solution, not human rights, in Colombo', 15 Aug. 2008. Wikileaks Cable 08COLOMBO766.

118. US Embassy Colombo, 'UN Chief reports humanitarian situation in North worse than expected', 2 Sept. 2008. Wikileaks Cable 08COLOMBO825.

119. Interestingly, Buhne also noted that 'UN conversations' with IDPs indicated that—at this point at least—'most' did not want to move out of LTTE-controlled areas, and for a 'variety' of reasons. Many were farmers unwilling to leave their land, had relatives fighting with the LTTE they did not want to abandon, or were genuinely fearful about their prospective treatment in government-controlled areas. Ibid.

120. Ibid.

121. I. Athas, 'Defining moments in Eelam War IV', *Sunday Times*, 7 Sept 2008; 'Battle for Kilinochchi reaches crucial phase', *Sunday Times*, 21 Sept. 2008.

122. Ibid.

123. Unmanned Aerial Vehicles, commonly referred to as drones.

124. UN Embassy Colombo, 'GSL orders all INGOs and UN out of Vanni for security reasons', 9 Sept. 2009.

125. Interview in *Sri Lanka's Killing Fields* (UK Channel 4 TV Documentary, 2011). https://www.youtube.com/watch?v=Mbl-Elax9uo

126. Ibid.

127. D.B.S. Jeyaraj, 'Civilians of Wanni are wretched of Lankan earth', *Daily Mirror*, 4 Oct. 2008. Gordon Weiss suggests that the LTTE 'angrily' informed UN officials that this 'relatively privileged class of Vanni Tamils should share the fate of their people, whatever that might be.' See Gordon Weiss, *The Cage: The Fight for Sri Lanka and the Last Days of the Tamil Tigers*, London: Bodley Head, 2011, p. 104.

128. Some sources suggest that the evacuation was far from orderly, and more a case of the civilian population starting to flee town as shelling drew closer. A member of the UN team present in the area has stated that already in early Sept. he had seen the LTTE withdrawing heavy weaopns and other military equipment from the town at night.

129. I. Athas, 'Fierce battles rage, flashpoint ahead', *Sunday Times*, 5 Oct. 2008.

130. Quoted in S. Bell, 'Inside Sri Lanka: A Life Given Over to War', *National Post*, 23 Sept. 2008. http://www.nationalpost.com/Inside+Lanka+life+given+over/832374/story.html

131. Quoted in M. Reddy, 'Indian concerns', *Frontline*, 25 Oct.–7 Nov. 2008.

132. M. Reddy, 'Political compulsions', *Frontline*, 25 Oct.–7 Nov. 2008. A new political party participant in the APRC meeting was the TMVP, led by its now reinstalled leader Karuna, who had duly been sworn into parliament as a National List MP for the ruling United People's Freedom Alliance (UPFA) on 8 Oct.

133. D.B.S. Jeyaraj, 'Delhi demarche more important than Tamil Nadu tempest', *Daily Mirror*, 18 Oct. 2008.

134. Ibid.

135. US Embassy Colombo, 'Rajapaksa and Ambassador discuss political solution, slower military progress and likelihood of reduced Indian pressure', 27 Oct. 2008. Wikileaks Cable 08COLOMBO976.

136. M. Reddy, 'New Delhi's dual approach', *Frontline*, 8–21 Nov. 2008.

137. Ibid.

138. 'Will there be a "mother of all battles" for Kilinochchi?', *Daily Mirror*, 25 Oct. 2008.

139. US Embassy Colombo, 'Government forces taking control of strategic peninsula', 18 Nov. 2008. Wikileaks Cable 08COLOMBO1042. Concerning access to sea supply routes the cable notes that following the fall of Pooneryn, the Tigers would be forced to send boats all the way round the Jaffna peninsula, past Point Pedro and down to the Mullaitivu coastal area still under its control, thereby 'greatly increasing' the risk of being detected by Sri Lanka Navy patrols.

140. Ibid.

141. University Teachers for Human Rights-Jaffna, *Pawns of an Unheroic War*, Special Report No. 31, 28 Oct. 2008. http://www.uthr.org/SpecialReports/spreport31. htm. For an eyewitness-based report on conditions facing civilians across the Vanni by the second half of 2008, see the Human Rights Watch Report. 'Besieged, Displaced and Detained: The Right of Civilians in Sri Lanka's Vanni Region'. http://www.hrw.org/sites/default/files/reports/srilanka1208webwcover.pdf

142. I. Athas, 'Prabhakaran strikes a defiant note', *Sunday Times*, 30 Nov. 2008.

143. US Embassy Colombo, 'LTTE chief praises India, calls Sri Lankan government 'genocidal' as Army near Kilinochchi', 28 Nov. 2008. Wikileaks Cable 08COLOMBO1079.

144. Ibid.

145. I. Athas, 'Troops capture land, face growing resistance', *Sunday Times*, 16 Dec. 2008.

146. Drawn from the Sri Lanka Army's 57th and 58th Divisions.

147. I. Athas, 'Mortar monsoon, fiercest battles knee-deep in mud', *Sunday Times*, 21 Dec. 2008. Commenting on casualty figures, having given the offical figures for LTTE dead and wounded, in a nod to military censorship he goes on to state that, 'For reasons that are now obvious, casualty figures of troops cannot be discussed. Suffice to say the numbers are substantial'. 'Eelam War IV: Which way the last phases next year?', *Sunday Times*, Dec. 28 2008. A later report indicates that on the LTTE side, 'sources with links to some [Tiger] leaders' stated that '2,000 cadres were killed in defence of Kilinochchi, pointing to similar losses among the army'. University Teachers for Human Rights-Jaffna (UTHR-J), Special Report No. 34, 'Let Them Speak: Truth about Sri Lanka's Victims of War', 13 Dec. 2009. p. 16. http://www.uthr.org/SpecialReports/Special%20rep34/ Uthr-sp.rp34.htm

147. M. Reddy, 'Stranded in the Wanni', *Frontline*, 30 Jan.–13 Feb. 2009.

148. Indian National Security Adviser (2005–2010). The author's concerted attempts to secure an interview with Narayanan for the purposes of this book ultimately proved fruitless.

149. I. Athas, 'Prabha's day-dream turns into Tiger nightmare', *Sunday Times*, 4 Jan. 2008. See also A. Perera, 'Troops enter Kilinochchi with multi pronged attack', *Sunday Leader*, 4 Jan. 2008.

11. ENDGAME

1. The LTTE had previously been banned in the aftermath of the notorious 1998 attack on the Temple of the Tooth in Kandy. The ban was lifted in early 2002 to allow talks between the two sides to go ahead.
2. M. Reddy, 'Presidential salvo', *Frontline*, 3–16 Jan. 20009.
3. US Embassy Colombo, 'Sri Lanka bans LTTE', 8 Jan. 2009. Wikileaks Cable 09COLOMBO26.
4. Eyewitness reports indicated that a group of armed men on motorbikes had blocked Wickrematunge's car before smashing the window screen, shooting him and rapidly disappearing. The part of town where the attack occurred was under High Security surveillance—an indication that the attackers almost certainly must have had official licence to proceed. 'A deadly drive to work', *Sunday Leader*, 11 Jan. 2009; 'Top Sri Lankan editor shot dead', *BBC News*, 8 Jan. 2009.
5. At one point in 2008 an incensed President Rajapaksa had reportedly called Wickrematunge, shouting that he would be killed if the paper did not change its editorial stance. In the meantime Gotabhaya had filed—and won—a defamation suit against the paper, as a result of which *The Sunday Leader* was forbidden to print his name. In the weeks before Wickrematunge's assassination a funeral wreath was delivered to him, as well as a copy of the paper with the words 'If you write you will be killed' emblazoned across it in red paint. A few days later opposition leader Ranil Wickremasinghe held a meeting with a number of diplomats to discuss the mounting assault on media freedom. Wickremasinghe stated he had convincing proof that a 'group in army intelligence' that reported directly to Army Commander Sarath Fonseka, and through him to Gotabhaya Rajapaksa, was responsible both for the killing of Wickrematunge and other earlier high-profile assassinations. The publication of a series of articles alleging high-level corruption in military procurement deals had unquestionably annoyed the president and Gotabhaya. But the decisive factor that lead to Wickrematunge's death, it was alleged, was evidence he had reportedly acquired of serious human rights violations in which both Gotabhaya and Fonseka were directly implicated, revolving around the actions of special military intelligence units. Reportedly, Wickrematunge had planned to publish some of this evidence in the paper's 11 Jan. edition. US Embassy Colombo, 'UNP accuses government of ordering attacks on media', 13 Jan. 2009. Wikileaks Cable 09COLOMBO47.
6. D. de Alwis, S de Silva, 'Armed attack on MTV', *Daily Mirror*, 7 Jan. 2009.
7. US Embassy Colombo, 'Journalists flee country amid continuing attacks, arrests and threats', 23 Jan. 2009. Wikileaks Cable 09COLOMBO81.
8. The fact that, as in Kilinochchi, the army's final advances were aided and abetted by the LTTE's decision to evacuate the area once the leadership came round to the view that Tiger positions on the Jaffna peninsula could no longer be

defended was not something that occasioned much comment in the Sri Lankan media. D.B.S. Jeyaraj, 'Dunkirk-type evacuation from Jaffna Peninsula', 6 Jan. 2009. http://dbsjeyaraj.com/dbsj/archives/92

9. US Embassy Colombo, 'Army takes Elephant Pass; now controls entire land route to Jaffna', 12 Jan. 2009. Wikileaks Cable 09COLOMBO44.

10. See, for example, 'AI, HRW call for probe on Lasantha's killing', *Daily Mirror*, 9 Jan. 2009

11. See US Embassy Colombo, 'Army takes Elephant Pass; now controls entire land route to Jaffna', 12 Jan. 2009. Wikileaks Cable 09COLOMBO44.

12. 'LTTE at 32: Whither LTTE?', *The Sunday Leader*, 19 Jan. 2009.

13. As cited in US Embassy Colombo, 'UNP accuses government of ordering attacks on media', 13 Jan. 2009. Wikileaks Cable 09COLOMBO47.

14. UTHR-J Special Report No. 34, 'Let Them Speak: Truth about Sri Lanka's Victims of War', 13 Dec. 2009, pp. 12–13. http://www.uthr.org/SpecialReports/Special%20rep34/Uthr-sp.rp34.htm

15. US Embassy Colombo, 'Vanni's civilians squeezed as Army pushes on; LTTE leadership gone underground', 20 Jan. 2009. Wikileaks Cable 09COLOMBO65.

16. Frances Harrison, 'UN: The Scene at First Light Was Devastating', *Huffington Post*, 20 May 2014.

17. Gordon Weiss, *The Cage*, pp. 97–98. A little later Weiss provides an even more harrowing account of the consequences of relentless shelling in and around PTK as witnessed by senior international members of the UN relief convoy attempting to negotiate an exit from the war zone. One of them, retired Bangladeshi Colonel Harum Khan, an experienced counterinsurgency soldier, reported that he was convinced that the artillery fire had come 'overwhelmingly from government forces'. p. 118. International Crisis Group's 'War Crimes in Sri Lanka', Asia Report No. 191, 17 May 2010, pp. 9–14 gives a more measured and forensic—but no less disturbing—account of 'Convoy 11's' experiences while attempting to exit the combat zone. 'The Report of the Secretary-General's Review Panel on United Nations Action in Sri Lanka'—the Petrie Report—Annex 1, Section 60, provides another chilling, first-hand account of events on the night of 24 Jan. 2009.

18. US Embassy Colombo, 'Vanni's civilians squeezed as Army pushes on; LTTE leadership gone underground', 20 Jan. 2009. Cable 09COLOMBO65.

19. See UTHR-J Special Report No. 34, 'Let Them Speak: Truth about Sri Lanka's Victims of War', p. 23.

20. US Embassy Colombo, 'Army captures Mullaitivu; both sides violate GSL-declared NFZ', 26 Jan. 2009. Wikileaks Cable 09COLOMBO86; K. Bandara, 'Liberation of North by Feb. 4: Minister', *Daily Mirror*, 28 Jan. 2009.

21. 'New configurations and constraints', *Frontline*, 4–17 Feb. 2009.

22. Even at this early stage after the NFZ's creation UN offices in Colombo were receiving reports of shelling damage to one of the UN compounds in PTK, as well as hospitals within the 'safe area' itself being hit.

23. Despite this, hundreds of patients reportedly remained in the PTK hospital, with

more arriving on the morning of 29 Jan. See International Crisis Group, 'War Crimes in Sri Lanka', Asia Report No. 191 (17 May 2010), p. 16.

24. 'Sri Lanka U.N. staff come under fire while in "safe zone"', Associated Press, 28 Jan. 2009, cited in ibid., p. 14.

25. Ibid., p. 16; UTHR-J Special Report No. 34, 'Let Them Speak: Truth about Sri Lanka's Victims of War', p. 25.

26. 'Nowhere people', *Frontline*, 4–17 Feb. 2009.

27. US Embassy Colombo, 'Declared safe zone inoperative; ICRC contemplates full withdrawal', 27 Jan. 2009. Wikileaks Cable 09COLOMBO95.

28. US Embassy Colombo, 'Indian External Affairs Minister stresses humanitarian concerns to Sri Lankan leadership', 27 Jan. 2009. Cable 09COLOMBO106

29. 'Hundreds escape fighting', *Sunday Leader*, 8 Feb. 2009. Associated Press also quoted a witness as saying, 'there's heavy shelling where there are civilians[. The shells] are coming from the [Sri Lankan] army side.' By now government troops were reportedly within 1km of PTK, and witnesses reported that while the Army was not directly targeting the hospital it was also not taking any specific precautions to avoid hitting it. Shelling continued for fourteen to sixteen hours, the hospital sustaining three direct hits in less than eight hours. The following day (3 Feb.), the hospital was reportedly shelled again, killing two people, and was evacuated the next day in the midst of heavy shelling. 'Report to Congress on Incidents During the Recent Conflict in Sri Lanka', U.S. Dept. of State, 2009, p. 20. www.state.gov/documents/organization/131025.pdf

30. 'Packed Sri Lanka hospital shelled', Sky News, 2 Feb. 2009. http://news.sky.com/story/667068/packed-sri-lanka-hospital-shelled

31. For a list of over thirty Army attacks on hospitals documented between Dec. 2008 and May 2009, see F. Harrison *Still Counting the Dead: Survivors of Sri Lanka's Hidden War*, London: Portobello, 2012, pp. 90–91.

32. US Embassy Colombo, 'Presidential Advisor welcomes Co-Chair statement; Gotabhaya labels it 'ridiculous', 5 Feb. 2009. Wikileaks Cable 09COLOMBO127.

33. 'Lanka rejects move to throw lifeline to LTTE', *The Island*, 5 Feb. 2009.

34. A. Perera, 'Plight of the civilians in Wanni', *The Sunday Leader*, 8 Feb. 2009.

35. The text of Hattrem's note is cited in Shamindra Ferdinando, 'Norwegians believed LTTE won't release hostages: Secret missive to Basil Rajapaksa revealed', *The Island*, 1 April 2015.

36. For a full discussion of this incident see UTHR-J Special Report No. 34, 'Let Them Speak: Truth about Sri Lanka's Victims of War', pp. 30–33.

37. 'Exodus from the Wanni', *The Sunday Leader*, 15 Feb. 2009. Other sources put the death toll higher.

38. Shakti, 'International focus on civilians amidst information rationing', *The Sunday Leader*, 15 Feb. 2009.

39. See F. Harrison, *Still Counting the Dead*, p. 77. Harrison quotes a UN official on the subject of the new 'safe zone': 'The intention was not so much to protect civilians as to cause pandemonium behind the Tiger lines. If the government had been really serious about saving lines, it wouldn't have located the "safe

zone" on the front line. It would have been as far away from the fighting as possible'.

40. M. Reddy, 'Electoral gains', *Frontline*, 28 Feb.-13 March 2009. 'Electoral victories of Mahinda government justify partition', *TamilNet*, 15 Feb. 2009.

41. 'UN concerned for civilian welfare', *Daily Mirror*, 16 Feb. 2009, quoted in M. Reddy, 'Helping hand', *Frontline*, 28 Feb.–13 March 2009. The UN statement also noted that the LTTE were continuing to prevent people from leaving the area; reports that those who tried to do so were fired on and, often, killed; and 'indications' that 'children as young as 14' were now being conscripted into the LTTE's ranks.

42. 'LTTE has intensified conscription—UNICEF', *Daily Mirror*, 17 Feb. 2009. The UNICEF statement also noted that from 2003 to the end of 2008, the organisation had recorded no less than 6,000 cases of LTTE child soldier recruitment.

43. US Embassy Colombo, 'Northern Sri Lanka Sit Rep 17', 20 Feb. 2009. Wikileaks Cable 09COLOMBO186.

44. M. Reddy, 'Close encounters', *Frontline*, 14–27 March 2009; A. Fuard, 'Tigers go kamikaze but attacks fail', *Sunday Times*, 22 Feb. 2009.

45. A. Wamanan, 'Holmes calls on Govt. and LTTE to avoid bloodbath', *The Sunday Leader*, 22 Feb. 2009; M. Reddy, 'Close encounters', *Frontline*, 14–27 March 2009.

46. 'UN nods "fight to the finish"', *TamilNet*, 28 Feb. 2009.

47. UN Security Council Briefing, 27 Feb. 2009. Full text of his briefing in 'UN nods "fight to the finish"', *TamilNet*, 28 Feb. 2009.

48. 'Ceasefire, solution first; laying down arms irrelevant: LTTE appeals to Co-Chairs, UN', *TamilNet*, 23 Feb. 2009.

49. 'Plans to evacuate civilians: Donor Co-Chairs working out "coalition humanitarian task force"', *Sunday Times*, 22 Feb. 2009.

50. Jay Maheshwaran and V. Rudrakumaran.

51. The message sent to Tore Hattrem by Basil Rajapaksa in early Jan. 2009 outlining an amnesty offer to the LTTE.

52. On 7 Aug. 2009 Sri Lankan authorities announced that KP had been kidnapped in a South East Asian country—which later turned out to have been Malaysia—and flown to Colombo. After his arrest KP began co-operating with the Colombo authorities and in Oct. 2012 it was announced that he was being released from custody. Currently KP is said to be living in the Vanni and running a relief organisation—the North-East Rehabilitation and Development Organisation (NERDO)—which he established in 2010.

53. 'Unending End Game', *The Sunday Leader*, 8 March 2009.

54. US Embassy Colombo, 'Northern Sri Lanka Sit Rep 28', 9 March 2009. Wikileaks Cable 09COLOMBO265.

55. US Embassy Colombo, 'Karuna joins the SLFP and becomes a government minister', 11 March 2009. Wikileaks Cable 09COLOMBO278.

56. See UTHR-J Special Report No. 34, 'Let Them Speak: Truth about Sri Lanka's Victims of War', p. 65, quoting 'What happened in the Vanni? An Experience from the Battleground', published by *Kalachchuvadu*, Aug. 2009 (UTHR-J's English translation).

57. One of the government doctors who stayed in the conflict area and who, despite the dwindling stocks of medical supplies available due to government restrictions, treated thousands of sick and injured Tamil civilians under the most appalling, often mortally dangerous, conditions testifies to having himself experienced the army's use of white phosphorous—the use of which is prohibited under international law in civilian-populated areas. See F. Harrison, *Still Counting the Dead*, pp. 82–83.

58. US Embassy Colombo, N. Sri Lanka Sit Rep 29', 11 March 2009. Wikileaks Cable 09COLOMBO277. There were also continuing reports of LTTE artillery fire from within the 'safe zone'.

59. See 'Report to Congress on Incidents During the Recent Conflict in Sri Lanka', U.S. Dept. of State, 2009', p. 31.

60. 'Report of the Secretary-General's Review Panel on United Nations Action in Sri Lanka', Annex 1, pp. 67–68, http://www.un.org/News/dh/infocus/Sri_Lanka/The_Internal_Review_Panel_report_on_Sri_Lanka.pdf. The email communications quoted come in a subsection of the report titled 'Fundamental disagreements in UNHQ on strategy and responsibilities' under the broader rubric '1 February–16 April 2009: Situation becomes catastrophic as UN equivocates'. Furthermore, there appears to be good reason to believe that at the time of Commissioner Pillay's statement the UN mission in Colombo did not provide her with all the information at its disposal regarding casualty levels inside the conflict zone. http://blog.srilankacampaign.org/2012/11/the-un-internal-petrie-report-into-sri.html

61. 'Serious violations of international law committed in Sri Lanka conflict: UN human rights chief', Office of the High Commissioner for Human Rights (OHCHR), 12 March 2009, http://www.ohchr.org/EN/NewsEvents/Pages/DisplayNews.aspx?NewsID=9499&LangID=E; 'Pillay slams violations of international law in Sri Lanka', *Daily Mirror*, 13 March 2009; M. Reddy, 'Nerves on test', *Frontline*, 11–24 April 2009.

62. 'Pillay's report: Govt. on diplomatic offensive', *Sunday Times*, 15 March 2009.

63. 'Politics of the plight of the civilians', *Sunday Times*, 15 March 2009. See also Robert Blake's comments below. For a full treatment of the background to the US-led humanitarian rescue plan see US Embassy Colombo, 'A suggestion for getting many of Sri Lanka's civilians out of the conflict zone', 19 March 2009. Wikileaks Cable 09COLOMBO308. The cable also details continuing Norwegian efforts to persuade the LTTE leadership to accept the release of civilians and a broader 'organised end to the conflict'.

64. See 'Pillay's report: Govt. on diplomatic offensive', *Sunday Times*, 15 March 2009.

65. US Embassy Colombo, 'Foreign Minister expresses GSL discomfort over UNSC briefing', 24 March 2009. Wikileaks Cable 09COLOMBO322.

66. As detailed in International Crisis Group's 'War Crimes in Sri Lanka', Asia Report No. 191, 17 May 2010, p. 26.

67. As quoted in US Embassy Colombo, 'Northern Sri Lanka Sit Rep 42', 30 March 2009. Wikileaks Cable 09COLOMBO357.

68. L. Berenger, 'Rambukwella says Govt. ready to consider 'humanitarian pause'", Sunday Times, 29 March 2009.

69. See US Embassy Colombo, 'Northern Sri Lanka Sit Rep 42', 30 March 2009. Wikileaks Cable 09COLOMBO357.

70. 'Erik Solheim discusses Vanni civilian plight with LTTE', TamilNet, 2 April 2009.

71. D.B.S. Jeyaraj, 'Wanni and the humanitarian catastrophe', 31 March 2009. http://dbsjeyaraj.com/dbsj/archives/235. Mohini Rohan offers another trenchant description of LTTE tactics: 'Exodus was the very foundation of the Vanni. [LTTE] Cadres internalised the practice: if civilians were removed from the picture, the army would have a free hand to bomb the fighters. And if the fighters lost and ceded territory, inch by inch, the dream of a Tamil homeland would go up in smoke. Keeping civilians around them was the way these guerrillas fought. It bought them time and, often, resources.' The Seasons Of Trouble: Life Amid The Ruins of Sri Lanka's Civil War, London: Verso, 2014, p. 90.

72. 'Statement attributable to the Spokesperson for the Secretary-General on Sri Lanka', 3 April 2009. http://www.un.org/sg/statements/index.asp?nid=3768 See also 'UN chief tells LTTE to free civilians', Daily Mirror, 3 April 2009. The paper's source for its coverage of a statement of obvious domestic concern is a Chinese official news agency (Xinhua) news report. Via AFP, The Island reproduces the original statement in full: 'UN chief urges LTTE to free civilians from war zone', The Island, 3 April 2009.

73. See UTHR-J Special Report No. 34, 'Let Them Speak', p. 37.

74. By this stage of the conflict more than 50,000 government soldiers were estimated to be involved in operations in the Vanni. D.B.S. Jeyaraj, 'Anatomy of the LTTE military debacle at Aanandapuram', 10 April 2009. http://dbsjeyaraj.com/dbsj/archives/315

75. Reportedly there were several attempts to rescue surrounded LTTE cadres. Sea Tiger leader Soosai launched several unsuccessful rescue attempts from the coast as did senior Tiger commander Bhanu, who together with a number of cadre had managed to escape from area on 3 April. See Jeyaraj, 'Anatomy of the LTTE military debacle at Aanandapuram'.

76. Ibid.

77. D.B.S. Jeyaraj, 'Top Tiger leaders killed in a major debacle for LTTE', 6 April 2009. http://dbsjeyaraj.com/dbsj/archives/293; A. Fuard, 'Tigers caught in a noose', Sunday Times, 5 April 2009.

78. D.B.S. Jeyaraj, 'Theepan of the LTTE: Heroic saga of a Northern warrior', 15 April 2009, http://dbsjeyaraj.com/dbsj/archives/318. Jeyaraj reports that before Bhanu and a 'sizable number' of cadres succeeded in escaping the area on 3 April, Bhanu had offered to carry an injured Theepan to safety. Theepan reportedly refused, and in a conversation intercepted by the Sri Lankan military, told him 'If I come out I'll come out with the cadres. Otherwise I'll die with them.'

79. 'Report to Congress on Incidents During the Recent Conflict in Sri Lanka', U.S. Dept. of State, 2009, p. 35; ICG, 'War Crimes in Sri Lanka', Asia Report No. 191, 17 May 2010, p. 15; UTHR-J Special Report No. 34, 'Let Them Speak', p. 49.

80. US Embassy Colombo, N. Sri Lanka Sit Rep 51', 13 April 2009. Wikileaks Cable 09COLOMBO413.

81. 'Secretary-General's Statement on Sri Lanka', 12 April 2009. Available at: http://www.un.org/sg/statements/index.asp?nid=3787

82. See US Embassy Colombo, N. Sri Lanka Sit Rep 51', 13 April 2009. Wikileaks Cable 09COLOMBO413.

83. 'Fighting resumes after 48-hour ceasefire', *Daily Mirror*, 13 April 2009. Reports in some sources, for example 'Report to Congress on Incidents During the Recent Conflict in Sri Lanka', U.S. Dept. of State, 2009, suggest that government forces commenced firing at around 9PM—3 hours before the ceasefire formally terminated.

84. 'Two day pause not long enough—Holmes', *Daily Mirror*, 16 April 2009.

85. 'LTTE reiterates need for permanent ceasefire', *TamilNet*, 13 April 2009.

86. 'Govt. tells LTTE to lay down arms', *Daily Mirror*, 16 April 2009.

87. US Embassy Colombo, N. Sri Lanka Sit Rep 53', 15 April 2009. Wikileaks Cable 09COLOMBO418.

88. US Embassy Colombo, 'Visit by UNSG Chief of Staff Nambiar yields mixed results', 17 April 2009. Wikileaks Cable 09COLOMBO431. See also 'UN call for pause in fighting rejected', Sunday Times, 19 April 2009.

89. Ibid.

90. See for example 'Norway's continued "facilitation" of LTTE', *Daily Mirror*, 20 April 2009; 'Norwegian Ambassador denies brokering top Tigers' escape', *The Sunday Leader*, 19 April 2009.

91. Ibid.

92. 'Expel Norwegian Ambassador from Colombo—Wimal Weerawamsa', *TamilNet*, 20 April 2009.

93. 'End of the way for Norway', *Sunday Times*, 19 April 2009.

94. At the same time, a lengthy opinion piece argued that since Norway had been formally invited to serve as peace facilitator by former President Kumaratunga, to be valid a dismissal would have to come directly from President Rajapaksa—something that never occurred. 'Norway's role has no way?', *Daily Mirror*, 23 April 2009.

95. 'Sri Lanka will not accept compensation for damage to mission in Oslo', *The Island*, 19 April 2009.

96. US Embassy Colombo, 'N. Sri Lanka Sit Rep 59', 23 April 2009. Wikileaks Cable 09COLOMBO456. By the end of the war upwards of 300,000 civilians had emerged from the combat zone: a figure to which, when calculating the total Tamil population in the area, the number of people killed in the final months of the war needs to be added—itself a subject of continued controversy.

97. 'Daya Master surrenders', *Daily Mirror*, 22 April 2009.

98. 'Hidden Reality', Parts 1–3. Available at http://defence.lk/new.asp?fname=HiddenReality

99. The pro-LTTE *TamilNet* gave figures of over 300 dead and 600 injured for the same period—considerably lower than those suggested by other pro-Tiger

sources. D.B.S. Jeyaraj, 'The "human" costs of the "humanitarian" rescue operation', 21 April 2009. http://dbsjeyaraj.com/dbsj/archives/365

100. D.B.S. Jeyaraj, 'Wretched of the Wanni earth break free of bondage', 26 April
2009. http://dbsjeyaraj.com/dbsj/archives/380 It is also important to note that
several well-informed Tamil sources estimate that up to a quarter of all civilian deaths were the result of their being targeted by the LTTE when trying to
escape the NFZ. See UTHR-J Special Report No. 34, 'Let Them Speak: Truth
about Sri Lanka's Victims of War', p. 67.

101. See UTHR-J Special Report No. 34, 'Let Them Speak: Truth about Sri Lanka's
Victims of War', p. 72.

102. The UN's estimate as of 25 April. On the same day, UNHCR reported a total of
over 120,000 civilian arrivals from the conflict zone since 20 April. US Embassy
Colombo, 'Northern Sri Lanka Sit Rep 61', 27 April 2009. Wikileaks Cable
09COLOMBO464.

103. See Jeyaraj, 'The "human" costs of the "humanitarian" rescue operation', 21 April
2009. http://dbsjeyaraj.com/dbsj/archives/365

104. 'India trips Lanka at the winning post?', Sunday Times, 26 April 2009.

105. See US Embassy Colombo, 'Northern Sri Lanka Sit Rep 61', 27 April 2009.
Wikileaks Cable 09COLOMBO464.

106. Ibid.

107. See UTHR-J Special Report No. 34, 'Let Them Speak', pp. 80–81. Or as a US
Embassy cable noted somewhat more drily: 'Despite the government's 27 April
promise to end the use of heavy weapons ... post continues to receive reports
from multiple reliable Embassy sources with access to first-hand information,
of firing causing civilian deaths and injured in the government-designated 'safe
zone'. See US Embassy Colombo, 'Northern Sri Lanka Sit Rep 61', 27 April 2009.
Wikileaks Cable 09COLOMBO464.

108. Translated from Tamil by D.B.S. Jeyaraj, 'More civilians killed and injured as
fighting continues', 1 May 2009. http://dbsjeyaraj.com/dbsj/archives/423

109. US Embassy Colombo, 'Government attempts to exclude Norway from the
Co-Chairs', 27 April 2009. Wikileaks Cable 09COLOMBO466.

110. See US Embassy Colombo, 'Northern Sri Lanka Sit Rep 61', 27 April 2009.
Wikileaks Cable 09COLOMBO464.

111. R. Wickrematunge, 'Concern over civilian casualties', The Sunday Leader, 3 May
2009.

112. D.B.S. Jeyaraj, 'Mullivaaikaal hit as shelling continues'. 29 April 2009. http://
dbsjeyaraj.com/dbsj/archives/418

113. In the UK some took the view that Miliband's visit was primarily a pre-election ploy to gain international attention—a view supported by a US Embassy
London cable later published by Wikileaks recording a senior Foreign Office
official's view that 'ministerial attention to Sri Lanka' was due to the 'very
vocal UK Tamil diaspora ... who have been protesting in front of parliament
since 6 April'. 'David Miliband focused on Sri Lankan war to win votes', The
Guardian, 1 Dec. 2010. Others pointed to the UK's position as a major arms

exporter to Sri Lanka—second only to the Czech Republic within the EU—as a major question mark against its credentials as a prospective peace broker.

114. US Embassy Colombo, 'Northern Sri Lanka Sit Rep 64', 30 April 2009. Wikileaks Cable 09COLOMBO477.

115. US Embassy Colombo, 'Few results from high-level visits', 30 April 2009. Wikileaks Cable 09COLOMBO479.

116. There appears to be disagreement between Solheim and KP over whether Prabhakaran and LTTE intelligence chief Pottu Amman were included in the proposal or not. KP maintains they were, Solheim maintains the opposite. See Jeyaraj, 'Top Tiger leaders killed in a major debacle for LTTE', 6 April 2009, for KP's view, and 'Prabhakaran to blame for final losses—Solheim', *Sri Lanka Mirror*, 10 Oct. 2012 for Solheim's.

117. See Jeyaraj, 'Top Tiger leaders killed in a major debacle for LTTE', 6 April 2009, as well as a more extended treatment of the ceasefire proposal by the same author: 'The Last Days of Thiruvenkadam Veluppillai Prabhakaran', 22 May 2009. http://dbsjeyaraj.com/dbsj/archives/615

118. 'Sri Lanka admits bombing safe zone', Al-Jazeera, 2 May 2009; 'Sri Lanka admits bombing safe haven', *The Guardian*, 2 May 2009.

119. 'Sri Lanka: Repeated Shelling of Hospitals Evidence of War Crimes', Human Rights Watch, 8 May 2009. http://www.hrw.org/news/2009/05/08/sri-lanka-repeated-shelling-hospitals-evidence-war-crimes

120. 'Sri Lanka army shells hospital', Al-Jazeera, 2 May 2009; 'Shells hit hospital in no fire zone', *Daily Mirror*, 2 May 2009.

121. US Embassy Colombo, 'Embassy shares images of safe zone with the President', 5 May 2009. Wikileaks Cable 09COLOMBO495.

122. US Embassy Colombo, 'Northern Sri Lanka Sit Rep 68', 7 May 2009. Wikileaks Cable 09COLOMBO507.

123. 'Report to Congress on Incidents During the Recent Conflict in Sri Lanka', U.S. Dept. of State, 2009, p. 41. The government doctor interviewed in Harrison, *Still Counting the Dead*, gives a more detailed account of the central allegation that efforts to provide the Army with GPS coordinates for hospitals and other medical installations inside the 'safe zone' consistently led to their being shelled. In the end doctors stopped providing coordinates. By the end stages of the war, the only medical units that were not attacked were those whose location doctors working inside the 'safe zone' did not disclose to the Army. See Ch. 10, pp. xx.

124. D.B.S. Jeyaraj, 'At least 378 killed an 1,122 injured in shelling and bombing', 10 May 2009. http://dbsjeyaraj.com/dbsj/archives/496

125. US Embassy Colombo, 'Northern Sri Lanka Sit Rep 69', 11 May 2009. Wikileaks Cable 09COLOMBO514.

126. 'Sri Lanka denies 'war crimes' claim', *Daily Mirror*, 9 May 2009.

127. See US Embassy Colombo, 'Northern Sri Lanka Sit Rep 69', 11 May 2009. Wikileaks Cable 09COLOMBO514.

128. 'Statement by the President on the situation in Sri Lanka', 13 May 2009. http://www.whitehouse.gov/the_press_office/

Statement-by-the-President-on-the-Situation-in-Sri-Lanka-and-Detainee-Photographs

129. See 'Report to Congress on Incidents During the Recent Conflict in Sri Lanka', U.S. Dept. of State, 2009, p. 44.

130. UTHR-J Special Report No. 34, 'Let Them Speak', pp. 87–88.

131. Ibid., p. 90.

132. Ibid., p. 86.

133. Ibid., p. 91.

134. UTHR-J, Special Report no. 32, 'A Marred Victory and a Defeat Pregnant with Foreboding', 10 June 2009, p. 7. Available at: http://uthr.org/SpecialReports/spreport32.htm

135. Ibid., p. 7.

136. M. Reddy, 'Final hours', *Frontline*, 23 May–5 June 2009.

137. D.B.S. Jeyaraj, 'Has Praba embraced death?', 16 May 2009. http://dbsjeyaraj.com/dbsj/archives/date/2009/05/16

138. See Reddy, 'Final hours', *Frontline*, 23 May–5 June 2009.

139. US Embassy Colombo. 'Northern Sri Lanka Sit Rep 74', 17 May 2009. Wikileaks Cable 09COLOMBO535. The following day, however, the US Embassy reported that despite 'helpful efforts' by the Norwegians, the LTTE were yet to provide such a list.

140. Ibid.

141. Later the same day, the Bishop of Mannar indicated that the small group of priests still inside the conflict zone estimated the remaining civilian population at 60–75,000. Another credible source puts the figure for civilians still within the combat zone at 35,000. UTHR-J, 'A Marred Victory and a Defeat Pregnant with Foreboding', 10 June 2009, p. 96.

142. See US Embassy Colombo. 'Northern Sri Lanka Sit Rep 74', 17 May 2009. Wikileaks Cable 09COLOMBO535.

143. D.B.S. Jeyaraj, 'Army wants to end "stand-off" and finish off Tigers', 17 May 2009. http://dbsjeyaraj.com/dbsj/archives/562

144. 'Dignity and respect for our people is all we ask—Pathmanathan', *TamilNet*, 17 May 2009.

145. D.B.S. Jeyaraj, 'KP, Soosai and Nadesan try for "ceasefire" while Praba and Pottu Amman become silent', 17 May 2009. http://dbsjeyaraj.com/dbsj/archives/590; 'The last days of Thiruvenkadam Veluppillai Prabhakaran', 22 May 2009. http://dbsjeyaraj.com/dbsj/archives/615. As noted above, however, it should be emphasised that Jeyaraj's account of these developments is not accepted by all independent expert sources.

146. See for example 'Balachandran Prabhakaran: Sri Lanka army accused over death', BBC News, 19 Feb. 2013. http://www.bbc.com/news/world-asia-21509656

147. See 'Report to Congress on Incidents During the Recent Conflict in Sri Lanka', U.S. Dept. of State, 2009, pp. 45–46; UTHR-J, Special Report no. 32, 'A Marred Victory and a Defeat Pregnant with Foreboding', 10 June 2009, p. 8.

148. See '5 years On: The White Flag Incident 2009–2014', www.white-flags.org

149. Ibid.

150. Ibid.

151. See Jeyaraj, 'KP, Soosai and Nadesan try for "ceasefire" while Praba and Pottu Amman become silent', 17 May 2009. http://dbsjeyaraj.com/dbsj/archives/590; 'The last days of Thiruvenkadam Veluppillai Prabhakaran', 22 May 2009. http://dbsjeyaraj.com/dbsj/archives/615

152. US Embassy Cable, 'Northern Sri Lanka Sit Rep 76', 19 May 2009. Wikileaks Cable 09COLOMBO543.

153. US Embassy Cable, 'Northern Sri Lanka Sit Rep 77', 20 May 2009. Wikileaks Cable 09COLOMBO549.

154. UTHR-J, Special Report no. 32, 'A Marred Victory and a Defeat Pregnant with Foreboding', 10 June 2009.

155. Ibid., p. 102.

156. http://www.channel4.com/programmes/sri-lankas-killing-fields

157. United Nations, 'The Report of the Secretary-General's Review Panel on United Nations Action in Sri Lanka', Nov. 2012.

158. The first Indian medical team arrived on 9 March to set up a field hospital at Pulmoddai, located some way south of the combat zone, to treat ICRC-assisted evacuees from the 'safe zone'. US Embassy Colombo, 'Northern Sri Lanka Sit Rep 28', 9 March 2009. Wikileaks Cable 09COLOMBO265.

159. 'House of the People', the Lower House of the Indian parliament to which elections are held every five years.

12. LESSONS LEARNED

1. See ICG, Asia Report No. 191, 'War Crimes in Sri Lanka', 17 May 2010, pp. 1–2, www.crisisgroup.org/en/regions/asia/south-asia/sri-lanka/191-war-crimes-in-sri-lanka.aspx

2. 'Nigeria, Boko Haram and the "Sri Lankan Model" of counter-insurgency', Transconflict, 7 Aug. 2014. www.transconflict.com/2014/08/nigeria-boko-haram-sri-lankan-model-counter-insurgency-078/. The Defence Chief of Staff's press release is reported in N. Ndahi & U. Upkong, 'B'Haram demands 800 cows for Chibok women', National Mirror, 13 June 2014. http://nationalmirroronline.net/new/bharam-demands-800-cows-for-chibok-women/

3. 'Report of the Secretary-General's Internal Review Panel on United Nations Action in Sri Lanka', http://www.un.org/News/dh/infocus/Sri_Lanka/The_Internal_Review_Panel_report_on_Sri_Lanka.pdf

4. 'Following report on activities in Sri Lanka war, Ban determined to strengthen UN responses to crises', UN News Centre, 14 Nov. 2012. www.un.org/apps/news/story.asp?NewsID=43496#.VFy2VtbF-1Q

5. Excerpted from Petrie Report Executive Summary, pp. 1–2. At http://www.innercitypress.com/sri16banpetrie111512.html The full report is at: http://www.un.org/News/dh/infocus/Sri_Lanka/The_Internal_Review_Panel_report_on_Sri_Lanka.pdf

6. M.R. Lee, 'Sri Lanka Report, UN Outright Removed Over 5,000 Dead & Summary', *Inner City Press*, 15 Nov. 2011.

7. See chapter annex for a summary of the Evaluation Report.

8. M. Lehti (ed.), *Nordic Approaches To Mediation: Research, Practices and Policies*, Tampere, Finland: TAPRI, 2014, p. 61, citing K. Höglund & I. Svensson, 'Mediating between Tigers and Lions: Norwegian Peace Diplomacy in Sri Lanka's Civil War' *Contemporary South Asia*, Vol. 17, No. 2, 2009.

9. The interview from which this quotation is taken was conducted in late 2013, when Mahinda Rajapaksa was still President.

10. Interview conducted while the Rajapaksa administration was still in power.

11. Interview conducted while the Rajapaksa administration was still in power.

12. An [unpublished] personal reflection written a couple of days after the end of the war in May 2009.

13. http://www.norad.no/en/tools-and-publications/publications/evaluations/publication?key=386346

EPILOGUE

1. Erik Solheim, 'Shock and Joy in Sri Lanka', *Huffington Post*, 29 Jan. 2015. Available at: http://www.huffingtonpost.com/erik-solheim/shock-and-joy-in-sri-lank_b_6574240.html

2. Rajapaksa had earlier altered the Constitution to allow himself to run for a third term of office.

3. Jayaveda Uyangoda, 'Revival of democracy', *The Gulf Today*, 11 Jan. 2015. Rajapaksa's second term in office is further characterised as involving a 'semi-authoritarian and family-centric style of governance'.

4. By way of example, the following are excerpts from an interview with Erik Solheim conducted in Nov. 2014: 'Five years after the war things have moved in a very bad direction. It's an enormous missed opportunity: after such a victory, no reaching out to Tamils, no interest in resolving the Tamil question. Mahinda is completely focused on consolidating his personal power. Why do the killings continue? Why is Mahinda choosing such a dictatorial path? He does not believe anyone can be trusted. He wants to keep the Sinhala vote. That's it: he has no other political strategy. But strong leaders do not necessarily stay forever. He is going against the current of the region. He has an ally in China, but only in economic terms. They are not interested in keeping him in power: China does not interfere in internal matters. If Mahinda had gone on TV to say we are a multi-cultural society, this would have stopped the upsurge in anti-Muslim feeling. There are genuine extremists out there, not funded by the regime but allowed to be there. But if you want to keep this government coalition together, you need enemies.'

5. '"Even Nostradamus got things wrong" says astrologer who advised Sri Lanka's president to call election', AFP, 13 Jan. 2015. Amusingly, two months later reports emerged that the self-same soothsayer, styling himself the 'royal astrologer', had written to President Sirisena lamenting the fact he hadn't been invited to assist

and offering his services to the new president. Shamindra Ferdinando, 'Rajapaksa's Key Astrologer now wants to Serve Sirisena', *The Island*, 10 March 2015.

6. The Buddhist *Jathika Hela Urumaya* (National Heritage Party) and leftist-nationalist *Janathā Vimukthi Peramuṇa* (People's Liberation Front), both previously allied with Rajapaksa.

7. Dharisha Bastians, 'When Democracy Stood Upon Razor's Edge', *Colombo Telegraph*, 17 Jan. 2015. Also alleged to have been among those present at the meeting were ex-Foreign Minister G.I. Peiris and Navy Commander Vice Admiral Jayantha Perera.

8. Ibid.

9. The composition of the new government was announced on 14 Jan. 2015.

10. 'Sri Lankan president appoints civilian governor in Tamil-controlled north', *The Guardian*, 15 Jan 2015.

11. Before the end of Jan., the appointment of a non-military replacement for the incumbent Eastern province governor was also announced. Human Rights Watch, 'Letter to President Sirisena Re. Human Rights Situation in Sri Lanka', 28 Feb. 2015. http://www.hrw.org/news/2015/02/26/president-sirisena-re-human-rights-situation-sri-lanka

12. Dharisha Bastians & Gardiner Harris, 'Sri Lanka to Free Tamils and Return Their Land', *New York Times*, 29 Jan. 2015. As of mid-July 2015, however, with the exception of one high-profile female human rights activist, the promise to move towards releasing Tamil political detainees remains unfulfilled.

13. At the time of writing the precise shape and form such a process might take remains unclear. During a March 2015 visit to the UK for a Commonwealth Meeting, President Sirisena stated he hoped to establish an 'investigative committee' within a month. In addition Sirisena argued that it would function 'efficiently' and in 'a balanced, legal and impartial manner', while also reiterating his previously-voiced position that, while they might be consulted, UN investigators would not be asked to participate in the new domestic process. 'Sri Lanka President Sirisena pledges war crimes inquiry', BBC News, 12 March 2015. Nonetheless, by mid-June 2015 there was till no clear indication from the government of the shape the promised 'domestic mechanism' would take, or indeed when specifically it would begin functioning.

14. http://www.priu.gov.lk/news_update/Current_Affairs/ca201112/FINAL%20 LLRC%20REPORT.pdf

15. As quoted in Jehan Perera, 'Balancing Change With Continuity To Ensure Public Support', *The Island*, 2 Feb. 2015.

16. 'The Time and Peace Required for Healing and Building Sustainable Peace and Security for all is Upon us', Statement of Peace by Sri Lankan Govt., 4 Feb 2015. Available at: http://dbsjeyaraj.com/dbsj/archives/38414#more-38414

17. One of the surprises of the 2014 presidential campaign was the TNA's eventual decision to endorse Sirisena as the 'Common Candidate' at the polls, although the party stopped short of joining the alliance formally backing him. At the same time, the decision to attend Independence Day celebrations sparked controversy within the TNA, with Northern Province Chief Minister C.V.

Wigneswaran reportedly among those vigorously opposed to the move. Defending the decision, TNA Parliamentry Leader R. Sampathan argued that while previous Independence Day celebrations had essentially been 'military exhibition[s]', this year's event had highlighted the need for 'true reconciliation'. 'Rift in TNA Over Sampanthan and Sumanthiran Attending 67th Independence Day Celebrations Without Party Taking Decision', *Asian Mirror*, 5 Feb. 2015. For an arresting description of the celebrations and their marked difference from previous years, see Dharisha Bastians, 'Independence Day with Difference as Sirisena Shapes a Different Type of Presidency in First 30 Days', *DailyFT*, 5 Feb. 2015.

18. The report is the responsibility of the UN's official human rights organ, the Office of the High Commissioner for Human Rights (OHCHR). The investigation on which is based—known as the OISL—was initiated on the basis of a March 2014 Human Rights Council decision to mandate such a process. Details are available at: www.ohchr.org/EN/HRBodies/HRC/Pages/OISL.aspx

19. The allies were India, the USA, and not long after, China.

20. 'UNHRC agrees to delay the report', *Daily Mirror*, 16 Feb. 2015.

21. Jason Burke, '"The fear has gone"—Sri Lankans hope for peace and reform under new president', *The Guardian*, 19 Feb. 2015. As this book goes to press, parliamentary elections have been announced for 17 Aug. 2015—meaning that the result will be clear before the OISL UN Report's official release and most probably before advance copies are forwarded to the government, as is suggested will occur according to July press reports.

22. 'Letter to President Sirisena Re. Human Rights Situation in Sri Lanka', *Human Rights Watch*, 26 Feb. 2015. http://www.hrw.org/print/news/2015/02/26/letter-president-sirisena-re-human-rights-situation-sri-lanka. Interestingly, in this context HRW urge the government to consider 'credible models of domestic-hybrid courts' such as those established in Sierra Leone and Bosnia-Herzegovina in the aftermath of their respective conflicts.

23. See, for example, Dharisha Bastians, '"Don't Shout at me. I Understand Your Issues"—Ranil Tells TNA in Stormy Meeting', *DailyFT*, 26 Feb. 2015. Concerns regarding the ruling coalition's stability are expressed by seasoned political commentator Jayaveda Uyangoda in 'National Democratic Front Coalition Seems to be Disintegrating within Three Months of Being in Power', *The Island*, 20 March 2015. For a more upbeat reading of the government's future prospects, particularly following the mid-March formation of a SLFP-UNP national government, see Rasika Jayakody, 'Maithri-Ranil-Chandrika Trinity Checkmates Mahinda by Forming National Govt Comprising UNP and SLFP', *Daily News*, 25 March 2015.

24. That said, the potential difficulties raised by this approach are highlighted by comments by President Sirisena regarding the issue of war crimes in a BBC Sinhala interview held during a state visit to the UK in March 2015. In the interview, Sirisena reportedly stated that he 'did not believe' the documented allegations of wartime atrocities contained in Callum Macrae's widely-viewed documentary 'No Fire Zone', now released in Sinhalese. While Chandrika

Kumaratunga's contention that Sirisena had been 'misunderstood' may have calmed some nerves on this issue, her parallel contention that the 'whole country' was against a UN war crimes enquiry, as the implied suggestion that Sri Lanka was unable to carry out its 'own investigation in a transparent manner' was 'insulting', will doubtless have proved rather less reassuring. 'Calls for international war crimes probe "insulting": CBK', *Daily Mirror*, 16 March 2015.

25. Landmark, because it was the first visit by an Indian political leader in twenty-eight years—the last having been by Rajiv Gandhi in 1987. Among other things, in his speech to the Sri Lankan parliament Modi argued that opting for 'early and full implementation', of the 13th Amendment to the Constitution 'and beyond' would greatly facilitate the reconciliation process in Sri Lanka, as well as overall efforts to 'build a future' that accommodates the 'aspirations of all sections of society, including the Sri Lankan Tamil community' within a 'united Sri Lanka'. 'Going beyond 13-A will expedite reconciliation', *Daily Mirror*, 13 March 2015. That said, the irony of a former Chief Minister of Gujarat accused of direct complicity in the Feb. 2002 anti-Muslim pogrom during which thousands were slaughtered, extolling the virtues of ethnic tolerance and co-existence to Sri Lankans did not go unremarked. See Latheeth Farook, 'Modi Preaching Sri Lanka On Treating Minorities!', *Colombo Telegraph*, 18 March 2015.

26. Importantly in this context, in his March 2015 speech to the Colombo parliament Prime Minister Modi underlined that he was a 'firm believer' in what he termed 'cooperative federalism'. India was engaged in 'devolving more power and more resources to the states', he argued, and 'we are making them formal partners in national decision making processes'. The implicit message will not have been missed by his Sri Lankan audience. For the text of Modi's speech, see 'Going beyond 13-A will expedite reconciliation', *Daily Mirror*, 13 March 2015.

27. Mark Salter, 'Democracy For All? Minority Rights And Minorities' Participation and Representation In Democratic Politics', International IDEA, Nov. 2011, pp. 19–20.

POSTSCRIPT

1. After two weeks of tantalising silence following the initial announcement of Rajapaksa's nomination, in mid July Sirisena finally made a public statement on the issue. And quite a statement it was too: focused on stinging criticism of Rajapaksa, whom Sirisena depicted as the country's only sitting president to have contested and lost an election; and a stern rebuke for seeking to regain the power he had lost at the beginning of the year. Implicitly pointing to the fact that it was internal party pressures that had forced his hand on the Rajapaksa nomination issue, the president's speech paved the way for what is likely to be a no-holds barred struggle between the Rajapaksa and Sirisena factions for control of the SLFP in the run-up to the 17 Aug. elections.

SELECT BIBLIOGRAPHY

Below is a list of sources referred to or otherwise used in the course of researching and writing this book.

Books

Balasingham, Adele, *The Will to Freedom: An Inside View of Tamil Resistance*, Mitcham: Fairmax, 2001.

Balasingham, Anton, *War and Peace: Armed Struggle and Peace Efforts of Liberation Tigers*, Mitcham: Fairmax, 2004.

Champion, Stephen, *Sri Lanka War Stories*, London: HotShoe Books, 2008.

Chandraprema, C. A., *Gota's War: The Crushing of Tamil Tiger Terrorism in Sri Lanka*, Colombo: Ranjan Wijeratne Foundation, 2012.

——, *Sri Lanka: The Years of Terror. The JVP Insurrection 1987–1989*, Colombo: Lake House, 1991.

De Silva, K.M., *Reaping The Whirlwind: Ethnic Conflict, Ethnic Politics In Sri Lanka*, New Delhi: Penguin India, 2000.

——, *A History of Sri Lanka*, New Delhi: Penguin India, 2008.

——, *Sri Lanka And The Defeat Of The LTTE*, New Delhi: Penguin India, 2012.

DeVotta, Neil, *Blowback: Linguistic Nationalism, Institutional Decay and Ethnic Conflict in Sri Lanka*, Redwood, CA: Stanford University Press, 2004.

Dixit, J. D., *Assignment Colombo*, New Delhi: Konark, 2002.

Fernando, Austin, *My Belly Is White: Reminiscences of a Peacetime Secretary of Defence*, Colombo: Vijitha Yapa, 2008.

Fjørtoft, Arne, *Rapport frå paradis—Ein Idé om Fred og Utvickling*, Oslo: Commentium Forlag, 2007.

Gooneratne, John, *Negotiating With The Tigers (LTTE) 2002—2005*, Colombo: Stamford Lake, 2007.

Harrison, Frances, *Still Counting the Dead: Survivors of Sri Lanka's Hidden War*, London: Portobello Books, 2012.

Herath, Dhammika and Kalinga Tudor Silva (eds), *Healing the Wounds: Rebuilding Sri Lanka after the War*, Colombo: ICES, 2012.

Hoole, Rajan, *Palmyra Broken: From Rajani to War's End*, Colombo: UTHR-J, 2015.

SELECT BIBLIOGRAPHY

Jayatilleka, Dayan, *Long War, Cold Peace; Conflict and Crisis in Sri Lanka,* Colombo: Vijitha Yapa, 2013.

Karunatilaka, Shenan, *Chinaman: The Legend of Pradeep Matthew,* New Delhi: Random House India, 2011.

Keethaponcalan, S. I., *Conflict and Peace in Sri Lanka: Major Documents,* Chennai: Kumaran, 2009.

——, *Sri Lanka: Politics of Power, Crisis and Peace,* Chennai: Kumaran, 2008.

Keethaponcalan, S.I. and R. Jayawardana (eds), *Sri Lanka: Perspectives on the Ceasefire Agreement of 2002,* New Delhi: South Asia Peace Institute, 2009.

McGowan, William, *Only Man Is Vile: The Tragedy Of Sri Lanka,* London: Picador, 1993.

Mohan, Rohini, *The Seasons Of Trouble: Life Amid The Ruins Of Sri Lanka's Civil War,* London: Verso, 2014.

Moragoda, Milinda, *With a Warm Heart, a Cool Head and a Deep Breath: Speeches by Milinda Moragoda,* Oslo: International Democrat Union, 2003.

Oondatje, Michael, *Anil's Ghost,* London: Vintage, 2000.

Orjuela, Camilla, *The Identity Politics of Peacebuilding: Civil Society In War-Torn Sri Lanka,* New Delhi: Sage, 2008.

Patten, Chris, *What Next? Surviving The Twenty-First Century,* London: Penguin, 2009.

Peiris, G. H., *Twilight of the Tigers: Peace Efforts and Power Struggles in Sri Lanka,* New Delhi: Oxford University Press, 2009.

Perera, Jehan, *A Dove Sits on My Shoulder: Analysis of the Continuing Ethnic Conflict in Sri Lanka 2007–2008,* Colombo: National Peace Council, 2008.

Pratap, Anita, *Island of Blood: Frontline Reports from Sri Lanka, Afghanistan and other South Asian Flashpoints,* New Delhi: Penguin India, 2001.

Richardson, J., *Paradise Poisoned: Learning about Conflict, Terrorism and Development from Sri Lanka's Civil Wars,* Colombo: ICES, 2005.

Roberts, Michael W., *Confrontations in Sri Lanka: Sinhalese, LTTE and Others,* Colombo: Vijitha Yapa, 2009.

Rupesinghe, Kumar, *Expressions of an Unequivocal Mind: Interviews with Kumar Rupesinghe 1991–2007,* Colombo: Foundation for Co-Existence, 2008.

—— (ed.), *Negotiating Peace in Sri Lanka: Efforts, Failures & Lessons, Vols. 1 & 2,* Colombo: Foundation for Co-Existence, 2006.

Sivanandan, A., *When Memory Dies,* London: Arcadia, 2007.

Solheim, Erik, *Nærmere,* Oslo: Cappelen Damm/Milennium, 1999.

——, *Politikk Er Å Ville,* Oslo: Cappelen Damm, 2013.

Solnes, Jon Oskar, *A Powderkeg in Paradise: Lost Opportunity for Peace in Sri Lanka,* New Delhi: Konark, 2010.

Subramanian, Nirupama, *Sri Lanka: Voices From a War Zone,* New Delhi: Penguin India, 2005.

Subramanian, Samanth, *The Divided Island: Stories From The Sri Lankan War,* London: Atlantic, 2015.

Sundarji, Padma Rao, *Sri Lanka: The New Country,* New Delhi: Harper Collins India, 2015.

SELECT BIBLIOGRAPHY

Svensson, Isaak and Peter Wallensteen, *The Go-Between: Jan Eliasson and the Styles of Mediation*, Washington, D.C.: USIP, 2010.

Swamy, M. R. Narayan, *Inside An Elusive Mind: Prabhakaran*, Colombo: Vijitha Yapa, 2003.

——, *Tigers of Lanka: From Boys to Guerillas*, Colombo: Vijitha Yapa, 2008.

——, *The Tiger Vanquished: LTTE's Story*, New Delhi: Sage Publications, 2010.

Thiranagama, Rajani (ed.), *The Broken Palmyra: the Tamil Crisis in Sri Lanka; an Inside Account*, Colombo: Sri Lanka Studies Institute, 1992.

Uyangoda, Jayaveda (ed.), *Matters of Violence: Reflections on Social and Political Violence in Sri Lanka*, Colombo: Social Scientists' Association, 2008.

Weerakoon, Bernard, *Rendering Unto Caesar: A fascinating story of one man's tenure under nine Prime Ministers and Presidents of Sri Lanka*, Elgin, IL: New Dawn Press, 2006.

Weiss, Gordon, *The Cage: The Fight for Sri Lanka and the Last Days of the Tamil Tigers*, London: Bodley Head, 2011.

Wickramasinghe, Nira, *Sri Lanka in the Modern Age: A History*, London: Hurst, 2014.

Journals, reports, media & online resources

Details of journals, news and other media reports consulted in the course of writing this book are provided in the footnotes. Below is a listing only of some of the most notable additional reports consulted.

Civil Wars, Sri Lanka Special Issue, Vol. 7, No. 2, (Summer 2005).

DeVotta, Neil, 'The Liberation Tigers of Tamil Eelam and the Lost Quest for Separatism in Sri Lanka', *Asian Survey*, Vol. 49, No. 6 (Nov/Dec. 2009), www.jstor.org/stable/10.1525/as.2009.49.6.1021

Groundviews, http://groundviews.org/ (An excellent general source of analysis and commentary on Sri Lankan current affairs produced by the Colombo-based NGO Centre for Policy Alternatives (CPA) www.cpalanka.org)

——*Groundviews Special Edition: The End of The War*, May 2009.

International Crisis Group (ICG) 'Sri Lanka: The Failure of the Peace Process', Asia Report no. 124, 8 Nov. 2006.

—— 'Sri Lanka's Return to War: Limiting the Damage', Asia Report no. 146, 20 Feb 2008.

—— 'War Crimes in Sri Lanka', Asia Report no. 191, 17 May 2010.

—— 'Sri Lanka's North I: The Denial of Minority Rights', Asia Report no. 219, 16 Mar 2012.

—— 'Sri Lanka's North II: Rebuilding under the Military', Asia Report no. 220, 16 Mar 2012.

—— 'Sri Lanka: Tamil Politics and the Quest for a Political Solution', Asia Report no. 239, 20 Nov 2012.

—— 'Sri Lanka's Potemkin Peace: Democracy Under Fire', Asia Report no. 253, 13 Nov. 2013.

—— 'Sri Lanka's Presidential Election: Risks and Opportunities', Asia Briefing no. 145, 9 Dec. 2014.

SELECT BIBLIOGRAPHY

Manikkalingham, Ram, 'A Unitary State, A Federal State Or Two Separate States?', Colombo: Social Scientists' Association Pamphlet, 2003.

Nadarajah Sutharan, and Luxshi Vimalarajah, 'The Politics of Transformation: The LTTE and the 2002–2006 Peace Process in Sri Lanka', Berlin: Berghof Centre, 2008.

Ropers, Norbert, 'Systemic Conflict Transformation: Reflections on the Conflict and Peace Process in Sri Lanka', Berlin: Berghof Centre, July 2008.

'Sri Lanka Monitoring Mission, The SLMM Report 2002–2008', Oslo: Norwegian MFA, 2010. Available at www.slmm-history.info

Stokke, Kristian, 'Building the Tamil Eelam State: Emerging State Institutions and Forms of Governance in LTTE-controlled Areas in Sri Lanka', *Third World Quarterly*, Vol. 26, No. 6 (2006).

TamilNet, www.tamilnet.com. A well-organised Tamil news site that has traditionally been strongly sympathetic to the LTTE. A frequently indispensible (although biased) source of news and information during the course of the conflict.

TransCurrents, *www.transcurrents.com*. News website maintained by veteran Tamil journalist D.B.S. Jeyaraj, alongside www.dbsjeyaraj.com which carries most of his referenced commentary and analysis.

United Nations, 'UN Secretary-General's Panel of Experts (POE) Report on Accountability in Sri Lanka', www.un.org/News/dh/infocus/Sri_Lanka/POE_Report_Executive_Summary.pdf (Mar 2011)

——,'UN Internal Review Panel Report (Petrie Report)', Nov. 2012, http://cl.ly/05042e2R3031 (unredacted version)

University Teachers for Human Rights-Jaffna (UTHR-J). All UTHR-J bulletins, reports and special reports—some of which are referred to extensively in this text—are available at www.uthr.org.

'US State Dept., Report to Congress on Incidents During the Recent Conflict in Sri Lanka (2009)', http://www.state.gov/documents/organization/131025.pdf

Uyangoda, Jayaveda, 'Ethnic Conflict in Sri Lanka: Changing Dynamics', Report No. 32, Washington, D.C.: East-West Center, 2007.

Wikileaks, www.wikileaks.org.

'5 Years on: the White Flag Incident 2009–2014', http://white-flags.org/. The most detailed, carefully researched study to date of the evidence surrounding the infamous May 2009 'White Flag Incident'.

English-language newspapers and weeklies

While not an exhaustive list of the Sri Lankan media outlets consulted in the course of researching this book—most are websites of daily print newspapers, some are weekend papers, one is a web-only production—it includes those that consistently yielded useful information and insights. In addition, although they began publishing after the war's end, both *Ceylon Today* (www.ceylontoday.lk) owned by Rajapaksa's presidential advisor-turned-politician Tiran Alles (see Chapter 8), and the finance-focused *DailyFT* (www.dailyft.lk), part of the Wijeya newspaper group that includes *The Daily Mirror* and *The Sunday Times*, proved useful further sources of reference.

SELECT BIBLIOGRAPHY

Colombo Telegraph www.colombotelegraph.lk
Daily Mirror www.dailymirror.lk
Sunday Leader www.thesundayleader.lk
Sunday Observer www.sundayobserver.lk
Sunday Times www.sundaytimes.lk
The Nation www.nation.lk
The Island www.island.lk

India

All three publications listed below—the first an excellent bi-weekly which frequently proved invaluable in researching this book—are produced in Chennai, which goes a long way to explaining their particular focus on Sri Lankan affairs. Generally speaking, an appreciation of Indian perspectives and insights remains indispensible to understanding the regional context of both the Sri Lankan conflict and its aftermath.

Frontline www.frontline.in
New Indian Express www.newindianexpress.com
The Hindu www.thehindu.in

INDEX

INDEX

INDEX

INDEX

INDEX